PHILIP'S

WORLD ATLAS

PHILIP'S

WORLD ATLAS

2004 EDITION

ICELAND
UNITED KINGDOM
NORWAY
SWEDEN
FINLAND
Murmansk
White Sea
GERMANY
Berlin
Prague
Vienna
Warsaw
ST.PETERSBURG
UKRAINE
Belgrade
Odessa
Danube
Rostov
Athens
ISTANBUL
Bursa
Izmir
Ankara
Konya
Adana
TURKEY
GEORGIA
Yerevan
ARMENIA
Nicosia
CYPRUS
Beirut
LEBANON
Aleppo
SYRIA
Mosul
Tabriz
Alexandria
ISRAEL
Damascus
CAIRO
Suez
JORDAN
IRAQ
Baghdad
Basra
EGYPT
Nile
Aswan
KUWAIT
Kuwait
Shiraz
SAUDI ARABIA
Medina
Riyadh
BAHRAIN
QATAR
Doha
Al Manamah
Abu Dhabi
UNITED ARAB EMIRATES
Jedda
Mecca
Port Sudan
Khartoum
ERITREA
Muscat
OMAN
YEMEN
Aden
DJIBOUTI
Addis Ababa
ETHIOPIA
SOMALI REP.
KENYA
Mogadishu
Nairobi
TANZANIA
KARACHI
Ahmadabad
Vadodara
Indore
Surat
BOMBAY
Nagpur
CALCUTTA
Khatanga
Norilsk
Verkhoyansk
Lena
Yakutsk
Okhotsk
Magadan
Sakhalin
Komsomolsk
Khabarovsk
Yuzhno-Sakhalinsk
L. Baikal
Chita
Amur
Blagoveshchensk
Hailar
Qiqihar
Harbin
Changchun
Vladivostok
Jilin
SHENYANG
Jinzhou
Anshan
Dalian
NORTH KOREA
P'yongyang
SEOUL
SOUTH KOREA
Pusan
Hiroshima
Kitakyushu
Baotou
BEIJING
TIANJIN
Taiyuan
Jinan
Lanzhou
Hwang-ho
Xi'an
Nanjing
SHANGHAI
Wuhan
HANGZHOU
Nanchang
Fuzhou
Chengdu
CHONGQING
Yangtze
Changsha
Kunming
GUANGZHOU
Si Kiang
HONG KONG
Macau
Brahmaputra
BURMA
(MYANMAR)
Chittagong
Hanoi
Haiphong
Hainan
LAOS
Vientiane
VIETNAM
Rangoon
THAILAND
BANGKOK
CAMBODIA
Phnom Penh
Ho Chi Minh City
Luzon
MANILA
Cebu
Palawan
Zamboanga
SABAH
Bandar Seri Begawan
SARAWAK
PEN. MALAYSIA
Kuala Lumpur
Str. of Malacca
Medan
SINGAPORE
Borneo
Celebes

THE EARTH IN SPACE
Cartography by Philip's

Text
Keith Lye

Illustrations
Stefan Chabluk

Star Charts
Wil Tirion

PICTURE ACKNOWLEDGEMENTS
Corbis /*Ed Eckstein* 42, /*Colin Garratt; Milepost 92 1/2* 44, /*Wolfgang Kaehler* 21, /*Gunter Marx Photography* 45, /*Galen Rowell* 46, /*Royalty-Free* 31, /*Peter Turnley* 35
Corbis Saba /*Shepard Sherbell* 40
Corbis Sygma /*Thorne Anderson* 47
Akira Fujii/David Malin Images 11
Getty Images/The Image Bank /*Peter Hendrie* 20, /*Pete Turner* 39
Getty Images/Stone /*James Balog* 16, /*Simeone Huber* 33, /*Gary John Norman* 36, /*Frank Oberle* 25 top, /*Dennis Oda* 17, /*Donovan Reese* 18–19, /*Hugh Sitton* 32, /*Michael Townsend* 29, /*World Perspectives* 10
Robert Harding Picture Library /*Bill Ross* 41, /*Adam Woolfitt* 43
Images Colour Library Limited 15
NASA /*Hubble Heritage Team (STScI/AURA)/R.G. French (Wellesley College)/ J. Cuzzi and J. Lissauer (NASA/Ames Research Center)/L. Dones (SwRI)* 9 bottom left, /*JPL* 8 centre left, 8 bottom, 9 centre right, /*JPL/Caltech* 9 top, /*JPL/Univ. Arizona* 9 centre left, /*JPL/USGS* 8 centre right, /*A. Stern (SwRI), M. Buie (Lowell Observatory)/ESA* 9 bottom right, /*R. Williams (STScI)/the Hubble Deep Field Team* 2
NPA Group, Edenbridge, UK 12, 13, 48
Chris Rayner 19 top
Rex Features /*Sipa* 34
Science Photo Library /*Martin Bond* 14, /*CNES, 1992 Distribution SPOT Image* 27 top, /*Luke Dodd* 3, 6, /*Earth Satellite Corporation* 25 bottom, /*ESA/PLI* 8 top, /*Simon Fraser* 38, /*NASA* 22, 23, 24, /*David Parker* 26, /*Peter Ryan* 27 bottom, /*Jerry Schad* 4
Still Pictures /*François Pierrel* 28
Tony Stone Images /*Neil Beer* 30, /*Nigel Press* 37

Published in Great Britain in 2003
by Philip's,
a division of Octopus Publishing Group Limited,
2–4 Heron Quays, London E14 4JP

This edition produced for Lomond Books, 2003

Cartography by Philip's

ISBN 0-540-08536-7

A CIP catalogue record for this book is available from the British Library.

Printed in Hong Kong

Details of other Philip's titles and services can be found on our website at:
www.philips-maps.co.uk

Philip's World Maps

The reference maps which form the main body of this atlas have been prepared in accordance with the highest standards of international cartography to provide an accurate and detailed representation of the Earth. The scales and projections used have been carefully chosen to give balanced coverage of the world, while emphasizing the most densely populated and economically significant regions. A hallmark of Philip's mapping is the use of hill shading and relief colouring to create a graphic impression of landforms: this makes the maps exceptionally easy to read. However, knowledge of the key features employed in the construction and presentation of the maps will enable the reader to derive the fullest benefit from the atlas.

MAP SEQUENCE

The atlas covers the Earth continent by continent: first Europe; then its land neighbour Asia (mapped north before south, in a clockwise sequence), then Africa, Australia and Oceania, North America and South America. This is the classic arrangement adopted by most cartographers since the 16th century. For each continent, there are maps at a variety of scales. First, physical relief and political maps

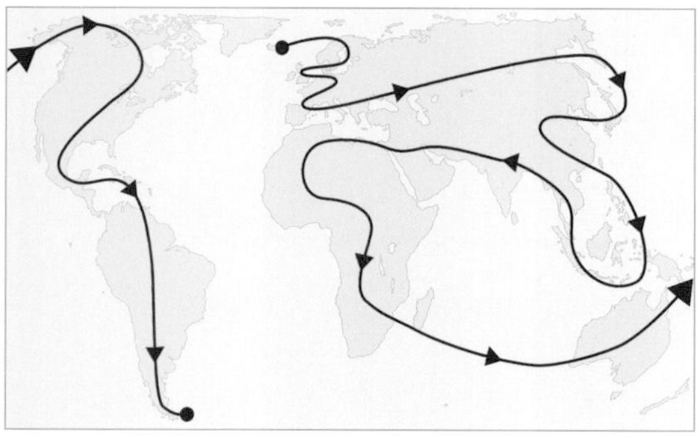

of the whole continent; then a series of larger-scale maps of the regions within the continent, each followed, where required, by still larger-scale maps of the most important or densely populated areas. The governing principle is that by turning the pages of the atlas, the reader moves steadily from north to south through each continent, with each map overlapping its neighbours.

MAP PRESENTATION

With very few exceptions (e.g. for the Arctic and Antarctica), the maps are drawn with north at the top, regardless of whether they are presented upright or sideways on the page. In the borders will be found the map title; a locator diagram showing the area covered; continuation arrows showing the page numbers for maps of adjacent areas; the scale; the projection used; the degrees of latitude and longitude; and the letters and figures used in the index for locating place names and geographical features. Physical relief maps also have a height reference panel identifying the colours used for each layer of contouring.

MAP SYMBOLS

Each map contains a vast amount of detail which can only be conveyed clearly and accurately by the use of symbols. Points and circles of varying sizes locate and identify the relative importance of towns and cities; different styles of type are employed for administrative, geographical and regional place names to aid identification. A variety of pictorial symbols denote landscape features such as glaciers, marshes and coral reefs, and man-made structures including roads, railways, airports, canals and dams. International borders are shown by red lines. Where neighbouring countries are in dispute, for example in parts of the Middle East, the maps show the *de facto* boundary between nations, regardless of the legal or historical situation. The symbols are explained on the first page of the *World Maps* section of the atlas.

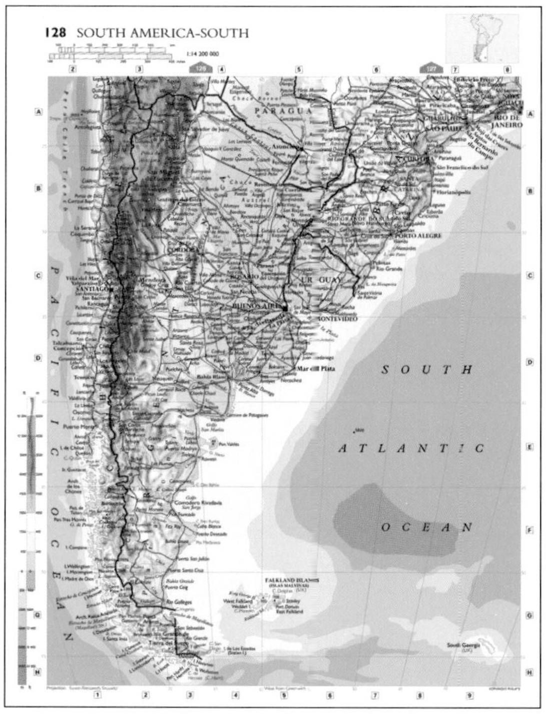
128 SOUTH AMERICA-SOUTH
S O U T H
A T L A N T I C
O C E A N

MAP SCALES

1:16 000 000
1 inch = 252 statute miles

The scale of each map is given in the numerical form known as the 'representative fraction'. The first figure is always one, signifying one unit of distance on the map; the second figure, usually in millions, is the number by which the map unit must be multiplied to give the equivalent distance on the Earth's surface. Calculations can easily be made in centimetres and kilometres, by dividing the Earth units figure by 100 000 (i.e. deleting the last five 0s). Thus 1:1 000 000 means 1 cm = 10 km. The calculation for inches and miles is more laborious, but 1 000 000 divided by 63 360 (the number of inches in a mile) shows that 1:1 000 000 means approximately 1 inch = 16 miles. The table below provides distance equivalents for scales down to 1:50 000 000.

LARGE SCALE

1:1 000 000	1 cm = 10 km	1 inch = 16 miles
1:2 500 000	1 cm = 25 km	1 inch = 39.5 miles
1:5 000 000	1 cm = 50 km	1 inch = 79 miles
1:6 000 000	1 cm = 60 km	1 inch = 95 miles
1:8 000 000	1 cm = 80 km	1 inch = 126 miles
1:10 000 000	1 cm = 100 km	1 inch = 158 miles
1:15 000 000	1 cm = 150 km	1 inch = 237 miles
1:20 000 000	1 cm = 200 km	1 inch = 316 miles
1:50 000 000	1 cm = 500 km	1 inch = 790 miles

SMALL SCALE

MEASURING DISTANCES

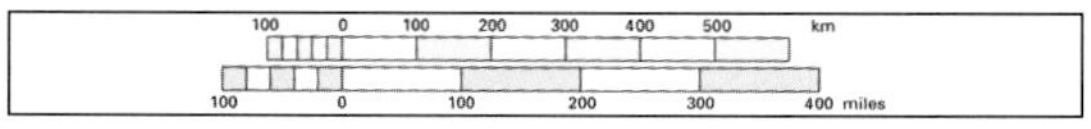
100 0 100 200 300 400 500 km
100 0 100 200 300 400 miles

Although each map is accompanied by a scale bar, distances cannot always be measured with confidence because of the distortions involved in portraying the curved surface of the Earth on a flat page. As a general rule, the larger the map scale (i.e. the lower the number of Earth units in the representative fraction), the more accurate and reliable will be the distance measured. On small-scale maps such as those of the world and of entire continents, measurement may only be accurate along the 'standard parallels', or central axes, and should not be attempted without considering the map projection.

MAP PROJECTIONS

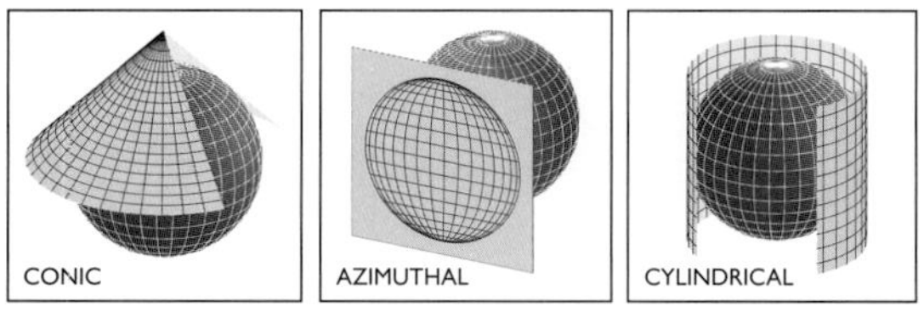
CONIC
AZIMUTHAL
CYLINDRICAL

Unlike a globe, no flat map can give a true scale representation of the world in terms of area, shape and position of every region. Each of the numerous systems that have been devised for projecting the curved surface of the Earth on to a flat page involves the sacrifice of accuracy in one or more of these elements. The variations in shape and position of landmasses such as Alaska, Greenland and Australia, for example, can be quite dramatic when different projections are compared.

For this atlas, the guiding principle has been to select projections that involve the least distortion of size and distance. The projection used for each map is noted in the border. Most fall into one of three categories – conic, azimuthal or cylindrical – whose basic concepts are shown above. Each involves plotting the forms of the Earth's surface on a grid of latitude and longitude lines, which may be shown as parallels, curves or radiating spokes.

LATITUDE AND LONGITUDE

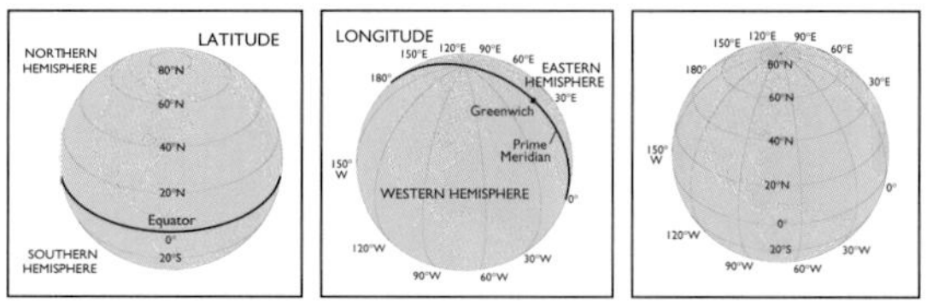
NORTHERN HEMISPHERE
LATITUDE
Equator
SOUTHERN HEMISPHERE
LONGITUDE
EASTERN HEMISPHERE
Greenwich
Prime Meridian
WESTERN HEMISPHERE

Accurate positioning of individual points on the Earth's surface is made possible by reference to the geometrical system of latitude and longitude. Latitude *parallels* are drawn west–east around the Earth and numbered by degrees north and south of the Equator, which is designated 0° of latitude. Longitude *meridians* are drawn north–south and numbered by degrees east and west of the *prime meridian*, 0° of longitude, which passes through Greenwich in England. By referring to these co-ordinates and their subdivisions of minutes (1/60th of a degree) and seconds (1/60th of a minute), any place on Earth can be located to within a few hundred metres. Latitude and longitude are indicated by blue lines on the maps; they are straight or curved according to the projection employed. Reference to these lines is the easiest way of determining the relative positions of places on different maps, and for plotting compass directions.

NAME FORMS

For ease of reference, both English and local name forms appear in the atlas. Oceans, seas and countries are shown in English throughout the atlas; country names may be abbreviated to their commonly accepted form (e.g. Germany, not The Federal Republic of Germany). Conventional English forms are also used for place names on the smaller-scale maps of the continents. However, local name forms are used on all large-scale and regional maps, with the English form given in brackets only for important cities – the large-scale map of Russia and Central Asia thus shows Moskva (Moscow). For countries which do not use a Roman script, place names have been transcribed according to the systems adopted by the British and US Geographic Names Authorities. For China, the Pin Yin system has been used, with some more widely known forms appearing in brackets, as with Beijing (Peking). Both English and local names appear in the index, the English form being cross-referenced to the local form.

Contents

World Statistics

The Earth In Space

World Maps

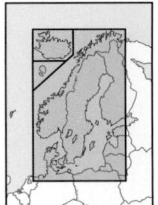

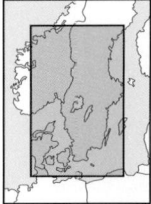

Europe

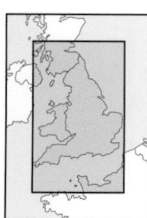

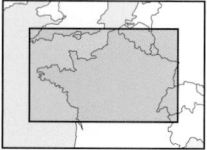

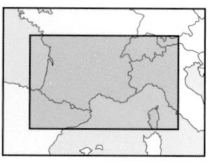

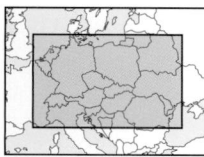

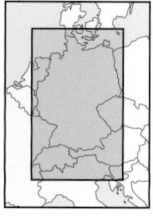

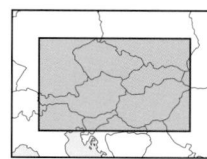

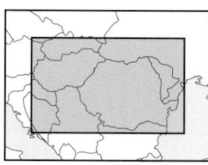

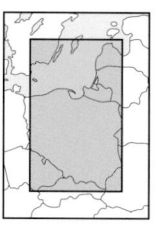

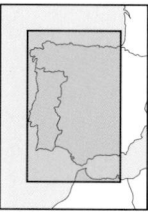

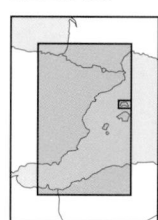

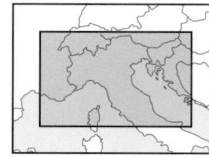

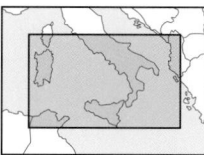

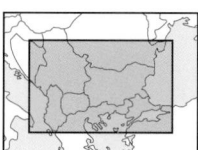

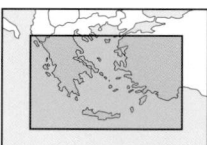

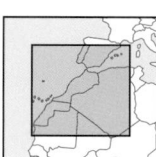

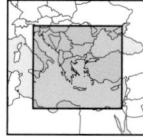

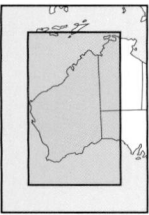

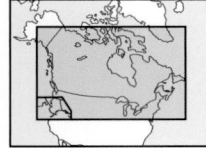

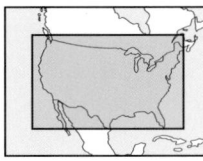

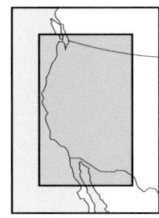

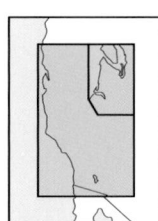

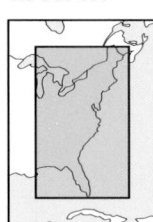

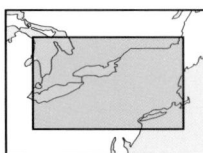

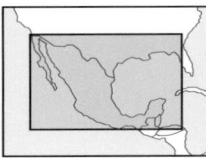

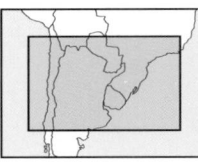

World Statistics: Countries

This alphabetical list includes all the countries and territories of the world. If a territory is not completely independent, the country it is associated with is named. The area figures give the total area of land, inland water and ice.

The population figures are 2002 estimates. The annual income is the Gross Domestic Product per capita† in US dollars. The figures are the latest available, usually 2001 estimates.

Country/Territory	Area km^2 Thousands	Area miles^2 Thousands	Population Thousands	Capital	Annual Income US $
Afghanistan	652	252	27,756	Kabul	800
Albania	28.8	11.1	3,545	Tirana	3,800
Algeria	2,382	920	32,278	Algiers	5,600
American Samoa (US)	0.2	0.08	69	Pago Pago	8,000
Andorra	0.45	0.17	68	Andorra La Vella	19,000
Angola	1,247	481	10,593	Luanda	1,330
Anguilla (UK)	0.1	0.04	12	The Valley	8,600
Antigua & Barbuda	0.44	0.17	67	St John's	10,000
Argentina	2,767	1,068	37,813	Buenos Aires	12,000
Armenia	29.8	11.5	3,330	Yerevan	3,350
Aruba (Netherlands)	0.19	0.07	70	Oranjestad	28,000
Australia	7,687	2,968	19,547	Canberra	24,000
Austria	83.9	32.4	8,170	Vienna	27,000
Azerbaijan	86.6	33.4	7,798	Baku	3,100
Azores (Portugal)	2.2	0.87	234	Ponta Delgada	12,600
Bahamas	13.9	5.4	301	Nassau	16,800
Bahrain	0.68	0.26	656	Manama	13,000
Bangladesh	144	56	133,377	Dhaka	1,750
Barbados	0.43	0.17	277	Bridgetown	14,500
Belarus	207.6	80.1	10,335	Minsk	8,200
Belgium	30.5	11.8	10,275	Brussels	26,100
Belize	23	8.9	263	Belmopan	3,250
Benin	113	43	6,788	Porto-Novo	1,040
Bermuda (UK)	0.05	0.02	64	Hamilton	34,800
Bhutan	47	18.1	2,094	Thimphu	1,200
Bolivia	1,099	424	8,445	La Paz/Sucre	2,600
Bosnia-Herzegovina	51	20	3,964	Sarajevo	1,800
Botswana	582	225	1,591	Gaborone	7,800
Brazil	8,512	3,286	176,030	Brasília	7,400
Brunei	5.8	2.2	351	Bandar Seri Begawan	18,000
Bulgaria	111	43	7,621	Sofia	6,200
Burkina Faso	274	106	12,603	Ouagadougou	1,040
Burma (= Myanmar)	677	261	42,238	Rangoon	1,500
Burundi	27.8	10.7	6,373	Bujumbura	600
Cambodia	181	70	12,775	Phnom Penh	1,500
Cameroon	475	184	16,185	Yaoundé	1,700
Canada	9,976	3,852	31,902	Ottawa	27,700
Canary Is. (Spain)	7.3	2.8	1,694	Las Palmas/Santa Cruz	18,200
Cape Verde Is.	4	1.6	409	Praia	1,500
Cayman Is. (UK)	0.26	0.1	36	George Town	30,000
Central African Republic	623	241	3,643	Bangui	1,300
Chad	1,284	496	8,997	Ndjaména	1,030
Chile	757	292	15,499	Santiago	10,000
China	9,597	3,705	1,284,304	Beijing	4,300
Colombia	1,139	440	41,008	Bogotá	6,300
Comoros	2.2	0.86	614	Moroni	710
Congo	342	132	2,958	Brazzaville	900
Congo (Dem. Rep. of the)	2,345	905	55,225	Kinshasa	590
Cook Is. (NZ)	0.24	0.09	21	Avarua	5,000
Costa Rica	51.1	19.7	3,835	San José	8,500
Croatia	56.5	21.8	4,391	Zagreb	8,300
Cuba	111	43	11,224	Havana	2,300
Cyprus	9.3	3.6	767	Nicosia	11,500
Czech Republic	78.9	30.4	10,257	Prague	14,400
Denmark	43.1	16.6	5,369	Copenhagen	28,000
Djibouti	23.2	9	473	Djibouti	1,400
Dominica	0.75	0.29	70	Roseau	3,700
Dominican Republic	48.7	18.8	8,722	Santo Domingo	5,800
East Timor	14.9	5.7	953	Dili	500
Ecuador	284	109	13,447	Quito	3,000
Egypt	1,001	387	70,712	Cairo	3,700
El Salvador	21	8.1	6,354	San Salvador	4,600
Equatorial Guinea	28.1	10.8	498	Malabo	2,100
Eritrea	94	36	4,466	Asmara	740
Estonia	44.7	17.3	1,416	Tallinn	10,000
Ethiopia	1,128	436	67,673	Addis Ababa	700
Faroe Is. (Denmark)	1.4	0.54	46	Tórshavn	20,000
Fiji	18.3	7.1	856	Suva	5,200
Finland	338	131	5,184	Helsinki	25,800
France	552	213	59,766	Paris	25,400
French Guiana (France)	90	34.7	182	Cayenne	6,000
French Polynesia (France)	4	1.5	258	Papeete	5,000
Gabon	268	103	1,233	Libreville	5,500
Gambia, The	11.3	4.4	1,456	Banjul	1,770
Gaza Strip (OPT)*	0.36	0.14	1,226	–	630
Georgia	69.7	26.9	4,961	Tbilisi	3,100
Germany	357	138	83,252	Berlin	26,200
Ghana	239	92	20,244	Accra	1,980
Gibraltar (UK)	0.007	0.003	28	Gibraltar Town	17,500
Greece	132	51	10,645	Athens	17,900
Greenland (Denmark)	2,176	840	56	Nuuk (Godthåb)	20,000
Grenada	0.34	0.13	89	St George's	4,750
Guadeloupe (France)	1.7	0.66	436	Basse-Terre	9,000
Guam (US)	0.55	0.21	161	Agana	21,000
Guatemala	109	42	13,314	Guatemala City	3,700
Guinea	246	95	7,775	Conakry	1,970
Guinea-Bissau	36.1	13.9	1,345	Bissau	900
Guyana	215	83	698	Georgetown	3,600
Haiti	27.8	10.7	7,064	Port-au-Prince	1,700
Honduras	112	43	6,561	Tegucigalpa	2,600
Hong Kong (China)	1.1	0.4	7,303	–	25,000
Hungary	93	35.9	10,075	Budapest	12,000
Iceland	103	40	279	Reykjavik	24,800
India	3,288	1,269	1,045,845	New Delhi	2,500
Indonesia	1,890	730	231,328	Jakarta	3,000
Iran	1,648	636	66,623	Tehran	6,400
Iraq	438	169	24,002	Baghdad	2,500
Ireland	70.3	27.1	3,883	Dublin	27,300
Israel	20.6	7.96	6,030	Jerusalem	20,000
Italy	301	116	57,716	Rome	24,300
Ivory Coast (= Côte d'Ivoire)	322	125	16,805	Yamoussoukro	1,550
Jamaica	11	4.2	2,680	Kingston	3,700
Japan	378	146	126,975	Tokyo	27,200
Jordan	89.2	34.4	5,307	Amman	4,200
Kazakhstan	2,717	1,049	16,742	Astana	5,900
Kenya	580	224	31,139	Nairobi	1,000
Kiribati	0.72	0.28	96	Tarawa	840
Korea, North	121	47	22,224	Pyŏngyang	1,000
Korea, South	99	38.2	48,324	Seoul	18,000
Kuwait	17.8	6.9	2,112	Kuwait City	15,100
Kyrgyzstan	198.5	76.6	4,822	Bishkek	2,800
Laos	237	91	5,777	Vientiane	1,630
Latvia	65	25	2,367	Riga	7,800
Lebanon	10.4	4	3,678	Beirut	5,200
Lesotho	30.4	11.7	2,208	Maseru	2,450
Liberia	111	43	3,288	Monrovia	1,100
Libya	1,760	679	5,369	Tripoli	7,600
Liechtenstein	0.16	0.06	33	Vaduz	23,000
Lithuania	65.2	25.2	3,601	Vilnius	7,600
Luxembourg	2.6	1	449	Luxembourg	43,400
Macau (China)	0.02	0.006	462	–	17,600
Macedonia (FYROM)	25.7	9.9	2,055	Skopje	4,400
Madagascar	587	227	16,473	Antananarivo	870
Madeira (Portugal)	0.81	0.31	241	Funchal	16,800
Malawi	118	46	10,702	Lilongwe	660
Malaysia	330	127	22,662	Kuala Lumpur/Putrajaya	9,000
Maldives	0.3	0.12	320	Malé	3,870
Mali	1,240	479	11,340	Bamako	840
Malta	0.32	0.12	397	Valletta	15,000
Marshall Is.	0.18	0.07	74	Dalap-Uliga-Darrit	1,600
Martinique (France)	1.1	0.42	422	Fort-de-France	11,000
Mauritania	1,030	398	2,829	Nouakchott	1,800
Mauritius	2	0.72	1,200	Port Louis	10,800
Mayotte (France)	0.37	0.14	171	Mamoundzou	600
Mexico	1,958	756	103,400	Mexico City	9,000
Micronesia, Fed. States of	0.7	0.27	136	Palikir	2,000
Moldova	33.7	13	4,435	Chişinău	2,550
Monaco	0.002	0.001	32	Monaco	27,000
Mongolia	1,567	605	2,694	Ulan Bator	1,770
Montserrat (UK)	0.1	0.04	8	Plymouth	2,400
Morocco	447	172	31,168	Rabat	3,700
Mozambique	802	309	19,608	Maputo	900
Namibia	825	318	1,821	Windhoek	4,500
Nauru	0.02	0.008	12	Yaren District	5,000
Nepal	141	54	25,874	Katmandu	1,400
Netherlands	41.5	16	16,068	Amsterdam/The Hague	25,800
Netherlands Antilles (Neths)	0.99	0.38	214	Willemstad	11,400
New Caledonia (France)	18.6	7.2	208	Nouméa	15,000
New Zealand	269	104	3,908	Wellington	19,500
Nicaragua	130	50	5,024	Managua	2,500
Niger	1,267	489	10,640	Niamey	820
Nigeria	924	357	129,935	Abuja	840
Northern Mariana Is. (US)	0.48	0.18	77	Saipan	12,500
Norway	324	125	4,525	Oslo	30,800
Oman	212	82	2,713	Muscat	8,200
Pakistan	796	307	147,663	Islamabad	2,100
Palau	0.46	0.18	19	Koror	9,000
Panama	77.1	29.8	2,882	Panamá	5,900
Papua New Guinea	463	179	5,172	Port Moresby	2,400
Paraguay	407	157	5,884	Asunción	4,600
Peru	1,285	496	27,950	Lima	4,800
Philippines	300	116	84,526	Manila	4,000
Poland	313	121	38,625	Warsaw	8,800
Portugal	92.4	35.7	9,609	Lisbon	17,300
Puerto Rico (US)	9	3.5	3,958	San Juan	11,200
Qatar	11	4.2	793	Doha	21,200
Réunion (France)	2.5	0.97	744	St-Denis	4,800
Romania	238	92	22,318	Bucharest	6,800
Russia	17,075	6,592	144,979	Moscow	8,300
Rwanda	26.3	10.2	7,398	Kigali	1,000
St Kitts & Nevis	0.36	0.14	39	Basseterre	8,700
St Lucia	0.62	0.24	160	Castries	4,400
St Vincent & Grenadines	0.39	0.15	116	Kingstown	2,900
Samoa	2.8	1.1	179	Apia	3,500
San Marino	0.06	0.02	28	San Marino	34,600
São Tomé & Príncipe	0.96	0.37	170	São Tomé	1,200
Saudi Arabia	2,150	830	23,513	Riyadh	10,600
Senegal	197	76	10,590	Dakar	1,580
Serbia & Montenegro	102.3	39.5	10,657	Belgrade	2,250
Seychelles	0.46	0.18	80	Victoria	7,600
Sierra Leone	71.7	27.7	5,615	Freetown	500
Singapore	0.62	0.24	4,453	Singapore	24,700
Slovak Republic	49	18.9	5,422	Bratislava	11,500
Slovenia	20.3	7.8	1,933	Ljubljana	16,000
Solomon Is.	28.9	11.2	495	Honiara	1,700
Somalia	638	246	7,753	Mogadishu	550
South Africa	1,220	471	43,648	C. Town/Pretoria/Bloem.	9,400
Spain	505	195	38,383	Madrid	18,900
Sri Lanka	65.6	25.3	19,577	Colombo	3,250
Sudan	2,506	967	37,090	Khartoum	1,360
Suriname	163	63	436	Paramaribo	3,500
Swaziland	17.4	6.7	1,124	Mbabane	4,200
Sweden	450	174	8,877	Stockholm	24,700
Switzerland	41.3	15.9	7,302	Bern	31,100
Syria	185	71	17,156	Damascus	3,200
Taiwan	36	13.9	22,548	Taipei	17,200
Tajikistan	143.1	55.2	6,720	Dushanbe	1,140
Tanzania	945	365	37,188	Dodoma	610
Thailand	513	198	62,354	Bangkok	6,600
Togo	56.8	21.9	5,286	Lomé	1,500
Tonga	0.75	0.29	106	Nuku'alofa	2,200
Trinidad & Tobago	5.1	2	1,164	Port of Spain	9,000
Tunisia	164	63	9,816	Tunis	6,600
Turkey	779	301	67,309	Ankara	6,700
Turkmenistan	488.1	188.5	4,689	Ashkhabad	4,700
Turks & Caicos Is. (UK)	0.43	0.17	19	Cockburn Town	7,300
Tuvalu	0.03	0.01	11	Fongafale	1,100
Uganda	236	91	24,699	Kampala	1,200
Ukraine	603.7	233.1	48,396	Kiev	4,200
United Arab Emirates	83.6	32.3	2,446	Abu Dhabi	21,100
United Kingdom	243.3	94	59,778	London	24,700
United States of America	9,373	3,619	280,562	Washington, DC	36,300
Uruguay	177	68	3,387	Montevideo	9,200
Uzbekistan	447.4	172.7	25,563	Tashkent	2,500
Vanuatu	12.2	4.7	196	Port-Vila	1,300
Vatican City	0.0004	0.0002	1	Vatican City	N/A
Venezuela	912	352	24,288	Caracas	6,100
Vietnam	332	127	81,098	Hanoi	2,100
Virgin Is. (UK)	0.15	0.06	21	Road Town	16,000
Virgin Is. (US)	0.34	0.13	123	Charlotte Amalie	15,000
Wallis & Futuna Is. (France)	0.2	0.08	16	Mata-Utu	2,000
West Bank (OPT)*	5.86	2.26	2,164	–	1,000
Western Sahara	266	103	256	El Aaiún	N/A
Yemen	528	204	18,701	Sana	820
Zambia	753	291	9,959	Lusaka	870
Zimbabwe	391	151	11,377	Harare	2,450

*OPT = Occupied Palestinian Territory   N/A = Not Available

† Gross Domestic Product per capita has been measured using the purchasing power parity method. This enables comparisons to be made between countries through their purchasing power (in US dollars), showing real price levels of goods and services rather than using currency exchange rates.

World Statistics: Cities

This list shows the principal cities with more than 500,000 inhabitants (only cities with more than 1 million inhabitants are included for Brazil, China, India, Indonesia, Japan and Russia). The figures are taken from the most recent census or estimate available, and as far as possible are the population of the metropolitan area, e.g. greater New York, Mexico or Paris. All the figures are in thousands. Local name forms have been used for the smaller cities (e.g. Kraków).

AFGHANISTAN	
Kabul	1,565
ALGERIA	
Algiers	1,722
Oran	664
ANGOLA	
Luanda	2,250
ARGENTINA	
Buenos Aires	10,990
Córdoba	1,198
Rosario	1,096
Mendoza	775
La Plata	640
San Miguel de Tucumán	622
Mar del Plata	520
ARMENIA	
Yerevan	1,256
AUSTRALIA	
Sydney	4,041
Melbourne	3,417
Brisbane	1,601
Perth	1,364
Adelaide	1,093
AUSTRIA	
Vienna	1,560
AZERBAIJAN	
Baku	1,713
BANGLADESH	
Dhaka	7,832
Chittagong	2,041
Khulna	877
Rajshahi	517
BELARUS	
Minsk	1,717
Homyel	502
BELGIUM	
Brussels	948
BENIN	
Cotonou	537
BOLIVIA	
La Paz	1,126
Santa Cruz	767
BOSNIA-HERZEGOVINA	
Sarajevo	526
BRAZIL	
São Paulo	10,434
Rio de Janeiro	5,858
Salvador	2,443
Belo Horizonte	2,239
Fortaleza	2,141
Brasília	2,051
Curitiba	1,587
Recife	1,423
Manaus	1,406
Pôrto Alegre	1,361
Belém	1,281
Goiânia	1,093
Guarulhos	1,073
BULGARIA	
Sofia	1,139
BURKINA FASO	
Ouagadougou	690
BURMA (MYANMAR)	
Rangoon	2,513
Mandalay	533
CAMBODIA	
Phnom Penh	570
CAMEROON	
Douala	1,200
Yaoundé	800
CANADA	
Toronto	4,881
Montréal	3,511
Vancouver	2,079
Ottawa–Hull	1,107
Calgary	972
Edmonton	957
Québec	693
Winnipeg	685
Hamilton	681
CENTRAL AFRICAN REPUBLIC	
Bangui	553
CHAD	
Ndjaména	530
CHILE	
Santiago	4,691
CHINA	
Shanghai	15,082
Beijing	12,362
Tianjin	10,687
Hong Kong (SAR)*	6,502
Chongqing	3,870
Shenyang	3,762
Wuhan	3,520
Guangzhou	3,114
Harbin	2,505
Nanjing	2,211
Xi'an	2,115
Chengdu	1,933
Dalian	1,855
Changchun	1,810
Jinan	1,660
Taiyuan	1,642
Qingdao	1,584
Zibo	1,346
Zhengzhou	1,324
Lanzhou	1,296
Anshan	1,252
Fushun	1,246
Kunming	1,242
Changsha	1,198
Hangzhou	1,185
Nanchang	1,169
Shijiazhuang	1,159
Guiyang	1,131
Ürümqi	1,130
Jilin	1,118
Tangshan	1,110
Qiqihar	1,104
Baotou	1,033
COLOMBIA	
Bogotá	6,005
Cali	1,986
Medellín	1,971
Barranquilla	1,158
Cartagena	813
Cúcuta	589
Bucaramanga	508
CONGO	
Brazzaville	938
Pointe-Noire	576
CONGO (DEM. REP.)	
Kinshasa	2,664
Lubumbashi	565
CROATIA	
Zagreb	868
CUBA	
Havana	2,204
CZECH REPUBLIC	
Prague	1,203
DENMARK	
Copenhagen	1,362
DOMINICAN REPUBLIC	
Santo Domingo	2,135
Stgo. de los Caballeros	691
ECUADOR	
Guayaquil	2,070
Quito	1,574
EGYPT	
Cairo	6,800
Alexandria	3,339
El Gîza	2,222
Shubra el Kheima	871
EL SALVADOR	
San Salvador	1,522
ETHIOPIA	
Addis Ababa	2,316
FINLAND	
Helsinki	532
FRANCE	
Paris	11,175
Lyons	1,648
Marseilles	1,516
Lille	1,143
Toulouse	965
Nice	933
Bordeaux	925
Nantes	711
Strasbourg	612
Toulon	565
Douai	553
Rennes	521
Rouen	518
Grenoble	515
GEORGIA	
Tbilisi	1,253
GERMANY	
Berlin	3,426
Hamburg	1,705
Munich	1,206
Cologne	964
Frankfurt	644
Essen	609
Dortmund	595
Stuttgart	585
Düsseldorf	571
Bremen	547
Duisburg	529
Hanover	521
GHANA	
Accra	1,781
GREECE	
Athens	3,097
GUATEMALA	
Guatemala	1,167
GUINEA	
Conakry	1,508
HAITI	
Port-au-Prince	885
HONDURAS	
Tegucigalpa	814
HUNGARY	
Budapest	1,885
INDIA	
Mumbai (Bombay)	16,368
Kolkata (Calcutta)	13,217
Delhi	12,791
Chennai (Madras)	6,425
Bangalore	5,687
Hyderabad	5,534
Ahmadabad	4,519
Pune	3,756
Surat	2,811
Kanpur	2,690
Jaipur	2,324
Lucknow	2,267
Nagpur	2,123
Patna	1,707
Indore	1,639
Vadodara	1,492
Bhopal	1,455
Coimbatore	1,446
Ludhiana	1,395
Cochin	1,355
Vishakhapatnam	1,329
Agra	1,321
Varanasi	1,212
Madurai	1,195
Meerut	1,167
Nasik	1,152
Jabalpur	1,117
Jamshedpur	1,102
Asansol	1,090
Faridabad	1,055
Allahabad	1,050
Amritsar	1,011
Vijayawada	1,011
Rajkot	1,002
INDONESIA	
Jakarta	11,500
Surabaya	2,701
Bandung	2,368
Medan	1,910
Semarang	1,366
Palembang	1,352
Tangerang	1,198
Ujung Pandang	1,092
IRAN	
Tehran	6,759
Mashhad	1,887
Esfahan	1,266
Tabriz	1,191
Shiraz	1,053
Karaj	941
Ahvaz	805
Qom	778
Bakhtaran	693
IRAQ	
Baghdad	3,841
As Sulaymaniyah	952
Arbil	770
Al Mawsil	664
Al Kazimiyah	521
IRELAND	
Dublin	1,024
ISRAEL	
Tel Aviv-Yafo	1,880
Jerusalem	591
ITALY	
Rome	2,654
Milan	1,306
Naples	1,050
Turin	923
Palermo	689
Genoa	659
IVORY COAST	
Abidjan	2,500
JAMAICA	
Kingston	644
JAPAN	
Tokyo	17,950
Yokohama	3,427
Osaka	2,599
Nagoya	2,171
Sapporo	1,822
Kobe	1,494
Kyoto	1,468
Fukuoka	1,341
Kawasaki	1,250
Hiroshima	1,126
Kitakyushu	1,011
Sendai	1,008
JORDAN	
Amman	1,752
KAZAKHSTAN	
Almaty	1,151
Qaraghandy	574
KENYA	
Nairobi	2,000
Mombasa	600
KOREA, NORTH	
Pyŏngyang	2,741
Hamhung	710
Chŏngjin	583
KOREA, SOUTH	
Seoul	10,231
Pusan	3,814
Taegu	2,449
Inch'on	2,308
Taejŏn	1,272
Kwangju	1,258
Ulsan	967
Sŏngnam	869
Puch'on	779
Suwŏn	756
Anyang	590
Chŏnju	563
Chŏngju	531
Ansan	510
P'ohang	509
KYRGYZSTAN	
Bishkek	589
LAOS	
Vientiane	532
LATVIA	
Riga	811
LEBANON	
Beirut	1,500
Tripoli	500
LIBERIA	
Monrovia	962
LIBYA	
Tripoli	960
LITHUANIA	
Vilnius	580
MACEDONIA	
Skopje	541
MADAGASCAR	
Antananarivo	1,053
MALAYSIA	
Kuala Lumpur	1,145
MALI	
Bamako	810
MAURITANIA	
Nouakchott	735
MEXICO	
Mexico City	15,643
Guadalajara	2,847
Monterrey	2,522
Puebla	1,055
León	872
Ciudad Juárez	798
Tijuana	743
Culiacán	602
Mexicali	602
Acapulco	592
Mérida	557
Chihuahua	530
San Luis Potosí	526
Aguascalientés	506
MOLDOVA	
Chişinău	658
MONGOLIA	
Ulan Bator	673
MOROCCO	
Casablanca	2,943
Rabat-Salé	1,220
Marrakesh	602
Fès	564
MOZAMBIQUE	
Maputo	2,000
NEPAL	
Katmandu	535
NETHERLANDS	
Amsterdam	1,115
Rotterdam	1,086
The Hague	700
Utrecht	557
NEW ZEALAND	
Auckland	1,090
NICARAGUA	
Managua	864
NIGERIA	
Lagos	10,287
Ibadan	1,432
Ogbomosho	730
Kano	674
NORWAY	
Oslo	502
PAKISTAN	
Karachi	9,269
Lahore	5,064
Faisalabad	1,977
Rawalpindi	1,406
Multan	1,182
Hyderabad	1,151
Gujranwala	1,125
Peshawar	988
Quetta	560
Islamabad	525
PARAGUAY	
Asunción	945
PERU	
Lima	6,601
Arequipa	620
Trujillo	509
PHILIPPINES	
Manila	8,594
Quezon City	1,989
Caloocan	1,023
Davao	1,009
Cebu	662
Zamboanga	511
POLAND	
Warsaw	1,626
Łódź	815
Kraków	740
Wroclaw	641
Poznań	580
PORTUGAL	
Lisbon	2,561
Oporto	1,174
ROMANIA	
Bucharest	2,028
RUSSIA	
Moscow	8,405
St Petersburg	4,216
Nizhniy Novgorod	1,371
Novosibirsk	1,367
Yekaterinburg	1,275
Samara	1,170
Omsk	1,158
Kazan	1,085
Chelyabinsk	1,084
Ufa	1,082
Perm	1,025
Rostov	1,023
Volgograd	1,005
SAUDI ARABIA	
Riyadh	1,800
Jedda	1,500
Mecca	630
SENEGAL	
Dakar	1,905
SIERRA LEONE	
Freetown	505
SINGAPORE	
Singapore	3,866
SOMALIA	
Mogadishu	997
SOUTH AFRICA	
Cape Town	2,350
Johannesburg	1,196
Durban	1,137
Pretoria	1,080
Port Elizabeth	853
Vanderbijlpark–Vereeniging	774
Soweto	597
Sasolburg	540
SPAIN	
Madrid	3,030
Barcelona	1,615
Valencia	763
Sevilla	720
Zaragoza	608
Málaga	532
SRI LANKA	
Colombo	1,863
SUDAN	
Omdurman	1,271
Khartoum	925
Khartoum North	701
SWEDEN	
Stockholm	727
SWITZERLAND	
Zürich	733
SYRIA	
Aleppo	1,813
Damascus	1,394
Homs	659
TAIWAN	
T'aipei	2,596
Kaohsiung	1,435
T'aichung	858
T'ainan	708
Panch'iao	539
TAJIKISTAN	
Dushanbe	524
TANZANIA	
Dar-es-Salaam	1,361
THAILAND	
Bangkok	7,507
TOGO	
Lomé	590
TUNISIA	
Tunis	1,827
TURKEY	
Istanbul	8,506
Ankara	3,294
Izmir	2,554
Bursa	1,485
Adana	1,273
Konya	1,140
Mersin (Içel)	956
Gaziantep	867
Antalya	867
Kayseri	862
Diyarbakir	833
Urfa	785
Manisa	696
Kocaeli	629
Antalya	591
Samsun	590
Kahramanmaras	551
Balikesir	538
Eskisehir	519
Erzurum	512
Malatya	510
TURKMENISTAN	
Ashkhabad	536
UGANDA	
Kampala	954
UKRAINE	
Kiev	2,621
Kharkov	1,521
Dnepropetrovsk	1,122
Donetsk	1,065
Odessa	1,027
Zaporizhzhya	863
Lviv	794
Kryvyy Rih	720
Mykolayiv	518
Mariupol	500
UNITED ARAB EMIRATES	
Abu Dhabi	928
Dubai	674
UNITED KINGDOM	
London	8,089
Birmingham	2,373
Manchester	2,353
Liverpool	852
Glasgow	832
Sheffield	661
Nottingham	649
Newcastle	617
Bristol	552
Leeds	529
UNITED STATES	
New York	21,200
Los Angeles	16,374
Chicago–Gary	9,158
Washington–Baltimore	7,608
San Francisco–San Jose	7,039
Philadelphia–Atlantic City	6,188
Boston–Worcester	5,819
Detroit–Flint	5,456
Dallas–Fort Worth	5,222
Houston–Galveston	4,670
Atlanta	4,112
Miami–Fort Lauderdale	3,876
Seattle–Tacoma	3,554
Phoenix–Mesa	3,252
Minneapolis–St Paul	2,969
Cleveland–Akron	2,946
San Diego	2,814
St Louis	2,604
Denver–Boulder	2,582
San Juan	2,450
Tampa–Saint Petersburg	2,396
Pittsburgh	2,359
Portland–Salem	2,265
Cincinnati–Hamilton	1,979
Sacramento–Yolo	1,797
Kansas City	1,776
Milwaukee–Racine	1,690
Orlando	1,645
Indianapolis	1,607
San Antonio	1,592
Norfolk–Virginia Beach –Newport News	1,570
Las Vegas	1,563
Columbus, OH	1,540
Charlotte–Gastonia	1,499
New Orleans	1,338
Salt Lake City	1,334
Greensboro–Winston Salem–High Point	1,252
Austin–San Marcos	1,250
Nashville	1,231
Providence–Fall River	1,189
Raleigh–Durham	1,188
Hartford	1,183
Buffalo–Niagara Falls	1,170
Memphis	1,136
West Palm Beach	1,131
Jacksonville, FL	1,100
Rochester	1,098
Grand Rapids	1,089
Oklahoma City	1,083
Louisville	1,026
Richmond–Petersburg	997
Greenville	962
Dayton–Springfield	951
Fresno	923
Birmingham	921
Honolulu	876
Albany–Schenectady	876
Tucson	844
Tulsa	803
Syracuse	732
Omaha	717
Albuquerque	713
Knoxville	687
El Paso	680
Bakersfield	662
Allentown	638
Harrisburg	629
Scranton	625
Toledo	618
Baton Rouge	603
Youngstown–Warren	595
Springfield, MA	592
Sarasota	590
Little Rock	584
McAllen	569
Stockton–Lodi	564
Charleston	549
Wichita	545
Mobile	540
Columbia, SC	537
Colorado Springs	517
Fort Wayne	502
URUGUAY	
Montevideo	1,379
UZBEKISTAN	
Tashkent	2,118
VENEZUELA	
Caracas	1,975
Maracaibo	1,706
Valencia	1,263
Barquisimeto	811
Ciudad Guayana	642
VIETNAM	
Ho Chi Minh City	4,322
Hanoi	3,056
Haiphong	783
YEMEN	
Sana'	972
Aden	562
YUGOSLAVIA	
Belgrade	1,598
ZAMBIA	
Lusaka	982
ZIMBABWE	
Harare	1,189
Bulawayo	622

* SAR = Special Administrative Region of China

World Statistics: Climate

Rainfall and temperature figures are provided for more than 70 cities around the world. As climate is affected by altitude, the height of each city is shown in metres beneath its name. For each location, the top row of figures shows the total rainfall or snow in millimetres, and the bottom row the average temperature in degrees Celsius; the average annual temperature and total annual rainfall are at the end of the rows. The map opposite shows the city locations.

CITY	JAN.	FEB.	MAR.	APR.	MAY	JUNE	JULY	AUG.	SEPT.	OCT.	NOV.	DEC.	YEAR
EUROPE													
Athens, Greece	62	37	37	23	23	14	6	7	15	51	56	71	402
107 m	10	10	12	16	20	25	28	28	24	20	15	11	18
Berlin, Germany	46	40	33	42	49	65	73	69	48	49	46	43	603
55 m	–1	0	4	9	14	17	19	18	15	9	5	1	9
Istanbul, Turkey	109	92	72	46	38	34	34	30	58	81	103	119	816
14 m	5	6	7	11	16	20	23	23	20	16	12	8	14
Lisbon, Portugal	111	76	109	54	44	16	3	4	33	62	93	103	708
77 m	11	12	14	16	17	20	22	23	21	18	14	12	17
London, UK	54	40	37	37	46	45	57	59	49	57	64	48	593
5 m	4	5	7	9	12	16	18	17	15	11	8	5	11
Málaga, Spain	61	51	62	46	26	5	1	3	29	64	64	62	474
33 m	12	13	16	17	19	29	25	26	23	20	16	13	18
Moscow, Russia	39	38	36	37	53	58	88	71	58	45	47	54	624
156 m	–13	–10	–4	6	13	16	18	17	12	6	–1	–7	4
Odesa, Ukraine	57	62	30	21	34	34	42	37	37	13	35	71	473
64 m	–3	–1	2	9	15	20	22	22	18	12	9	1	10
Paris, France	56	46	35	42	57	54	59	64	55	50	51	50	619
75 m	3	4	8	11	15	18	20	19	17	12	7	4	12
Rome, Italy	71	62	57	51	46	37	15	21	63	99	129	93	744
17 m	8	9	11	14	18	22	25	25	22	17	13	10	16
Shannon, Ireland	94	67	56	53	61	57	77	79	86	86	96	117	929
2 m	5	5	7	9	12	14	16	16	14	11	8	6	10
Stockholm, Sweden	43	30	25	31	34	45	61	76	60	48	53	48	554
44 m	–3	–3	–1	5	10	15	18	17	12	7	3	0	7
ASIA													
Bahrain	8	18	13	8	<3	0	0	0	0	0	18	18	81
5 m	17	18	21	25	29	32	33	34	31	28	24	19	26
Bangkok, Thailand	8	20	36	58	198	160	160	175	305	206	66	5	1,397
2 m	26	28	29	30	29	29	28	28	28	28	26	25	28
Beirut, Lebanon	191	158	94	53	18	3	<3	<3	5	51	132	185	892
34 m	14	14	16	18	22	24	27	28	26	24	19	16	21
Colombo, Sri Lanka	89	69	147	231	371	224	135	109	160	348	315	147	2,365
7 m	26	26	27	28	28	27	27	27	27	27	26	26	27
Harbin, China	6	5	10	23	43	94	112	104	46	33	8	5	488
160 m	–18	–15	–5	6	13	19	22	21	14	4	–6	–16	3
Ho Chi Minh, Vietnam	15	3	13	43	221	330	315	269	335	269	114	56	1,984
9 m	26	27	29	30	29	28	28	28	27	27	27	26	28
Hong Kong, China	33	46	74	137	292	394	381	361	257	114	43	31	2,162
33 m	16	15	18	22	26	28	28	28	27	25	21	18	23

CITY	JAN.	FEB.	MAR.	APR.	MAY	JUNE	JULY	AUG.	SEPT.	OCT.	NOV.	DEC.	YEAR
ASIA (continued)													
Jakarta, Indonesia	300	300	211	147	114	97	64	43	66	112	142	203	1,798
8 m	26	26	27	27	27	27	27	27	27	27	27	26	27
Kabul, Afghanistan	31	36	94	102	20	5	3	3	<3	15	20	10	338
1,815 m	–3	–1	6	13	18	22	25	24	20	14	7	3	12
Karachi, Pakistan	13	10	8	3	3	18	81	41	13	<3	3	5	196
4 m	19	20	24	28	30	31	30	29	28	28	24	20	26
Kazalinsk, Kazakhstan	10	10	13	13	15	5	5	8	8	10	13	15	125
63 m	–12	–11	–3	6	18	23	25	23	16	8	–1	–7	7
Kolkata (Calcutta), India	10	31	36	43	140	297	325	328	252	114	20	5	1,600
6 m	20	22	27	30	30	30	29	29	29	28	23	19	26
Mumbai (Bombay), India	3	3	3	<3	18	485	617	340	264	64	13	3	1,809
11 m	24	24	26	28	30	29	27	27	27	28	27	26	27
New Delhi, India	23	18	13	8	13	74	180	172	117	10	3	10	640
218 m	14	17	23	28	33	34	31	30	29	26	20	15	25
Omsk, Russia	15	8	8	13	31	51	51	51	28	25	18	20	318
85 m	–22	–19	–12	–1	10	16	18	16	10	1	–11	–18	–1
Shanghai, China	48	58	84	94	94	180	147	142	130	71	51	36	1,135
7 m	4	5	9	14	20	24	28	28	23	19	12	7	16
Singapore	252	173	193	188	173	173	170	196	178	208	254	257	2,413
10 m	26	27	28	28	28	28	28	27	27	27	27	27	27
Tehran, Iran	46	38	46	36	13	3	3	3	3	8	20	31	246
1,220 m	2	5	9	16	21	26	30	29	25	18	12	6	17
Tokyo, Japan	48	74	107	135	147	165	142	152	234	208	97	56	1,565
6 m	3	4	7	13	17	21	25	26	23	17	11	6	14
Ulan Bator, Mongolia	<3	<3	3	5	10	28	76	51	23	5	5	3	208
1,325 m	–26	–21	–13	–1	6	14	16	14	8	–1	–13	–22	–3
Verkhoyansk, Russia	5	5	3	5	8	23	28	25	13	8	8	5	134
100 m	–50	–45	–32	–15	0	12	14	9	2	–15	–38	–48	–17
AFRICA													
Addis Ababa, Ethiopia	<3	3	25	135	213	201	206	239	102	28	<3	0	1,151
2,450 m	19	20	20	20	19	18	18	19	21	22	21	20	20
Antananarivo, Madag.	300	279	178	53	18	8	8	10	18	61	135	287	1,356
1,372 m	21	21	21	19	18	15	14	15	17	19	21	21	19
Cairo, Egypt	5	5	5	3	3	<3	0	0	<3	<3	3	5	28
116 m	13	15	18	21	25	28	28	28	26	24	20	15	22
Cape Town, S. Africa	15	8	18	48	79	84	89	66	43	31	18	10	508
17 m	21	21	20	17	14	13	12	13	14	16	18	19	17
Jo'burg, S. Africa	114	109	89	38	25	8	8	8	23	56	107	125	709
1,665 m	20	20	18	16	13	10	11	13	16	18	19	20	16

CITY	JAN.	FEB.	MAR.	APR.	MAY	JUNE	JULY	AUG.	SEPT.	OCT.	NOV.	DEC.	YEAR
AFRICA (continued)													
Khartoum, Sudan	<3	<3	<3	<3	3	8	53	71	18	5	<3	0	158
390 m	24	25	28	31	33	34	32	31	32	32	28	25	29
Kinshasa, Congo (D.R.)	135	145	196	196	158	8	3	3	31	119	221	142	1,354
325 m	26	26	27	27	26	24	23	24	25	26	26	26	25
Lagos, Nigeria	28	46	102	150	269	460	279	64	140	206	69	25	1,836
3 m	27	28	29	28	28	26	26	25	26	26	28	28	27
Lusaka, Zambia	231	191	142	18	3	<3	<3	0	<3	10	91	150	836
1,277 m	21	22	21	21	19	16	16	18	22	24	23	22	21
Monrovia, Liberia	31	56	97	216	516	973	996	373	744	772	236	130	5,138
23 m	26	26	27	27	26	25	24	25	25	25	26	26	26
Nairobi, Kenya	38	64	125	211	158	46	15	23	31	53	109	86	958
820 m	19	19	19	19	18	16	16	16	18	19	18	18	18
Timbuktu, Mali	<3	<3	3	<3	5	23	79	81	38	3	<3	<3	231
301 m	22	24	28	32	34	35	32	30	32	31	28	23	29
Tunis, Tunisia	64	51	41	36	18	8	3	8	33	51	48	61	419
66 m	10	11	13	16	19	23	26	27	25	20	16	11	18
Walvis Bay, Namibia	<3	5	8	3	3	<3	<3	3	<3	<3	<3	<3	23
7 m	19	19	19	18	17	16	15	14	14	15	17	18	18
AUSTRALIA, NEW ZEALAND AND ANTARCTICA													
Alice Springs, Aust.	43	33	28	10	15	13	8	8	8	18	31	38	252
579 m	29	28	25	20	15	12	12	14	18	23	26	28	21
Christchurch, N.Z.	56	43	48	48	66	66	69	48	46	43	48	56	638
10 m	16	16	14	12	9	6	6	7	9	12	14	16	11
Darwin, Australia	386	312	254	97	15	3	<3	3	13	51	119	239	1,491
30 m	29	29	29	29	28	26	25	26	28	29	30	29	28
Mawson, Antarctica	11	30	20	10	44	180	4	40	3	20	0	0	362
14 m	0	–5	–10	–14	–15	–16	–18	–18	–19	–13	–5	–1	–11
Perth, Australia	8	10	20	43	130	180	170	149	86	56	20	13	881
60 m	23	23	22	19	16	14	13	13	15	16	19	22	18
Sydney, Australia	89	102	127	135	127	117	117	76	73	71	73	73	1,181
42 m	22	22	21	18	15	13	12	13	15	18	19	21	17
NORTH AMERICA													
Anchorage, USA	20	18	15	10	13	18	41	66	66	56	25	23	371
40 m	–11	–8	–5	2	7	12	14	13	9	2	–5	–11	2
Chicago, USA	51	51	66	71	86	89	84	81	79	66	61	51	836
251 m	–4	–3	2	9	14	20	23	22	19	12	5	–1	10
Churchill, Canada	15	13	18	23	32	44	46	58	51	43	39	21	402
13 m	–28	–26	–20	–10	–2	6	12	11	5	–2	–12	–22	–7
Edmonton, Canada	25	19	19	22	43	77	89	78	39	17	16	25	466
676 m	–15	–10	–5	4	11	15	17	16	11	6	–4	–10	3
Honolulu, USA	104	66	79	48	25	18	23	28	36	48	64	104	643
12 m	23	18	19	20	22	24	25	26	26	24	22	19	22
Houston, USA	89	76	84	91	119	117	99	99	104	94	89	109	1,171
12 m	12	13	17	21	24	27	28	29	26	22	16	12	21

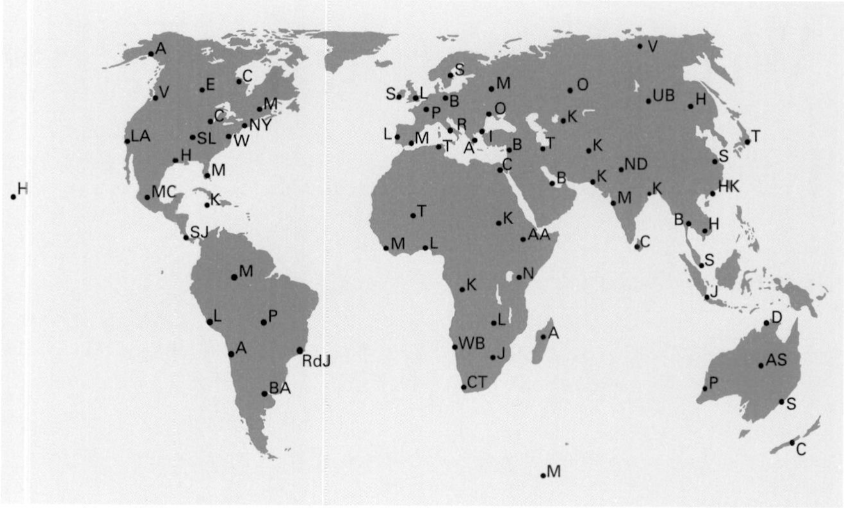

CITY	JAN.	FEB.	MAR.	APR.	MAY	JUNE	JULY	AUG.	SEPT.	OCT.	NOV.	DEC.	YEAR
NORTH AMERICA (continued)													
Kingston, Jamaica	23	15	23	31	102	89	38	91	99	180	74	36	800
34 m	25	25	25	26	26	28	28	28	27	27	26	26	26
Los Angeles, USA	79	76	71	25	10	3	<3	<3	5	15	31	66	381
95 m	13	14	14	16	17	19	21	22	21	18	16	14	17
Mexico City, Mexico	13	5	10	20	53	119	170	152	130	51	18	8	747
2,309 m	12	13	16	18	19	19	17	18	18	16	14	13	16
Miami, USA	71	53	64	81	173	178	155	160	203	234	71	51	1,516
8 m	20	20	22	23	25	27	28	28	27	25	22	21	24
Montréal, Canada	72	65	74	74	66	82	90	92	88	76	81	87	946
57 m	–10	–9	–3	–6	13	18	21	20	15	9	2	–7	6
New York City, USA	94	97	91	81	81	84	107	109	86	89	76	91	1,092
96 m	–1	–1	3	10	16	20	23	23	21	15	7	2	11
St Louis, USA	58	64	89	97	114	114	89	86	81	74	71	64	1,001
173 m	0	1	7	13	19	24	26	26	22	15	8	2	14
San José, Costa Rica	15	5	20	46	229	241	211	241	305	300	145	41	1,798
1,146 m	19	19	21	21	22	21	21	21	21	20	20	19	20
Vancouver, Canada	154	115	101	60	52	45	32	41	67	114	150	182	1,113
14 m	3	5	6	9	12	15	17	17	14	10	6	4	10
Washington, DC, USA	86	76	91	84	94	99	112	109	94	74	66	79	1,064
22 m	1	2	7	12	18	23	25	24	20	14	8	3	13
SOUTH AMERICA													
Antofagasta, Chile	0	0	0	<3	<3	3	5	3	<3	3	<3	0	13
94 m	21	21	20	18	16	15	14	14	15	16	18	19	17
Buenos Aires, Arg.	79	71	109	89	76	61	56	61	79	86	84	99	950
27 m	23	23	21	17	13	9	10	11	13	15	19	22	16
Lima, Peru	3	<3	<3	<3	5	5	8	8	8	3	3	<3	41
120 m	23	24	24	22	19	17	17	16	17	18	19	21	20
Manaus, Brazil	249	231	262	221	170	84	58	38	46	107	142	203	1,811
44 m	28	28	28	27	28	28	28	28	29	29	29	28	28
Paraná, Brazil	287	236	239	102	13	<3	3	5	28	127	231	310	1,582
260 m	23	23	23	23	23	21	21	22	24	24	24	23	23
Rio de Janeiro, Brazil	125	122	130	107	79	53	41	43	66	79	104	137	1,082
61 m	26	26	25	24	22	21	21	21	21	22	23	25	23

World Statistics: Physical Dimensions

Each topic list is divided into continents and within a continent the items are listed in order of size. The bottom part of many of the lists is selective in order to give examples from as many different countries as possible. The order of the continents is as in the atlas, Europe through to South America. The world top ten are shown in square brackets; in the case of mountains this has not been done because the world top 30 are all in Asia. The figures are rounded as appropriate.

WORLD, CONTINENTS, OCEANS

THE WORLD	km²	miles²	%
The World	509,450,000	196,672,000	–
Land	149,450,000	57,688,000	29.3
Water	360,000,000	138,984,000	70.7
Asia	44,500,000	17,177,000	29.8
Africa	30,302,000	11,697,000	20.3
North America	24,241,000	9,357,000	16.2
South America	17,793,000	6,868,000	11.9
Antarctica	14,100,000	5,443,000	9.4
Europe	9,957,000	3,843,000	6.7
Australia & Oceania	8,557,000	3,303,000	5.7
Pacific Ocean	179,679,000	69,356,000	49.9
Atlantic Ocean	92,373,000	35,657,000	25.7
Indian Ocean	73,917,000	28,532,000	20.5
Arctic Ocean	14,090,000	5,439,000	3.9

SEAS

PACIFIC	km²	miles²
South China Sea	2,974,600	1,148,500
Bering Sea	2,268,000	875,000
Sea of Okhotsk	1,528,000	590,000
East China & Yellow	1,249,000	482,000
Sea of Japan	1,008,000	389,000
Gulf of California	162,000	62,500
Bass Strait	75,000	29,000

ATLANTIC	km²	miles²
Caribbean Sea	2,766,000	1,068,000
Mediterranean Sea	2,516,000	971,000
Gulf of Mexico	1,543,000	596,000
Hudson Bay	1,232,000	476,000
North Sea	575,000	223,000
Black Sea	462,000	178,000
Baltic Sea	422,170	163,000
Gulf of St Lawrence	238,000	92,000

INDIAN	km²	miles²
Red Sea	438,000	169,000
The Gulf	239,000	92,000

MOUNTAINS

EUROPE		m	ft
Elbrus	Russia	5,642	18,510
Mont Blanc	France/Italy	4,807	15,771
Monte Rosa	Italy/Switzerland	4,634	15,203
Dom	Switzerland	4,545	14,911
Liskamm	Switzerland	4,527	14,852
Weisshorn	Switzerland	4,505	14,780
Taschorn	Switzerland	4,490	14,730
Matterhorn/Cervino	Italy/Switz.	4,478	14,691
Mont Maudit	France/Italy	4,465	14,649
Dent Blanche	Switzerland	4,356	14,291
Nadelhorn	Switzerland	4,327	14,196
Grandes Jorasses	France/Italy	4,208	13,806
Jungfrau	Switzerland	4,158	13,642
Barre des Ecrins	France	4,103	13,461
Gran Paradiso	Italy	4,061	13,323
Piz Bernina	Italy/Switzerland	4,049	13,284
Eiger	Switzerland	3,970	13,025
Monte Viso	Italy	3,841	12,602
Grossglockner	Austria	3,797	12,457
Wildspitze	Austria	3,772	12,382
Monte Disgrazia	Italy	3,678	12,066
Mulhacén	Spain	3,478	11,411
Pico de Aneto	Spain	3,404	11,168
Marmolada	Italy	3,342	10,964
Etna	Italy	3,340	10,958
Zugspitze	Germany	2,962	9,718
Musala	Bulgaria	2,925	9,596
Olympus	Greece	2,917	9,570
Triglav	Slovenia	2,863	9,393
Monte Cinto	France (Corsica)	2,710	8,891
Galdhöpiggen	Norway	2,468	8,100
Ben Nevis	UK	1,343	4,406

ASIA		m	ft
Everest	China/Nepal	8,850	29,035
K2 (Godwin Austen)	China/Kashmir	8,611	28,251
Kanchenjunga	India/Nepal	8,598	28,208
Lhotse	China/Nepal	8,516	27,939
Makalu	China/Nepal	8,481	27,824
Cho Oyu	China/Nepal	8,201	26,906
Dhaulagiri	Nepal	8,172	26,811
Manaslu	Nepal	8,156	26,758
Nanga Parbat	Kashmir	8,126	26,660
Annapurna	Nepal	8,078	26,502
Gasherbrum	China/Kashmir	8,068	26,469
Broad Peak	China/Kashmir	8,051	26,414
Xixabangma	China	8,012	26,286
Kangbachen	India/Nepal	7,902	25,925
Jannu	India/Nepal	7,902	25,925
Gayachung Kang	Nepal	7,897	25,909
Himalchuli	Nepal	7,893	25,896
Disteghil Sar	Kashmir	7,885	25,869
Nuptse	Nepal	7,879	25,849
Khunyang Chhish	Kashmir	7,852	25,761
Masherbrum	Kashmir	7,821	25,659
Nanda Devi	India	7,817	25,646
Rakaposhi	Kashmir	7,788	25,551
Batura	Kashmir	7,785	25,541
Namche Barwa	China	7,756	25,446
Kamet	India	7,756	25,446
Soltoro Kangri	Kashmir	7,742	25,400
Gurla Mandhata	China	7,728	25,354
Trivor	Pakistan	7,720	25,328
Kongur Shan	China	7,719	25,324
Tirich Mir	Pakistan	7,690	25,229
K'ula Shan	Bhutan/China	7,543	24,747
Pik Kommunizma	Tajikistan	7,495	24,590
Demavend	Iran	5,604	18,386
Ararat	Turkey	5,165	16,945
Gunong Kinabalu	Malaysia (Borneo)	4,101	13,455
Yu Shan	Taiwan	3,997	13,113
Fuji-San	Japan	3,776	12,388

AFRICA		m	ft
Kilimanjaro	Tanzania	5,895	19,340
Mt Kenya	Kenya	5,199	17,057
Ruwenzori (Margherita)	Uganda/Congo (D.R.)	5,109	16,762
Ras Dashan	Ethiopia	4,620	15,157
Meru	Tanzania	4,565	14,977
Karisimbi	Rwanda/Congo (D.R.)	4,507	14,787
Mt Elgon	Kenya/Uganda	4,321	14,176
Batu	Ethiopia	4,307	14,130
Guna	Ethiopia	4,231	13,882
Toubkal	Morocco	4,165	13,665
Irhil Mgoun	Morocco	4,071	13,356
Mt Cameroon	Cameroon	4,070	13,353
Amba Ferit	Ethiopia	3,875	13,042
Pico del Teide	Spain (Tenerife)	3,718	12,198
Thabana Ntlenyana	Lesotho	3,482	11,424
Emi Koussi	Chad	3,415	11,204
Mt aux Sources	Lesotho/S. Africa	3,282	10,768
Mt Piton	Réunion	3,069	10,069

OCEANIA		m	ft
Puncak Jaya	Indonesia	5,030	16,503
Puncak Trikora	Indonesia	4,750	15,584
Puncak Mandala	Indonesia	4,702	15,427
Mt Wilhelm	Papua NG	4,508	14,790
Mauna Kea	USA (Hawaii)	4,205	13,796
Mauna Loa	USA (Hawaii)	4,169	13,681
Mt Cook (Aoraki)	New Zealand	3,753	12,313
Mt Balbi	Solomon Is.	2,439	8,002
Orohena	Tahiti	2,241	7,352
Mt Kosciuszko	Australia	2,237	7,339

NORTH AMERICA		m	ft
Mt McKinley (Denali)	USA (Alaska)	6,194	20,321
Mt Logan	Canada	5,959	19,551
Pico de Orizaba	Mexico	5,610	18,405
Mt St Elias	USA/Canada	5,489	18,008
Popocatepetl	Mexico	5,452	17,887

NORTH AMERICA (continued)		m	ft
Mt Foraker	USA (Alaska)	5,304	17,401
Ixtaccihuatl	Mexico	5,286	17,342
Lucania	Canada	5,227	17,149
Mt Steele	Canada	5,073	16,644
Mt Bona	USA (Alaska)	5,005	16,420
Mt Blackburn	USA (Alaska)	4,996	16,391
Mt Sanford	USA (Alaska)	4,940	16,207
Mt Wood	Canada	4,848	15,905
Nevado de Toluca	Mexico	4,670	15,321
Mt Fairweather	USA (Alaska)	4,663	15,298
Mt Hunter	USA (Alaska)	4,442	14,573
Mt Whitney	USA	4,418	14,495
Mt Elbert	USA	4,399	14,432
Mt Harvard	USA	4,395	14,419
Mt Rainier	USA	4,392	14,409
Blanca Peak	USA	4,372	14,344
Longs Peak	USA	4,345	14,255
Tajumulco	Guatemala	4,220	13,845
Grand Teton	USA	4,197	13,770
Mt Waddington	Canada	3,994	13,104
Mt Robson	Canada	3,954	12,972
Chirripó Grande	Costa Rica	3,837	12,589
Pico Duarte	Dominican Rep.	3,175	10,417

SOUTH AMERICA		m	ft
Aconcagua	Argentina	6,962	22,841
Bonete	Argentina	6,872	22,546
Ojos del Salado	Argentina/Chile	6,863	22,516
Pissis	Argentina	6,779	22,241
Mercedario	Argentina/Chile	6,770	22,211
Huascaran	Peru	6,768	22,204
Llullaillaco	Argentina/Chile	6,723	22,057
Nudo de Cachi	Argentina	6,720	22,047
Yerupaja	Peru	6,632	21,758
N. de Tres Cruces	Argentina/Chile	6,620	21,719
Incahuasi	Argentina/Chile	6,601	21,654
Cerro Galan	Argentina	6,600	21,654
Tupungato	Argentina/Chile	6,570	21,555
Sajama	Bolivia	6,542	21,463
Illimani	Bolivia	6,485	21,276
Coropuna	Peru	6,425	21,079
Ausangate	Peru	6,384	20,945
Cerro del Toro	Argentina	6,380	20,932
Siula Grande	Peru	6,356	20,853
Chimborazo	Ecuador	6,267	20,561
Alpamayo	Peru	5,947	19,511
Cotapaxi	Ecuador	5,896	19,344
Pico Colon	Colombia	5,800	19,029
Pico Bolivar	Venezuela	5,007	16,427

ANTARCTICA		m	ft
Vinson Massif		4,897	16,066
Mt Kirkpatrick		4,528	14,855
Mt Markham		4,349	14,268

OCEAN DEPTHS

ATLANTIC OCEAN	m	ft	
Puerto Rico (Milwaukee) Deep	9,220	30,249	[7]
Cayman Trench	7,680	25,197	[10]
Gulf of Mexico	5,203	17,070	
Mediterranean Sea	5,121	16,801	
Black Sea	2,211	7,254	
North Sea	660	2,165	
Baltic Sea	463	1,519	
Hudson Bay	258	846	

INDIAN OCEAN	m	ft
Java Trench	7,450	24,442
Red Sea	2,635	8,454
Persian Gulf	73	239

PACIFIC OCEAN	m	ft	
Mariana Trench	11,022	36,161	[1]
Tonga Trench	10,882	35,702	[2]
Japan Trench	10,554	34,626	[3]
Kuril Trench	10,542	34,587	[4]
Mindanao Trench	10,497	34,439	[5]
Kermadec Trench	10,047	32,962	[6]

PACIFIC OCEAN (continued)	m	ft	
Peru–Chile Trench	8,050	26,410	[8]
Aleutian Trench	7,822	25,662	[9]

ARCTIC OCEAN	m	ft
Molloy Deep	5,608	18,399

LAND LOWS

		m	ft
Dead Sea	Asia	–411	–1,348
Lake Assal	Africa	–156	–512
Death Valley	N. America	–86	–282
Valdés Peninsula	S. America	–40	–131
Caspian Sea	Europe	–28	–92
Lake Eyre North	Oceania	–16	–52

RIVERS

EUROPE		km	miles
Volga	Caspian Sea	3,700	2,300
Danube	Black Sea	2,850	1,770
Ural	Caspian Sea	2,535	1,575
Dnepr (Dnipro)	Black Sea	2,285	1,420
Kama	Volga	2,030	1,260
Don	Black Sea	1,990	1,240
Petchora	Arctic Ocean	1,790	1,110
Oka	Volga	1,480	920
Belaya	Kama	1,420	880
Dnister (Dniester)	Black Sea	1,400	870
Vyatka	Kama	1,370	850
Rhine	North Sea	1,320	820
N. Dvina	Arctic Ocean	1,290	800
Desna	Dnepr (Dnipro)	1,190	740
Elbe	North Sea	1,145	710
Wisla	Baltic Sea	1,090	675
Loire	Atlantic Ocean	1,020	635

ASIA		km	miles	
Yangtze	Pacific Ocean	6,380	3,960	[3]
Yenisey–Angara	Arctic Ocean	5,550	3,445	[5]
Huang He	Pacific Ocean	5,464	3,395	[6]
Ob–Irtysh	Arctic Ocean	5,410	3,360	[7]
Mekong	Pacific Ocean	4,500	2,795	[9]
Amur	Pacific Ocean	4,400	2,730	[10]
Lena	Arctic Ocean	4,400	2,730	
Irtysh	Ob	4,250	2,640	
Yenisey	Arctic Ocean	4,090	2,540	
Ob	Arctic Ocean	3,680	2,285	
Indus	Indian Ocean	3,100	1,925	
Brahmaputra	Indian Ocean	2,900	1,800	
Syrdarya	Aral Sea	2,860	1,775	
Salween	Indian Ocean	2,800	1,740	
Euphrates	Indian Ocean	2,700	1,675	
Vilyuy	Lena	2,650	1,645	
Kolyma	Arctic Ocean	2,600	1,615	
Amudarya	Aral Sea	2,540	1,575	
Ural	Caspian Sea	2,535	1,575	
Ganges	Indian Ocean	2,510	1,560	
Si Kiang	Pacific Ocean	2,100	1,305	
Irrawaddy	Indian Ocean	2,010	1,250	
Tarim–Yarkand	Lop Nor	2,000	1,240	
Tigris	Indian Ocean	1,900	1,180	

AFRICA		km	miles	
Nile	Mediterranean	6,670	4,140	[1]
Congo	Atlantic Ocean	4,670	2,900	[8]
Niger	Atlantic Ocean	4,180	2,595	
Zambezi	Indian Ocean	3,540	2,200	
Oubangi/Uele	Congo (D.R.)	2,250	1,400	
Kasai	Congo (D.R.)	1,950	1,210	
Shaballe	Indian Ocean	1,930	1,200	
Orange	Atlantic Ocean	1,860	1,155	
Cubango	Okavango Delta	1,800	1,120	
Limpopo	Indian Ocean	1,600	995	
Senegal	Atlantic Ocean	1,600	995	
Volta	Atlantic Ocean	1,500	930	

AUSTRALIA		km	miles
Murray–Darling	Indian Ocean	3,750	2,330
Darling	Murray	3,070	1,905
Murray	Indian Ocean	2,575	1,600
Murrumbidgee	Murray	1,690	1,050

NORTH AMERICA		km	miles	
Mississippi–Missouri	Gulf of Mexico	6,020	3,740	[4]
Mackenzie	Arctic Ocean	4,240	2,630	
Mississippi	Gulf of Mexico	3,780	2,350	
Missouri	Mississippi	3,780	2,350	
Yukon	Pacific Ocean	3,185	1,980	
Rio Grande	Gulf of Mexico	3,030	1,880	

NORTH AMERICA (continued)		km	miles
Arkansas	Mississippi	2,340	1,450
Colorado	Pacific Ocean	2,330	1,445
Red	Mississippi	2,040	1,270
Columbia	Pacific Ocean	1,950	1,210
Saskatchewan	Lake Winnipeg	1,940	1,205
Snake	Columbia	1,670	1,040
Churchill	Hudson Bay	1,600	990
Ohio	Mississippi	1,580	980
Brazos	Gulf of Mexico	1,400	870
St Lawrence	Atlantic Ocean	1,170	730

SOUTH AMERICA		km	miles	
Amazon	Atlantic Ocean	6,450	4,010	[2]
Paraná–Plate	Atlantic Ocean	4,500	2,800	
Purus	Amazon	3,350	2,080	
Madeira	Amazon	3,200	1,990	
São Francisco	Atlantic Ocean	2,900	1,800	
Paraná	Plate	2,800	1,740	
Tocantins	Atlantic Ocean	2,750	1,710	
Paraguay	Paraná	2,550	1,580	
Orinoco	Atlantic Ocean	2,500	1,550	
Pilcomayo	Paraná	2,500	1,550	
Araguaia	Tocantins	2,250	1,400	
Juruá	Amazon	2,000	1,240	
Xingu	Amazon	1,980	1,230	
Ucayali	Amazon	1,900	1,180	
Maranón	Amazon	1,600	990	
Uruguay	Plate	1,600	990	

LAKES

EUROPE		km²	miles²
Lake Ladoga	Russia	17,700	6,800
Lake Onega	Russia	9,700	3,700
Saimaa system	Finland	8,000	3,100
Vänern	Sweden	5,500	2,100
Rybinskoye Res.	Russia	4,700	1,800

ASIA		km²	miles²	
Caspian Sea	Asia	371,800	143,550	[1]
Lake Baykal	Russia	30,500	11,780	[8]
Aral Sea	Kazakhstan/Uzbekistan	28,687	11,086	[10]
Tonlé Sap	Cambodia	20,000	7,700	
Lake Balqash	Kazakhstan	18,500	7,100	
Lake Dongting	China	12,000	4,600	
Lake Ysyk	Kyrgyzstan	6,200	2,400	
Lake Orumiyeh	Iran	5,900	2,300	
Lake Koko	China	5,700	2,200	
Lake Poyang	China	5,000	1,900	
Lake Khanka	China/Russia	4,400	1,700	
Lake Van	Turkey	3,500	1,400	

AFRICA		km²	miles²	
Lake Victoria	E. Africa	68,000	26,000	[3]
Lake Tanganyika	C. Africa	33,000	13,000	[6]
Lake Malawi/Nyasa	E. Africa	29,600	11,430	[9]
Lake Chad	C. Africa	25,000	9,700	
Lake Turkana	Ethiopia/Kenya	8,500	3,300	
Lake Volta	Ghana	8,500	3,300	
Lake Bangweulu	Zambia	8,000	3,100	
Lake Rukwa	Tanzania	7,000	2,700	
Lake Mai-Ndombe	Congo (D.R.)	6,500	2,500	
Lake Kariba	Zambia/Zimbabwe	5,300	2,000	
Lake Albert	Uganda/Congo (D.R.)	5,300	2,000	
Lake Nasser	Egypt/Sudan	5,200	2,000	
Lake Mweru	Zambia/Congo (D.R.)	4,900	1,900	
Lake Cabora Bassa	Mozambique	4,500	1,700	
Lake Kyoga	Uganda	4,400	1,700	
Lake Tana	Ethiopia	3,630	1,400	

AUSTRALIA		km²	miles²
Lake Eyre	Australia	8,900	3,400
Lake Torrens	Australia	5,800	2,200
Lake Gairdner	Australia	4,800	1,900

NORTH AMERICA		km²	miles²	
Lake Superior	Canada/USA	82,350	31,800	[2]
Lake Huron	Canada/USA	59,600	23,010	[4]
Lake Michigan	USA	58,000	22,400	[5]
Great Bear Lake	Canada	31,800	12,280	[7]
Great Slave Lake	Canada	28,500	11,000	
Lake Erie	Canada/USA	25,700	9,900	
Lake Winnipeg	Canada	24,400	9,400	
Lake Ontario	Canada/USA	19,500	7,500	
Lake Nicaragua	Nicaragua	8,200	3,200	
Lake Athabasca	Canada	8,100	3,100	
Smallwood Reservoir	Canada	6,530	2,520	
Reindeer Lake	Canada	6,400	2,500	
Nettilling Lake	Canada	5,500	2,100	
Lake Winnipegosis	Canada	5,400	2,100	

SOUTH AMERICA		km²	miles²
Lake Titicaca	Bolivia/Peru	8,300	3,200
Lake Poopo	Bolivia	2,800	1,100

ISLANDS

EUROPE		km²	miles²	
Great Britain	UK	229,880	88,700	[8]
Iceland	Atlantic Ocean	103,000	39,800	
Ireland	Ireland/UK	84,400	32,600	
Novaya Zemlya (N.)	Russia	48,200	18,600	
W. Spitzbergen	Norway	39,000	15,100	
Novaya Zemlya (S.)	Russia	33,200	12,800	
Sicily	Italy	25,500	9,800	
Sardinia	Italy	24,000	9,300	
N.E. Spitzbergen	Norway	15,000	5,600	
Corsica	France	8,700	3,400	
Crete	Greece	8,350	3,200	
Zealand	Denmark	6,850	2,600	

ASIA		km²	miles²	
Borneo	S. E. Asia	744,360	287,400	[3]
Sumatra	Indonesia	473,600	182,860	[6]
Honshu	Japan	230,500	88,980	[7]
Sulawesi (Celebes)	Indonesia	189,000	73,000	
Java	Indonesia	126,700	48,900	
Luzon	Philippines	104,700	40,400	
Mindanao	Philippines	101,500	39,200	
Hokkaido	Japan	78,400	30,300	
Sakhalin	Russia	74,060	28,600	
Sri Lanka	Indian Ocean	65,600	25,300	
Taiwan	Pacific Ocean	36,000	13,900	
Kyushu	Japan	35,700	13,800	
Hainan	China	34,000	13,100	
Timor	Indonesia	33,600	13,000	
Shikoku	Japan	18,800	7,300	
Halmahera	Indonesia	18,000	6,900	
Ceram	Indonesia	17,150	6,600	
Sumbawa	Indonesia	15,450	6,000	
Flores	Indonesia	15,200	5,900	
Samar	Philippines	13,100	5,100	
Negros	Philippines	12,700	4,900	
Bangka	Indonesia	12,000	4,600	
Palawan	Philippines	12,000	4,600	
Panay	Philippines	11,500	4,400	
Sumba	Indonesia	11,100	4,300	
Mindoro	Philippines	9,750	3,800	

AFRICA		km²	miles²	
Madagascar	Indian Ocean	587,040	226,660	[4]
Socotra	Indian Ocean	3,600	1,400	
Réunion	Indian Ocean	2,500	965	
Tenerife	Atlantic Ocean	2,350	900	
Mauritius	Indian Ocean	1,865	720	

OCEANIA		km²	miles²	
New Guinea	Indon./Papua NG	821,030	317,000	[2]
New Zealand (S.)	Pacific Ocean	150,500	58,100	
New Zealand (N.)	Pacific Ocean	114,700	44,300	
Tasmania	Australia	67,800	26,200	
New Britain	Papua NG	37,800	14,600	
New Caledonia	Pacific Ocean	19,100	7,400	
Viti Levu	Fiji	10,500	4,100	
Hawaii	Pacific Ocean	10,450	4,000	
Bougainville	Papua NG	9,600	3,700	
Guadalcanal	Solomon Is.	6,500	2,500	
Vanua Levu	Fiji	5,550	2,100	
New Ireland	Papua NG	3,200	1,200	

NORTH AMERICA		km²	miles²	
Greenland	Atlantic Ocean	2,175,600	839,800	[1]
Baffin Is.	Canada	508,000	196,100	[5]
Victoria Is.	Canada	212,200	81,900	[9]
Ellesmere Is.	Canada	212,000	81,800	[10]
Cuba	Caribbean Sea	110,860	42,800	
Newfoundland	Canada	110,680	42,700	
Hispaniola	Dom. Rep./Haiti	76,200	29,400	
Banks Is.	Canada	67,000	25,900	
Devon Is.	Canada	54,500	21,000	
Melville Is.	Canada	42,400	16,400	
Vancouver Is.	Canada	32,150	12,400	
Somerset Is.	Canada	24,300	9,400	
Jamaica	Caribbean Sea	11,400	4,400	
Puerto Rico	Atlantic Ocean	8,900	3,400	
Cape Breton Is.	Canada	4,000	1,500	

SOUTH AMERICA		km²	miles²
Tierra del Fuego	Argentina/Chile	47,000	18,100
Falkland Is. (East)	Atlantic Ocean	6,800	2,600
South Georgia	Atlantic Ocean	4,200	1,600
Galapagos (Isabela)	Pacific Ocean	2,250	870

World: Regions in the News

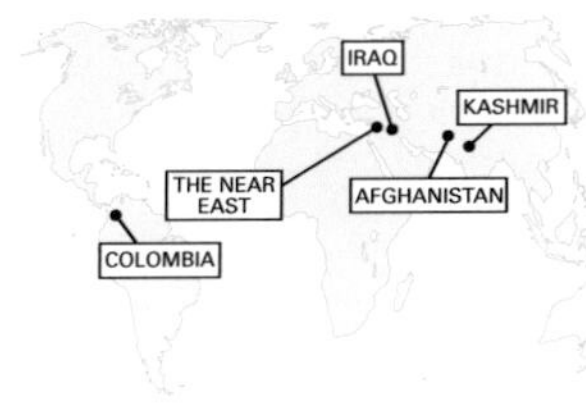

IRAQ
KASHMIR
THE NEAR EAST
AFGHANISTAN
COLOMBIA

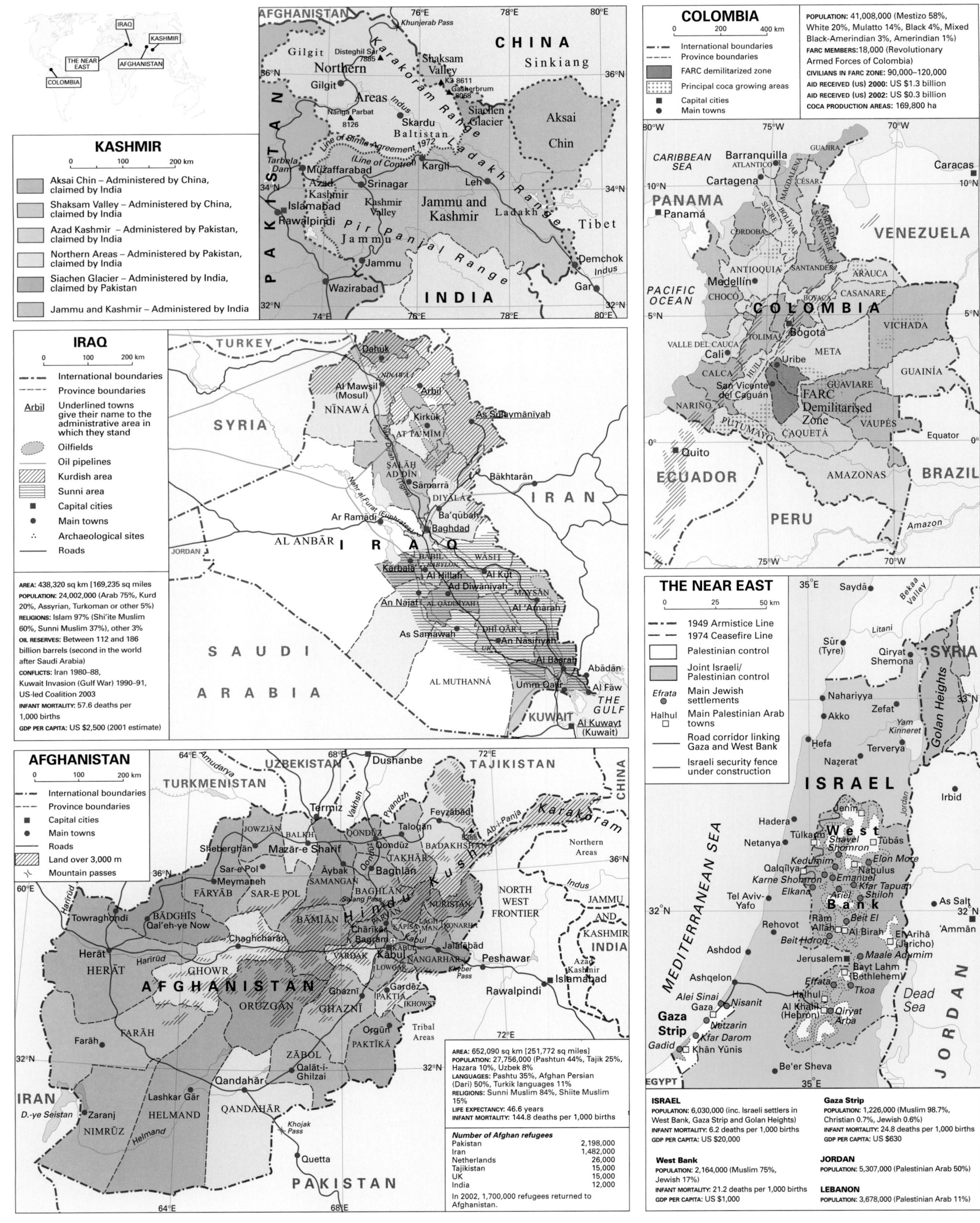

KASHMIR
0 100 200 km
Aksai Chin – Administered by China, claimed by India
Shaksam Valley – Administered by China, claimed by India
Azad Kashmir – Administered by Pakistan, claimed by India
Northern Areas – Administered by Pakistan, claimed by India
Siachen Glacier – Administered by India, claimed by Pakistan
Jammu and Kashmir – Administered by India
AFGHANISTAN
CHINA
Sinkiang
Khunjerab Pass
Gilgit
Northern Areas
Disteghil Sar 7885
Shaksam Valley
K2 8611
Gasherbrum 8068
Siachen Glacier
Aksai Chin
Nanga Parbat 8126
Skardu
Baltistan
Karakoram Range
Ladakh Range
Line of Simla Agreement 1972
(Line of Control)
Tarbela Dam
Muzaffarabad
Azad Kashmir
Srinagar
Kargil
Leh
Islamabad
Rawalpindi
Kashmir Valley
Jammu and Kashmir
Ladakh
Tibet
Pir Panjal Range
Jammu
Demchok
Indus
Gar
Wazirabad
PAKISTAN
INDIA

COLOMBIA
0 200 400 km
International boundaries
Province boundaries
FARC demilitarized zone
Principal coca growing areas
Capital cities
Main towns
CARIBBEAN SEA
Barranquilla
Cartagena
Caracas
PANAMA
Panamá
VENEZUELA
PACIFIC OCEAN
Medellín
COLOMBIA
Bogotá
Cali
Uribe
San Vicente del Caguán
FARC Demilitarised Zone
Quito
ECUADOR
PERU
BRAZIL
Amazon
Equator

POPULATION: 41,008,000 (Mestizo 58%, White 20%, Mulatto 14%, Black 4%, Mixed Black-Amerindian 3%, Amerindian 1%)
FARC MEMBERS: 18,000 (Revolutionary Armed Forces of Colombia)
CIVILIANS IN FARC ZONE: 90,000–120,000
AID RECEIVED (US) 2000: US $1.3 billion
AID RECEIVED (US) 2002: US $0.3 billion
COCA PRODUCTION AREAS: 169,800 ha

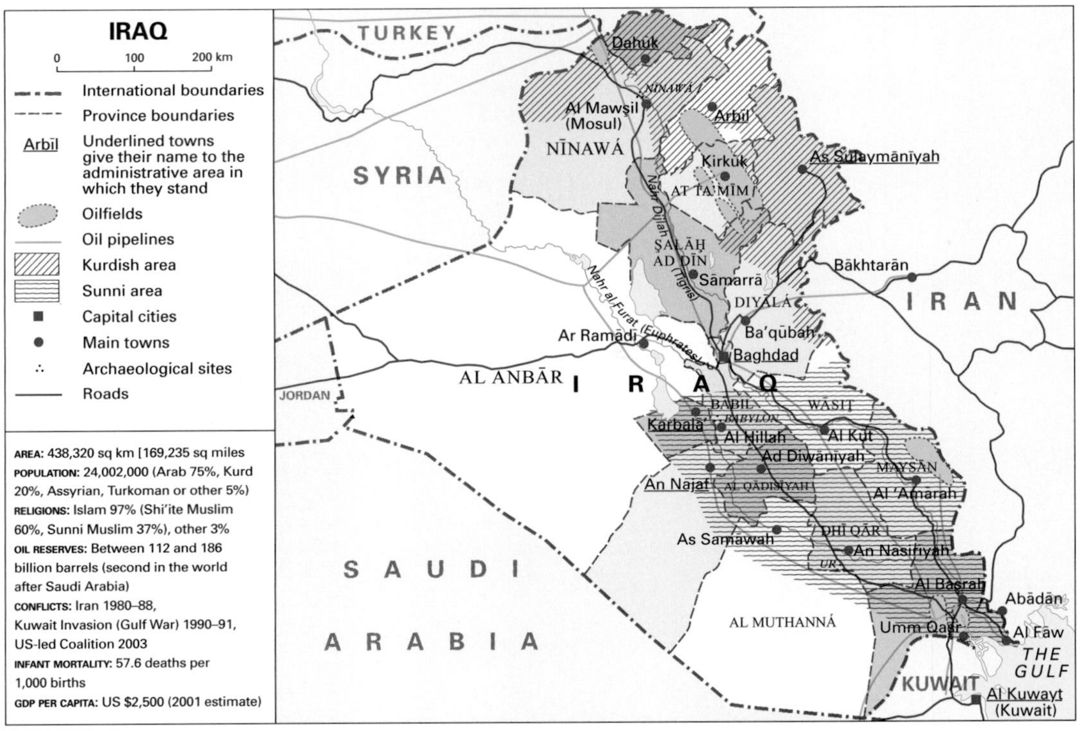

IRAQ
0 100 200 km
International boundaries
Province boundaries
Arbīl Underlined towns give their name to the administrative area in which they stand
Oilfields
Oil pipelines
Kurdish area
Sunni area
Capital cities
Main towns
Archaeological sites
Roads
TURKEY
SYRIA
IRAN
IRAQ
SAUDI ARABIA
JORDAN
KUWAIT
THE GULF
Dahūk
Al Mawşil (Mosul)
Arbīl
Kirkūk
As Sulaymānīyah
Sāmarrā
Ba'qūbah
Baghdad
Ar Ramādi
Karbalā
Al Ḩillah
Al Kūt
Ad Dīwānīyah
An Najaf
Al 'Amārah
As Samāwah
An Nāşirīyah
Al Başrah
Umm Qaşr
Abādān
Al Fāw
Bākhtarān
Al Kuwayt (Kuwait)

AREA: 438,320 sq km [169,235 sq miles]
POPULATION: 24,002,000 (Arab 75%, Kurd 20%, Assyrian, Turkoman or other 5%)
RELIGIONS: Islam 97% (Shi'ite Muslim 60%, Sunni Muslim 37%), other 3%
OIL RESERVES: Between 112 and 186 billion barrels (second in the world after Saudi Arabia)
CONFLICTS: Iran 1980–88, Kuwait Invasion (Gulf War) 1990–91, US-led Coalition 2003
INFANT MORTALITY: 57.6 deaths per 1,000 births
GDP PER CAPITA: US $2,500 (2001 estimate)

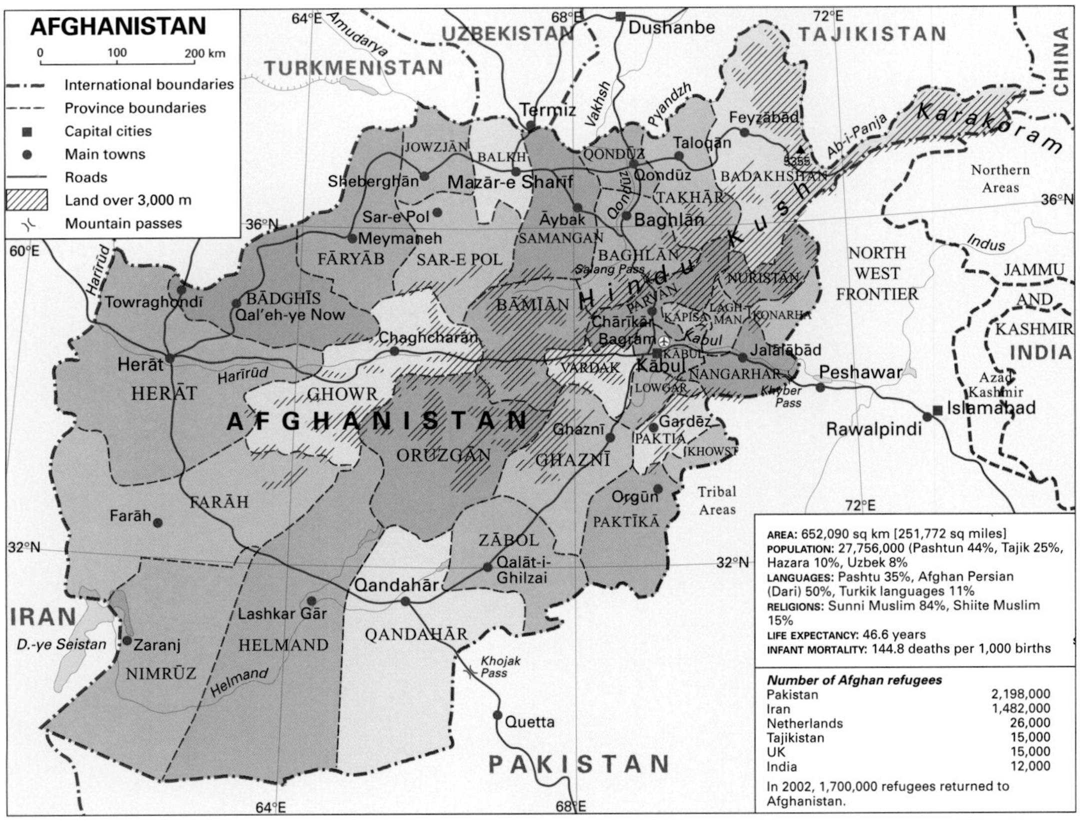

AFGHANISTAN
0 100 200 km
International boundaries
Province boundaries
Capital cities
Main towns
Roads
Land over 3,000 m
Mountain passes
UZBEKISTAN
TAJIKISTAN
TURKMENISTAN
CHINA
Dushanbe
Termiz
Mazār-e Sharīf
Konduz
Feyzābād
Baghlān
Sheberghān
Meymaneh
Hindu Kush
Karakoram
Towraghondi
Qal'eh-ye Now
Chaghcharān
Herāt
Bagrām
Chārīkar
Kabul
Jalālābād
Peshawar
Islamabad
Rawalpindi
Khyber Pass
AFGHANISTAN
Ghaznī
Gardēz
Orgūn
Farāh
Qalāt-i-Ghilzai
Qandahār
Lashkar Gāh
Zaranj
Khojak Pass
Quetta
IRAN
PAKISTAN
NORTH WEST FRONTIER
Tribal Areas

AREA: 652,090 sq km [251,772 sq miles]
POPULATION: 27,756,000 (Pashtun 44%, Tajik 25%, Hazara 10%, Uzbek 8%
LANGUAGES: Pashtu 35%, Afghan Persian (Dari) 50%, Turkik languages 11%
RELIGIONS: Sunni Muslim 84%, Shiite Muslim 15%
LIFE EXPECTANCY: 46.6 years
INFANT MORTALITY: 144.8 deaths per 1,000 births

Number of Afghan refugees	
Pakistan	2,198,000
Iran	1,482,000
Netherlands	26,000
Tajikistan	15,000
UK	15,000
India	12,000

In 2002, 1,700,000 refugees returned to Afghanistan.

THE NEAR EAST
0 25 50 km
1949 Armistice Line
1974 Ceasefire Line
Palestinian control
Joint Israeli/ Palestinian control
Efrata Main Jewish settlements
Halhul Main Palestinian Arab towns
Road corridor linking Gaza and West Bank
Israeli security fence under construction
Saydā
Bekaa Valley
Litani
Sūr (Tyre)
Qiryat Shemona
SYRIA
Golan Heights
Nahariyya
Akko
Zefat
Hefa
Nazerat
Terverya
ISRAEL
Irbid
MEDITERRANEAN SEA
Hadera
Jenin
Netanya
Tulkarm
West Bank
Nablus
Tel Aviv-Yafo
Ramallah
Rehovot
Ashdod
Jerusalem
Bayt Lahm (Bethlehem)
Ashqelon
Gaza
Gaza Strip
Al Khalil (Hebron)
Be'er Sheva
Dead Sea
JORDAN
'Ammān
As Salt
EGYPT

ISRAEL
POPULATION: 6,030,000 (inc. Israeli settlers in West Bank, Gaza Strip and Golan Heights)
INFANT MORTALITY: 6.2 deaths per 1,000 births
GDP PER CAPITA: US $20,000

Gaza Strip
POPULATION: 1,226,000 (Muslim 98.7%, Christian 0.7%, Jewish 0.6%)
INFANT MORTALITY: 24.8 deaths per 1,000 births
GDP PER CAPITA: US $630

West Bank
POPULATION: 2,164,000 (Muslim 75%, Jewish 17%)
INFANT MORTALITY: 21.2 deaths per 1,000 births
GDP PER CAPITA: US $1,000

JORDAN
POPULATION: 5,307,000 (Palestinian Arab 50%)

LEBANON
POPULATION: 3,678,000 (Palestinian Arab 11%)

THE EARTH IN SPACE

The Universe

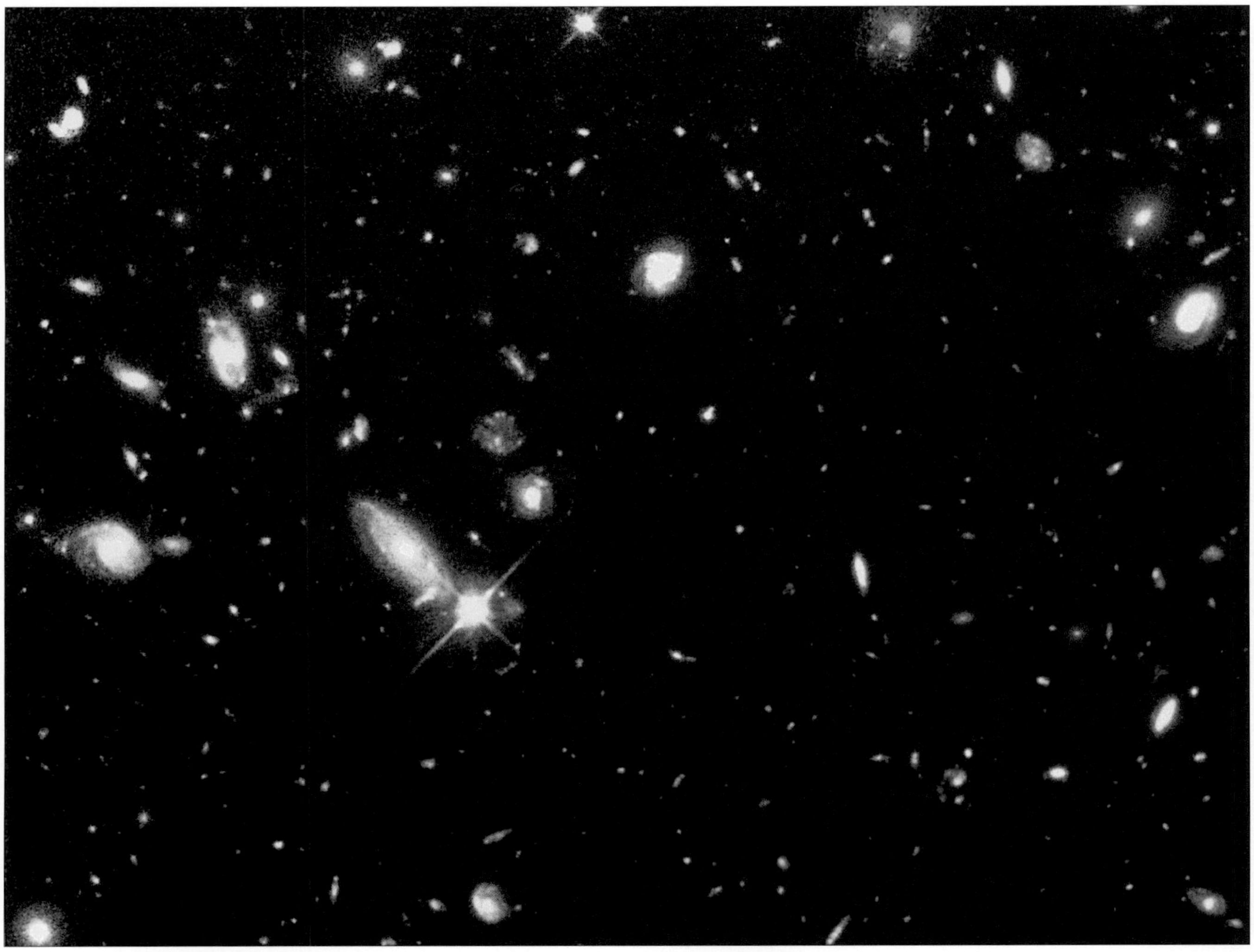

The depths of the Universe
This photograph shows some of the 1,500 or more galaxies that were recorded in the montage of photographs taken by the Hubble Space Telescope in 1995–6.

THE NEAREST STARS

The 20 nearest stars, excluding the Sun, with their distance from the Earth in light-years.*

Proxima Centauri	4.2
Alpha Centauri A	4.3
Alpha Centauri B	4.3
Barnard's Star	6.0
Wolf 359	7.8
Lalande 21185	8.3
Sirius A	8.7
Sirius B	8.7
UV Ceti A	8.7
UV Ceti B	8.7
Ross 154	9.4
Ross 248	10.3
Epsilon Eridani	10.7
Ross 128	10.9
61 Cygni A	11.1
61 Cygni B	11.1
Epsilon Indi	11.2
Groombridge 34 A	11.2
Groombridge 34 B	11.2
L789-6	11.2

** A light-year equals approximately 9,500 billion km [5,900 billion miles].*

In early 2003, NASA scientists produced an image of the Universe as it was about 380,000 years after its creation. The image was produced by an American satellite called the Wilkinson Microwave Anisotropy Probe (WMAP), which has been supplying data since its launch in June 2001.

The probe measures small variations in the cosmic wave radiation (CMB). By measuring the size of hot and cold spots in the CMB, scientists have calculated how far away they are, and this data has enabled them to calculate the age of the Universe. It has also established the proportions of its three ingredients, namely 4% ordinary matter (made up of atoms), 23% of 'cold dark matter', whose nature is unknown, and 73% of the mysterious 'dark energy', which seems to be accelerating the expansion of space.

Armed with the new data, scientists have established that our Universe was created, or 'time' began, about 13.7 billion years ago (disproving earlier estimates that ranged from 8 billion to 24 billion years), that it is flat, and that the first stars did not appear until it was 200 million years old.

The Big Bang

Most scientists agree that the Universe was formed by a colossal explosion, called the 'Big Bang'. In the first millionth of a second after the Big Bang, the Universe expanded from a dimensionless point of infinite mass and

The end of the Universe
The diagram shows two theories concerning the fate of the Universe. One theory, top, suggests that the Universe will expand indefinitely, moving into an immense dark graveyard. Another theory, bottom, suggests that the galaxies will fall back until everything is again concentrated in one point in a so-called 'Big Crunch'. This might then be followed by a new 'Big Bang'.

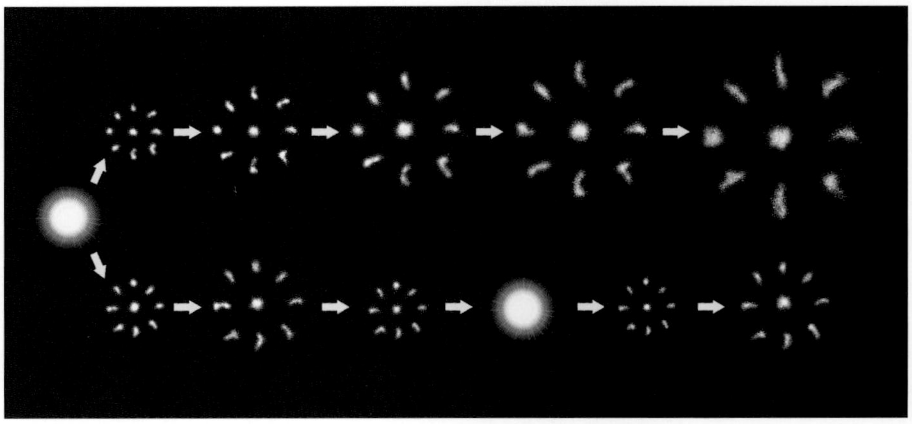

density into a fireball about 30 billion km [19 billion miles] across. The Universe has been expanding ever since, as demonstrated in the 1920s by Edwin Hubble, the American astronomer after whom the Hubble Space Telescope, which has also been shedding light on the origins of the Universe, was named.

The temperature at the end of the first second was perhaps 10 billion degrees – far too hot for composite atomic nuclei to exist. As a result, the fireball consisted mainly of radiation mixed with microscopic particles of matter. Almost a million years passed before the Universe was cool enough for atoms to form.

In regions where matter was relatively dense, atoms began, under the influence of gravity, to move together to form proto-galaxies – masses of gas separated by empty space. The protogalaxies were dark, because the Universe had cooled. But 200 million years after its creation, stars began to form within the protogalaxies as particles were drawn together. The internal pressure produced as matter condensed created the high temperatures required to cause nuclear fusion. Stars were born and later destroyed. Each generation of stars fed on the debris of extinct ones. Each generation produced larger atoms, increasing the number of different chemical elements.

Solar System

The Home Galaxy
This schematic plan shows that our Solar System is located in one of the spiral arms of the Milky Way galaxy, a little less than 30,000 light-years from its centre. The centre of the Milky Way galaxy is not visible from Earth. Instead, it is masked by light-absorbing clouds of interstellar dust.

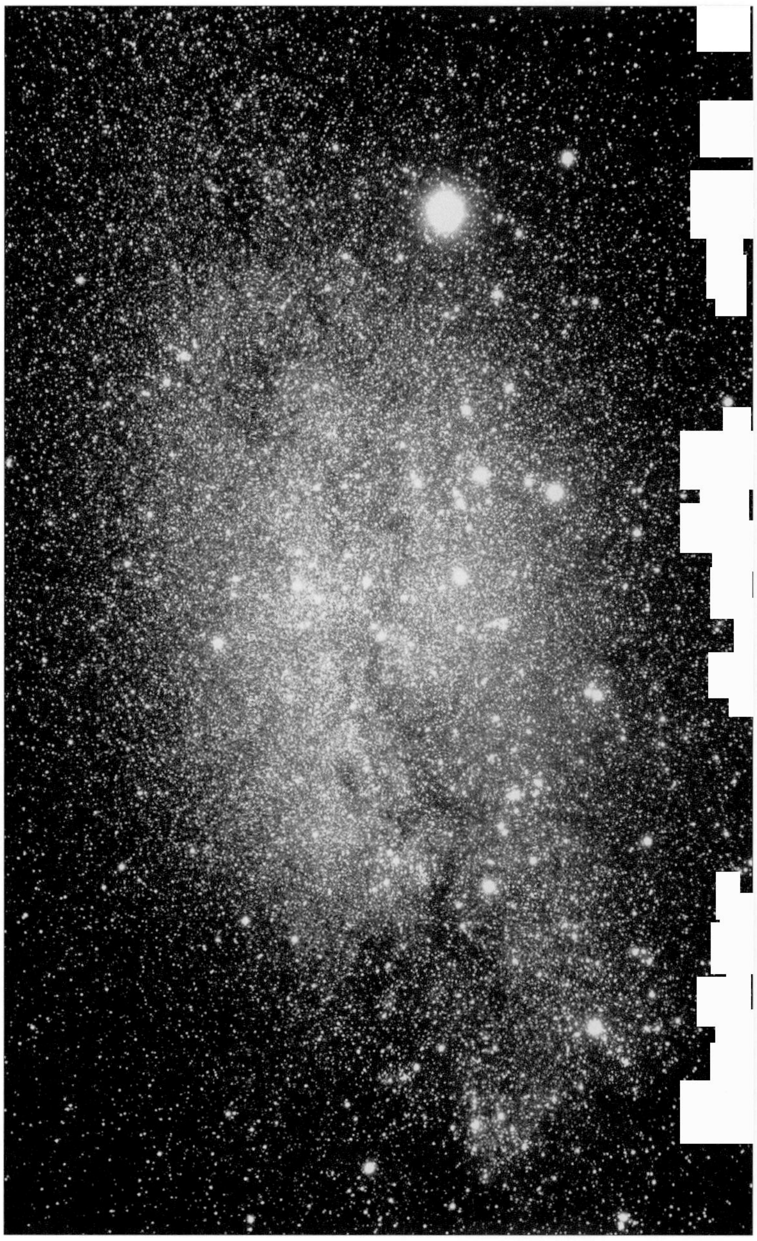

The Milky Way
This section of the Milky Way is dominated by Sirius, the Dog Star, top centre, in the constellation of Canis Major. Sirius is the brightest star in the sky.

The Galaxies

At least a billion galaxies are scattered through the Universe, though the discoveries made by the Hubble Space Telescope suggest that there may be far more than once thought, and some estimates are as high as 100 billion. The largest galaxies contain trillions of stars, while small ones contain less than a billion.

Galaxies tend to occur in groups or clusters, while some clusters appear to be grouped in vast superclusters. Our Local Cluster includes the spiral Milky Way galaxy, whose diameter is about 100,000 light-years; one light-year, the distance that light travels in one year, measures about 9,500 billion km [5,900 billion miles]. The Milky Way is a huge galaxy, shaped like a disk with a bulge at the centre. It is larger, brighter and more massive than many other known galaxies. It contains about 100 billion stars which rotate around the centre of the galaxy in the same direction as the Sun does.

One medium-sized star in the Milky Way galaxy is the Sun. After its formation, about 5 billion years ago, there was enough leftover matter around it to create the planets, asteroids, moons and other bodies that together form our Solar System. The Solar System rotates around the centre of the Milky Way galaxy approximately every 225 million years.

Stars similar to our Sun are known to have planets orbiting around them. By the start of 2003, 100 or so extrasolar planets had been reported, and evidence from the Hubble Space Telescope suggests that the raw materials from which planets are formed is common in dusty disks around many stars. This provokes one of the most intriguing questions that has ever faced humanity. If other planets exist in the Universe, then are they home to living organisms?

Before the time of Galileo, people thought that the Earth lay at the centre of the Universe. But we now know that our Solar System and even the Milky Way galaxy are tiny specks in the Universe as a whole. Perhaps our planet is also not unique in being the only one to support intelligent life.

Star Charts and Constellations

The Plough

The Plough, or Big Dipper, above glowing yellow clouds lit by city lights. It is part of a larger group called Ursa Major, one of the best-known constellations of the northern hemisphere. The two bright stars to the lower right of the photograph (Merak and Dubhe) are known as the Pointers because they show the way to the Pole Star.

THE BRIGHTEST STARS

The 15 brightest stars visible from northern Europe. Magnitudes are given to the nearest tenth.

Sirius	−1.5
Arcturus	0.0
Vega	0.0
Capella	0.1
Rigel	0.1
Procyon	0.4
Betelgeuse	0.4
Altair	0.8
Aldebaran	0.8
Antares	1.0
Spica	1.0
Pollux	1.1
Fomalhaut	1.2
Deneb	1.2
Regulus	1.3

On a clear night, under the best conditions and far away from the glare of city lights, a person in northern Europe can look up and see about 2,500 stars. In a town, however, light pollution can reduce visibility to 200 stars or less. Over the whole celestial sphere it is possible to see about 8,500 stars with the naked eye and it is only when you look through a telescope that you begin to realize that the number of stars is countless.

Small and Large Stars

Stars come in several sizes. Some, called neutron stars, are compact, with the same mass as the Sun but with diameters of only about 20 km [12 miles]. Larger than neutron stars are the small white dwarfs. Our Sun is a medium-sized star, but many visible stars in the night sky are giants with diameters between 10 and 100 times that of the Sun, or supergiants with diameters over 100 times that of the Sun.

Two bright stars in the constellation Orion are Betelgeuse (also known as Alpha Orionis) and Rigel (or Beta Orionis). Betelgeuse is an orange-red supergiant, whose diameter is about 400 times that of the Sun. Rigel is also a supergiant. Its diameter is about 50 times that of the Sun, but its luminosity is estimated to be over 100,000 times that of the Sun.

The stars we see in the night sky all belong to our home galaxy, the Milky Way. This name is also used for the faint, silvery band that arches across the sky. This band, a slice through our

THE CONSTELLATIONS

The constellations and their English names. Constellations visible from both hemispheres are listed.

Andromeda	Andromeda	Delphinus	Dolphin	Perseus	Perseus
Antlia	Air Pump	Dorado	Swordfish	Phoenix	Phoenix
Apus	Bird of Paradise	Draco	Dragon	Pictor	Easel
Aquarius	Water Carrier	Equuleus	Little Horse	Pisces	Fishes
Aquila	Eagle	Eridanus	River Eridanus	Piscis Austrinus	Southern Fish
Ara	Altar	Fornax	Furnace	Puppis	Ship's Stern
Aries	Ram	Gemini	Twins	Pyxis	Mariner's Compass
Auriga	Charioteer	Grus	Crane	Reticulum	Net
Boötes	Herdsman	Hercules	Hercules	Sagitta	Arrow
Caelum	Chisel	Horologium	Clock	Sagittarius	Archer
Camelopardalis	Giraffe	Hydra	Water Snake	Scorpius	Scorpion
Cancer	Crab	Hydrus	Sea Serpent	Sculptor	Sculptor
Canes Venatici	Hunting Dogs	Indus	Indian	Scutum	Shield
Canis Major	Great Dog	Lacerta	Lizard	Serpens*	Serpent
Canis Minor	Little Dog	Leo	Lion	Sextans	Sextant
Capricornus	Sea Goat	Leo Minor	Little Lion	Taurus	Bull
Carina	Ship's Keel	Lepus	Hare	Telescopium	Telescope
Cassiopeia	Cassiopeia	Libra	Scales	Triangulum	Triangle
Centaurus	Centaur	Lupus	Wolf	Triangulum Australe	Southern Triangle
Cepheus	Cepheus	Lynx	Lynx	Tucana	Toucan
Cetus	Whale	Lyra	Lyre	Ursa Major	Great Bear
Chamaeleon	Chameleon	Mensa	Table	Ursa Minor	Little Bear
Circinus	Compasses	Microscopium	Microscope	Vela	Ship's Sails
Columba	Dove	Monoceros	Unicorn	Virgo	Virgin
Coma Berenices	Berenice's Hair	Musca	Fly	Volans	Flying Fish
Corona Australis	Southern Crown	Norma	Level	Vulpecula	Fox
Corona Borealis	Northern Crown	Octans	Octant		
Corvus	Crow	Ophiuchus	Serpent Bearer		
Crater	Cup	Orion	Hunter		
Crux	Southern Cross	Pavo	Peacock		
Cygnus	Swan	Pegasus	Winged Horse		

* *In two halves: Serpens Caput, the head, and Serpens Cauda, the tail.*

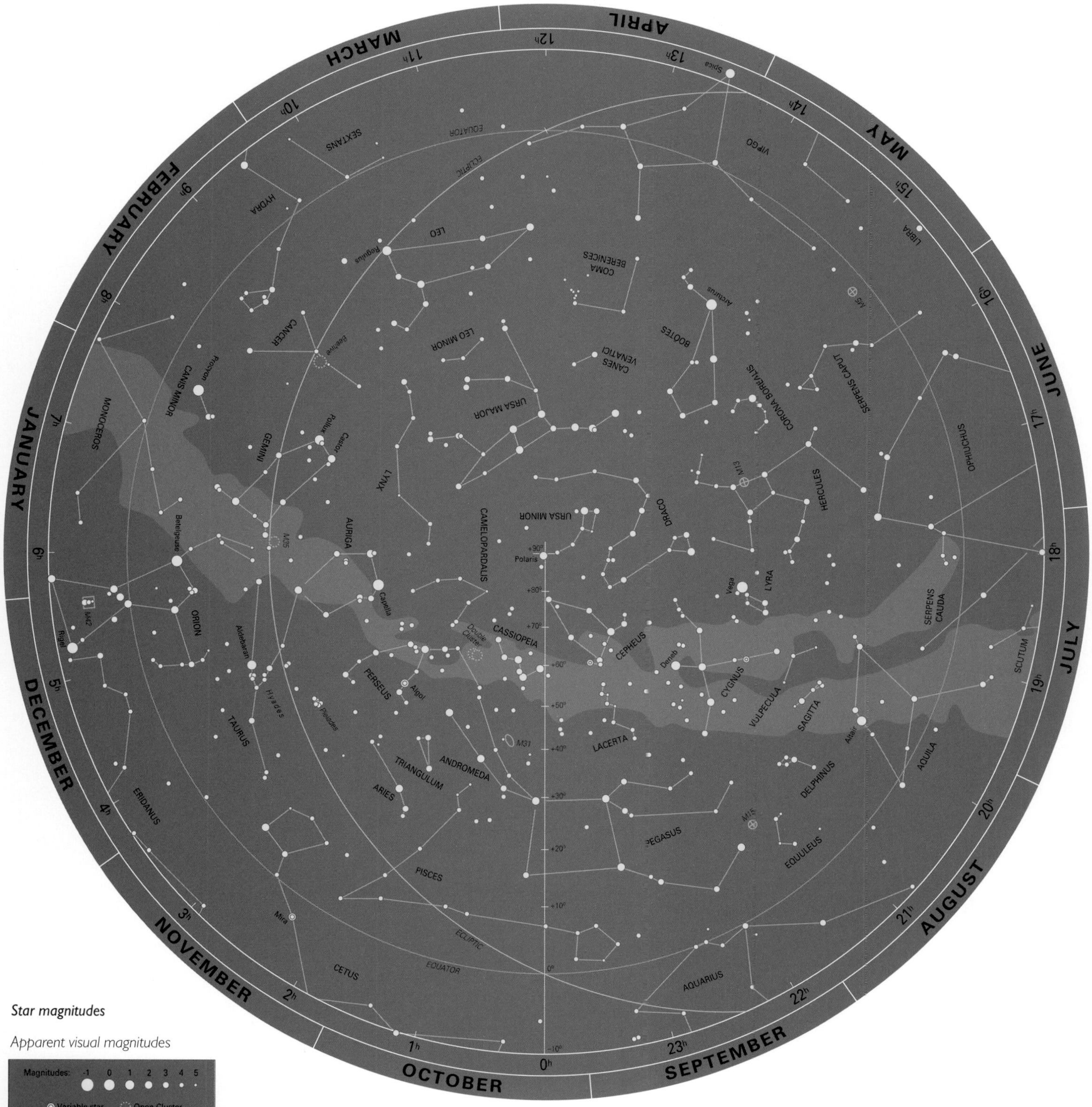
MARCH
APRIL
MAY
JUNE
JULY
AUGUST
SEPTEMBER
OCTOBER
NOVEMBER
DECEMBER
JANUARY
FEBRUARY
SEXTANS
HYDRA
LEO
LEO MINOR
COMA BERENICES
CANES VENATICI
URSA MAJOR
URSA MINOR
BOÖTES
VIRGO
LIBRA
CORONA BOREALIS
SERPENS CAPUT
OPHIUCHUS
HERCULES
DRACO
LYRA
SERPENS CAUDA
SCUTUM
AQUILA
SAGITTA
VULPECULA
CYGNUS
CEPHEUS
CASSIOPEIA
CAMELOPARDALIS
LYNX
GEMINI
CANCER
CANIS MINOR
MONOCEROS
ORION
AURIGA
PERSEUS
TAURUS
ERIDANUS
ANDROMEDA
TRIANGULUM
ARIES
PISCES
CETUS
PEGASUS
LACERTA
DELPHINUS
EQUULEUS
AQUARIUS
Polaris
Vega
Deneb
Altair
Arcturus
Spica
Regulus
Procyon
Pollux
Castor
Betelgeuse
Rigel
Aldebaran
Capella
Algol
Mira
Hyades
Pleiades
M31
ECLIPTIC
EQUATOR

Star magnitudes

Apparent visual magnitudes

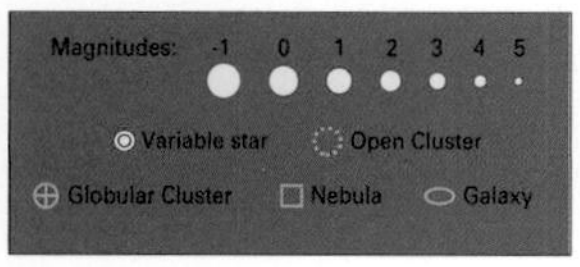
Magnitudes: -1 0 1 2 3 4 5
Variable star
Open Cluster
Globular Cluster
Nebula
Galaxy

The Milky Way is shown in light blue on the above chart.

Star chart of the northern hemisphere

When you look into the sky, the stars seem to be on the inside of a huge dome. This gives astronomers a way of mapping them. This chart shows the sky as it would appear from the North Pole. To use the star chart above, an observer in the northern hemisphere should face south and turn the chart so that the current month appears at the bottom. The chart will then show the constellations on view at approximately 11 p.m. Greenwich Mean Time. The map should be rotated clockwise 15° for each hour before 11 p.m. and anticlockwise for each hour after 11 p.m.

galaxy, contains an enormous number of stars. The nucleus of the Milky Way galaxy cannot be seen from Earth. Lying in the direction of the constellation Sagittarius in the southern hemisphere, it is masked by clouds of dust.

The Brightness of Stars

Astronomers use a scale of magnitudes to measure the brightness of stars. The brightest visible to the naked eye were originally known as first-magnitude stars, ones not so bright were second-magnitude, down to the faintest visible, which were rated as sixth-magnitude. The brighter the star, the lower the magnitude. With the advent of telescopes and the development of accurate instruments for measuring brightnesses, the magnitude scale has been refined and extended.

Very bright bodies such as Sirius, Venus and the Sun have negative magnitudes. The nearest star is Proxima Centauri, part of a multiple star system, which is 4.2 light-years away. Proxima Centauri is very faint and has a magnitude of 11.3. Alpha Centauri A, one of the two brighter members of the system, is the nearest visible star to Earth. It has a magnitude of 1.7.

These magnitudes are known as apparent magnitudes – measures of the brightnesses of the stars as they appear to us. These are the magnitudes shown on the charts on these pages. But the stars are at very different distances. The star Deneb, in the constellation Cygnus, for example, is over 1,200 light-years away. So astronomers also use absolute magnitudes – measures of how bright the stars really are. A star's absolute magnitude is the apparent magnitude it would have if it could be placed 32.6 light-years away. So Deneb, with an apparent magnitude of 1.2, has an absolute magnitude of –7.2.

The brightest star in the night sky is Sirius, the Dog Star, with a magnitude of –1.5. This medium-sized star is 8.64 light-years distant but it gives out about 20 times as much light as the Sun. After the Sun and the Moon, the brightest objects in the sky are the planets Venus, Mars and Jupiter. For example, Venus has a magnitude of up to –4. The planets have no light of their own, however, and shine only because they reflect the Sun's rays. But whilst stars have fixed positions, the planets shift nightly in relation to the constellations, following a path called the Ecliptic (shown on the star charts). As they follow their orbits around the Sun, their distances from the Earth vary, and therefore so also do their magnitudes.

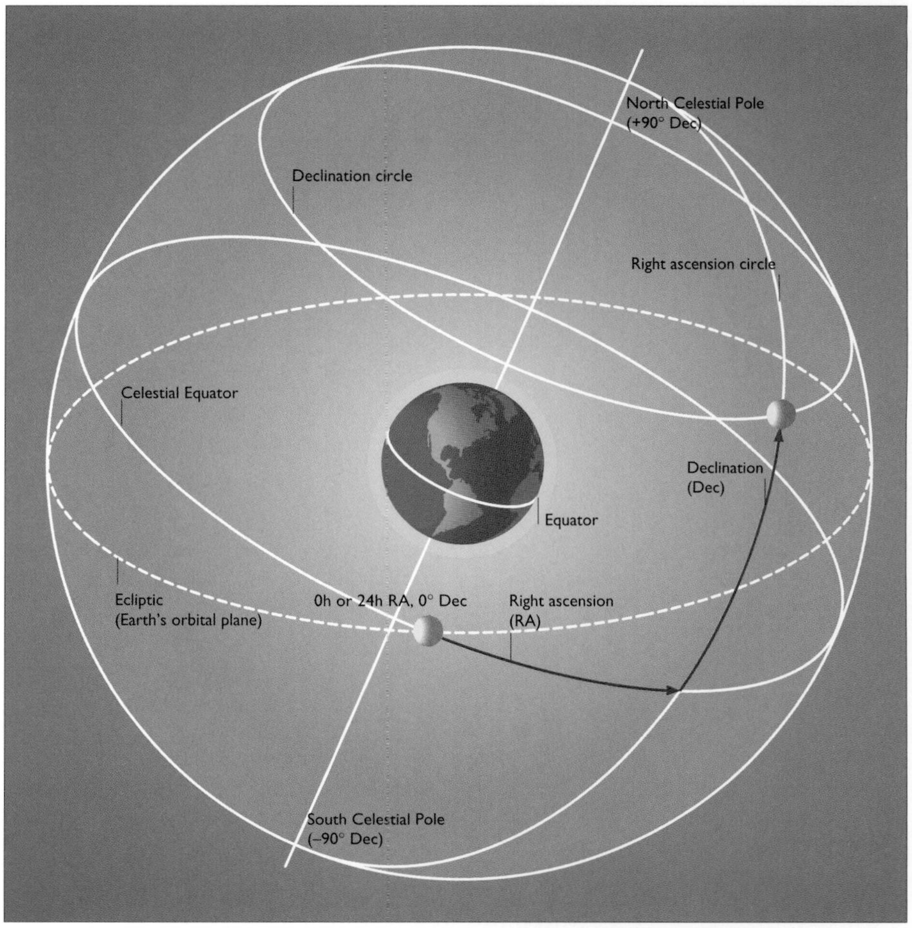
North Celestial Pole
(+90° Dec)
Declination circle
Right ascension circle
Celestial Equator
Declination
(Dec)
Equator
Ecliptic
(Earth's orbital plane)
0h or 24h RA, 0° Dec
Right ascension
(RA)
South Celestial Pole
(–90° Dec)

Celestial sphere

The diagram shows the imaginary surface on which astronomical positions are measured. The celestial sphere appears to rotate about the celestial poles, as though an extension of the Earth's own axis. The Earth's axis points towards the celestial poles.

While atlas maps record the details of the Earth's surface, star charts are a guide to the heavens. An observer at the Equator can see the entire sky at some time during the year, but an observer at the poles can see only the stars in a single hemisphere. As a result, star charts of both hemispheres are produced. The northern hemisphere chart is centred on the North Celestial Pole, while the southern hemisphere chart is centred on the South Celestial Pole.

In the northern hemisphere, the North Pole is marked by the star Polaris, or North Star. Polaris lies within a degree of the point where an extension of the Earth's axis meets the sky. Polaris appears to be stationary and navigators throughout history have used it as a guide. Unfortunately, the South Pole has no convenient reference point.

Star charts of the two hemispheres are bounded by the Celestial Equator, an imaginary line in the sky directly above the terrestrial Equator. Astronomical co-ordinates, which give the location of stars, are normally stated in terms of right ascension (the equivalent of longitude) and declination (the equivalent of latitude). Because the stars appear to rotate around the Earth every 24 hours, right ascension is measured eastwards in hours and minutes. Declination is measured in degrees north or south of the Celestial Equator.

The Southern Cross

The Southern Cross, or Crux, in the southern hemisphere, was classified as a constellation in the 17th century. It is as familiar to Australians and New Zealanders as the Plough (or Big Dipper) is to people in the northern hemisphere. The vertical axis of the Southern Cross points towards the South Celestial Pole.

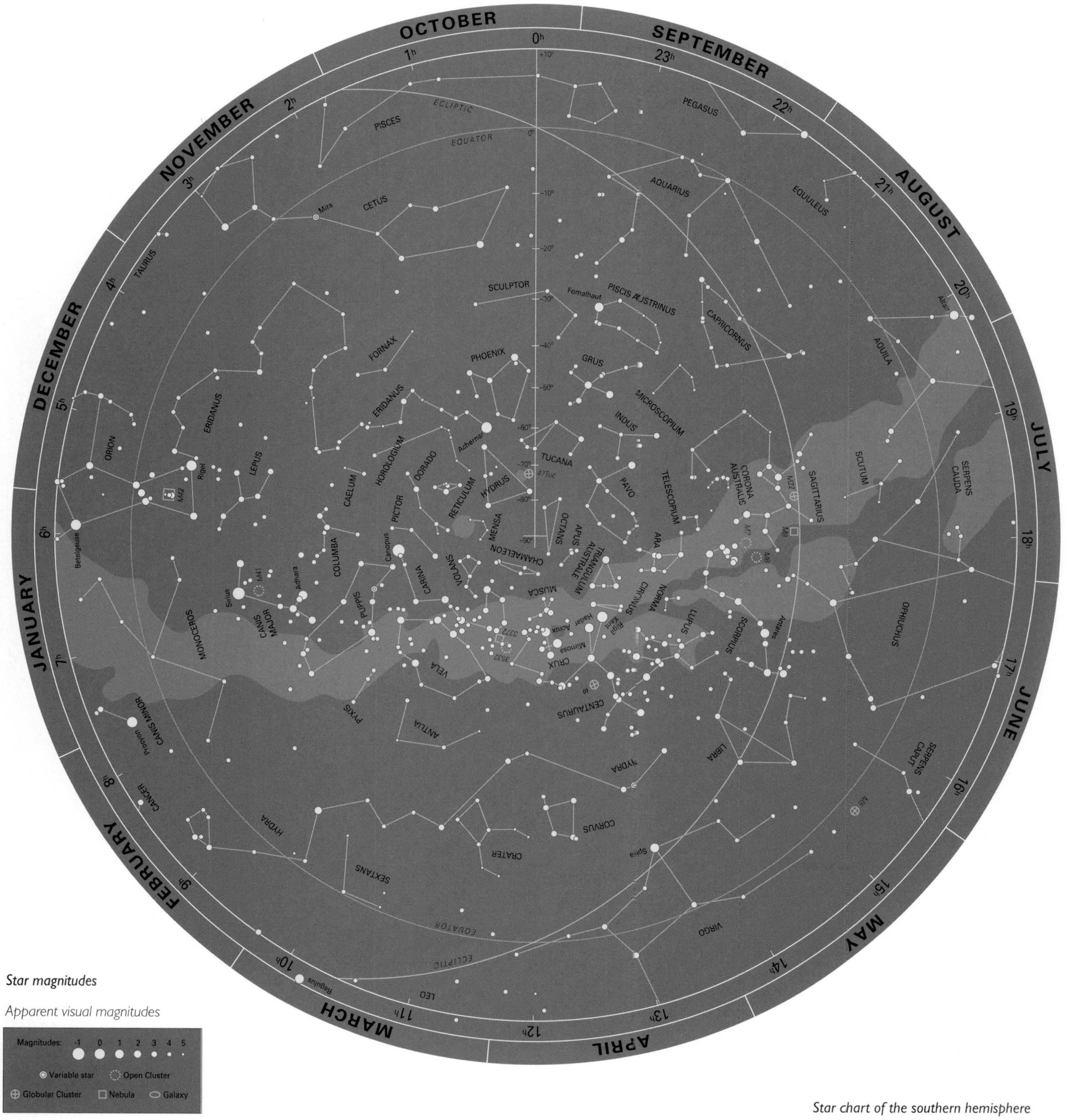
OCTOBER
SEPTEMBER
AUGUST
JULY
JUNE
MAY
APRIL
MARCH
FEBRUARY
JANUARY
DECEMBER
NOVEMBER
ECLIPTIC
EQUATOR
PISCES
PEGASUS
AQUARIUS
EQUULEUS
CETUS
Mira
TAURUS
SCULPTOR
Fomalhaut
PISCIS AUSTRINUS
CAPRICORNUS
AQUILA
Altair
FORNAX
PHOENIX
GRUS
MICROSCOPIUM
INDUS
ERIDANUS
ORION
Rigel
Betelgeuse
LEPUS
CAELUM
HOROLOGIUM
DORADO
Achernar
TUCANA
PAVO
TELESCOPIUM
CORONA AUSTRALIS
SAGITTARIUS
SCUTUM
SERPENS CAUDA
RETICULUM
HYDRUS
PICTOR
COLUMBA
MENSA
OCTANS
APUS
TRIANGULUM AUSTRALE
ARA
Canopus
CHAMAELEON
VOLANS
CARINA
PUPPIS
MUSCA
CIRCINUS
NORMA
LUPUS
SCORPIUS
Antares
OPHIUCHUS
Sirius
Adhara
CANIS MAJOR
MONOCEROS
CRUX
Mimosa
Acrux
Hadar
Rigil Kent
VELA
PYXIS
ANTLIA
CENTAURUS
LIBRA
CANIS MINOR
Procyon
CANCER
HYDRA
SEXTANS
CRATER
CORVUS
Spica
SERPENS CAPUT
VIRGO
LEO
Regulus
Magnitudes: -1 0 1 2 3 4 5
Variable star
Open Cluster
Globular Cluster
Nebula
Galaxy

Star magnitudes

Apparent visual magnitudes

The Milky Way is shown in light blue on the above chart.

Star chart of the southern hemisphere

Many constellations in the southern hemisphere were named not by the ancients but by later astronomers. Some, including Antila (Air Pump) and Microscopium (Microscope), have modern names. The Large and Small Magellanic Clouds (LMC, SMC) are small 'satellite' galaxies of the Milky Way. To use the chart, an observer in the southern hemisphere should face north and turn the chart so that the current month appears at the bottom. The map will then show the constellations on view at approximately 11 p.m. Greenwich Mean Time. The chart should be rotated clockwise 15° for each hour before 11 p.m. and anticlockwise for each hour after 11 p.m.

Constellations

Every star is identifiable as a member of a constellation. The night sky contains 88 constellations, many of which were named by the ancient Greeks, Romans and other early peoples after animals and mythological characters, such as Orion and Perseus. More recently, astronomers invented names for constellations seen in the southern hemisphere, in areas not visible around the Mediterranean Sea.

Some groups of easily recognizable stars form parts of a constellation. For example, seven stars form the shape of the Plough, or Big Dipper, within the constellation Ursa Major. Such groups are called asterisms.

The stars in constellations lie in the same direction in space, but normally at vastly different distances. Hence, there is no real connection between them. The positions of stars seem fixed, but in fact the shapes of the constellations are changing slowly over very long periods of time. This is because the stars have their own 'proper motions', which because of the huge distances involved are imperceptible to the naked eye.

The Solar System

Although the origins of the Solar System are still a matter of debate, many scientists believe that it was formed from a cloud of gas and dust, the debris from some long-lost, exploded star. Around 5 billion years ago, material was drawn towards the hub of the rotating disk of gas and dust, where it was compressed to thermonuclear fusion temperatures. A new star, the Sun, was born, containing 99.8% of the mass of the Solar System. The remaining material was later drawn together to form the planets and the other bodies in the Solar System. Spacecraft, manned and unmanned, have greatly increased our knowledge of the Solar System since the start of the Space Age in 1957, when the Soviet Union launched the satellite Sputnik I.

The Planets

Mercury is the closest planet to the Sun and the fastest moving. Space probes have revealed that its surface is covered by craters, and looks much like our Moon. Mercury is a hostile place, with no significant atmosphere and temperatures ranging between 400°C [750°F] by day and –170°C [–275°F] by night. It seems unlikely that anyone will ever want to visit this planet.

Venus is much the same size as Earth, but it is the hottest of the planets, with temperatures reaching 475°C [885°F], even at night. The reason for this scorching heat is the atmosphere, which consists mainly of carbon dioxide, a gas that traps heat thus creating a greenhouse effect. The density of the atmosphere is about 90 times that of Earth and dense clouds permanently mask the surface. Active volcanic regions discharging sulphur dioxide may account for the haze of sulphuric acid droplets in the upper atmosphere.

From planet Earth, Venus is brighter than any other star or planet and is easy to spot. It is often the first object to be seen in the evening sky and the last to be seen in the morning sky. It can even be seen in daylight.

Earth, seen from space, looks blue (because of the oceans which cover more than 70% of the planet) and white (a result of clouds in the atmosphere). The atmosphere and water make Earth the only planet known to support life. The Earth's hard outer layers, including the crust and the top of the mantle, are divided into rigid plates. Forces inside the Earth move the plates, modifying the landscape and causing earthquakes and volcanic activity. Weathering and erosion also change the surface.

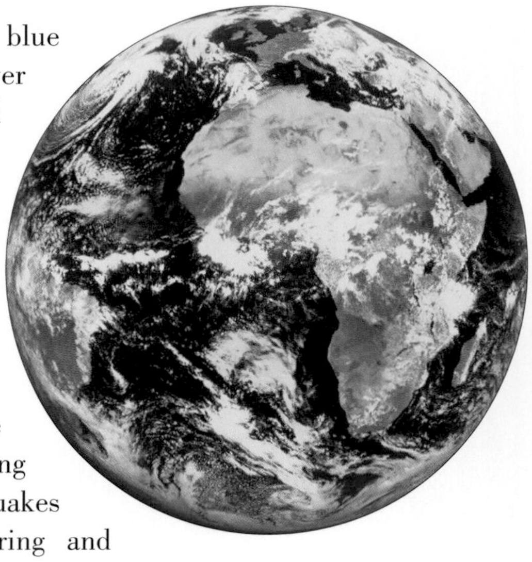

Mars has many features in common with Earth, including an atmosphere with clouds and polar caps that partly melt in summer. Scientists once considered that it was the most likely planet on which other life might exist, but the two Viking space probes that went there in the 1970s found only a barren rocky surface with no trace of water. But data from NASA's probe Mars Odyssey, launched in 2001, suggests that vast quantities of water may lie only a few centimetres below the surface.

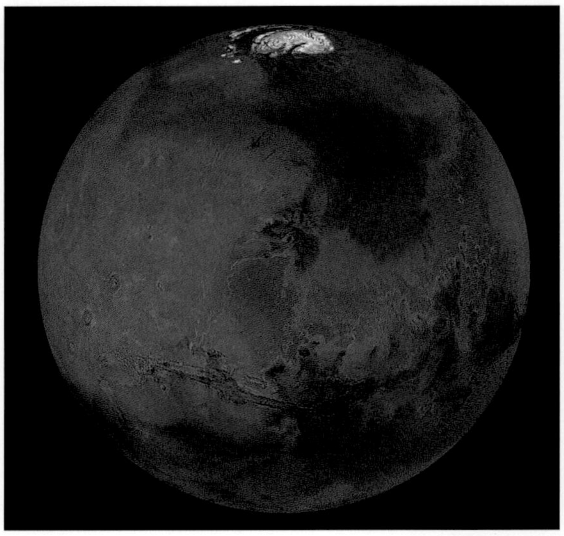

PLANETARY DATA

Planet	Mean distance from Sun (million km)	Mass (Earth=1)	Period of orbit (Earth days/yrs)	Period of rotation (Earth days)	Equatorial diameter (km)	Average density (water=1)	Surface gravity (Earth=1)	Number of known satellites
Sun	–	*332,946*	–	*25.4*	*1,392,000*	*1.41*	*27.9*	–
Mercury	57.9	0.055	87.97d	58.67	4,878	5.44	0.38	0
Venus	108.2	0.815	224.7d	243.00	12,104	5.25	0.90	0
Earth	149.6	1.0	365.3d	1.00	12,756	5.52	1.00	1
Mars	227.9	0.11	687.0d	1.028	6,794	3.94	0.38	2
Jupiter	778	317.9	11.86y	0.411	143,884	1.33	2.64	60
Saturn	1,427	95.2	29.46y	0.427	120,536	0.71	1.16	31
Uranus	2,870	14.6	84.01y	0.748	51,118	1.27	0.79	21
Neptune	4,497	17.2	164.8y	0.710	50,538	1.77	0.98	11
Pluto	5,900	0.002	247.7y	6.39	2,324	2.02	0.06	1

Asteroids are small, rocky bodies. Most of them orbit the Sun between Mars and Jupiter, but some small ones can approach the Earth. The largest is Ceres, 913 km [567 miles] in diameter. There may be around a million asteroids bigger than 1 km [0.6 miles].

Jupiter, the giant planet, lies beyond Mars and the asteroid belt. Its mass is almost three times as much as all the other planets combined and, because of its size, it shines more brightly than any other planet apart from Venus and, occasionally, Mars. The four largest moons of Jupiter were discovered by Galileo. Jupiter is made up mostly of hydrogen and helium, covered by a layer of clouds. Its Great Red Spot is a high-pressure storm. Jupiter made headline news when it was struck by fragments of Comet Shoemaker–Levy 9 in July 1994. This was the greatest collision ever seen by scientists between a planet and another heavenly body. The fragments of the comet that crashed into Jupiter created huge fireballs that caused scars on the planet that remained visible for months after the event.

Saturn is structurally similar to Jupiter but it is best known for its rings. The rings measure about 270,000 km [170,000 miles] across, yet they are no more than a few hundred metres thick. Seen from Earth, the rings seem divided into three main bands of varying brightness, but photographs sent back by the Voyager space probes in 1980 and 1981 showed that they are broken up into thousands of thin ringlets composed of ice particles ranging in size from a snowball to an iceberg. The origin of the rings is still a matter of debate.

Uranus was discovered in 1781 by William Herschel, who first thought it was a comet. It is broadly similar to Jupiter and Saturn in composition, though its distance from the Sun makes its surface even colder. Uranus is circled by thin rings which were discovered in 1977. Unlike the rings of Saturn, the rings of Uranus are black, which explains why they cannot be seen from Earth.

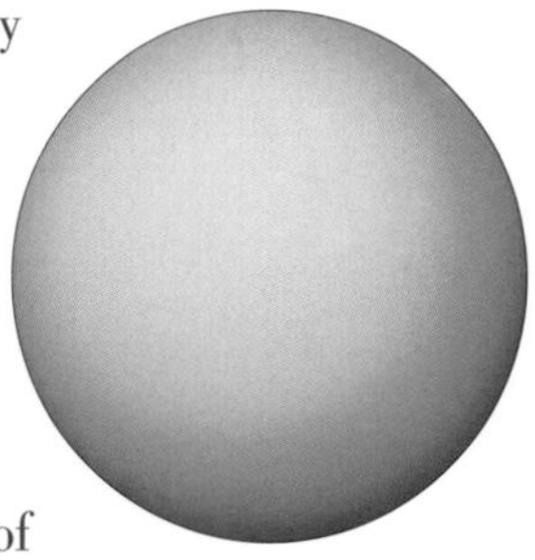

Neptune, named after the mythological sea god, was discovered in 1846 as the result of mathematical predictions made by astronomers to explain irregularities in the orbit of Uranus, its near twin. Little was known about this distant body until Voyager 2 came close to it in 1989. Neptune has thin rings, like those of Uranus. Among its blue-green clouds is a prominent dark spot, which rotates anticlockwise every 18 hours or so.

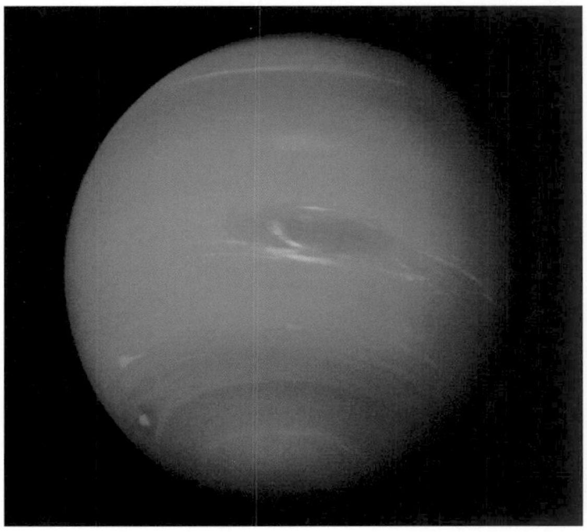

Pluto is the smallest planet in the Solar System, even smaller than our Moon. The American astronomer Clyde Tombaugh discovered Pluto in 1930. Its orbit is odd and it sometimes comes closer to the Sun than Neptune. The nature of Pluto, a gloomy planet appropriately named after the Greek and Roman god of the underworld, is uncertain. At Pluto's distance and beyond are many small, asteroid-like bodies, the first of which was found in 1992.

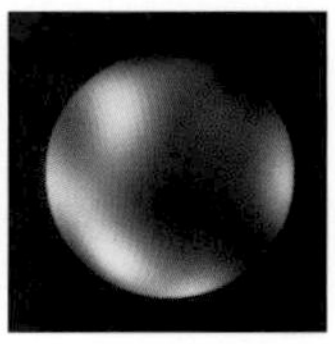

Comets are small icy bodies that orbit the Sun in highly elliptical orbits. When a comet swings in towards the Sun some of its ice evaporates, and the comet brightens and may become visible from Earth. The best known is Halley's Comet, which takes 76 years to orbit the Sun.

The Earth: Time and Motion

The Earth is constantly moving through space like a huge, self-sufficient spaceship. First, with the rest of the Solar System, it moves around the centre of the Milky Way galaxy. Second, it rotates around the Sun at a speed of more than 100,000 km/h [more than 60,000 mph], covering a distance of nearly 1,000 million km [600 million miles] in a little over 365 days. The Earth also spins on its axis, an imaginary line joining the North and South Poles, via the centre of the Earth, completing one turn in a day. The Earth's movements around the Sun determine our calendar, though accurate observations of the stars made by astronomers help to keep our clocks in step with the rotation of the Earth around the Sun.

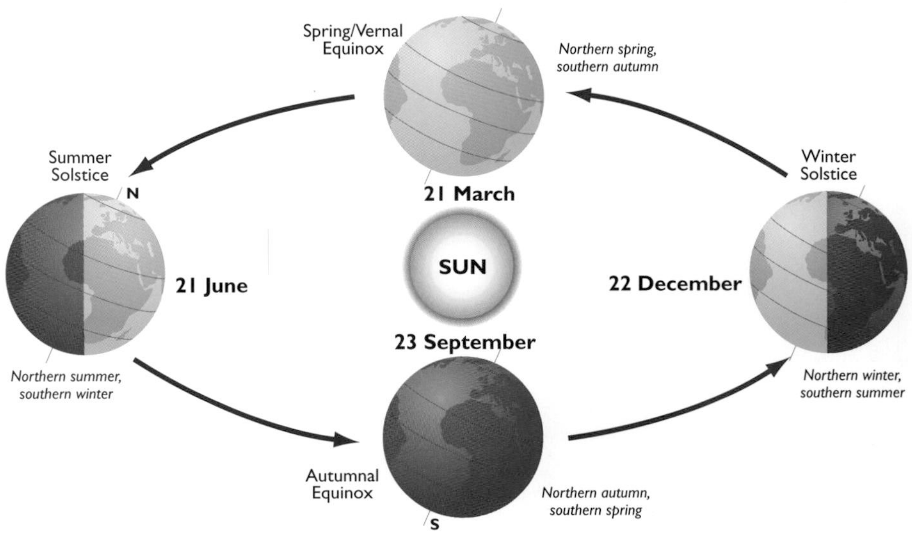
Spring/Vernal Equinox
Northern spring, southern autumn
Summer Solstice
N
21 March
Winter Solstice
21 June
SUN
22 December
23 September
Northern summer, southern winter
Northern winter, southern summer
Autumnal Equinox
Northern autumn, southern spring
S

The Seasons
The 23½° tilt of the Earth's axis remains constant as the Earth orbits around the Sun. As a result, first the northern and then the southern hemispheres lean towards the Sun. Annual variations in the amount of sunlight received in turn by each hemisphere are responsible for the four seasons experienced in the middle latitudes.

The Earth from the Moon
In 1969, Neil Armstrong and Edwin 'Buzz' Aldrin, Junior, were the first people to set foot on the Moon. The photographs forming this composite view of the Earth and Moon were taken by the crew of Apollo 11.

The Changing Year

The Earth takes 365 days, 6 hours, 9 minutes and 9.54 seconds to complete one orbit around the Sun. We have a calendar year of 365 days, so allowance has to be made for the extra time over and above the 365 days. This is allowed for by introducing leap years of 366 days. Leap years are generally those, such as 1992 and 1996, which are divisible by four. Century years, however, are not leap years unless they are divisible by 400. Hence, 1700, 1800 and 1900 were not leap years, but the year 2000 was one. Leap years help to make the calendar conform with the solar year.

Because the Earth's axis is tilted by 23½°, the middle latitudes enjoy four distinct seasons. On 21 March, the vernal or spring equinox in the northern hemisphere, the Sun is directly overhead at the Equator and everywhere on Earth has about 12 hours of daylight and 12 hours of darkness. But as the Earth continues on its journey around the Sun, the northern hemisphere tilts more and more towards the Sun. Finally, on 21 June, the Sun is overhead at the Tropic of Cancer (latitude 23½° North). This is

Tides
The daily rises and falls of the ocean's waters are caused by the gravitational pull of the Moon and the Sun. The effect is greatest on the hemisphere facing the Moon, causing a 'tidal bulge'. The diagram below shows that the Sun, Moon and Earth are in line when the spring tides occur. This causes the greatest tidal ranges. On the other hand, the neap tides occur when the pull of the Moon and the Sun are opposed. Neap tides, when tidal ranges are at their lowest, occur near the Moon's first and third quarters.

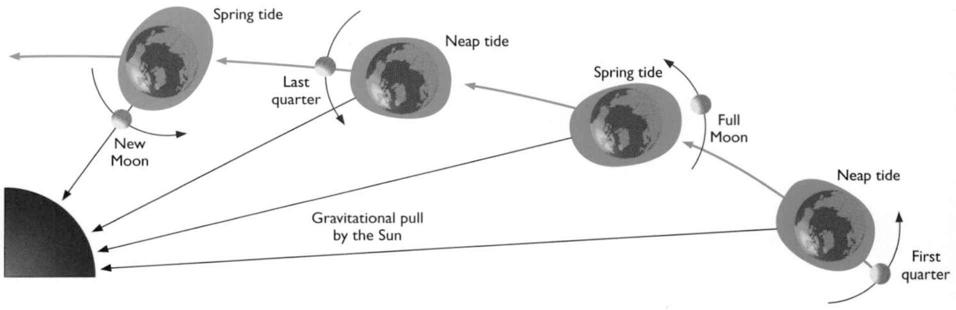
Spring tide
Neap tide
Last quarter
Spring tide
New Moon
Full Moon
Neap tide
Gravitational pull by the Sun
First quarter

SUN DATA

DIAMETER	1.391 x 10^6 km
VOLUME	1.412 x 10^{18} km^3
VOLUME (EARTH = 1)	1.303 x 10^6
MASS	1.989 x 10^{30} kg
MASS (EARTH = 1)	3.329 x 10^6
MEAN DENSITY (WATER = 1)	1.409
ROTATION PERIOD	
AT EQUATOR	25.4 days
AT POLES	about 35 days
SURFACE GRAVITY (EARTH = 1)	28
MAGNITUDE	
APPARENT	–26.9
ABSOLUTE	+4.71
TEMPERATURE	
AT SURFACE	5,400°C [5,700 K]
AT CORE	15 x 10^6 K

MOON DATA

DIAMETER	3,476 km
MASS (EARTH = 1)	0.0123
DENSITY (WATER = 1)	3.34
MEAN DISTANCE FROM EARTH	384,402 km
MAXIMUM DISTANCE (APOGEE)	406,740 km
MINIMUM DISTANCE (PERIGEE)	356,410 km
SIDEREAL ROTATION AND REVOLUTION PERIOD	27.322 days
SYNODIC MONTH (NEW MOON TO NEW MOON)	29.531 days
SURFACE GRAVITY (EARTH = 1)	0.165
MAXIMUM SURFACE TEMPERATURE	+130°C [403 K]
MINIMUM SURFACE TEMPERATURE	–158°C [115 K]

the summer solstice in the northern hemisphere.

The overhead Sun then moves south again until on 23 September, the autumn equinox in the northern hemisphere, the Sun is again overhead at the Equator. The overhead Sun then moves south until, on around 22 December, it is overhead at the Tropic of Capricorn. This is the winter solstice in the northern hemisphere, and the summer solstice in the southern, where the seasons are reversed.

At the poles, there are two seasons. During half of the year, one of the poles leans towards the Sun and has continuous sunlight. For the other six months, the pole leans away from the Sun and is in continuous darkness.

Regions around the Equator do not have marked seasons. Because the Sun is high in the sky throughout the year, it is always hot or warm. When people talk of seasons in the tropics, they are usually referring to other factors, such as rainy and dry periods.

Day, Night and Tides

As the Earth rotates on its axis every 24 hours, first one side of the planet and then the other faces the Sun and enjoys daylight, while the opposite side is in darkness.

The length of daylight varies throughout the year. The longest day in the northern hemisphere falls on the summer solstice, 21 June, while the longest day in the southern hemisphere is on 22 December. At 40° latitude, the length of daylight on the longest day is 14 hours, 30 minutes. At 60° latitude, daylight on that day lasts 18 hours, 30 minutes. On the shortest day, 22 December in the northern hemisphere and 21 June in the southern, daylight hours at 40° latitude total 9 hours and 9 minutes. At latitude 60°, daylight lasts only 5 hours, 30 minutes in the 24-hour period.

Tides are caused by the gravitational pull of the Moon and, to a lesser extent, the Sun on the waters in the world's oceans. Tides occur twice every 24 hours, 50 minutes – one complete orbit of the Moon around the Earth.

Total eclipse of the Sun

A total eclipse is caused when the Moon passes between the Sun and the Earth. With the Sun's bright disk completely obscured, the Sun's corona, or outer atmosphere, can be viewed.

The highest tides, the spring tides, occur when the Earth, Moon and Sun are in a straight line, so that the gravitational pulls of the Moon and Sun are combined. The lowest, or neap, tides occur when the Moon, Earth and Sun form a right angle. The gravitational pull of the Moon is then opposed by the gravitational pull of the Sun. The greatest tidal ranges occur in the Bay of Fundy in North America. The greatest mean spring range is 14.5 m [47.5 ft].

The speed at which the Earth is spinning on its axis is gradually slowing down, because of the movement of tides. As a result, experts have calculated that, in about 200 million years, the day will be 25 hours long.

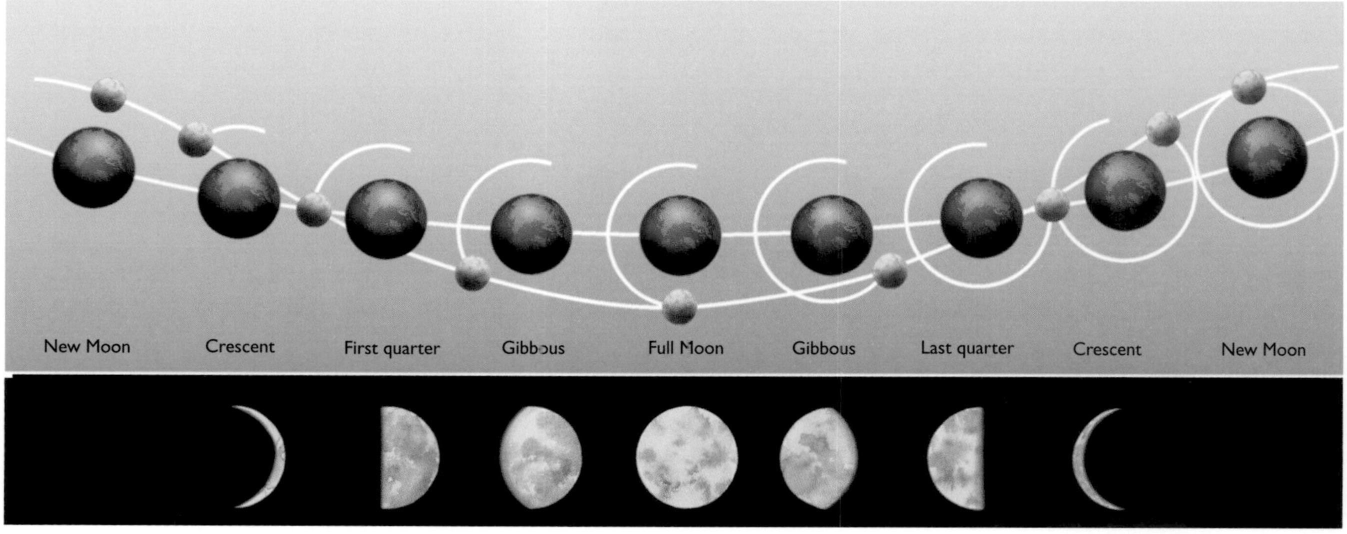
New Moon
Crescent
First quarter
Gibbous
Full Moon
Gibbous
Last quarter
Crescent
New Moon

Phases of the Moon

The Moon rotates more slowly than the Earth, making one complete turn on its axis in just over 27 days. This corresponds to its period of revolution around the Earth and, hence, the same hemisphere always faces us. The interval between one full Moon and the next (and also between new Moons) is about 29½ days, or one lunar month. The apparent changes in the appearance of the Moon are caused by its changing position in relation to Earth. Like the planets, the Moon produces no light of its own. It shines by reflecting the Sun's rays, varying from a slim crescent to a full circle and back again.

The Earth from Space

Any last doubts about whether the Earth was round or flat were finally resolved by the appearance of the first photographs of our planet taken at the start of the Space Age. Satellite images also confirmed that map- and globe-makers had correctly worked out the shapes of the continents and the oceans.

More importantly, images of our beautiful, blue, white and brown planet from space impressed on many people that the Earth and its resources are finite. They made people realize that if we allow our planet to be damaged by such factors as overpopulation, pollution and irresponsible over-use of resources, then its future and the survival of all the living things upon it may be threatened.

Views from Above

The first aerial photographs were taken from balloons in the mid-19th century and their importance in military reconnaissance was recognized as early as the 1860s during the American Civil War.

Vesuvius and the Bay of Naples

Space photographs have given us a new perspective on planet Earth. They vividly convey the dramatic quality of landforms, such as Vesuvius, the volcanic craters that lie just west of Naples and the isle of Capri to the south.

Since the end of World War II, photographs taken by aircraft have been widely used in map-making. The use of air photographs has greatly speeded up the laborious process of mapping land details and they have enabled cartographers to produce maps of the most remote parts of the world.

Aerial photographs have also proved useful because they reveal features that are not visible at ground level. For example, circles that appear on many air photographs do not correspond to visible features on the ground. Many of these mysterious shapes have turned out to be the sites of ancient settlements previously unknown to archaeologists.

Images from Space

Space probes equipped with cameras and a variety of remote-sensing instruments have sent back images of distant planets and moons. From these images, detailed maps have been produced, rapidly expanding our knowledge of the Solar System.

Photographs from space are also proving invaluable in the study of the Earth. One of the best known uses of space imagery is the study of the atmosphere. Polar-orbiting weather satellites that circle the Earth, together with geostationary satellites, whose motion is synchronized with the Earth's rotation, now regularly transmit images showing the changing patterns of weather systems from above. Forecasters use these images to track the development and the paths taken by hurricanes, enabling them to issue storm warnings to endangered areas, saving lives and reducing damage to property.

Remote-sensing devices are now monitoring changes in temperatures over the land and sea, while photographs indicate the melting of ice sheets. Such evidence is vital in the study of global warming. Other devices reveal polluted areas, patterns of vegetation growth, and areas suffering deforestation.

In recent years, remote-sensing devices have been used to monitor the damage being done to the ozone layer in the stratosphere, which prevents most of the Sun's harmful ultraviolet radiation from reaching the surface. The discovery of 'ozone holes', where the protective layer of ozone is being thinned by chlorofluorocarbons (CFCs), chemicals used in the manufacture of such things as air conditioners and refrigerators, has enabled governments to take concerted action to save our planet from imminent danger.

Earth Data

MAXIMUM DISTANCE FROM SUN (APHELION)
152,007,016 km

MINIMUM DISTANCE FROM SUN (PERIHELION)
147,000,830 km

LENGTH OF YEAR – SOLAR TROPICAL (EQUINOX TO EQUINOX)
365.24 days

LENGTH OF YEAR – SIDEREAL (FIXED STAR TO FIXED STAR)
365.26 days

LENGTH OF DAY – MEAN SOLAR DAY
24 hours, 03 minutes, 56 seconds

LENGTH OF DAY – MEAN SIDEREAL DAY
23 hours, 56 minutes, 4 seconds

SUPERFICIAL AREA
510,000,000 km^2

LAND SURFACE
149,000,000 km^2 (29.2%)

WATER SURFACE
361,000,000 km^2 (70.8%)

EQUATORIAL CIRCUMFERENCE
40,077 km

POLAR CIRCUMFERENCE
40,009 km

EQUATORIAL DIAMETER
12,756.8 km

POLAR DIAMETER
12,713.8 km

EQUATORIAL RADIUS
6,378.4 km

POLAR RADIUS
6,356.9 km

VOLUME OF THE EARTH
1,083,230 × 10^6 km^3

MASS OF THE EARTH
5.9 × 10^{21} tonnes

Satellite image of San Francisco Bay

Unmanned scientific satellites called ERTS (Earth Resources Technology Satellites), *or* Landsats, *were designed to collect information about the Earth's resources. The satellites transmitted images of the land using different wavelengths of light in order to identify, in false colours, such subtle features as areas that contain minerals or areas covered with growing crops, that are not identifiable on simple photographs using the visible range of the spectrum. They were also equipped to monitor conditions in the atmosphere and oceans, and also to detect pollution levels. This* Landsat *image of San Francisco Bay covers an area of great interest to geologists because it lies in an earthquake zone in the path of the San Andreas fault.*

The Dynamic Earth

The Earth was formed about 4.6 billion years [4,600 million years] ago from the ring of gas and dust left over after the formation of the Sun. As the Earth took shape, lighter elements, such as silicon, rose to the surface, while heavy elements, notably iron, sank towards the centre.

Gradually, the outer layers cooled to form a hard crust. The crust enclosed the dense mantle which, in turn, surrounded the even denser liquid outer and solid inner core. Around the Earth was an atmosphere, which contained abundant water vapour. When the surface cooled, rainwater began to fill hollows, forming the first lakes and seas. Since that time, our planet has been subject to constant change – the result of powerful internal and external forces that still operate today.

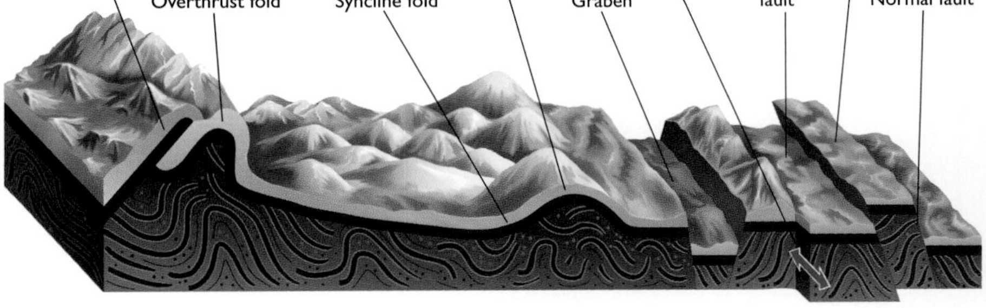
Nappe fold
Overthrust fold
Syncline fold
Symmetrical anticline fold
Graben
Strike-slip fault
Reverse fault
Horst
Normal fault

Mountain building
Lateral pressure, which occurs when plates collide, squeezes and compresses rocks into folds. Simple symmetrical upfolds are called anticlines, while downfolds are synclines. As the pressure builds up, strata become asymmetrical and they may be tilted over to form recumbent folds. The rocks often crack under the intense pressure and the folds are sheared away and pushed forward over other rocks. These features are called overthrust folds or nappes. Plate movements also create faults along which rocks move upwards, downwards and sideways. The diagram shows a downfaulted graben, or rift valley, and an uplifted horst, or block mountain.

Lulworth Cove, southern England
When undisturbed by earth movements, sedimentary rock strata are generally horizontal. But lateral pressure has squeezed the Jurassic strata at Lulworth Cove into complex folds.

The History of the Earth

From their study of rocks, geologists have pieced together the history of our planet and the life forms that evolved upon it. They have dated the oldest known crystals, composed of the mineral zircon, at 4.2 billion years. But the oldest rocks are younger, less than 4 billion years old. This is because older rocks have been weathered away by natural processes.

The oldest rocks that contain fossils, which are evidence of once-living organisms, are around 3.5 billion years old. But fossils are rare in rocks formed in the first 4 billion years of Earth history. This vast expanse of time is called the Precambrian. This is because it precedes the Cambrian period, at the start of which, about 590 million years ago, life was abundant in the seas.

The Cambrian is the first period in the Paleozoic (or ancient life) era. The Paleozoic era is followed by the Mesozoic (middle life) era, which witnessed the spectacular rise and fall of the dinosaurs, and the Cenozoic (recent life) era, which was dominated by the evolution of mammals. Each of the eras is divided into periods, and the periods in the Cenozoic era, covering the last 65 million years, are further divided into epochs.

The Earth's Changing Face

While life was gradually evolving, the face of the Earth was constantly changing. By piecing together evidence of rock structures and fossils, geologists have demonstrated that around 250 million years ago, all the world's land areas were grouped together in one huge landmass called Pangaea. Around 180 million years ago, the supercontinent Pangaea, began to break up. New oceans opened up as the continents began to move towards their present positions.

Evidence of how continents drift came from studies of the ocean floor in the 1950s and 1960s. Scientists discovered that the oceans are young features. By contrast with the continents, no part of the ocean floor is more than 200 million years old. The floors of oceans older than 200 million years have completely vanished.

Studies of long undersea ranges, called ocean ridges, revealed that the youngest rocks occur along their centres, which are the edges of huge plates – rigid blocks of the Earth's lithosphere, which is made up of the crust and the solid upper layer of the mantle. The Earth's lithosphere is split into six large and several smaller

The Himalayas seen from Nepal

The Himalayas are a young fold mountain range formed by a collision between two plates. The earthquakes felt in the region testify that the plate movements are still continuing.

plates. The ocean ridges are 'constructive' plate margins, because new crustal rock is being formed there from magma that wells up from the mantle as the plates gradually move apart. By contrast, the deep ocean trenches are 'destructive' plate edges. Here, two plates are pushing against each other and one plate is descending beneath the other into the mantle where it is melted and destroyed. Geologists call these areas subduction zones.

A third type of plate edge is called a transform fault. Here two plates are moving alongside each other. The best known of these plate edges is the San Andreas fault in California, which separates the Pacific plate from the North American plate.

Slow-moving currents in the partly molten asthenosphere, which underlies the solid lithosphere, are responsible for moving the plates, a process called plate tectonics.

Geological time scale

The geological time scale was first constructed by a study of the stratigraphic, or relative, ages of layers of rock. But the absolute ages of rock strata could not be fixed until the discovery of radioactivity in the early 20th century. Some names of periods, such as Cambrian (Latin for Wales), come from places where the rocks were first studied. Others, such as Carboniferous, refer to the nature of the rocks formed during the period. For example, coal seams (containing carbon) were formed from decayed plant matter during the Carboniferous period.

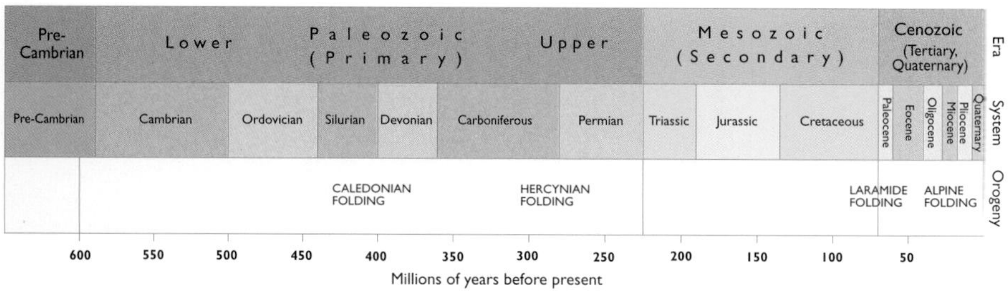
Pre-Cambrian
Lower
Paleozoic (Primary)
Upper
Mesozoic (Secondary)
Cenozoic (Tertiary, Quaternary)
Era
Pre-Cambrian
Cambrian
Ordovician
Silurian
Devonian
Carboniferous
Permian
Triassic
Jurassic
Cretaceous
Paleocene
Eocene
Oligocene
Miocene
Pliocene
Quaternary
System
CALEDONIAN FOLDING
HERCYNIAN FOLDING
LARAMIDE FOLDING
ALPINE FOLDING
Orogeny
600
550
500
450
400
350
300
250
200
150
100
50
Millions of years before present

Mountain Building

The study of plate tectonics has helped geologists to understand the mechanisms that are responsible for the creation of mountains. Many of the world's greatest ranges were created by the collision of two plates and the bending of the intervening strata into huge loops, or folds. For example, the Himalayas began to rise around 50 million years ago, when a plate supporting India collided with the huge Eurasian plate. Rocks on the floor of the intervening and long-vanished Tethys Sea were squeezed up to form the Himalayan Mountain Range.

Plate movements also create tension that cracks rocks, producing long faults along which rocks move upwards, downwards or sideways. Block mountains are formed when blocks of rock are pushed upwards along faults. Steep-sided rift valleys are formed when blocks of land sink down between faults. For example, the basin and range region of the south-western United States has both block mountains and downfaulted basins, such as Death Valley.

Earthquakes and Volcanoes

On 24 February 2003, an earthquake that registered 6.8 on the Richter scale struck north-western China. More than 260 people died and more than 1,000 houses collapsed in one village alone. Earthquakes are common in this part of China, but loss of life is limited because the region is thinly populated. However, when an earthquake struck the Chinese city of Tangshan in 1976, 250,000 people died.

The Restless Earth

Earthquakes can occur anywhere, whenever rocks move along faults. But the most severe and most numerous earthquakes occur near the edges of the plates that make up the Earth's lithosphere. Japan, for example, lies in a particularly unstable region above subduction zones, where plates are descending into the Earth's mantle. It lies in a zone encircling the Pacific Ocean, called the 'Pacific ring of fire'.

Plates do not move smoothly. Their edges are jagged and for most of the time they are locked together. However, pressure gradually builds up until the rocks break and the plates lurch forward, setting off vibrations ranging from slight tremors to terrifying earthquakes. The greater the pressure released, the more destructive the earthquake.

Earthquakes are also common along the ocean trenches where plates are moving apart, but they mostly occur so far from land that they do little damage. Far more destructive are the earthquakes that occur where plates are moving alongside each other. For example, the earthquakes that periodically rock south-western California are caused by movements along the San Andreas Fault.

The spot where an earthquake originates is called the focus, while the point on the Earth's surface directly above the focus is called the epicentre. Two kinds of waves, P-waves or compressional waves and S-waves or shear waves, travel from the focus to the surface where they make the ground shake. P-waves travel faster than S-waves and the time difference between their arrival at recording stations enables scientists to calculate the distance from a station to the epicentre.

Earthquakes are measured on the Richter scale, which indicates the magnitude of the shock. The most destructive earthquakes are shallow-focus, that is, the focus is within 60 km [37 miles] of the surface. A magnitude of 7.0 is a major earthquake, but earthquakes with a somewhat lower magnitude can cause tremendous damage if their epicentres are on or close to densely populated areas.

San Andreas Fault, United States

Geologists call the San Andreas fault in south-western California a transform, or strike-slip, fault. Sudden movements along it cause earthquakes. In 1906, shifts of about 4.5 metres [15 ft] occurred near San Francisco, causing a massive earthquake.

NOTABLE EARTHQUAKES *(since 1900)*

Year	Location	Mag.
1906	San Francisco, USA	8.3
1906	Valparaiso, Chile	8.6
1908	Messina, Italy	7.5
1915	Avezzano, Italy	7.5
1920	Gansu, China	8.6
1923	Yokohama, Japan	8.3
1927	Nan Shan, China	8.3
1932	Gansu, China	7.6
1934	Bihar, India/Nepal	8.4
1935	Quetta, India†	7.5
1939	Chillan, Chile	8.3
1939	Erzincan, Turkey	7.9
1964	Anchorage, Alaska	8.4
1968	N. E. Iran	7.4
1970	N. Peru	7.7
1976	Guatemala	7.5
1976	Tangshan, China	8.2
1978	Tabas, Iran	7.7
1980	El Asnam, Algeria	7.3
1980	S. Italy	7.2
1985	Mexico City, Mexico	8.1
1988	N. W. Armenia	6.8
1990	N. Iran	7.7
1993	Maharashtra, India	6.4
1994	Los Angeles, USA	6.6
1995	Kobe, Japan	7.2
1995	Sakhalin Is., Russia	7.5
1996	Yunnan, China	7.0
1997	N. E. Iran	7.1
1998	N. Afghanistan	6.1
1998	N. E. Afghanistan	7.0
1999	Izmit, Turkey	7.4
1999	Taipei, Taiwan	7.6
2001	El Salvador	7.7
2001	Gujarat, India	7.7
2002	Afyon, Turkey	6.0
2002	Baghlan, Afghanistan	6.1
2003	Mexico	7.8

† now Pakistan

Earthquakes in subduction zones

Along subduction zones, one plate is descending beneath another. The plates are locked together until the rocks break and the descending plate lurches forwards. From the point where the plate moves – the origin – seismic waves spread through the lithosphere, making the ground shake. The earthquake in Mexico City in 1985 occurred in this way.

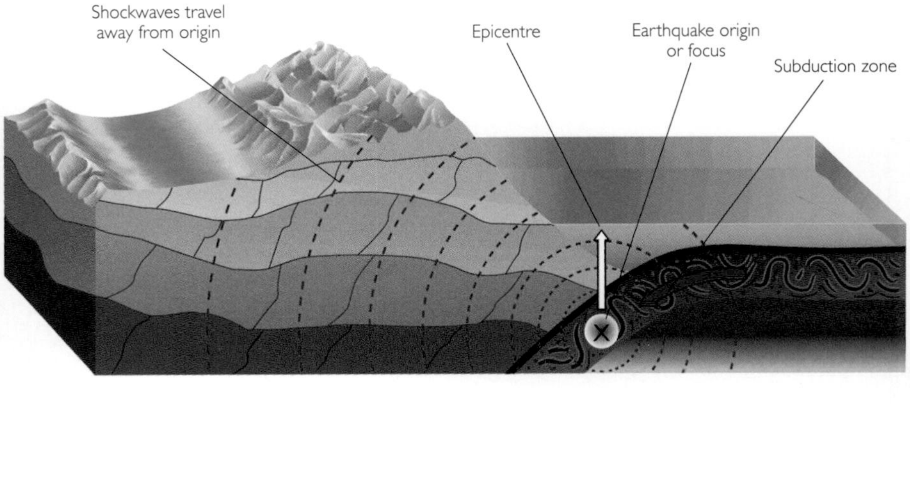
Shockwaves travel away from origin
Epicentre
Earthquake origin or focus
Subduction zone

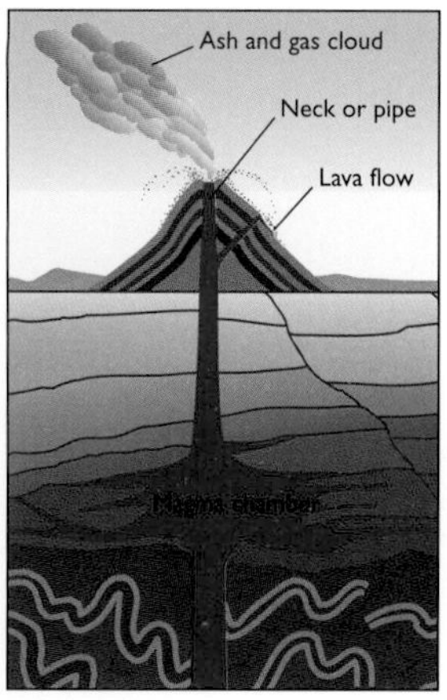
Ash and gas cloud
Neck or pipe
Lava flow
Magma chamber

Cross-section of a volcano
Volcanoes are vents in the ground, through which magma reaches the surface. The term volcano is also used for the mountains formed from volcanic rocks. Beneath volcanoes are pockets of magma derived from the semi-molten asthenosphere in the mantle. The magma rises under pressure through the overlying rocks until it reaches the surface. There it emerges through vents as pyroclasts, ranging in size from large lumps of magma, called volcanic bombs, to fine volcanic ash and dust. In quiet eruptions, streams of liquid lava run down the side of the mountain. Side vents sometimes appear on the flanks of existing volcanoes.

Scientists have been working for years to find effective ways of forecasting earthquakes but with very limited success. Following the Kobe earthquake in 1995, many experts argued that they would be better employed developing techniques of reducing the damage caused by earthquakes, rather than pursuing an apparently vain attempt to predict them.

Volcanic Eruptions

Most active volcanoes also occur on or near plate edges. Many undersea volcanoes along the ocean ridges are formed from magma that wells up from the asthenosphere to fill the gaps created as the plates, on the opposite sides of the ridges, move apart. Some of these volcanoes reach the surface to form islands. Iceland is a country which straddles the Mid-Atlantic Ocean Ridge. It is gradually becoming wider as magma rises to the surface through faults and vents. Other volcanoes lie alongside subduction zones. The magma that fuels them comes from the melted edges of the descending plates.

A few volcanoes lie far from plate edges. For example, Mauna Loa and Kilauea on Hawaii are situated near the centre of the huge Pacific plate. The molten magma that reaches the surface is created by a source of heat, called a 'hot spot', in the Earth's mantle.

Magma is molten rock at temperatures of about 1,100°C to 1,200°C [2,012°F to 2,192°F]. It contains gases and superheated steam. The chemical composition of magma varies. Viscous magma is rich in silica and superheated steam, while runny magma contains less silica and steam. The chemical composition of the magma affects the nature of volcanic eruptions.

Explosive volcanoes contain thick, viscous magma. When they erupt, they usually hurl clouds of ash (shattered fragments of cooled magma) into the air. By contrast, quiet volcanoes emit long streams of runny magma, or lava. However, many volcanoes are intermediate in type, sometimes erupting explosively and sometimes emitting streams of fluid lava. Explosive and intermediate volcanoes usually have a conical shape, while quiet volcanoes are flattened, resembling upturned saucers. They are often called shield volcanoes.

One dangerous type of eruption is called a *nuée ardente*, or 'glowing cloud'. It occurs when a cloud of intensely hot volcanic gases and dust particles and superheated steam are exploded from a volcano. They move rapidly downhill, burning everything in their path and choking animals and people. The blast that creates the *nuée ardente* may release the pressure inside the volcano, resulting in a tremendous explosion that hurls tall columns of ash into the air.

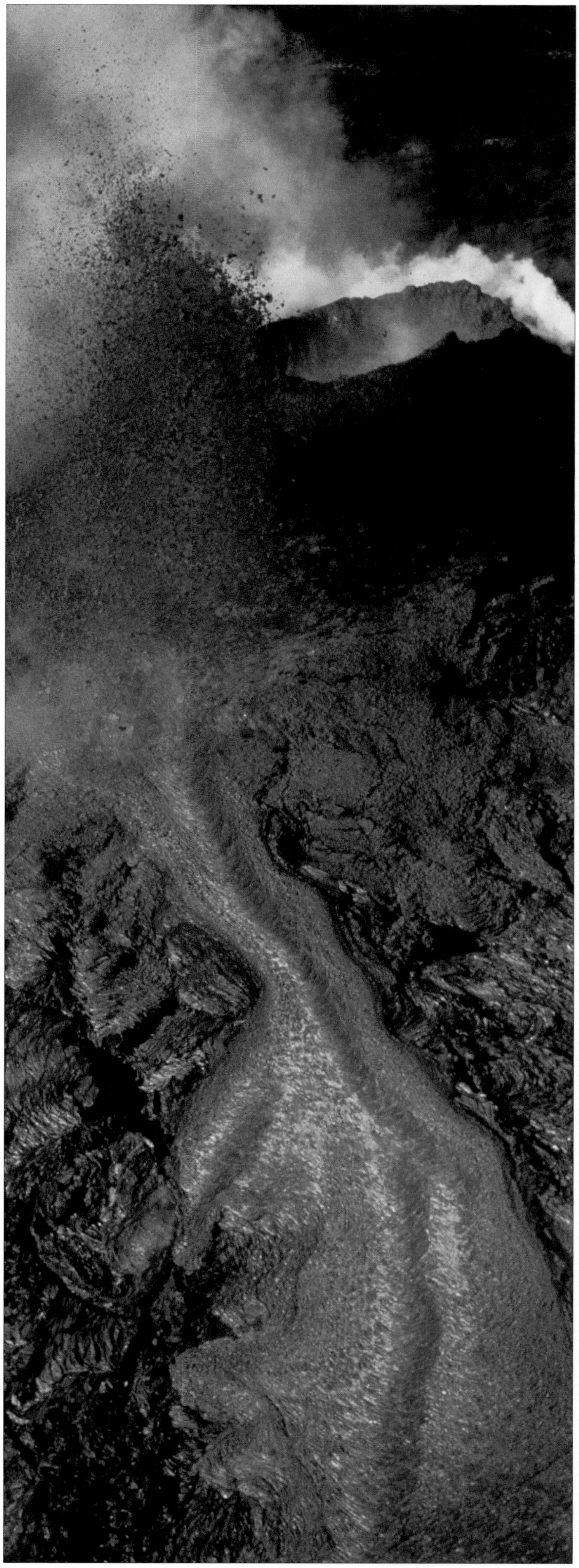

Kilauea Volcano, Hawaii
The volcanic Hawaiian islands in the North Pacific Ocean were formed as the Pacific plate moved over a 'hot spot' in the Earth's mantle. Kilauea on Hawaii emits blazing streams of liquid lava.

Forces of Nature

When the volcano Mount Pinatubo erupted in the Philippines in 1991, loose ash covered large areas around the mountain. During the 1990s and early 2000s, rainwater mixed with the ash on sloping land, creating *lahars*, or mudflows, which swept down river valleys burying many areas. Such incidents are not only reminders of the great forces that operate inside our planet but also of those natural forces operating on the surface, which can have dramatic effects on the land.

The chief forces acting on the surface of the Earth are weathering, running water, ice and winds. The forces of erosion seem to act slowly. One estimate suggests that an average of only 3.5 cm [1.4 in] of land is removed by natural processes every 1,000 years. This may not sound much, but over millions of years, it can reduce mountains to almost flat surfaces.

RATES OF EROSION

	WEATHERING RATE: SLOW ⟵		⟶ FAST
Mineral solubility	low (e.g. quartz)	moderate (e.g. feldspar)	high (e.g. calcite)
Rainfall	low	moderate	heavy
Temperature	cold	temperate	hot
Vegetation	sparse	moderate	lush
Soil cover	bare rock	thin to moderate soil	thick soil

Weathering is the breakdown and decay of rocks in situ. It may be mechanical (physical), chemical or biological.

Rates of erosion
The chart shows that the rates at which weathering takes place depend on the chemistry and hardness of rocks, climatic factors, especially rainfall and temperature, the vegetation and the nature of the soil cover in any area. The effects of weathering are increased by human action, particularly the removal of vegetation and the exposure of soils to the rain and wind.

Weathering

Weathering occurs in all parts of the world, but the most effective type of weathering in any area depends on the climate and the nature of the rocks. For example, in cold mountain areas, when water freezes in cracks in rocks, the ice occupies 9% more space than the water. This exerts a force which, when repeated over and over again, can split boulders apart. By contrast, in hot deserts, intense heating by day and cooling by night causes the outer layers of rocks to expand and contract until they break up and peel away like layers of an onion. These are examples of what is called mechanical weathering.

Other kinds of weathering include chemical reactions usually involving water. Rainwater containing carbon dioxide dissolved from the air or the soil is a weak acid which reacts with limestone, wearing out pits, tunnels and networks of caves in layers of limestone rock. Water also combines with some minerals, such as the feldspars in granite, to create kaolin, a white

Grand Canyon, Arizona, at dusk
The Grand Canyon in the United States is one of the world's natural wonders. Eroded by the Colorado River and its tributaries, it is up to 1.6 km [1 mile] deep and 29 km [18 miles] wide.

clay. These are examples of chemical weathering which constantly wears away rock.

Running Water, Ice and Wind

In moist regions, rivers are effective in shaping the land. They transport material worn away by weathering and erode the land. They wear out V-shaped valleys in upland regions, while vigorous meanders widen their middle courses. The work of rivers is at its most spectacular when earth movements lift up flat areas and rejuvenate the rivers, giving them a new erosive power capable of wearing out such features as the Grand Canyon. Rivers also have a constructive role. Some of the world's most fertile regions are deltas and flood plains composed of sediments periodically dumped there by such rivers as the Ganges, Mississippi and Nile.

Glaciers

During Ice Ages, ice spreads over large areas but, during warm periods, the ice retreats. The chart shows that the volume of ice in many glaciers is decreasing, possibly as a result of global warming. Experts estimate that, between 1850 and the early 21st century, more than half of the ice in Alpine glaciers has melted.

ANNUAL FLUCTUATIONS FOR SELECTED GLACIERS

Glacier name and location	Changes in the annual mass balance† 1970–1	1990–1	Cumulative total 1970–90
Alfotbreen, Norway	+940	+790	+12,110
Wolverine, USA	+770	–410	+2,320
Storglaciaren, Sweden	–190	+170	–120
Djankuat, Russia	–230	–310	–1,890
Grasubreen, Norway	+470	–520	–2,530
Ürümqi, China	+102	–706	–3,828
Golubin, Kyrgyzstan	–90	–722	–7,105
Hintereisferner, Austria	–600	–1,325	–9,081
Gries, Switzerland	–970	–1,480	–10,600
Careser, Italy	–650	–1,730	–11,610
Abramov, Tajikistan	–890	–420	–13,700
Sarennes, France	–1,100	–1,360	–15,020
Place, Canada	–343	–990	–15,175

† *The annual mass balance is defined as the difference between glacier accumulation and ablation (melting) averaged over the whole glacier. Balances are expressed as water equivalent in millimetres. A plus indicates an increase in the depth or length of the glacier; a minus indicates a reduction.*

Juneau Glacier, Alaska

Like huge conveyor belts, glaciers transport weathered debris from mountain regions. Rocks frozen in the ice give the glaciers teeth, enabling them to wear out typical glaciated land features.

Running water in the form of sea waves and currents shapes coastlines, wearing out caves, natural arches, and stacks. The sea also transports and deposits worn material to form such features as spits and bars.

Glaciers in cold mountain regions flow downhill, gradually deepening valleys and shaping dramatic landscapes. They erode steep-sided U-shaped valleys, into which rivers often plunge in large waterfalls. Other features include cirques, armchair-shaped basins bounded by knife-edged ridges called *arêtes*. When several glacial cirques erode to form radial *arêtes*, pyramidal peaks like the Matterhorn are created. Deposits of moraine, rock material dumped by the glacier, are further evidence that ice once covered large areas. The work of glaciers, like other agents of erosion, varies with the climate. In recent years, global warming has been making glaciers retreat in many areas, while several of the ice shelves in Antarctica have been breaking up.

Many land features in deserts were formed by running water at a time when the climate was much rainier than it is today. Water erosion also occurs when flash floods are caused by rare thunderstorms. But the chief agent of erosion in dry areas is wind-blown sand, which can strip the paint from cars, and undercut boulders to create mushroom-shaped rocks.

Oceans and Ice

Since the 1970s, oceanographers have found numerous hot vents on the ocean ridges. Called black smokers, the vents emit dark, mineral-rich water reaching 350°C [662°F]. Around the vents are chimney-like structures formed from minerals deposited from the hot water. The discovery of black smokers did not surprise scientists who already knew that the ridges were plate edges, where new crustal rock was being formed as molten magma welled up to the surface. But what was astonishing was that the hot water contained vast numbers of bacteria, which provided the base of a food chain that included many strange creatures, such as giant worms, eyeless shrimps and white clams. Many species were unknown to science.

Little was known about the dark world beneath the waves until about 50 years ago. But through the use of modern technology such as echo-sounders, magnetometers, research ships equipped with huge drills, submersibles that can carry scientists down to the ocean floor, and satellites, the secrets of the oceans have been gradually revealed.

The study of the ocean floor led to the discovery that the oceans are geologically young features – no more than 200 million years old. It also revealed evidence as to how oceans form and continents drift because of the action of plate tectonics.

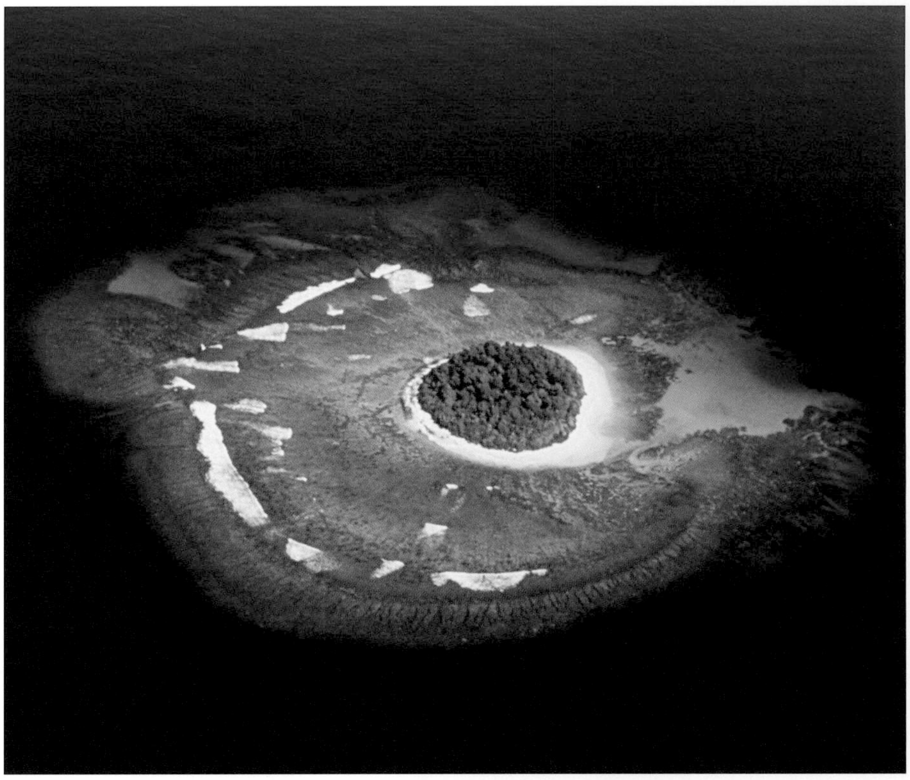

Vava'u Island, Tonga

This small coral atoll in northern Tonga consists of a central island covered by rainforest. Low coral reefs washed by the waves surround a shallow central lagoon.

The Blue Planet

Water covers almost 71% of the Earth, which makes it look blue when viewed from space. Although the oceans are interconnected, geographers divide them into four main areas: the Pacific, Atlantic, Indian and Arctic oceans. The average depth of the oceans is 3,370 m [12,238 ft], but they are divided into several zones.

Around most continents are gently sloping continental shelves, which are flooded parts of the continents. The shelves end at the continental slope, at a depth of about 200 m [656 ft]. This slope leads steeply down to the abyss. The deepest parts of the oceans are the trenches, which reach a maximum depth of 11,022 m [36,161 ft] in the Mariana Trench in the western Pacific.

Most marine life is found in the top 200 m [656 ft], where there is sufficient sunlight for plants, called phytoplankton, to grow. Below this zone, life becomes more and more scarce, though no part of the ocean, even at the bottom of the deepest trenches, is completely without living things.

Continental islands, such as the British Isles, are high parts of the continental shelves. For example, until about 7,500 years ago, when the ice sheets formed during the Ice Ages were melting, raising the sea level and filling the North Sea and the Strait of Dover, Britain was linked to mainland Europe.

By contrast, oceanic islands, such as the Hawaiian chain in the North Pacific Ocean, rise from the ocean floor. All oceanic islands are of volcanic origin, although many of them in warm parts of the oceans have sunk and are capped by layers of coral to form ring- or horseshoe-shaped atolls and coral reefs.

Ocean Water

The oceans contain about 97% of the world's water. Seawater contains more than 70 dissolved elements, but chloride and sodium make up 85% of the total. Sodium chloride is common salt and it makes seawater salty. The salinity of the oceans is mostly between 3.3–3.7%. Ocean water fed by icebergs or large rivers is less saline than shallow seas in the tropics, where the evaporation rate is high. Seawater is a source of salt but the water is useless for agriculture or drinking unless it is desalinated. However, land

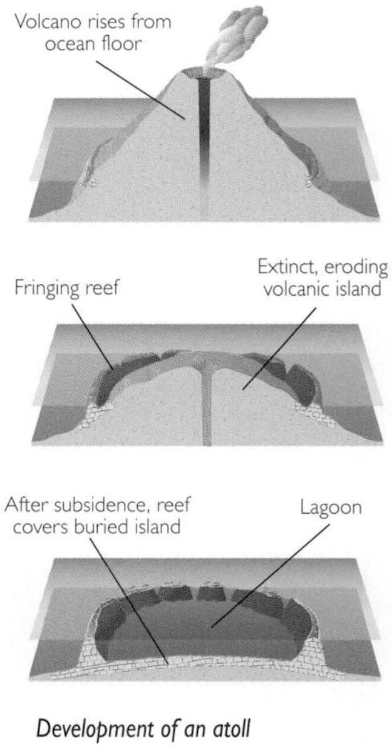
Volcano rises from ocean floor
Fringing reef
Extinct, eroding volcanic island
After subsidence, reef covers buried island
Lagoon

Development of an atoll

Some of the volcanoes that rise from the ocean floor reach the surface to form islands. Some of these islands subside and become submerged. As an island sinks, coral starts to grow around the rim of the volcano, building up layer upon layer of limestone deposits to form fringing reefs. Sometimes coral grows on the tip of a central cone to form an island in the middle of the atoll.

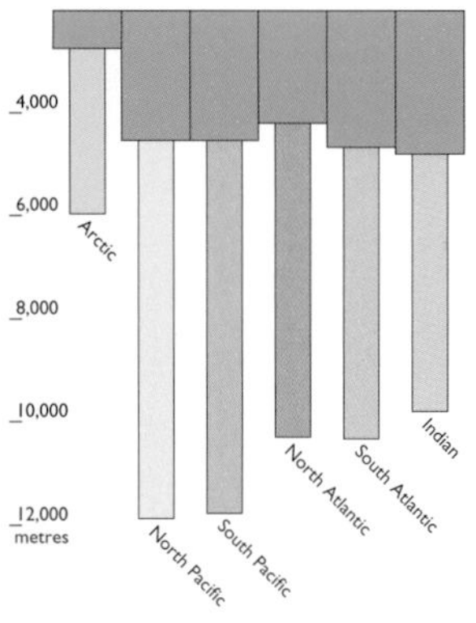
4,000
6,000
8,000
10,000
12,000
metres
Arctic
North Pacific
South Pacific
North Atlantic
South Atlantic
Indian

The ocean depths

The diagram shows the average depths (in dark blue) and the greatest depths in the four oceans. The North Pacific Ocean contains the world's deepest trenches, including the Mariana Trench, where the deepest manned descent was made by the bathyscaphe Trieste *in 1960. It reached a depth of 10,916 m [35,813 ft].*

Relative sizes of the world's oceans:

PACIFIC 49% ATLANTIC 26%
INDIAN 21% ARCTIC 4%

Some geographers distinguish a fifth ocean, the Southern or Antarctic Ocean, but most authorities regard these waters as the southern extension of the Pacific, Atlantic and Indian oceans.

areas get a regular supply of fresh water through the hydrological cycle (see page 26).

The density of seawater depends on its salinity and temperature. Temperatures vary from –2°C [28°F], the freezing point of seawater at the poles, to around 30°C [86°F] in parts of the tropics. Density differences help to maintain the circulation of the world's oceans, especially deep-sea currents. But the main cause of currents within 350 m [1,148 ft] of the surface is the wind. Because of the Earth's rotation, currents are deflected, creating huge circular motions of surface water – clockwise in the northern hemisphere and anticlockwise in the southern hemisphere.

Ocean currents transport heat from the tropics to the polar regions and thus form part of the heat engine that drives the Earth's climates. Ocean currents have an especially marked effect on coastal climates, such as north-western Europe. In the mid-1990s, scientists warned that global warming may be weakening currents, including the warm Gulf Stream which is responsible for the mild winters experienced in north-western Europe.

Ice Sheets, Ice Caps and Glaciers

Of the world's two ice sheets, the largest, covering most of Antarctica, has maximum depths of 4,800 m [15,748 ft]. Its volume is about nine times greater than the Greenland ice sheet. The ice sheets, together with smaller ice caps and glaciers together account for about 2% of the world's water. However, in many parts of the world, the ice is melting and many scientists think the cause is global warming. In March 2002, the vast Larsen ice shelf bordering the Antarctic peninsula collapsed and broke up into icebergs. Some scientists thought this was evidence of global warming, though some attributed the event to local factors.

Only about 11,000 years ago, during the final phase of the Pleistocene Ice Age, ice covered much of the northern hemisphere. The Ice Age, which began about 1.8 million years ago, was not a continuous period of cold. Instead, it consisted of glacial periods when the ice advanced and warmer interglacial periods when temperatures rose and the ice retreated.

Some scientists believe that we are now living in an interglacial period, and that glacial conditions will recur in the future. Others fear that global warming, caused mainly by pollution, may melt the world's ice, raising sea levels by up to 55 m [180 ft]. Many fertile and densely populated coastal plains, islands and cities would vanish from the map.

Weddell Sea, Antarctica

Antarctica contains two huge bays, occupied by the Ross and Weddell seas. Ice shelves extend from the ice sheet across parts of these seas. Researchers fear that warmer weather is melting Antarctica's ice sheets at a dangerous rate, after large chunks of the Larsen ice shelf and the Ronne ice shelf broke away in 1997 and 1998 respectively. This was followed in March 2002 by the disintegration of the Larsen B ice shelf.

The Earth's Atmosphere

Since the discovery in 1985 of a thinning of the ozone layer, creating a so-called 'ozone hole', over Antarctica, many governments have worked to reduce the emissions of ozone-eating substances, notably the chlorofluorocarbons (CFCs) used in aerosols, refrigeration, air conditioning and dry cleaning.

Following forecasts that the ozone layer would rapidly repair itself as a result of controls on these emissions, scientists were surprised in early 1996 when a marked thinning of the ozone layer occurred over the Arctic, northern Europe, Russia and Canada. The damage, which was recorded as far south as southern Britain, was due to pollution combined with intense cold in the stratosphere. It was another sharp reminder of the dangers humanity faces when it interferes with and harms the environment.

The ozone layer in the stratosphere blocks out most of the dangerous ultraviolet B radiation in the Sun's rays. This radiation causes skin cancer and cataracts, as well as harming plants on the land and plankton in the oceans. The ozone layer is only one way in which the atmosphere protects life on Earth. The atmosphere also provides the air we breathe and the carbon dioxide required by plants. It is also a shield against meteors and it acts as a blanket to prevent heat radiated from the Earth escaping into space.

Layers of Air

The atmosphere is divided into four main layers. The troposphere at the bottom contains about 85% of the atmosphere's total mass, where most weather conditions occur. The troposphere is about 15 km [9 miles] thick over the Equator and 8 km [5 miles] thick at the poles. Temperatures decrease with height by approximately 1°C [2°F] for every 100 m [328 ft]. At the top of the troposphere is a level called the tropopause where temperatures are stable at around –55°C [–67°F]. Above the tropopause is the stratosphere, which contains the ozone layer. Here, at about 50 km [30 miles] above the Earth's surface, temperatures rise to about 0°C [32°F].

The ionosphere extends from the stratopause to about 600 km [373 miles] above the surface. Here temperatures fall up to about 80 km

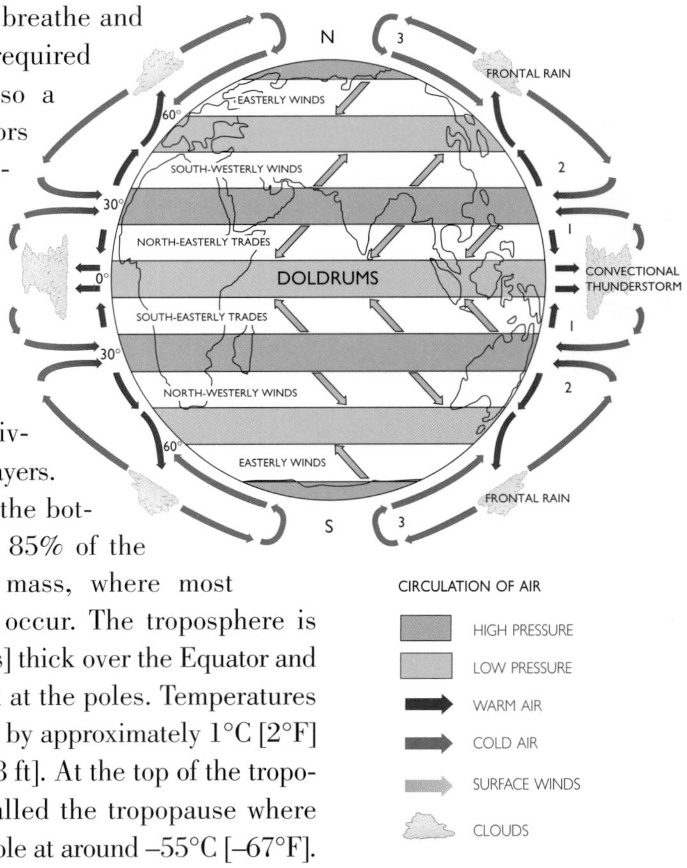
N
S
3
2
1
FRONTAL RAIN
CONVECTIONAL THUNDERSTORM
60°
30°
0°
EASTERLY WINDS
SOUTH-WESTERLY WINDS
NORTH-EASTERLY TRADES
DOLDRUMS
SOUTH-EASTERLY TRADES
NORTH-WESTERLY WINDS
CIRCULATION OF AIR
HIGH PRESSURE
LOW PRESSURE
WARM AIR
COLD AIR
SURFACE WINDS
CLOUDS

The circulation of the atmosphere can be divided into three rotating but interconnected air systems, or cells. The Hadley cell (figure 1 on the above diagram) is in the tropics; the Ferrel cell (2) lies between the subtropics and the mid-latitudes; and the Polar cell (3) is in the high latitudes.

Moonrise seen from orbit

This photograph taken by an orbiting Shuttle shows the crescent of the Moon. Silhouetted at the horizon is a dense cloud layer. The reddish-brown band is the tropopause, which separates the blue-white stratosphere from the yellow troposphere.

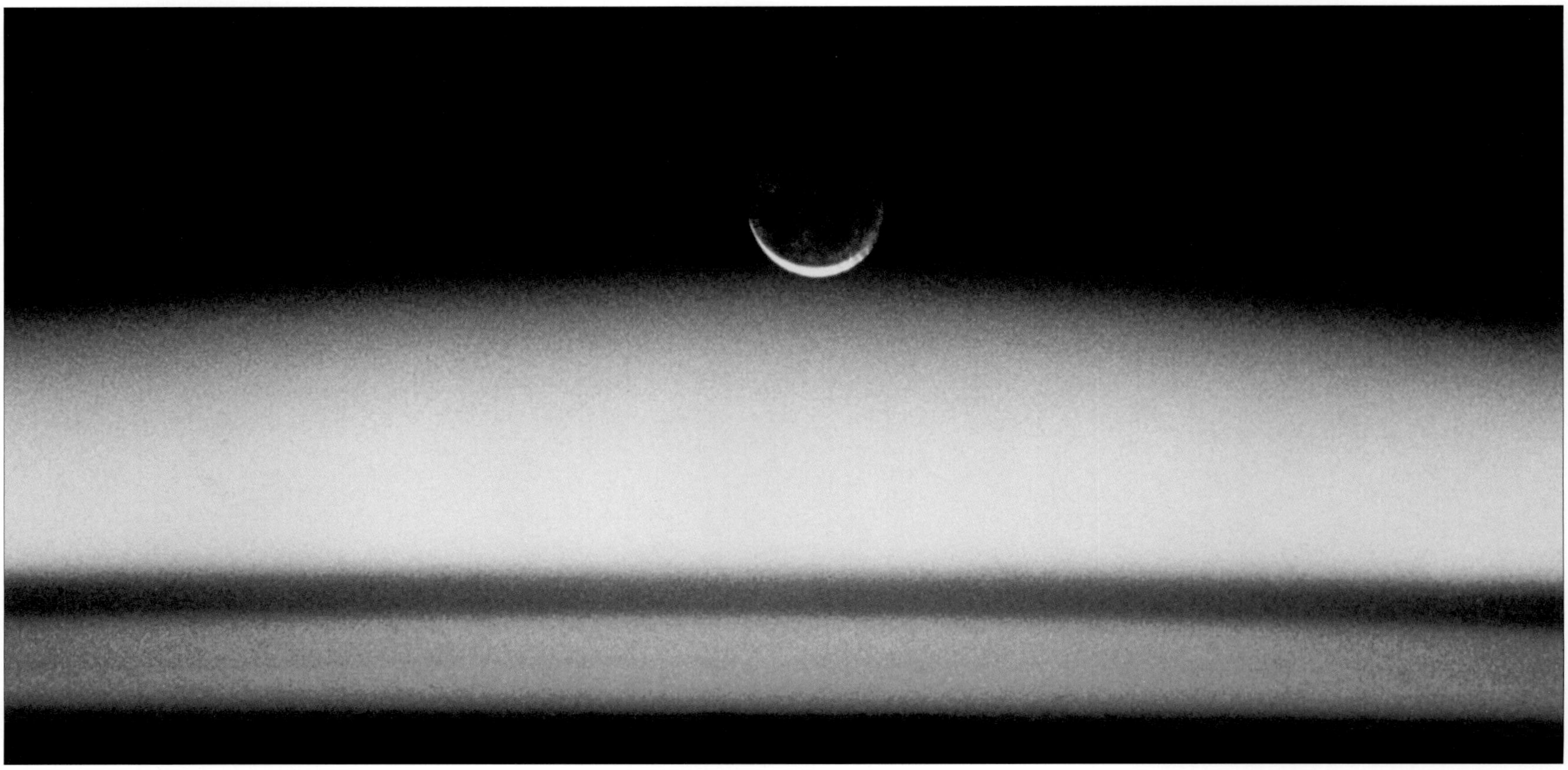

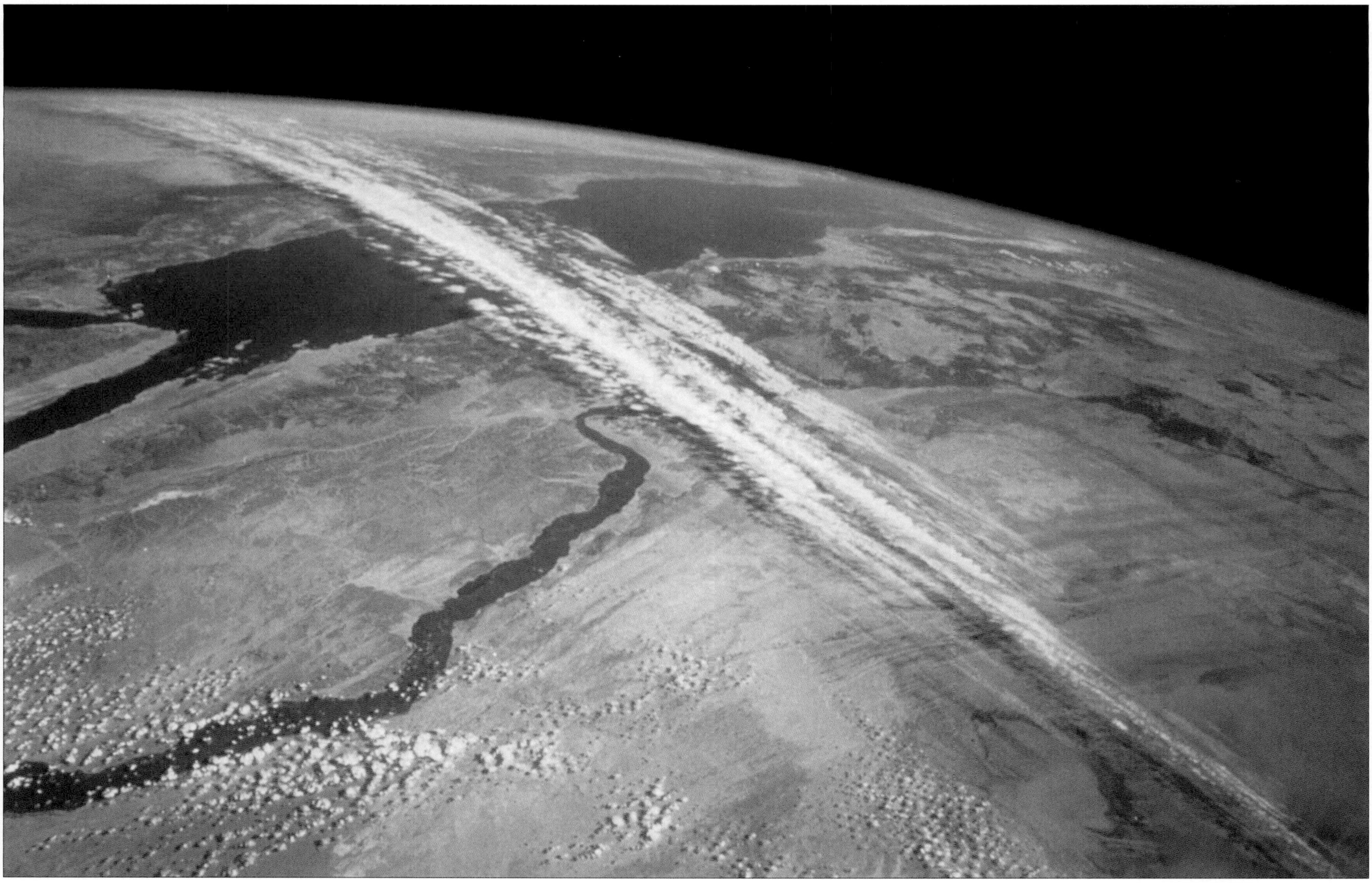

Jetstream from space
Jetstreams are strong winds that normally blow near the tropopause. Cirrus clouds mark the route of the jet stream in this photograph, which shows the Red Sea, North Africa and the Nile valley, which appears as a dark band crossing the desert.

[50 miles], but then rise. The aurorae, which occur in the ionosphere when charged particles from the Sun interact with the Earth's magnetic field, are strongest near the poles. In the exosphere, the outermost layer, the atmosphere merges into space.

Circulation of the Atmosphere

The heating of the Earth is most intense around the Equator where the Sun is high in the sky. Here warm, moist air rises in strong currents, creating a zone of low air pressure: the doldrums. The rising air eventually cools and spreads out north and south until it sinks back to the ground around latitudes 30° North and 30° South. This forms two zones of high air pressure called the horse latitudes.

From the horse latitudes, trade winds blow back across the surface towards the Equator, while westerly winds blow towards the poles. The warm westerlies finally meet the polar easterlies (cold dense air flowing from the poles). The line along which the warm and cold air streams meet is called the polar front. Depressions (or cyclones) are low air pressure frontal systems that form along the polar front.

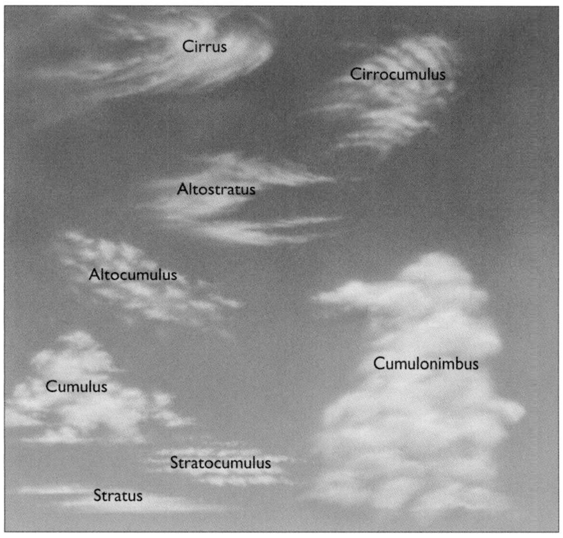
Cirrus
Cirrocumulus
Altostratus
Altocumulus
Cumulonimbus
Cumulus
Stratocumulus
Stratus

Classification of clouds
Clouds are classified broadly into cumuliform, or 'heap' clouds, and stratiform, or 'layer' clouds. Both types occur at all levels. The highest clouds, composed of ice crystals, are cirrus, cirrostratus and cirrocumulus. Medium-height clouds include altostratus, a grey cloud that often indicates the approach of a depression, and altocumulus, a thicker and fluffier version of cirrocumulus. Low clouds include stratus, which forms dull, overcast skies; nimbostratus, a dark grey layer cloud which brings almost continuous rain and snow; cumulus, a brilliant white heap cloud; and stratocumulus, a layer cloud arranged in globular masses or rolls. Cumulonimbus, a cloud associated with thunderstorms, lightning and heavy rain, often extends from low to medium altitudes. It has a flat base, a fluffy outline and often an anvil-shaped top.

Composition of the Atmosphere

The air in the troposphere is made up mainly of nitrogen (78%) and oxygen (21%). Argon makes up more than 0.9% and there are also minute amounts of carbon dioxide, helium, hydrogen, krypton, methane, ozone and xenon. The atmosphere also contains water vapour, the gaseous form of water, which, when it condenses around minute specks of dust and salt, forms tiny water droplets or ice crystals. Large masses of water droplets or ice crystals form clouds.

Climate and Weather

In 1992, Hurricane Andrew struck the Bahamas, Florida and Louisiana, causing record damage estimated at $30 billion. In September 1998, following heavy monsoon rains, floods submerged two-thirds of Bangladesh. The same month, in Central America, more than 7,000 people died in floods and mudslides caused by Hurricane Mitch. In December 2002, Cyclone Zoe battered some islands in the Solomon Islands. Amazingly, there were no deaths. However, because of the massive destruction, the islands were declared a disaster area.

Every year, exceptional weather conditions cause disasters around the world. Modern forecasting techniques now give people warning of advancing storms, but the toll of human deaths continues as people are powerless in the face of the awesome forces of nature.

Weather is the day-to-day condition of the atmosphere. In some places, the weather is normally stable, but in other areas, especially the middle latitudes, it is highly variable, changing with the passing of a depression. By contrast, climate is the average weather of a place, based on data obtained over a long period.

Hurricane Elena, 1985
Hurricanes form over warm oceans north and south of the Equator. Their movements are tracked by satellites, enabling forecasters to issue storm warnings as they approach land. In North America, forecasters identify them with boys' and girls' names.

Climatic Factors

Climate depends basically on the unequal heating of the Sun between the Equator and the poles. But ocean currents and terrain also affect climate. For example, despite their northerly positions, Norway's ports remain ice-free in winter. This is because of the warming effect of the North Atlantic Drift, an extension of the Gulf Stream which flows across the Atlantic Ocean from the Gulf of Mexico.

By contrast, the cold Benguela current which flows up the coast of south-western Africa cools the coast and causes arid conditions. This is because the cold onshore winds are warmed as they pass over the land. The warm air can hold more water vapour than cold air, giving the winds a drying effect.

The terrain affects climate in several ways. Because temperatures fall with altitude, highlands are cooler than lowlands in the same

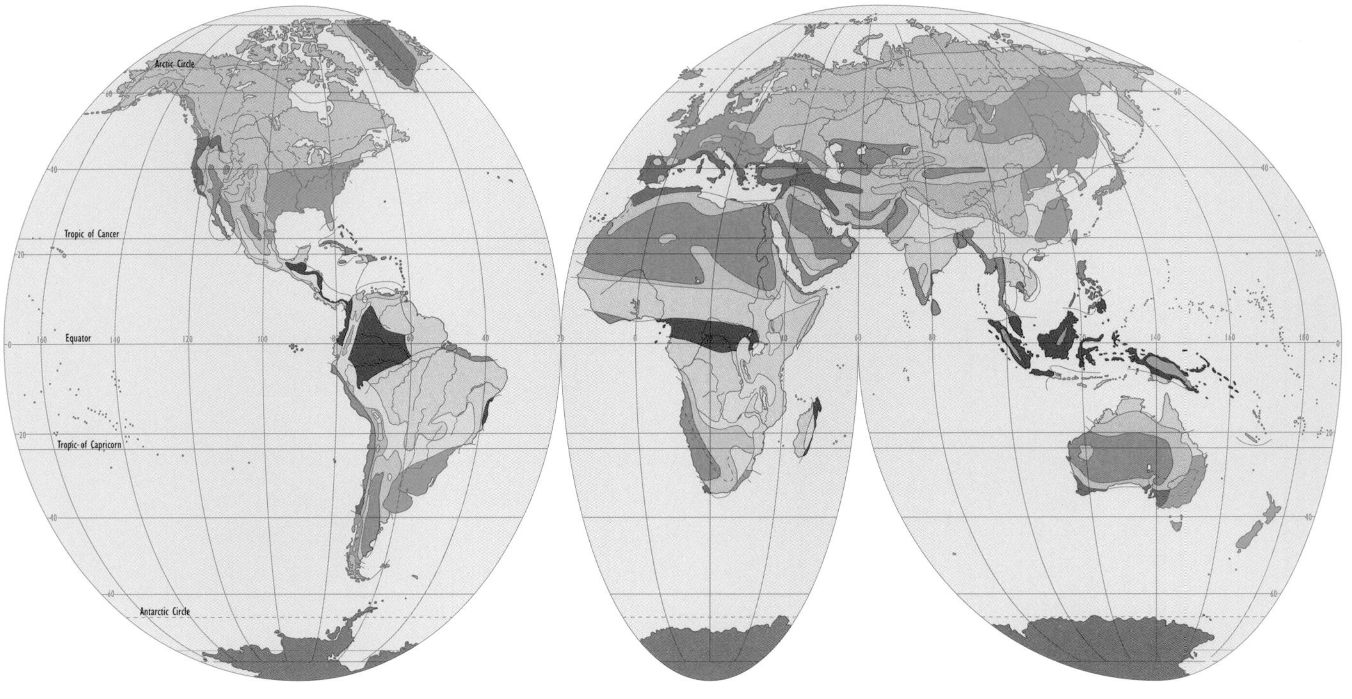

Arctic Circle
Tropic of Cancer
Equator
Tropic of Capricorn
Antarctic Circle

CLIMATIC REGIONS

Tropical rainy climates
All mean monthly temperatures above 18°C [64°F].

- RAINFOREST CLIMATE
- MONSOON CLIMATE
- SAVANNA CLIMATE

Dry climates
Low rainfall combined with a wide range of temperatures.

- STEPPE CLIMATE
- DESERT CLIMATE

Warm temperate rainy climates
The mean temperature is below 18°C [64°F] but above –3°C [26°F], and that of the warmest month is over 10°C [50°F].

- DRY WINTER CLIMATE
- DRY SUMMER CLIMATE
- CLIMATE WITH NO DRY SEASON

Cold temperate rainy climates
The mean temperature of the coldest month is below 3°C [37°F] but the warmest month is over 10°C [50°F].

- DRY WINTER CLIMATE
- CLIMATE WITH NO DRY SEASON

Polar climates
The temperature of the warmest month is below 10°C [50°F], giving permanently frozen subsoil.

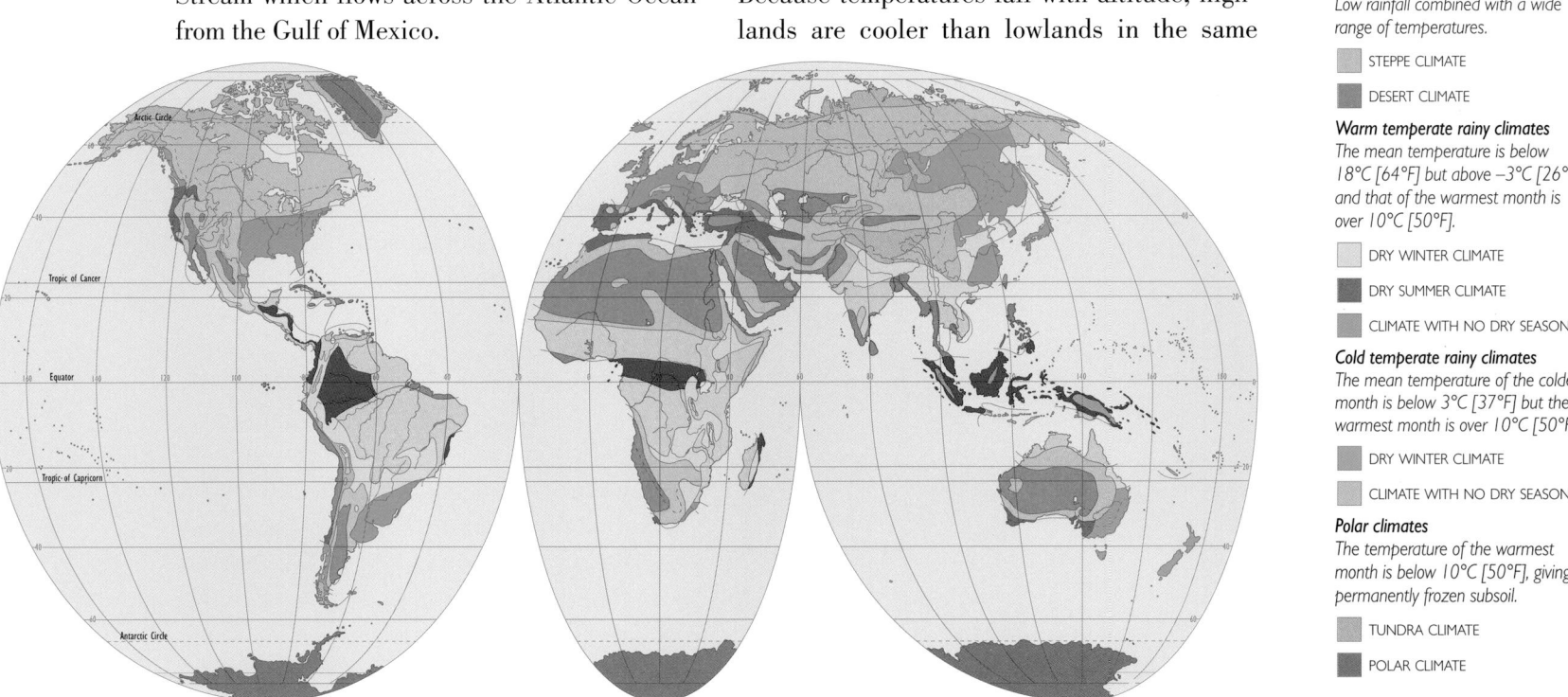

- TUNDRA CLIMATE
- POLAR CLIMATE

Flood damage in the United States
In June and July 1993, the Mississippi River basin suffered record floods. The photograph shows a sunken church in Illinois. The flooding along the Mississippi, Missouri and other rivers caused great damage, amounting to about $12 billion. At least 48 people died in the floods.

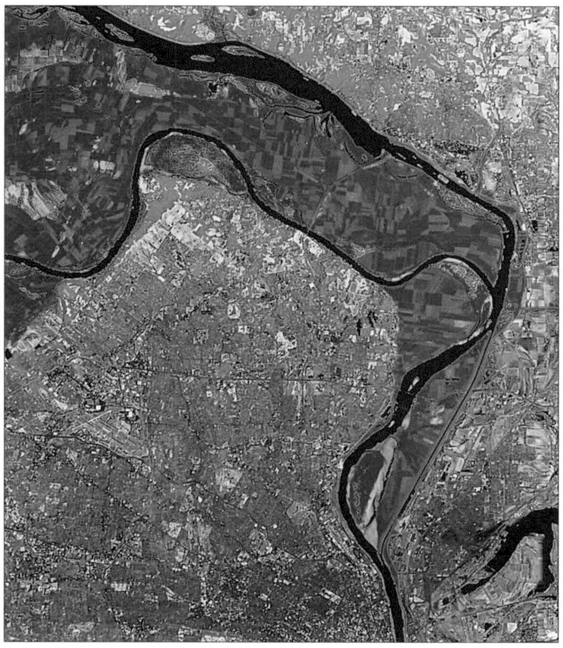

Floods in St Louis, United States
The satellite image, right, shows the extent of the floods at St Louis at the confluence of the Mississippi and the Missouri rivers in June and July 1993. The floods occurred when very heavy rainfall raised river levels by up to 14 m [46 ft]. The floods reached their greatest extent between Minneapolis in the north and a point approximately 150 km [93 miles] south of St Louis. In places, the width of the Mississippi increased to nearly 11 km [7 miles], while the Missouri reached widths of 32 km [20 miles]. In all, more than 28,000 sq km [10,800 sq miles] were inundated and hundreds of towns and cities were flooded. Damage to crops was estimated at $8 billion. The USA was hit again by flooding in early 1997, when heavy rainfall in North Dakota and Minnesota caused the Red River to flood. The flooding had a catastrophic effect on the city of Grand Forks, which was inundated for months.

latitude. Terrain also affects rainfall. When moist onshore winds pass over mountain ranges, they are chilled as they are forced to rise and the water vapour they contain condenses to form clouds which bring rain and snow. After the winds have crossed the mountains, the air descends and is warmed. These warm, dry winds create rain shadow (arid) regions on the lee side of the mountains.

Climatic Regions

The two major factors that affect climate are temperature and precipitation, including rain and snow. In addition, seasonal variations and other climatic features are also taken into account. Climatic classifications vary because of the weighting given to various features. Yet most classifications are based on five main climatic types: tropical rainy climates; dry climates; warm temperate rainy climates; cold temperate rainy climates; and very cold polar climates. Some classifications also allow for the effect of altitude. The main climatic regions are subdivided according to seasonal variations and also to the kind of vegetation associated with the climatic conditions. Thus, the rainforest climate, with rain throughout the year, differs from monsoon and savanna climates, which have marked dry seasons. Similarly, parched desert climates differ from steppe climates which have enough moisture for grasses to grow.

Water and Land Use

All life on land depends on fresh water. Yet about 80 countries now face acute water shortages. The world demand for fresh water is increasing by about 2.3% a year and this demand will double every 21 years. About a billion people, mainly in developing countries, do not have access to clean drinking water and around 10 million die every year from drinking dirty water. This problem is made worse in many countries by the pollution of rivers and lakes.

UN experts predict that water is becoming the most pressing environmental and development issue facing the world. By 2003, heavily populated regions in 26 countries were suffering serious water shortages. In 20 years, this number will probably rise to 65. As resources dwindle, conflicts over water are becoming more common. They are likely to increase.

However, experts stress that while individual countries face water crises, there is no global crisis. The chief global problems are the uneven distribution of water and its inefficient and wasteful use.

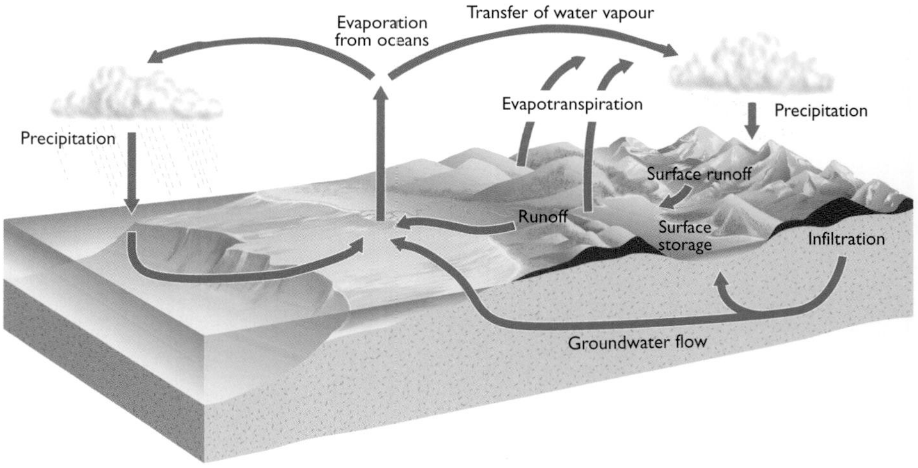
Evaporation from oceans
Transfer of water vapour
Precipitation
Evapotranspiration
Precipitation
Surface runoff
Runoff
Surface storage
Infiltration
Groundwater flow

The hydrological cycle
The hydrological cycle is responsible for the continuous circulation of water around the planet. Water vapour contains and transports latent heat, or latent energy. When the water vapour condenses back into water (and falls as rain, hail or snow), the heat is released. When condensation takes place on cold nights, the cooling effect associated with nightfall is offset by the liberation of latent heat.

Hoover Dam, United States
The Hoover Dam in Arizona controls the Colorado River's flood waters. Its reservoir supplies domestic and irrigation water to the south-west, while a hydroelectric plant produces electricity.

The World's Water Supply

Of the world's total water supply, 99.4% is in the oceans or frozen in bodies of ice. Most of the rest circulates through the rocks beneath our feet as groundwater. Water in rivers and lakes, in the soil and in the atmosphere together make up only 0.013% of the world's water.

The freshwater supply on land is dependent on the hydrological, or water cycle which is driven by the Sun's heat. Water is evaporated from the oceans and carried into the air as invisible water vapour. Although this vapour averages less than 2% of the total mass of the atmosphere, it is the chief component from the standpoint of weather.

When air rises, water vapour condenses into visible water droplets or ice crystals, which eventually fall to earth as rain, snow, sleet, hail or frost. Some of the precipitation that reaches the ground returns directly to the atmosphere through evaporation or transpiration via plants. Much of the rest of the water flows into the rocks to become groundwater, or across the surface into rivers and, eventually, back to the oceans, so completing the hydrological cycle.

WATER DISTRIBUTION
The distribution of planetary water, by percentage.

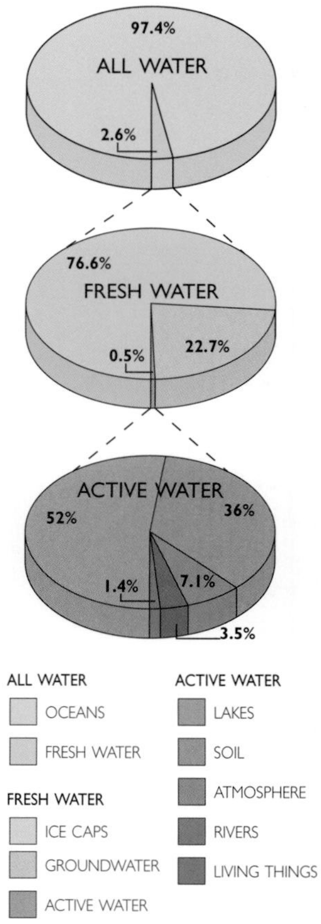
97.4%
ALL WATER
2.6%
76.6%
FRESH WATER
0.5%
22.7%
ACTIVE WATER
52%
36%
1.4%
7.1%
3.5%
ALL WATER
OCEANS
FRESH WATER
FRESH WATER
ICE CAPS
GROUNDWATER
ACTIVE WATER
ACTIVE WATER
LAKES
SOIL
ATMOSPHERE
RIVERS
LIVING THINGS

Water and Agriculture

Only about a third of the world's land area is used for growing crops, while another third

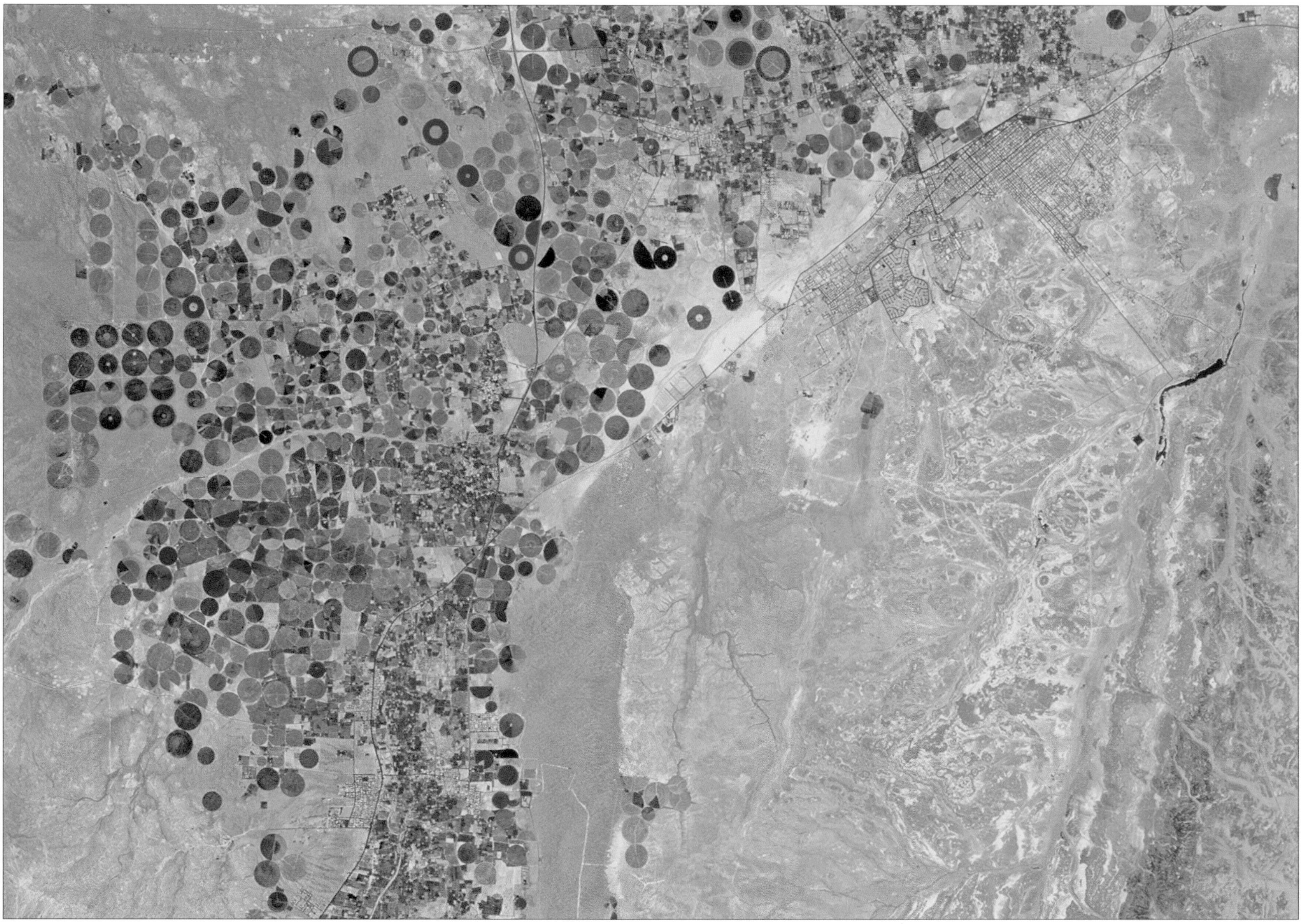

Irrigation in Saudi Arabia
Saudi Arabia is a desert country which gets its water from oases, which tap groundwater supplies, and desalination plants. The sale of oil has enabled the arid countries of south-western Asia to develop their agriculture. In the above satellite image, vegetation appears brown and red.

Irrigation boom
The photograph shows a pivotal irrigation boom used to sprinkle water over a wheat field in Saudi Arabia. Irrigation in hot countries often takes place at night so that water loss through evaporation is reduced. Irrigation techniques vary from place to place. In monsoon areas with abundant water, the fields are often flooded, or the water is led to the crops along straight furrows. Sprinkler irrigation has become important since the 1940s. In other types of irrigation, the water is led through pipes which are on or under the ground. Underground pipes supply water directly to the plant roots and, as a result, water loss through evaporation is minimized.

consists of meadows and pasture. The rest of the world is unsuitable for farming, being too dry, too cold, too mountainous, or covered by dense forests. Although the demand for food increases every year, problems arise when attempts are made to increase the existing area of farmland. For example, the soils and climates of tropical forest and semi-arid regions of Africa and South America are not ideal for farming. Attempts to work such areas usually end in failure. To increase the world's food supply, scientists now concentrate on making existing farmland more productive rather than farming marginal land.

To grow crops, farmers need fertile, workable land, an equable climate, including a frost-free growing period, and an adequate supply of fresh water. In some areas, the water falls directly as rain. But many other regions depend on irrigation.

Irrigation involves water conservation through the building of dams which hold back storage reservoirs. In some areas, irrigation water comes from underground aquifers, layers of permeable and porous rocks through which groundwater percolates. But in many cases, the water in the aquifers has been there for thousands of years, having accumulated at a time when the rainfall was much greater than it is today. As a result, these aquifers are not being renewed and will, one day, dry up.

Other sources of irrigation water are desalination plants, which remove salt from seawater and pump it to farms. This is a highly expensive process and is employed in areas where water supplies are extremely low, such as the island of Malta, or in the oil-rich desert countries around the Gulf, which can afford to build huge desalination plants.

LAND USE BY CONTINENT (2000)

	Forest	Permanent pasture	Permanent crops	Arable	Non-productive
N. & C. America	25.7%	17.2%	0.4%	12.1%	44.6%
S. America	50.5%	28.7%	1.1%	5.5%	14.2%
Europe	46.0%	8.0%	0.7%	12.8%	32.5%
Africa	21.8%	30.2%	0.9%	6.1%	41.0%
Asia	17.8%	35.8%	1.9%	15.7%	28.8%
Oceania	23.3%	49.3%	0.4%	6.2%	20.8%

The Natural World

In 2002, a United Nations report identified more than 11,000 plant and animal species known to face a high risk of extinction, including 24% of all mammals and 12% of birds. Human activities, ranging from habitat destruction to the introduction of alien species from one area to another, are the main causes of this devastating reduction of our planet's biodiversity, which might lead to the disappearance of unique combinations of genes that could be vital in improving food yields on farms or in the production of drugs to combat disease.

Extinctions of species have occurred throughout Earth history, but today the extinction rate is estimated to be about 10,000 times the natural average. Some scientists have even compared it with the mass extinction that wiped out the dinosaurs 65 million years ago. However, the main cause of today's high extinction rate is not some natural disaster, such as the impact of an asteroid a few kilometres across, but it is the result of human actions, most notably the destruction of natural habitats for farming and other purposes. In some densely populated areas, such as Western Europe, the natural habitats were destroyed long ago. Today, the greatest damage is occurring in tropical rainforests, which contain more than half of the world's known species.

Modern technology has enabled people to live comfortably almost anywhere on Earth. But most plants and many animals are adapted to particular climatic conditions, and they live in association with and dependent on each other. Plant and animal communities that cover large areas are called biomes.

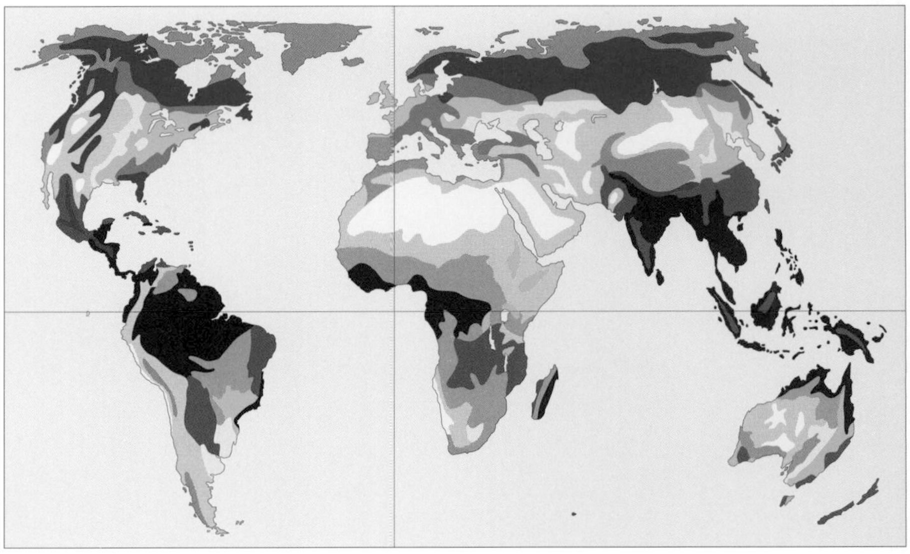

NATURAL VEGETATION

- TUNDRA & MOUNTAIN VEGETATION
- NEEDLELEAF EVERGREEN FOREST
- MIXED NEEDLELEAF EVERGREEN & BROADLEAF DECIDUOUS TREES
- BROADLEAF DECIDUOUS WOODLAND
- MID-LATITUDE GRASSLAND
- EVERGREEN BROADLEAF & DECIDUOUS TREES & SHRUBS
- SEMI-DESERT SCRUB
- DESERT
- TROPICAL GRASSLAND (SAVANNA)
- TROPICAL BROADLEAF RAINFOREST & MONSOON FOREST
- SUBTROPICAL BROADLEAF & NEEDLELEAF FOREST

The map shows the world's main biomes. The classification is based on the natural 'climax' vegetation of regions, a result of the climate and the terrain. But human activities have greatly modified this basic division. For example, the original deciduous forests of Western Europe and the eastern United States have largely disappeared. In recent times, human development of some semi-arid areas has turned former dry grasslands into barren desert.

The World's Biomes

The world's biomes are defined mainly by climate and vegetation. They range from the tundra, in polar regions and high mountain regions, to the lush equatorial rainforests.

The Arctic tundra covers large areas in the polar regions of the northern hemisphere. Snow covers the land for more than half of the year and the subsoil, called permafrost, is permanently frozen. Comparatively few species can survive in this harsh, treeless environment. The main plants are hardy mosses, lichens, grasses, sedges and low shrubs. However, in summer, the tundra plays an important part in world animal geography, when its growing plants and swarms of insects provide food for migrating animals and birds that arrive from the south.

The tundra of the northern hemisphere merges in the south into a vast region of needleleaf evergreen forest, called the boreal forest or taiga. Such trees as fir, larch, pine and spruce are adapted to survive the long, bitterly cold winters of this region, but the number of plant and animal species is again small. South of the boreal forests is a zone of mixed needleleaf evergreens and broadleaf deciduous trees, which

Rainforest in Rwanda

Rainforests are the most threatened of the world's biomes. Effective conservation policies must demonstrate to poor local people that they can benefit from the survival of the forests.

Tundra in subarctic Alaska
The Denali National Park, Alaska, contains magnificent mountain scenery and tundra vegetation which flourishes during the brief summer. The park is open between 1 June and 15 September.

shed their leaves in winter. In warmer areas, this mixed forest merges into broadleaf deciduous forest, where the number and diversity of plant species is much greater.

Deciduous forests are adapted to temperate, humid regions. Evergreen broadleaf and deciduous trees grow in Mediterranean regions, with their hot, dry summers. But much of the original deciduous forest has been cut down and has given way to scrub and heathland. Grasslands occupy large areas in the middle latitudes, where the rainfall is insufficient to support forest growth. The moister grasslands are often called prairies, while drier areas are called steppe.

NET PRIMARY PRODUCTION OF EIGHT MAJOR BIOMES

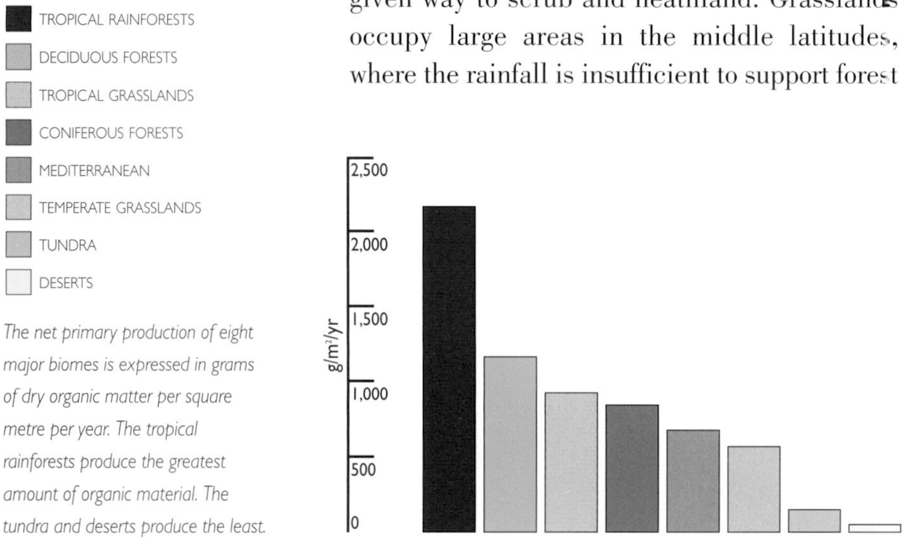
TROPICAL RAINFORESTS
DECIDUOUS FORESTS
TROPICAL GRASSLANDS
CONIFEROUS FORESTS
MEDITERRANEAN
TEMPERATE GRASSLANDS
TUNDRA
DESERTS
g/m²/yr
2,500
2,000
1,500
1,000
500
0

The net primary production of eight major biomes is expressed in grams of dry organic matter per square metre per year. The tropical rainforests produce the greatest amount of organic material. The tundra and deserts produce the least.

The tropics also contain vast dry areas of semi-desert scrub which merges into desert, as well as large areas of savanna, which is grassland with scattered trees. Savanna regions, with their marked dry season, support a wide range of mammals.

Tropical and subtropical regions contain three types of forest biomes. The tropical rainforest, the world's richest biome measured by its plant and animal species, experiences rain and high temperatures throughout the year. Similar forests occur in monsoon regions, which have a season of very heavy rainfall. They, too, are rich in plant species, though less so than the tropical rainforest. A third type of forest is the subtropical broadleaf and needleleaf forest, found in such places as south-eastern China, south-central Africa and eastern Brazil.

The Human World

Every minute, the world's population increases by around 140. Predictions of future growth vary. In 1999, UN demographers stated that the population, which passed the 6 billion mark in October 1999, would reach 8.9 million by 2050. It would level out after 2200 when it would peak at 11 million. But, in 2001, other demographers predicted that the world's population would peak at 9 billion in 2070, and then decline to 8.4 billion by 2100. However, all forecasters are agreed that the fastest rates of increase will take place in developing countries – the places least able to afford the high costs arising from a rapidly growing population.

Elevated view of Ki Lung Street, Hong Kong

Urban areas of Hong Kong, a Special Administrative Region on the southern coast of China, contain busy streets overlooked by crowded apartments.

Average world population growth rates have declined from about 2% a year in the early 1960s to 1.4% in 2002. This was partly due to a decline in fertility rates – that is, the number of births to the number of women of child-bearing age – especially in developed countries where, as income has risen, the average size of families has fallen.

Declining fertility rates were also evident in many developing countries. Even Africa shows signs of such change, though its population is expected to triple before it begins to fall. Population growth is also dependent on death rates, which are affected by such factors as famine, disease and the quality of medical care.

The Population Explosion

The world's population has grown steadily throughout most of human history, though certain events triggered periods of population growth. The invention of agriculture, around 10,000 years ago, led to great changes in human society. Before then, most people had obtained food by hunting animals and gathering plants. Average life expectancies were probably no more than 20 years and life was hard. However, when farmers began to produce food surpluses, people began to live settled lives. This major milestone in human history led to the development of the first cities and early civilizations.

From an estimated 8 million in 8000 BC, the world population rose to about 300 million by AD 1000. Between 1000 and 1750, the rate of world population increase was around 0.1% per year, but another period of major economic and social change – the Industrial Revolution – began in the late 18th century. The Industrial Revolution led to improvements in farm technology and increases in food production. The world population began to increase quickly as industrialization spread across Europe and into North America. By 1850, it had reached 1.2 billion. The 2 billion mark was passed in the 1920s, and then the population rapidly doubled to 4 billion by the 1970s.

Population Features

Population growth affects the structure of societies. In developing countries with high annual rates of population increase, the large majority of the people are young and soon to become parents themselves. For example, in Kenya, which had until recently an annual rate of population growth of around 4%, about 46%

Largest Cities

Within 10 years, for the first time ever, the majority of the world's population will live in urban areas. Almost all the urban growth will be in developing countries. Below is a list of cities with their estimated populations in the year 2015, in millions.

1	Tokyo	28.7
2	Mumbai (Bombay)	27.4
3	Lagos	24.1
4	Shanghai	23.2
5	Jakarta	21.5
6	São Paulo	21.0
7	Karachi	20.6
8	Beijing	19.6
9	Dhaka	19.2
10	Mexico City	19.1
11	Kolkata (Calcutta)	17.6
12	Delhi	17.5
13	New York City	17.4
14	Tianjin	17.1
15	Metro Manila	14.9
16	Cairo	14.7
17	Los Angeles	14.5
18	Seoul	13.1
19	Buenos Aires	12.5
20	Istanbul	12.1

These city populations are based on figures for urban agglomerations rather than actual city limits.

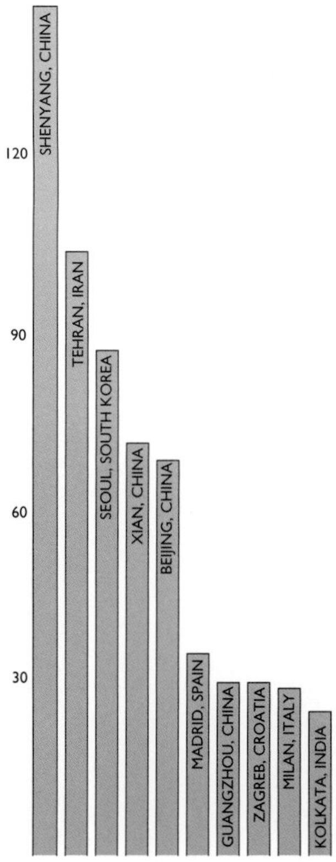
120
90
60
30
SHENYANG, CHINA
TEHRAN, IRAN
SEOUL, SOUTH KOREA
XIAN, CHINA
BEIJING, CHINA
MADRID, SPAIN
GUANGZHOU, CHINA
ZAGREB, CROATIA
MILAN, ITALY
KOLKATA, INDIA

Urban air pollution

This diagram of the world's most polluted cities indicates the number of days per year when sulphur dioxide levels exceed the WHO threshhold of 150 micrograms per cubic metre.

Hong Kong's business district
By contrast with the picturesque old streets of Hong Kong, the business district of Hong Kong City, on the northern shore of Hong Kong Island, is a cluster of modern high-rise buildings. The glittering skyscrapers reflect the success of this tiny region, which has one of the strongest economies in Asia.

of the population is under 15 years of age, as compared with 21% in the United States. Most developed countries have a fairly even spread across the age groups.

Such differences are reflected in average life expectancies. In a rich country, such as the USA, the average life expectancy in 2001 was 77 years (74 for men and 80 for women; women live longer, on average, than men). As a result, an increasing proportion of the people are elderly and retired. The reverse applies in many poor countries, where average life expectancies are below 60 years. In the early 21st century, life expectancies were falling in parts of southern Africa because of the spread of HIV and AIDS. In 2003, experts estimated that, in Botswana, if the epidemic continues, average life expectancies will fall to 27 years in 2010.

Paralleling the population explosion has been a rapid growth in the number and size of cities and towns, which contained nearly half of the world's people by the 1990s. This proportion is expected to rise to nearly two-thirds by 2025.

Urbanization occurred first in areas undergoing the industrialization of their economies, but today it is also a feature of the developing world. In developing countries, people are leaving impoverished rural areas hoping to gain access to the education, health and other services available in cities. But many cities cannot provide the facilities necessitated by rapid population growth. Slums develop and pollution, crime and disease become features of everyday life.

The population explosion poses another problem for the entire world. No one knows how many people the world can support or how consumer demand will damage the fragile environments on our planet. The British economist Thomas Malthus argued in the late 18th century that overpopulation would lead to famine and war. But an increase in farm technology in the 19th and 20th centuries, combined with a green revolution, in which scientists developed high-yield crop varieties, has greatly increased food production since Malthus' time.

However, some modern scientists argue that overpopulation may become a problem in the 21st century. They argue that food shortages leading to disastrous famines will result unless population growth can be halted. Such people argue in favour of birth control programmes. China, one of the two countries with more than a billion people, introduced a one-child family policy. Its action has slowed the growth of China's huge population.

POPULATION CHANGE 1990–2000

The population change for the years 1990–2000.

- OVER 40% POPULATION GAIN
- 20–40% POPULATION GAIN
- 10–20% POPULATION GAIN
- 0–10% POPULATION GAIN
- LOSS OR NO CHANGE
- NO DATA

TOP 5 COUNTRIES	
Kuwait	+75.9%
Namibia	+69.4%
Afghanistan	+60.1%
Mali	+55.5%
Tanzania	+54.6%

BOTTOM 5 COUNTRIES	
Belgium	–0.1%
Hungary	–0.2%
Grenada	–2.4%
Tonga	–3.2%
Germany	–3.2%

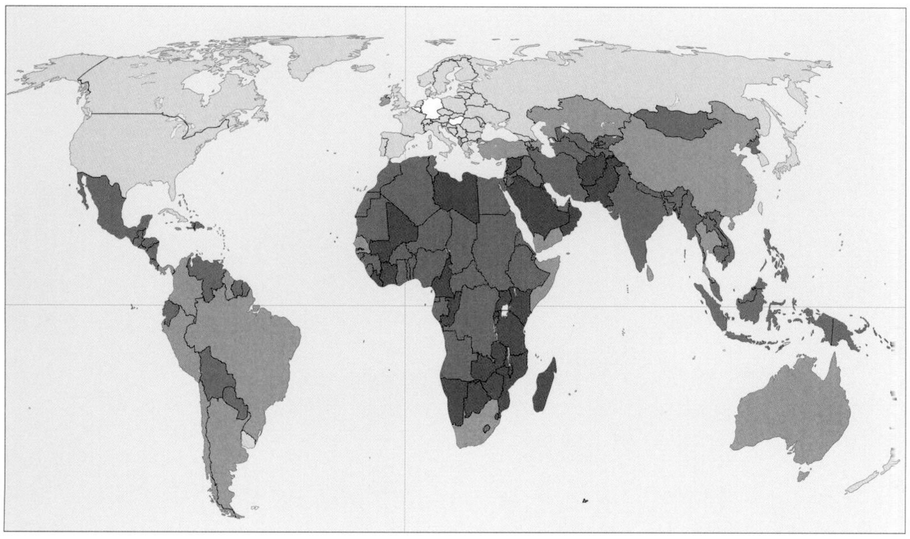

Languages and Religions

In 1995, 90-year-old Edna Guerro died in northern California. She was the last person able to speak Northern Pomo, one of about 50 Native American languages spoken in the state. Her death marked the extinction of one of the world's languages.

This event is not an isolated incident. Language experts regularly report the disappearance of languages and some of them predict that up to 90% of the world's languages will no longer exist by the end of the 21st century. Improved transport and communications are partly to blame, because they bring people from various cultures into closer and closer contact. Many children no longer speak the language of their parents, preferring instead to learn the language used at their schools. The pressures on children to speak dominant rather than minority languages are often great. In the first part of the 20th century, Native American children were punished if they spoke their native language.

The disappearance of a language represents the extinction of a way of thinking, a unique expression of the experiences and knowledge of a group of people. Language and religion together give people an identity and a sense of belonging. However, there are others who argue that the disappearance of minority languages is a step towards international understanding and economic efficiency.

The World's Languages

Definitions of what is a language or a dialect vary and, hence, estimates of the number of languages spoken around the world range from about 3,000 to 6,000. But whatever the figure, it is clear that the number of languages far exceeds the number of countries.

RELIGIOUS ADHERENTS

Number of adherents to the world's major religions, in millions (2001).

Christianity	**2,019**
Roman Catholic	1,067
Protestant	346
Orthodox	216
Anglican	80
Independent	392
Others	139
Islam	**1,207**
Sunni	1,002
Shiite	193
Others	12
Secular/Atheist/Agnostic/ Non-religious	**921**
Hinduism	**820**
Chinese folk	**387**
Buddhism	**362**
Ethnic religions	**242**
New religions	**103**
Sikhism	**24**
Judaism	**14**
Spiritism	**12**
Baha'i	**7**
Confucianism	**6**
Jainism	**4**
Shintoism	**3**

Buddhist monks in Katmandu, Nepal

Hinduism is Nepal's official religion, but the Nepalese observe the festivals of both Hinduism and Buddhism. They also regard Buddhist shrines and Hindu temples as equally sacred.

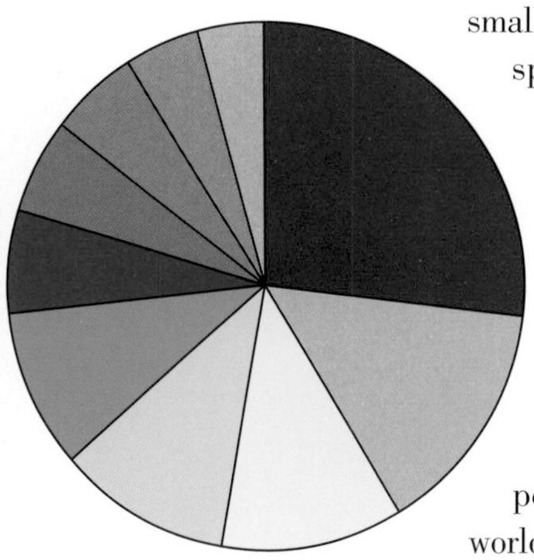

MOTHER TONGUES

First-language speakers of the major languages, in millions (1999).

- MANDARIN CHINESE 885M
- SPANISH 332M
- ENGLISH 322M
- BENGALI 189M
- HINDI 182M
- PORTUGUESE 170M
- RUSSIAN 170M
- JAPANESE 125M
- GERMAN 98M
- WU CHINESE 77M

Countries with only one language tend to be small. For example, in Liechtenstein, everyone speaks German. By contrast, more than 860 languages have been identified in Papua New Guinea, whose population is only about 5.1 million people. Hence, many of its languages are spoken by only small groups of people. In fact, scientists have estimated that about a third of the world's languages are now spoken by less than 1,000 people. By contrast, more than half of the world's population speak just seven languages.

The world's languages are grouped into families. The Indo-European family consists of languages spoken between Europe and the Indian subcontinent. The growth of European empires over the last 300 years led several Indo-European languages, most notably English, French, Portuguese and Spanish, to spread throughout much of North and South America, Africa, Australia and New Zealand.

English has become the official language in many countries which together contain more than a quarter of the world's population. It is now a major international language, surpassing in importance Mandarin Chinese, a member of the Sino-Tibetan family, which is the world's leading first language. Without a knowledge of English, businessmen face many problems when conducting international trade, especially with the United States or other English-speaking countries. But proposals that English, French, Russian or some other language should become a world language seem unlikely to be acceptable to a majority of the world's peoples.

The Church of San Giovanni, Dolomites, Italy

Christianity has done much to shape Western civilization. Christian churches were built as places of worship, but many of them are among the finest achievements of world architecture.

World Religions

Religion is another fundamental aspect of human culture. It has inspired much of the world's finest architecture, literature, music and painting. It has also helped to shape human cultures since prehistoric times and is responsible for the codes of ethics by which most people live.

The world's major religions were all founded in Asia. Judaism, one of the first faiths to teach that there is only one god, is one of the world's oldest. Founded in south-western Asia, it influenced the more recent Christianity and Islam, two other monotheistic religions which now have the greatest number of followers. Hinduism, the third leading faith in terms of the numbers of followers, originated in the Indian subcontinent and most Hindus are now found in India. Another major religion, Buddhism, was founded in the subcontinent partly as a reaction to certain aspects of Hinduism. But unlike Hinduism, it has spread from India throughout much of eastern Asia.

Religion and language are powerful creative forces. They are also essential features of nationalism, which gives people a sense of belonging and pride. But nationalism is often also a cause of rivalry and tension. Cultural differences have led to racial hatred, the persecution of minorities, and to war between national groups.

OFFICIAL LANGUAGES: % OF WORLD POPULATION

English	27.0%
Chinese	19.0%
Hindi	13.5%
Spanish	5.4%
Russian	5.2%
French	4.2%
Arabic	3.3%
Portuguese	3.0%
Malay	3.0%
Bengali	2.9%
Japanese	2.3%

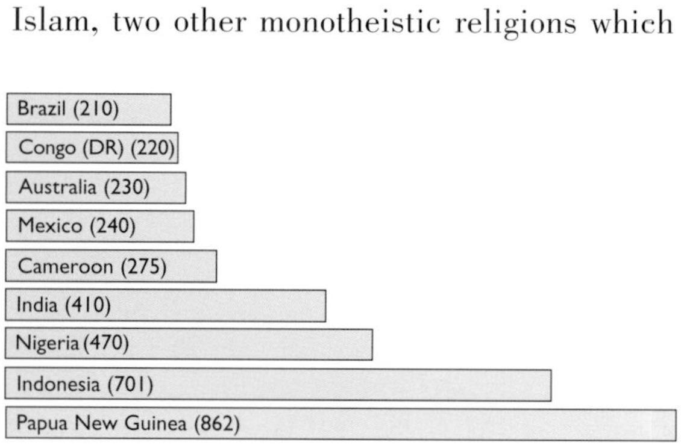
Brazil (210)
Congo (DR) (220)
Australia (230)
Mexico (240)
Cameroon (275)
India (410)
Nigeria (470)
Indonesia (701)
Papua New Guinea (862)

Polyglot nations

The graph, right, shows countries of the world with more than 200 languages. Although it has only about 5.1 million people, Papua New Guinea holds the record for the number of languages spoken.

International Organizations

Twelve days before the surrender of Germany and four months before the final end of World War II, representatives of 50 nations met in San Francisco to create a plan to set up a peace-keeping organization, the United Nations. Since its birth on 24 October 1945, its membership has grown from 51 to 191 in 2003.

Its first 50 years have been marked by failures as well as successes. While it has helped to prevent some disputes from flaring up into full-scale wars, the Blue Berets, as the UN troops are called, have been forced, because of their policy of neutrality, to stand by when atrocities are committed by rival warring groups.

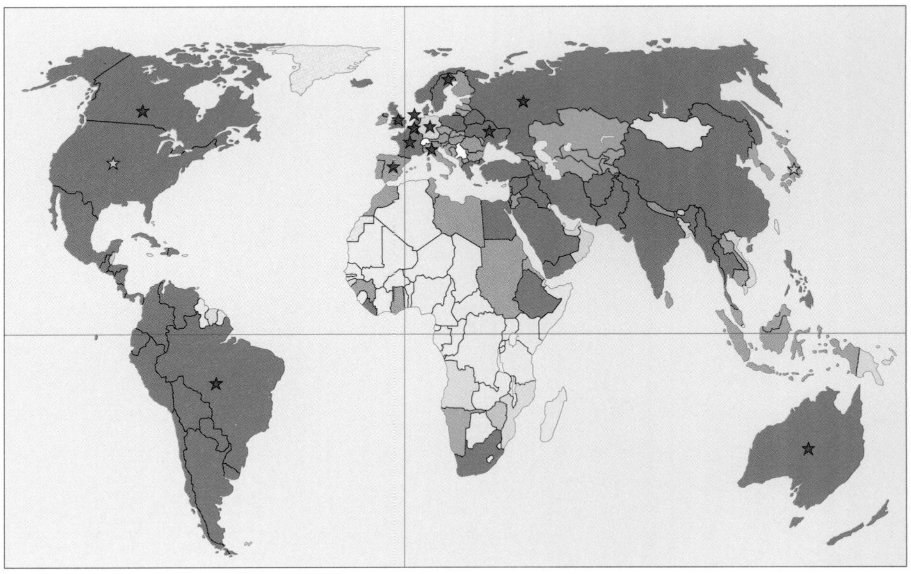

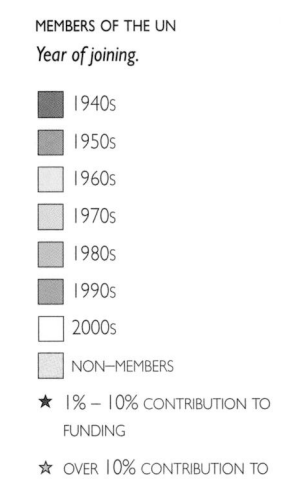

MEMBERS OF THE UN
Year of joining.

- 1940s
- 1950s
- 1960s
- 1970s
- 1980s
- 1990s
- 2000s
- NON–MEMBERS
- ★ 1% – 10% CONTRIBUTION TO FUNDING
- ☆ OVER 10% CONTRIBUTION TO FUNDING

The Work of the UN

The United Nations has six main organs. They include the General Assembly, where member states meet to discuss issues concerned with peace, security and development. The Security Council, containing 15 members, is concerned with maintaining world peace. The Secretariat, under the Secretary-General, helps the other organs to do their jobs effectively, while the Economic and Social Council works with specialized agencies to implement policies concerned with such matters as development, education and health. The International Court of Justice, or World Court, helps to settle disputes between member nations. The sixth organ of the UN, the Trusteeship Council, was designed to bring 11 UN trust territories to independence. Its task has now been completed.

The specialized agencies do much important work. For example, UNICEF (United Nations International Children's Fund) has provided health care and aid for children in many parts of the world. The ILO (International Labour Organization) has improved working conditions in many areas, while the FAO (Food and Agricultural Organization) has worked to improve the production and distribution of food. Among the other agencies are organizations to help refugees, to further human rights and to control the environment. The latest agency, set up in 1995, is the WTO (World Trade Organization), which took over the work of GATT (General Agreement on Tariffs and Trade).

Other Organizations

In a world in which nations have become increasingly interdependent, many other organizations have been set up to deal with a variety of problems. Some, such as NATO (the North Atlantic Treaty Organization), are defence alliances. In the early 1990s, the end of the Cold War suggested that NATO's role might be finished, but the civil war in the former Yugoslavia showed that it still has a role in maintaining peace and security.

Other organizations encourage social and economic co-operation in various regions. Some are NGOs (non-governmental organizations), such as the Red Cross and its Muslim equivalent, the Red Crescent. Other NGOs raise funds to provide aid to countries facing major crises, such as famine.

Some major international organizations aim at economic co-operation and the removal of trade barriers. For example, the European Union has 15 members. On 1 January 2001, 12 of the member states adopted a single currency, the

UN peace-keeping missions
In the 1990s, a UN peace-keeping mission worked to restore peace to Bosnia-Herzegovina, following the Dayton Peace Accord of 1995. By 2003, hopes of long-term stability were high and refugees were returning home in large numbers.

UN
UN
15

INTERNATIONAL AID AND GNP
Aid provided as a percentage of GNP, with total aid in brackets (latest available year).

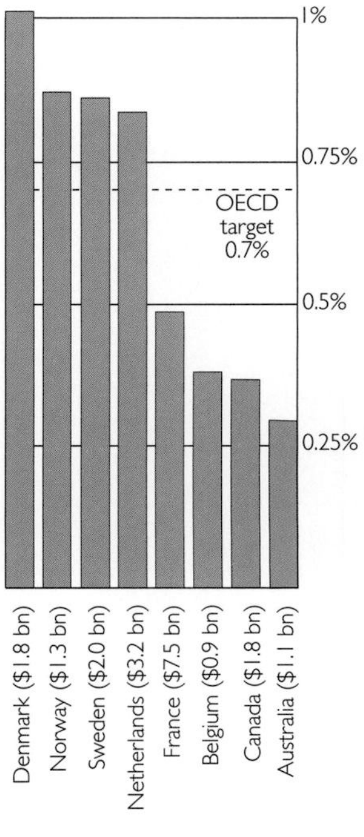
1%
0.75%
0.5%
0.25%
OECD target 0.7%
Denmark ($1.8 bn)
Norway ($1.3 bn)
Sweden ($2.0 bn)
Netherlands ($3.2 bn)
France ($7.5 bn)
Belgium ($0.9 bn)
Canada ($1.8 bn)
Australia ($1.1 bn)

Refugee camp, Sudan

In the late 20th and early 21st centuries, many people in the Horn of Africa and Sudan were displaced by war. Here, and in other parts of the world, refugees from war depended largely on aid from international organizations and NGOs.

euro. In 2002, the European Union announced that it planned to invite ten more countries in eastern and southern Europe to join its ranks on 1 May 2004.

Other groupings include ASEAN (the Association of South-east Asian Nations) which aims to reduce trade barriers between its members (Brunei, Burma [Myanmar], Cambodia, Indonesia, Laos, Malaysia, the Philippines, Singapore, Thailand and Vietnam). APEC (the Asia-Pacific Co-operation Group), founded in 1989, aims to create a free trade zone between the countries of eastern Asia, North America, Australia and New Zealand by 2020. Meanwhile, Canada, Mexico and the United States have formed NAFTA (the North American Free Trade Agreement), while other economic groupings link most of the countries in Latin America. Another grouping with a more limited but important objective is OPEC (the Organization of Oil-Exporting Countries). OPEC works to unify policies concerning trade in oil on the world markets.

Some organizations exist to discuss matters of common interest between groups of nations. The Commonwealth of Nations, for example, grew out of links created by the British Empire. In North and South America, the OAS (Organization of American States) aims to increase understanding in the Western hemisphere. The African Union, which replaced the Organization of African Unity in 2002, has a similar role in Africa, while the Arab League represents the Arab nations.

COUNTRIES OF THE EUROPEAN UNION

	Total land area (sq km)	Total population (2002 est.)	GDP per capita, US$ (2001 est.)	Unemployment rate, % (2001)	Year of accession to the EU	Seats in EU parliament (1999–2004)
Austria	83,850	8,170,000	27,000	3.4%	1995	21
Belgium	30,510	10,275,000	26,100	6.6%	1958	25
Denmark	43,070	5,369,000	28,000	4.4%	1973	15
Finland	338,130	5,184,000	25,800	9.1%	1995	16
France	551,500	59,766,000	25,400	8.5%	1958	87
Germany	356,910	83,252,000	26,200	7.8%	1958	99
Greece	131,990	10,645,000	17,900	10.2%	1981	25
Ireland	70,280	3,883,000	27,300	3.7%	1973	15
Italy	301,270	57,716,000	24,300	9.5%	1958	87
Luxembourg	2,590	449,000	43,400	2.4%	1958	6
Netherlands	41,526	16,068,000	25,800	2.3%	1958	3
Portugal	92,390	9,609,000	17,300	4.0%	1986	25
Spain	504,780	38,383,000	18,900	13.1%	1986	64
Sweden	449,960	8,877,000	24,700	5.1%	1995	22
United Kingdom	243,368	59,778,000	24,700	4.8%	1973	87

Agriculture

In the 1990s, partly as a result of the break-up of the former Soviet Union in 1991, the increase in world food production was less than the rise in the world's population, creating a small per capita fall in food production. Downward trends in world food production reopened an old debate – whether food production will be able to keep pace with the predicted rapid rises in the world population in the 21st century.

Some experts argue that the lower than expected production figures in the 1990s heralded a period of relative scarcity and high prices of food, which will be felt most in the poorer developing countries. Others are more optimistic. They point to the successes of the 'green revolution' which, through the use of new crop varieties produced by scientists, irrigation and the extensive use of fertilizers and pesticides, has revolutionized food production since the 1950s and 1960s.

The green revolution has led to a great expansion in the production of many crops, including such basic foods as rice, maize and wheat. In India, its effects have been spectacular. Between 1955 and 1995, grain production trebled, giving the country sufficient food reserves to prevent famine in years when droughts or floods reduce the harvest. While once India had to import food, it is now self-sufficient.

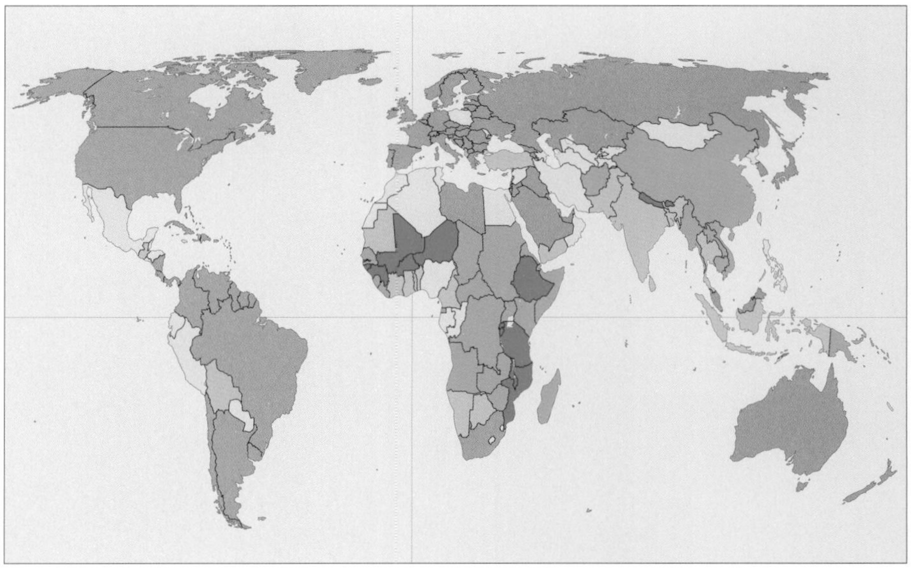

IMPORTANCE OF AGRICULTURE

Agricultural workforce as a percentage of the total workforce (2001).

- OVER 80%
- 60–80%
- 40–60%
- 20–40%
- UNDER 20%
- NO DATA

Rice harvest, Bali, Indonesia

More than half of the world's people eat rice as their basic food. Rice grows well in tropical and subtropical regions, such as in Indonesia, India and south-eastern China.

Food Production

Agriculture, which supplies most of our food, together with materials to make clothes and other products, is the world's most important economic activity. But its relative importance has declined in comparison with manufacturing and service industries. As a result, the end of the 20th century marked the first time for 10,000 years when the vast majority of the people no longer had to depend for their living on growing crops and herding animals.

However, agriculture remains the dominant economic activity in many developing countries in Africa and Asia. For example, in the early 21st century, 80% or more of the people of Bhutan, Burundi, Nepal and Rwanda depended on farming for their living.

Many people in developing countries eke out the barest of livings by nomadic herding or shifting cultivation, combined with hunting, fishing and gathering plant foods. A large proportion of farmers live at subsistence level, producing little more than they require to provide the basic needs of their families.

The world's largest food producer and exporter is the United States, although agriculture employs

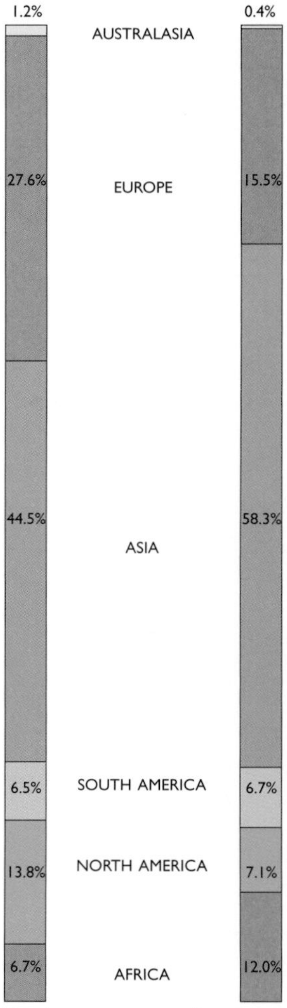
1.2%
0.4%
AUSTRALASIA
27.6%
EUROPE
15.5%
44.5%
ASIA
58.3%
6.5%
SOUTH AMERICA
6.7%
13.8%
NORTH AMERICA
7.1%
6.7%
AFRICA
12.0%
Food
Population

A comparison of world food production and population by continent.

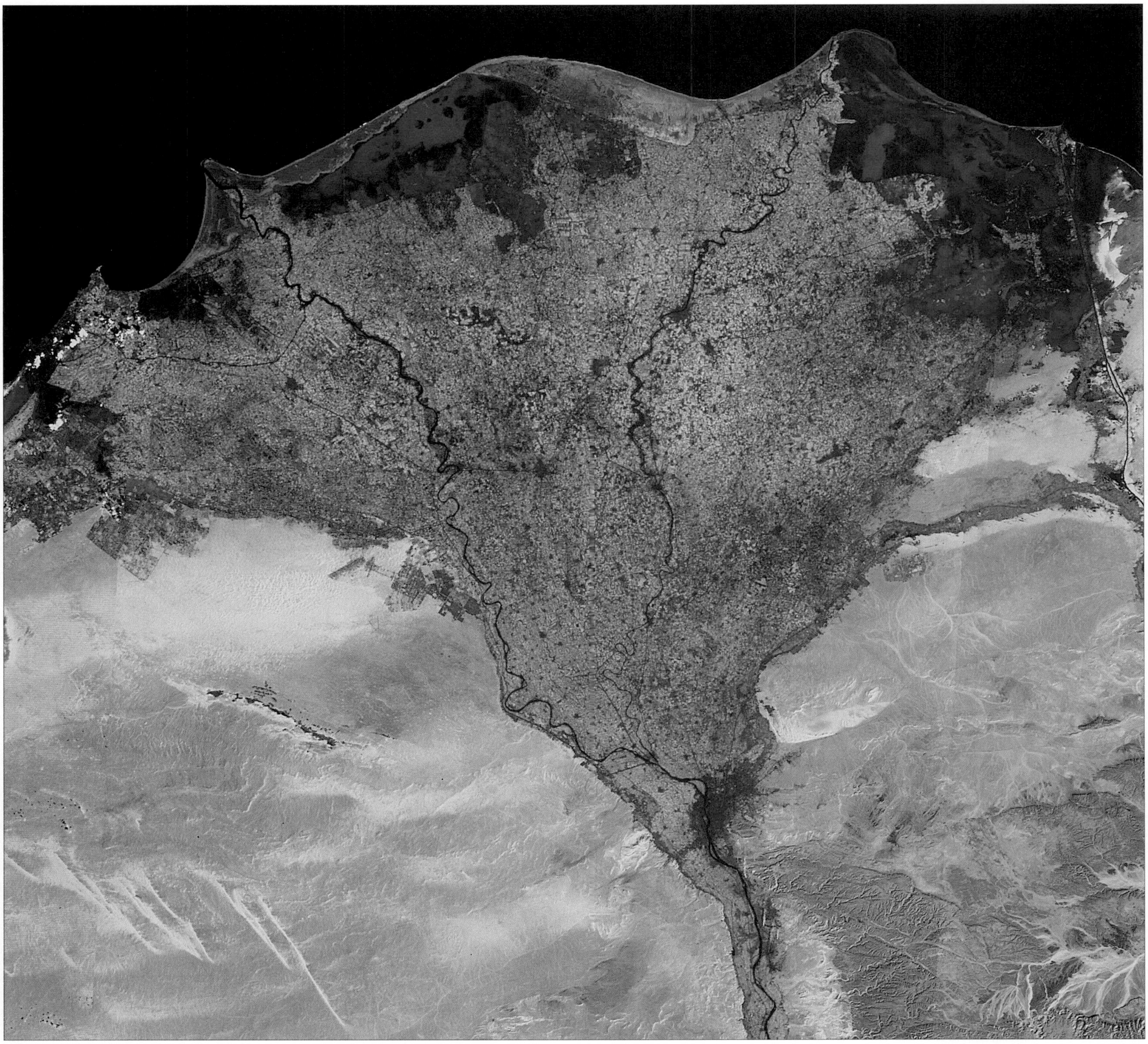

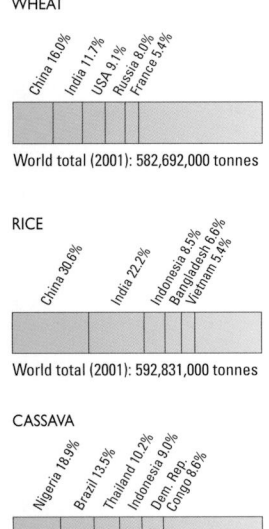

Landsat *image of the Nile delta, Egypt*

Most Egyptians live in the Nile valley and on its delta. Because much of the silt carried by the Nile now ends up on the floor of Lake Nasser, upstream of the Aswan Dam, the delta is now retreating and seawater is seeping inland. This eventuality was not foreseen when the Aswan High Dam was built in the 1960s.

WHEAT

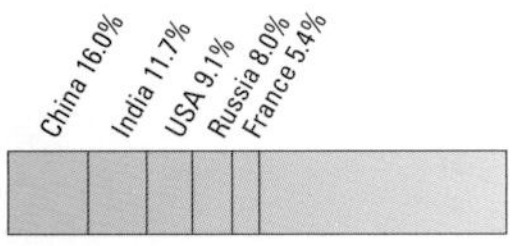
China 16.0%
India 11.7%
USA 9.1%
Russia 8.0%
France 5.4%

World total (2001): 582,692,000 tonnes

RICE

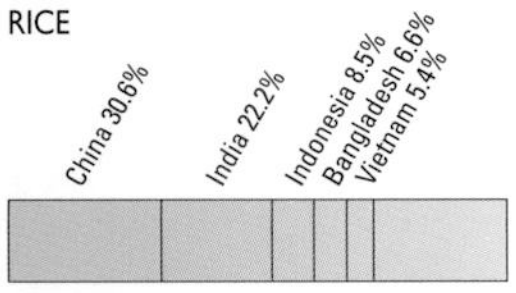
China 30.6%
India 22.2%
Indonesia 8.5%
Bangladesh 6.6%
Vietnam 5.4%

World total (2001): 592,831,000 tonnes

CASSAVA

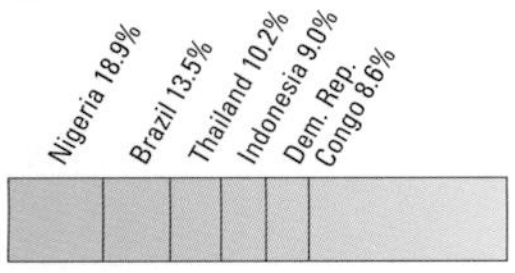
Nigeria 18.9%
Brazil 13.5%
Thailand 10.2%
Indonesia 9.0%
Dem. Rep. Congo 8.6%

World total (2001): 178,868,000 tonnes

around 1.2% of its total workforce. The high production of the United States is explained by its use of scientific methods and mechanization, which are features of agriculture throughout the developed world.

Intensive or Organic Farming

In the early 21st century, some people were beginning to question the dependence of farmers on chemical fertilizers and pesticides. Many people became concerned that the widespread use of chemicals was seriously polluting and damaging the environment.

Others objected to the intensive farming of animals to raise production and lower prices. For example, the suggestion in Britain in 1996 that BSE, or 'mad cow disease', might be passed on to people causing CJD (Creuzfeldt-Jakob Disease) caused widespread alarm. The introduction of GM (genetically modified) crops has also caused concern in many countries.

Some farmers have returned to organic farming, which is based on animal-welfare principles and the banning of chemical fertilizers and pesticides. Organic foods are more expensive to produce than those produced by intensive farming, but an increasing number of consumers are demanding them.

Energy and Minerals

In September 2000, Japan experienced its worst nuclear accident, when more than 400 people were exposed to harmful levels of radiation. This was the worst nuclear incident since the explosion at the Chernobyl nuclear power station, in Ukraine, in 1986. Nuclear power provides around 17% of the world's electricity and experts once thought that it would generate much of the world's energy supply. But concerns about safety and worries about the high costs make this seem unlikely. By 2002, five European countries were committed to abandoning nuclear energy.

Fossil Fuels

Huge amounts of energy are needed for heating, generating electricity and for transport. In the early years of the Industrial Revolution, coal, formed from organic matter buried beneath the Earth's surface, was the leading source of energy. It remains important as a raw material in the manufacture of drugs and other products and also as a fuel, despite the fact that burning coal causes air pollution and gives off carbon dioxide, an important greenhouse gas.

However, oil and natural gas, which came into wide use in the 20th century, are cheaper to produce and easier to handle than coal, while, kilogram for kilogram, they give out more heat. Oil is especially important in moving transport, supplying about 97% of the fuel required.

In the 1990s, proven reserves of oil were sufficient to supply the world, at current rates of production, for 43 years, while supplies of natural gas stood at about 66 years. Coal reserves are more abundant and known reserves would last 200 years at present rates of use. Although these figures must be regarded with caution, because they do not allow for future discoveries, it is clear that fossil fuel reserves will one day run out.

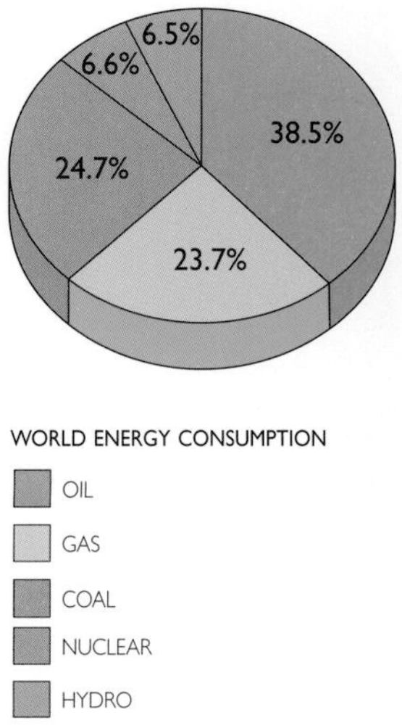
6.5%
6.6%
38.5%
24.7%
23.7%
WORLD ENERGY CONSUMPTION
OIL
GAS
COAL
NUCLEAR
HYDRO

The diagram shows the proportion of world energy consumption in 2001 by form. Total energy consumption was 9,124.8 million tonnes of oil equivalent. Such fuels as wood, peat and animal wastes, together with renewable forms of energy, such as wind and geothermal power, are not included, although they are important in some areas.

Wind farms in California, United States

Wind farms using giant turbines can produce electricity at a lower cost than conventional power stations. But in many areas, winds are too light or too strong for wind farms to be effective.

SELECTED MINERAL PRODUCTION STATISTICS (2000)

Bauxite		Diamonds	
Australia	39.9%	Australia	22.7%
Guinea	11.1%	Botswana	21.4%
Brazil	10.4%	Russia	19.7%
Jamaica	8.2%	Congo (D.R.)	15.0%
China	6.7%	S. Africa	9.2%
Gold		**Iron ore**	
S. Africa	16.9%	China	21.1%
USA	13.8%	Brazil	18.4%
Australia	11.6%	Australia	15.8%
China	7.1%	Russia	8.2%
Canada	6.0%	India	7.1%
Manganese		**Zinc**	
Ukraine	32.1%	China	19.6%
China	18.8%	Australia	16.3%
S. Africa	14.4%	Canada	10.7%
Gabon	10.9%	Peru	10.4%
Brazil	7.7%	USA	9.5%

Potash mines in Utah, United States

Potash is a mineral used mainly to make fertilizers. Much of it comes from mines where deposits formed when ancient seas dried up are exploited. Potash is also extracted from salt lakes.

Alternative Energy

Other sources of energy are therefore required. Besides nuclear energy, the main alternative to fossil fuels is water power. The costs of building dams and hydroelectric power stations is high, though hydroelectric production is comparatively cheap and it does not cause pollution. But the creation of reservoirs uproots people and, in tropical rainforests, it destroys natural habitats. Hydroelectricity is also suitable only in areas with plenty of rivers and steep slopes, such as Norway, while it is unsuitable in flat areas, such as the Netherlands.

In Brazil, alcohol made from sugar has been used to fuel cars. Initially, this government-backed policy met with success. However, it proved to be expensive and the production of ethanol-fuelled cars was halted until Brazil struck a deal with Germany in the early 2000s. Battery-run electric cars have been developed in the United States, but regular and time-consuming recharging is a major drawback.

Other forms of energy, which are renewable and cleaner than fossil fuels, are winds, sea waves, the rise and fall of tides, and geothermal power. In many Western countries seeking to reduce carbon dioxide emissions, these forms of energy seem to have a bright future.

Minerals for Industry

In addition to energy, manufacturing industries need raw materials, including minerals, and these natural resources, like fossil fuels, are being used in such huge quantities that some experts have predicted shortages of some of them before long.

Manufacturers depend on supplies of about 80 minerals. Some, such as bauxite (aluminium ore) and iron, are abundant, but others are scarce or are found only in deposits that are uneconomical to mine. Many experts advocate a policy of recycling scrap metal, including aluminium, chromium, copper, lead, nickel and zinc. This practice would reduce pollution and conserve the energy required for extracting and refining mineral ores.

MINERAL DISTRIBUTION

The map shows the richest sources of the most important minerals. Major mineral locations are named. Undersea deposits, most of which are considered inaccessible, are not shown.

- ▽ GOLD
- SILVER
- ♦ DIAMONDS
- ▽ TUNGSTEN
- ● IRON ORE
- ■ NICKEL
- CHROME
- ▲ MANGANESE
- □ COBALT
- ▲ MOLYBDENUM
- ■ COPPER
- ▲ LEAD
- ● BAUXITE
- ▽ TIN
- ♦ ZINC
- MERCURY

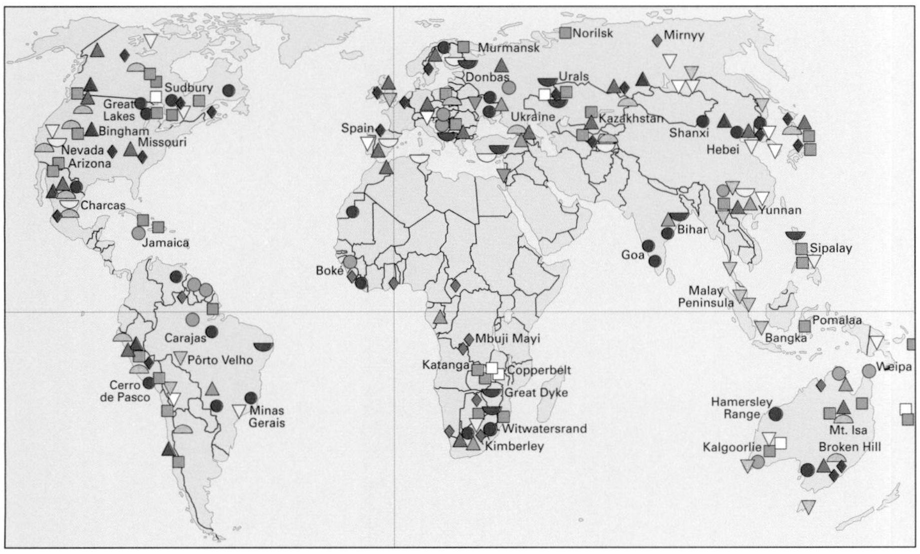

Murmansk
Norilsk
Mirnyy
Donbas
Urals
Sudbury
Great Lakes
Bingham
Missouri
Nevada
Arizona
Spain
Ukraine
Kazakhstan
Shanxi
Hebei
Charcas
Jamaica
Yunnan
Bihar
Goa
Sipalay
Boke
Malay Peninsula
Pomalaa
Bangka
Carajas
Pôrto Velho
Mbuji Mayi
Katanga
Copperbelt
Great Dyke
Weipa
Cerro de Pasco
Minas Gerais
Hamersley Range
Witwatersrand
Kimberley
Mt. Isa
Broken Hill
Kalgoorlie

World Economies

In 2000, Tanzania had a per capita GNI (Gross National Income) of US$270, as compared with Switzerland, whose per capita GNI stood at $38,140. These figures indicate the vast gap between the economies and standards of living of the two countries.

The GNI includes the GDP (Gross Domestic Product), which consists of the total output of goods and services in a country in a given year, plus net exports – that is, the value of goods and services sold abroad less the value of foreign goods and services used in the country in the same year. The GNI divided by the population gives a country's GNI per capita. In low-income developing countries, agriculture makes a high contribution to the GNI. For example, in Tanzania, 40% of the GDP in 1999 came from agriculture. On the other hand, manufacturing was small scale and contributed only 6.6% of the GDP. By comparison, in high-income economies, the percentage contribution of manufacturing far exceeds that of agriculture.

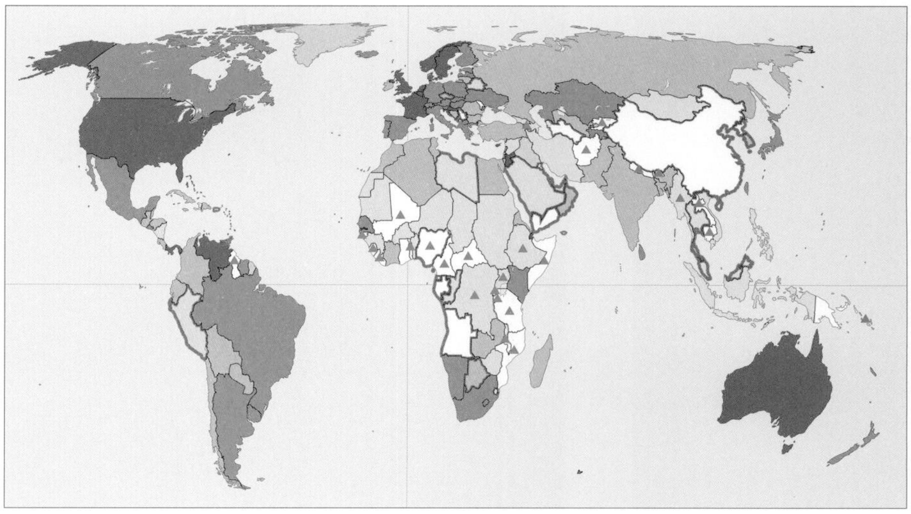

IMPORTANCE OF SERVICE INDUSTRY
Percentage of total GDP from the service sector (1999).

- OVER 70%
- 60–70%
- 50–60%
- 40–50%
- UNDER 40%
- NO DATA
- OVER 40% OF TOTAL GDP FROM INDUSTRIAL SECTOR
- OVER 40% OF TOTAL GDP FROM AGRICULTURAL SECTOR

INDUSTRIALIZATION

The Industrial Revolution began in Britain in the late 18th century. Before that time, most people worked on farms. But with the Industrial Revolution came factories, using machines that could manufacture goods much faster and more cheaply than those made by cottage industries which already existed.

The Industrial Revolution soon spread to several countries in mainland Europe and the United States and, by the late 19th century, it had reached Canada, Japan and Russia. At first,

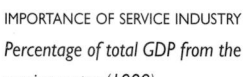

Hard-disk assembly factory
The manufacture of computers and computer software is a fairly new industrial phenomenon. In Asia, high-tech industries have developed quickly, helping relatively poor developing countries to achieve rapid economic growth.

GROSS NATIONAL INCOME PER CAPITA, US$ (2000)

1	Luxembourg	42,050
2	Switzerland	38,140
3	Japan	35,620
4	Norway	34,530
5	United States	34,100
6	Denmark	32,280
7	Iceland	30,390
8	Sweden	27,140
9	Austria	25,220
10	Finland	25,130
11	Germany	25,120
12	Netherlands	24,970
13	Singapore	24,740
14	Belgium	24,540
15	United Kingdom	24,430
16	France	24,090
17	Ireland	22,660
18	Canada	21,130
19	Australia	20,240
20	Italy	20,160

New cars awaiting transportation, Los Angeles, United States
Cars are the most important single manufactured item in world trade, followed by vehicle parts and engines. The world's leading car producers are Japan, the United States, Germany and France.

industrial development was based on such areas as coalfields or ironfields. But in the 20th century, the use of oil, which is easy to transport along pipelines, made it possible for industries to be set up anywhere.

Some nations, such as Switzerland, became industrialized even though they lacked natural resources. They depended instead on the specialized skills of their workers. This same pattern applies today. Some countries with rich natural resources, such as Mexico (with a per capita GNI in 2000 of US$5,070), lag far behind Japan ($35,620) and Cyprus ($12,370), which lack resources and have to import many of the materials they need for their manufacturing industries.

Service Industries

Experts often refer to high-income countries as industrial economies. But manufacturing employs only one in six workers in the United States, one in five in Britain, and one in three in Germany and Japan.

In most developed economies, the percentage of manufacturing jobs has fallen in recent years, while jobs in service industries have risen. For example, in Britain, the proportion of jobs in manufacturing fell from 37% in 1970 to 14% in 2001, while jobs in the service sector rose from just under 50% to 77%. While change in Britain was especially rapid, similar changes were taking place in most industrial economies. By the late 1990s, service industries accounted for well over half the jobs in the generally prosperous countries that made up the OECD (Organization for Economic Co-operation and Development). Instead of being called the 'industrial' economies, these countries might be better named the 'service' economies.

Service industries offer a wide range of jobs and many of them require high educational qualifications. These include finance, insurance and high-tech industries, such as computer programming, entertainment and telecommunications. Service industries also include marketing and advertising, which are essential if the cars and television sets made by manufacturers are to be sold. Another valuable service industry is tourism; in some countries, such as the Gambia, it is the major foreign exchange earner. Trade in services plays a crucial part in world economics. The share of services in world trade rose from 17% in 1980 to 22% in the 1990s.

THE WORKFORCE
Percentage of men and women over 15 years old in employment, selected countries (2001).
MEN
WOMEN

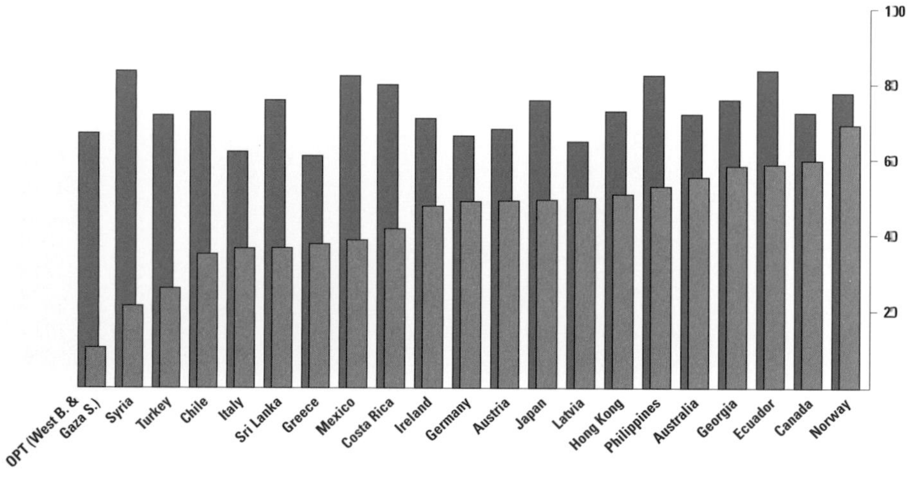
100
80
60
40
20
OPT (West B. & Gaza S.)
Syria
Turkey
Chile
Italy
Sri Lanka
Greece
Mexico
Costa Rica
Ireland
Germany
Austria
Japan
Latvia
Hong Kong
Philippines
Australia
Georgia
Ecuador
Canada
Norway

Trade and Commerce

The establishment of the WTO (World Trade Organization) on 1 January 1995 was the latest step in the long history of world trade. The WTO was set up by the eighth round of negotiations, popularly called the 'Uruguay round', conducted by the General Agreement on Tariffs and Trade (GATT). This treaty was signed by representatives of 125 governments in April 1994. By the start of 2003, the WTO had 145 members.

GATT was first established in 1948. Its initial aim was to produce a charter to create a body called the International Trade Organization. This body never came into being. Instead, GATT, acting as an *ad hoc* agency, pioneered a series of agreements aimed at liberalizing world trade by reducing tariffs on imports and other obstacles to free trade.

GATT's objectives were based on the belief that international trade creates wealth. Trade occurs because the world's resources are not distributed evenly between countries, and, in theory, free trade means that every country should concentrate on what it can do best and purchase from others goods and services that they can supply more cheaply. In practice, however, free trade may cause unemployment when imported goods are cheaper than those produced within the country.

Trade is sometimes an important factor in world politics, especially when trade sanctions are applied against countries whose actions incur the disapproval of the international community. For example, in the 1990s, worldwide trade sanctions were imposed on Serbia because of its involvement in the civil war in Bosnia-Herzegovina.

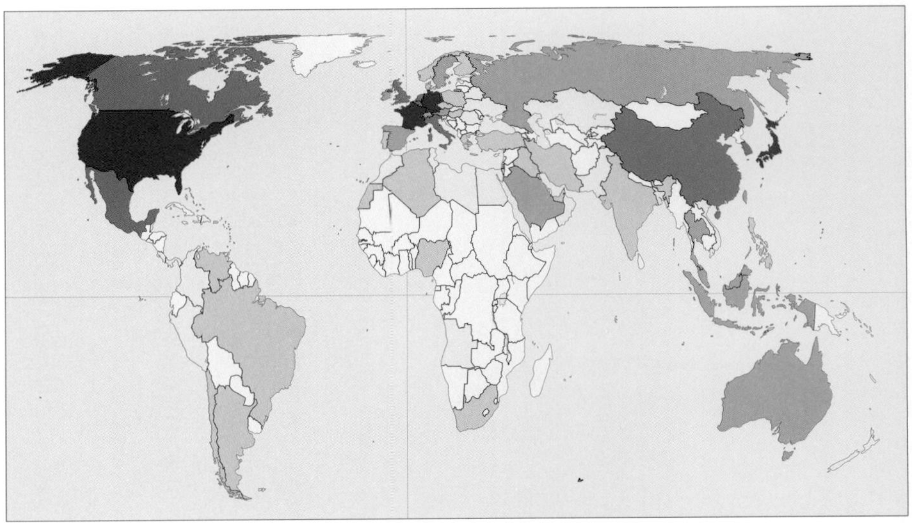

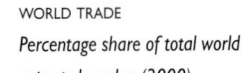

WORLD TRADE
Percentage share of total world exports by value (2000).

- OVER 5%
- 2.5–5%
- 1–2.5%
- 0.25–1%
- 0.1–0.25%
- UNDER 0.1%
- NO DATA

The world's leading trading nations, according to the combined value of their exports and imports, are the United States, Germany, Japan, France and the United Kingdom.

New York City Stock Exchange, United States
Stock exchanges, where stocks and shares are sold and bought, are important in channelling savings and investments to companies and governments. The world's largest stock exchange is in Tokyo, Japan.

Changing Trade Patterns

The early 16th century, when Europeans began to divide the world into huge empires, opened up a new era in international trade. By the 19th century, the colonial powers, who were among the first industrial powers, promoted trade with their colonies, from which they obtained unprocessed raw materials, such as food, natural fibres, minerals and timber. In return, they shipped clothes, shoes and other cheap items to the colonies.

From the late 19th century until the early 1950s, primary products dominated world trade, with oil becoming the leading item in the later part of this period. Many developing countries still depend heavily on the export of one or two primary products, such as coffee or iron ore, but overall the proportion of primary products in world trade has fallen since the 1950s. Today the most important elements in world trade are

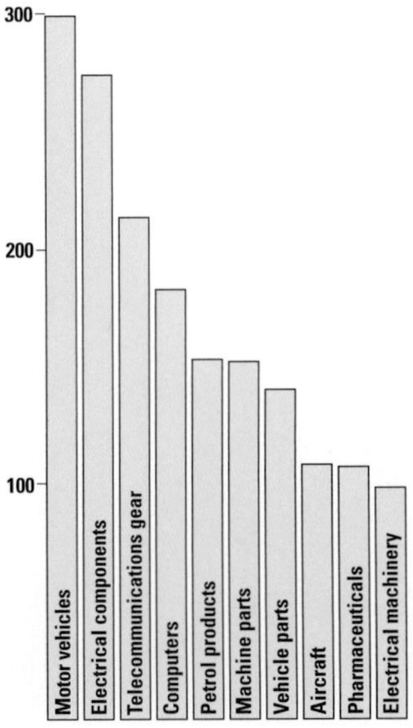
300
200
100
Motor vehicles
Electrical components
Telecommunications gear
Computers
Petrol products
Machine parts
Vehicle parts
Aircraft
Pharmaceuticals
Electrical machinery

Traded products
Major manufactures traded by value in billions of US$ (2000).

Rotterdam, Netherlands

World trade depends on transport. Rotterdam, the world's largest port, serves not only the Netherlands, but also industrial areas in parts of Germany, France and Switzerland.

manufactures and semi-manufactures, exchanged mainly between the industrialized nations.

The World's Markets

Private companies conduct most of world trade, but government policies affect it. Governments which believe that certain industries are strategic, or essential for the country's future, may impose tariffs on imports, or import quotas to limit the volume of imports, if they are thought to be undercutting the domestic industries.

For example, the United States has argued that Japan has greater access to its markets than the United States has to Japan's. This might have led the United States to resort to protectionism, but instead the United States remains committed to free trade despite occasional disputes.

Other problems in international trade occur when governments give subsidies to its producers, who can then export products at low prices. Another difficulty, called 'dumping', occurs when products are sold at below the market price in order to gain a market share. One of the aims of the newly-created WTO is the phasing out of government subsidies for agricultural products, though the world's poorest countries will be exempt from many of the WTO's most severe regulations.

Governments are also concerned about the volume of imports and exports and most countries keep records of international transactions. When the total value of goods and services imported exceeds the value of goods and services exported, then the country has a deficit in its balance of payments. Large deficits can weaken a country's economy.

DEPENDENCE ON TRADE

Value of exports as a percentage of GDP (latest available year).

- OVER 50% GDP FROM EXPORTS
- 40–50% GDP FROM EXPORTS
- 30–40% GDP FROM EXPORTS
- 20–30% GDP FROM EXPORTS
- 10–20% GDP FROM EXPORTS
- UNDER 10% GDP FROM EXPORTS
- MOST DEPENDENT ON INDUSTRIAL EXPORTS (OVER 75% OF TOTAL)
- MOST DEPENDENT ON FUEL EXPORTS (OVER 75% OF TOTAL)
- MOST DEPENDENT ON METAL & MINERAL EXPORTS (OVER 75% OF TOTAL)

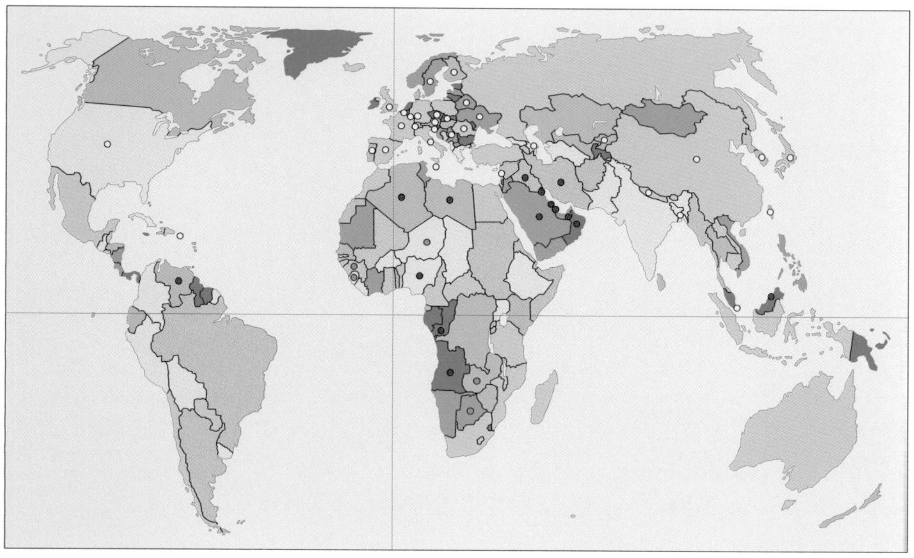

Travel and Communications

In the 1990s, millions of people became linked into an 'information superhighway' called the Internet. Equipped with a personal computer, an electricity supply, a telephone and a modem, people are able to communicate with others all over the world. People can now send messages by e-mail (electronic mail), they can engage in electronic discussions, contacting people with similar interests, and engage in 'chat lines', which are the latest equivalent of telephone conferences.

These new developments are likely to affect the working lives of people everywhere, enabling them to work at home whilst having many of the facilities that are available in an office. The Internet is part of an ongoing and astonishingly rapid evolution in the fields of communications and transport.

Transport

Around 200 years ago, most people never travelled far from their birthplace, but today we are much more mobile. Cars and buses now provide convenient forms of transport for many millions of people, huge ships transport massive cargoes around the world, and jet airliners, some travelling faster than the speed of sound, can transport high-value goods as well as holiday-makers to almost any part of the world.

Land transport of freight has developed greatly since the start of the Industrial Revolution. Canals, which became important in the 18th century, could not compete with rail transport in the 19th century. Rail transport remains important, but, during the 20th century, it suffered from competition with road transport, which is cheaper and has the advantage of carrying materials and goods from door to door.

Road transport causes pollution and the burning of fuels creates greenhouse gases that contribute to global warming. Yet privately owned cars are now the leading form of passenger traffic in developed nations, especially for journeys of less than around 400 km [250 miles]. Car owners do not have to suffer the inconvenience of waiting for public transport, such as buses, though they often have to endure traffic jams at peak travel times.

Ocean passenger traffic is now modest, but ships carry the bulk of international trade. Huge oil tankers and bulk grain carriers now ply the oceans with their cargoes, while container ships carry mixed cargoes. Containers are boxes built

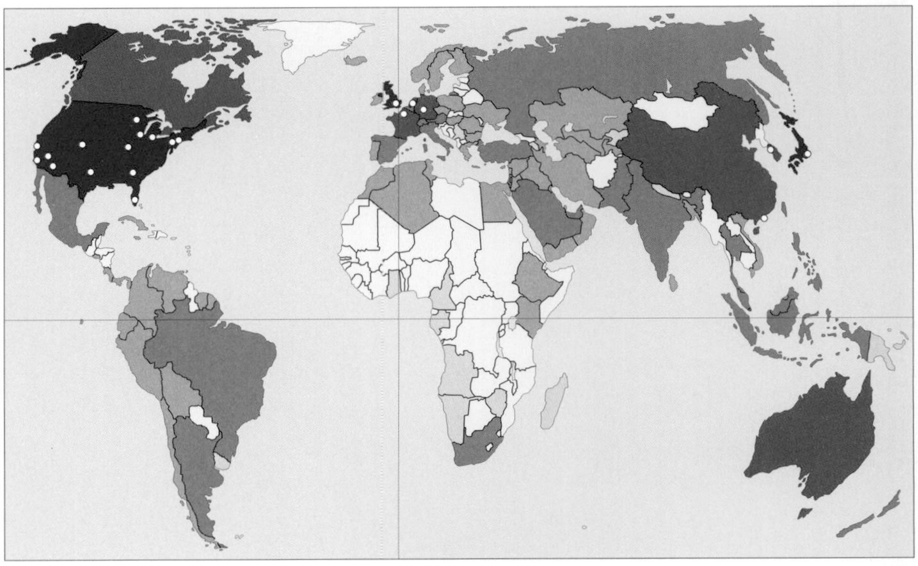

AIR TRAVEL – PASSENGER KILOMETRES* FLOWN *(latest available year).*

- OVER 100,000 MILLION
- 50,000–100,000 MILLION
- 10,000–50,000 MILLION
- 1,000–10,000 MILLION
- 500–1,000 MILLION
- UNDER 500 MILLION
- ∘ MAJOR AIRPORTS (HANDLING OVER 25 MILLION PASSENGERS IN 2000)

** Passenger kilometres are the number of passengers (both international and domestic) multiplied by the distance flown by each passenger from the airport of origin.*

Eurostar travel

High-speed Eurostar services connect London to Paris and Brussels via the $15 billion Channel Tunnel, linking the UK to mainland Europe. Only six years after the tunnel opened in 1994, Eurostar carried more than 7 million passengers.

SELECTED NEWSPAPER CIRCULATION FIGURES (LATEST AVAILABLE YEAR)

France		
Le Monde		357,362
Le Figaro		350,000
Germany		
Bild		4,500,000
Süddeutsche Zeitung		402,866
Italy		
Corriera Della Sella		676,904
La Republica		655,321
La Stampa		436,047
Japan		
Yomiuri Shimbun	(a.m. edition)	9,800,000
	(p.m. edition)	4,400,000
Manichi Shimbun	(a.m. edition)	3,200,000
	(p.m. edition)	1,900,000

Russia	
Pravda	1,373,795
Ivestia	700,000
Spain	
El Pais	407,629
United Kingdom	
The Sun	4,061,253
Daily Mirror	2,525,000
Daily Express	1,270,642
The Times	672,802
The Guardian	402,214
United States	
New York Times	1,724,705
Chicago Tribune	1,110,552
Houston Chronicle	605,343

JAL
Japan Airlines
JA8185
unicef

JAL Airways Boeing-747, Vancouver Airport, Canada
Air travel has transformed world tourism. However, the terrorist attacks on the United States in September 2001 and the spread of the SARS (Severe Acute Respiratory Syndrome) virus in 2003 led to large falls in passenger numbers.

to international standards that contain cargo. Containers are easy to handle, and so they reduce shipping costs, speed up deliveries and cut losses caused by breakages. Most large ports now have the facilities to handle containers.

Air transport is suitable for carrying goods that are expensive, light and compact, or perishable. However, because of the high costs of air freight, it is most suitable for carrying passengers along long-distance routes around the world. Through air travel, international tourism, with people sometimes flying considerable distances, has become a major and rapidly expanding industry.

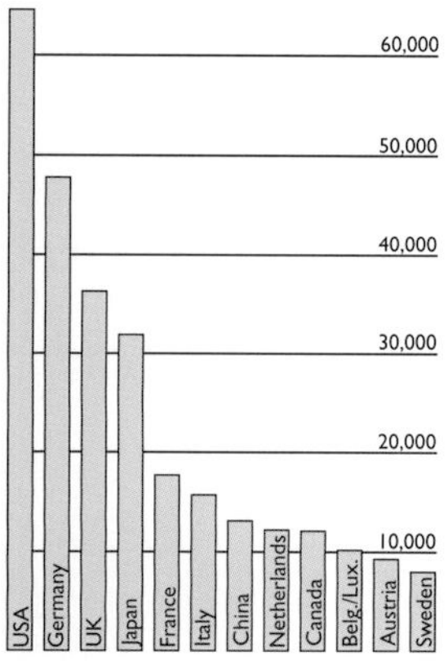
60,000
50,000
40,000
30,000
20,000
10,000
USA
Germany
UK
Japan
France
Italy
China
Netherlands
Canada
Belg./Lux.
Austria
Sweden

Spending on tourism
Countries spending the most on overseas tourism, US$ million (2000).

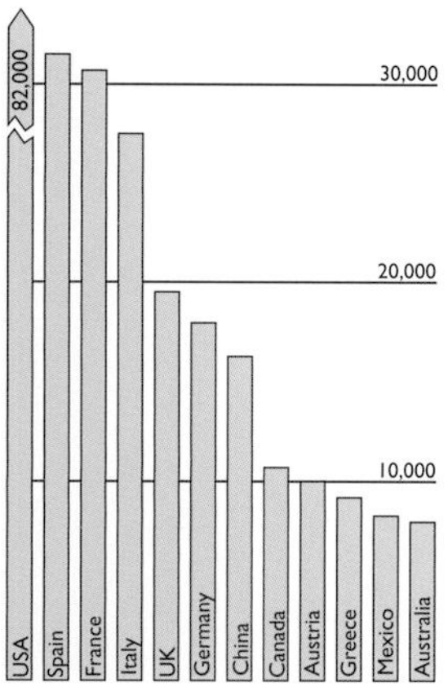
82,000
30,000
20,000
10,000
USA
Spain
France
Italy
UK
Germany
China
Canada
Austria
Greece
Mexico
Australia

Receipts from tourism
Countries receiving the most from overseas tourism, US$ million (2000).

Communications

After humans first began to communicate by using the spoken word, the next great stage in the development of communications was the invention of writing around 5,500 years ago.

The invention of movable type in the mid 15th century led to the mass production of books and, in the early 17th century, the first newspapers. Newspapers now play an important part in the mass communication of information, although today radio and, even more important, television have led to a decline in the circulation of newspapers in many parts of the world.

The most recent developments have occurred in the field of electronics. Artificial communications satellites now circle the planet, relaying radio, television, telegraph and telephone signals. This enables people to watch events on the far side of the globe as they are happening. Electronic equipment is also used in many other ways, such as in navigation systems used in air, sea and space, and also in modern weaponry, as shown vividly in the television coverage of such military actions as that in Iraq in 2003.

The Age of Computers

One of the most remarkable applications of electronics is in the field of computers. Computers are now making a huge contribution to communications. They are able to process data at incredibly high speeds and can store vast quantities of information. For example, the work of weather forecasters has been greatly improved now that computers can process the enormous amount of data required for a single weather forecast. They also have many other applications in such fields as business, government, science and medicine.

Through the Internet, computers provide a free interchange of news and views around the world. But the dangers of misuse, such as the exchange of pornographic images, have led to calls for censorship. Censorship, however, is a blunt weapon, which can be used by authoritarian governments to suppress the free exchange of information that the new information superhighway makes possible.

The World Today

The early years of the 20th century witnessed the exploration of Antarctica, the last uncharted continent. Today, less than 100 years later, tourists are able to take cruises to the icy southern continent, while almost no part of the globe is inaccessible to the determined traveller. Improved transport and images from space have made our world seem smaller.

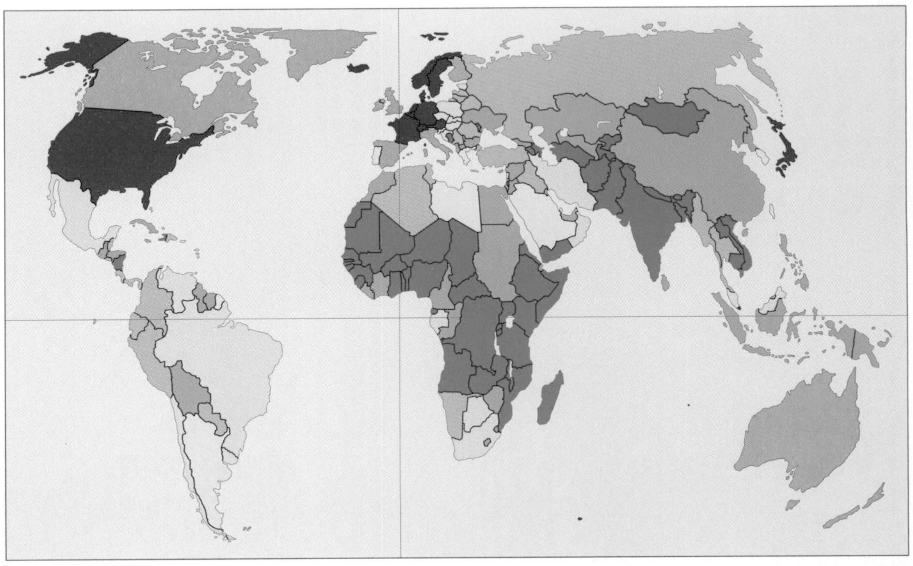

GROSS NATIONAL PRODUCT PER CAPITA

The value of total production divided by the population (1999).

- OVER 400% OF WORLD AVERAGE
- 200–400% OF WORLD AVERAGE
- 100–200% OF WORLD AVERAGE

[WORLD AVERAGE WEALTH PER PERSON US$6,316]

- 50–100% OF WORLD AVERAGE
- 25–50% OF WORLD AVERAGE
- 10–25% OF WORLD AVERAGE
- UNDER 10% OF WORLD AVERAGE

RICHEST COUNTRIES	
Liechtenstein	$44,640
Switzerland	$38,350
Bermuda	$35,590
Norway	$32,880
Japan	$32,230

POOREST COUNTRIES	
Ethiopia	$100
Burundi	$120
Sierra Leone	$130
Guinea-Bissau	$160
Niger	$190

A Divided World

Between the end of World War II in 1945 and the late 1980s, the world was divided, politically and economically, into three main groups: the developed countries or Western democracies, with their free enterprise or mixed economies; the centrally planned or Communist countries; and the developing countries or Third World.

This division became obsolete when the former Soviet Union and its old European allies, together with the 'special economic zones' in eastern China, began the transition from centrally planned to free enterprise economies. This left the world divided into two broad camps: the prosperous developed countries and the poorer developing countries. The simplest way of distinguishing between the groups is with reference to their per capita Gross National Products (per capita GNPs).

The World Bank divides the developing countries into three main groups. At the bottom are the low-income economies, which include China, India and most of sub-Saharan Africa. In 1999, this group contained about 40% of the world's population, but its average per capita GNP was only US$420. The other two groups are the lower-middle-income economies, with an average per capita GNP of $1,200, and the upper-middle-income economies with an average per capita GNP of $4,870. By contrast, the high-income economies, also called the developed countries, contain only 15% of the world's population but have the high (and rising) average GNP per capita of $26,440.

Economic and Social Contrasts

Economic differences are coupled with other factors, such as rates of population growth. For example, around the turn of the century, the low- and middle-income economies had a high population growth rate of 1.7%, while the growth rate in high-income economies was around 0.1%. Around 18 countries in Europe experienced a natural decrease in population in 1998.

Stark contrasts exist worldwide in the quality

East African tourism

Improved transport, including the use of four-wheel drive vehicles, has led to a boom in tourism in many developing regions, such as East Africa. But terrorist incidents may slow down the development of tourism in some areas.

Operation Enduring Freedom, Afghanistan
A joint patrol of US Marines and Army soldiers is seen here patrolling through the village of Cem, Afghanistan, some 10 km [6 miles] from the airport near Kandahar, in January 2002.

of life. Generally, the people in Western Europe and North America are better fed, healthier and have more cars and better homes than the people in low- and middle-income economies.

In 2000, the average life expectancy at birth in sub-Saharan Africa was 47 years. By contrast, the average life expectancy in the United States and the United Kingdom was 77 years. Illiteracy in low-income economies for people aged 15 and over was 39% in 1999. But for women, the percentage of those who could not read or write was 48%. Illiteracy is relatively rare for both sexes in high-income economies.

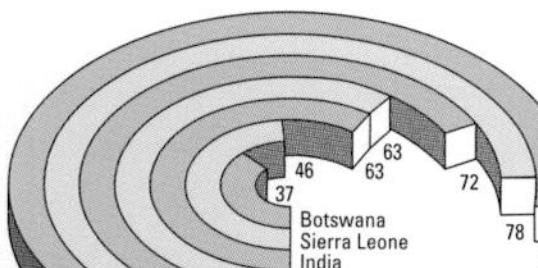
46
63
63
72
37
Botswana
Sierra Leone
India
Brazil
Hungary
UK
Japan
78
81

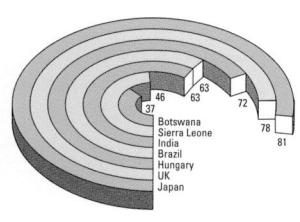

Years of life expectancy at birth, selected countries (2001).
The chart shows the contrasting range of average life expectancies at birth for a range of countries, including both low-income and high-income economies. Generally, improved health services are raising life expectancies. On average, women live longer than men, even in the poorer developing countries.

Future Development

In the last 50 years, despite all the aid supplied to developing countries, much of the world still suffers from poverty and economic backwardness. Some countries are even poorer now than they were a generation ago while others have become substantially richer.

However, several factors suggest that poor countries may find progress easier in the 21st century. For example, technology is now more readily transferable between countries, while improved transport and communications make it easier for countries to take part in the world economy. But industrial development could lead to an increase in global pollution. Hence, any strategy for global economic expansion must also take account of environmental factors.

A World In Conflict

The end of the Cold War held out hopes of a new world order. But ethnic, religious and other rivalries have subsequently led to appalling violence in places as diverse as the Balkan peninsula, Israel and the Palestinian territories, and Rwanda–Burundi. Then, on 11 September 2001, the attack on those symbols of the economic and military might of the United States – the World Trade Center and the Pentagon Building – demonstrated that nowhere on Earth is safe from attack by extremists prepared to sacrifice their lives in pursuit of their aims.

The danger posed by terrorist groups, such as al Qaida, or by rogue states, possibly in possession of nuclear or biological weapons, has forced many countries into new alliances to combat the terrorists and the governments that give them shelter. Many people also recognize a pressing need to understand and correct the wrongs, real or perceived, that lead people to acts of martyrdom or murderous destruction.

WESTERN CAPE, SOUTH AFRICA

WORLD MAPS

SETTLEMENTS

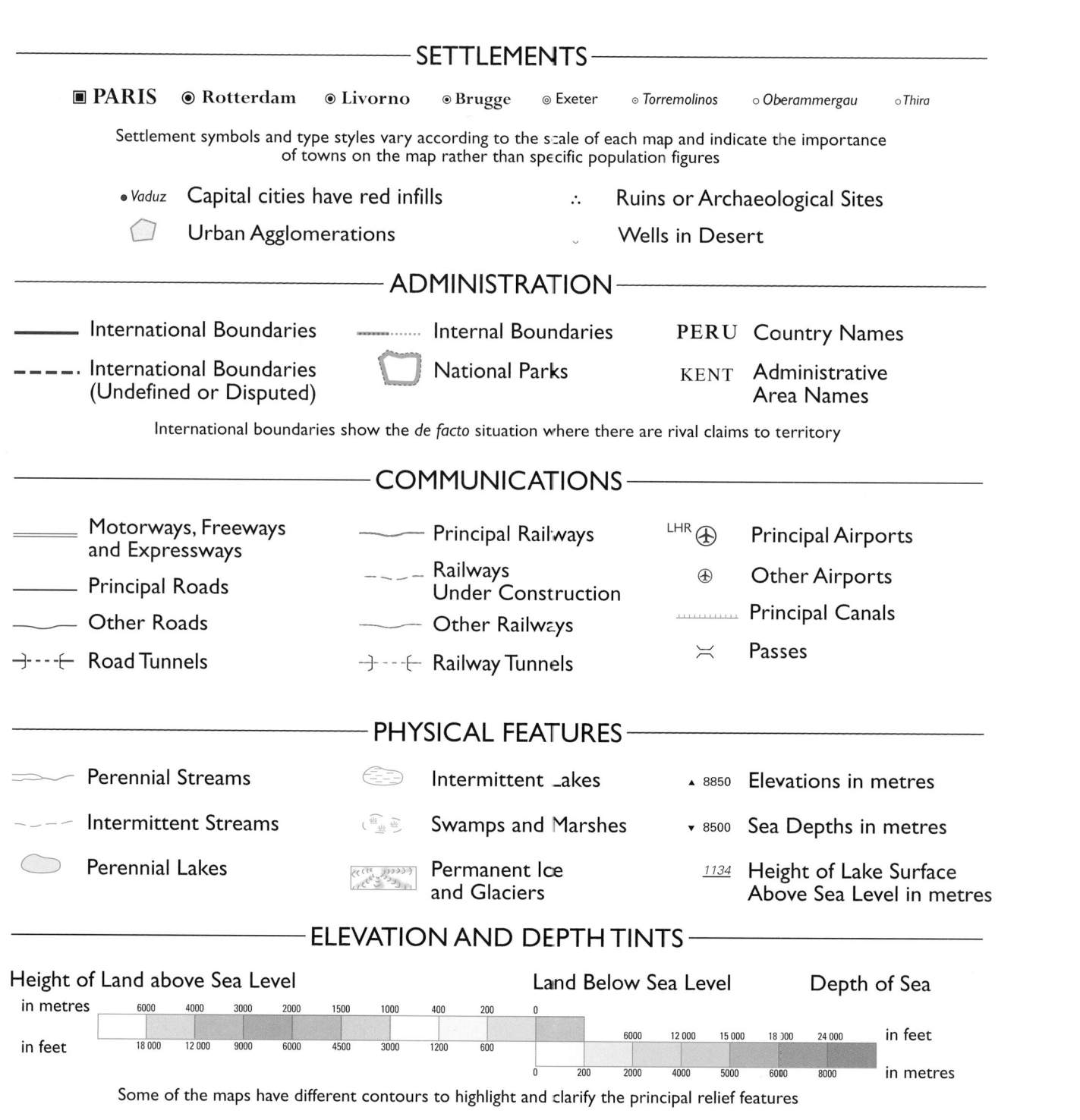

▣ **PARIS** ◉ **Rotterdam** ◉ **Livorno** ◉ **Brugge** ◎ Exeter ○ *Torremolinos* ○ *Oberammergau* ○ *Thira*

Settlement symbols and type styles vary according to the scale of each map and indicate the importance of towns on the map rather than specific population figures

Vaduz Capital cities have red infills

Urban Agglomerations

∴ Ruins or Archaeological Sites

Wells in Desert

ADMINISTRATION

International Boundaries

International Boundaries (Undefined or Disputed)

Internal Boundaries

National Parks

PERU Country Names

KENT Administrative Area Names

International boundaries show the *de facto* situation where there are rival claims to territory

COMMUNICATIONS

Motorways, Freeways and Expressways

Principal Roads

Other Roads

Road Tunnels

Principal Railways

Railways Under Construction

Other Railways

Railway Tunnels

LHR Principal Airports

Other Airports

Principal Canals

Passes

PHYSICAL FEATURES

Perennial Streams

Intermittent Streams

Perennial Lakes

Intermittent Lakes

Swamps and Marshes

Permanent Ice and Glaciers

▲ 8850 Elevations in metres

▼ 8500 Sea Depths in metres

1134 Height of Lake Surface Above Sea Level in metres

ELEVATION AND DEPTH TINTS

Height of Land above Sea Level

in metres	6000	4000	3000	2000	1500	1000	400	200	0
in feet	18 000	12 000	9000	6000	4500	3000	1200	600	

Land Below Sea Level

Depth of Sea

in feet		6000	12 000	15 000	18 000	24 000
in metres	0	200	2000	4000	5000	6000	8000

Some of the maps have different contours to highlight and clarify the principal relief features

Equatorial Scale 1:84 000 000

Beaufort Sea
Banks I.
Parry Is.
Queen Elizabeth Is.
Ellesmere I.
Devon I.
Victoria I.
Baffin Bay
Baffin I.
Davis Str.
GREENLAND
(Denmark)
Nuuk
Denmark Str.
ICELAND
Reykjavík
Faroe Is.
(Den.)
Arctic Circle
UNITED KINGDOM
Glasgow
Dublin
IRELAND
Bering Strait
St. Lawrence I.
ALASKA
(U.S.A.)
Yukon
Fairbanks
Anchorage
G. of Alaska
Kodiak I.
Aleutian Is. (U.S.A.)
Great Bear L.
Yellowknife
Great Slave L.
Hudson Bay
Churchill
Nelson
Queen Charlotte Is.
Edmonton
Calgary
CANADA
Vancouver
Vancouver I.
L. Winnipeg
Winnipeg
Schefferville
Newfoundland
St. John's
Seattle
Portland
Missouri
UNITED STATES OF AMERICA
L. Superior
Québec
Ottawa
Montreal
Minneapolis
Michigan
L. Huron
Toronto
Halifax
Milwaukee
Detroit
Boston
Salt Lake City
Denver
CHICAGO
Cleveland
Pittsburgh
NEW YORK
PHILADELPHIA
SAN FRANCISCO
Sacramento
Kansas City
St. Louis
Cincinnati
Baltimore
Washington D.C.
NORTH ATLANTIC OCEAN
Colorado
LOS ANGELES
San Diego
Phoenix
Memphis
Atlanta
Dallas
El Paso
Houston
Mississippi
New Orleans
Jacksonville
Bermuda
(U.K.)
Azores
(Port.)
PORTUGAL
Lisbon
Tangier
Rabat
Casablanca
Madeira
(Port.)
Marrakesh
MOROCCO
Canary Is.
(Sp.)
El Aaiun
WESTERN SAHARA
International Date Line
Midway Is.
Hawaiian Is.
(U.S.A.)
Honolulu
Oahu
Hawaii
Ciudad Juárez
Rio Grande
Guadalupe I.
(Mexico)
G. of California
Monterrey
MEXICO
Gulf of Mexico
Miami
BAHAMAS
Tropic of Cancer
Havana
CUBA
Turks & Caicos Is.
(U.K.)
León
Guadalajara
MÉXICO
Cayman Is. (U.K.)
HAITI
DOMINICAN REP.
Port-au-Prince
JAMAICA
Kingston
Santo Domingo
PUERTO RICO
Virgin Is. (U.S.A.)&(U.K.)
ANTIGUA & BARBUDA
ST. KITTS & NEVIS
Revilla Gigedo Is.
(Mexico)
Puebla
Belmopan
BELIZE
GUATEMALA
Guatemala
HONDURAS
Tegucigalpa
San Salvador
EL SALVADOR
NICARAGUA
Caribbean Sea
GUADELOUPE (Fr.)
DOMINICA
MARTINIQUE (Fr.)
ST. LUCIA
ST. VINCENT & THE GRENADINES
BARBADOS
GRENADA
NETH. ANTILLES
TRINIDAD & TOBAGO
Managua
Barranquilla
San José
Panamá
COSTA RICA
PANAMA
Caracas
Orinoco
Clipperton I.
(Fr.)
CAPE VERDE IS.
Nouakchott
MAURITANIA
Timbuktu
Dakar
SENEGAL
GAMBIA
GUINEA-BISSAU
Bamako
Bissau
GUINEA
Conakry
Freetown
SIERRA LEONE
Ouagadougou
IVORY COAST
Yamoussoukro
Monrovia
LIBERIA
Abidjan
Gulf of Guinea
PACIFIC OCEAN
VENEZUELA
Georgetown
Paramaribo
Cayenne
GUYANA
SURINAME
FRENCH GUIANA
Palmyra Is.
(U.S.A.)
Medellín
Coco I.
(C. Rica)
Cali
BOGOTÁ
COLOMBIA
Malpelo
(Colombia)
Kiritimati
Howland I. (U.S.A.)
Baker I. (U.S.A.)
Jarvis I.
(U.S.A.)
Equator
Negro
Japurá
Belém
São Paulo
(Brazil)
Galápagos Is.
(Ecuador)
Quito
ECUADOR
Guayaquil
Manaus
Amazon
Iquitos
Xingu
Fortaleza
Fernando de Noronha
(Brazil)
Abariringa
KIRIBATI
Malden I.
Phoenix Is.
Starbuck I.
Natal
Ascension I.
(U.K.)
Tokelau Is.
(N.Z.)
Penrhyn Is.
Marquesas Is.
BRAZIL
Recife
Madeira
Tocantins
Ucayali
Marañón
PERU
LIMA
São Francisco
Salvador
Manihiki
Flint I.
Wallis & Futuna
(Fr.)
SAMOA
AMERICAN SAMOA
FRENCH POLYNESIA
Callao
OCEAN
Tuamotu Is.
Society Is.
Tahiti
L. Titicaca
La Paz
BOLIVIA
Sucre
Brasília
St. Helena
(U.K.)
Arequipa
FIJI
TONGA
Niue
(N.Z.)
Cook Is.
(N.Z.)
Belo Horizonte
SOUTH ATLANTIC OCEAN
Trindade
(Brazil)
SÃO PAULO
RIO DE JANEIRO
Antofagasta
PARAGUAY
Tropic of Capricorn
Tubuai Is.
Asunción
Santos
Curitiba
Pitcairn I.
(U.K.)
Ducie I.
San Ambrosio
(Chile)
San Felix
(Chile)
Tucumán
Sala-y-Gomez
(Chile)
Easter I.
(Chile)
Rapa
Paraná
Uruguay
Córdoba
Pôrto Alegre
Rio Grande
Valparaíso
Rosario
URUGUAY
Kermadec Is. (N.Z.)
Juan Fernández
(Chile)
SANTIAGO
Talcahuano
BUENOS AIRES
ARGENTINA
Montevideo
Tristan da Cunha
(U.K.)
Bahía Blanca
Gough I.
(U.K.)
CHILE
Chiloé I.
Chatham Is.
(N.Z.)
Falkland Is.
(U.K.)
Punta Arenas
Tierra del Fuego
South Georgia
(U.K.)
C. Horn
Scotia Sea
South Sandwich Is.
(U.K.)
Drake Passage
South Orkney Is.
South Shetland Is.
Bellingshausen Sea
Weddell Sea
Antarctic Circle
Amundsen Sea
Antarctica
West from Greenwich
A
B
C
D
E
F
G
H
1
2
3
4
5
6
7
8
9
180
160
140
120
100
80
60
40
20

Projection: Hammer Equal Area

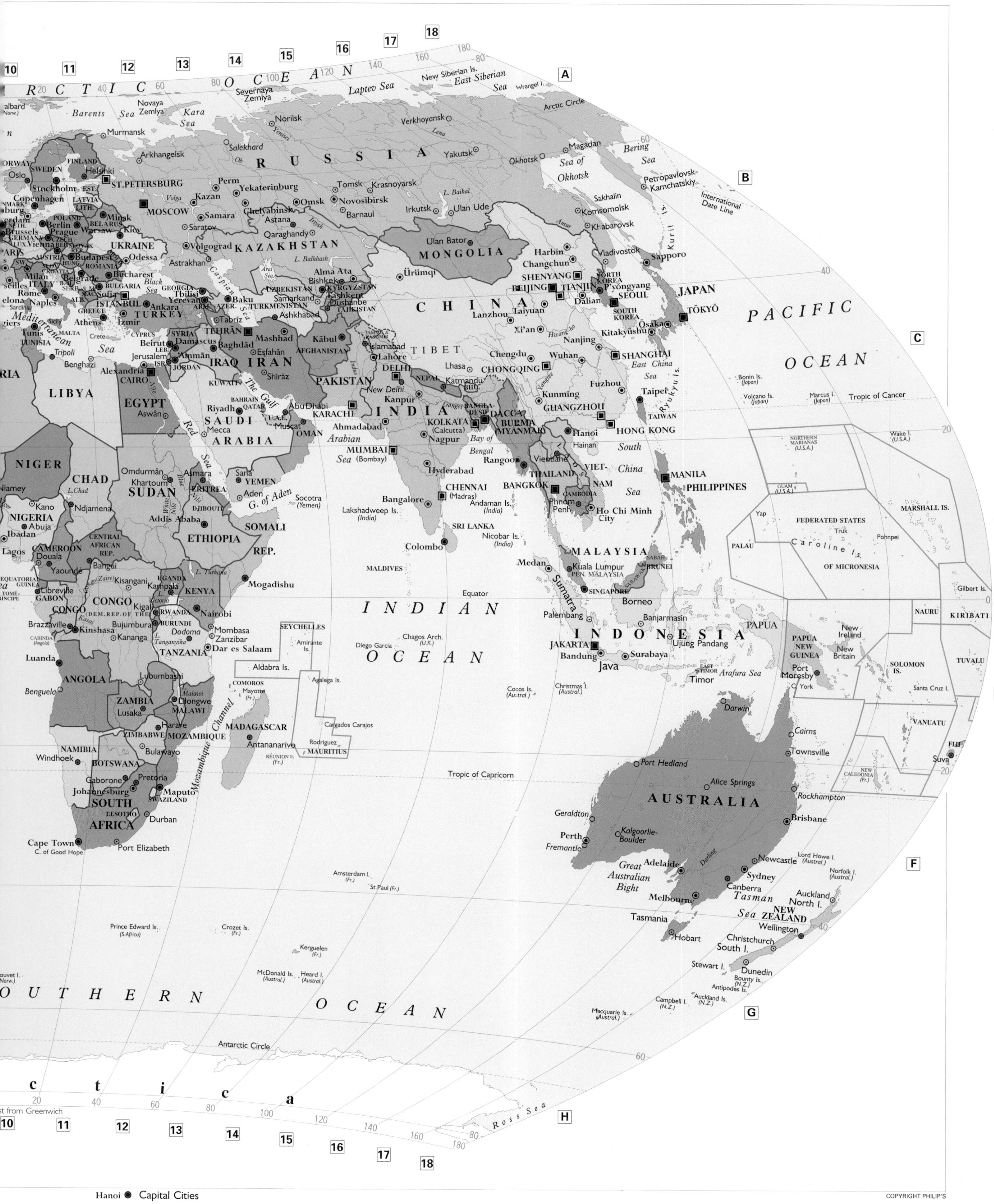
Arctic Ocean
Barents Sea
Kara Sea
Laptev Sea
East Siberian Sea
Novaya Zemlya
Severnaya Zemlya
New Siberian Is.
Wrangel I.
Arctic Circle
RUSSIA
Murmansk
Arkhangelsk
ST.PETERSBURG
MOSCOW
Norilsk
Salekhard
Verkhoyansk
Yakutsk
Okhotsk
Magadan
Sea of Okhotsk
Bering Sea
Petropavlovsk-Kamchatskiy
International Date Line
Sakhalin
Komsomolsk
Khabarovsk
Vladivostok
Perm
Yekaterinburg
Kazan
Samara
Saratov
Volgograd
Astrakhan
Chelyabinsk
Omsk
Novosibirsk
Tomsk
Krasnoyarsk
Barnaul
Irkutsk
L. Baikal
Ulan Ude
Astana
Qaraghandy
KAZAKHSTAN
L. Balkhash
Almaty
Bishkek
UZBEKISTAN
KYRGYZSTAN
TURKMENISTAN
TAJIKISTAN
Tashkent
Samarkand
Dushanbe
Ashkhabad
Aral Sea
Caspian Sea
MONGOLIA
Ulan Bator
CHINA
Ürümqi
TIBET
Lhasa
Lanzhou
Taiyuan
Xi'an
Chengdu
CHONGQING
Wuhan
Nanjing
SHANGHAI
Kunming
GUANGZHOU
HONG KONG
Fuzhou
Taipei
TAIWAN
Harbin
Changchun
SHENYANG
BEIJING
TIANJIN
Dalian
NORTH KOREA
P'yongyang
SEOUL
SOUTH KOREA
JAPAN
TŌKYŌ
Sapporo
Ōsaka
Kitakyushu
East China Sea
Ryukyu Is.
Kuril Is.
PACIFIC OCEAN
Tropic of Cancer
Bonin Is. (Japan)
Volcano Is. (Japan)
Marcus I. (Japan)
Wake I. (U.S.A.)
NORTHERN MARIANAS (U.S.A.)
GUAM (U.S.A.)
FEDERATED STATES OF MICRONESIA
Caroline Is.
Truk
Pohnpei
Yap
PALAU
MARSHALL IS.
Gilbert Is.
NAURU
KIRIBATI
TUVALU
SOLOMON IS.
Santa Cruz I.
VANUATU
NEW CALEDONIA (Fr.)
FIJI
Suva
PHILIPPINES
MANILA
South China Sea
VIETNAM
Hanoi
Hainan
Vientiane
THAILAND
BANGKOK
CAMBODIA
Phnom Penh
Ho Chi Minh City
BURMA (MYANMAR)
Rangoon
MALAYSIA
Kuala Lumpur
PEN. MALAYSIA
SINGAPORE
SABAH
BRUNEI
SARAWAK
Borneo
Sumatra
Medan
Palembang
INDONESIA
JAKARTA
Bandung
Java
Surabaya
Banjarmasin
Ujung Pandang
EAST TIMOR
Timor
Arafura Sea
PAPUA
PAPUA NEW GUINEA
Port Moresby
New Ireland
New Britain
C. York
Equator
INDIA
DELHI
New Delhi
Kanpur
KOLKATA (Calcutta)
Nagpur
Ahmadabad
MUMBAI (Bombay)
Hyderabad
CHENNAI (Madras)
Bangalore
SRI LANKA
Colombo
NEPAL
Katmandu
BHUTAN
BANGLADESH
DACCA
Ganges
Bay of Bengal
Andaman Is. (India)
Nicobar Is. (India)
Lakshadweep Is. (India)
MALDIVES
Arabian Sea
PAKISTAN
KARACHI
Lahore
Islamabad
JAMMU & KASHMIR
Kābul
AFGHANISTAN
IRAN
TEHRĀN
Mashhad
Tabrīz
Esfahān
Shīrāz
IRAQ
Baghdād
KUWAIT
The Gulf
BAHRAIN
QATAR
Abu Dhabi
U.A.E.
Muscat
OMAN
SAUDI ARABIA
Riyadh
Mecca
Red Sea
YEMEN
Sana
Aden
G. of Aden
Socotra (Yemen)
SYRIA
Damascus
LEB.
Beirut
Jerusalem
ISR.
Ammān
JORDAN
CYPRUS
TURKEY
Ankara
ISTANBUL
Izmir
GEORGIA
Tbilisi
ARM.
Yerevan
AZER.
Baku
Black Sea
UKRAINE
Kiev
Odessa
BELARUS
Minsk
POLAND
Warsaw
Berlin
Prague
CZECH REP.
SLOVAK REP.
AUSTRIA
Vienna
HUNG.
Budapest
ROMANIA
Bucharest
BULGARIA
Sofia
SERB. & M.
Belgrade
MAC.
ALB.
GREECE
Athens
Crete
ITALY
Rome
Naples
Milan
Sardinia
Sicily
MALTA
Tunis
TUNISIA
Tripoli
Benghazi
Mediterranean Sea
LIBYA
EGYPT
CAIRO
Alexandria
Aswân
Nile
SUDAN
Khartoum
Omdurmân
White Nile
Blue Nile
ERITREA
Asmara
DJIBOUTI
ETHIOPIA
Addis Ababa
SOMALI REP.
Mogadishu
KENYA
Nairobi
Mombasa
L. Turkana
UGANDA
Kampala
RWANDA
BURUNDI
Kigali
Bujumbura
TANZANIA
Dodoma
Zanzibar
Dar es Salaam
L. Tanganyika
L. Victoria
CONGO
DEM. REP. OF THE CONGO
Kisangani
Kinshasa
Brazzaville
Kananga
Lubumbashi
Congo (Zaïre)
GABON
Libreville
EQUATORIAL GUINEA
SÃO TOMÉ & PRINCIPE
CAMEROON
Douala
Yaoundé
CENTRAL AFRICAN REP.
Bangui
CHAD
L. Chad
Ndjamena
NIGER
Niamey
NIGERIA
Kano
Abuja
Ibadan
Lagos
CABINDA (Angola)
ANGOLA
Luanda
Benguela
ZAMBIA
Lusaka
MALAWI
L. Malawi
Lilongwe
ZIMBABWE
Harare
Bulawayo
MOZAMBIQUE
Maputo
Mozambique Channel
NAMIBIA
Windhoek
BOTSWANA
Gaborone
Pretoria
Johannesburg
SWAZILAND
LESOTHO
SOUTH AFRICA
Durban
Cape Town
C. of Good Hope
Port Elizabeth
MADAGASCAR
Antananarivo
COMOROS
Mayotte (Fr.)
Aldabra Is.
SEYCHELLES
Amirante Is.
Agalega Is.
Cargados Carajos
Rodriguez
MAURITIUS
RÉUNION (Fr.)
Chagos Arch. (U.K.)
Diego Garcia
INDIAN OCEAN
Cocos Is. (Austral.)
Christmas I. (Austral.)
Tropic of Capricorn
AUSTRALIA
Darwin
Cairns
Townsville
Port Hedland
Alice Springs
Rockhampton
Brisbane
Geraldton
Kalgoorlie-Boulder
Perth
Fremantle
Great Australian Bight
Adelaide
Darling
Newcastle
Sydney
Canberra
Melbourne
Tasmania
Hobart
Tasman Sea
Lord Howe I. (Austral.)
Norfolk I. (Austral.)
NEW ZEALAND
Auckland
North I.
Wellington
Christchurch
South I.
Dunedin
Stewart I.
Bounty Is. (N.Z.)
Antipodes Is.
Auckland Is. (N.Z.)
Campbell I. (N.Z.)
Macquarie Is. (Austral.)
Amsterdam I. (Fr.)
St. Paul (Fr.)
Prince Edward Is. (S.Africa)
Crozet Is. (Fr.)
Kerguelen (Fr.)
McDonald Is. (Austral.)
Heard I. (Austral.)
Bouvet I. (Norw.)
SOUTHERN OCEAN
Antarctic Circle
Antarctica
Ross Sea
East from Greenwich
SWEDEN
FINLAND
Helsinki
Stockholm
Oslo
EST.
LATVIA
LITH.
Copenhagen
Brussels
PARIS
Svalbard (Norw.)
A
B
C
D
E
F
G
H
10
11
12
13
14
15
16
17
18

Hanoi ● Capital Cities

4 ARCTIC OCEAN

1:31 100 000

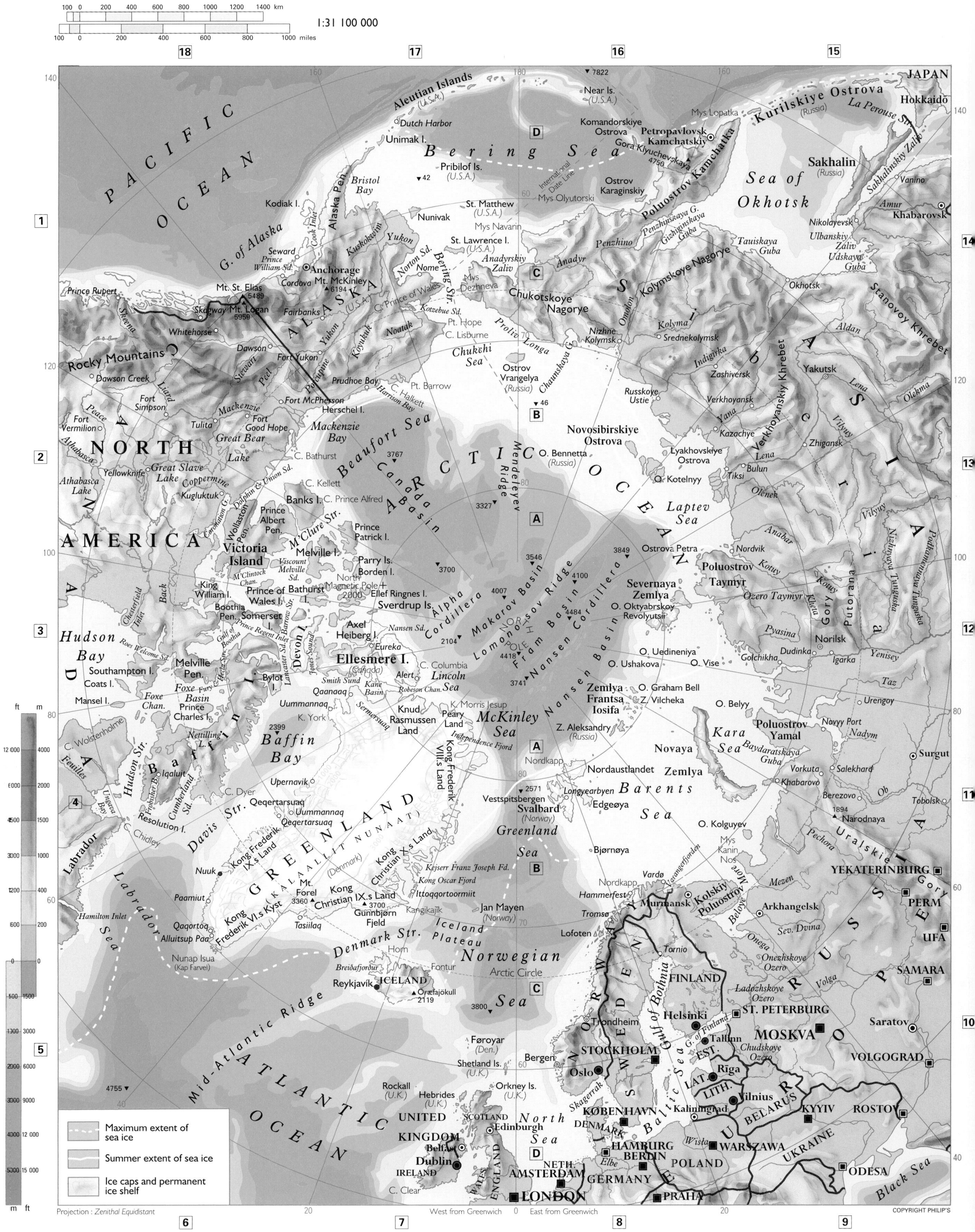

100 0 200 400 600 800 1000 1200 1400 km
100 0 200 400 600 800 1000 miles
PACIFIC OCEAN
Aleutian Islands (U.S.A.)
Dutch Harbor
Unimak I.
Near Is. (U.S.A.)
Komandorskiye Ostrova
Petropavlovsk Kamchatskiy
Gora Klyuchevskaya 4750
Mys Lopatka
Kurilskiye Ostrova (Russia)
JAPAN
Hokkaido
La Perouse Str.
Bering Sea
Pribilof Is. (U.S.A.)
International Date Line
Poluostrov Kamchatka
Ostrov Karaginskiy
Mys Olyutorski
Sea of Okhotsk
Sakhalin (Russia)
Sakhalinskiy Zaliv
Vanino
Amur
Khabarovsk
Bristol Bay
Kodiak I.
Alaska Pen.
Cook Inlet
G. of Alaska
St. Matthew (U.S.A.)
Nunivak
Mys Navarin
St. Lawrence I. (U.S.A.)
Anadyrskiy Zaliv
Anadyr
Penzhino
Penzhinskaya G.
Gizhiginskaya Guba
Tauiskaya Guba
Nikolayevsk
Ulbanskiy Zaliv
Udskaya Guba
Seward
Prince William Sd.
Anchorage
Cordova
Mt. McKinley 6194
Kuskokwim
Yukon
Norton Sd.
Nome
Bering Str.
Mys Dezhneva
Chukotskoye Nagorye
Kolymskoye Nagorye
Okhotsk
Stanovoy Khrebet
Prince Rupert
Mt. St. Elias 5489
Skagway
Mt. Logan 5959
Whitehorse
Fairbanks
ALASKA (U.S.A.)
C. Prince of Wales
Kotzebue Sd.
Pt. Hope
C. Lisburne
Noatak
Koyukuk
Chukchi Sea
Proliv Longa
Nizhne Kolymsk
Srednekolymsk
Kolyma
Omolon
Aldan
Rocky Mountains
Dawson Creek
Dawson
Fort Yukon
Porcupine
Stewart
Peel
Liard
Prudhoe Bay
Pt. Barrow
C. Halkett
Harrison Bay
Ostrov Vrangelya (Russia)
Chaunskaya G.
Indigirka
Zashiversk
Yakutsk
Lena
Olekma
Fort Simpson
Fort McPherson
Herschel I.
Russkoye Ustie
Verkhoyansk
Verkhoyanskiy Khrebet
Fort Vermilion
Peace
Mackenzie
Tulita
Fort Good Hope
Great Bear Lake
Mackenzie Bay
Beaufort Sea
Mendeleyev Ridge
Novosibirskiye Ostrova
Yana
Kazachye
Vilyuy
Zhigansk
NORTH AMERICA
Athabasca
Yellowknife
Great Slave Lake
Athabasca Lake
Coppermine
C. Bathurst
3767
Canada Basin
ARCTIC OCEAN
O. Bennetta (Russia)
Lyakhovskiye Ostrova
Bulun
Tiksi
O. Kotelnyy
Kugluktuk
Dolphin & Union Sd.
C. Kellett
Banks I.
C. Prince Alfred
3327
Laptev Sea
Olenek
Coronation G.
Wollaston Pen.
Prince Albert Pen.
M'Clure Str.
Prince Patrick I.
Anabar
Nordvik
Victoria Island
Melville I.
Viscount Melville Sd.
Parry Is.
Borden I.
3700
3546
3849
Ostrova Petra
Poluostrov Taymyr
Kotuy
Kheta
Ozero Taymyr
Putorana
Gory
Nizhnyaya Tunguska
Podkamennaya Tunguska
Chesterfield Inlet
Back
King William I.
M'Clintock Chan.
North Magnetic Pole 2000
Prince of Wales I.
Bathurst I.
Ellef Ringnes I.
Sverdrup Is.
4007
Makarov Basin
Lomonosov Ridge
4100
Severnaya Zemlya
O. Oktyabrskoy Revolyutsii
Boothia Pen.
Somerset I.
Alpha Cordillera
NORTH POLE
Fram Basin
4484
Nansen Cordillera
Pyasina
Norilsk
Hudson Bay
Roes Welcome Sd.
Gulf of Boothia
Prince Regent Inlet
Barrow Str.
Lancaster Sd.
Devon I.
Jones Sound
Axel Heiberg I.
Nansen Sd.
Eureka
2104
4418
O. Uedineniya
Dudinka
Golchikha
Igarka
Yenisey
Southampton I.
Coats I.
Melville Pen.
Fury & Hecla Str.
Bylot I.
Ellesmere I. (Canada)
Alert
C. Columbia
Lincoln Sea
Robeson Chan.
3741
Nansen Basin
O. Ushakova
O. Vise
Smith Sund
Kane Basin
Qaanaaq
Mansel I.
Foxe Chan.
Foxe Basin
Prince Charles I.
Uummannaq
K. Morris Jesup
Peary Land
Zemlya Frantsa Iosifa
O. Graham Bell
Z. Vilcheka
O. Belyy
Taz
Urengoy
K. York
Sermersuaq
Knud Rasmussen Land
McKinley Sea
Z. Aleksandry (Russia)
Kara Sea
Poluostrov Yamal
Novyy Port
Nadym
2399
Baffin Bay
Independence Fjord
Kong Frederik VIII.s Land
Nordkapp
Nordaustlandet
Novaya Zemlya
Baydaratskaya Guba
Surgut
C. Wolstenholme
Nettilling L.
Baffin I.
Hudson Str.
Feuilles
Iqaluit
Frobisher B.
Cumberland Sd.
Upernavik
2571
Vestspitsbergen
Longyearbyen
Svalbard (Norway)
Edgeøya
Barents Sea
Vorkuta
Khabarovo
Salekhard
Ob
Berezovo
Tobolsk
C. Dyer
Ungava Bay
Qeqertarsuaq
Uummannaq
Qeqertarsuaq
GREENLAND (KALAALLIT NUNAAT) (Denmark)
Davis Str.
Resolution I.
Chidley
1894
Narodnaya
Greenland Sea
O. Kolguyev
Mys Kanin Nos
Pechora
Uralskie Gory
Labrador
Kong Frederik IX.s Land
Kong Christian X.s Land
Kejserr Franz Joseph Fd.
Kong Oscar Fjord
Ittoqqortoormiit
Bjørnøya
Varangerfjorden
Vardø
Nordkapp
Hammerfest
Murmansk
Kolskiy Poluostrov
More
Mezen
YEKATERINBURG
PERM
Nuuk
Paamiut
Mt. Forel 3360
Kong Christian IX.s Land
3700
Gunnbjørn Fjeld
Kangikajik
Jan Mayen (Norway)
Tromsø
Beloye
Arkhangelsk
Sev. Dvina
UFA
Hamilton Inlet
Labrador Sea
Qaqortoq
Alluitsup Paa
Kong Frederik VI.s Kyst
Tasiilaq
Denmark Str.
Iceland Plateau
Lofoten
Onega
Onezhskoye Ozero
Nunap Isua (Kap Farvel)
Horn
Breiðafjörður
Fontur
Norwegian Sea
Arctic Circle
Tornio
Gulf of Bothnia
FINLAND
Ladozhskoye Ozero
Volga
SAMARA
Reykjavík
ICELAND
Öræfajökull 2119
3800
Mid-Atlantic Ridge
Trondheim
NORWAY
SWEDEN
Helsinki
G. of Finland
ST. PETERBURG
MOSKVA
RUSSIA
Saratov
Føroyar (Den.)
Bergen
STOCKHOLM
Tallinn
EST.
Chudskoye Ozero
VOLGOGRAD
Shetland Is. (U.K.)
Oslo
Rīga
LAT.
LITH.
4755
Rockall (U.K.)
Hebrides (U.K.)
Orkney Is. (U.K.)
Skagerrak
Baltic Sea
Vilnius
Kaliningrad
BELARUS
KYYIV
ROSTOV
ATLANTIC OCEAN
UNITED KINGDOM
SCOTLAND
Edinburgh
North Sea
KØBENHAVN
DENMARK
EUROPE
Belfast
Dublin
IRELAND
HAMBURG
BERLIN
Wisła
WARSZAWA
UKRAINE
NETH.
AMSTERDAM
Elbe
POLAND
GERMANY
ODESA
Black Sea
WALES
ENGLAND
LONDON
C. Clear
PRAHA
Maximum extent of sea ice
Summer extent of sea ice
Ice caps and permanent ice shelf
Projection : Zenithal Equidistant
West from Greenwich
East from Greenwich
ft m
12 000 4000
6000 2000
4500 1500
3000 1000
1200 400
600 200
0 0
500 1500
1000 3000
2000 6000
3000 9000
4000 12 000
5000 15 000
m ft

1:31 100 000

100 0 200 400 600 800 1000 1200 1400 km

100 0 200 400 600 800 1000 miles

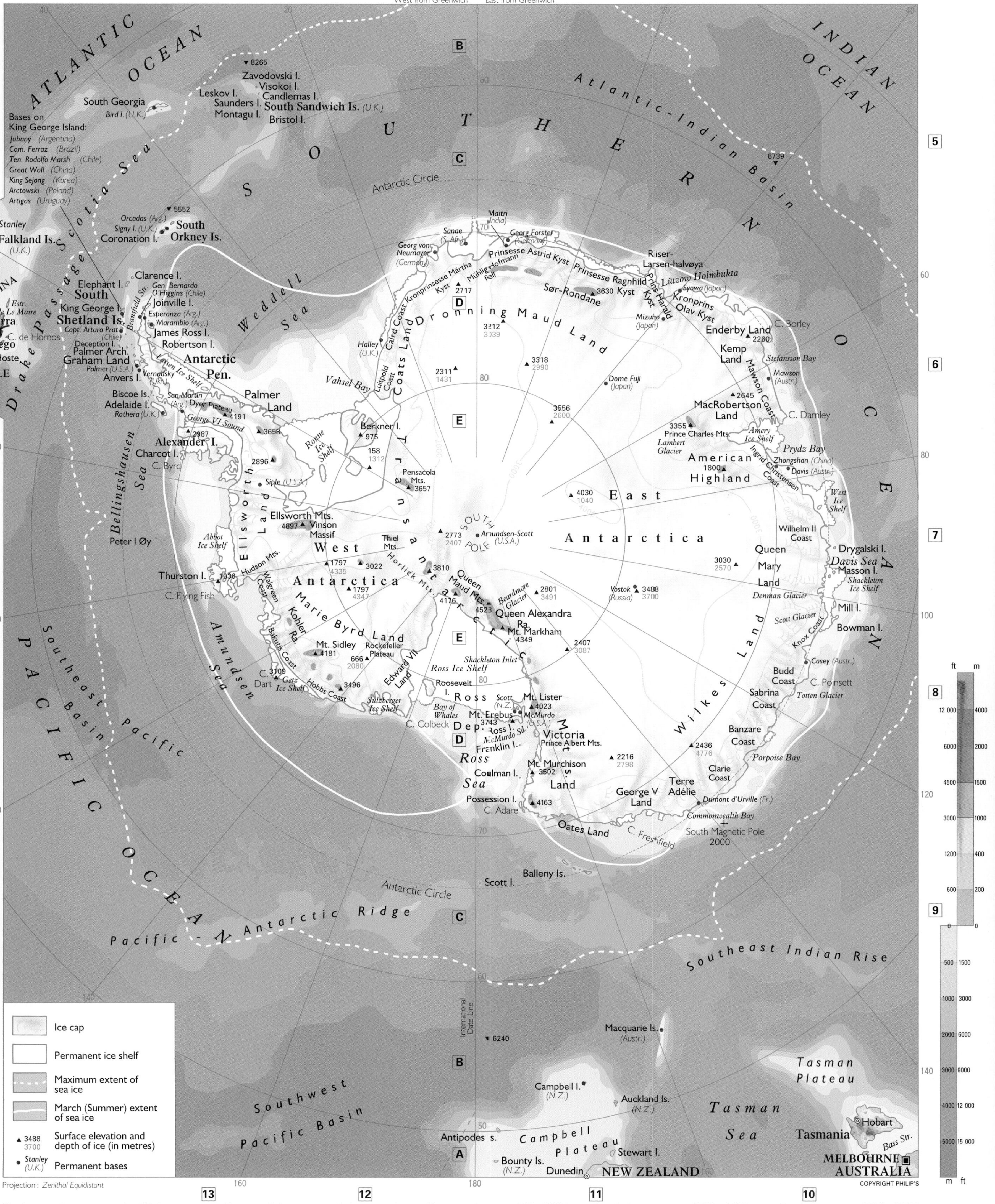
West from Greenwich
East from Greenwich
ATLANTIC OCEAN
INDIAN OCEAN
SOUTHERN OCEAN
PACIFIC OCEAN
Atlantic-Indian Basin
Scotia Sea
Drake Passage
Weddell Sea
Bellingshausen Sea
Amundsen Sea
Ross Sea
Southeast Pacific Basin
Pacific-Antarctic Ridge
Southeast Indian Rise
Southwest Pacific Basin
Campbell Plateau
Tasman Plateau
Tasman Sea
Antarctic Circle
South Georgia
Bird I. (U.K.)
Zavodovski I.
Visokoi I.
Candlemas I.
Leskov I.
Saunders I.
Montagu I.
South Sandwich Is. (U.K.)
Bristol I.
Bases on King George Island:
Jubany (Argentina)
Com. Ferraz (Brazil)
Ten. Rodolfo Marsh (Chile)
Great Wall (China)
King Sejong (Korea)
Arctowski (Poland)
Artigas (Uruguay)
Stanley
Falkland Is. (U.K.)
Orcadas (Arg.)
Signy I. (U.K.)
Coronation I.
South Orkney Is.
Tierra del Fuego
C. de Hornos
CHILE
Elephant I.
Clarence I.
South Shetland Is.
King George I.
Gen. Bernardo O'Higgins (Chile)
Joinville I.
Esperanza (Arg.)
Marambio (Arg.)
Capt. Arturo Prat (Chile)
Deception I.
James Ross I.
Robertson I.
Palmer Arch.
Graham Land
Palmer (U.S.A.)
Anvers I.
Vernadsky (Ukr.)
Antarctic Pen.
Larsen Ice Shelf
Biscoe Is.
Adelaide I.
Rothera (U.K.)
San Martín (Arg.)
Dyer Plateau
George VI Sound
Palmer Land
Alexander I.
Charcot I.
C. Byrd
Peter I Øy
Abbot Ice Shelf
Thurston I.
C. Flying Fish
Ellsworth Land
Siple (U.S.A.)
Ellsworth Mts.
Vinson Massif
Hudson Mts.
Walgreen Coast
West Antarctica
Marie Byrd Land
Kohler Ra.
Mt. Sidley
Rockefeller Plateau
Bakutis Coast
C. Dart
Getz Ice Shelf
Hobbs Coast
Sulzberger Ice Shelf
Edward VII Land
C. Colbeck
Roosevelt I.
Ross Ice Shelf
Bay of Whales
Ross Dep.
Shackleton Inlet
Ronne Ice Shelf
Berkner I.
Vahsel Bay
Luitpold Coast
Coats Land
Caird Coast
Halley (U.K.)
Transantarctic Mts.
Pensacola Mts.
Thiel Mts.
Horlick Mts.
Queen Maud Mts.
Beardmore Glacier
Queen Alexandra Ra.
Mt. Markham
SOUTH POLE
Amundsen-Scott (U.S.A.)
Georg von Neumayer (Germany)
Sanae (S. Afr.)
Maitri (India)
Georg Forster (Germany)
Kronprinsesse Märtha Kyst
Mühlig-Hofmann fell
Prinsesse Astrid Kyst
Prinsesse Ragnhild Kyst
Sør-Rondane
Dronning Maud Land
Riser-Larsen-halvøya
Lützow Holmbukta
Prins Harald Kyst
Syowa (Japan)
Kronprins Olav Kyst
Mizuho (Japan)
Dome Fuji (Japan)
Enderby Land
C. Borley
Kemp Land
Stefansson Bay
Mawson Coast
Mawson (Austr.)
MacRobertson Land
C. Darnley
Prince Charles Mts.
Lambert Glacier
Amery Ice Shelf
Prydz Bay
Zhongshan (China)
Davis (Austr.)
Ingrid Christensen Coast
American Highland
East Antarctica
West Ice Shelf
Wilhelm II Coast
Queen Mary Land
Drygalski I.
Davis Sea
Masson I.
Shackleton Ice Shelf
Denman Glacier
Mill I.
Bowman I.
Scott Glacier
Knox Coast
Casey (Austr.)
Budd Coast
C. Poinsett
Totten Glacier
Sabrina Coast
Wilkes Land
Banzare Coast
Porpoise Bay
Clarie Coast
Vostok (Russia)
Terre Adélie
Dumont d'Urville (Fr.)
Commonwealth Bay
South Magnetic Pole 2000
George V Land
C. Freshfield
Oates Land
Victoria Land
Prince Albert Mts.
Mt. Lister
Scott (N.Z.)
McMurdo (U.S.A.)
Mt. Erebus
Ross I.
McMurdo Sd.
Franklin I.
Mt. Murchison
Coulman I.
Possession I.
C. Adare
Balleny Is.
Scott I.
International Date Line
Macquarie Is. (Austr.)
Campbell I. (N.Z.)
Auckland Is. (N.Z.)
Antipodes Is.
Bounty Is. (N.Z.)
Stewart I.
Dunedin
NEW ZEALAND
Tasmania
Hobart
Bass Str.
MELBOURNE
AUSTRALIA
8265
5552
6739
2717
3312
3039
3630
3318
2990
2311
1431
3556
2600
2260
2645
3355
1800
4191
2987
3658
975
158
1312
3657
2896
4030
1040
4897
2773
2407
1797
4335
3022
3810
1797
4347
4176
4523
2801
3491
3488
3700
3030
2570
4181
666
2080
3105
3496
4349
2407
3087
4023
3743
3502
2216
2798
2436
4776
4163
6240
Ice cap
Permanent ice shelf
Maximum extent of sea ice
March (Summer) extent of sea ice
Surface elevation and depth of ice (in metres)
Permanent bases
ft m
12 000 4000
6000 2000
4500 1500
3000 1000
1200 400
600 200
0 0
500 1500
1000 3000
2000 6000
3000 9000
4000 12 000
5000 15 000
m ft
Projection: Zenithal Equidistant

The Antarctic Treaty was signed in Washington in 1959 so that scientific and technical research could continue unhampered by international politics.

All territorial claims covering land areas south of latitude 60°S have been suspended. Those claims were:

Norwegian claim (Dronning Maud Land)	45°E - 20°W
Australian claims	45°E - 136°E, 142°E - 160°E
French claim (Terre Adélie)	136°E - 142°E
New Zealand claim (Ross Dependency)	160°E - 150°W
British claim	80°W - 20°W
Argentine claim	74°W - 53°W
Chilean claim	90°W - 53°W

1:17 800 000

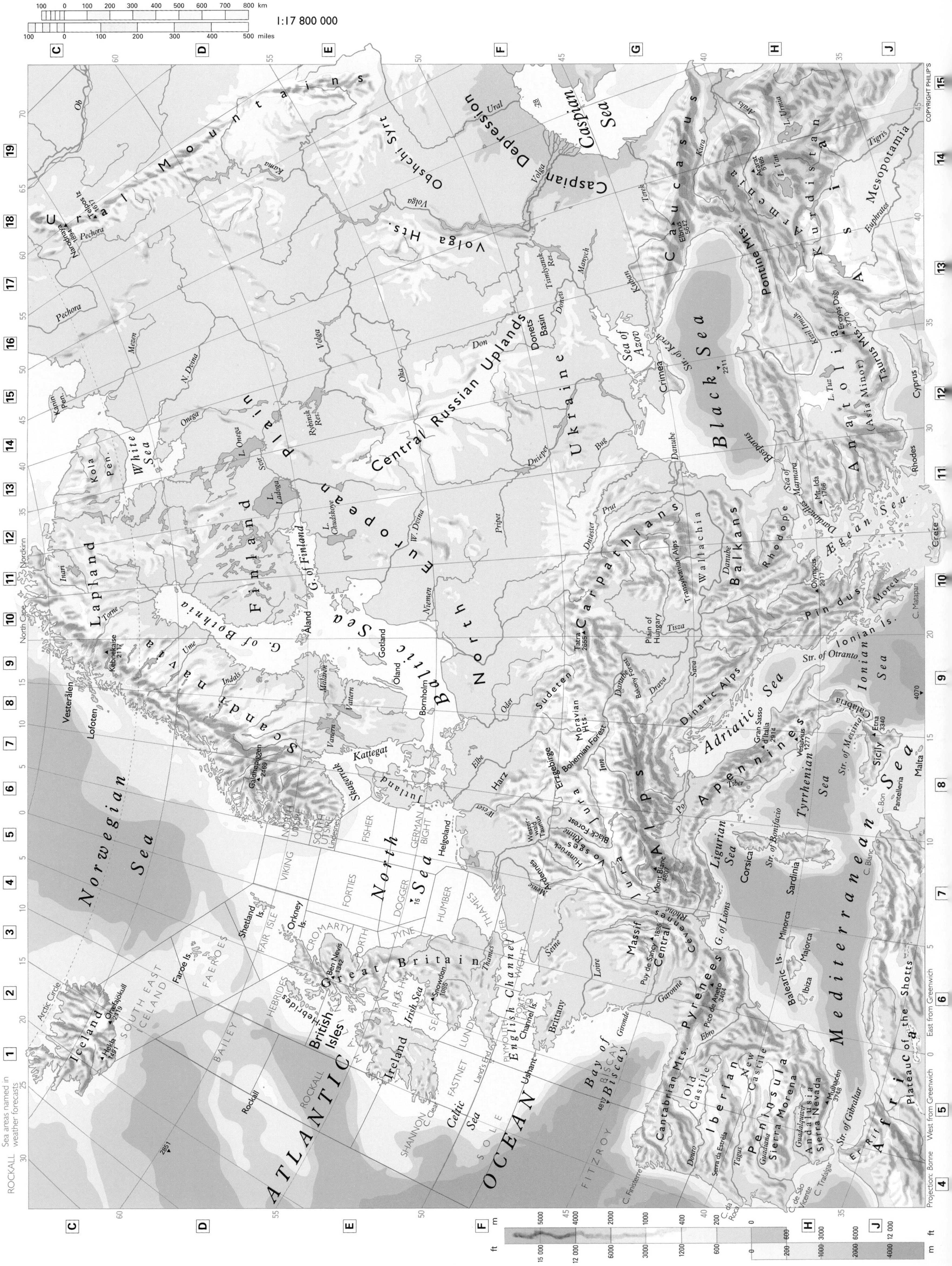

100 0 100 200 300 400 500 600 700 800 km
100 0 100 200 300 400 500 miles
Ural Mountains
Obshchi Syrt
Caspian Depression
Caspian Sea
Volga Hts.
Caucasus
Elbrus 5642
Armenia
Kurdistan
Mesopotamia
Pontine Mts.
Anatolia (Asia Minor)
Taurus Mts.
Cyprus
Black Sea
Sea of Azov
Crimea
Ukraine
Donets Basin
Central Russian Uplands
European Plain
North European Plain
Finland
Lapland
Kola Pen.
White Sea
Kanin Pen.
L. Ladoga
L. Onega
G. of Finland
G. of Bothnia
Baltic Sea
Scandinavia
Carpathians
Transylvanian Alps
Wallachia
Balkans
Rhodope
Aegean Sea
Pindus
Ionian Sea
Adriatic Sea
Dinaric Alps
Apennines
Tyrrhenian Sea
Alps
Mont Blanc 4807
Jura
Massif Central
Pyrenees
Iberian Peninsula
Sierra Nevada
Mediterranean Sea
Plateau of the Shotts
Norwegian Sea
North Sea
Great Britain
British Isles
Ireland
Iceland
Faroe Is.
Shetland Is.
Orkney Is.
English Channel
Bay of Biscay
Celtic Sea
ATLANTIC OCEAN
Plain of Hungary
Sudeten
Harz
Erzgebirge
Bohemian Forest
Black Forest
Vosges
Ardennes
Brittany
Corsica
Sardinia
Sicily
Balearic Is.
Crete
Rhodes
Sea areas named in weather forecasts
m ft
5000 15 000
4000 12 000
2000 6000
1000 3000
400 1200
200 600
0 0
200 600
1000 3000
2000 6000
4000 12 000
Projection: Bonne
West from Greenwich
East from Greenwich
COPYRIGHT PHILIP'S

1:17 800 000

100 0 100 200 300 400 500 600 700 800 km

100 0 100 200 300 400 500 miles

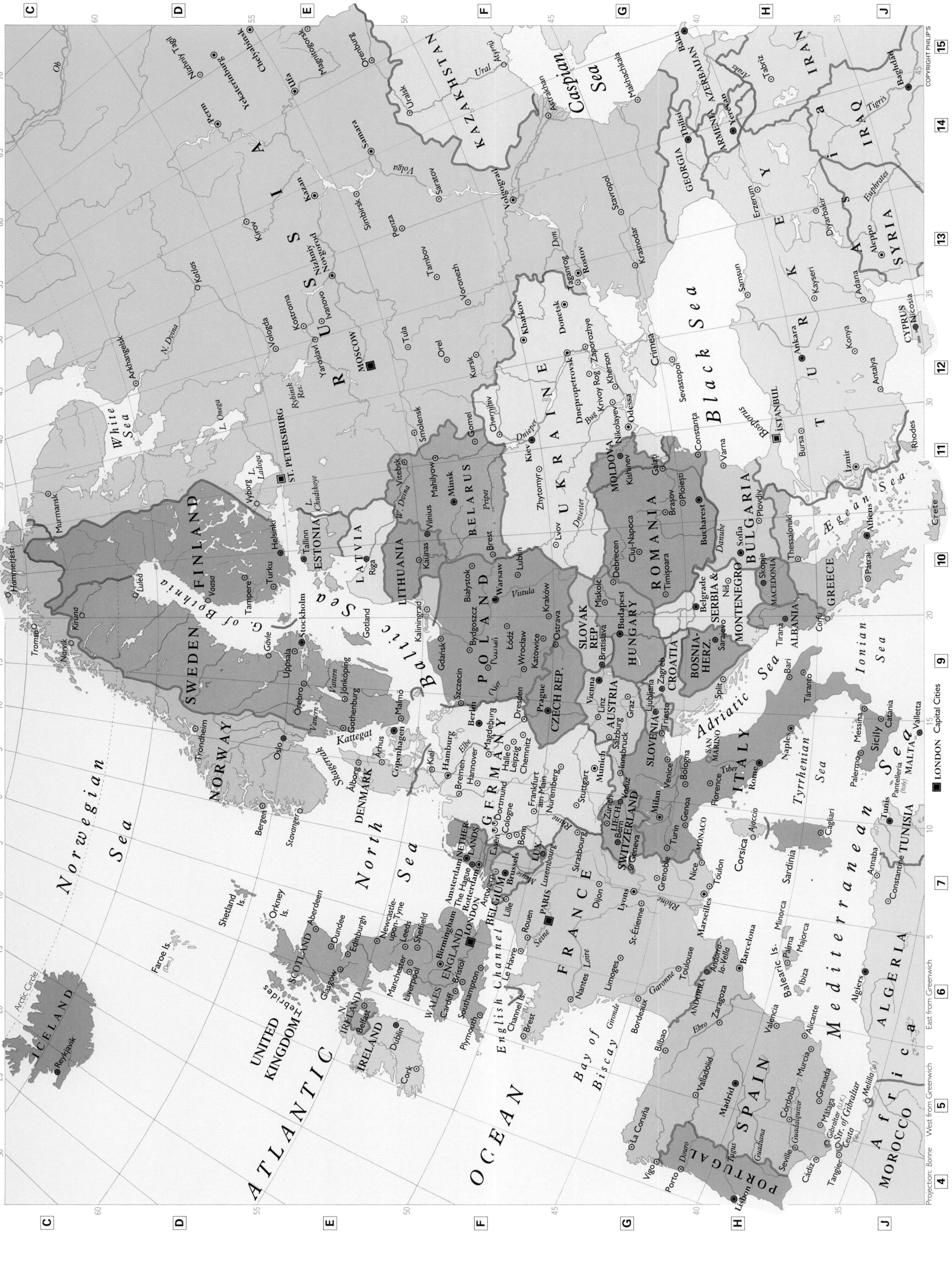

ICELAND
Reykjavík
Arctic Circle
Norwegian Sea
NORWAY
Oslo
Bergen
Stavanger
Trondheim
Narvik
Tromsø
Hammerfest
SWEDEN
Stockholm
Uppsala
Gävle
Göteborg
Gothenburg
Malmö
Jönköping
Örebro
Vänern
Vättern
Kiruna
Luleå
FINLAND
Helsinki
Turku
Tampere
Vaasa
G. of Bothnia
Baltic Sea
Gotland
Kattegat
Skagerrak
DENMARK
Copenhagen
Århus
Ålborg
ESTONIA
Tallinn
LATVIA
Riga
LITHUANIA
Vilnius
Kaunas
Kaliningrad
BELARUS
Minsk
Brest
Gomel
Vitebsk
Mahilyow
POLAND
Warsaw
Gdańsk
Szczecin
Poznań
Łódź
Wrocław
Kraków
Katowice
Białystok
Bydgoszcz
Lublin
GERMANY
Berlin
Hamburg
Bremen
Hannover
Kiel
Magdeburg
Leipzig
Halle
Dresden
Chemnitz
Dortmund
Essen
Cologne
Bonn
Frankfurt am Main
Nuremberg
Stuttgart
Munich
NETHERLANDS
Amsterdam
The Hague
Rotterdam
BELGIUM
Brussels
Antwerp
LUX.
Luxembourg
UNITED KINGDOM
LONDON
ENGLAND
SCOTLAND
WALES
Birmingham
Manchester
Liverpool
Leeds
Sheffield
Newcastle-upon-Tyne
Edinburgh
Glasgow
Dundee
Aberdeen
Bristol
Cardiff
Southampton
Plymouth
Belfast
IRELAND
Dublin
Cork
Hebrides
Orkney Is.
Shetland Is.
Faroe Is. (Den.)
North Sea
English Channel
Channel Is.
ATLANTIC OCEAN
Bay of Biscay
FRANCE
PARIS
Lille
Rouen
Le Havre
Brest
Nantes
Strasbourg
Dijon
Lyons
Grenoble
St-Étienne
Limoges
Bordeaux
Toulouse
Marseilles
Toulon
Nice
MONACO
Seine
Loire
Garonne
Gironde
Rhône
Rhine
Corsica
Ajaccio
SWITZERLAND
Bern
Zürich
Geneva
LIECH.
Vaduz
AUSTRIA
Vienna
Linz
Salzburg
Innsbruck
Graz
CZECH REP.
Prague
Ostrava
SLOVAK REP.
Bratislava
HUNGARY
Budapest
Miskolc
Debrecen
SLOVENIA
Ljubljana
CROATIA
Zagreb
Split
BOSNIA-HERZ.
Sarajevo
SERBIA & MONTENEGRO
Belgrade
Niš
ALBANIA
Tirana
MACEDONIA
Skopje
BULGARIA
Sofia
Plovdiv
Varna
ROMANIA
Bucharest
Cluj-Napoca
Timişoara
Braşov
Ploieşti
Galati
Constanţa
Danube
MOLDOVA
Kishinev
GREECE
Athens
Thessaloniki
Patrai
Corfu
Crete
Ægean Sea
Ionian Sea
ITALY
Rome
Milan
Turin
Genoa
Venice
Bologna
Florence
Trieste
Naples
Bari
Taranto
Messina
Palermo
Catania
Cagliari
Sardinia
Sicily
Tiber
SAN MARINO
Adriatic Sea
Tyrrhenian Sea
MALTA
Valletta
Pantelleria (Italy)
SPAIN
Madrid
Barcelona
Valencia
Zaragoza
Bilbao
Valladolid
Seville
Córdoba
Granada
Málaga
Murcia
Alicante
Cádiz
La Coruña
Vigo
Ebro
Tagus
Douro
Guadiana
Guadalquivir
ANDORRA
Andorra-la-Vella
Balearic Is.
Majorca
Minorca
Ibiza
Palma
Gibraltar (U.K.)
Str. of Gibraltar
Ceuta (Sp.)
Melilla (Sp.)
PORTUGAL
Lisbon
Porto
Mediterranean Sea
Africa
MOROCCO
Tangier
ALGERIA
Algiers
Constantine
Annaba
TUNISIA
Tunis
RUSSIA
MOSCOW
ST. PETERSBURG
Murmansk
Arkhangelsk
White Sea
L. Onega
L. Ladoga
L. Chudskoye
Vyborg
Rybinsk Res.
N. Dvina
Kotlas
Vologda
Yaroslavl
Kostroma
Ivanovo
Nizhniy Novgorod
Kirov
Perm
Kazan
Samara
Simbirsk
Penza
Saratov
Volgograd
Tambov
Voronezh
Tula
Orel
Kursk
Smolensk
Rostov
Taganrog
Krasnodar
Stavropol
Astrakhan
Makhachkala
Ufa
Orenburg
Magnitogorsk
Chelyabinsk
Yekaterinburg
Nizhniy Tagil
Ob
Volga
Ural
Don
UKRAINE
Kiev
Kharkov
Donetsk
Dnepropetrovsk
Zaporozhye
Krivoy Rog
Kherson
Nikolayev
Odessa
Sevastopol
Crimea
Lvov
Zhytomyr
Chernihiv
Dnieper
Dniester
Bug
Pripet
KAZAKHSTAN
Uralsk
Caspian Sea
Black Sea
Bosporus
GEORGIA
Tbilisi
ARMENIA
Yerevan
AZERBAIJAN
Baku
IRAN
Tabriz
IRAQ
Baghdad
Tigris
Euphrates
SYRIA
Aleppo
TURKEY
Ankara
İstanbul
Bursa
İzmir
Konya
Antalya
Adana
Kayseri
Samsun
Erzurum
Diyarbakir
Rhodes
CYPRUS
Nicosia
LONDON Capital Cities
Projection: Bonne
West from Greenwich
East from Greenwich
COPYRIGHT PHILIP'S

8 SCANDINAVIA

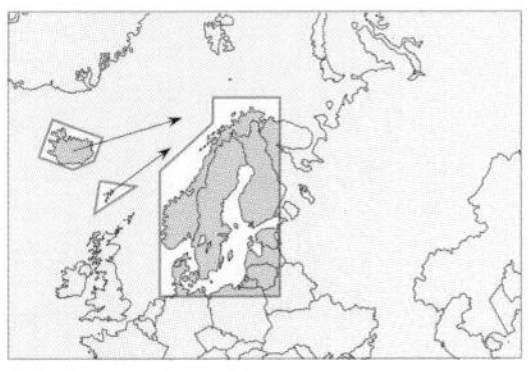

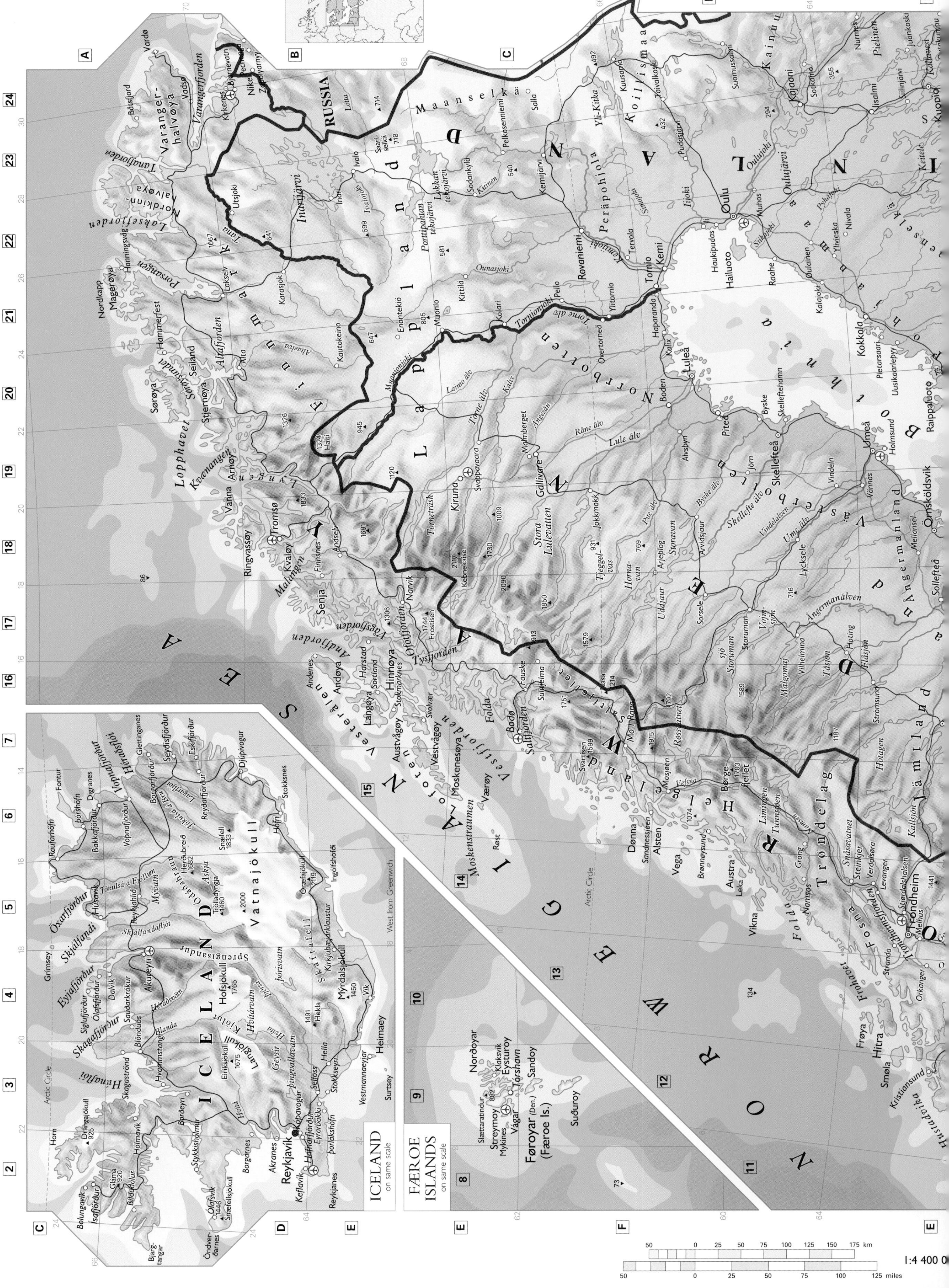

RUSSIA
Lapland
Finnmarksvidda
Norrbotten
Västerbotten
Ångermanland
Jämtland
Trøndelag
Nordland
Lofoten
Vesterålen
Senja
Tromsø
Narvik
Bodø
Hammerfest
Nordkapp
Kiruna
Gällivare
Luleå
Umeå
Oulu
Kemi
Tornio
Rovaniemi
Kajaani
Kokkola
Trondheim
Steinkjer
Namsos
ICELAND
Vatnajökull
Hofsjökull
Langjökull
Reykjavík
Akureyri
Hekla
ICELAND on same scale
FÆROE ISLANDS on same scale
Føroyar (Den.) (Færoe Is.)
Tórshavn
Streymoy
Eysturoy
Vágar
Sandoy
Suðuroy
Arctic Circle
West from Greenwich
1:4 400 0
50 0 25 50 75 100 125 150 175 km
50 0 25 50 75 100 125 miles

Gulf of Bothnia
Gulf of Finland
Gulf of Riga
Ålands hav
BALTIC SEA
Skagerrak
Kattegat
ESTONIA
LATVIA
LITHUANIA
POLAND
GERMANY
DENMARK
NORWAY
SWEDEN
FINLAND
STOCKHOLM
KØBENHAVN (Copenhagen)
Oslo
Helsinki (Helsingfors)
Tallinn
Riga
Vilnius
Gotland
Öland
Bornholm
Saaremaa (Ösel)
Hiiumaa (Dagö)
Åland (Ahvenanmaa)
Göteborg (Gothenburg)
Kaliningrad (Russia)
Projection: Conical with two standard parallels
East from Greenwich
COPYRIGHT PHILIP'S

10 DENMARK AND SOUTHERN SWEDEN

10 0 10 20 30 40 50 60 70 80 90 km

10 0 10 20 30 40 50 60 miles

1:2 200 000

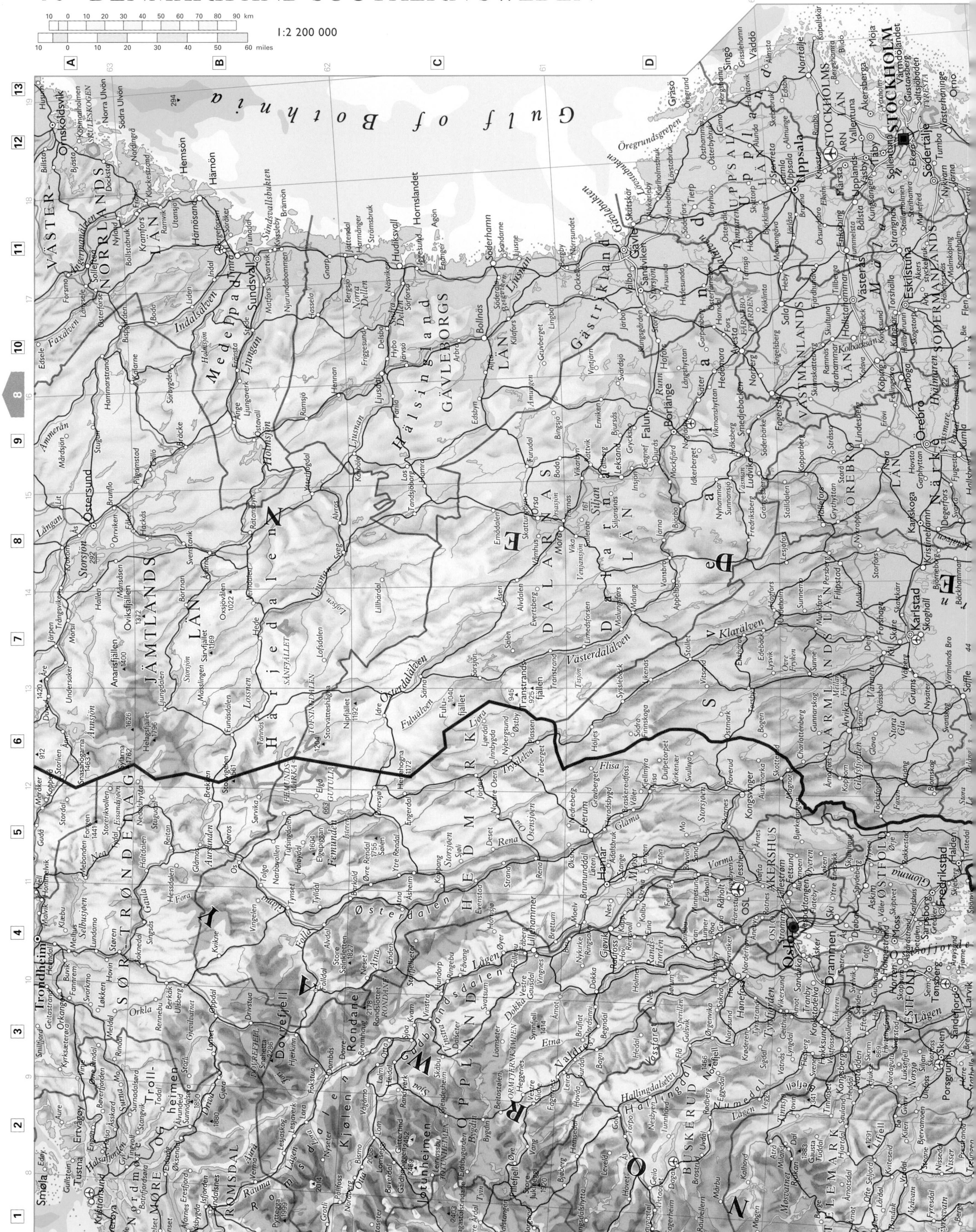
Gulf of Bothnia
STOCKHOLM
Uppsala
UPPSALA LÄN
STOCKHOLMS LÄN
SÖDERMANLANDS LÄN
VÄSTMANLANDS LÄN
ÖREBRO LÄN
VÄRMLANDS LÄN
KOPPARBERGS LÄN
GÄVLEBORGS LÄN
JÄMTLANDS LÄN
VÄSTERNORRLANDS LÄN
Gästrikland
Hälsingland
Härjedalen
Medelpad
Dalarna
Uppland
Närke
Östersund
Sundsvall
Gävle
Falun
Borlänge
Örebro
Västerås
Eskilstuna
Karlstad
Trondheim
Oslo
Drammen
Lillehammer
Hamar
Fredrikstad
Halden
Skien
Tønsberg
Larvik
Kongsberg
Kristiansund
SØR-TRØNDELAG
HEDMARK
OPPLAND
BUSKERUD
AKERSHUS
ØSTFOLD
VESTFOLD
TELEMARK
MØRE OG ROMSDAL
Dovrefjell
Rondane
Jotunheimen
Mjøsa
Siljan
Klarälven
Glåma
Lågen
Österdalälven
Västerdalälven
Ljusnan
Indalsälven
Ljungan

m 2000 1500 1000 500 200 0 50 150

ft 6000 4500 3000 1500 600 0 150 300 600 1500

Skagerrak
Kattegat
BALTIC SEA
DENMARK
SWEDEN
NORWAY
GERMANY
POLAND
Göteborg
København
Malmö
Helsingborg
Århus
Aalborg
Odense
Esbjerg
Jönköping
Norrköping
Linköping
Nyköping
Västervik
Kalmar
Växjö
Karlskrona
Halmstad
Borås
Trollhättan
Vänersborg
Uddevalla
Lidköping
Skövde
Visby
Gotland (Sweden)
Öland (Sweden)
Bornholm (Denmark)
Rønne
Læsø (Denmark)
Anholt (Denmark)
Flensburg
Kiel
Sylt
Fehmarn
Lolland
Falster
Møn
Sjælland
Fyn
Jylland
Øresund
Store Bælt
Lille Bælt
Kalmarsund
Hanöbukten
Bornholmsgattet
Fehmarn Belt
Ålborg Bugt
Småland
Götaland
Skåne
Vättern
ÖSTERGÖTLANDS LÄN
VÄSTRA GÖTALANDS LÄN
JÖNKÖPINGS LÄN
KRONOBERGS LÄN
KALMAR LÄN
BLEKINGE LÄN
SKÅNE LÄN
HALLANDS LÄN
GOTLANDS LÄN
NORDJYLLANDS AMT.
VIBORG AMT.
RINGKØBING AMT.
ÅRHUS AMT.
VEJLE AMT.
RIBE AMT.
SØNDERJYLLANDS AMT.
FYNS AMT.
VESTSJÆLLANDS AMT.
STORSTRØMS AMT.
ROSKILDE AMT.
FREDERIKSBORG AMT.
KØBENHAVNS AMT.
BORNHOLMS AMT.
Projection : Lambert's Conformal Conic
East from Greenwich
COPYRIGHT PHILIP'S
24
30
National Parks

IRELAND

10 0 10 20 30 40 50 60 70 80 km

10 0 10 20 30 40 50 miles

1:1 800 000

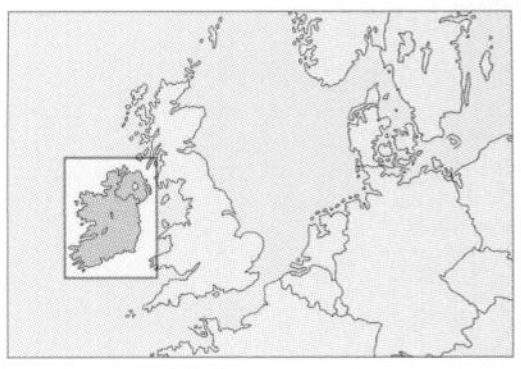

1
2
3
4
5
6
A
B
C
D
E
ATLANTIC OCEAN
CELTIC SEA
IRISH SEA
North Channel
St. George's Channel
SCOTLAND
WALES
NORTHERN IRELAND
IRELAND
Ulster
Connacht
Leinster
Munster
DONEGAL
LONDONDERRY
ANTRIM
TYRONE
FERMANAGH
ARMAGH
DOWN
MONAGHAN
CAVAN
LEITRIM
SLIGO
MAYO
ROSCOMMON
LONGFORD
MEATH
LOUTH
WESTMEATH
GALWAY
OFFALY
KILDARE
DUBLIN
WICKLOW
LAOIS
CARLOW
KILKENNY
WEXFORD
TIPPERARY
CLARE
LIMERICK
KERRY
CORK
WATERFORD
Kintyre
Campbeltown
Arran
Brodick
Firth of Clyde
Mull of Oa
Mull of Kintyre
Ailsa Craig
L. Ryan
Cairnryan
Stranraer
Portpatrick
Rathlin I.
Giants Causeway
Fair Hd.
Ballycastle
Portrush
Portstewart
Coleraine
Limavady
Ballymoney
Trostan
Garron Pt.
GLENARIFF
Mts. of Antrim
Ballymena
Larne
Carrickfergus
Ballyclare
Randalstown
Antrim
Newtownabbey
Belfast
Bangor
Donaghadee
Newtownards
Belfast L.
Ards Pen.
Strangford L.
Comber
Lisburn
Saintfield
Ballynahinch
Portaferry
Ballyquintin Pt.
Downpatrick
Dundrum
Dundrum B.
St. John's Pt.
Newcastle
Slieve Donard
Mourne Mts.
Warrenpoint
Kilkeel
Carlingford L.
Greenore
Newry
Slieve Gullion
Banbridge
Portadown
Craigavon
Lurgan
Tandragee
Armagh
Middletown
Keady
Lough Neagh
Coalisland
Dungannon
Cookstown
Moneymore
Magherafelt
Sperrin Mts.
Sawel Mt.
Londonderry
Strabane
Sion Mills
Newtownstewart
Castlederg
Omagh
Dromore
Irvinestown
Aughnacloy
Blackwater
Enniskillen
Lower L. Erne
Upper L. Erne
Monaghan
Clones
Castleblaney
Cootehill
Annalee
Belturbet
Cavan
Carrickmacross
Kingscourt
Dundalk
Dundalk Bay
Ardee
Dunleer
Clogher Hd.
Drogheda
Balbriggan
Inishtrahull
Malin Hd.
Malin Pen.
Carndonagh
Inishowen Pen.
Moville
Buncrana
L. Foyle
Lough Swilly
Fanad Hd.
Mulroy B.
Sheep Haven
Horn Hd.
Tory I.
Bloody Foreland
Inishfree B.
Gweedore
Errigal
Derryveagh Mts.
Rathmelton
GLENVEAGH
Letterkenny
Lifford
Aran I.
The Rosses
Crohy Hd.
Gweebarra B.
Dawros Hd.
Glenties
Finn
Loughros More B.
Lavagh More
Rossan Pt.
Slieve League
Killybegs
Donegal
St. John's Pt.
Donegal Bay
Ballyshannon
Bundoran
Erne
Sligo Bay
Sligo
Dromore West
Collooney
Ox Mts.
Ballymote
L. Arrow
L. Allen
Leitrim
Carrick-on-Shannon
Boyle
Killala B.
Killala
Ballina
Downpatrick Hd.
Broad Haven
Erris Hd.
Belmullet
Mullet Pen.
Inishkea North
Inishkea South
Blacksod Bay
Achill Hd.
Achill I.
Corraun Pen.
Nephin
L. Conn
Newport
Clew Bay
Clare I.
Westport
Castlebar
Swinford
Charlestown
Ballaghaderreen
Knock
Ballyhaunis
Castlerea
Claremorris
Inishturk
Croagh Patrick
Killary Harbour
Mweelrea
Inishbofin
Inishshark
Ballinrobe
Lough Mask
Glennamaddy
Connemara
CONNEMARA
Clifden
Slyne Hd.
Tuam
Lough Corrib
Oughterard
Bertraghboy B.
Kilkieran B.
Galway
Athenry
Galway Bay
Black Hd.
Aran Is.
Inishmore
Inishmaan
Inisheer
Loughrea
Slieve Aughty
Gort
Portumna
BURREN
Cliffs of Moher
Hags Hd.
Liscannor Bay
Ennistimon
Lough Derg
Tulla
Ennis
Mal Bay
Milltown Malbay
Mutton I.
Kilkee
Shannon Airport
Sixmilebridge
Killaloe
Kilrush
Loop Hd.
Mouth of the Shannon
Kerry Hd.
Ballybunion
Foynes
Limerick
Rathkeale
Listowel
Newcastle West
Feale
Golden Vale
Tipperary
Kilfinnane
Galtymore
Galty Mts.
Roscommon
Lough Ree
Athlone
Ballinasloe
Shannon
Suck
Longford
Granard
Castlepollard
L. Gowna
L. Sheelin
Oldcastle
Ceanannus Mor (Kells)
An Uaimh (Navan)
Trim
Athboy
Boyne
Mullingar
Royal Canal
Moate
Clara
Tullamore
Grand Canal
Daingean
Bog of Allen
Edenderry
Maynooth
Swords
Malahide
Lambay I.
Howth Hd.
Dublin
Dun Laoghaire
Clondalkin
Liffey
Naas
Droichead Nua
Kildare
Kilcoole
Bray
Greystones
Monasterevin
Portarlington
Birr
Mountmellick
Slieve Bloom
Arderin
Port Laoise
Athy
Poulaphouca Res.
Wicklow Mts.
WICKLOW MTS.
Lugnaquillia
Wicklow
Wicklow Hd.
Rathdrum
Avoca
Mizen Hd.
Arklow
Roscrea
Mountrath
Durrow
Nenagh
Templemore
Keeper Hill
Thurles
Carlow
Tullow
Muine Bheag
Shillelagh
Gorey
Bunclody
Mt. Leinster
Slaney
Enniscorthy
Cahore Pt.
Kilkenny
Callan
Nore
Barrow
New Ross
Wexford
Wexford Harbour
Rosslare
Rosslare Harbour
Greenore Pt.
Carnsore Pt.
Saltee Is.
Hook Hd.
Cashel
Slievenamon
Carrick-on-Suir
Suir
Caher
Clonmel
Comeragh Mts.
Knockmealdown Mts.
Waterford
Tramore
Tramore B.
Waterford Harbour
Dungarvan
Dungarvan Harbour
Lismore
Fermoy
Blackwater
Mitchelstown
Rath Luirc
Buttevant
Kanturk
Newmarket
Mallow
Boggeragh Mts.
Youghal
Youghal B.
Midleton
Cork
Blarney
Macroom
Lee
Passage West
Cobh
Crosshaven
Cork Harbour
Bandon
Kinsale
Old Head of Kinsale
Clonakilty
Clonakilty B.
Dunmanway
Skibbereen
Galley Hd.
Baltimore
Sherkin I.
Clear I.
C. Clear
Fastnet Rock
Skull
Long I.
Mizen Hd.
Dunmanus B.
Bantry Bay
Bantry
Glengarriff
Caha Mts.
Kenmare River
Kenmare
Castletown Bearhaven
Bear I.
Dursey I.
Crow Hd.
Scariff I.
Ballinskelligs B.
Great Skellig
Puffin I.
Valencia I.
Caherciveen
Macgillycuddy's Reeks
Carrauntoohill
KILLARNEY
L. Leane
Killarney
Killorglin
Dingle Bay
Dingle
Inishvickillane
Great Blasket I.
Dunmore Hd.
Brandon Mt.
Slieve Mish
Maine
Tralee
Tralee B.
Brandon B.
Smerwick Harbour
Laune
St. David's Hd.
St. David's
St. Brides Bay
West from Greenwich
ft
m
1500
500
600
200
300
100
0
50
150
100
300
200
600
500
1500
1000
3000
2000
6000
National Parks

Projection : Lambert's Conformal Conic

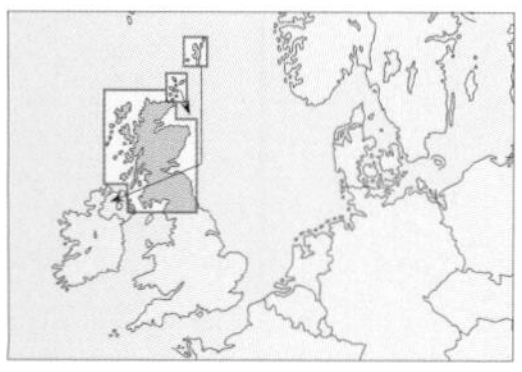

1:1 800 000

10 0 10 20 30 40 50 60 70 80 km

10 0 10 20 30 40 50 miles

Key to Scottish unitary authorities on map
1 CITY OF ABERDEEN
2 DUNDEE CITY
3 WEST DUNBARTONSHIRE
4 EAST DUNBARTONSHIRE
5 CITY OF GLASGOW
6 INVERCLYDE
7 RENFREWSHIRE
8 EAST RENFREWSHIRE
9 NORTH LANARKSHIRE
10 FALKIRK
11 CLACKMANNANSHIRE
12 WEST LOTHIAN
13 CITY OF EDINBURGH
14 MIDLOTHIAN
ORKNEY IS.
on same scale
SHETLAND IS.
on same scale
SCOTLAND
ENGLAND
NORTHERN IRELAND
NORTH SEA
ATLANTIC OCEAN
WESTERN ISLES
Outer Hebrides
Inner Hebrides
Sea of the Hebrides
North Minch
Little Minch
Pentland Firth
Moray Firth
Firth of Forth
Firth of Tay
Firth of Clyde
Firth of Lorn
Solway Firth
North Channel
Sutherland
Caithness
Lewis
Harris
North Uist
South Uist
Benbecula
Barra
Skye
Mull
Islay
Jura
Arran
Kintyre
HIGHLAND
MORAY
ABERDEENSHIRE
ANGUS
PERTH AND KINROSS
FIFE
STIRLING
ARGYLL AND BUTE
NORTH AYRSHIRE
EAST AYRSHIRE
SOUTH AYRSHIRE
SOUTH LANARKSHIRE
DUMFRIES & GALLOWAY
SCOTTISH BORDERS
EAST LOTHIAN
NORTHUMBERLAND
CUMBRIA
DURHAM
North West Highlands
Grampian Mountains
Cairngorm Mts.
Monadhliath Mts.
Southern Uplands
Cheviot Hills
Lammermuir Hills
Ochil Hills
Sidlaw Hills
Buchan
Glen Mor
Ben Nevis 1342
Ben Macdhui 1309
Ben Lawers 1214
Lochnagar 1154
Ben More 1174
Ben Hope 927
Ben More Assynt 998
Goat Fell 874
Broad Law 840
The Cheviot 816
Cross Fell 893
Skiddaw 931
Helvellyn 950
Stornoway
Thurso
Wick
Inverness
Aberdeen
Dundee
Perth
Stirling
Glasgow
Edinburgh
Oban
Fort William
Kirkwall
Lerwick
Ayr
Dumfries
Carlisle
Newcastle-upon-Tyne
Belfast
Berwick-upon-Tweed
Fraserburgh
Peterhead
Montrose
Arbroath
St. Andrews
Campbeltown
Stranraer
L. Ness
L. Lomond
L. Tay
L. Rannoch
Tweed
Forest Parks in Scotland
Projection : Lambert's Conformal Conic
West from Greenwich
COPYRIGHT PHILIP'S
ft m
3000 1000
1500 500
600 200
300 100
0 0
50 150
100 300
200 600
500 1500
1000 3000
m ft

12 14

Forest Parks in Scotland

ENGLAND AND WALES

10 0 10 20 30 40 50 60 70 80 km

1:1 800 000

10 0 10 20 30 40 50 miles

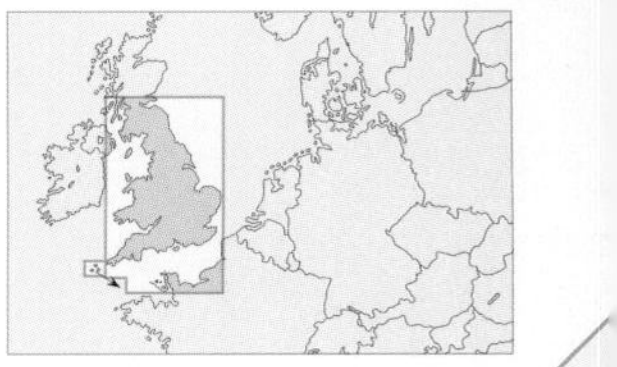

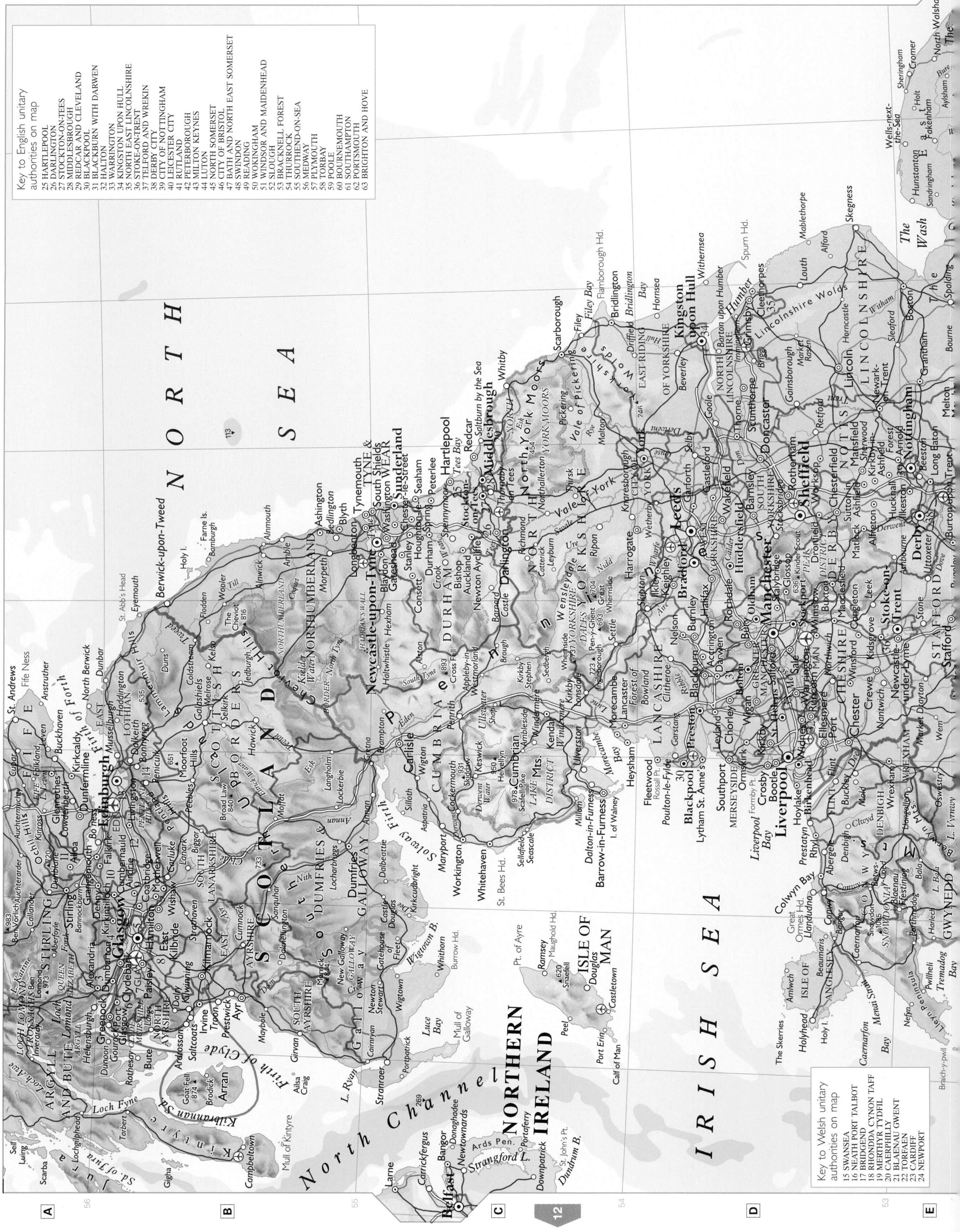
Key to English unitary authorities on map
25 HARTLEPOOL
26 DARLINGTON
27 STOCKTON-ON-TEES
28 MIDDLESBROUGH
29 REDCAR AND CLEVELAND
30 BLACKPOOL
31 BLACKBURN WITH DARWEN
32 HALTON
33 WARRINGTON
34 KINGSTON UPON HULL
35 NORTH EAST LINCOLNSHIRE
36 STOKE-ON-TRENT
37 TELFORD AND WREKIN
38 DERBY CITY
39 CITY OF NOTTINGHAM
40 LEICESTER CITY
41 RUTLAND
42 PETERBOROUGH
43 MILTON KEYNES
44 LUTON
45 NORTH SOMERSET
46 CITY OF BRISTOL
47 BATH AND NORTH EAST SOMERSET
48 SWINDON
49 READING
50 WOKINGHAM
51 WINDSOR AND MAIDENHEAD
52 SLOUGH
53 BRACKNELL FOREST
54 THURROCK
55 SOUTHEND-ON-SEA
56 MEDWAY
57 PLYMOUTH
58 TORBAY
59 POOLE
60 BOURNEMOUTH
61 SOUTHAMPTON
62 PORTSMOUTH
63 BRIGHTON AND HOVE
Key to Welsh unitary authorities on map
15 SWANSEA
16 NEATH PORT TALBOT
17 BRIDGEND
18 RHONDDA CYNON TAFF
19 MERTHYR TYDFIL
20 CAERPHILLY
21 BLAENAU GWENT
22 TORFAEN
23 CARDIFF
24 NEWPORT
NORTH SEA
IRISH SEA
North Channel
NORTHERN IRELAND
ISLE OF MAN
SCOTLAND
NORTHUMBERLAND
CUMBRIA
DURHAM
LANCASHIRE
Newcastle-upon-Tyne
Edinburgh
Glasgow
Liverpool
Manchester
Leeds
Sheffield
Kingston upon Hull
Middlesbrough
Carlisle
Blackpool
Nottingham
Derby
Stoke-on-Trent

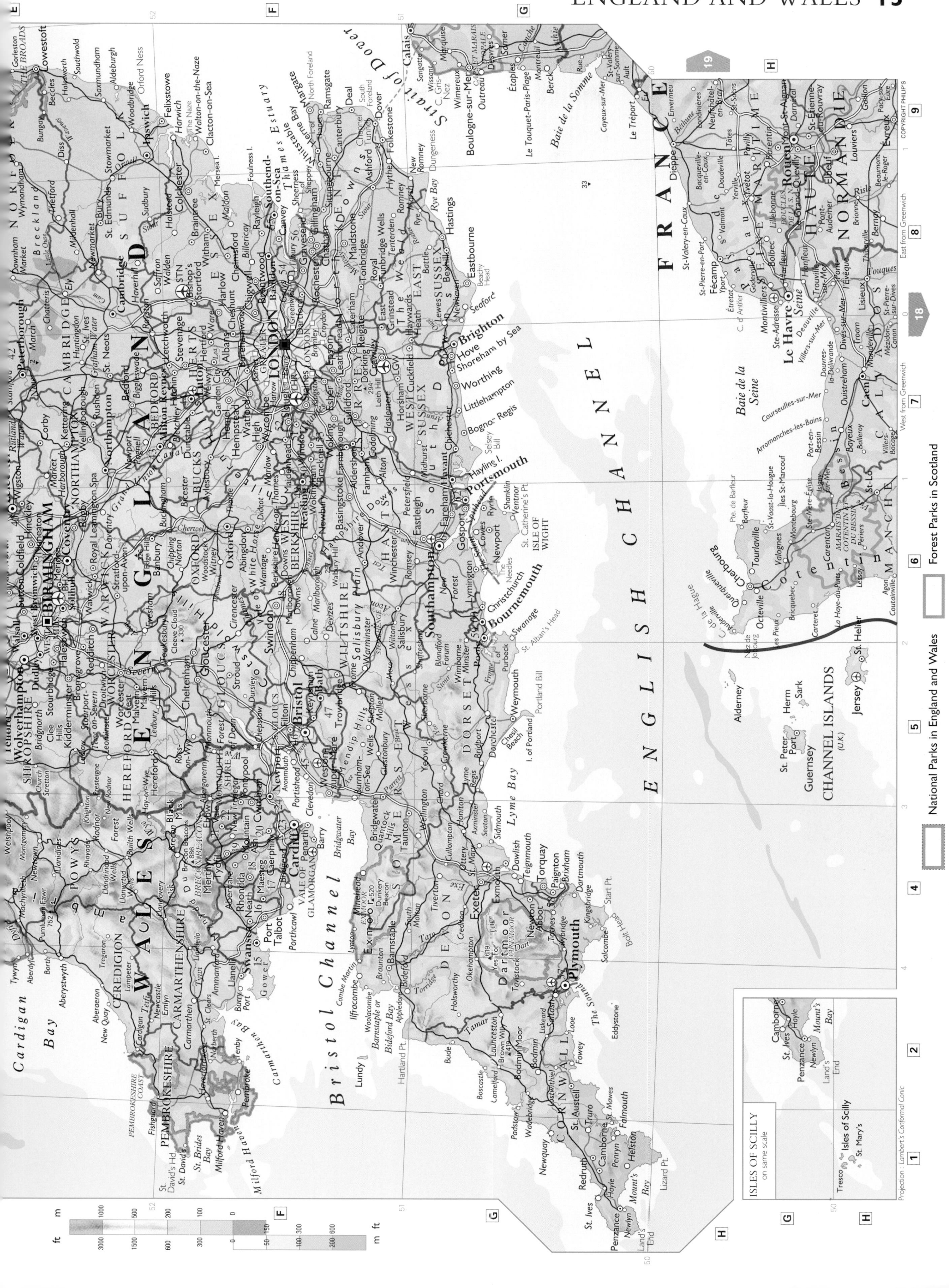
ENGLAND
WALES
FRANCE
ENGLISH CHANNEL
Bristol Channel
Cardigan Bay
Strait of Dover
Thames Estuary
Lyme Bay
Baie de la Seine
Baie de la Somme
CHANNEL ISLANDS (U.K.)
ISLES OF SCILLY on same scale
LONDON
BIRMINGHAM
Bristol
Cardiff
Southampton
Portsmouth
Plymouth
Brighton
Bournemouth
Oxford
Cambridge
Ipswich
Norwich
Exeter
Swansea
Newport
Gloucester
Swindon
Reading
Northampton
Peterborough
Dover
Calais
Boulogne-sur-Mer
Dieppe
Le Havre
Rouen
Caen
Cherbourg
Guernsey
Jersey
Alderney
Sark
Herm
ISLE OF WIGHT
NORMANDIE
HAUTE-NORMANDIE
National Parks in England and Wales
Forest Parks in Scotland
Projection : Lambert's Conformal Conic
West from Greenwich
East from Greenwich
COPYRIGHT PHILIP'S
ft
m
3000
1500
600
300
1000
500
200
100
0
50
150
100
300
200
600

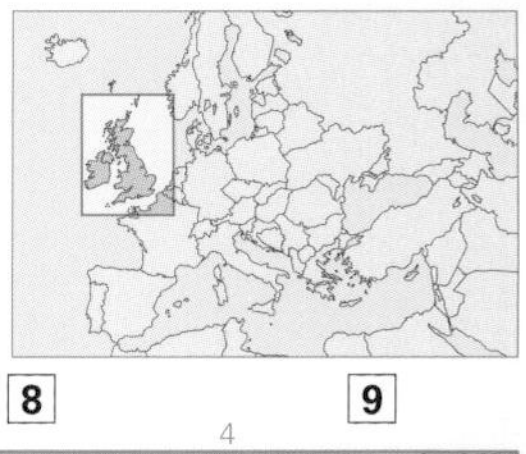

1:4 400 000
km
miles
ft
m
ATLANTIC OCEAN
NORTH SEA
IRISH SEA
CELTIC SEA
English Channel
St. George's Channel
North Channel
Bristol Channel
Cardigan Bay
Shetland Is.
Yell
Unst
Fetlar
Mainland
Lerwick
Foula
Fair Isle
Orkney Is.
Westray
Sanday
Stronsay
Kirkwall
Hoy
South Ronaldsay
Pentland Firth
C. Wrath
Thurso
Wick
Helmsdale
Moray Firth
Outer Hebrides
Lewis
Stornoway
Harris
St. Kilda
North Uist
Benbecula
South Uist
Barra
Inner Hebrides
Skye
Rhum
Eigg
Coll
Tiree
Mull
Colonsay
Jura
Islay
North Minch
North West Highlands
SCOTLAND
Grampian Mts.
Southern Uplands
Cheviot Hills
Ullapool
Lairg
Golspie
Tain
Invergordon
Dingwall
Portree
L. Ness
Inverness
Nairn
Elgin
Buckie
Banff
Fraserburgh
Peterhead
Huntly
Inverurie
Aberdeen
Stonehaven
Aviemore
Mallaig
Ben Nevis
Fort William
Tobermory
Oban
Ballater
Montrose
Arbroath
Forfar
Dundee
St. Andrews
Perth
Glenrothes
Kirkcaldy
L. Lomond
Stirling
Dunfermline
Dunbar
Greenock
Glasgow
Edinburgh
Paisley
East Kilbride
Hamilton
Irvine
Kilmarnock
Ayr
Arran
Campbeltown
Galashiels
Berwick-upon-Tweed
Jedburgh
Hawick
Alnwick
Girvan
Dumfries
Stranraer
Kirkcudbright
Annan
Firth of Clyde
Malin Hd.
Buncrana
Coleraine
Aran I.
Letterkenny
Lifford
Londonderry
Ballymena
Larne
NORTHERN IRELAND
Antrim
Bangor
Belfast
Lough Neagh
Donegal
Omagh
Bundoran
Lower L. Erne
Portadown
Lisburn
Lurgan
Enniskillen
Armagh
Newry
Clones
Sligo
Ballina
Achill I.
L. Conn
Leitrim
Cavan
Castlebar
Westport
Dundalk
Roscommon
Longford
Ceanannus Mor
Drogheda
Lough Mask
Lough Ree
Mullingar
Boyne
Connemara
Lough Corrib
Athlone
Connacht
Ballinasloe
Tullamore
Liffey
Dublin
Dun Laoghaire
Bray
Galway B.
Galway
Aran Is.
Birr
IRELAND
Leinster
Wicklow Mts.
Lough Derg
Port Laoise
Athy
Ennis
Nenagh
Carlow
Arklow
Kilrush
Limerick
Thurles
Kilkenny
Shannon
Listowel
Tipperary
Munster
Tralee
Clonmel
Carrick-on-Suir
Wexford
Rosslare
Dingle
Mallow
Waterford
Carrauntoohill
Killarney
Blackwater
Dungarvan
Valencia I.
Macgillycuddy's Reeks
Cork
Youghal
Cobh
Bandon
Bantry
Kinsale
C. Clear
UNITED KINGDOM
I. of Man
Douglas
Mull of Galloway
Workington
Whitehaven
Cumbrian Mts.
Carlisle
Hexham
Newcastle-upon-Tyne
South Shields
Sunderland
Gateshead
Durham
Pennines
Hartlepool
Redcar
Middlesbrough
Darlington
Stockton-on-Tees
Scarborough
Barrow-in-Furness
Lancaster
Harrogate
York
Bridlington
Blackpool
Keighley
Burnley
Leeds
Bradford
Beverley
Kingston upon Hull
Preston
Blackburn
Halifax
Huddersfield
Barnsley
Scunthorpe
Humber
Bolton
Doncaster
Grimsby
Manchester
Oldham
Rotherham
Liverpool
Warrington
Stockport
Sheffield
Lincoln
Louth
Holyhead
Anglesey
Bangor
Colwyn Bay
Chester
Chesterfield
Skegness
Crewe
Mansfield
Boston
The Wash
Snowdon
Wrexham
Stoke on Trent
Derby
Nottingham
Grantham
Trent
Cromer
Pwllheli
Stafford
ENGLAND
King's Lynn
Norwich
Great Yarmouth
Lowestoft
Shrewsbury
Welshpool
Telford
Nuneaton
Leicester
Aberystwyth
Cambrian Mts.
Wolverhampton
BIRMINGHAM
Coventry
Corby
Peterborough
Thetford
Rugby
Redditch
Ely
Bury St. Edmunds
Worcester
Royal Leamington Spa
Northampton
Cambridge
Ipswich
Felixstowe
Harwich
WALES
Hereford
Bedford
Milton Keynes
Luton
Stevenage
Fishguard
Carmarthen
Brecon
Cheltenham
Cotswold Hills
Colchester
Haverfordwest
Milford Haven
Merthyr Tydfil
Gloucester
Oxford
Hemel Hempstead
Harlow
Chelmsford
Pembroke
Llanelli
Neath
Swansea
Rhondda
Cwmbran
Newport
High Wycombe
Watford
Basildon
Southend-on-Sea
Port Talbot
Barry
Cardiff
Bristol
Swindon
Slough
LONDON
Thames
Chatham
Margate
Bath
Newbury
Reading
Canterbury
Weston-super-Mare
Basingstoke
Reigate
Maidstone
Dover
Barnstaple
Exmoor
Salisbury
Guildford
Crawley
Ashford
Folkestone
Str. of Dover
Taunton
Winchester
Hastings
Yeovil
Southampton
Fareham
Havant
Brighton
Worthing
Eastbourne
Bude
Exeter
Bournemouth
Poole
Portsmouth
Dartmoor
Exmouth
Weymouth
Newport
Isle of Wight
Torbay
Newquay
Truro
St. Austell
Plymouth
Falmouth
Land's End
Penzance
Isles of Scilly
Channel Is.
(U.K.)
Alderney
Guernsey
St. Peter Port
Sark
Jersey
St. Helier
C. de la Hague
Cotentin
Cherbourg
Valognes
Pte. de Barfleur
Bayeux
Caen
Le Havre
Trouville-sur-Mer
Bolbec
Fécamp
Pays de Caux
Lisieux
Seine
Elbeuf
Rouen
FRANCE
Dieppe
Le Tréport
Abbeville
Somme
Amiens
Picardie
St-Quentin
Cambrai
Valenciennes
Lens
Douai
Arras
Béthune
Bruay-la-Buissière
Lille
Villeneuve-d'Ascq
Tourcoing
Tournai
St-Omer
Boulogne-sur-Mer
Le Touquet-Paris-Plage
C. Gris-Nez
Calais
Dunkerque
Flandre
BELGIUM
BRUSSEL (Bruxelles)
Gent
Brugge
Mechelen
Oostende
Zeebrugge
Antwerpen
Vlissingen
NETHERLANDS
's-Gravenhage (Den Haag)
Hoek van Holland
ROTTERDAM
Dordrecht
Haarlem
Alkmaar
Den Helder
Texel
NORWAY
Askøy
Bergen
Os
Stord
Bømlo
Haugesund
Kopervik
Åkrahamn
Stavanger
Sandnes
Bryne
Nærbø
Projection: Conical with two standard parallels
East from Greenwich
West from Greenwich
COPYRIGHT PHILIP'S

9 18 19 17

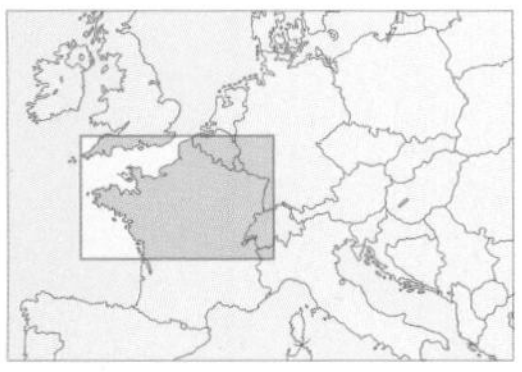

17
BELGIUM
GERMANY
LUXEMBOURG
SWITZERLAND
ITALY
PARIS
Brussel (Bruxelles)
Lille
Amiens
Reims
Metz
Nancy
Strasbourg
Dijon
Lyon
Genève
Orléans
Bourges
Clermont-Ferrand
Besançon
Mulhouse
Köln
Frankfurt
Luxembourg
Troyes
PICARDIE
CHAMPAGNE-ARDENNE
LORRAINE
ALSACE
BOURGOGNE
FRANCHE-COMTÉ
RHÔNE-ALPES
NORD-PAS-DE-CALAIS
SAARLAND
East from Greenwich
21
25

Underlined towns give their name to the administrative area in which they stand.

National Parks

Regional Nature Parks in France

20 SOUTHERN FRANCE

1:2 200 000

10 0 10 20 30 40 50 60 70 80 90 km
10 0 10 20 30 40 50 60 miles
18
38
ATLANTIC OCEAN
Golfe de Gascogne
FRANCE
SPAIN
ANDORRA
POITOU-CHARENTES
LIMOUSIN
AQUITAINE
MIDI-PYRÉNÉES
LANGUEDOC-ROUSSILLON
AUVERGNE
NAVARRA
HUESCA
LLEIDA
CATALUÑA
ZARAGOZA
GIRONA
BARCELONA
Massif Central
PYRÉNÉES
Cholet
Poitiers
Niort
La Rochelle
Rochefort
Île de Ré
Île d'Oléron
Île d'Yeu
La Roche-sur-Yon
Les Sables-d'Olonne
Angoulême
Cognac
Saintes
Royan
Limoges
Châteauroux
Bourges
Nevers
Montluçon
Moulins
Vichy
Clermont-Ferrand
Périgueux
Brive-la-Gaillarde
Bordeaux
Arcachon
Bergerac
Agen
Cahors
Rodez
Aurillac
Millau
Albi
Montauban
Toulouse
Castres
Carcassonne
Narbonne
Béziers
Sète
Perpignan
Pau
Tarbes
Lourdes
Bayonne
Biarritz
Mont-de-Marsan
Auch
Foix
Donostia-San Sebastián
Pamplona
Huesca
Zaragoza
Lleida
Manresa
Girona
Figueres
Terrassa
Sabadell
Badalona
Costa Brava
Golfe du Lion
Projection : Lambert's Conformal Conic
West from Greenwich
East from Greenwich
ft m

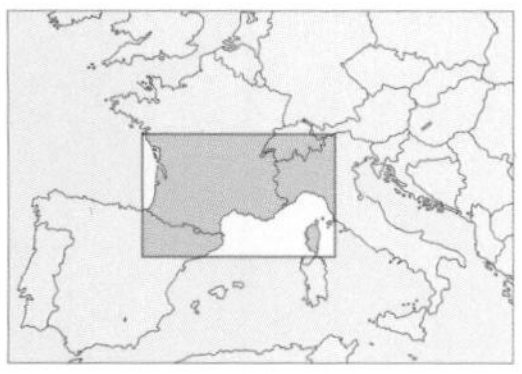

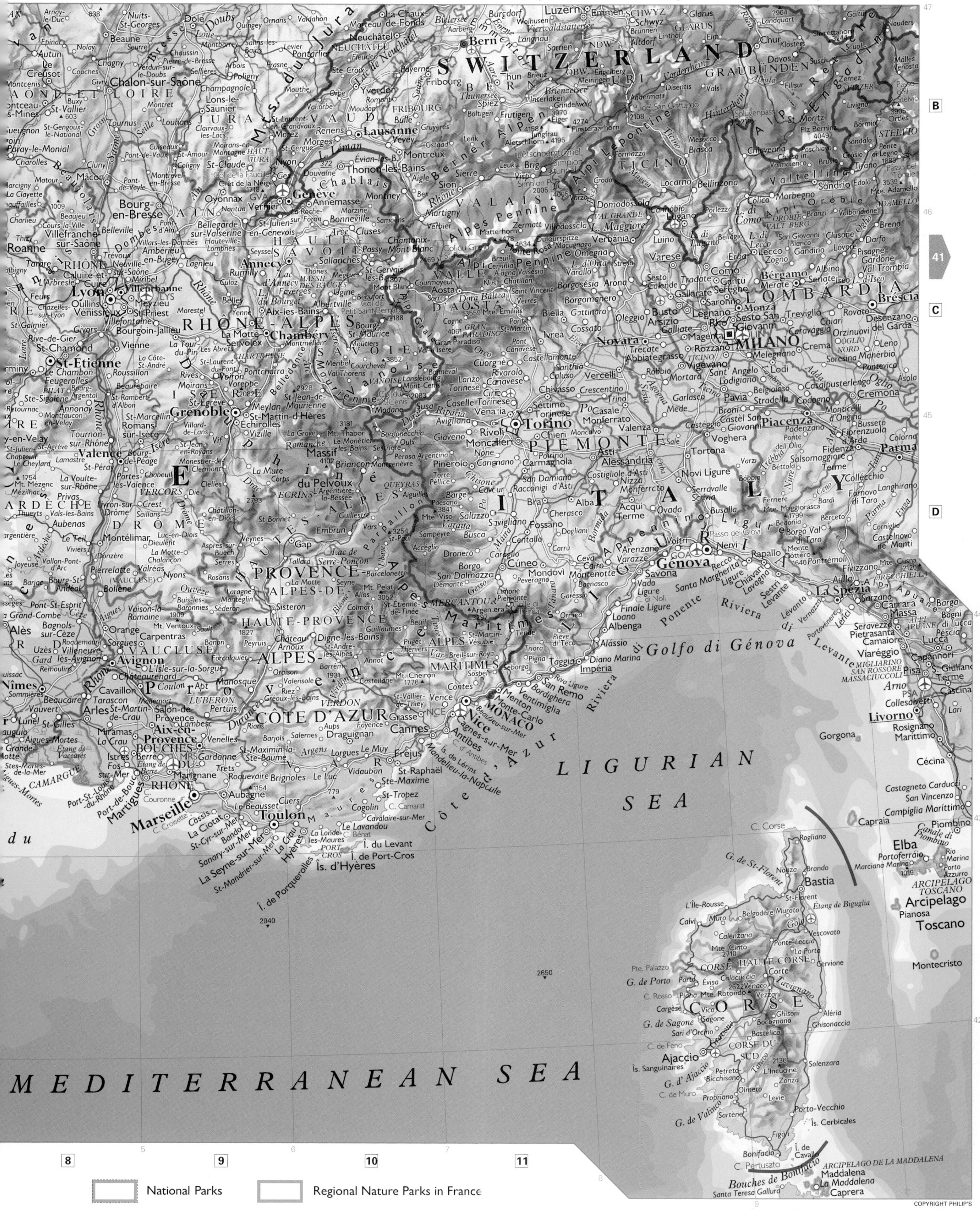
SWITZERLAND
ITALY
MEDITERRANEAN SEA
LIGURIAN SEA
Golfo di Génova
Riviera di Ponente
Riviera di Levante
Côte d'Azur
RHÔNE-ALPES
PROVENCE-ALPES-CÔTE D'AZUR
PIEMONTE
LOMBARDIA
LIGURIA
VALLE D'AOSTA
CORSE
HAUTE-CORSE
CORSE-DU-SUD
SAVOIE
HAUTE SAVOIE
ISÈRE
DRÔME
ARDÈCHE
VAUCLUSE
BOUCHES-DU-RHÔNE
ALPES-DE-HAUTE-PROVENCE
ALPES-MARITIMES
HAUTES-ALPES
JURA
AIN
VAUD
VALAIS
TICINO
GRAUBÜNDEN
Bern
Lausanne
Genève
Lyon
Grenoble
Chambéry
Annecy
St-Étienne
Valence
Avignon
Nîmes
Marseille
Toulon
Nice
MONACO
Torino
Milano
Genova
Ajaccio
Bastia
Livorno
Parma
Brescia
Piacenza
Novara
Cannes
Alpes Maritimes
Alpi Pennine
Alpi Lepontine
Berner Alpen
Mts. du Jura
Dauphiné
Vanoise
Massif du Pelvoux
Monts de Vaucluse
Elba
Arcipelago Toscano
Bouches de Bonifacio
ARCIPELAGO DE LA MADDALENA
Is. d'Hyères
8
9
19
10
11
12
13
14
41
42
B
C
D

National Parks

Regional Nature Parks in France

CENTRAL EUROPE

50 0 25 50 75 100 125 150 175 km

50 0 25 50 75 100 125 miles

1:4 400 000

NORTH SEA
BALTIC SEA
UNITED KINGDOM
NETHERLANDS
BELGIUM
LUXEMBOURG
DENMARK
GERMANY
FRANCE
SWITZERLAND
LIECHTENSTEIN
AUSTRIA
CZECH R
SLOVENIA
ITALY
MONACO
SAN MARINO
ADRIATIC SEA
Golfo di Venézia
Golfo di Génova
AMSTERDAM
'S-Gravenhage (Den Haag)
ROTTERDAM
BRUSSEL (Bruxelles)
PARIS
LUXEMBOURG
BERLIN
HAMBURG
MÜNCHEN (Munich)
PRAHA (Prague)
Bern
Zürich
MILANO
TORINO (Turin)
LYON
MARSEILLE
Genova
Venézia (Venice)
Ljubljana
Zagreb
Frankfurt
Köln (Cologne)
Stuttgart
Hannover
Bremen
Leipzig
Dresden
Nürnberg
Strasbourg
Dijon
Grenoble
Nice
Firenze (Florence)
Bologna
Innsbruck
Salzburg
Linz
Graz
Szczecin
Deutsche Bucht
Kieler Bucht
Mecklenburger Bucht
Nordfriesische Inseln
Ostfriesische Inseln
Niedersachsen
Nordrhein-Westfalen
Hessen
Rheinland-Pfalz
Bayern
Sachsen
Sachsen-Anhalt
Brandenburg
Mecklenburg
Thüringer Wald
Schwarzwald
Schwäbische Alb
Böhmerwald
Erzgebirge
Harz
Ardennes
Vosges
Jura
Alpes Maritimes
Massif Central
Provence
Dauphiné
Savoie
Lombardia
Piemonte
Liguria
Tirol
Dolomiti
Karawanken
Istra

Projection: *Conical with two standard parallels*

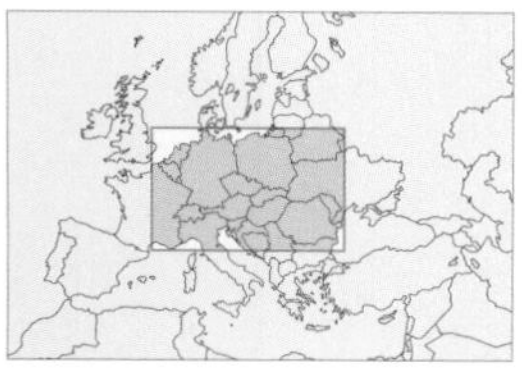

9
10
11
12
13
14
15
32
16
LITHUANIA
Vilnius
Kaliningrad (Russia)
Zatoka Gdańska
Gdynia
Gdańsk
Elbląg
Olsztyn
Hrodna
MINSK
B E L A R U S
Babruysk
Homyel
Baranavichy
Białystok
Bydgoszcz
Toruń
Włocławek
Płock
WARSZAWA (Warsaw)
Brest
Pinsk
P O L A N D
Łódź
Radom
Lublin
Kielce
Częstochowa
Wrocław
Opole
Katowice
Kraków
Tarnów
Rzeszów
Przemyśl
Lviv (Lvov)
Kovel
Lutsk
Rivne
Zhytomyr
KYYIV (Kiev)
U K R A I N E
Ternopil
Khmelnytskyy
Vinnytsya
Ivano-Frankivsk
Chernivtsi
Uzhhorod
Košice
Prešov
SLOVAK REP.
Bratislava
Ostrava
Miskolc
Debrecen
Nyíregyháza
BUDAPEST
H U N G A R Y
Szeged
Pécs
Oradea
Cluj-Napoca
Satu Mare
Baia Mare
Suceava
Iași
Chișinău
MOLDOVA
Tiraspol
Bacău
Galați
Brăila
Constanța
BUCUREȘTI (Bucharest)
Ploiești
Brașov
Sibiu
Timișoara
Arad
R O M A N I A
Craiova
Pitești
Transilvania
Carpații Meridionali
Walachia
Subotica
Novi Sad
BEOGRAD (Belgrade)
SERBIA & MONTENEGRO
BOSNIA-HERZEGOVINA
Sarajevo
CROATIA
Osijek
BULGARIA
Ruse
Varna
Dobrich
Dunav
Dnister
Prut
Siret
Tisza
Wisła
Pripet Marshes
Podilska vysochyna
Carpathians
B
C
D
E
F
G
34
East from Greenwich
44
45
COPYRIGHT PHILIP'S

10 0 10 20 30 40 50 60 70 80 90 km

10 0 10 20 30 40 50 60 miles

1:2 200 000

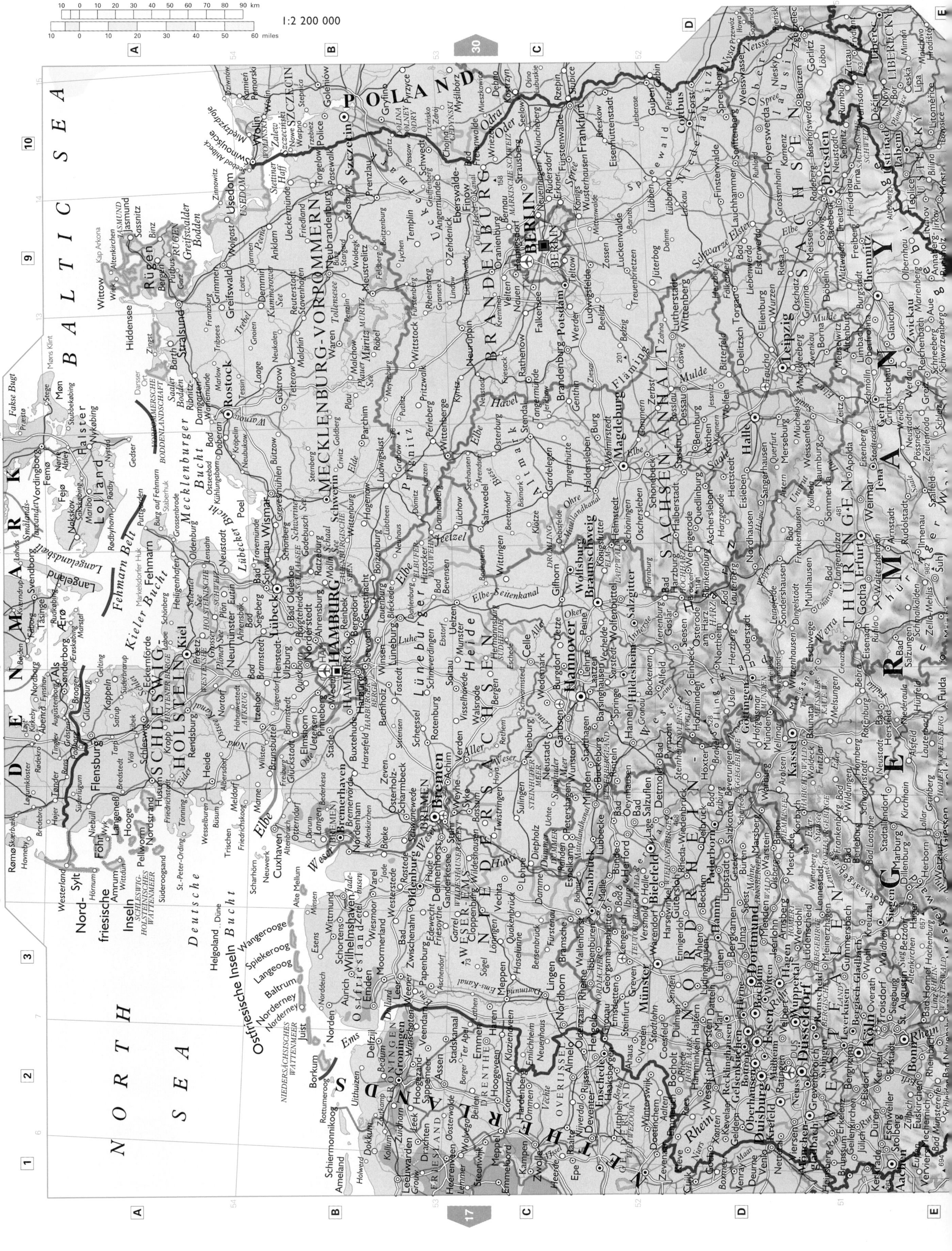
NORTH SEA
BALTIC SEA
DENMARK
POLAND
GERMANY
NETHERLANDS
SCHLESWIG-HOLSTEIN
MECKLENBURG-VORPOMMERN
BRANDENBURG
NIEDERSACHSEN
SACHSEN-ANHALT
SACHSEN
THÜRINGEN
NORDRHEIN-WESTFALEN
HAMBURG
BREMEN
BERLIN
Hannover
Magdeburg
Leipzig
Dresden
Kiel
Lübeck
Rostock
Schwerin
Szczecin
Potsdam
Bremerhaven
Osnabrück
Münster
Bielefeld
Dortmund
Essen
Düsseldorf
Köln
Bonn
Kassel
Erfurt
Halle
Chemnitz
Braunschweig
Wolfsburg
Göttingen
Groningen
Flensburg
Cuxhaven
Oldenburg
Rügen
Fehmarn
Helgoland
Ostfriesische Inseln
Nordfriesische Inseln
Lüneburger Heide
Elbe
Weser
Ems
Rhein
Oder
Spree
Havel
Saale
Mulde
Kieler Bucht
Mecklenburger Bucht
Lübecker Bucht
Deutsche Bucht
Fehmarn Belt
Lolland
Falster
Møn
Sylt
Föhr
Usedom
Harz
30
17
11

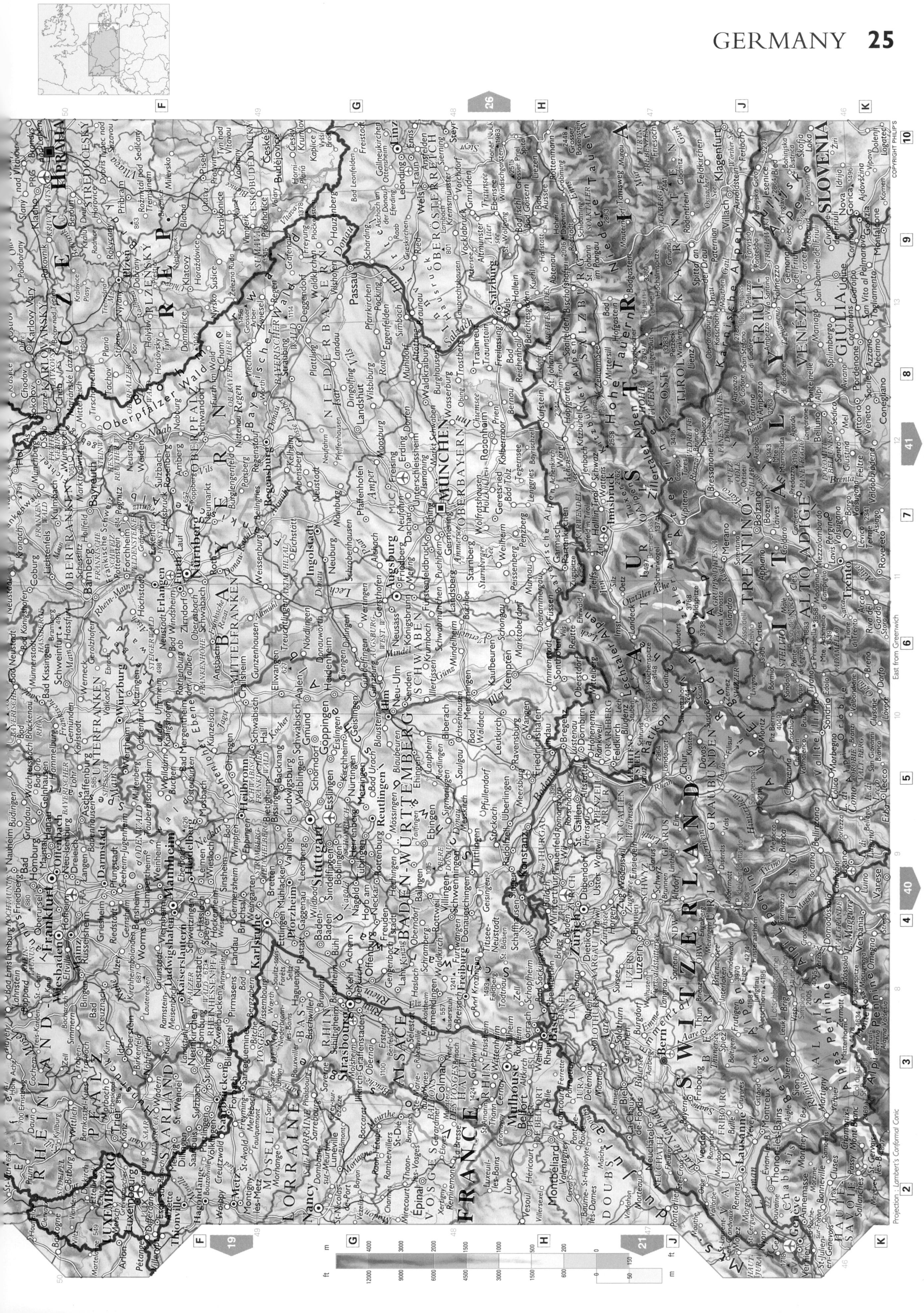
Projection: Lambert's Conformal Conic
COPYRIGHT PHILIPS
East from Greenwich

Underlined towns give their name to the administrative area in which they stand.

National Parks

Nature Parks in Germany

1:2 200 000

km
miles
GERMANY
THÜRINGEN
Dresden
Chemnitz
Erfurt
Weimar
Jena
Gera
Zwickau
Plauen
Hof
Coburg
Bamberg
Bayreuth
Würzburg
Schweinfurt
Aschaffenburg
UNTERFRANKEN
OBERFRANKEN
MITTELFRANKEN
OBERPFALZ
Nürnberg
Fürth
Erlangen
Regensburg
Ingolstadt
Augsburg
Ulm
Stuttgart
Heilbronn
München
OBERBAYERN
NIEDERBAYERN
SCHWABEN
BAYERN
Passau
Landshut
Rosenheim
Kempten
Friedrichshafen
Salzburg
Linz
Graz
Innsbruck
Klagenfurt
Villach
Leoben
Wels
Steyr
OBERÖSTERREICH
NIEDERÖSTERREICH
STEIERMARK
SALZBURG
TIROL
KÄRNTEN
VORARLBERG
Bregenz
Dornbirn
Feldkirch
AUSTRIA
PRAHA
Plzeň
České Budějovice
Karlovy Vary
Liberec
Ústí nad Labem
Hradec Králové
Pardubice
Jihlava
Kladno
CZECH REP.
STŘEDOČESKÝ
PLZEŇSKÝ
KARLOVARSKÝ
LIBERECKÝ
ÚSTECKÝ
JIHLAVSKÝ
ČESKOBUDĚJOVICKÝ
SWITZERLAND
Chur
Davos
St. Moritz
ITALY
TRENTINO-ALTO ADIGE
FRIULI-VENEZIA GIULIA
VENETO
LOMBARDIA
Bolzano
Trento
Merano
Udine
Trieste
Venézia
Vicenza
Treviso
Padova
Brescia
Bérgamo
Golfo di Venézia
SLOVENIA
Ljubljana
Maribor
Kranj
Koper
Zagreb
Bodensee
Donau
Inn
Salzach
Mur
Drau
Vltava
Labe
Lech
Isar
Böhmer Wald
Bayerischer Wald
Hohe Tauern
Niedere Tauern
Zillertaler Alpen
Karnische Alpen
Karawanken
Erzgebirge
Grossglockner 3797
ft
m
12000
9000
6000
4500
3000
1500
600
4000
3000
2000
1500
1000
500
200

Projection : *Lambert's Conformal Conic*

POLAND
ŚLĄSKIE
OPOLSKIE
ŚWIĘTOKRZYSKIE
MAŁOPOLSKIE
PODKARPACKIE
SLOVAK REP.
HUNGARY
ROMANIA
SERBIA & MONTENEGRO
CROATIA
UKRAINE
Wrocław
Częstochowa
Kielce
Katowice
Kraków
Rzeszów
Ostrava
Olomouc
Brno
WIEN
Bratislava
Žilina
Košice
Miskolc
Nyíregyháza
Debrecen
BUDAPEST
Győr
Székesfehérvár
Pécs
Szeged
Kecskemét
Oradea
Arad
Timişoara
Subotica
Tatry
Nízke Tatry
Matra
Bükk
Dunaj
Duna
Tisza
Dráva
Maros
Mureş
Balaton
BORSOD-ABAÚJ-ZEMPLÉN
SZABOLCS-SZATMÁR-BEREG
HAJDÚ-BIHAR
JÁSZ-NAGYKUN-SZOLNOK
PEST
BÁCS-KISKUN
CSONGRÁD
BÉKÉS
HEVES
NÓGRÁD
KOMÁROM-ESZTERGOM
GYŐR-MOSON-SOPRON
VESZPRÉM
FEJÉR
VAS
ZALA
SOMOGY
TOLNA
BARANYA
BIHOR
SATU MARE
TIMIŞ
TRENČIANSKY
TRNAVSKÝ
NITRIANSKY
BANSKOBYSTRICKÝ
ŽILINSKÝ
PREŠOVSKÝ
KOŠICKÝ
BRATISLAVSKÝ
ZLÍNSKÝ
OLOMOUCKÝ
MORAVSKOSLEZSKÝ
BRNĚNSKÝ
BJELOVARSKO-BILOGORSKA
East from Greenwich

National Parks

Underlined towns give their name to the administrative area in which they stand.

31 33 29 28

1:2 200 000

0 10 20 30 40 50 60 70 80 90 km
0 10 20 30 40 50 60 miles
SLOVAK REP.
HUNGARY
CROATIA
BOSNIA-HERZEGOVINA
SERBIA & MONTENEGRO
AUSTRIA
BUDAPEST
WIEN
Bratislava
BEOGRAD (Belgrade)
Sarajevo
Debrecen
Szeged
Timişoara
Oradea
Arad
Novi Sad
Osijek
Košice
Miskolc
Pécs
Győr
Kecskemét
Nyíregyháza
Subotica
Balaton
Duna
Tisza
Dunav
Sava
Drava
VOJVODINA
Projection : Lambert's Conformal Conic
East from Greenwich

Administrative divisions in Croatia:

1 Brodsko-Posavska
2 Koprivničko-Križevačka
4 Medimurska
5 Osječko-Baranjska
6 Požeško-Slavonska
8 Virovitičko-Podravska
9 Vukovarsko-Srijemska

Inter-entity boundaries as agreed at the 1995 Dayton Peace Agreement

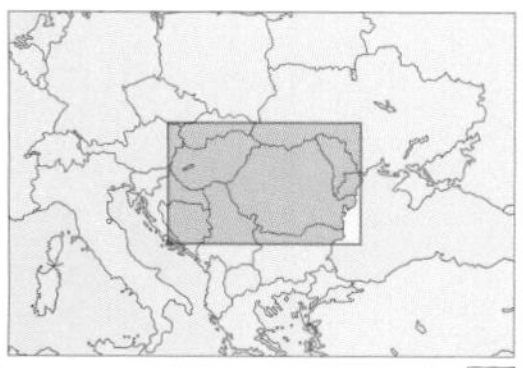

33
45
UKRAINE
MOLDOVA
ROMANIA
BULGARIA
BLACK SEA
Ivano-Frankivsk
Chernivtsi
Kamyanets-Podilskyy
Mohyliv-Podilskyy
Bălți
Chișinău (Kishinev)
Tiraspol
Tighina
Cluj-Napoca
Târgu Mureș
Sibiu
Brașov
Piatra Neamț
Bacău
Suceava
Botoșani
Iași
Vaslui
Focșani
Galați
Brăila
Tulcea
Ploiești
Pitești
Craiova
BUCUREȘTI (Bucharest)
Constanța
Călărași
Slobozia
Giurgiu
Ruse
Pleven
Dobrich
Mangalia
Dunărea
Dunărea (Danube)
DELTA DUNĂREA
Lacul Razim
Karpatskyy
Munții Rodnei
Munții Călimani
Munții Harghita
Munții Făgăraș
Transilvania
Valahia
Dobrogea
Moldova
Prut
Siret
Nistru
Olt
Mureș
Argeș
Ialomița
COPYRIGHT PHILIP'S

National Parks

Underlined towns give their name to the administrative area in which they stand.

1:2 200 000

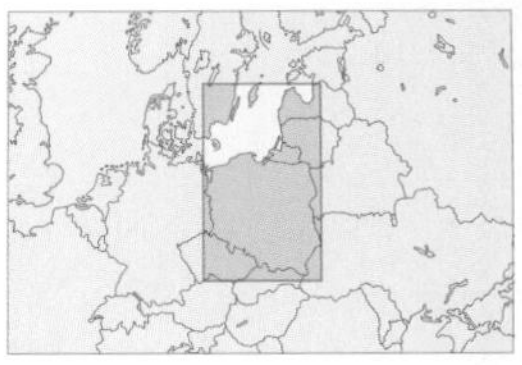

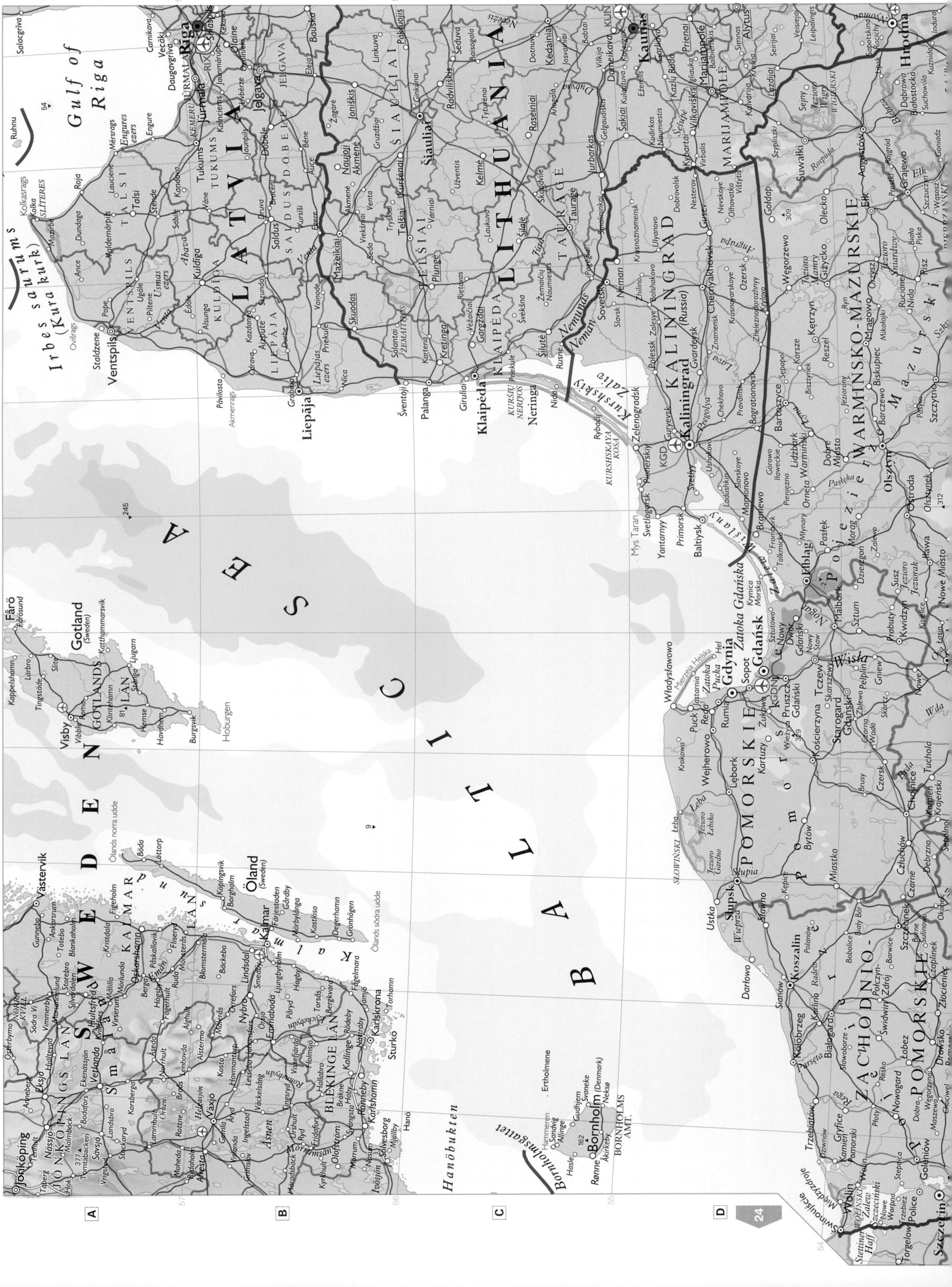
BALTIC SEA
SWEDEN
LATVIA
LITHUANIA
KALININGRAD (Russia)
Gulf of Riga
Gotland (Sweden)
Öland (Sweden)
Bornholm (Denmark)
Riga
Kaunas
Klaipėda
Liepāja
Ventspils
Kaliningrad
Gdańsk
Gdynia
Zatoka Gdańska
Elbląg
Olsztyn
Słupsk
Koszalin
Kołobrzeg
Szczecin
Hrodna
Šiauliai
Karlskrona
Kalmar
Växjö
Visby
POMORSKIE
WARMIŃSKO-MAZURSKIE
ZACHODNIO-POMORSKIE
Hanöbukten
Kurshskiy Zaliv
Irbes šaurums (Kura kurk)

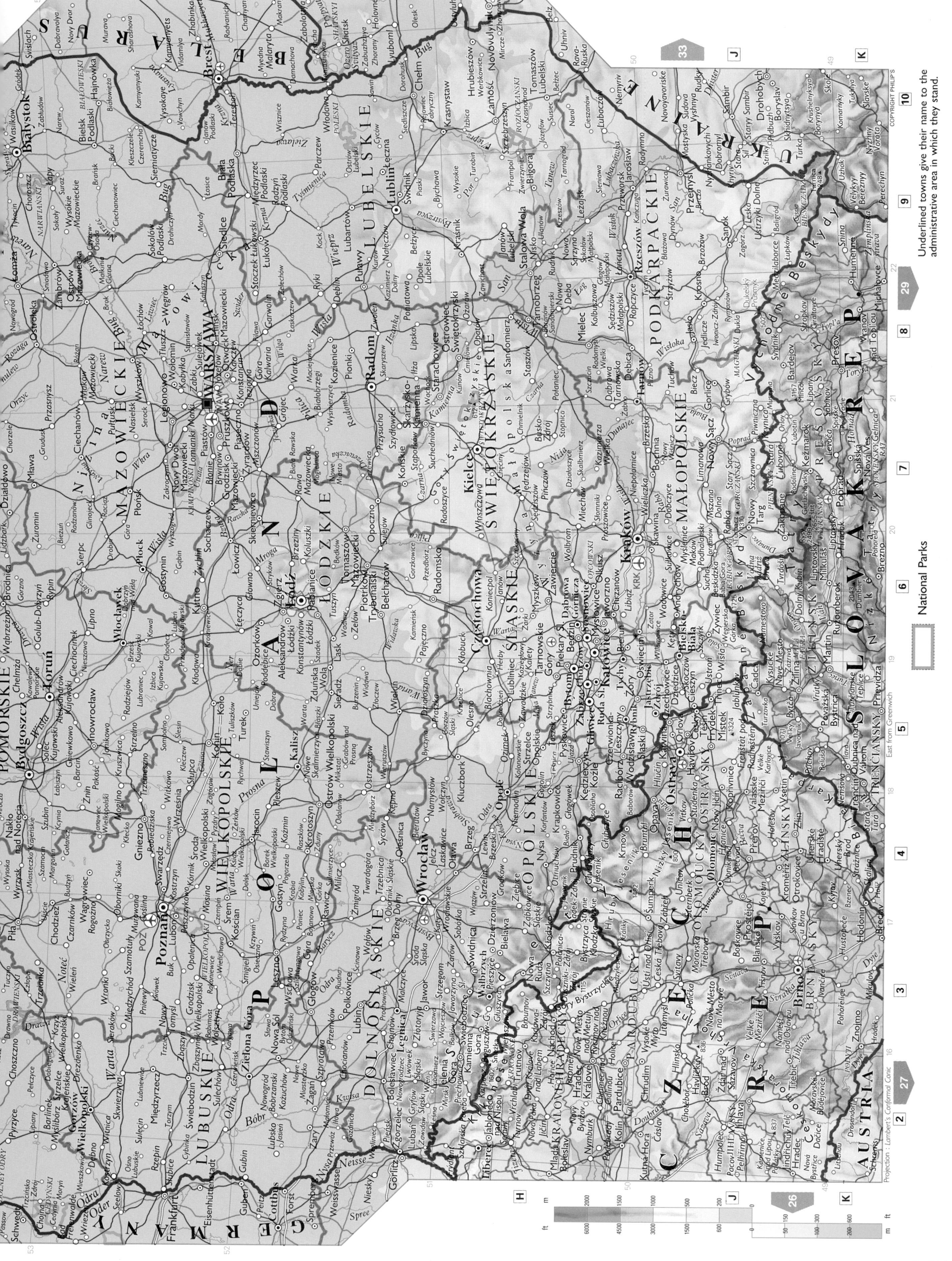
POLAND
GERMANY
CZECH REPUBLIC
SLOVAK REPUBLIC
AUSTRIA
UKRAINE
BELARUS
POMORSKIE
MAZOWIECKIE
WIELKOPOLSKIE
LUBUSKIE
DOLNOŚLĄSKIE
OPOLSKIE
ŚLĄSKIE
ŁÓDZKIE
ŚWIĘTOKRZYSKIE
MAŁOPOLSKIE
PODKARPACKIE
LUBELSKIE
WARSZAWA
National Parks
Underlined towns give their name to the administrative area in which they stand.
Projection : Lambert's Conformal Conic
East from Greenwich
COPYRIGHT PHILIP'S

1:4 400 000

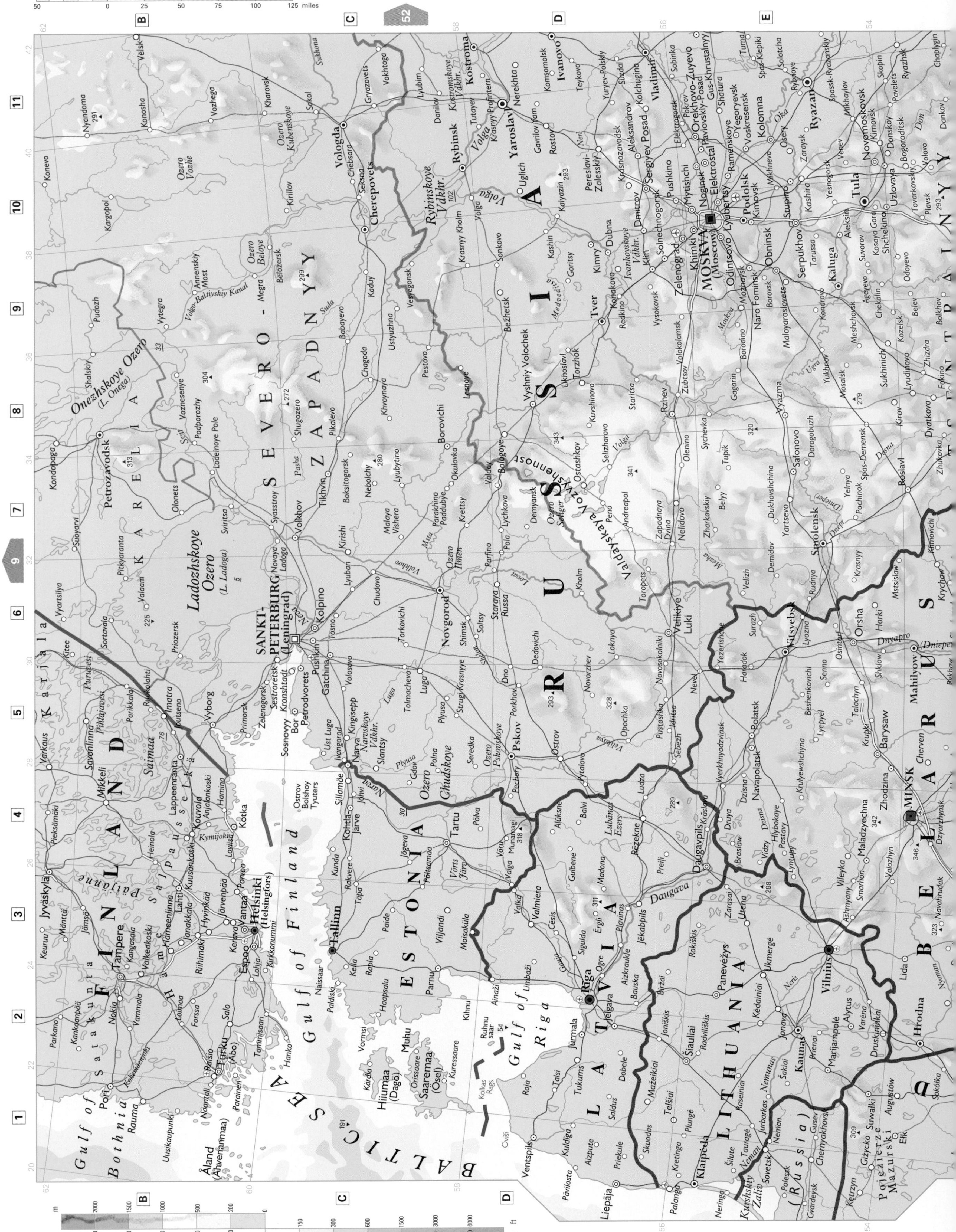
50 0 25 50 75 100 125 150 175 km
50 0 25 50 75 100 125 miles
52
9
FINLAND
ESTONIA
LATVIA
LITHUANIA
BELARUS
RUSSIA
KARELIA
SEVERO - ZAPADNY
Gulf of Finland
Gulf of Riga
Gulf of Bothnia
BALTIC SEA
Ladozhskoye Ozero (L. Ladoga)
Onezhskoye Ozero (L. Onega)
Ozero Chudskoye
Ozero Pskovskoye
Ozero Il'men
Rybinskoye Vdkhr.
Valdayskaya Vozvyshennost
Saimaa
SANKT-PETERBURG (Leningrad)
MOSKVA (Moscow)
MINSK
Helsinki (Helsingfors)
Tallinn
Riga
Vilnius
Kaunas
Daugavpils
Tartu
Pskov
Novgorod
Tver
Smolensk
Vitsyebsk
Mahilyow
Hrodna
Klaipeda
Liepaja
Ventspils
Turku (Åbo)
Tampere
Vologda
Cherepovets
Yaroslavl
Kostroma
Ivanovo
Vladimir
Ryazan
Tula
Kaluga
Orsha
Petrozavodsk
Vyborg
Narva
Pärnu
Šiauliai
Panevėžys
Saaremaa (Ösel)
Hiiumaa (Dagö)
Åland (Ahvenanmaa)
Daugava
Dnyapro
Neman

m	ft
2000	6000
1500	4500
1000	3000
500	1500
200	600
0	0
50	150
100	300
200	600
500	1500
1000	3000
2000	6000

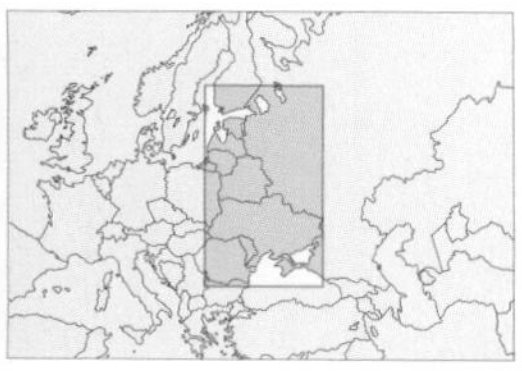

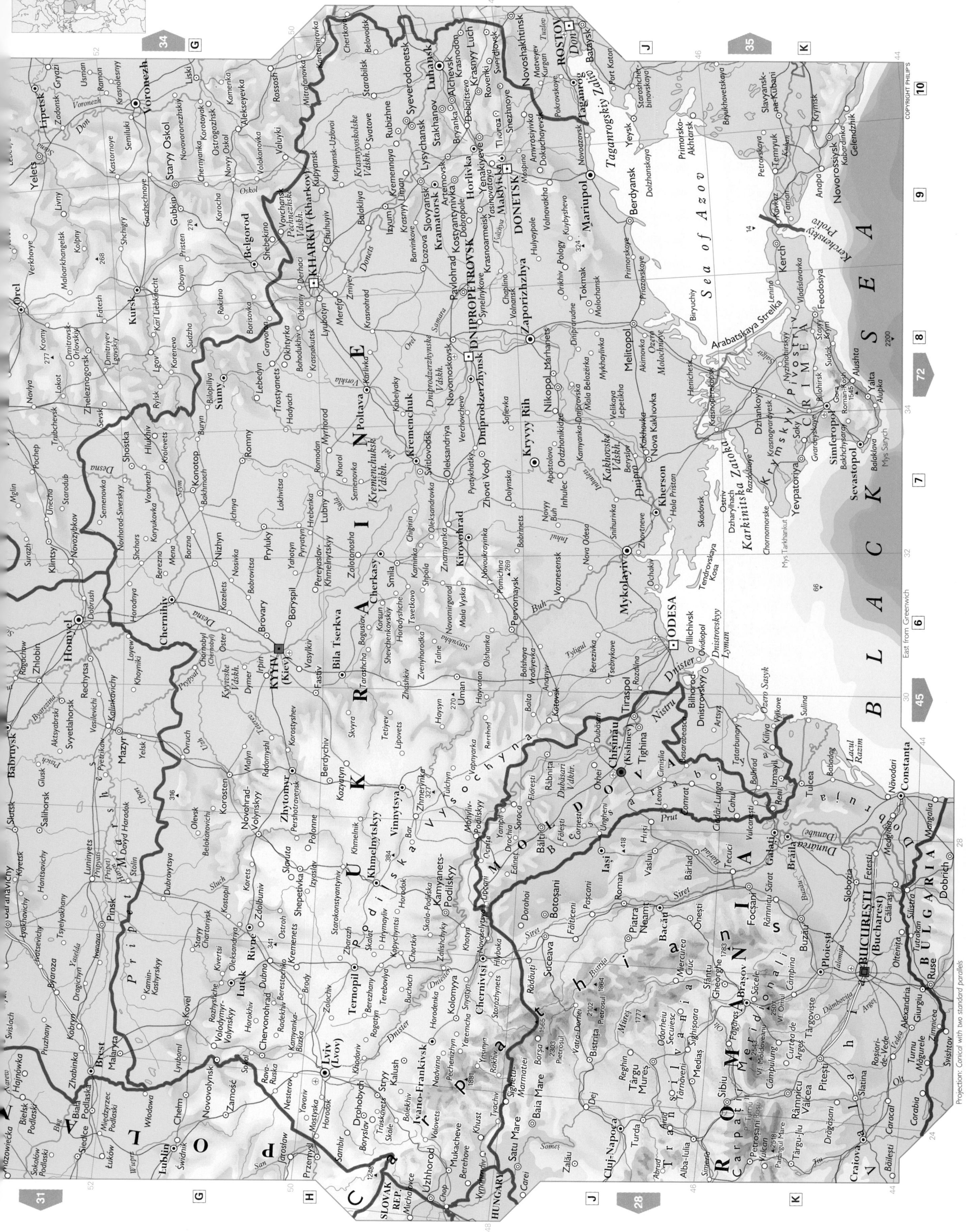
UKRAINE
MOLDOVA
ROMANIA
POLAND
BULGARIA
SLOVAK REP.
HUNGARY
BLACK SEA
Sea of Azov
CRIMEA
KYIV (Kiev)
KHARKIV (Kharkov)
DNIPROPETROVSK
DONETSK
ODESA
ROSTOV
BUCUREȘTI (Bucharest)
Chișinău (Kishinev)
Lviv (Lvov)
Homyel
Voronezh
Kursk
Belgorod
Orel
Lipetsk
Yelets
Zaporizhzhya
Mariupol
Mykolayiv
Kherson
Sevastopol
Simferopol
Poltava
Cherkasy
Vinnytsya
Zhytomyr
Chernihiv
Sumy
Kryvyy Rih
Kirovohrad
Kremenchuk
Luhansk
Constanța
Iași
Galați
Brăila
Lublin
Brest
Pinsk
Mazyr
Taganrogskiy Zaliv
Kerchenskiy Proliv
Karkinitska Zatoka
Dnister
Dnipro
Prut
Siret
Pripet Marshes
Podilska Vysochyna
Carpathians
Projection: Conical with two standard parallels
East from Greenwich
COPYRIGHT PHILIP'S
31
34
35
72
45
28

50 0 25 50 75 100 125 150 175 km

50 0 25 50 75 100 125 miles

1:4 400 000

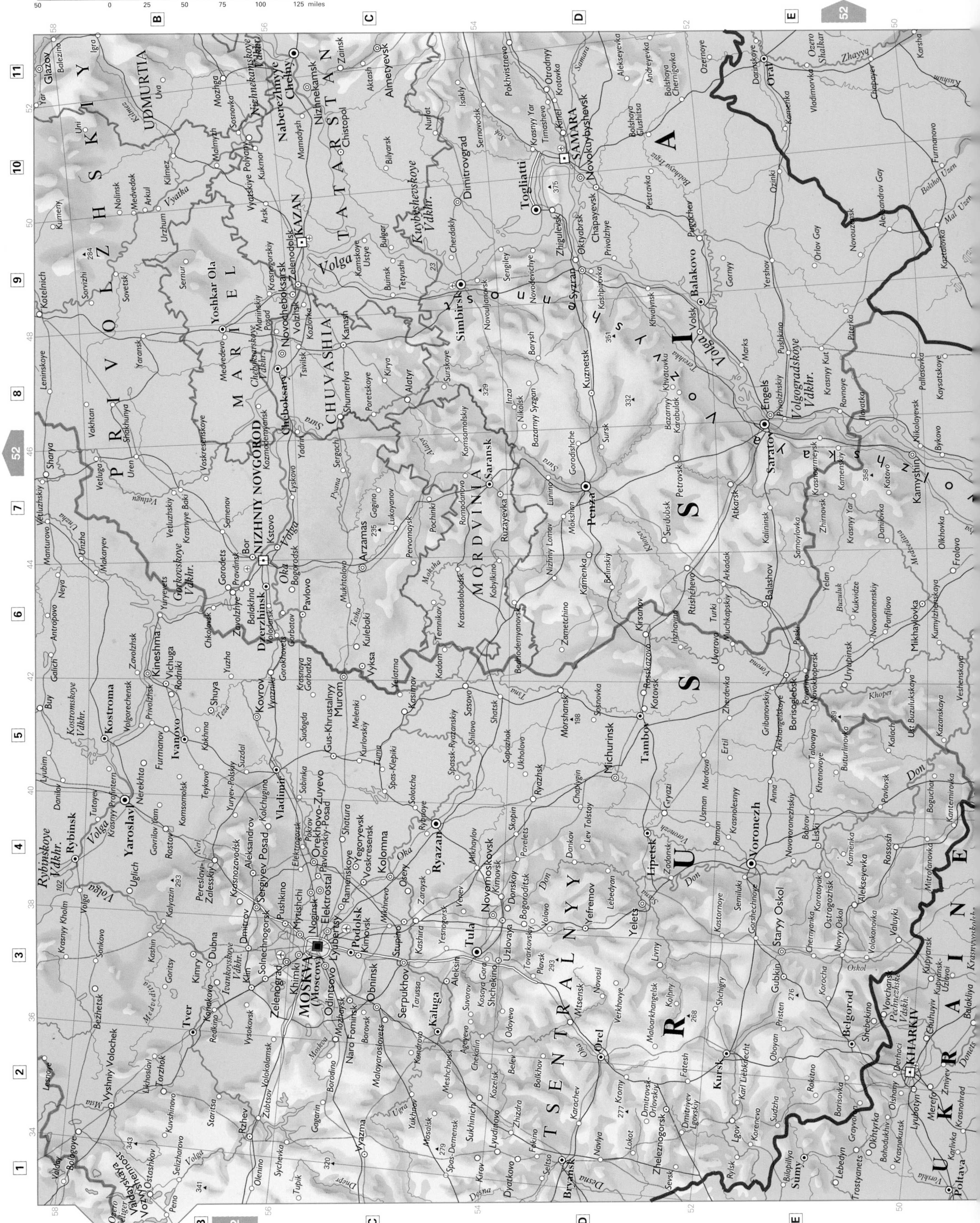
PRIVOLZHSKIY
UDMURTIA
MARI EL
TATARSTAN
CHUVASHIA
MORDVINIA
TSENTRALNYY
RUSSIA
UKRAINE
KAZAN
SAMARA
NIZHNIY NOVGOROD
MOSKVA (Moscow)
KHARKIV
Naberezhnyye Chelny
Nizhnekamsk
Izhevsk
Yoshkar Ola
Cheboksary
Novocheboksarsk
Simbirsk
Togliatti
Syzran
Novokuybyshevsk
Saransk
Penza
Saratov
Engels
Balakovo
Kamyshin
Tambov
Michurinsk
Voronezh
Lipetsk
Yelets
Kursk
Belgorod
Staryy Oskol
Orel
Bryansk
Kaluga
Tula
Ryazan
Vladimir
Ivanovo
Kostroma
Yaroslavl
Rybinsk
Tver
Dzerzhinsk
Arzamas
Murom
Kovrov
Podolsk
Zelenograd
Elektrostal
Kolomna
Serpukhov
Obninsk
Novomoskovsk
Sumy
Poltava
Oral
Volga
Oka
Don
Sura
Khoper
Kuybyshevskoye Vdkhr.
Volgogradskoye Vdkhr.
Rybinskoye Vdkhr.
Gorkovskoye Vdkhr.
Ivankovskoye Vdkhr.
Kostromskoye Vdkhr.
Cheboksarskoye Vdkhr.
52
32

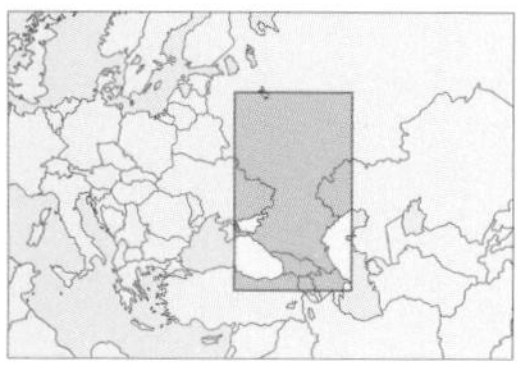

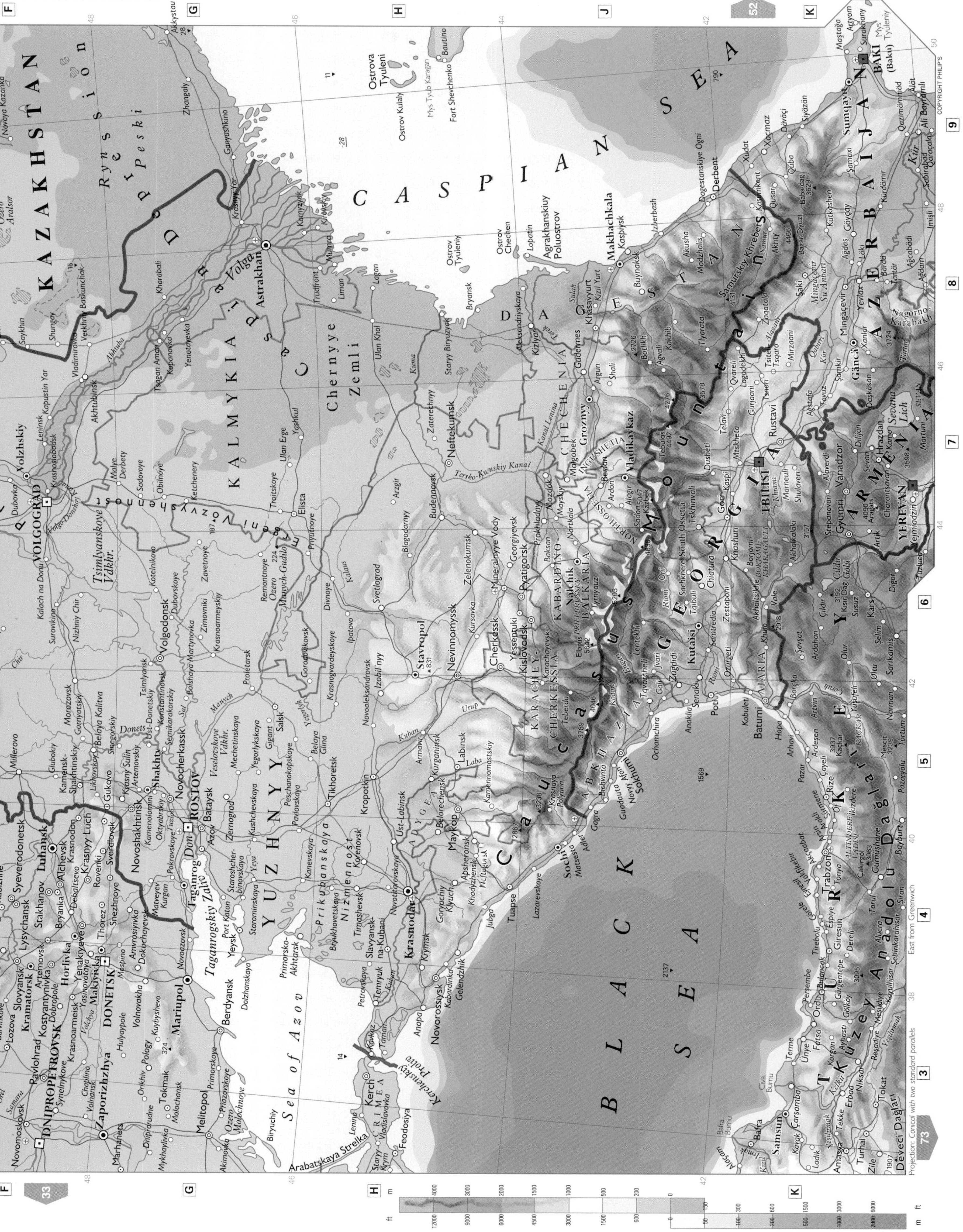
CASPIAN SEA
BLACK SEA
Sea of Azov
KAZAKHSTAN
GEORGIA
ARMENIA
AZERBAIJAN
KALMYKIA
CHECHENIA
DAGESTAN
VOLGOGRAD
ROSTOV
DONETSK
TBILISI
YEREVAN
BAKI (Baku)
Astrakhan
Grozny
Krasnodar
Stavropol
Projection: Conical with two standard parallels
East from Greenwich
COPYRIGHT PHILIP'S

1:2 200 000
10 0 10 20 30 40 50 60 70 80 90 km
10 0 10 20 30 40 50 60 miles
38
Bay of Biscay
Costa Verde
GALICIA
ASTURIAS
CANTABRIA
PAÍS VASCO
LA RIOJA
CASTILLA Y LEÓN
ESPAÑA
MADRID
A Coruña (La Coruña)
Santiago de Compostela
Lugo
Ourense (Orense)
Pontevedra
Vigo
Ferrol
Oviedo
Gijón
Santander
Bilbao
Donostia-San Sebastián
Vitoria-Gasteiz
Logroño
Burgos
León
Palencia
Valladolid
Zamora
Salamanca
Segovia
Ávila
Soria
Guadalajara
Toledo
Plasencia
Porto
Braga
Viana do Castelo
Aveiro
Coimbra
Viseu
Guarda
Bragança
Vila Real
Castelo Branco
Leiria
Ponferrada
Astorga
Benavente
Talavera de la Reina
Picos de Europa
Cordillera Cantábrica
Sierra de Guadarrama
Sierra de Gredos
Serra da Estrela
Douro
Duero
Miño
Tajo

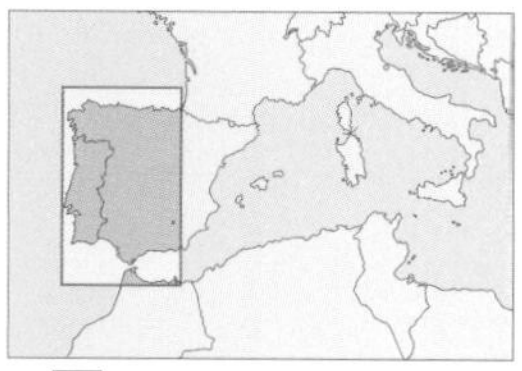

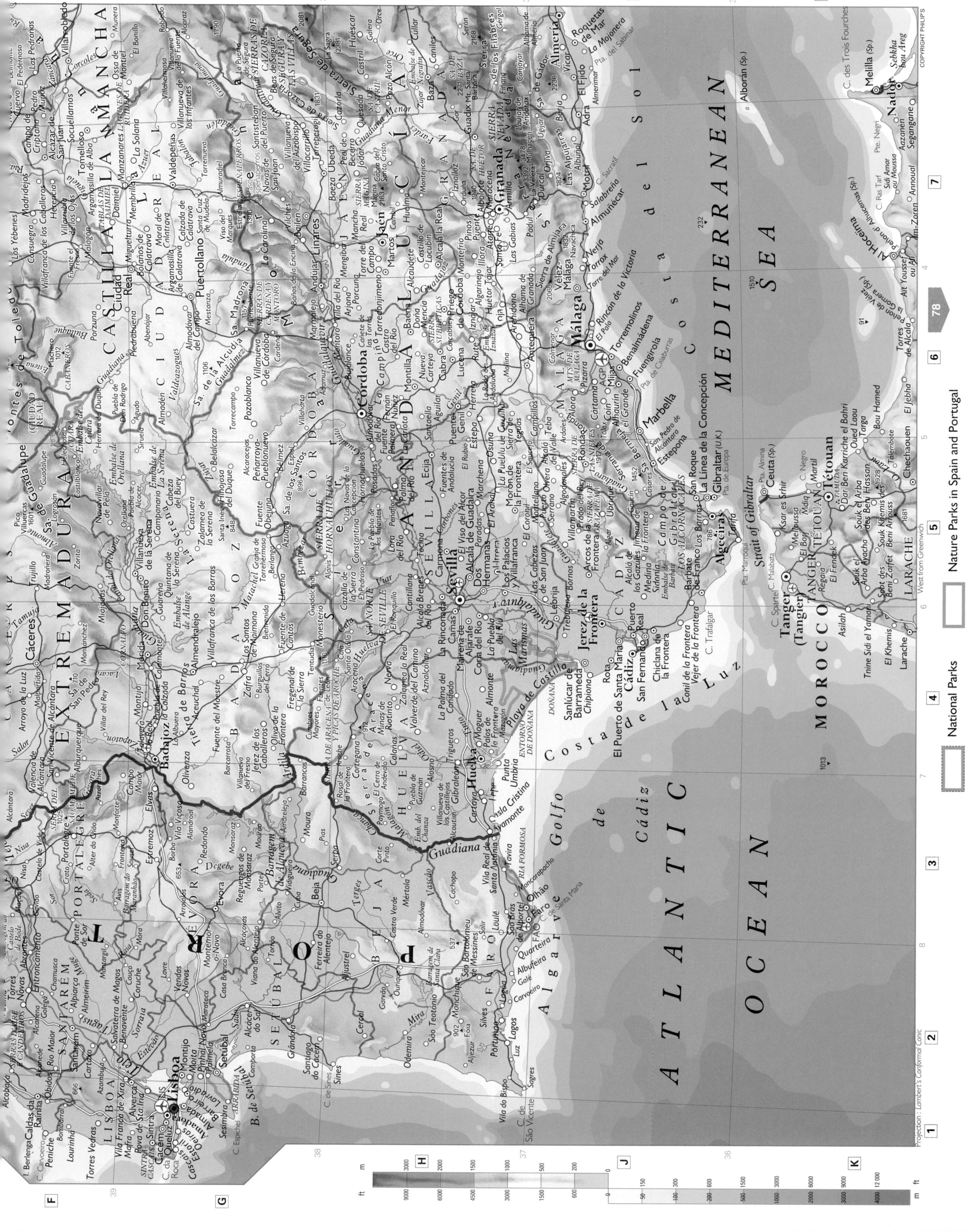
ATLANTIC
OCEAN
MEDITERRANEAN
SEA
Golfo de Cádiz
Costa de la Luz
Costa del Sol
Strait of Gibraltar
MOROCCO
EXTREMADURA
CASTILLA-LA MANCHA
ANDALUCÍA
SEVILLA
CÓRDOBA
HUELVA
CÁDIZ
MÁLAGA
GRANADA
JAÉN
BADAJOZ
CIUDAD REAL
LISBOA
SANTARÉM
PORTALEGRE
ÉVORA
SETÚBAL
BEJA
FARO
Lisboa
Sevilla
Córdoba
Málaga
Granada
Cádiz
Huelva
Badajoz
Cáceres
Jaén
Almería
Gibraltar (U.K.)
Ceuta (Sp.)
Melilla (Sp.)
Tanger (Tangier)
Tétouan
Faro
Évora
Setúbal
Beja
Guadiana
Guadalquivir
Tejo
Sierra Nevada
Sierra Morena
Algarve
National Parks
Nature Parks in Spain and Portugal
West from Greenwich
Projection: Lambert's Conformal Conic
COPYRIGHT PHILIP'S

10 0 10 20 30 40 50 60 70 80 90 km

1:2 200 000

10 0 10 20 30 40 50 60 miles

FRANCE
PYRÉNÉES
ANDORRA
CATALUÑA
ARAGÓN
NAVARRA
PAÍS VASCO
LA RIOJA
CASTILLA Y LEÓN
BARCELONA
Zaragoza
Toulouse
Pamplona
Bilbao
Vitoria-Gasteiz
Logroño
Lleida
Tarragona
Girona
Perpignan
MADRID
Guadalajara
Cuenca
Teruel
Castelló de la Plana
Golfe de Gascogne
Donostia-San Sebastián
Costa Brava
MENORCA
MALLORCA
BALEARES

20

36

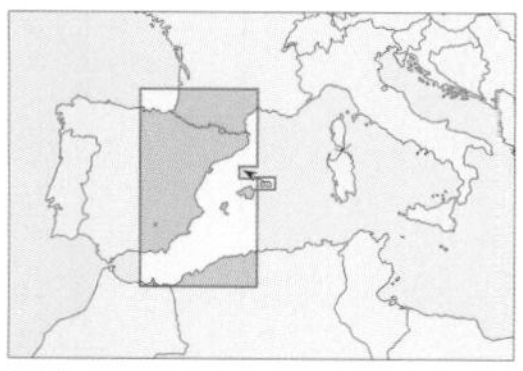

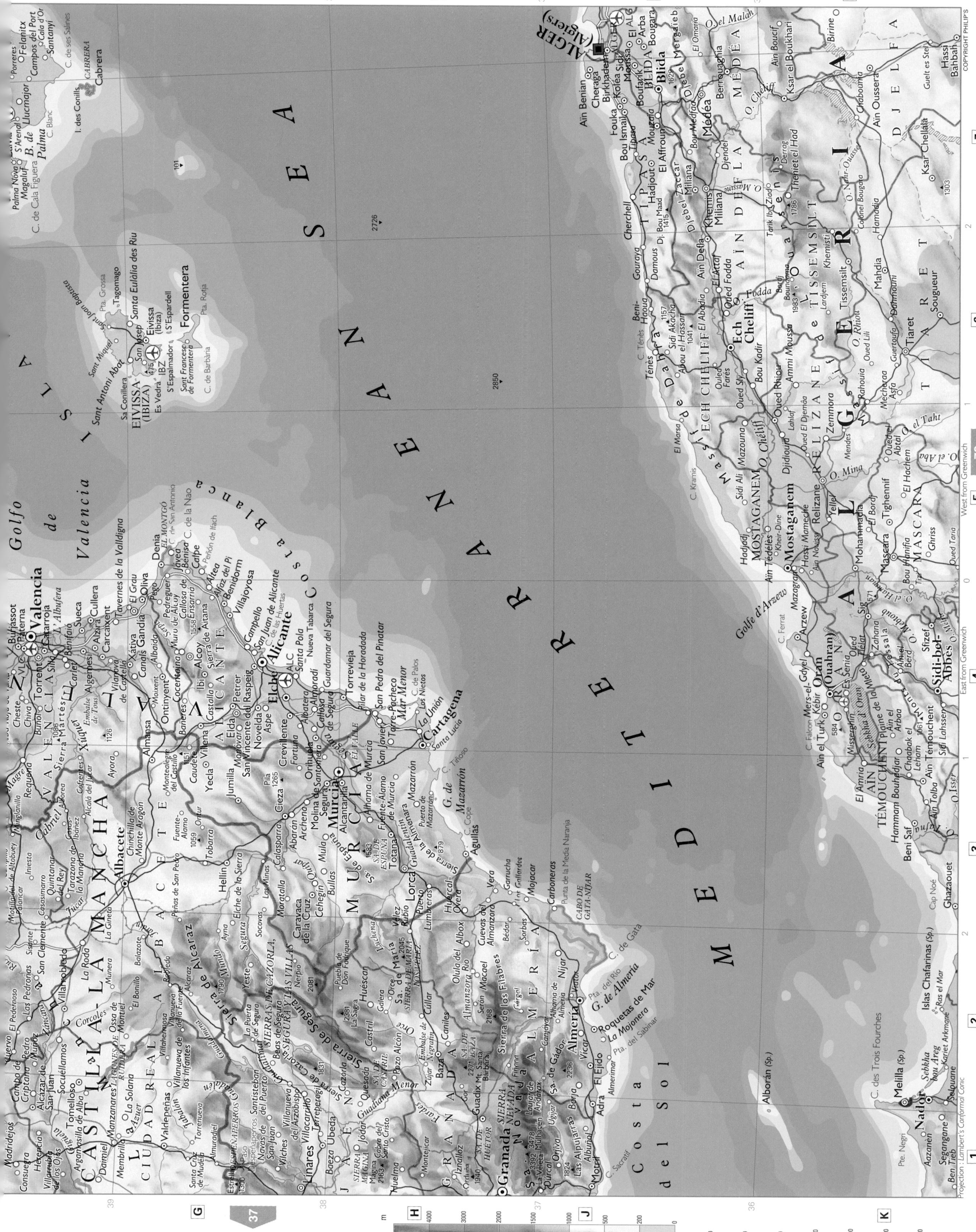
MEDITERRANEAN SEA
Golfo de Valencia
Costa Blanca
Costa del Sol
ISLAS BALEARES
Valencia
Alicante
Murcia
Cartagena
Albacete
Almería
Granada
Linares
Elche
Benidorm
Gandia
Lorca
Eivissa (Ibiza)
Formentera
EIVISSA (IBIZA)
CASTILLA-LA MANCHA
VALENCIA
MURCIA
ANDALUCÍA
ALGER (Algiers)
Blida
Médéa
Ech Cheliff
Mostaganem
Oran (Ouahran)
Sidi-bel-Abbès
Relizane
Tiaret
Mascara
Melilla (Sp.)
Nador
ALGERIA
Alborán (Sp.)
Islas Chafarinas (Sp.)
G. de Almería
G. de Mazarrón
Golfe d'Arzew
Sierra Nevada
Sierra de Segura
Sierra de Alcaraz
Projection: Lambert's Conformal Conic
COPYRIGHT PHILIP'S
National Parks
Nature Parks in Spain
East from Greenwich
West from Greenwich
37
78

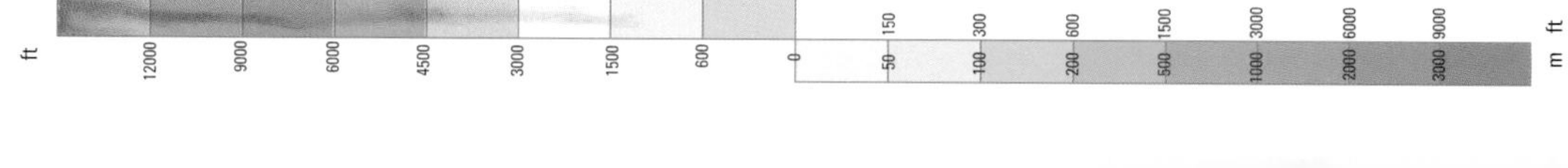
m
4000
3000
2000
1500
1000
500
200
0
ft
12000
9000
6000
4500
3000
1500
600
0
50
100
200
500
1000
2000
3000
150
300
600
1500
3000
6000
9000
m
ft

10 0 10 20 30 40 50 60 70 80 90 km

10 0 10 20 30 40 50 60 miles

1:2 200 000

25

SWITZERLAND
FRANCE
LIGURIAN SEA
Golfo di Génova
RHÔNE-ALPES
PROVENCE-ALPES-CÔTE D'AZUR
LOMBARDIA
PIEMONTE
VALLE D'AOSTA
LIGURIA
CORSE
Milano
Torino
Genova
Lyon
Marseille
Nice
Toulon
Grenoble
Genève
Lausanne
Bern
Luzern
Avignon
Bastia
Ajaccio
Livorno
Parma
La Spezia
MONACO
Elba
Arcipelago Toscano
Riviera di Ponente
Riviera di Levante
Côte d'Azur

Projection : Lambert's Conformal Conic

East from Greenwich

42

21

m	4000	3000	2000	1500	1000	500	200	0
ft	12 000	9000	6000	4500	3000	1500	600	0

ft	150	300	600	1500	3000	6000
m	50	100	200	500	1000	2000

National Parks

Underlined towns give their name to t administrative area in which they stan

AUSTRIA
SLOVENIA
CROATIA
HUNGARY
BOSNIA-HERZEGOVINA
SAN MARINO
VATICAN CITY
ROMA
ADRIATIC SEA
Golfo di Venézia
VÉNETO
FRIULI-VENEZIA GIULIA
EMILIA-ROMAGNA
TOSCANA
MARCHE
UMBRIA
LAZIO
ABRUZZO
Ljubljana
Zagreb
Graz
Klagenfurt
Maribor
Rijeka
Trieste
Venézia
Pádova
Ferrara
Bologna
Ravenna
Rímini
Ancona
Pescara
Firenze
Perúgia
Zadar
Split
Šibenik
Banja Luka
Innsbruck
Pula
Istra
Krk
Cres
Pag
Brač
Hvar
Korčula
Vis
Lastovo
Mljet
Palagruža (Croatia)
Trémiti
Pianosa
Dinara Planina
Velebit
Appennino Umbro-Marchigiano
Karawanken
Hohe Tauern
COPYRIGHT PHILIP'S

Administrative divisions in Croatia:
Brodsko-Posavska
Koprivničko-Križevačka
Krapinsko-Zagorska
4 Međimurska
6 Požeško-Slavonska
7 Varaždinska
8 Virovitičko-Podravska
10 Zagreba čka

Nature Parks in Italy

Inter-entity boundaries as agreed at the 1995 Dayton Peace Agreement

1:2 200 000

40

CORSE
(France)
CORSE-DU-SUD
G. d' Ajaccio
G. de Valinco
Solenzara
Porto-Vecchio
Ìs. Cerbicales
Bonifacio
Bouches de Bonifacio
ARCIPELAGO DE LA MADDALENA
La Maddalena
Caprera
Asinara
Golfo dell' Asinara
Costa Smeralda
Porto Torres
Sássari
Alghero
Tempio Pausania
Ólbia
G. di Ólbia
Tavolara
Ozieri
Siniscóla
Núoro
Orosei
Golfo di Orosei
GOLFO DI OROSEI E DEL GENNARGENTU
Macomer
SARDEGNA
Monti del Gennargentu
Oristano
Golfo di Oristano
Tortolì
Arbatax
Lanusei
Iglésias
Villacidro
San Pietro
Carbónia
Assemini
Cágliari
Golfo di Cágliari
Quartu Sant' Élena
Sant' Antioco
G. di Pálmas
C. Carbonara
C. Spartivento
Teulada
Santa Margherita
ROMA
VATICAN CITY
Tívoli
Lido di Óstia
Pomèzia
Anzio
Nettuno
Latina
Frosinone
Terracina
Gaeta
Golfo di Gaeta
Ísole Ponziane
Ponza
Palmarola
Zannone
Ventotène
Íschia
Fondi
Formia
Sabáudia
Mte. Circeo
TYRRHENIAN SEA
3589
Ústica
Palermo
Bagheria
Trápani
Ísole Égadi
Favignana
Maréttimo
Lévanzo
Marsala
Mazara del Vallo
Castelvetrano
Alcamo
Sciacca
Agrigento
Porto Empédocle
Palma di Montechiaro
Licata
Strait of Sicily
Pantelleria
(Italy)
Ìs. de la Galite
(Tunisia)
Canal de la Galite
Bizerte
BIZERTE
Lac de Bizerte
Menzel-Bourguiba
Golfe de Tunis
Zembra
C. Bon
KERKOUANE
Kelibia
Ariana
La Marsa
CARTHAGE
La Goulette
Tunis
Hammam-Lif
NABEUL
Nabeul
Hammamet
Menzel-Temime
Korba
Grombalia
TUNISIA
Béja
BÉJA
JENDOUBA
Jendouba
Tabarka
El Kala
Ain Draham
Mateur
ZAGHOUAN
MEDITE
Projection : Lambert's Conformal Conic
East from Greenwich

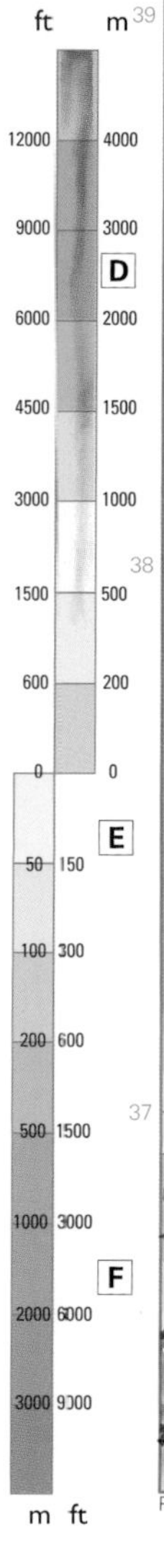

ft
m
12000
4000
9000
3000
6000
2000
4500
1500
3000
1000
1500
500
600
200
0
0
50
150
100
300
200
600
500
1500
1000
3000
2000
6000
3000
9300
m
ft

78

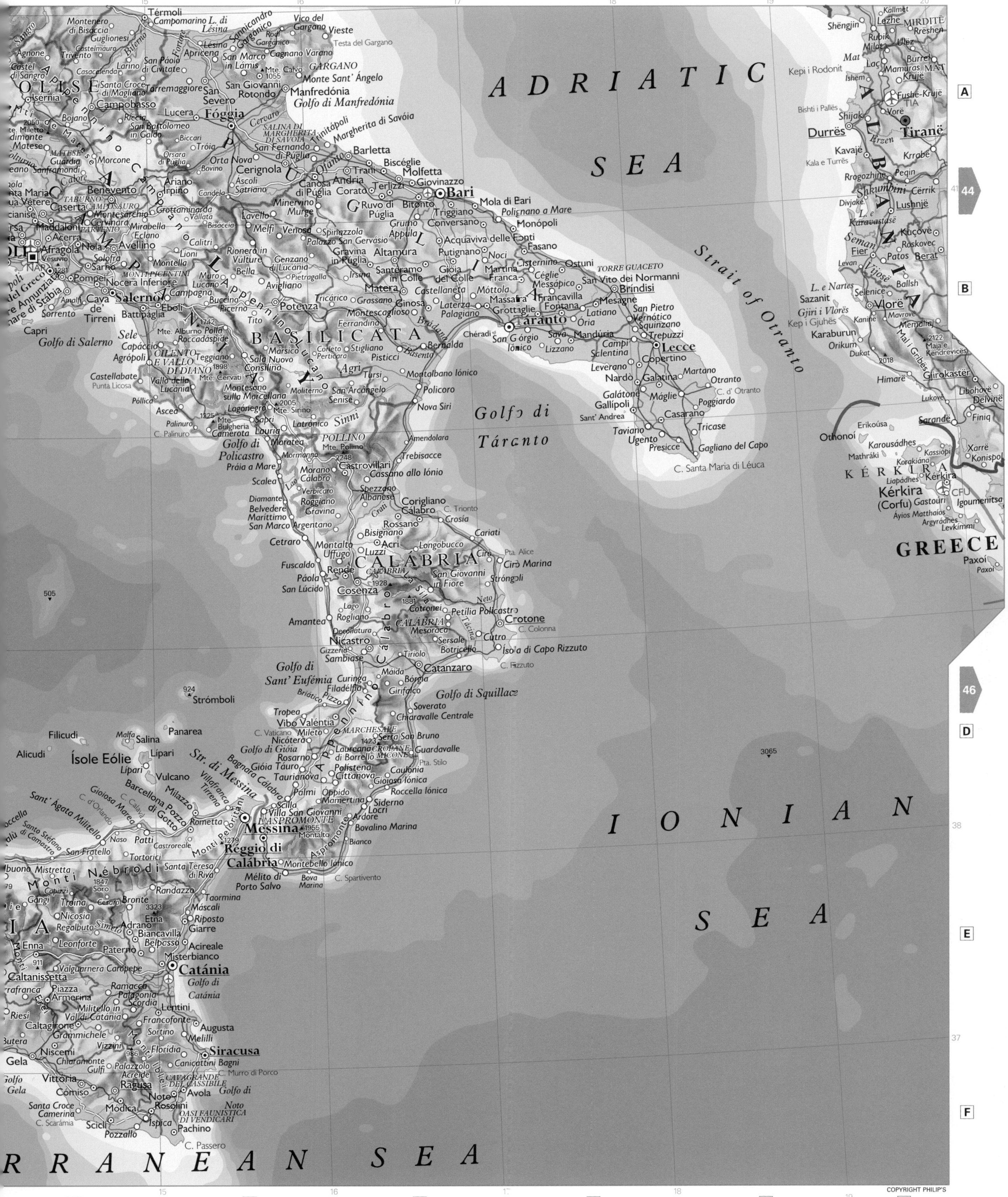
ADRIATIC SEA
IONIAN SEA
MEDITERRANEAN SEA
Strait of Otranto
Golfo di Táranto
Golfo di Manfredónia
Golfo di Salerno
Golfo di Policastro
Golfo di Sant' Eufémia
Golfo di Squillace
Golfo di Gióia
Golfo di Catánia
Golfo di Noto
Golfo di Gela
Str. di Messina
GREECE
ALBANIA
Kérkira (Corfu)
Durrës
Tiranë
Vlorë
Sarandë
Gjirokastër
PUGLIA
BASILICATA
CALÁBRIA
CAMPANIA
MOLISE
SICILIA
GARGANO
Vieste
Manfredónia
Monte Sant' Ángelo
Fóggia
Lucera
Cerignola
Barletta
Trani
Bisceglie
Molfetta
Andria
Bari
Mola di Bari
Polignano a Mare
Monópoli
Fasano
Ostuni
Bríndisi
Lecce
Otranto
Gallípoli
Nardò
Táranto
Martina Franca
Altamura
Gravina in Púglia
Matera
Potenza
Melfi
Avellino
Benevento
Caserta
Nápoli
Salerno
Eboli
Battipáglia
Capri
Campobasso
Isérnia
Termoli
Policoro
Castrovillari
Rossano
Corigliano Cálabro
Cosenza
Crotone
Catanzaro
Vibo Valéntia
Tropea
Reggio di Calábria
Messina
Ísole Eólie
Lípari
Vulcano
Strómboli
Salina
Panarea
Filicudi
Alicudi
Catánia
Acireale
Etna 3323
Enna
Caltanissetta
Piazza Armerina
Caltagirone
Ragusa
Módica
Noto
Siracusa
Augusta
Gela
Vittória
Pachino
Pozzallo
C. Passero
C. Santa Maria di Léuca
C. Spartivento
C. Colonna
C. Rizzuto
C. Vaticano
Nature Parks in Italy
National Parks
COPYRIGHT PHILIP'S

Nature Parks in Italy

National Parks

Underlined towns give their name to the administrative area in which they stand.

10 0 10 20 30 40 50 60 70 80 90 km

1:2 200 000

10 0 10 20 30 40 50 60 miles

28
41
43
46
1 2 3 4 5 6 7
A B C D E F G
CROATIA
BOSNIA-HERZEGOVINA
SERBIA & MONTENEGRO
VOJVODINA
SERBIA
MONTENEGRO
KOSOVO
MACEDONIA
ALBANIA
ITALY
RO
ADRIATIC SEA
Strait of Otranto
Thermaïkós Kólpos
BEOGRAD (Belgrade)
Novi Sad
Sarajevo
Podgorica
Priština
Skopje
Tiranë
SOFIYA GRAD
Thessaloníki (Salonica)
Niš
Kragujevac
Shkodër
Durrës
Vlorë
Bitola
Craiova
Vidin
KENTRIKÍ MAKEDHONÍA
DYTIKÍ MAKEDHONÍA
Kérkira (Corfu)
Lecce
Brindisi
Dubrovnik
Projection : Lambert's Conformal Conic
East from Greenwich

28 41 43 46

Inter-entity boundaries as agreed at the 1995 Dayton Peace Agreement

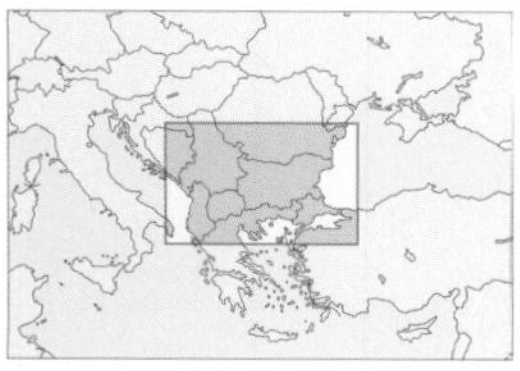

BLACK SEA
TURKEY
BULGARIA
ROMANIA
Marmara Denizi
(Sea of Marmara)
BUCUREŞTI
(Bucharest)
İSTANBUL
Constanţa
Varna
Burgas
Plovdiv
Ruse
Pleven
Shumen
Dobrich
Sliven
Stara Zagora
Haskovo
Edirne
Tekirdağ
Bursa
Çanakkale
Brăila
Galaţi
Tulcea
Ploieşti
Piteşti
Kavála
Thásos
Samothráki
Límnos
Gökçeada
Thrakikón Pélagos
Dunărea
Dunav
Stara Planina
Rodopi
COPYRIGHT PHILIP'S

National Parks

Underlined towns give their name to the administrative area in which they stand.

29
47
72

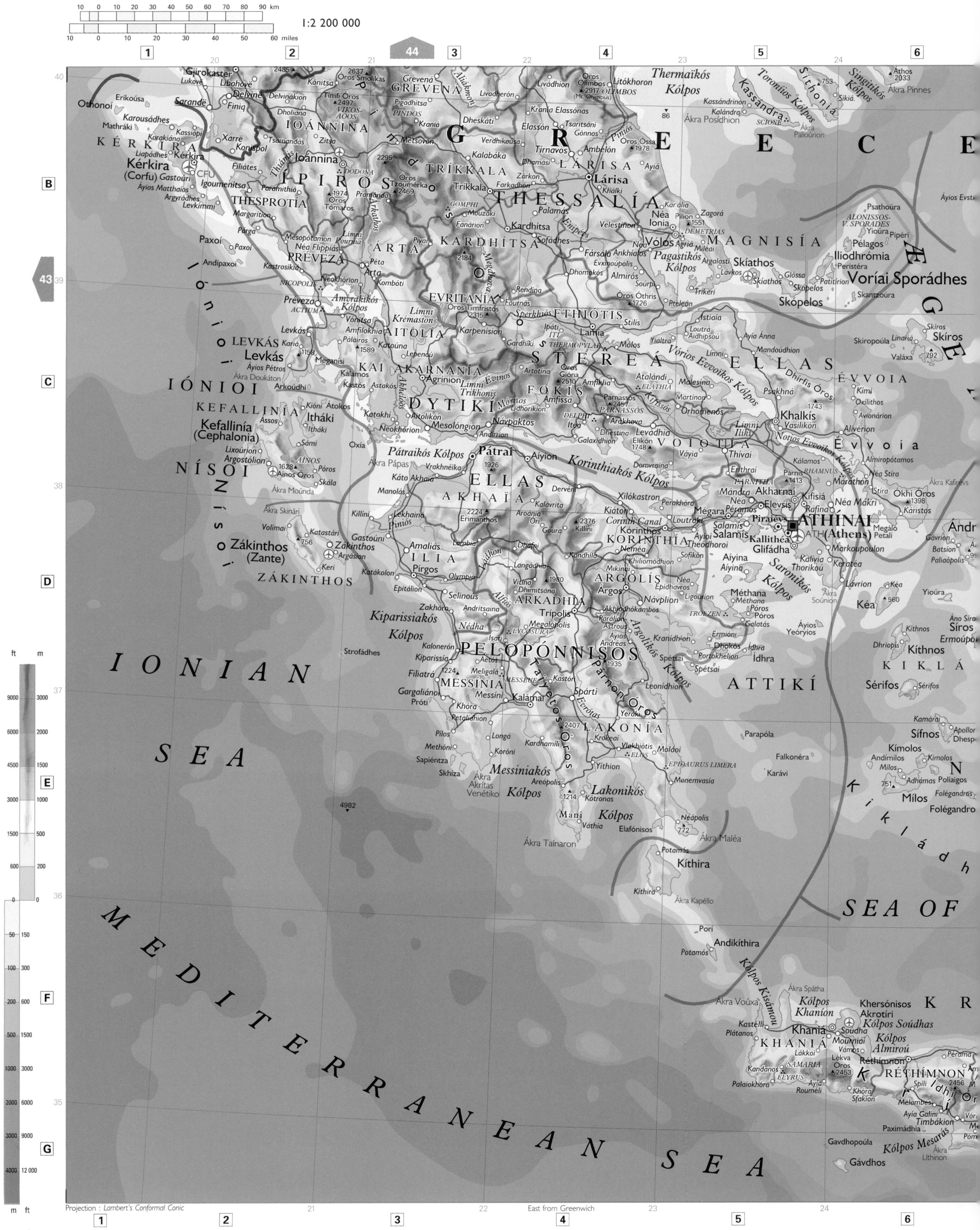

1:2 200 000
10 0 10 20 30 40 50 60 70 80 90 km
10 0 10 20 30 40 50 60 miles
44
43
IONIAN SEA
MEDITERRANEAN SEA
SEA OF
GREECE
Thermaïkós Kólpos
Kassándra
Toronaíos Kólpos
Sithonía
Singitikós Kólpos
Áthos 2033
Ákra Pínnes
Gjirokastër
Sarandë
Othonoí
Erikoúsa
Mathráki
KÉRKIRA
Kérkira (Corfu)
Paxoí
Andípaxoi
IOÁNNINA
Ioánnina
ÍPIROS
THESPROTÍA
PRÉVEZA
Préveza
ÁRTA
Árta
Amvrakikós Kólpos
GREVENÁ
Grevená
TRÍKKALA
Tríkkala
KARDHÍTSA
Kardhítsa
THESSALÍA
LÁRISA
Lárisa
Vólos
MAGNISÍA
Pagastikós Kólpos
Skíathos
Vóriai Sporádhes
Skópelos
Iliodhrómia
EVRITANÍA
FTHIÓTIS
Lamía
STEREÁ ELLÁS
AITOLÍA KAI AKARNANÍA
Agrínion
FOKÍS
VOIOTÍA
Thívai
ÉVVOIA
Évvoia
Khalkís
Skíros
LEVKÁS
Levkás
IÓNIOI NÍSOI
KEFALLINÍA
Itháki
Kefallinía (Cephalonia)
Zákinthos (Zante)
ZÁKINTHOS
Pátraikós Kólpos
Pátrai
Korinthiakós Kólpos
DYTIKÍ ELLÁS
AKHAÏA
ILÍA
Pírgos
KORINTHÍA
Kórinthos
ATHÍNAI (Athens)
Piraiévs
Sarōnikós Kólpos
ARGOLÍS
Árgos
ARKADHÍA
Trípolis
PELOPÓNNISOS
MESSÍNIA
Kalámai
LAKONÍA
Spárti
Kiparissiakós Kólpos
Messiniakós Kólpos
Lakonikós Kólpos
Ákra Taínaron
Ákra Maléa
Kíthira
Andikíthira
ATTIKÍ
Kéa
Kíthnos
Sérifos
Sífnos
Mílos
KIKLÁDHES
Kíklådhes
Khaniá
Kólpos Khaniōn
Kólpos Soúdhas
Rethímnon
RÉTHIMNON
Gávdhos
Gavdhopoúla
Kólpos Mesarás
Strofádhes
4982
Projection : Lambert's Conformal Conic
East from Greenwich

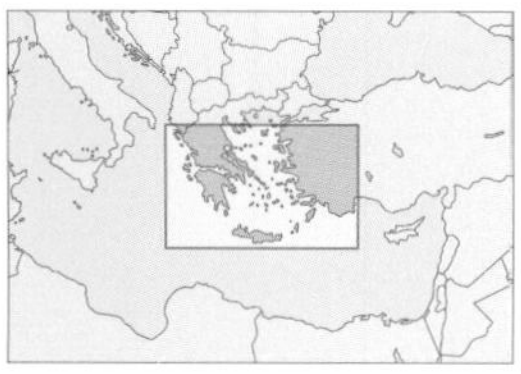

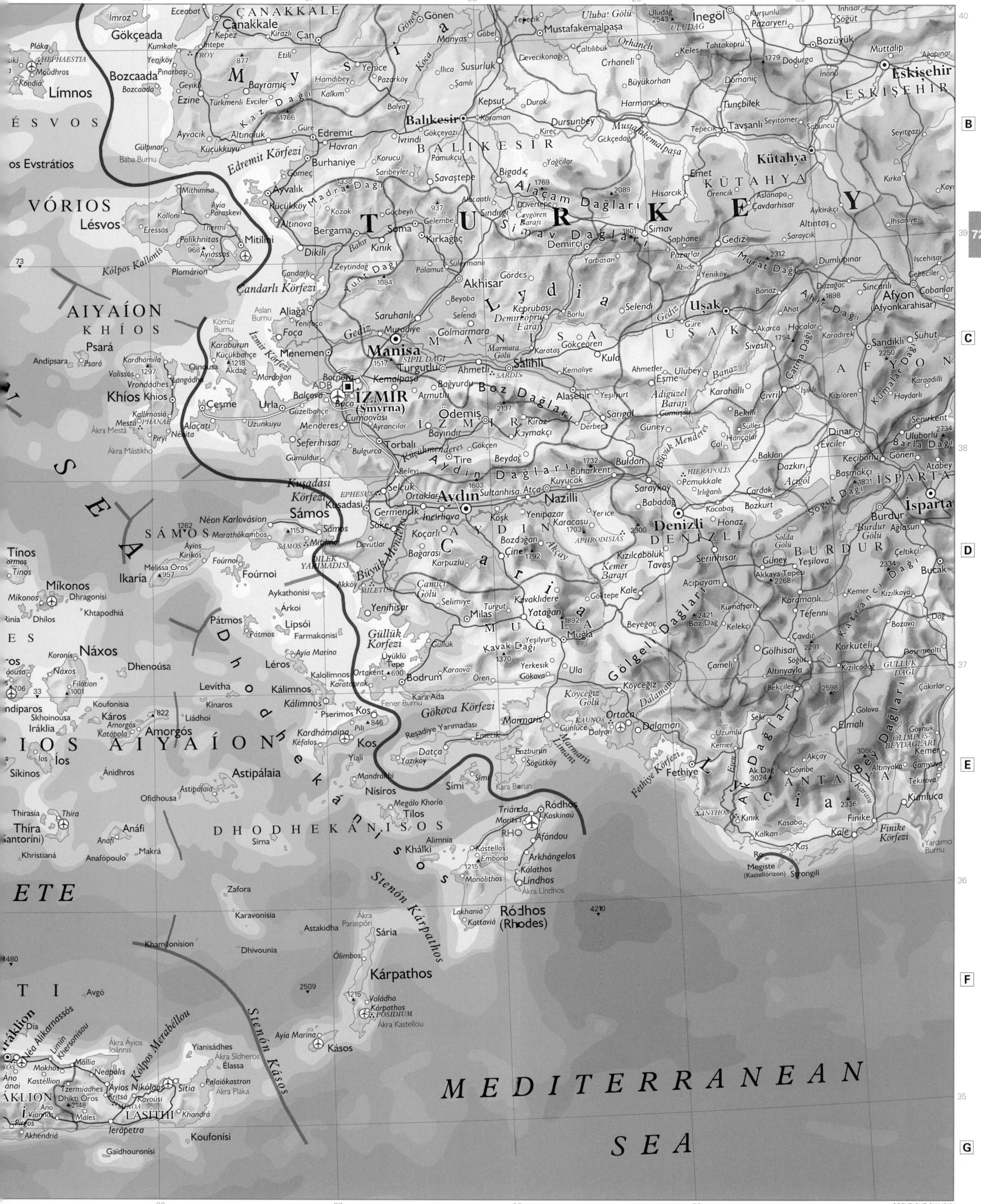
T U R K E Y
AIYAÍON
S E A
MEDITERRANEAN
SEA
DHODHEKÁNISOS
Ródhos (Rhodes)
Kárpathos
Kásos
Sámos
Ikaría
Khíos
Psará
VÓRIOS
Lésvos
Límnos
Gökçeada
Bozcaada
Çanakkale
ÇANAKKALE
Edremit
Edremit Körfezi
Ayvalık
Balıkesir
BALIKESİR
Bergama
Dikili
Çandarlı Körfezi
Aliağa
Foça
Menemen
Manisa
MANİSA
İZMİR
(Smyrna)
İZMİR
Çeşme
Urla
Kuşadası
Kuşadası Körfezi
Selçuk
Aydın
AYDIN
Nazilli
Denizli
DENİZLİ
Uşak
UŞAK
Afyon
(Afyonkarahisar)
AFYON
Kütahya
KÜTAHYA
Eskişehir
ESKİŞEHİR
İnegöl
Bozüyük
Isparta
ISPARTA
Burdur
BURDUR
Muğla
MUĞLA
Milas
Bodrum
Marmaris
Fethiye
Antalya
Kaş
Finike
Gökova Körfezi
Güllük Körfezi
Akhisar
Salihli
Alaşehir
Ödemiş
Söke
Didim
Datça
Kos
Kálimnos
Léros
Pátmos
Náxos
Mílos
Amorgós
Astipálaia
Thíra
Sími
Tílos
Khálki
Líndhos
Lydia
Caria
Lycia
Mysia
Boz Dağları
Simav Dağları
Aydın Dağları
Murat Dağı
Büyük Menderes
Gediz
Stenón Kárpathos
Stenón Kásos
Kólpos Merabéllou
Iráklion
Áyios Nikólaos
Sitía
Ierápetra
Koufonísi
Gaidhouronísi
Dhíkti Óros
2148
4210
2509
Uludağ
2543
SIPIL DAĞI
SARDIS
EPHESUS
MILETUS
APHRODISIAS
HIERAPOLIS
TROY
PHANAE
XANTHOS
POSIDIUM
7 8 9 10 11 12
26 27 28 29 30
40 39 38 37 36 35
B C D E F G
45
72

National Parks

Balearic Islands
Madeira
Canary Islands

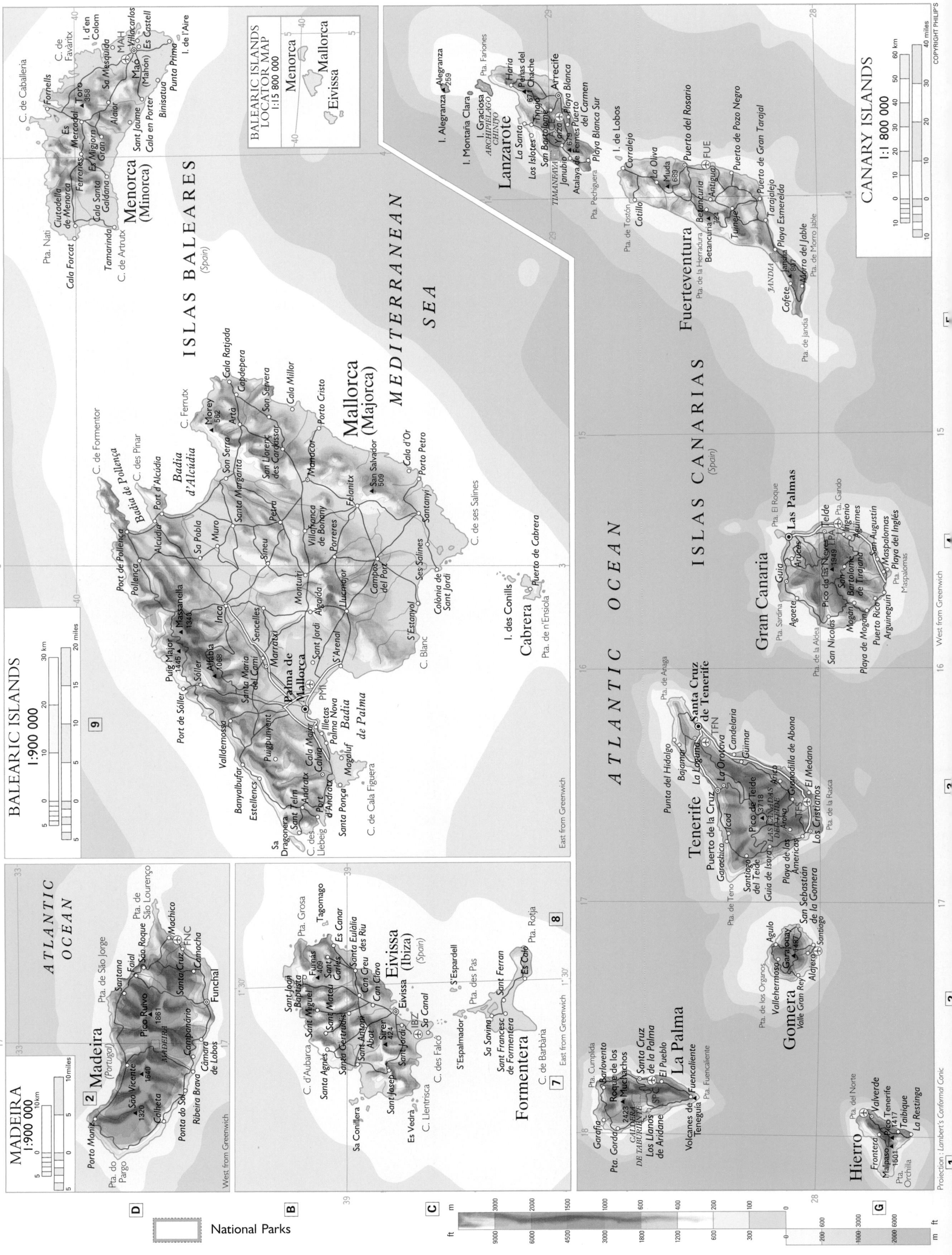

BALEARIC ISLANDS
1:900 000
ISLAS BALEARES
(Spain)
Menorca
(Minorca)
Mallorca
(Majorca)
Eivissa
(Ibiza)
Formentera
Cabrera
MEDITERRANEAN
SEA
BALEARIC ISLANDS
LOCATOR MAP
1:15 800 000
Palma de Mallorca
Badia de Palma
Badia de Pollença
Badia d'Alcúdia
Mao (Mahón)
Ciutadella de Menorca
Alcúdia
Manacor
Inca
Sóller
Puig Major
Eivissa
Sant Antoni
CANARY ISLANDS
1:1 800 000
ISLAS CANARIAS
(Spain)
ATLANTIC OCEAN
Lanzarote
Fuerteventura
Gran Canaria
Tenerife
Gomera
La Palma
Hierro
Arrecife
Puerto del Rosario
Las Palmas
Santa Cruz de Tenerife
Pico de Teide
San Sebastián de la Gomera
Santa Cruz de la Palma
Valverde
MADEIRA
1:900 000
Madeira
(Portugal)
ATLANTIC OCEAN
Funchal
Pico Ruivo
Projection : Lambert's Conformal Conic
COPYRIGHT PHILIP'S

National Parks

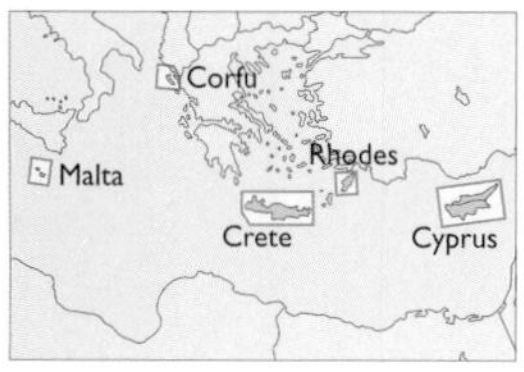
Corfu
Malta
Rhodes
Crete
Cyprus

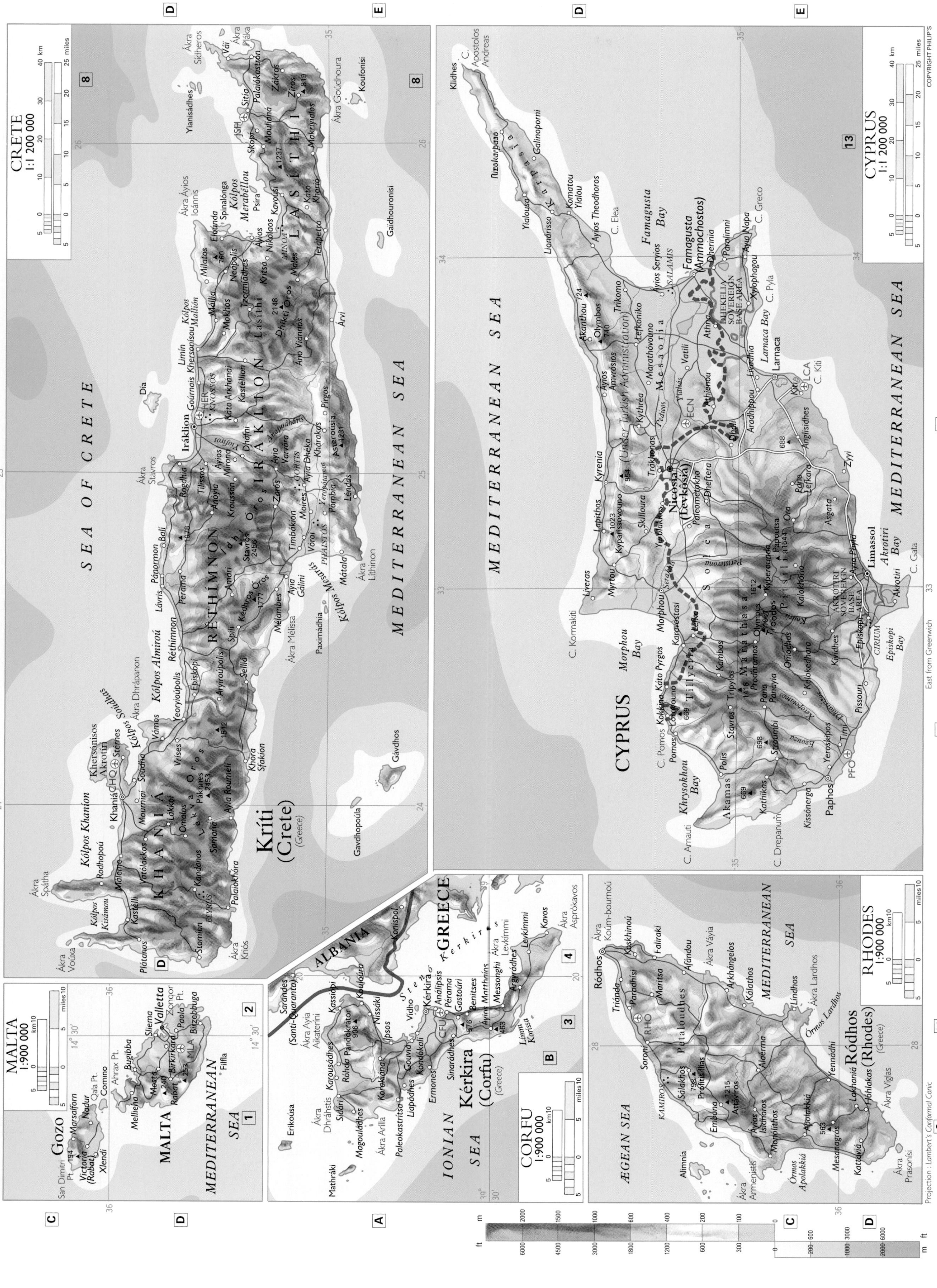
CRETE
1:1 200 000
Kríti
(Crete)
(Greece)
SEA OF CRETE
MEDITERRANEAN SEA
CYPRUS
1:1 200 000
CYPRUS
MEDITERRANEAN SEA
MALTA
1:900 000
Gozo
MALTA
MEDITERRANEAN SEA
CORFU
1:900 000
Kérkira
(Corfu)
(Greece)
IONIAN SEA
ALBANIA
GREECE
RHODES
1:900 000
Ródhos
(Rhodes)
(Greece)
ÆGEAN SEA
MEDITERRANEAN SEA
Projection : Lambert's Conformal Conic
East from Greenwich
COPYRIGHT PHILIP'S

1:44 400 000

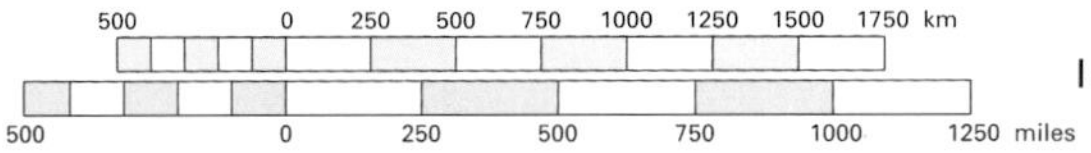
500 0 250 500 750 1000 1250 1500 1750 km
500 0 250 500 750 1000 1250 miles

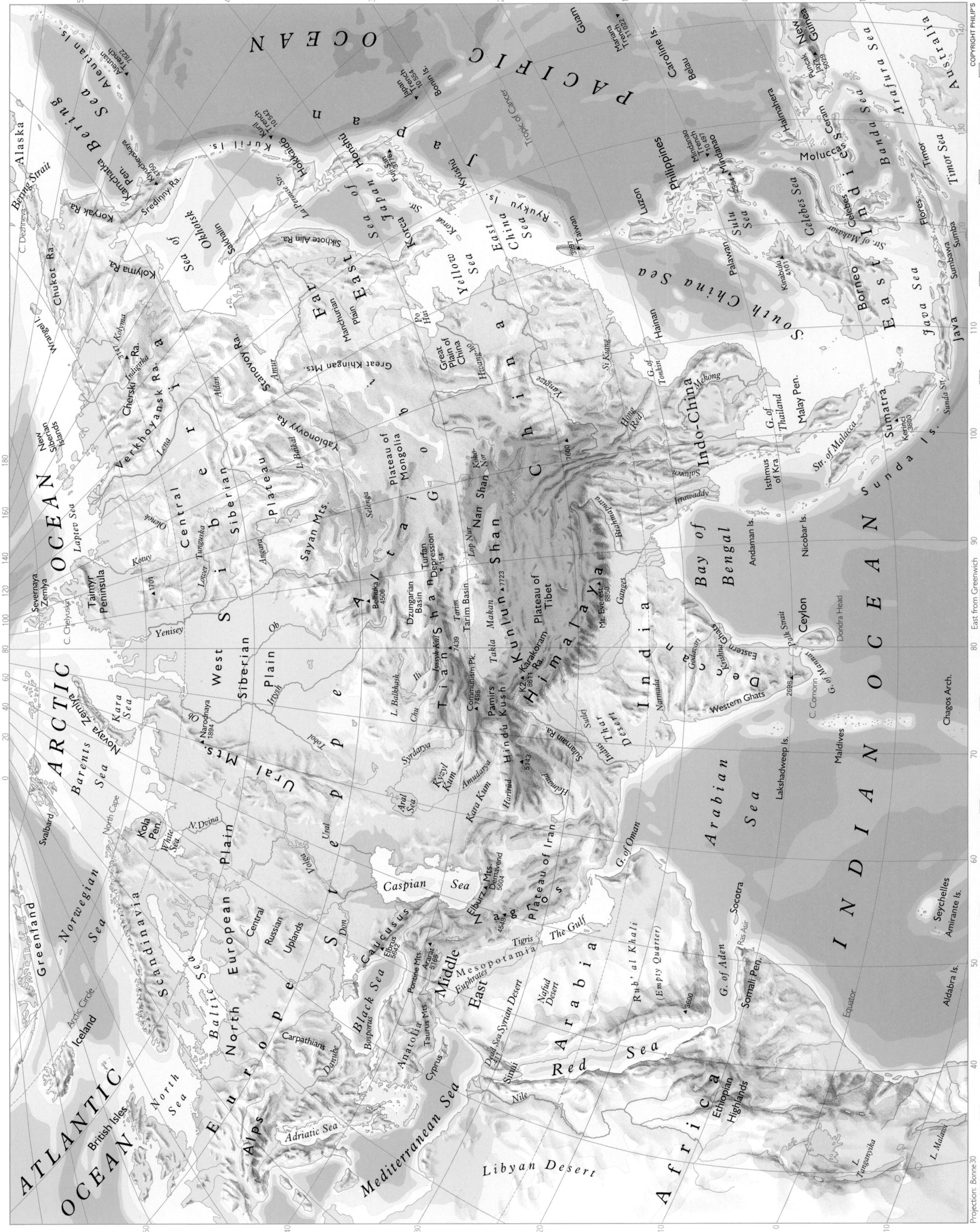
ARCTIC OCEAN
PACIFIC OCEAN
INDIAN OCEAN
ATLANTIC OCEAN
Bay of Bengal
Arabian Sea
South China Sea
East China Sea
Yellow Sea
Sea of Japan
Sea of Okhotsk
Bering Sea
Barents Sea
Kara Sea
Laptev Sea
Norwegian Sea
North Sea
Baltic Sea
Black Sea
Caspian Sea
Mediterranean Sea
Red Sea
Aral Sea
The Gulf
G. of Oman
G. of Aden
Java Sea
Banda Sea
Arafura Sea
Timor Sea
Celebes Sea
Sulu Sea
Himalaya
Plateau of Tibet
Kunlun Shan
Tian Shan
Altai
Gobi
Plateau of Mongolia
Central Siberian Plateau
West Siberian Plain
Ural Mts.
North European Plain
Steppe
Arabia
India
China
Indo-China
Europe
Africa
Libyan Desert
Mt. Everest 8850
K2 8611
Japan
Philippines
Borneo
Sumatra
Java
New Guinea
Ceylon
Maldives
Tropic of Cancer
Arctic Circle
Equator
East from Greenwich
Projection: Bonne
COPYRIGHT PHILIP'S

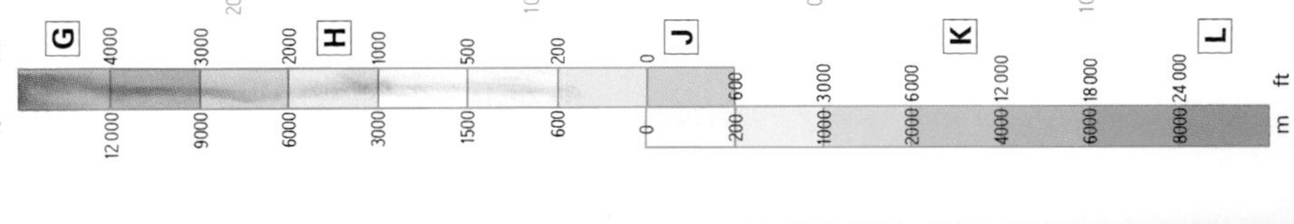
m 4000 3000 2000 1000 500 200 0
ft 12 000 9000 6000 3000 1500 600 0
200 600 | 1000 3000 | 2000 6000 | 4000 12 000 | 6000 18 000 | 8000 24 000
m ft

1:44 400 000

500 0 250 500 750 1000 1250 1500 1750 km

500 0 250 500 750 1000 1250 miles

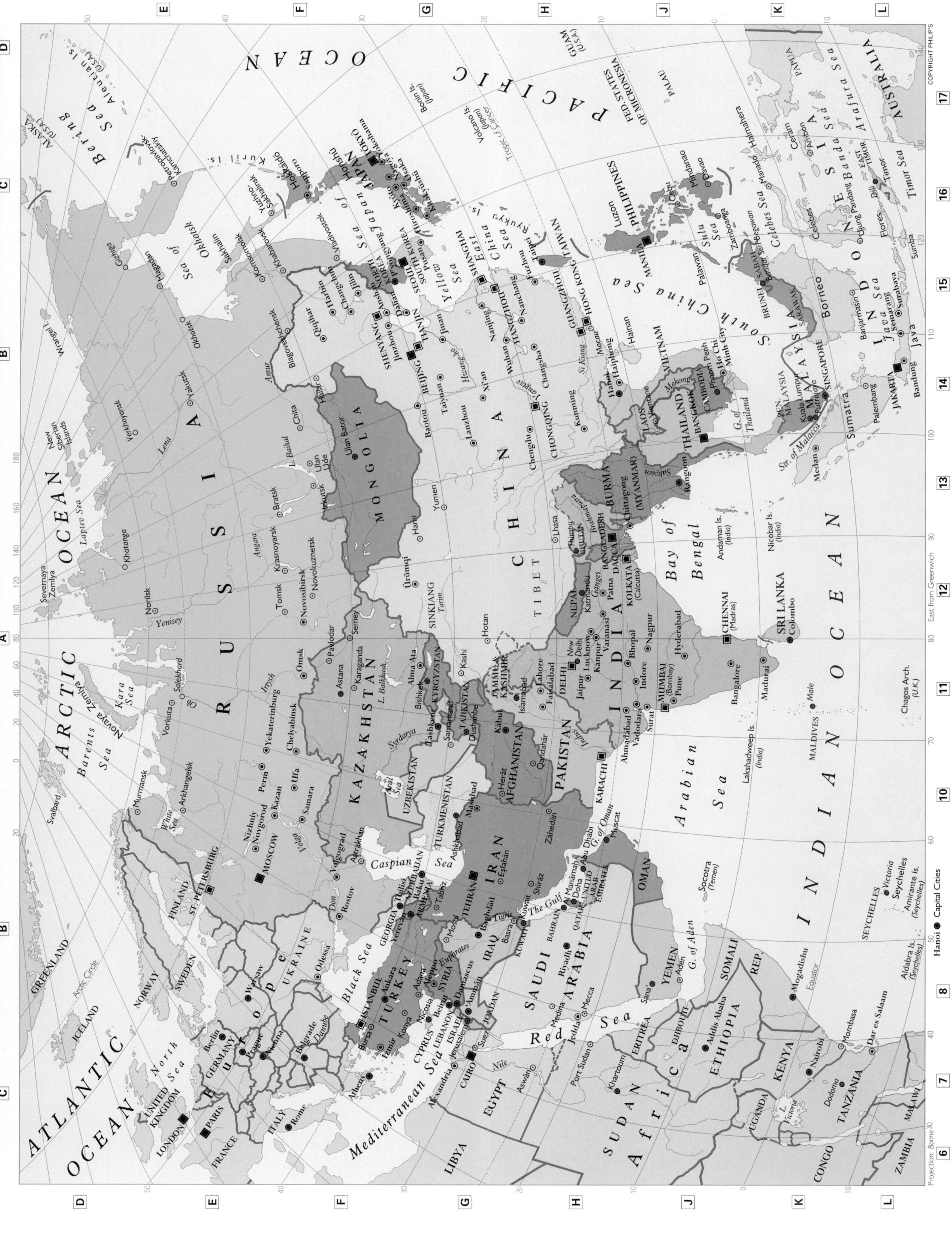
ARCTIC OCEAN
PACIFIC OCEAN
INDIAN OCEAN
ATLANTIC OCEAN
R U S S I A
C H I N A
I N D I A
K A Z A K H S T A N
M O N G O L I A
I N D O N E S I A
MALAYSIA
JAPAN
NORTH KOREA
SOUTH KOREA
TAIWAN
PHILIPPINES
VIETNAM
LAOS
THAILAND
CAMBODIA
BURMA (MYANMAR)
BANGLADESH
BHUTAN
NEPAL
SRI LANKA
MALDIVES
PAKISTAN
AFGHANISTAN
IRAN
IRAQ
SAUDI ARABIA
YEMEN
OMAN
UNITED ARAB EMIRATES
QATAR
BAHRAIN
KUWAIT
JORDAN
ISRAEL
LEBANON
SYRIA
CYPRUS
TURKEY
GEORGIA
ARMENIA
AZERBAIJAN
TURKMENISTAN
UZBEKISTAN
TAJIKISTAN
KYRGYZSTAN
JAMMU & KASHMIR
TIBET
SINKIANG
E u r o p e
A f r i c a
EGYPT
SUDAN
ERITREA
DJIBOUTI
ETHIOPIA
SOMALI REP.
KENYA
TANZANIA
UGANDA
LIBYA
FRANCE
UNITED KINGDOM
GERMANY
ITALY
UKRAINE
FINLAND
SWEDEN
NORWAY
ICELAND
GREENLAND
ALASKA (USA)
AUSTRALIA
PAPUA
BRUNEI
SABAH
SARAWAK
SINGAPORE
EAST TIMOR
FED. STATES OF MICRONESIA
PALAU
GUAM (USA)
SEYCHELLES
Caspian Sea
Black Sea
Mediterranean Sea
Red Sea
Arabian Sea
Bay of Bengal
South China Sea
East China Sea
Yellow Sea
Sea of Japan
Sea of Okhotsk
Bering Sea
Laptev Sea
Kara Sea
Barents Sea
North Sea
Java Sea
Banda Sea
Celebes Sea
Sulu Sea
Arafura Sea
Timor Sea
G. of Aden
G. of Oman
G. of Thailand
The Gulf
Aral Sea
L. Baikal
L. Balkhash
MOSCOW
ST. PETERSBURG
BEIJING
SHANGHAI
TIANJIN
CHONGQING
HONG KONG
TOKYO
SEOUL
PYONGYANG
MANILA
BANGKOK
JAKARTA
SINGAPORE
DELHI
New Delhi
MUMBAI (Bombay)
KOLKATA (Calcutta)
CHENNAI (Madras)
DACCA
KARACHI
TEHRAN
ISTANBUL
CAIRO
LONDON
PARIS
Ulan Bator
Kabul
Islamabad
Katmandu
Colombo
Rangoon
Hanoi
Kuala Lumpur
Riyadh
Baghdad
Ankara
Damascus
Beirut
Amman
Jerusalem
Tbilisi
Yerevan
Baku
Ashkhabad
Tashkent
Dushanbe
Bishkek
Astana
Rome
Athens
Berlin
Warsaw
Prague
Vienna
Belgrade
Nairobi
Addis Ababa
Khartoum
Mogadishu
Sana
Muscat
Abu Dhabi
Doha
Manamah
Kuwait
Hanoi ● Capital Cities
Projection: Bonne
East from Greenwich
Equator
Arctic Circle
Tropic of Cancer
COPYRIGHT PHILIP'S

1:17 800 000

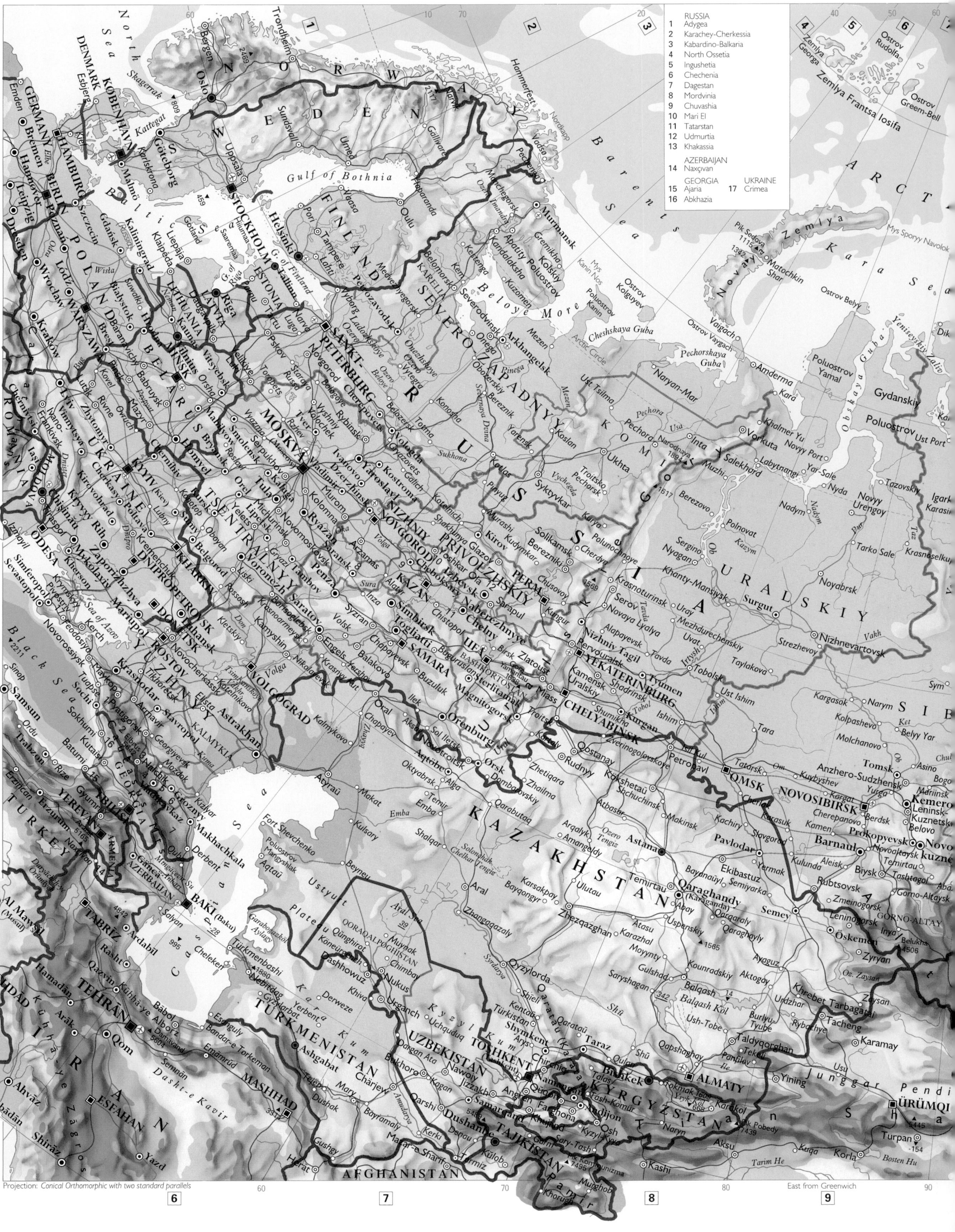
RUSSIA
1 Adygea
2 Karachey-Cherkessia
3 Kabardino-Balkaria
4 North Ossetia
5 Ingushetia
6 Chechenia
7 Dagestan
8 Mordvinia
9 Chuvashia
10 Mari El
11 Tatarstan
12 Udmurtia
13 Khakassia
AZERBAIJAN
14 Naxçıvan
GEORGIA
15 Ajaria
16 Abkhazia
UKRAINE
17 Crimea
NORWAY
SWEDEN
FINLAND
ESTONIA
LATVIA
LITHUANIA
BELARUS
POLAND
UKRAINE
MOLDOVA
ROMANIA
GERMANY
DENMARK
TURKEY
GEORGIA
ARMENIA
AZERBAIJAN
IRAQ
IRAN
TURKMENISTAN
UZBEKISTAN
TAJIKISTAN
KYRGYZSTAN
AFGHANISTAN
KAZAKHSTAN
RUSSIA
SEVERO-ZAPADNYY
TSENTRALNYY
PRIVOLZHSKIY
YUZHNYY
URALSKIY
KOMI
Barents Sea
Kara Sea
Beloye More
Gulf of Bothnia
Baltic Sea
Black Sea
Sea of Azov
Caspian Sea
Aral Sea
North Sea
MOSKVA
SANKT-PETERBURG
KYIV
ASTANA
ALMATY
TEHRAN
BAKI
TBILISI
YEREVAN
BISHKEK
TASHKENT
DUSHANBE
ASHGABAT
Projection: Conical Orthomorphic with two standard parallels
East from Greenwich

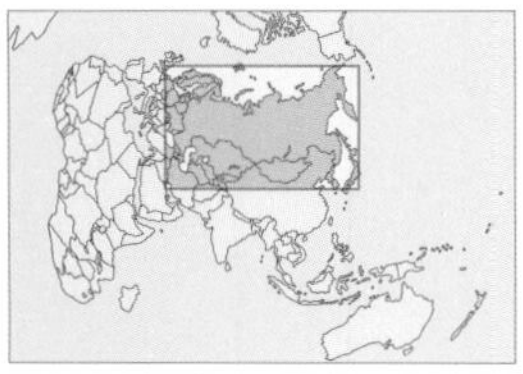

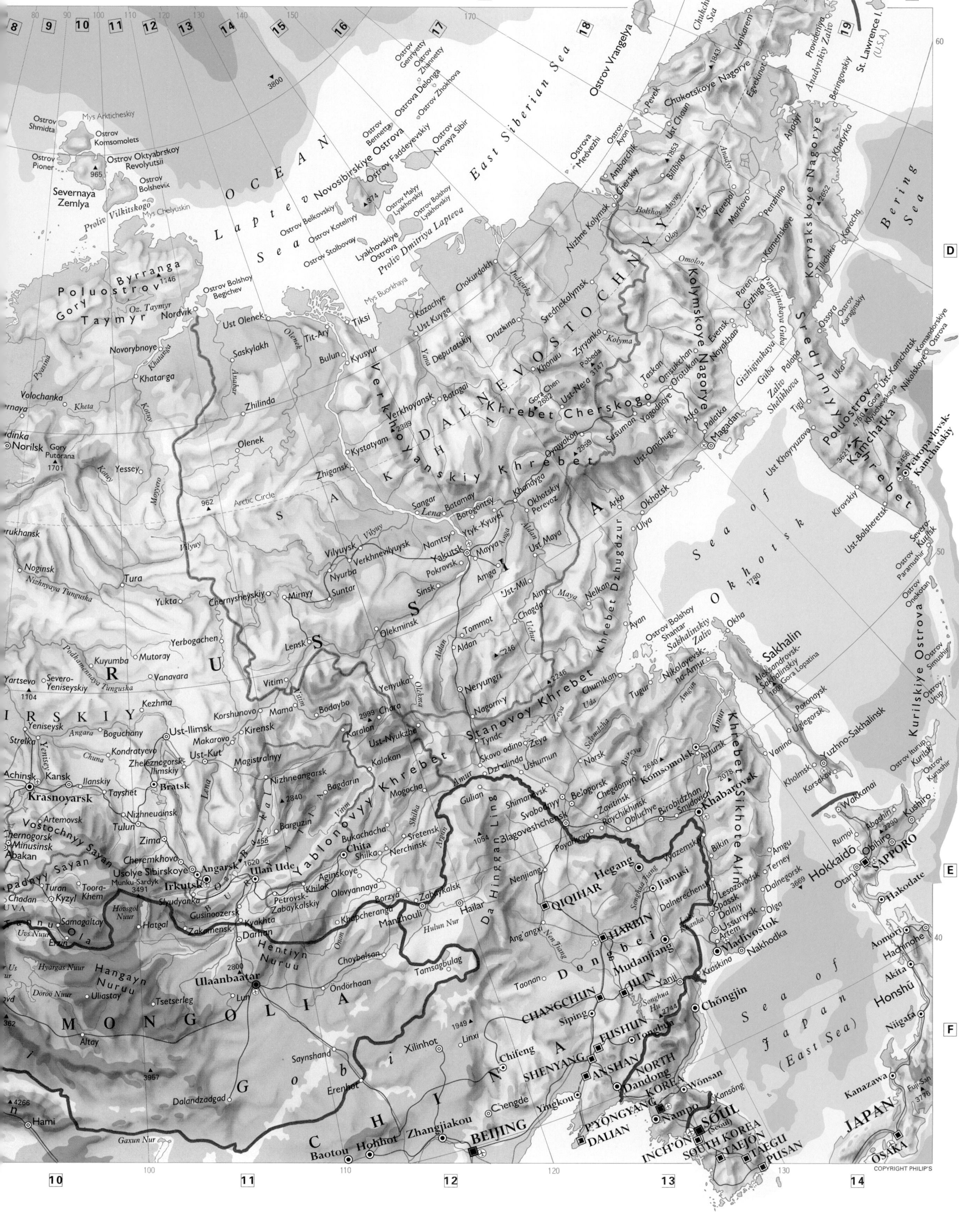
A
B
C
D
E
F
10
11
12
13
14
East Siberian Sea
Laptev Sea
Sea of Okhotsk
Sea of Japan (East Sea)
Bering Sea
Chukchi Sea
Severnaya Zemlya
Ostrov Vrangelya
Novosibirskiye Ostrova
Poluostrov Taymyr
Poluostrov Kamchatka
Sakhalin
Hokkaidō
Honshū
Kurilskiye Ostrova
Verkhoyanskiy Khrebet
Khrebet Cherskogo
Kolymskoye Nagorye
Chukotskoye Nagorye
Koryakskoye Nagorye
Sredinnyy Khrebet
Stanovoy Khrebet
Yablonovyy Khrebet
Khrebet Dzhugdzur
Khrebet Sikhote Alin
Da Hinggan Ling
Vostochnyy Sayan
Hangayn Nuruu
Hentiyn Nuruu
Gobi
MONGOLIA
CHINA
RUSSIA
NORTH KOREA
SOUTH KOREA
JAPAN
Ulaanbaatar
BEIJING
HARBIN
CHANGCHUN
SHENYANG
P'YONGYANG
SŎUL
Vladivostok
Khabarovsk
Yakutsk
Magadan
Petropavlovsk-Kamchatskiy
Irkutsk
Krasnoyarsk
Norilsk
Bratsk
Chita
Ulan Ude
SAPPORO
Arctic Circle
Mys Dezhneva (East C.)
St. Lawrence I. (U.S.A.)
COPYRIGHT PHILIP'S

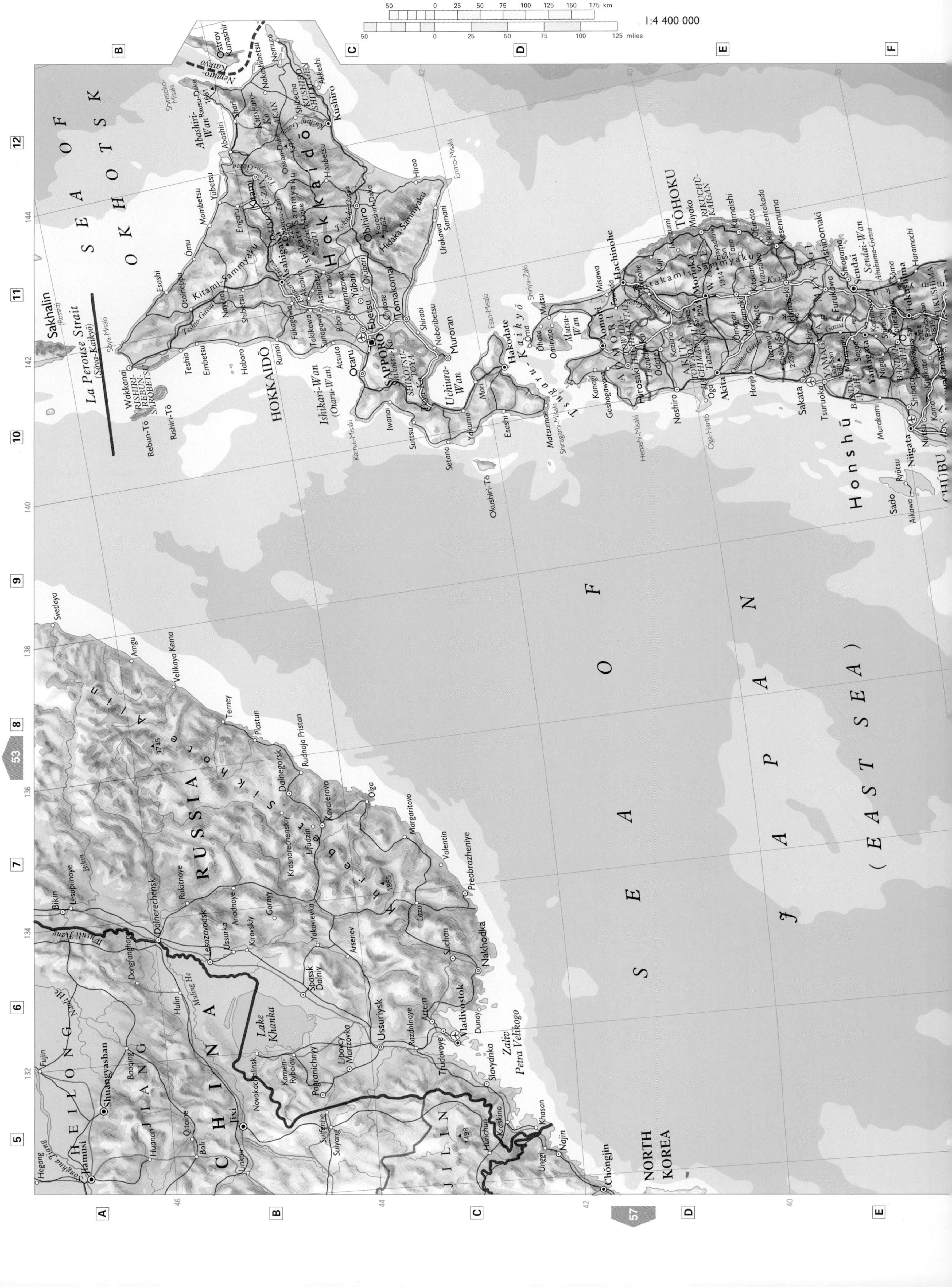
1:4 400 000
km
miles
SEA OF OKHOTSK
SEA OF JAPAN (EAST SEA)
HOKKAIDŌ
Hokkaidō
Honshū
TŌHOKU
RUSSIA
CHINA
NORTH KOREA
HEILONGJIANG
JILIN
Sakhalin
La Perouse Strait (Sōya-Kaikyō)
Tsugaru-Kaikyō
SAPPORO
Asahikawa
Hakodate
Muroran
Otaru
Kushiro
Obihiro
Abashiri
Nemuro
Wakkanai
Aomori
Hachinohe
Morioka
Akita
Sendai
Yamagata
Sakata
Niigata
Fukushima
Ishinomaki
Miyako
Kamaishi
Hirosaki
Noshiro
Sado
Okushiri-Tō
Rishiri-Tō
Rebun-Tō
Vladivostok
Nakhodka
Ussuriysk
Dalnerechensk
Lesozavodsk
Spassk-Dalniy
Arsenev
Olga
Terney
Plastun
Svetlaya
Lake Khanka
Zaliv Petra Velikogo
Jiamusi
Shuangyashan
Jixi
Chŏngjin
Najin
Hunchun

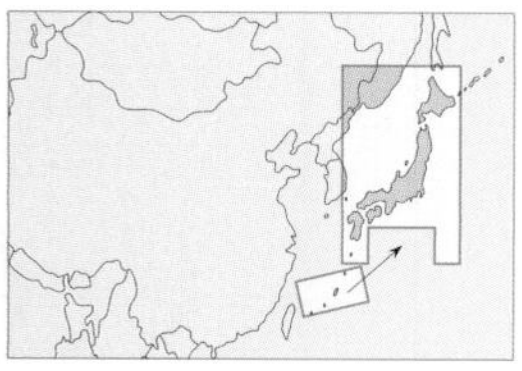

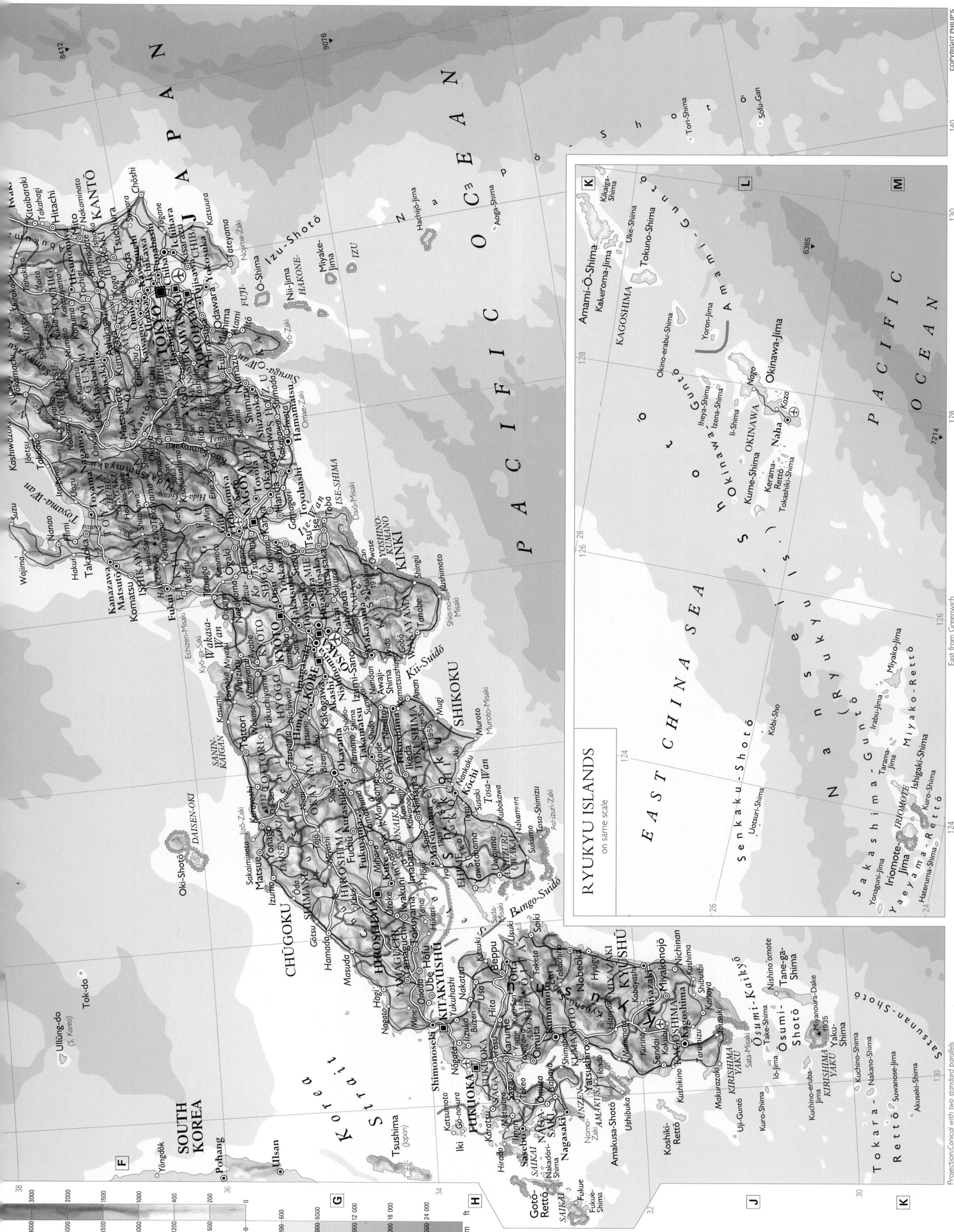
PACIFIC OCEAN
SEA OF JAPAN
EAST CHINA SEA
RYUKYU ISLANDS
on same scale
SOUTH KOREA
Korea Strait
CHŪGOKU
SHIKOKU
KYŪSHŪ
KINKI
KANTŌ
TŌKYŌ
YOKOHAMA
NAGOYA
ŌSAKA
KŌBE
KYŌTO
HIROSHIMA
FUKUOKA
KITAKYŪSHŪ
Nagasaki
Kagoshima
Okinawa-Jima
Naha
Amami-Ō-Shima
Izu-Shotō
Hachijō-Jima
Tokara-Rettō
Ōsumi-Shotō
Satsunan-Shotō
Nansei-Shotō (Ryukyu Is.)
Sakishima-Guntō
Yaeyama-Rettō
Miyako-Rettō
Tsushima (Japan)
Ullŭng-do (S. Korea)
Tok-do
Oki-Shotō
Projection: Conical with two standard parallels
East from Greenwich
COPYRIGHT PHILIP'S
m
ft

1:5 300 000

50 0 50 100 150 200 km

50 0 50 100 150 miles

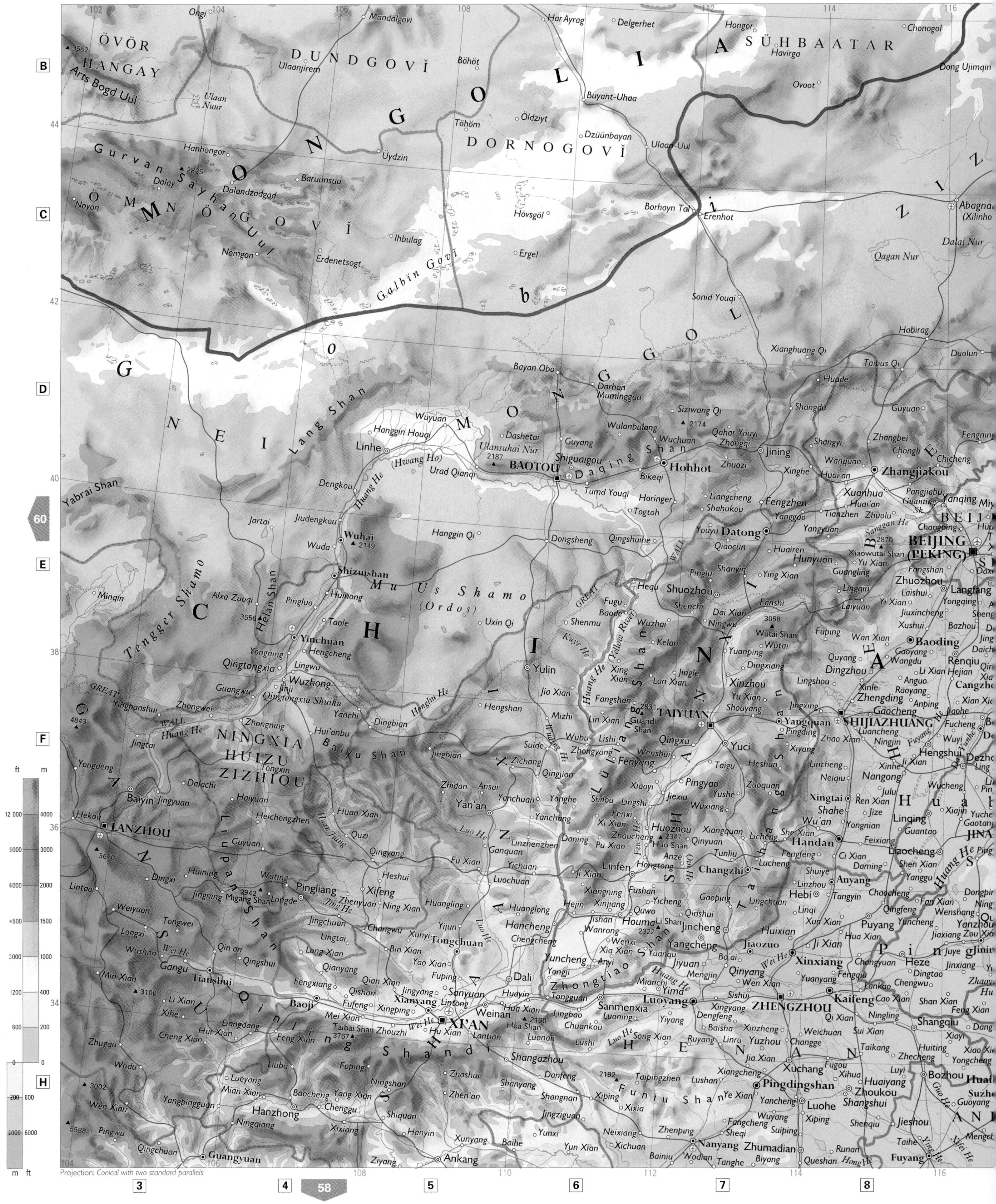

2 3 4 5 6 7 8
53
B C D E F G H
60
58
102 104 106 108 110 112 114 116
44 42 40 38 36 34
ÖVÖR HANGAY
Arts Bogd Uul
DUNDGOVĬ
Mandalgovĭ
Ulaanjirem
Ongi
Ulaan Nuur
Böhöt
Har Ayrag
Delgerhet
Hongor
SÜHBAATAR
Havirga
Chonogol
Dong Ujimqin
Ovoot
Buyant-Uhaa
Töhöm
Öldziyt
Dzüünbayan
DORNOGOVĬ
Ulaan-Uul
Üydzin
Hanhongor
Gurvan Sayhan Uul
Dalay
Dalandzadgad
Baruunsuu
ÖMNÖGOVĬ
Noyon
Nomgon
Ihbulag
Erdenetsogt
Galbïn Govĭ
Hövsgöl
Ergel
Borhoyn Tal
Erenhot
Abagnar Qi (Xilinhot)
Dalai Nur
Qagan Nur
Sonid Youqi
MONGOLIA
NEI MONGGOL
Habirag
Xianghuang Qi
Taibus Qi
Duolun
Bayan Obo
Darhan Muminggan
Huade
Shangdu
Guyuan
Siziwang Qi
Wulanbulang
Wuchuan
Qahar Youyi Zhongqi
Jining
Shangyi
Zhangbei
Chongli
Fengning
Chicheng
Lang Shan
Wuyuan
Hanggin Houqi
Dashetai
Ulansuhai Nur
Linhe
Huang He (Hwang Ho)
Urad Qianqi
BAOTOU
Shiguaigou
Daqing Shan
Hohhot
Zhuozi
Xinghe
Wanquan
Huai'an
Zhangjiakou
Yabrai Shan
Dengkou
Tumd Youqi
Bikeqi
Horinger
Liangcheng
Shahukou
Fengzhen
Yanggao
Tianzhen
Xuanhua
Zhuolu
Yanqing
Jartai
Jiudengkou
Wuhai
Wuda
Hanggin Qi
Dongsheng
Qingshuihe
Togtoh
Youyu
Datong
Yangyuan
BEIJING (PEKING)
Changping
Sanggan He
Qiaocun
Huairen
Hunyuan
Xiaowutai Shan
Yu Xian
Guangling
Fangshan
Zhuozhou
Langfang
Yongqing
Shizuishan
Mu Us Shamo (Ordos)
Huinong
Pingluo
Alxa Zuoqi
Helan Shan
Minqin
Tengger Shamo
Hequ
Fugu
Baode
Shuozhou
Shenchi
Pinglu
Shanyin
Ying Xian
Fanshi
Dai Xian
Ningwu
Wutai Shan
Wutai
Lingqiu
Laiyuan
Yi Xian
Laishui
Jiuxincheng
Xushui
Baoding
Fuping
Wan Xian
Gaoyang
Wangdu
Renqiu
Dingzhou
Quyang
Li Xian
Hejian
Cangzhou
Taole
Yinchuan
Uxin Qi
Shenmu
Wuzhai
Kelan
Yuanping
Dingxiang
Xinzhou
Yongning
Hengcheng
Qingtongxia
Lingwu
Wuzhong
Guangwu
Jinji
Qingtongxia Shuiku
Yulin
Jia Xian
Xing Xian
Lan Xian
Jingle
Yu Xian
Shouyang
Yangquan
Pingding
SHIJIAZHUANG
Luancheng
Zhengding
Xinle
Gaocheng
Anping
Raoyang
Anguo
Lingshou
Jingxing
Fucheng
Hengshui
Wuyi
Zhao Xian
Ningjin
Yingpanshui
Zhongwei
Zhongning
Yanchi
Dingbian
Honglui He
Hengshan
Mizhi
Fangshan
Guandi Shan
TAIYUAN
Qingxu
Yuci
Lin Xian
Lishi
Wenshui
Fenyang
Taigu
Heshun
Xiyang
NINGXIA HUIZU ZIZHIQU
Huang He
Jingtai
Hui'anbu
Baiyu Shan
Jingbian
Suide
Wubu
Zichang
Qingjian
Zhongyang
Lüliang Shan
Xiaoyi
Pingyao
Jiexiu
Zuoquan
Yushe
Wuxiang
Lincheng
Neiqiu
Nangong
Xingtai
Shahe
Ren Xian
Jize
Yongnian
Wu'an
Handan
She Xian
Licheng
Feixiang
Ci Xian
Fengfeng
Daming
Yongdeng
Tongxin
Dalachi
Baiyin
Jingyuan
Haiyuan
Heichengzhen
Huan Xian
Zhidan
Ansai
Yan'an
Yanchuan
Yonghe
Shilou
Lingshi
Fenxi
Zhaocheng
Huozhou
Huo Shan
Xiangquan
Qinyuan
Tunliu
Changzhi
Lucheng
Hekou
LANZHOU
Guyuan
Quzi
Qingyang
Yanchang
Linzhenzhen
Ganquan
Daning
Xi Xian
Pu Xian
Anze
Liupan Shan
Fu Xian
Yichuan
Luochuan
Ji Xian
Linfen
Hongtong
Huining
Wating
Pingliang
Xifeng
Heshui
Lintao
Dingxi
Jingning
Migang Shan
Longde
Zhenyuan
Ning Xian
Huangling
Huanglong
Hancheng
Xiangning
Fushan
Xinjiang
Yicheng
Quwo
Houma
Qinshui
Jincheng
Gaoping
Lingchuan
Hebi
Tangyin
Anyang
Linqi
Xun Xian
Puyang
Weiyuan
Tongwei
Longxi
Wushan
Wei He
Gangu
Qin'an
Qingshui
Tianshui
Jingchuan
Lingtai
Changwu
Xunyi
Yijun
Tongchuan
Long Xian
Bin Xian
Yao Xian
Qianyang
Fengxiang
Qishan
Fufeng
Baoji
Mei Xian
Qian Xian
Xianyang
Xingping
Lintong
Sanyuan
Fuping
Dali
Weinan
Huayin
Hua Xian
Hua Shan
XI'AN
Hu Xian
Lantian
Zhouzhi
Taibai Shan
Chengcheng
Heyang
Yuncheng
Anyi
Wenxi
Wanrong
Jishan
Xia Xian
Zhongtiao Shan
Yongji
Ruicheng
Mianchi
Sanmenxia
Lingbao
Luoning
Yiyang
Luoyang
Yima
Mengjin
Jiyuan
Qinyang
Wen Xian
Jiaozuo
Huixian
Xinxiang
Ji Xian
Yangcheng
Zhengzhou
ZHENGZHOU
Kaifeng
Xingyang
Dengfeng
Xinzheng
Sishui
Min Xian
Li Xian
Xihe
Liangdang
Hui Xian
Cheng Xian
Feng Xian
Qinling Shandi
Zhugqu
Wudu
Liuba
Foping
Ningshan
Zhashui
Shanyang
Danfeng
Shangzhou
Shangnan
Xiping
Xixia
Funiu Shan
Lueyang
Mian Xian
Baocheng
Yang Xian
Chenggu
Hanzhong
Xixiang
Shiquan
Hanyin
Zhen'an
Xunyang
Baihe
Yunxi
Yun Xian
Ankang
Ziyang
Pingwu
Qingchuan
Guangyuan
Wen Xian
Ningqiang
Yangpingguan
Neixiang
Xichuan
Zhenping
Nanyang
Fangcheng
Sheqi
Tanghe
Biyang
Zhumadian
Bainiu
Wodian
Ruyang
Linru
Yuzhou
Jia Xian
Xuchang
Pingdingshan
Lushan
Ye Xian
Xiangcheng
Taipingzhen
Yancheng
Luohe
Wuyang
Suiping
Xiping
Shangshui
Zhoukou
Huaiyang
Xihua
Fugou
Luyi
Bozhou
Zhecheng
Taikang
Sui Xian
Weichuan
Changge
Qi Xian
Ningling
Shangqiu
Shan Xian
Heze
Dingtao
Chengwu
Lankao
Fengqiu
Changyuan
Yuanyang
Queshan
Runan
Shenqiu
Jieshou
Taihe
Fuyang
Mengcheng
Xiayi
Yongcheng
Huiting
Guoyang
Dongming
Juye
Jinxiang
Zou Xian
Fan Xian
Wenshang
Qingfeng
Nanle
Guantao
Linqing
Liaocheng
Shen Xian
Yanggu
Huang He
Jiaxiang
Yuncheng
Hua Xian
Xiajin
Yucheng
Julu
Wucheng
Dezhou
Jingxian
Gucheng
HEBEI
HENAN
SHANXI
SHAANXI
GANSU
SHANDONG
3582 2825 2187 2174 2149 2870 3058 3556 4843 2831 2347 2322 2942 3670 3100 3767 2160 2192 3002 5588
GREAT WALL
Fen He
Luo He
Jing He
Huan Jiang
Kuye He
Wuding He
Qin He
Yellow River
ft m
12 000 4000
9000 3000
6000 2000
4500 1500
3000 1000
1200 400
600 200
0 0
200 600
2000 6000
m ft

Projection: Conical with two standard parallels

3 4 58 5 6 7 8

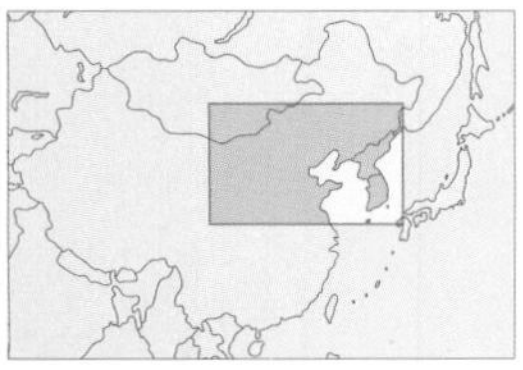

9 10 11 12 13 14 15 16

HARBIN
Bin Xian
Acheng
Shuangcheng
Yanshou
Shangzhi
Lalin
Wuchang
Yimianpo
Hengdaohezi
Mudanjiang
Hailin
Ning'an
Zhangguangcai Ling
Linkou
Jixi
Muling
Turiy Rog
Lake Khanka
Maqiaohe
Xiachengzi
Pogranichnyy
Suifenhe
Suiyang
Dongning
Golenki
Ussuriysk
Razdolnoye
Artem
Tavrichanka
Vladivostok
Slavyanka
Posyet
Kraskino
Hunchun
Tumen
Shixian
Daxinggou
Dunhua
Wangqing
Yanji
Longjing
Helong
Mingyuegue
Antu
Baihe
Changbai Shan
Paektu-san
Hoeryong
Unggi
Sŏsura
Najin
Musan
Puryong
Pugŏdong
Nanam
Chŏngjin
Kyŏngsŏng
Chuuronjang
Ondaejin
Hyesan
Kilchu
Musudan
Kimch'aek (Songjin)
Tanch'ŏn
Pukch'ŏng
Sinch'ang
Hongwon
Hamhung
Hŭngnam
NORTH KOREA
SEA OF JAPAN (EAST SEA)
Tongjosŏn Man
Wŏnsan
Anbyŏn
Kosŏng
Kansŏng
Sokch'o
Yangyang
Kangnŭng
Samch'ŏk
Ullŭng-do (S. Korea)
Ulchin
P'YŎNGYANG
Namp'o
Sariwŏn
Haeju
Kaesŏng
Panmunjŏm
Ongjin
SOUL
INCH'ŎN
Suwŏn
Wŏnju
SOUTH KOREA
TAEJŎN
Chŏngju
Andong
P'ohang
Kyŏngju
TAEGU
Ulsan
PUSAN
Masan
Chinju
KWANGJU
Chŏnju
Kunsan
Mokp'o
Yŏsu
Tsushima
Korea Strait
Hŭksan-chedo (S. Korea)
Cheju-do (S. Korea)
Cheju
Halla-san
Sŏgwipo
JAPAN
Sasebo
Nagasaki
Fukue-Shima
Nakadōri-Shima
Karatsu
Iki
HEILONGJIANG
JILIN
CHANGCHUN
Jiutai
Dehui
Nong'an
Fuyu
Songyuan
Qian'an
Da'an
Baicheng
Taonan
Tuquan
Horqin Youyi Qianqi (Ulanhot)
Hulingol
Jarud Qi
Tongliao
Shuangliao
Siping
Gongzhuling
Liaoyuan
Meihekou
Tonghua
Ji'an
Manp'o
Kanggye
Siping
Tieling
Kaiyuan
SHENYANG
FUSHUN
Benxi
Liaoyang
ANSHAN
Haicheng
Dandong
Sinŭiju
Yingkou
Fuxin
Chifeng
Chaoyang
Jinzhou
Huludao
Xingcheng
Suizhong
Qinhuangdao
Chengde
Tangshan
Tianjin Shi
TIANJIN
Tanggu
LIAONING
Liaodong Wan
Liaodong Bandao
Wafangdian
Pulandian
Jin Xian
DALIAN
Lüshun
Korea Bay
Bo Hai
Miaodao Qundao
Yantai
Weihai
Wendeng
Rongcheng
Chengshan Jiao
Laizhou Wan
Longkou
Laiyang
Shandong Bandao
Weifang
ZIBO
Dongying
Binzhou
Qingdao
Jimo
Jiaozhou
Zhucheng
Rizhao
Linyi
Lianyungang
Xuzhou
Zaozhuang
JIANGSU
Huaiyin
Yancheng
Dongtai
YELLOW SEA (Huang Hai)
East from Greenwich
COPYRIGHT PHILIP'S

9 10 11 12 13 14 15

55

59

50 0 50 100 150 200 km

1:5 300 000

50 0 50 100 150 miles

1 2 3 4 5 6 7

56

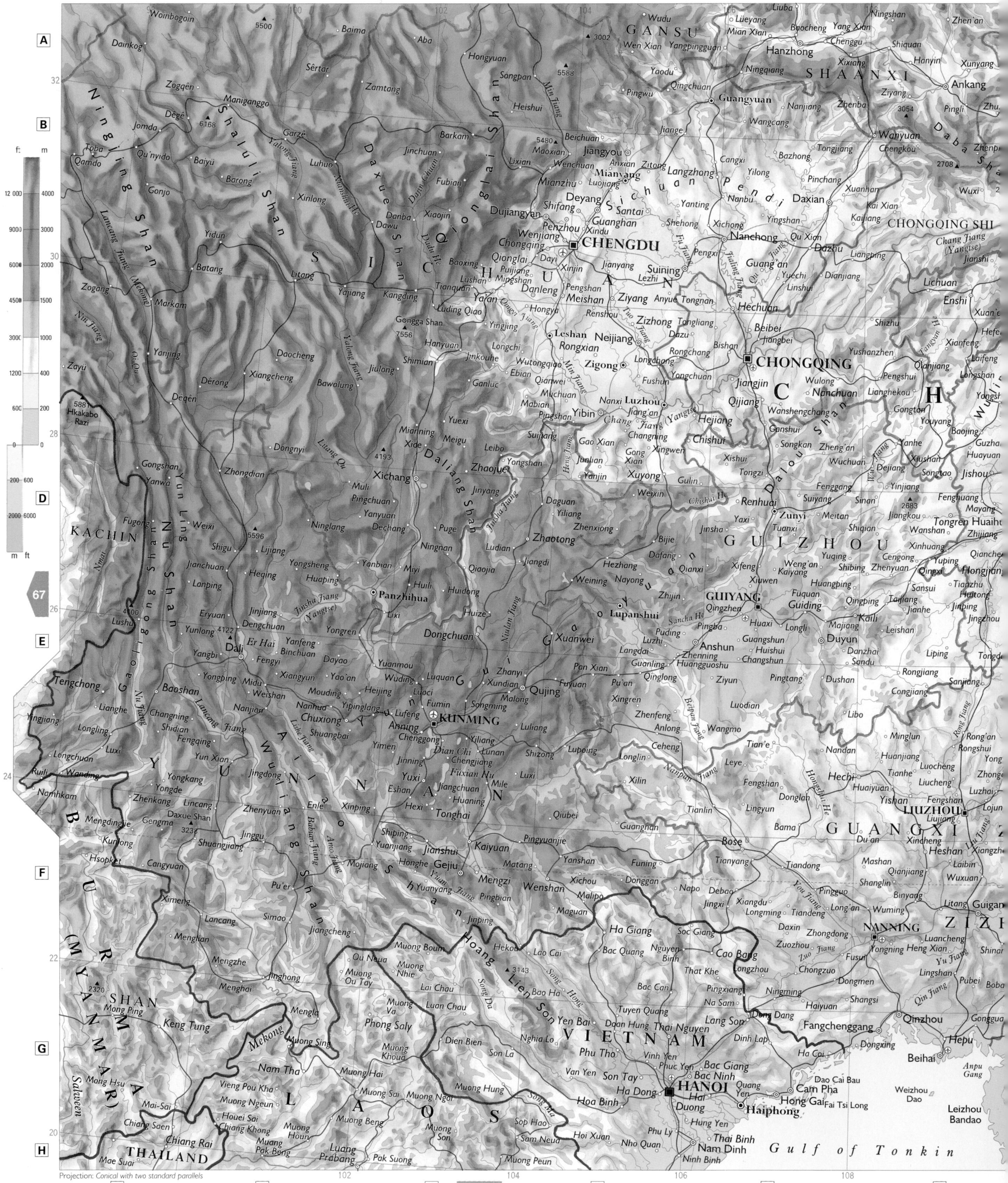
ft m
12 000 4000
9000 3000
6000 2000
4500 1500
3000 1000
1200 400
600 200
0 0
200 600
2000 6000
m ft
67
A
B
D
E
F
G
H
GANSU
SHAANXI
SICHUAN
CHONGQING SHI
GUIZHOU
YUNNAN
GUANGXI
KACHIN
SHAN
BURMA (MYANMAR)
LAOS
VIETNAM
THAILAND
Sichuan Pendi
Gulf of Tonkin
CHENGDU
CHONGQING
KUNMING
GUIYANG
NANNING
HANOI
LIUZHOU
Panzhihua
Xichang
Zigong
Leshan
Yibin
Luzhou
Neijiang
Mianyang
Deyang
Suining
Nanchong
Guangyuan
Hanzhong
Ankang
Dazhou
Daxian
Wanyuan
Zunyi
Anshun
Duyun
Kaili
Qujing
Dali
Baoshan
Tengchong
Lijiang
Gejiu
Kaiyuan
Mengzi
Wenshan
Jinghong
Simao
Bose
Hechi
Beihai
Qinzhou
Fangchenggang
Haiphong
Hong Gai
Nam Dinh
Lao Cai
Ha Giang
Cao Bang
Lang Son
Dien Bien
Luang Prabang
Chiang Rai
Chiang Saen
Keng Tung
Ningjing Shan
Shaluli Shan
Daxue Shan
Qionglai Shan
Daliang Shan
Dalou Shan
Daba Shan
Wuliang Shan
Ailao Shan
Nu Shan
Yun Ling
Gaoligong Shan
Min Shan
Wumeng Shan
Hoang Lien Son
Chang Jiang (Yangtse)
Jinsha Jiang (Yangtse)
Lancang Jiang (Mekong)
Mekong
Nu Jiang
Salween
Yalong Jiang
Dadu He
Min Jiang
Jialing Jiang
Wu Jiang
Hongshui He
Nanpan Jiang
Beipan Jiang
Song Hong
Song Da
Yuan Jiang
Er Hai
Dian Chi
Fuxian Hu
Hkakabo Razi
5881
Gongga Shan
7556
5596
5588
6168
5500
3143
3054
4193
2683
3002
2708
2320
3233
4122
5480
4200
Leizhou Bandao
Weizhou Dao
Anpu Gang
Dao Cai Bau
Fai Tsi Long
32
30
28
26
24
22
20
100
102
104
106
108

2 3 4 5 6 7

64

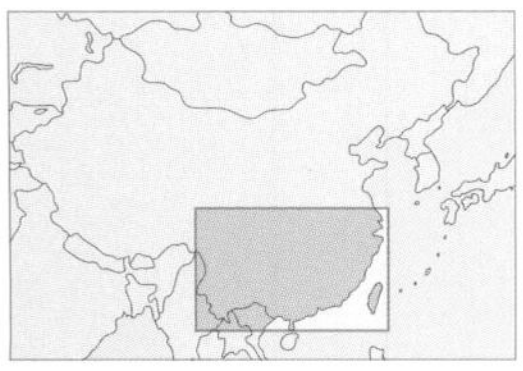

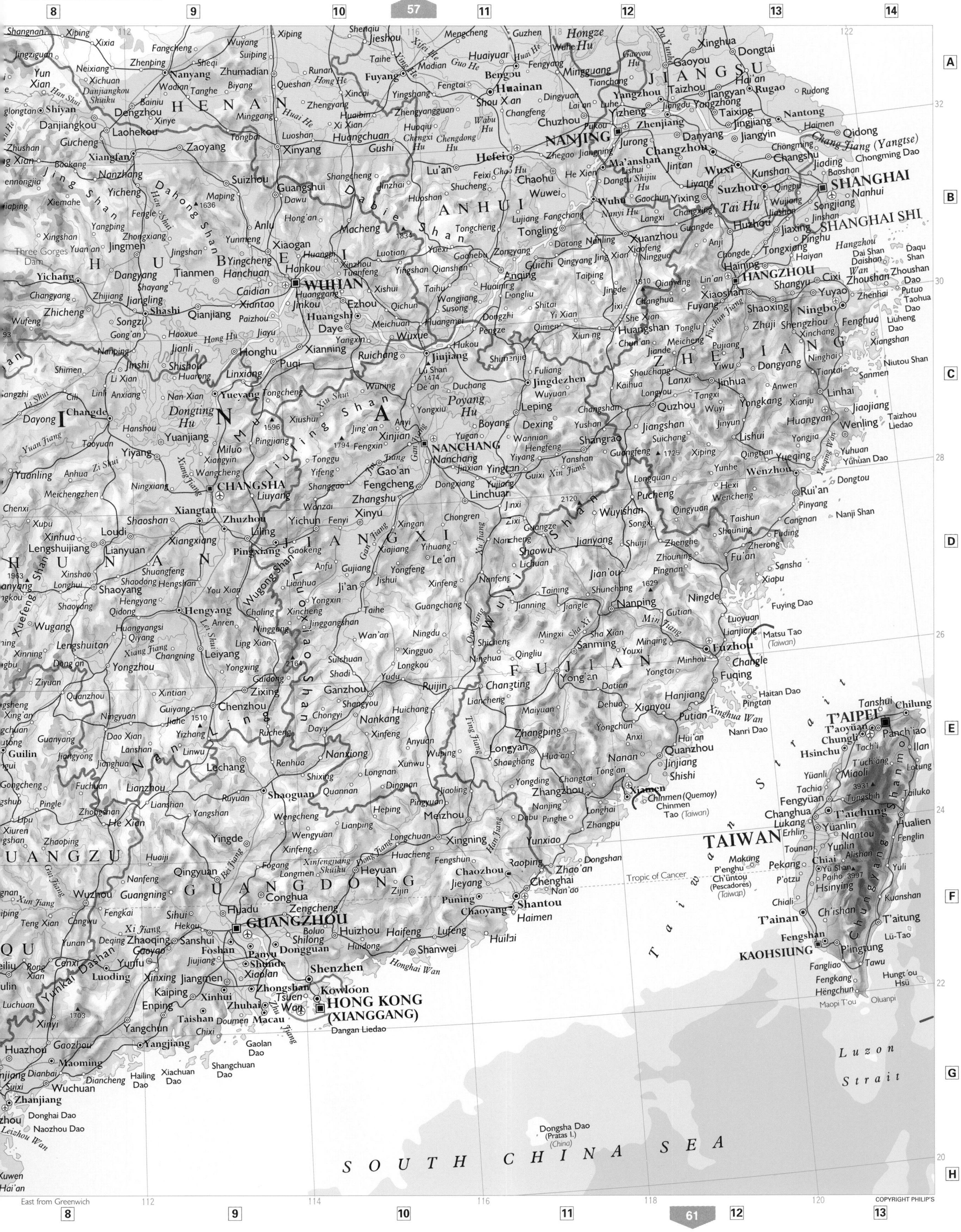
8
9
10
57
11
12
13
14
A
B
C
D
E
F
G
H
HENAN
HUBEI
ANHUI
JIANGSU
SHANGHAI SHI
ZHEJIANG
JIANGXI
HUNAN
FUJIAN
GUANGDONG
TAIWAN
SHANGHAI
NANJING
WUHAN
HANGZHOU
NANCHANG
CHANGSHA
GUANGZHOU
HONG KONG (XIANGGANG)
T'AIPEI
KAOHSIUNG
Hefei
Fuzhou
Xiamen
Shantou
Shenzhen
Kowloon
Macau
Zhuhai
Ningbo
Wenzhou
Suzhou
Wuxi
Changzhou
Zhenjiang
Yangzhou
Nantong
Jiujiang
Ganzhou
Shaoguan
Hengyang
Zhuzhou
Xiangtan
Yueyang
Yichang
Shashi
Jingdezhen
Huainan
Bengbu
Wuhu
Anqing
Zhanjiang
Maoming
Jiangmen
Foshan
Huizhou
Chaozhou
Quanzhou
Zhangzhou
T'aichung
T'ainan
Chilung
Hsinchu
Hualien
T'aitung
Chang Jiang (Yangtze)
Tai Hu
Poyang Hu
Dongting Hu
Hongze Hu
Chao Hu
Hong Hu
Dabie Shan
Wuyi Shan
Nan Ling
Luoxiao Shan
Jiuling Shan
Wugong Shan
Dahong Shan
Jing Shan
Chungyang Shanmo
Xiang Jiang
Gan Jiang
Min Jiang
Han Shui
Zhujiang
Huai He
Three Gorges Dam
Hangzhou Wan
Zhoushan Dao
Chongming Dao
Matsu Tao (Taiwan)
Chinmen (Quemoy)
Haitan Dao
Nanri Dao
Dongshan
Makung
P'enghu
Ch'üntou (Pescadores) (Taiwan)
Tropic of Cancer
Taiwan Strait
Luzon Strait
Lü-Tao
Hungt'ou Hsü
Dongsha Dao (Pratas I.) (China)
Shangchuan Dao
Xiachuan Dao
Hailing Dao
Gaolan Dao
Dangan Liedao
Donghai Dao
Naozhou Dao
Leizhou Wan
Honghai Wan
SOUTH CHINA SEA
Yushan 3997
3931
1834
1810
2120
2164
1725
1794
1596
1636
1510
1474
1629
1703
1963
112
114
116
118
120
122
32
30
28
26
24
22
20
East from Greenwich
61

100 0 100 200 300 400 500 600 700 800 km

1:17 800 000

100 0 100 200 300 400 500 miles

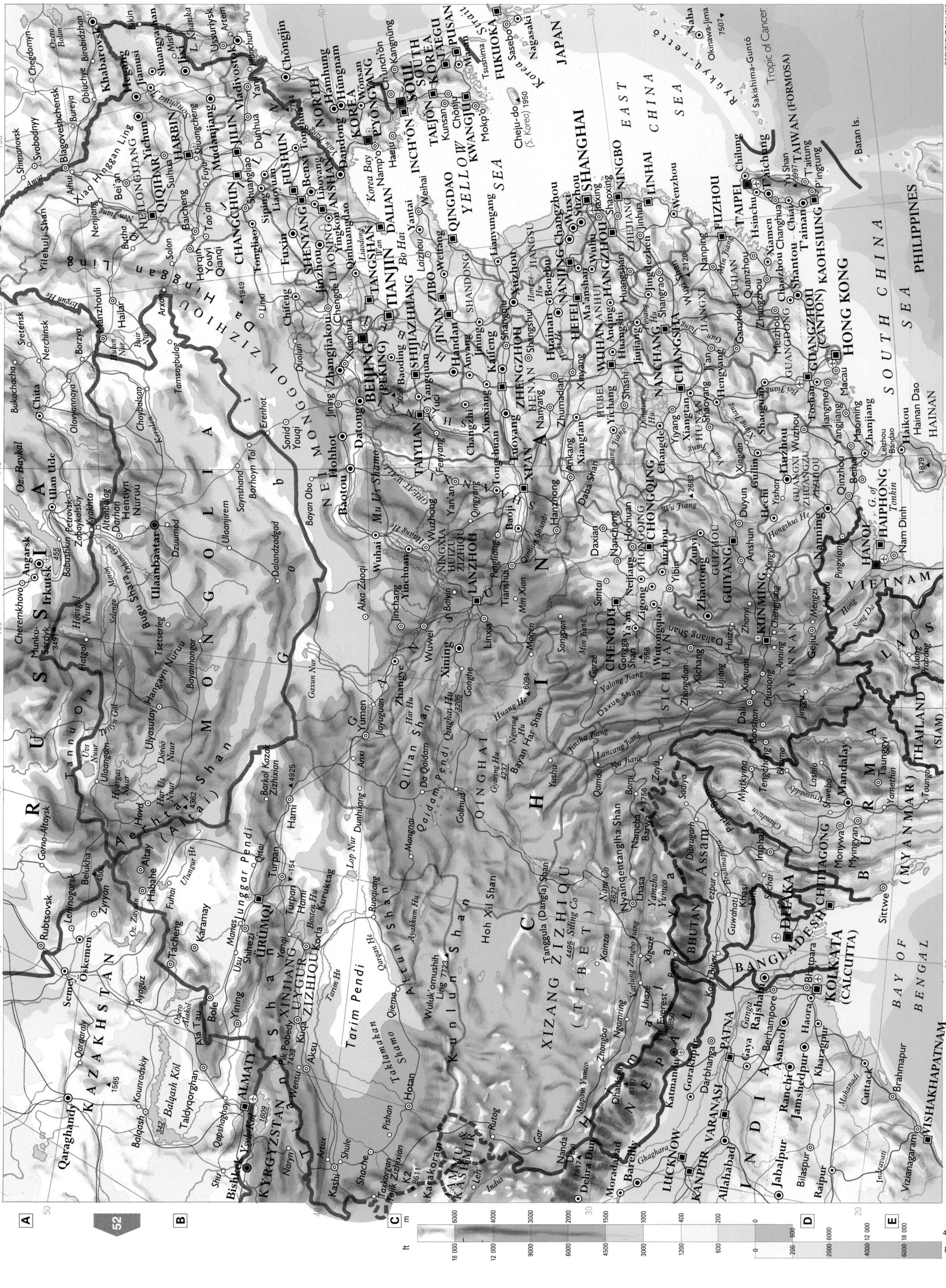
RUSSIA
MONGOLIA
CHINA
KAZAKHSTAN
KYRGYZSTAN
INDIA
NEPAL
BHUTAN
BANGLADESH
BURMA (MYANMAR)
THAILAND (SIAM)
LAOS
VIETNAM
PHILIPPINES
JAPAN
NORTH KOREA
SOUTH KOREA
TAIWAN (FORMOSA)
HONG KONG
BEIJING (PEKING)
SHANGHAI
TIANJIN
CHONGQING
CHENGDU
WUHAN
GUANGZHOU (CANTON)
XI'AN
LANZHOU
ÜRÜMQI
HARBIN
SHENYANG
KUNMING
ULAANBAATAR
ALMATY
KOLKATA (CALCUTTA)
DHAKA
HANOI
SEOUL
PYONGYANG
YELLOW SEA
EAST CHINA SEA
SOUTH CHINA SEA
BAY OF BENGAL
Tropic of Cancer
East from Greenwich
Projection: Bonne
COPYRIGHT PHILIP'S
m 6000 4000 3000 2000 1500 1000 400 200 0
ft 18 000 12 000 9000 6000 4500 3000 1200 600 0
200 600 2000 6000 4000 12 000 6000 18 000

53
52
62

1:6 700 000

50 0 100 150 200 250 300 km

50 0 50 100 150 200 miles

1 2 3 4 5 6 7 8

59

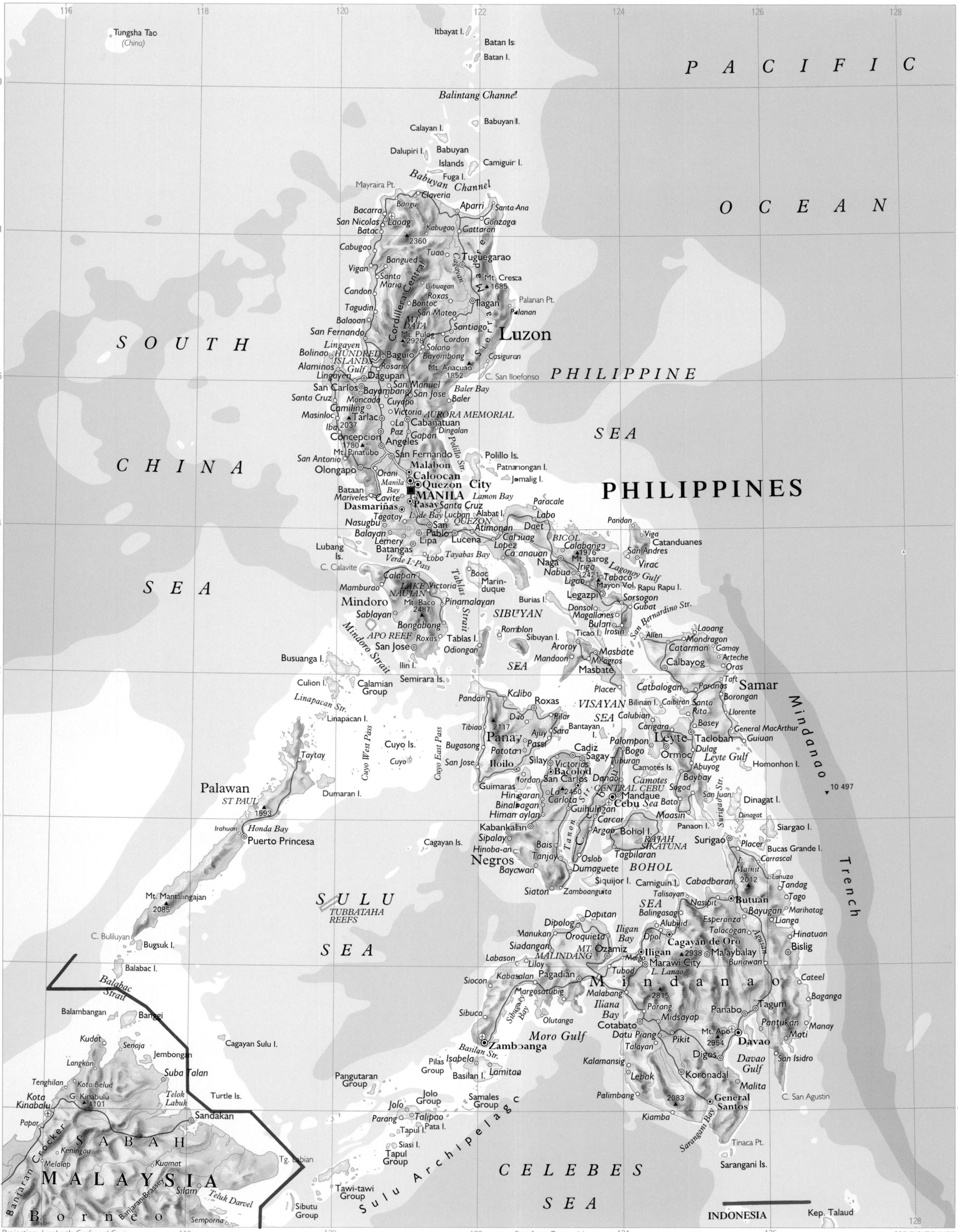

P A C I F I C
O C E A N
S O U T H
C H I N A
S E A
PHILIPPINE
SEA
PHILIPPINES
SULU
SEA
TUBBATAHA REEFS
CELEBES
SEA
SIBUYAN
SEA
VISAYAN
SEA
Luzon
Mindoro
Palawan
Panay
Negros
Samar
Leyte
Bohol
Mindanao
Sulu Archipelago
Mindanao Trench
10 497
Tungsha Tao
(China)
Itbayat I.
Batan Is.
Batan I.
Balintang Channel
Babuyan I.
Calayan I.
Dalupiri I.
Babuyan Islands
Camiguin I.
Fuga I.
Babuyan Channel
Mayraira Pt.
Claveria
Aparri
Santa Ana
Bacarra
Laoag
San Nicolas
Batac
Gonzaga
Gattaran
Kabugao
2360
Cabugao
Tuguegarao
Vigan
Bangued
Candon
Santa Maria
Mt. Cresta
1685
Cordillera Central
Sierra Madre
Tagudin
Bontoc
Roxas
Ilagan
Palanan Pt.
Palanan
Balaoan
San Mateo
Santiago
San Fernando
Mt. Pulog
2928
Cordon
Lingayen Gulf
HUNDRED ISLANDS
Bolinao
Baguio
Bayombong
Casiguran
Alaminos
Rosario
Solano
Lingayen
Dagupan
Mt. Anacuao
1852
C. San Ildefonso
San Carlos
Bayambang
San Manuel
San Jose
Baler Bay
Baler
Santa Cruz
Moncada
Cuyapo
Camiling
Victoria
AURORA MEMORIAL
Masinloc
Tarlac
Cabanatuan
Iba
2037
Dingalan
Paz
Concepcion
Gapan
Angeles
Mt. Pinatubo
1780
San Fernando
Polillo Is.
San Antonio
Malabon
Polillo Str.
Patnanungan I.
Olongapo
Caloocan
Jomalig I.
Orani
Quezon City
Manila Bay
MANILA
Lamon Bay
Bataan
Mariveles
Cavite
Pasay
Santa Cruz
Dasmariñas
Paracale
Labo
Nasugbu
Tagaytay
Laguna de Bay
Lucban
Alabat I.
Daet
QUEZON
Pandan
Viga
Balayan
San Pablo
Atimonan
Calauag
BICOL
Catanduanes
Lubang Is.
Lemery
Lipa
Lucena
Lopez
Calabanga
1976
San Andres
Batangas
Lobo
Tayabas Bay
Caramoan
Mt. Isarog
Virac
C. Calavite
Verde I. Pass
Naga
Iriga
Lagonoy Gulf
Nabua
2421
Tabaco
Calapan
Boac
Ligao
Mayon Vol.
Rapu Rapu I.
Marinduque
Tablas Strait
Mamburao
LAKE NAUJAN
Victoria
Burias I.
Legazpi
Sorsogon
Gubat
Mt. Baco
2487
Pinamalayan
Donsol
San Bernardino Str.
Sablayan
Magallanes
Bulan
Bongabong
Romblon
Ticao I.
Irosin
Laoang
APO REEF
Roxas
Tablas I.
Sibuyan I.
Allen
Mondragon
Mindoro Strait
San Jose
Odiongan
Aroroy
Masbate
Catarman
Gamay
Arteche
Busuanga I.
Mandaon
Milagros
Calbayog
Oras
Ilin I.
Semirara Is.
Masbate
Taft
Culion I.
Calamian Group
Placer
Catbalogan
Paranas
Borongan
Linapacan Str.
Pandan
Kalibo
Roxas
Bilinan I.
Caibiran
Santa Rita
Llorente
Linapacan I.
Dao
Pilar
Calubian
Basey
General MacArthur
Tibiao
2117
Ajuy
Sara
Bantayan I.
Tacloban
Guiuan
Cuyo West Pass
Cuyo East Pass
Bugasong
Passi
Palompon
Cuyo Is.
Pototan
Cadiz
Bogo
Ormoc
Leyte Gulf
Taytay
Cuyo
San Jose
Iloilo
Silay
Sagay
Tuburan
Dulag
Abuyog
Homonhon I.
Bacolod
Victorias
Camotes Is.
Baybay
Guimaras
San Carlos
Danao
Camotes Sea
Palawan
Hinigaran
Iordan
La Carlota
2450
CENTRAL CEBU
Sogod
ST PAUL
Dumaran I.
Binalbagan
Guihulngan
Tañon Strait
Cebu
Sea Bato
San Juan
Dinagat I.
1593
Himamaylan
Carcar
Maasin
Surigao Str.
Irahuan
Honda Bay
Kabankalan
Argao
Bohol I.
Panaon I.
Dinagat
Siargao I.
Puerto Princesa
Cagayan Is.
Sipalay
RAJAH SIKATUNA
Surigao
Placer
Bucas Grande I.
Hinoba-an
Bais
Tagbilaran
Carrascal
Tanjay
Oslob
BOHOL
Mainit
Lanuza
Baywan
Dumaguete
2012
Tandag
Siquijor I.
Camiguin I.
Cabadbaran
Tago
Siaton
Zamboanguita
Talisayan
Butuan
Mt. Mantalingajan
2085
Nasipit
Bayugan
Marihatag
Dipolog
Dapitan
Balingasag
Alubijid
Esperanza
Lianga
Manukan
Oroquieta
Iligan Bay
Talacogon
Hinatuan
C. Buliluyan
Sindangan
MT. MALINDANG
Ozamiz
Opol
Cagayan de Oro
Agusan
Bislig
Bugsuk I.
Labason
Liloy
Iligan
Malaybalay
Balabac I.
Tubod
2938
Marawi City
Bunawan
Kabasalan
Pagadian
L. Lanao
Cateel
Balabac Strait
Siocon
Margosatubig
Malabang
2815
Baganga
Sibuguey Bay
Illana Bay
Parang
Tagum
Balambangan
Banggi
Sibuco
Panabo
Olutanga
Midsayap
Cotabato
Pantukan
Manay
Kudat
Moro Gulf
Mt. Apo
2954
Mati
Senaja
Datu Piang
Pikit
Jembongan
Zamboanga
Talayan
Davao
Cagayan Sulu I.
Basilan Str.
Davao Gulf
Langkon
Isabela
Digos
San Isidro
Suba Talan
Kalamansig
Pilas Group
Lamitan
Tenghilan
Kota Belud
Pangutaran Group
Basilan I.
Lebak
Koronadal
Malita
Kota Kinabalu
G. Kinabalu
4101
Telok Labuk
Turtle Is.
Jolo
Samales Group
Palimbang
General Santos
C. San Agustin
Papar
Sandakan
Jolo Group
2083
SABAH
Parang
Talipao
Kiamba
Crocker
Keningau
Pata I.
Tapul I.
Sarangani Bay
Tinaca Pt.
Siasi I.
Kuamat
Tg. Labian
Tapul Group
Sarangani Is.
Melalap
Banjaran Crocker
MALAYSIA
Silam
Tawi-tawi Group
Teluk Darvel
Banjaran Brassey
Sibutu Group
Borneo
Semporna
INDONESIA
Kep. Talaud

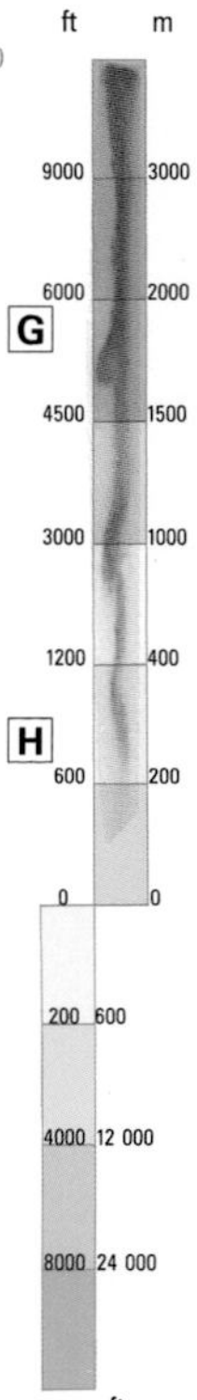

ft
m
9000
3000
6000
2000
4500
1500
3000
1000
1200
400
600
200
0
0
200
600
4000
12 000
8000
24 000
m
ft

Projection: Lambert's Conformal Conic

East from Greenwich

1 2 3 4 5 6 7 8

63

National Parks

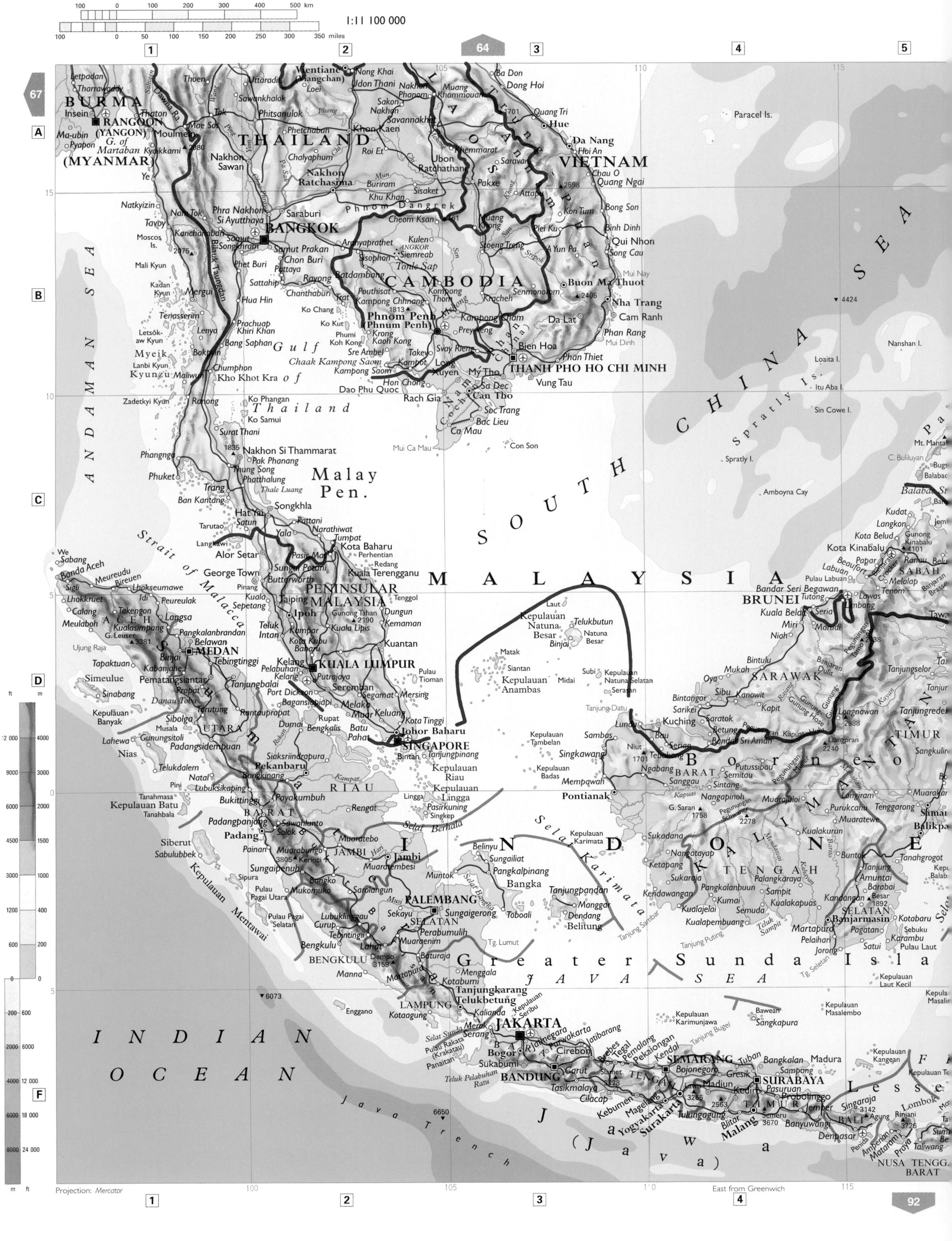

1:11 100 000
100 0 100 200 300 400 500 km
100 0 50 100 150 200 250 300 350 miles
1
2
64
3
4
5
67
A
B
C
D
E
F
BURMA
RANGOON (YANGON)
(MYANMAR)
G. of Martaban
THAILAND
BANGKOK
Vientiane (Viangchan)
LAOS
VIETNAM
Hue
Da Nang
Dong Hoi
CAMBODIA
Phnom Penh (Phnum Penh)
THANH PHO HO CHI MINH
Gulf of Thailand
ANDAMAN SEA
SOUTH CHINA SEA
Paracel Is.
Spratly Is.
Malay Pen.
MALAYSIA
PENINSULAR MALAYSIA
KUALA LUMPUR
SINGAPORE
Strait of Malacca
MEDAN
BRUNEI
Bandar Seri Begawan
SABAH
SARAWAK
Kota Kinabalu
Kuching
Pontianak
Kepulauan Natuna
Kepulauan Anambas
Borneo
KALIMANTAN
Sumatera
INDONESIA
PALEMBANG
Bangka
Belitung
Greater Sunda Islands
JAVA SEA
JAKARTA
BANDUNG
SEMARANG
SURABAYA
Madura
BALI
Denpasar
NUSA TENGGARA BARAT
Jawa (Java)
INDIAN OCEAN
Java Trench
Kepulauan Mentawai
Siberut
Nias
Simeulue
Selat Karimata
Selat Sunda
Projection: Mercator
East from Greenwich
100
105
110
115

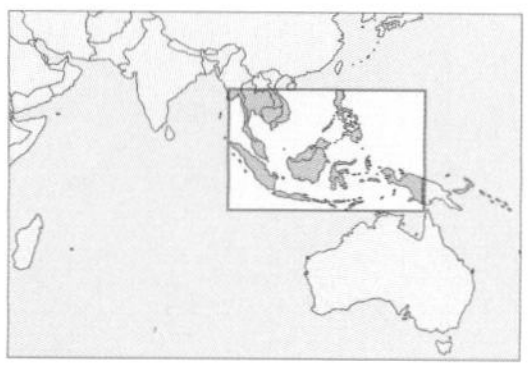

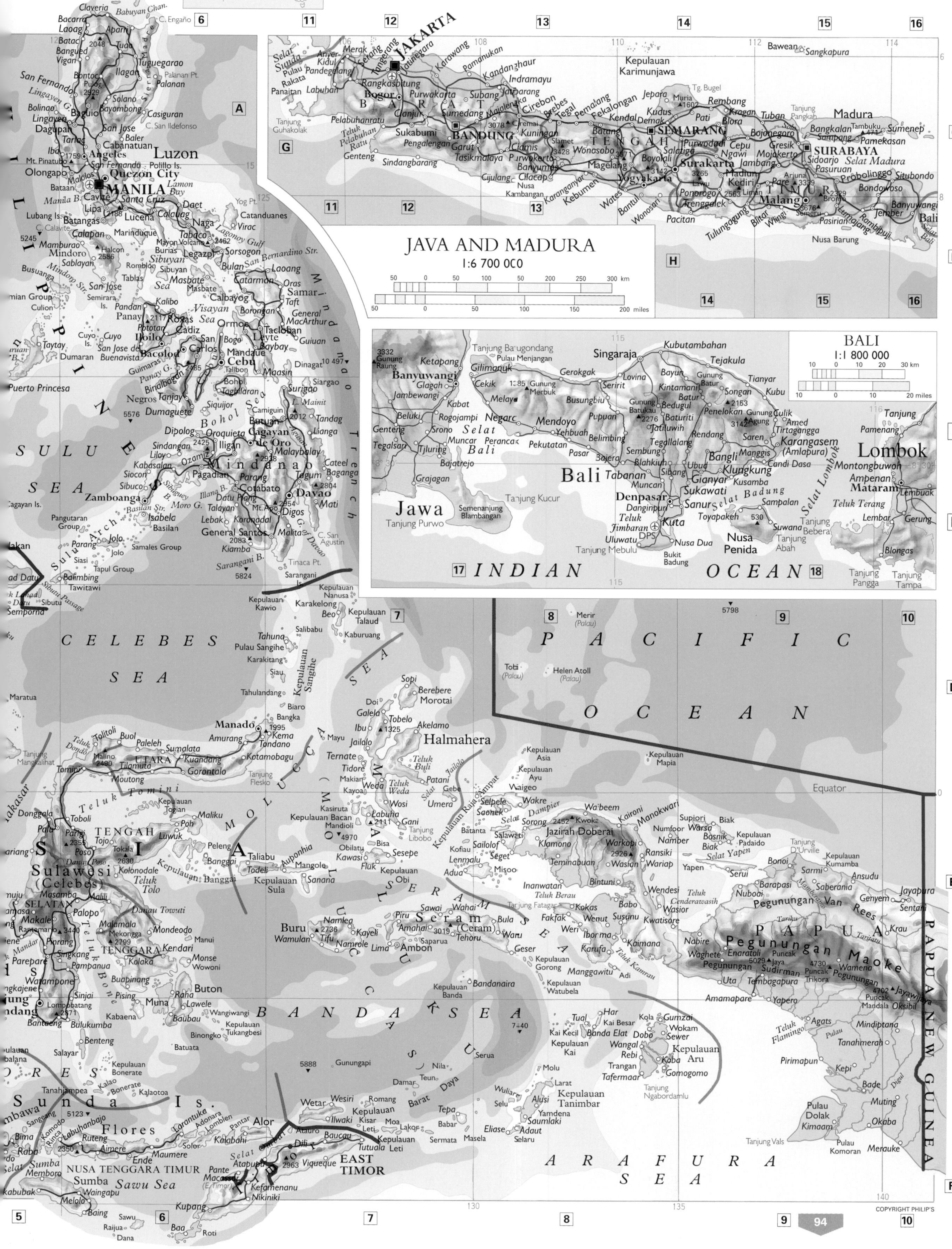
JAVA AND MADURA
1:6 700 000
km
miles
BALI
1:1 800 000
km
miles
Luzon
MANILA
Quezon City
Mindoro
Panay
Negros
Cebu
Bohol
Mindanao
Zamboanga
Davao
Cagayan de Oro
S U L U
S E A
C E L E B E S
S E A
Sulawesi
(Celebes)
Manado
Halmahera
Ternate
P A C I F I C
O C E A N
Equator
B A N D A
S E A
A R A F U R A
S E A
Buru
Seram
(Ceram)
Ambon
Flores
Sunda Is.
Sumba
Sawu Sea
Kupang
EAST
TIMOR
Dili
Alor
Wetar
Kepulauan
Tanimbar
Kepulauan
Aru
Kepulauan
Kai
Jazirah Doberai
P A P U A
Pegunungan Maoke
Jayapura
Merauke
PAPUA NEW GUINEA
JAKARTA
Bogor
BANDUNG
SEMARANG
Yogyakarta
Surakarta
SURABAYA
Malang
Madura
Kepulauan
Karimunjawa
Bali
Denpasar
Singaraja
Lombok
Mataram
Jawa
INDIAN
OCEAN
Nusa
Penida
Pulau
Dolak
COPYRIGHT PHILIP'S

50 0 50 100 150 200 km

50 0 50 100 150 miles

1:5 300 000

BURMA (MYANMAR)
THAILAND
CAMBODIA
LAOS
YUNNAN
GUANGXI ZHUANGZU ZIZHIQU
HAINAN
G. of Tonkin
G. of Martaban
RANGOON (YANGON)
BANGKOK
HANOI
Vientiane (Viangchan)
Phnom Penh
Mandalay
Moulmein
Chiang Mai
Luang Prabang
Haiphong
Da Nang
Haikou
Nanning
Mekong
Salween
Khorat
Phnom Dangrek
Bilauk Taung Range
TENASSERIM
Dawna Range
KAYAH
MON
SHAN
PEGU
58
67

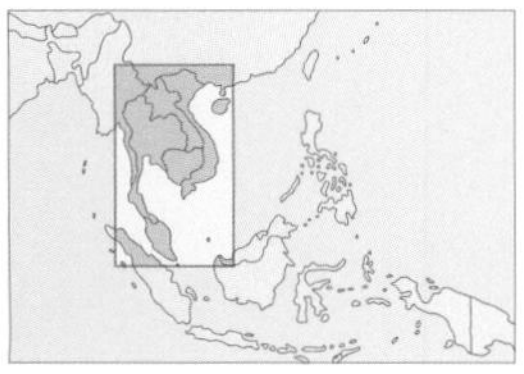

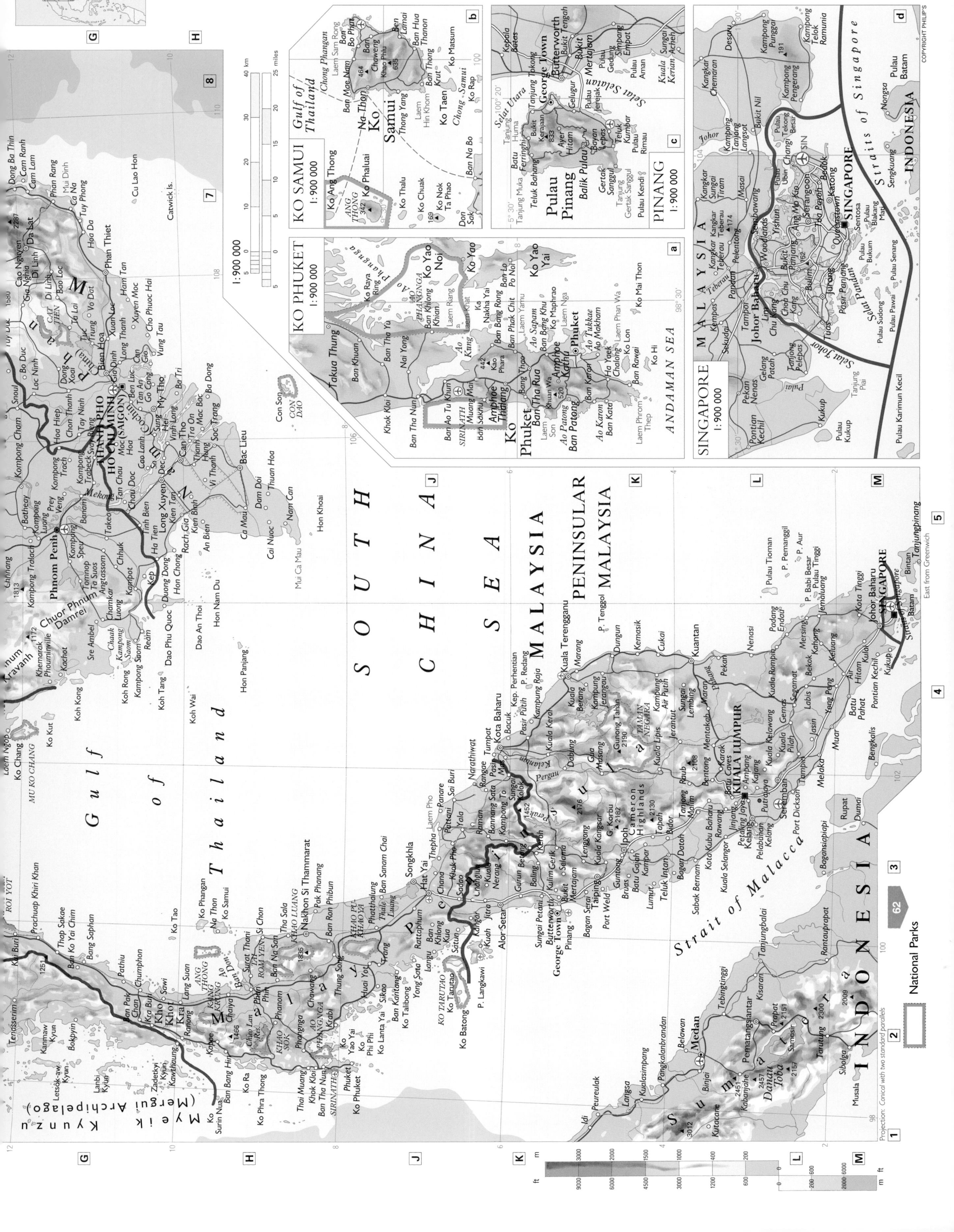
KO PHUKET
1:900 000
KO SAMUI
1:900 000
PINANG
1:900 000
SINGAPORE
1:900 000
1:900 000
Gulf of Thailand
SOUTH CHINA SEA
Strait of Malacca
ANDAMAN SEA
MALAYSIA
PENINSULAR MALAYSIA
INDONESIA
SINGAPORE
Phnom Penh
KUALA LUMPUR
THANH PHO HO CHI MINH (SAIGON)
Mekong
National Parks
Projection: Conical with two standard parallels
East from Greenwich
COPYRIGHT PHILIP'S

1:8 900 000
km
miles
TURKMENISTAN
AFGHANISTAN
PAKISTAN
IRAN
INDIA
SRI LANKA
ARABIAN SEA
Gulf of Kachchh
Gulf of Khambhat
Gulf of Mannar
Palk Strait
Adam's Bridge
Rann of Kachchh
Thar or Great Indian Desert
Makran Coast Range
Central Makran Range
Siahan Range
Chāh Gay Hills
Kirthar Range
Sulaiman Range
Toba Kakar
Hindu Kush
Karakoram
Safīd Kūh
Rīgestān
Dasht-e Khāsh
Dasht-e Mārgow
Northern Areas
NORTH WEST FRONTIER
Tribal Areas
JAMMU & KASHMIR
PUNJAB
SIND
BALUCHISTAN
RAJASTHAN
GUJARAT
MADHYA PRADESH
MAHARASHTRA
KARNATAKA
KERALA
TAMIL NADU
ANDHRA PRADESH
HIMACHAL PRADESH
HARYANA
UTTARANCHAL
Kathiawar
Vindhya Range
Satpura Range
Western Ghats
Eastern Ghats
Coromandel Coast
Malabar Coast
Aksai Chin
Kābul
Herāt
Qandahār
Quetta
Islamabad
Rawalpindi
Peshawar
Lahore
Faisalabad
Multan
Hyderabad
KARACHI
Srinagar
Amritsar
Delhi
New Delhi
Jaipur
Agra
Ahmadabad
Vadodara (Baroda)
Surat
MUMBAI (BOMBAY)
PUNE (Poona)
Bhopal
Indore
Nagpur
Solapur
Hubli
Belgaum
BANGALORE
CHENNAI (Madras)
Madurai
Pondicherry
Mangalore
Cochin (Kochi)
Trivandrum (Thiruvananthapuram)
Colombo
Kandy
Jaffna
Trincomalee
C. Comorin
Dondra Head
Tropic of Cancer
Continuation Southwards on same scale
Projection: Conical with two standard parallels

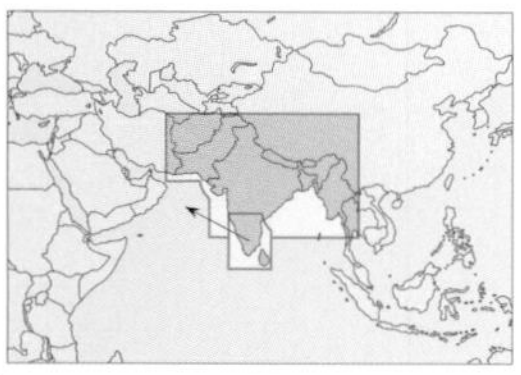

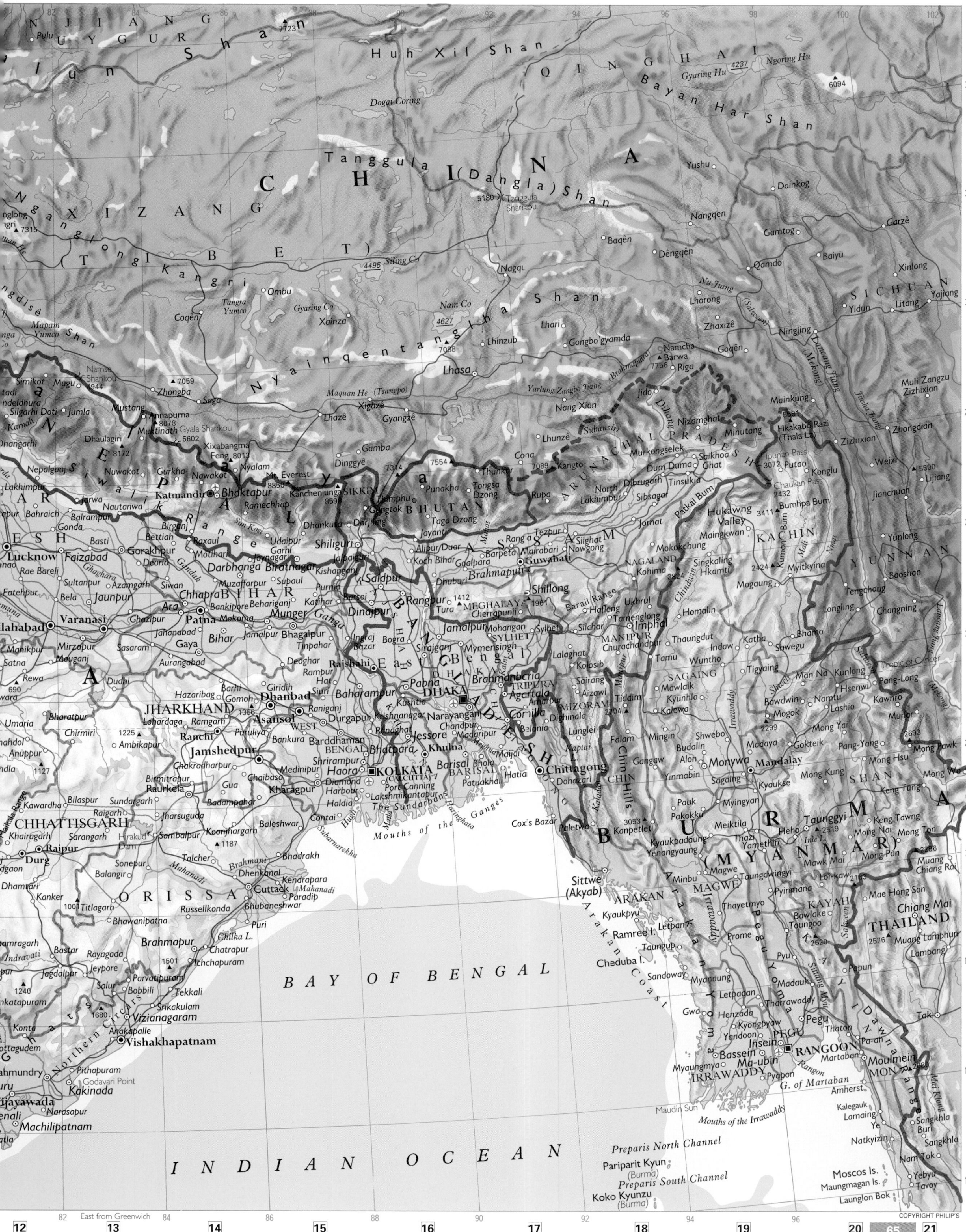
CHINA
XIZANG (TIBET)
QINGHAI
SICHUAN
YUNNAN
NEPAL
BHUTAN
BANGLADESH
BURMA (MYANMAR)
THAILAND
INDIA
BIHAR
JHARKHAND
WEST BENGAL
ORISSA
CHHATTISGARH
ASSAM
ARUNACHAL PRADESH
MEGHALAYA
NAGALAND
MANIPUR
MIZORAM
TRIPURA
SIKKIM
SAGAING
KACHIN
SHAN
MANDALAY
MAGWE
KAYAH
KAYIN
MON
IRRAWADDY
ARAKAN
CHIN
BAY OF BENGAL
INDIAN OCEAN
Kunlun Shan
Huh Xil Shan
Bayan Har Shan
Tanggula (Dangla) Shan
Nyainqentanglha Shan
Tonglkangri
Gangdisê Shan
Siwalik Range
Khasi Hills
Patkai Bum
Chin Hills
Arakan Yoma
Pegu Yoma
Arakan Coast
Dawna Range
Northern Circars
Eastern Ghats
Mouths of the Ganges
Mouths of the Irrawaddy
The Sundarbans
G. of Martaban
Preparis North Channel
Preparis South Channel
Mt. Everest 8850
Kanchenjunga 8598
Lhasa
Kathmandu
Thimphu
DHAKA
KOLKATA (CALCUTTA)
RANGOON
Mandalay
Patna
Varanasi
Lucknow
Allahabad
Guwahati
Shillong
Imphal
Chittagong
Khulna
Dhanbad
Jamshedpur
Cuttack
Bhubaneshwar
Vishakhapatnam
Raipur
Sittwe (Akyab)
Moulmein
Pegu
Bassein
Cox's Bazar
Taunggyi
Chiang Mai
Tavoy
East from Greenwich
COPYRIGHT PHILIP'S

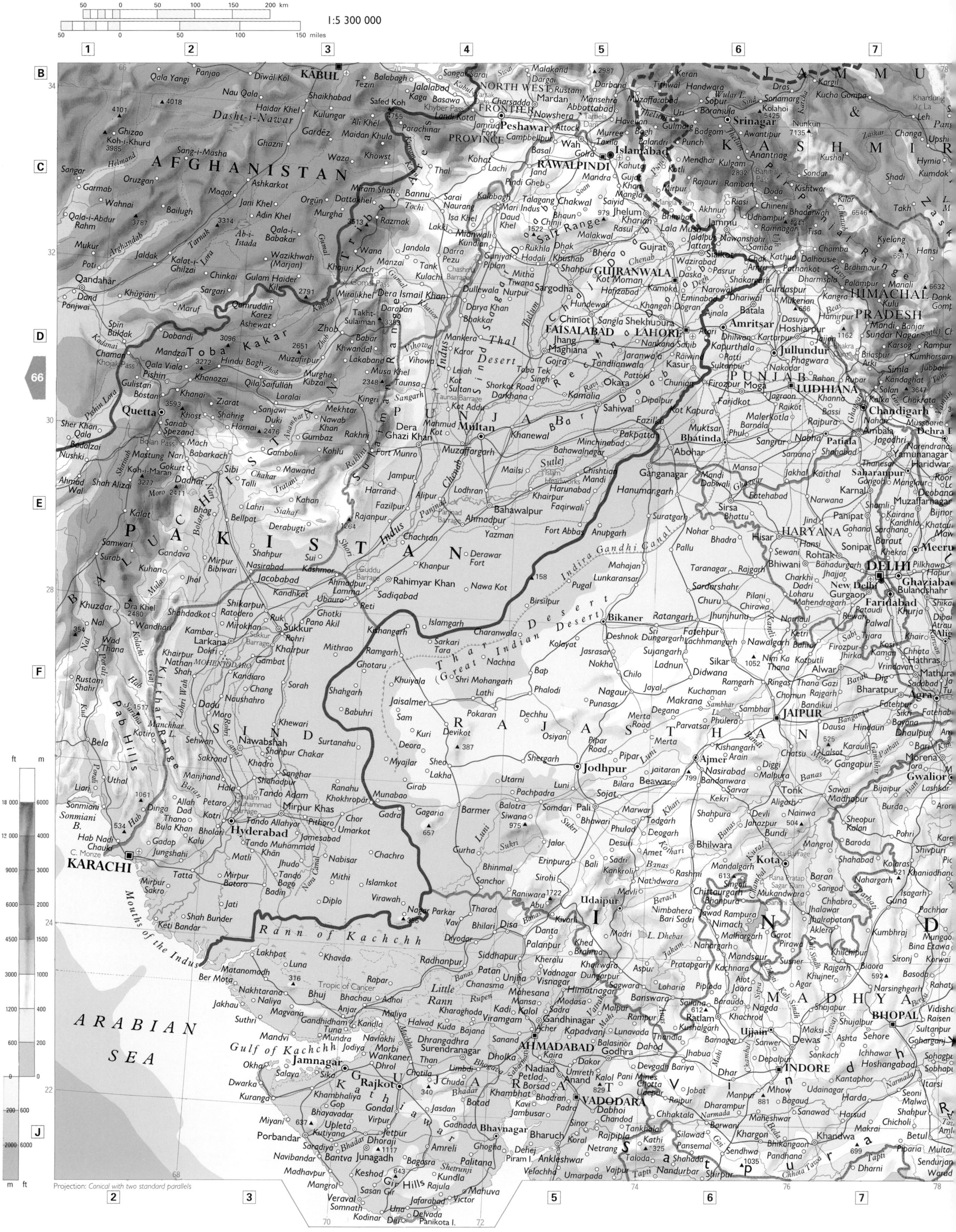
1:5 300 000
km
miles
Projection: Conical with two standard parallels
AFGHANISTAN
PAKISTAN
INDIA
BALUCHISTAN
PUNJAB
SIND
RAJASTHAN
HARYANA
HIMACHAL PRADESH
JAMMU & KASHMIR
MADHYA PRADESH
NORTH WEST FRONTIER PROVINCE
KATHIAWAR
ARABIAN SEA
Gulf of Kachchh
Rann of Kachchh
Little Rann
Mouths of the Indus
Thar Desert (Great Indian Desert)
Thal Desert
Dasht-i-Nawar
Toba Kakar
Sulaiman Range
Kirthar Range
Pab Hills
Salt Range
Pir Panjal Range
Indira Gandhi Canal
Tropic of Cancer
KABUL
Qandahar
Quetta
Peshawar
Islamabad
RAWALPINDI
Srinagar
Jammu
GUJRANWALA
FAISALABAD
LAHORE
Amritsar
Jullundur
LUDHIANA
Chandigarh
Multan
Bahawalpur
Sukkur
Hyderabad
KARACHI
Bikaner
Jodhpur
JAIPUR
Ajmer
DELHI
New Delhi
Faridabad
Ghaziabad
Agra
Gwalior
Kota
Udaipur
AHMADABAD
VADODARA
Rajkot
Jamnagar
Bhavnagar
Ujjain
INDORE
BHOPAL
1
2
3
4
5
6
7
B
C
D
E
F
J
66

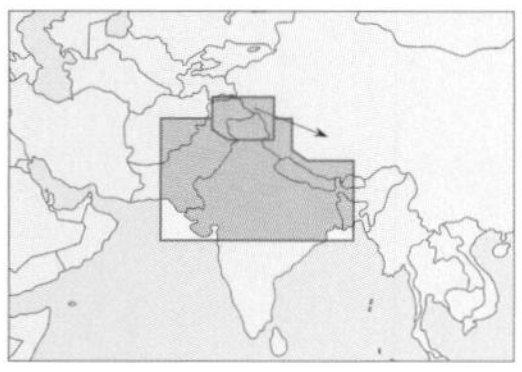

JAMMU AND KASHMIR
on same scale
AFGHANISTAN
CHINA
NORTH WEST FRONTIER
Northern Areas
Azad Kashmir
PUNJAB
ISLAMABAD
RAWALPINDI
Srinagar
JAMMU & KASHMIR
HIMACHAL PRADESH
Karakoram Range
Zaskar Mountains
Ladakh Range
Kunlun Shan
Aksai Chin
Leh
Kargil
Gilgit
Nanga Parbat
K2
Siachen Glacier
Karakoram Pass
CHINA
XIZANG ZIZHIQU (TIBET)
Nganglong Kangri
Gangdisê Shan
NEPAL
Katmandu
Mt. Everest (Chomolungma or Sagarmatha)
Annapurna
Himalchuli
Makalu
Kanchenjunga
SIKKIM
BHUTAN
Thimphu
BANGLADESH
DHAKA
UTTAR PRADESH
LUCKNOW
KANPUR
Allahabad
VARANASI
PATNA
BIHAR
JHARKHAND
Ranchi
Jamshedpur
Dhanbad
WEST BENGAL
KOLKATA
Haora
CHHATTISGARH
Bilaspur
MADHYA PRADESH
Jabalpur
Kaimur Hills
Panna Hills
Mahabharat Lekh
Siwalik Range
Yarlung Zangbo Jiang (Brahmaputra)
Ganga
Mouths of the Ganges
The Sandheads
Sundarbans
Rajshahi
Khulna
Darjiling
Gangtok
East from Greenwich

1:6 200 000

35 72 80

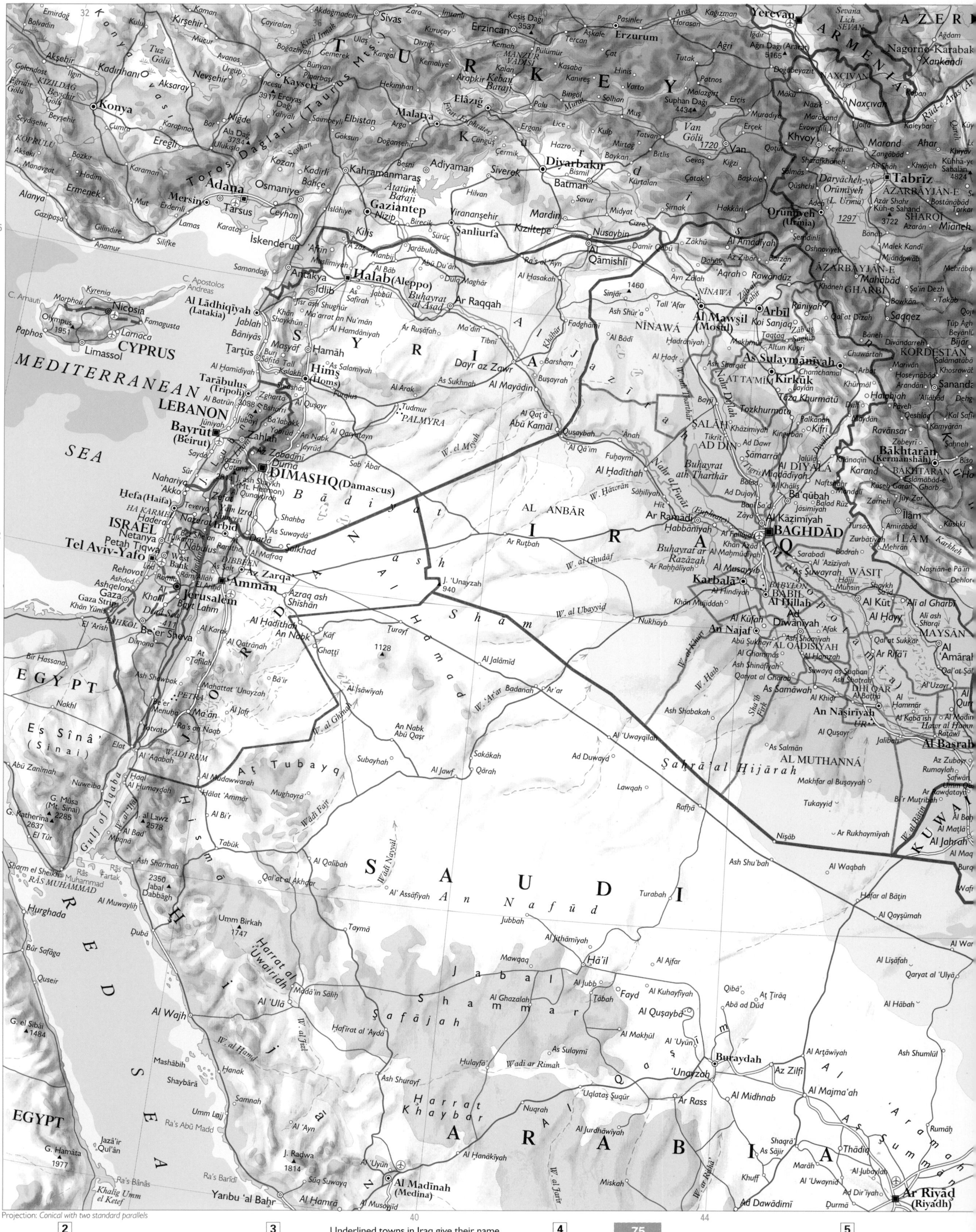
TURKEY
SYRIA
IRAQ
JORDAN
LEBANON
ISRAEL
CYPRUS
EGYPT
SAUDI ARABIA
ARMENIA
MEDITERRANEAN SEA
RED SEA
Konya
Kayseri
Adana
Mersin
Gaziantep
Şanliurfa
Diyarbakır
Erzurum
Elazığ
Malatya
Kahramanmaraş
İskenderun
Antakya
Halab (Aleppo)
Al Lādhiqīyah (Latakia)
Hims (Homs)
Hamāh
Tarābulus (Tripoli)
Bayrūt (Beirut)
DIMASHQ (Damascus)
Nicosia
Limassol
Larnaca
Famagusta
Hefa (Haifa)
Tel Aviv-Yafo
Jerusalem
'Ammān
Irbid
Az Zarqā'
Be'er Sheva
Gaza
Al 'Aqabah
Dayr az Zawr
Ar Raqqah
Al Mawşil (Mosul)
Arbīl
Kirkūk
As Sulaymānīyah
BAGHDĀD
Karbalā'
An Najaf
Al Ḩillah
An Nāşirīyah
Al Başrah
Tabrīz
Orūmīyeh (Urmia)
Yerevan
Ḩā'il
Buraydah
Al Madīnah (Medina)
Ar Riyāḑ (Riyadh)
Tabūk
Al Wajh
An Nafūd
Bādiyat ash Shām
Es Sînâ' (Sinai)
Gulf of Aqaba
G. Mûsa (Mt. Sinai) 2285
Van Gölü
Tuz Gölü
Toros Dağları (Taurus Mts.)

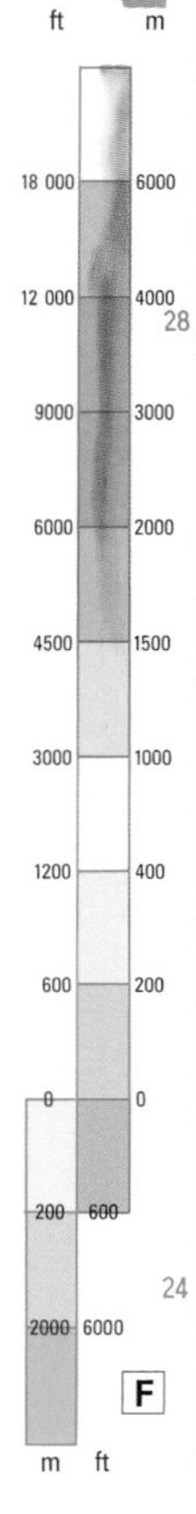
ft
m
18 000
6000
12 000
4000
9000
3000
6000
2000
4500
1500
3000
1000
1200
400
600
200
0
0
200
600
2000
6000

Projection: Conical with two standard parallels

Underlined towns in Iraq give their name to the administrative area in which they stand

75

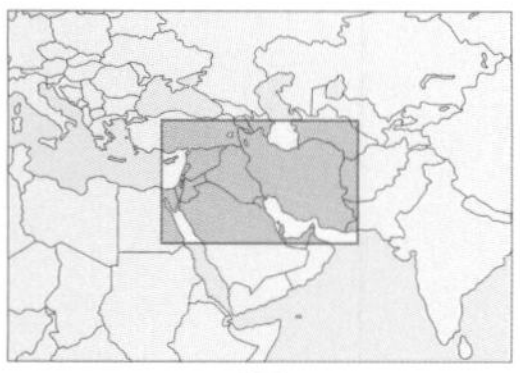

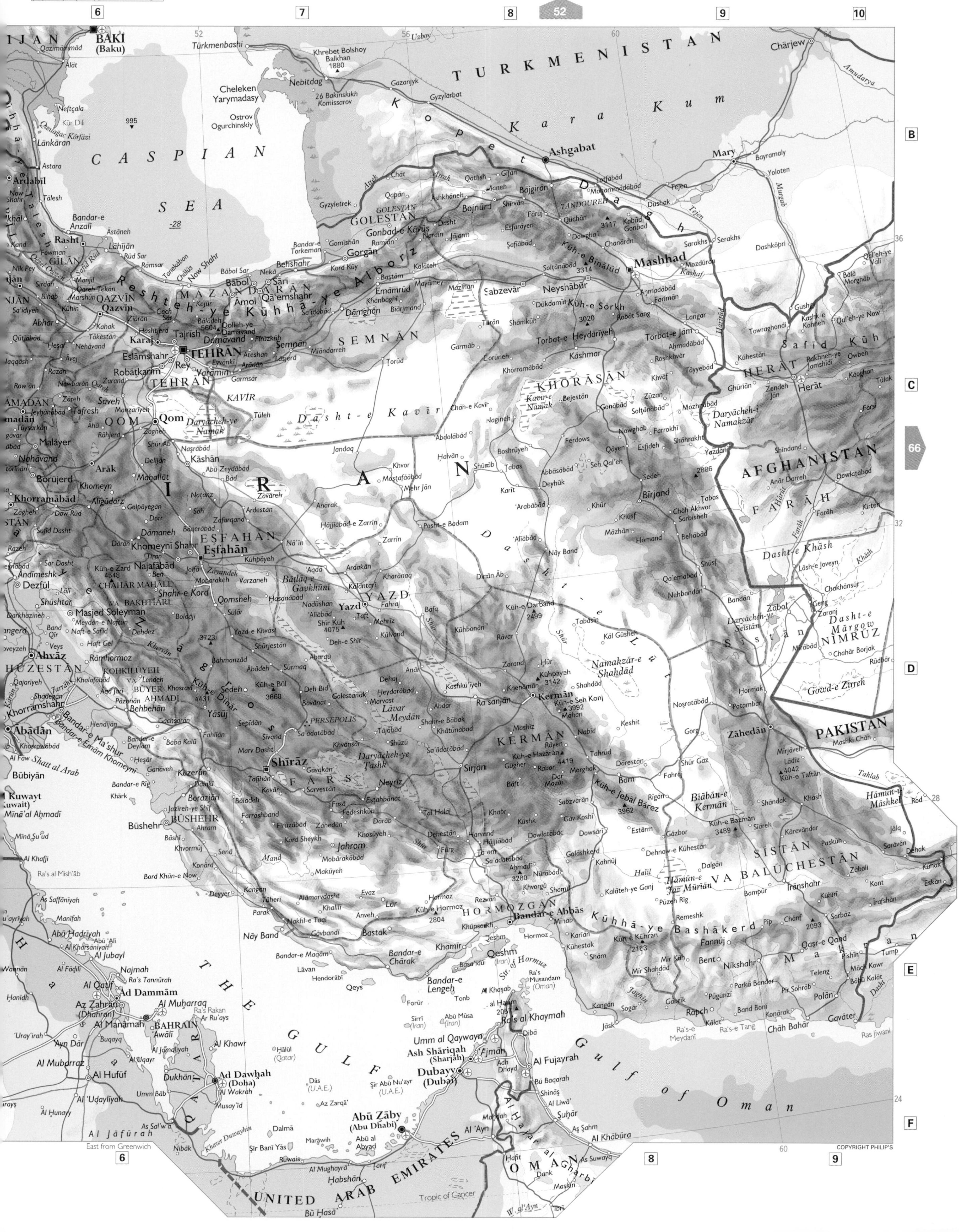
6
7
8
52
9
10
TURKMENISTAN
Kara Kum
Kopet Dagh
CASPIAN SEA
BAKI (Baku)
Türkmenbashi
Cheleken Yarymadasy
Ostrov Ogurchinskiy
Nebitdag
Ashgabat
Mary
Chärjew
Amudarya
Bayramaly
Yoloten
Tejen
Serakhs
Länkäran
Astara
Ardabīl
Rasht
Bandar-e Anzalī
GĪLĀN
QAZVĪN
Qazvīn
Reshteh-ye Kūhhā-ye Alborz
MĀZANDARĀN
GOLESTĀN
Gorgān
Gonbad-e Kāvūs
Bojnūrd
Quchān
Mashhad
Neyshābūr
Sabzevār
Semnān
SEMNĀN
Sārī
Bābol
Āmol
Qā'emshahr
Damāvand
5604
TEHRĀN
Karaj
Tajrish
Rey
Varāmīn
Qom
QOM
Dasht-e Kavīr
Kavir-e Namak
KHORĀSĀN
Kāshān
Arāk
Malāyer
Nahāvand
Borūjerd
Khorramābād
I R A N
Esfahān
ESFAHĀN
Khomeynī Shahr
Najafabad
Nā'īn
Zavāreh
Yazd
YAZD
Bāfq
Ardakān
Tabas
Dasht-e Lūt
Bīrjand
Ferdows
Gonābād
Torbat-e Heydārīyeh
Torbat-e Jām
Kāshmar
Herāt
HERAT
Safīd Kūh
AFGHANISTAN
FARĀH
Farāh
Daryācheh-ye Namakzār
Shīndand
Dasht-e Khāsh
Zābol
Daryācheh-ye Sīstān
Dasht-e Mārgow
NĪMRŪZ
Gowd-e Zirreh
Zāhedān
PAKISTAN
Hāmūn-i Māshkel
Dezfūl
Shūshtar
Ahvāz
KHŪZESTĀN
Khorramshahr
Ābādān
Shatt al Arab
Kūh-e Zard
4548
CHAHĀR MAHALL VA BAKHTĪARĪ
Shahr-e Kord
KOHKĪLŪYEH VA BŪYER AHMADĪ
Yāsūj
Kūh-e Dīnār
4431
Zagros
Shīrāz
FĀRS
PERSEPOLIS
Kāzerūn
Būshehr
BŪSHEHR
Jahrom
Fasā
Lār
Kermān
KERMĀN
Kūh-e Hazārān
4419
Rafsanjān
Sīrjān
Bam
Kūh-e Jebāl Bārez
3962
Kūh-e Taftān
4042
Jāz Mūriān
Hāmūn-e Jaz Mūriān
SĪSTĀN VA BALŪCHESTĀN
Īrānshahr
Bandar-e Abbās
HORMOZGĀN
Minab
Qeshm
Str. of Hormuz
Kūhhā-ye Bashākerd
Makran
Chāh Bahār
Gavāter
Jāsk
Gulf of Oman
THE GULF
Kuwayt (Kuwait)
Mīnā' al Ahmadī
Būbiyān
Al Jubayl
Ad Dammām
Al Qatīf
Az Zahrān (Dhahran)
Al Manāmah
BAHRAIN
QATAR
Ad Dawhah (Doha)
Al Hufūf
Al Mubarraz
Al Jāfūrah
Ra's al Khaymah
Umm al Qaywayn
Ash Shāriqah (Sharjah)
Dubayy (Dubai)
Al Fujayrah
Abū Zāby (Abu Dhabi)
Al 'Ayn
UNITED ARAB EMIRATES
OMAN
Suhār
Tropic of Cancer
East from Greenwich
6
8
9
COPYRIGHT PHILIP'S

50 0 25 50 75 100 125 150 175 km

50 0 25 50 75 100 125 miles

1: 4 400 000

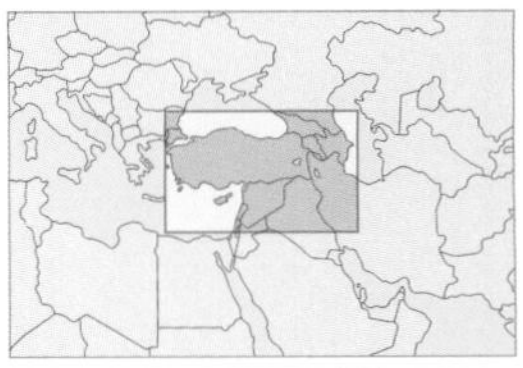

1
2
3
33
4
5
6
7
A
B
C
D
E
F
G
45
47
BLACK SEA
MEDITERRANEAN SEA
BULGARIA
GREECE
CYPRUS
LEBANON
ISRAEL
TURKEY
Stara Zagora
Aytos
Yambol
Burgas
Nos Emine
Elkhovo
Michurin
Kırklareli
Edirne
Orestiás
Yıldız Dağları
Demirköy
İğneada Burnu
Babaeski
Lüleburgaz
Uzunköprü
Çorlu
Silivri
Tekirdağ
Thrace
İpsala
Keşan
Enez
Saros Körfezi
Gelibolu
Samothráki
Gökçeada
Çanakkale
Marmara Denizi (Sea of Marmara)
İSTANBUL
İstanbul Boğazı (Bosporus)
Kocaeli (İzmit)
Sakarya (Adapazarı)
Gebze
Yalova
Gölcük
İznik Gölü
Bandırma
Bursa
Uludağ
İnegöl
Bilecik
Bozcaada
Ayvacık
Edremit
Edremit Körfezi
Balıkesir
Ayvalık
Midilli
Lésvos
Bergama
Soma
Dursunbey
Alaçam Dağları
Kütahya
Eskişehir
Manisa
Lydia
Foça
Khíos
Menemen
Turgutlu
İZMİR (Smyrna)
Çeşme
Boz Dağlar
Ödemiş
Selçuk
Sámos
Kuşadası
Aydın
Nazilli
Büyük Menderes
Denizli
Caria
Ikaría
Pátmos
Fournoi
Dhodhekánisos
Milas
Muğla
Bodrum
Kálimnos
Kos
Gökova Körfezi
Marmaris
Datça
Ródhos (Rhodes)
Astipálaia
Tilos
Simi
Kárpathos
Kásos
Fethiye
Lycia
Kaş
Kalkan
Megiste
Finike
Kemer
Antalya
Antalya Körfezi
Manavgat
Alanya
Pamphylia
Gazipaşa
Anamur
Anamur Burnu
Bey Dağları
Burdur
Isparta
Eğridir Gölü
Beyşehir Gölü
Pisidia
Afyon
Phrygia
Uşak
Akşehir Gölü
Sultan Dağları
Konya
Konya Ovası
Lycaonia
Karaman
Toros Dağları
Ereğli
Karapınar
Tuz Gölü
Anadolu
Polatlı
ANKARA
Kırıkkale
Kırşehir
Nevşehir
Kapadokya
Aksaray
Niğde
Kayseri
Tahtalı Dağları
Adana
Tarsus
Mersin (İçel)
Silifke
Cilicia
İskenderun Körfezi
İskenderun
Antakya
Osmaniye
Gaziantep
Kahramanmaraş
Kilis
Sivas
Tokat
Amasya
Çorum
Samsun
Bafra
Sinop
İnce Burun
Kastamonu
Küre Dağları
Paphlagonia
Zonguldak
Bartın
Karabük
Ereğli
Düzce
Bolu
Bithynia
Köroğlu Dağları
Ilgaz Dağları
Çankırı
Yozgat
Kerempe Burnu
Çatalzeytin
Ünye
Terme
Çarşamba
Merzifon
Turhal
Zile
Deveci Dağları
Ak Dağlar
Tecer Dağları
Al Lādhiqīyah (Latakia)
C. Apostolos Andreas
Rizokarpaso
Kyrenia
Nicosia
Famagusta
Morphou
Troodos
Olympus 1951
Paphos
Akrotiri
Larnaca
Limassol
Ţarţūs
Ḩimş (Homs)
Ḩamāh
Ţarābulus (Tripoli)
BAYRŪT (Beirut)
Zaḩlah
Şaydā
Şūr
DIMASHQ (Damascus)
Ḩefa (Haifa)
Netanya
Tel Aviv-Yafo
Jerusalem
West Bank
'AMMĀN
Az Zarqā'
Irbid
Halab (Aleppo)

Projection: Conical with two standard parallels

3 80 4 5 74 6 7

Division between Greeks and Turks in Cyprus; Turks to the North.

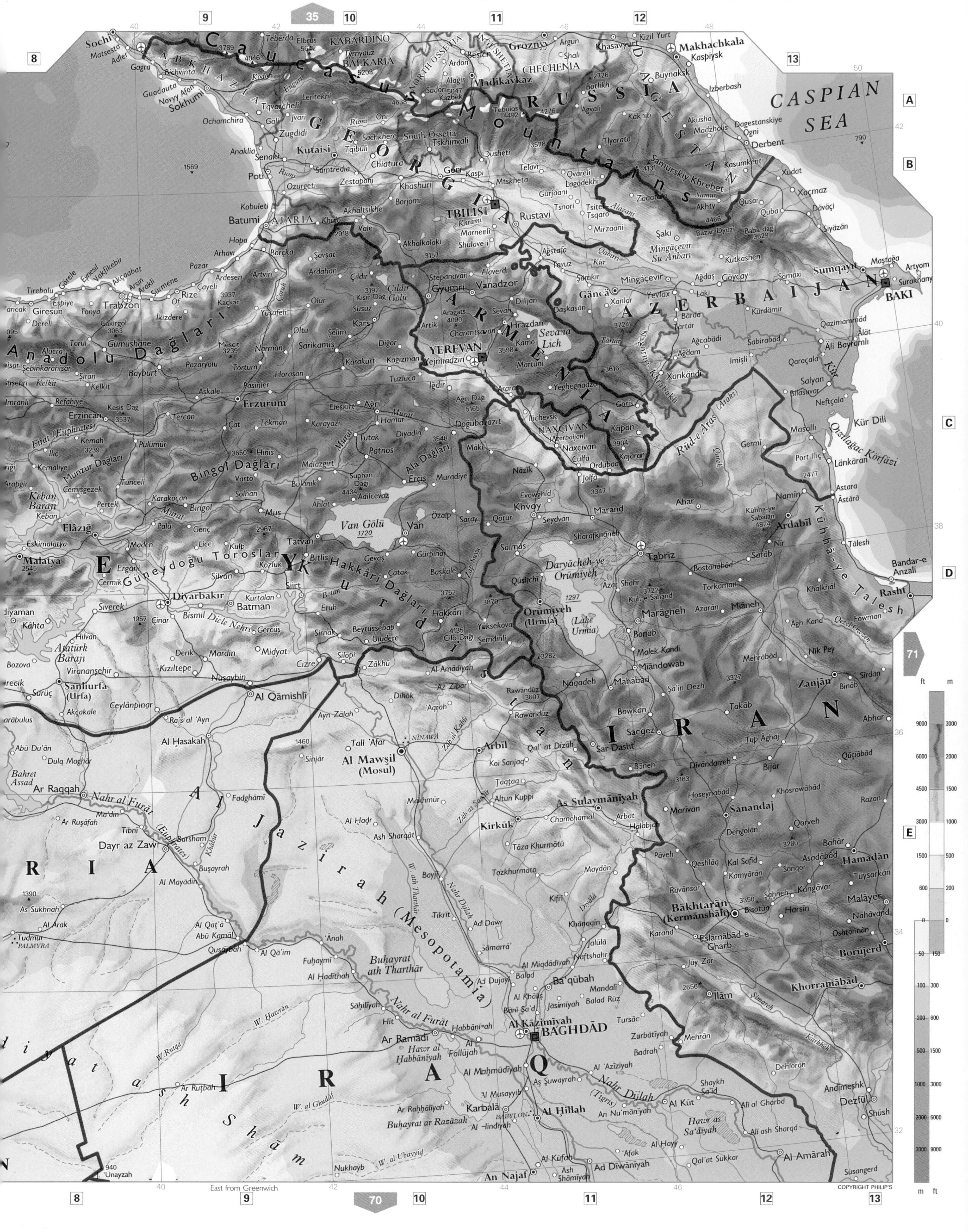

Caucasus Mountains
RUSSIA
GEORGIA
ARMENIA
AZERBAIJAN
DAGESTAN
CHECHENIA
INGUSHETIA
NORTH OSSETIA
KABARDINO-BALKARIA
ABKHAZIA
AJARIA
South Ossetia
NAXÇIVAN (Azerbaijan)
Nagorno-Karabakh
CASPIAN SEA
TURKEY
IRAN
IRAQ
SYRIA
Kurdistan
Al Jazīrah (Mesopotamia)
Bādiyat ash Shām
Anadolu Dağları
Güneydoğu Toroslar
Hakkâri Dağları
Bingöl Dağları
Munzur Dağları
Ala Dağları
Kūhhā-ye Talesh
Samurskiy Khrebet
Van Gölü
Daryācheh-ye Orūmīyeh (Lake Urmia)
Sevana Lich
Çıldır Gölü
Mingäçevir Su Anbarı
Keban Barajı
Atatürk Barajı
Buhayrat ath Tharthār
Buhayrat ar Razāzah
Hawr al Ḩabbānīyah
Hawr as Sa'dīyah
Qızılağac Körfäzi
Kür Dili
Nahr al Furāt (Euphrates)
Fırat (Euphrates)
Nahr Dijlah (Tigris)
Dicle Nehri
Rūd-e Aras (Araks)
Kür
Murat
Zāb al Kabīr
Zāb aş Şaghīr
Khābūr
Diyālā
Karkheh
TBILISI
YEREVAN
BAKI
BAGHDĀD
Sochi
Sokhumi
Batumi
Poti
Kutaisi
Gori
Rustavi
Vladikavkaz
Groznyy
Makhachkala
Derbent
Gyumri
Vanadzor
Gäncä
Sumqayıt
Mingäçevir
Trabzon
Rize
Giresun
Erzurum
Erzincan
Kars
Ağrı
Iğdır
Van
Muş
Bitlis
Elâzığ
Malatya
Diyarbakır
Batman
Siirt
Mardin
Şanlıurfa (Urfa)
Hakkâri
Tabrīz
Orūmīyeh (Urmia)
Ardabīl
Rasht
Zanjān
Sanandaj
Bākhtarān (Kermānshāh)
Hamadān
Khorramābād
Dezfūl
Al Mawşil (Mosul)
Arbīl
Kirkūk
As Sulaymānīyah
Dayr az Zawr
Ar Raqqah
Al Ḩasakah
Al Qāmishlī
Ar Ramādī
Al Fallūjah
Karbalā
Al Ḩillah
An Najaf
Al Kūt
Al 'Amārah
Ad Dīwānīyah
Ba'qūbah
Sāmarrā'
Tikrīt
Palmyra
Elbrus 5642
Kazbek 5047
Ağrı Dağı 5165
Aragats 4090
Süphan Dağı 4434
Kūh-e Sabalān 4824
East from Greenwich
COPYRIGHT PHILIP'S
ft
m

10 0 10 20 30 40 50 60 70 80 100 km

10 0 10 20 30 40 50 60 miles

1:2 200 000

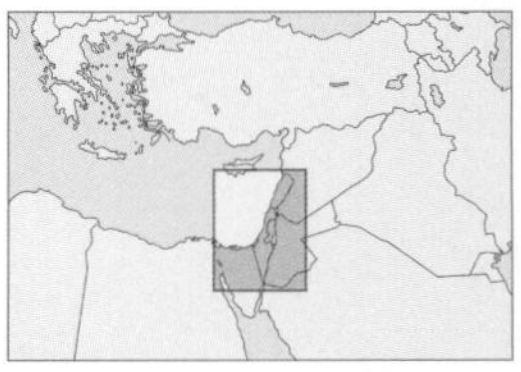

1 2 3 4 5 6
72
A B C D E F
70
80
CYPRUS
Paphos
Episkopi
Limassol
Akrotiri Bay
Episkopi Bay
C. Gata
MEDITERRANEAN
SEA
LEBANON
SYRIA
ISRAEL
JORDAN
EGYPT
SAUDI ARABIA
Gaza Strip
West Bank
BAYRŪT (Beirut)
DIMASHQ (Damascus)
Tarābulus (Tripoli)
Jerusalem (Yerushalayim) (Al Quds)
'AMMĀN
Tel Aviv-Yafo
Hefa (Haifa)
Irbid
Az Zarqā
Ḩimş (Homs)
Sayda (Sidon)
Sūr (Tyre)
Gaza
Khān Yūnis
Rafah
Bûr Sa'îd (Port Said)
Bûr Fu'ad
Ismâ'ilîya
El Suweis (Suez)
Elat
Al 'Aqabah
Be'er Sheva (Beersheba)
Ashdod
Ashqelon
Netanya
Nābulus
Al Khalīl (Hebron)
Bayt Lahm (Bethlehem)
El Arīḩā (Jericho)
Dead Sea
Gulf of Aqaba
Sinai
HADAROM
Hanegev
SHAMÂL SÎNÂ'
JANŪB SÎNÎ
Gebel el Tih
Khalig el Suweis
Ḩims
AS SUWAYDĀ'
AL MAFRAQ
AZ ZARQĀ
'AMMAN
AL KARAK
AT ṬAFĪLAH
MA'ĀN
AL 'AQABAH
Ma'ān
Petra
Wadi Rum
Golan Heights
Jabal Lubnān
Al Biqā'
Qurnat as Sawdā' 3088
2814
1942
2628
2464
2616
1435
1736
1754
1592
1272
1165
948
892
1094
1072
1305
-411
-210
-289
-333
-121
Suez Canal
Great Bitter Lakes
Projection: Polyconic
East from Greenwich
33 34 35 36 37
COPYRIGHT PHILIP'S
ft m
9000 3000
6000 2000
4500 1500
3000 1000
1200 400
600 200
0 0
200 600
2000 6000

1974 Cease Fire Lines

National Parks

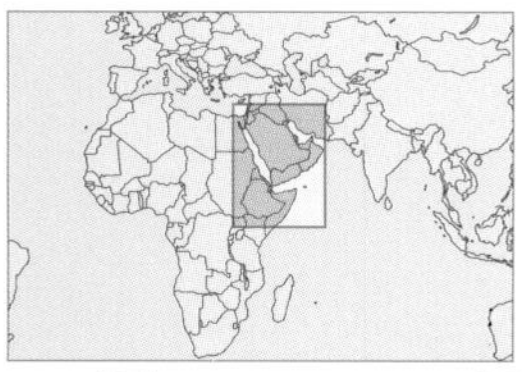

1:13 300 000

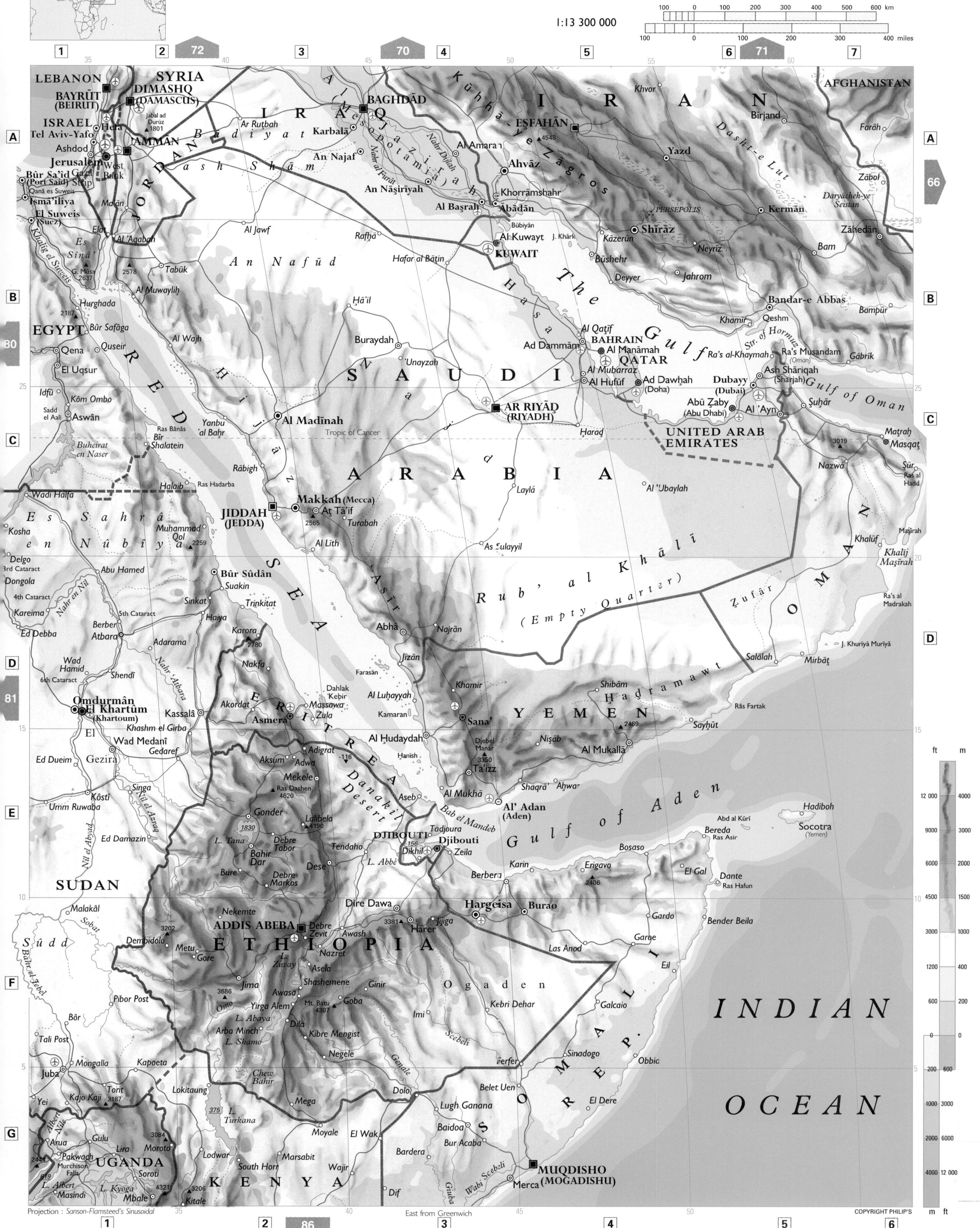

100 0 100 200 300 400 500 600 km
100 0 100 200 300 400 miles
1 2 72 3 70 4 5 6 71 7
A B C D E F G
66 80 81 86
LEBANON
SYRIA
BAYRŪT (BEIRUT)
DIMASHQ (DAMASCUS)
ISRAEL
Tel Aviv-Yafo
Ashdod
Jerusalem
West Bank
Gaza Strip
AMMĀN
JORDAN
Jabal ad Durūz 1801
Bûr Sa'îd (Port Said)
Qanâ es Suweis
Ismâ'ilîya
El Suweis (Suez)
Ma'ān
Elat
Al 'Aqabah
Es Sînâ'
G. Mûsa 2637
2578
Tabūk
Khalîg el Suweis
Hurghada
2187
EGYPT
Bûr Safâga
Qena
Quseir
El Uqsur
Idfû
Kôm Ombo
Sadd el Aali
Aswân
Ras Bânâs
Bir Shalatein
Buheirat en Naser
Halaib
Ras Hadarba
Wadi Halfa
Es Sahrâ en Nûbîya
Kosha
Muhammad Qol
2259
Delgo
3rd Cataract
Dongola
4th Cataract
Nahr en Nil
Kareima
Abu Hamed
5th Cataract
Ed Debba
Berber
Atbara
Adarama
Nahr 'Atbara
Wad Hamid
6th Cataract
Shendî
Omdurmân
El Khartûm (Khartoum)
Kassalā
Khashm el Girba
El Gezira
Wad Medanî
Gedaref
Ed Dueim
Singa
Kôstî
Umm Ruwaba
Nil el Azraq
Nil el Abyad
Ed Damazin
SUDAN
Malakâl
Sobat
Sûdd
Bahr el Jebel
Pibor Post
Bôr
Tali Post
Juba
Mongalla
Kapoeta
Torit
Kajo Kaji
3187
Yei
Albert Nile
Arua
Gulu
Lira
Moroto
3084
Pakwach
Murchison Falls
UGANDA
Soroti
L. Albert
Masindi
L. Kyoga
Mbale
4321
2444
619
Kitale
3206
Lodwar
Lokitaung
L. Turkana
375
South Horr
Marsabit
KENYA
Moyale
Wajir
El Wak
Dif
Ar Rutbah
IRAQ
Bādiyat ash Shām
Karbalā
An Najaf
BAGHDĀD
Al Jazīrah
Mesopotamia
Nahr Dijlah
Nahr al Furāt
Al 'Amarah
An Nāsirīyah
Al Basrah
Khorramshahr
Ābādān
Ahvāz
Būbiyān
Al Kuwayt
KUWAIT
J. Khārk
Al Jawf
Rafhā
An Nafūd
Hafar al Bātin
Al Muwaylih
Al Wajh
Hā'il
Buraydah
'Unayzah
SAUDI ARABIA
Hijāz
Najd
Al Madīnah
Yanbu 'al Bahr
Tropic of Cancer
AR RIYĀD (RIYADH)
Harad
Rābigh
JIDDAH (JEDDA)
Makkah (Mecca)
At Tā'if
2565
Turabah
Laylá
Al Līth
As Sulayyil
'Asīr
Al 'Ubaylah
Rub' al Khālī (Empty Quarter)
Abhā
Najrān
Jīzān
Farasān
Al Hasa
Al Qatīf
Ad Dammām
BAHRAIN
Al Manāmah
QATAR
Al Mubarraz
Al Hufūf
Ad Dawhah (Doha)
The Gulf
IRAN
Khvor
Kūhhā-ye Zāgros
EŞFAHĀN
4548
Yazd
Bīrjand
Dasht-e Lut
Persepolis
Shīrāz
Kāzerūn
Būshehr
Deyyer
Jahrom
Neyrīz
Kermān
Bam
Zābol
Daryācheh-ye Sīstan
Zāhedān
Farāh
AFGHANISTAN
Bandar-e Abbās
Bampūr
Khamīr
Qeshm
Str. of Hormuz
Ra's al-Khaymah
Ra's Musandam (Oman)
Gābrīk
Ash Shāriqah (Sharjah)
Dubayy (Dubai)
Abū Zaby (Abu Dhabi)
Al 'Ayn
UNITED ARAB EMIRATES
Şuhār
Gulf of Oman
Matrah
Masqat
3019
Nazwa
Şūr
Ras al Hadd
OMAN
Maşīrah
Khalūf
Khalīj Maşīrah
Ra's al Madrakah
Zufār
Salālah
Mirbāt
J. Khurīyā Murīyā
Hadramawt
Shibām
Rās Fartak
Sayhūt
YEMEN
Sana'
Khamir
2469
Al Mukallā
Nişāb
Djebel Manār 3350
Ta'izz
Al Hudaydah
Hanish
Kamaran
Al Luhayyah
Al Mukhā
Shaqrā'
Ahwar
Al' Adan (Aden)
Bab el Mandeb
Gulf of Aden
Hadiboh
Abd al Kūrī
Socotra (Yemen)
Dahlak Kebir
Massawa
Zula
Asmera
ERITREA
Akordat
Nakfa
Karora
2780
Sinkat
Haiya
Bûr Sûdân
Suakin
Trinkitat
RED SEA
Adigrat
Aksum
Adwa
Mekele
-116
Danakil Desert
Ras Dashen 4620
Gonder
1830
Lalibela
4190
L. Tana
Debre Tabor
Bahir Dar
Tendaho
Aseb
DJIBOUTI
Tadjoura
Djibouti
Dikhil
156
L. Abbé
Zeila
Dese
Bure
Debre Markos
Nekemte
ADDIS ABEBA
Debre Zevit
Awash
Dire Dawa
3381
Harer
Jijiga
Hargeisa
Burao
Berbera
Karin
Erigavo
2406
Bosaso
Bereda
Ras Asir
El Gal
Dante
Ras Hafun
Gardo
Bender Beila
Garoe
Eil
Las Anod
3202
Dembidolo
Metu
Gore
ETHIOPIA
L. Zaway
Nazret
Asela
Shashemene
Ginir
Goba
Mt. Batu 4307
Jima
Awasa
3686
Omo
Yirga Alem
L. Abaya
Dila
Arba Minch
L. Shamo
Kibre Mengist
Negele
Imi
Ogaden
Kebri Dehar
Galcaio
Scebeli
Genale
Chew Bahir
Ferfer
Sinadogo
Obbia
SOMALI REP.
Dolo
Belet Uen
El Dere
Lugh Ganana
Baidoa
Bur Acaba
Bardera
Giuba
Wabi Scebeli
Merca
MUQDISHO (MOGADISHU)
INDIAN OCEAN
ft m
12 000 4000
9000 3000
6000 2000
4500 1500
3000 1000
1200 400
600 200
0 0
200 600
1000 3000
2000 6000
4000 12 000
m ft

Projection : Sanson-Flamsteed's Sinusoidal

East from Greenwich

200 0 200 400 600 800 1000 1200 1400 1600 1800 km

1:37 300 000

200 0 200 400 600 800 1000 1200 miles

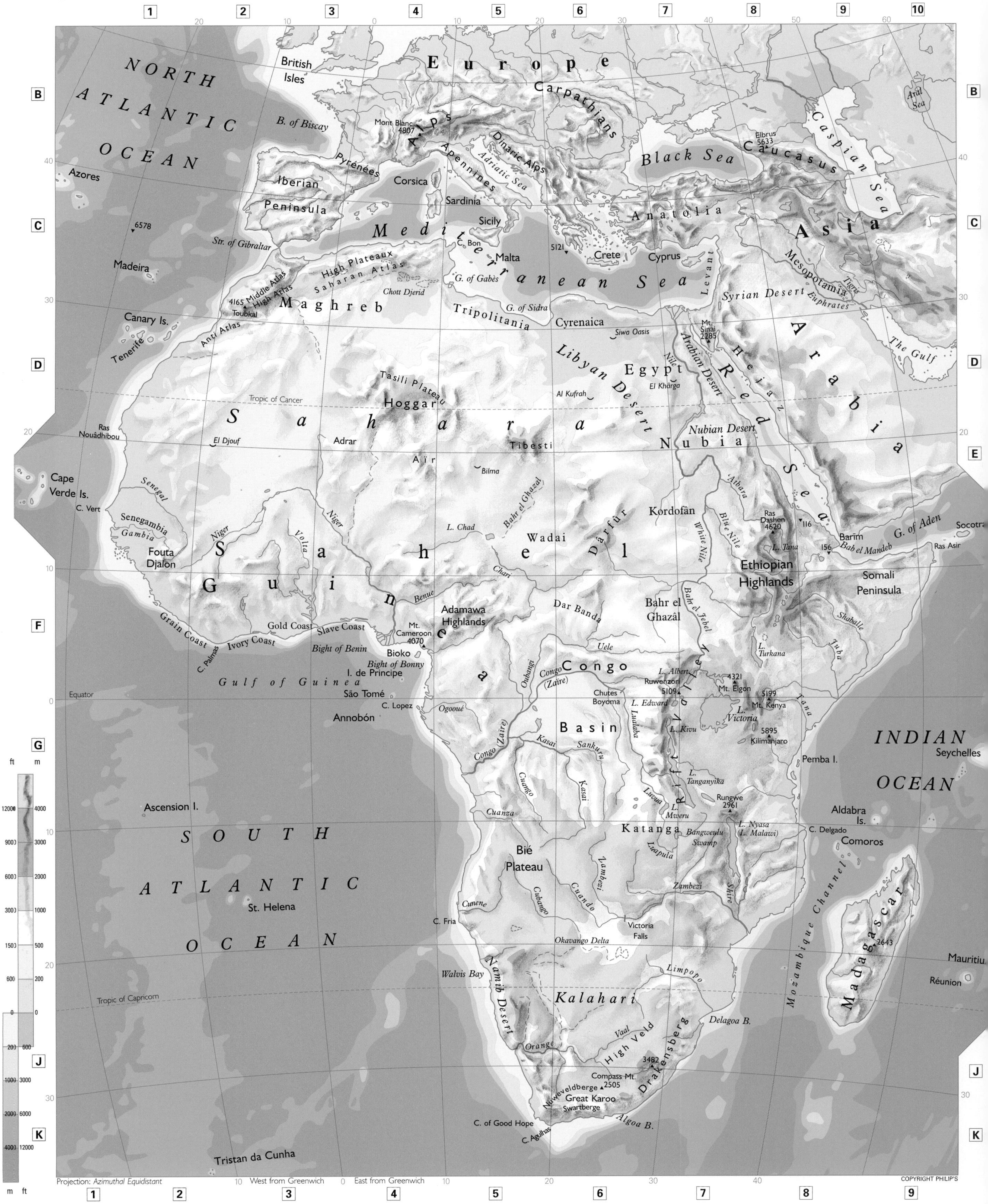
NORTH ATLANTIC OCEAN
British Isles
Europe
Carpathians
B. of Biscay
Mont Blanc 4807
Alps
Dinaric Alps
Apennines
Adriatic Sea
Elbrus 5633
Caucasus
Caspian Sea
Aral Sea
Black Sea
Azores
Pyrénées
Iberian Peninsula
Corsica
Sardinia
Sicily
Anatolia
Asia
6578
Mediterranean Sea
Str. of Gibraltar
C. Bon
Malta
5121
Crete
Cyprus
Levant
Mesopotamia
Tigris
Euphrates
Syrian Desert
Madeira
High Plateaux
Saharan Atlas
Middle Atlas
High Atlas
4165 Toubkal
Chott Djerid
G. of Gabès
G. of Sidra
Maghreb
Tripolitania
Cyrenaica
Siwa Oasis
Mt. Sinai 2285
Canary Is.
Tenerife
Anti Atlas
Libyan Desert
Egypt
Nile
El Khârga
Arabian Desert
Hejaz
Red Sea
Arabia
The Gulf
Tasili Plateau
Hoggar
Tropic of Cancer
Al Kufrah
Sahara
Ras Nouâdhibou
El Djouf
Adrar
Tibesti
Nubian Desert
Nubia
Aïr
Bilma
Cape Verde Is.
C. Vert
Senegal
Niger
'Atbara
Ras Dashen 4620
116
Barim
G. of Aden
Socotra
Bab el Mandeb
156
Ras Asir
Senegambia
Gambia
Fouta Djalon
Volta
L. Chad
Bahr el Ghazal
Wadai
Dârfûr
Kordofân
White Nile
Blue Nile
L. Tana
Ethiopian Highlands
Somali Peninsula
Sahel
Guinea
Chari
Benue
Adamawa Highlands
Dar Banda
Bahr el Ghazâl
Bahr el Jebel
Shaballe
Juba
Grain Coast
Gold Coast
Slave Coast
Ivory Coast
C. Palmas
Bight of Benin
Mt. Cameroon 4070
Bioko
Bight of Bonny
I. de Principe
Gulf of Guinea
São Tomé
Equator
C. Lopez
Annobón
Ogooué
Oubangi
Uele
Congo (Zaïre)
Congo Basin
Chutes Boyoma
L. Albert
Ruwenzori 5109
Rift Valley
4321 Mt. Elgon
5199 Mt. Kenya
L. Turkana
Tana
L. Edward
Lualaba
L. Kivu
L. Victoria
5895 Kilimanjaro
INDIAN OCEAN
Seychelles
Kasai
Sankuru
Pemba I.
Cuango
L. Tanganyika
Lucua
L. Mweru
Rungwe 2961
Ascension I.
Cuanza
Katanga
Bangweulu Swamp
Luapula
L. Nyasa (L. Malawi)
C. Delgado
Aldabra Is.
Comoros
SOUTH ATLANTIC OCEAN
Bié Plateau
Zambezi
Cuando
Cubango
Shire
Cunene
Mozambique Channel
St. Helena
C. Fria
Victoria Falls
Okavango Delta
Madagascar
2643
Mauritius
Réunion
Walvis Bay
Namib Desert
Limpopo
Kalahari
Tropic of Capricorn
Delagoa B.
Vaal
High Veld
Drakensberg
Orange
3482
Compass Mt. 2505
Nuweveldberge
Great Karoo
Swartberge
C. of Good Hope
C. Agulhas
Algoa B.
Tristan da Cunha
Projection: Azimuthal Equidistant
West from Greenwich
East from Greenwich
COPYRIGHT PHILIP'S
ft m
12000 4000
9000 3000
6000 2000
3000 1000
1500 500
600 200
0 0
200 600
1000 3000
2000 6000
4000 12000
m ft

1:37 300 000

200 0 200 400 600 800 1000 1200 1400 1600 1800 km

200 0 200 400 600 800 1000 1200 miles

NORTH ATLANTIC OCEAN
B. of Biscay
Azores (Port.)
Madeira (Port.)
Canary Is. (Sp.)
UNITED KINGDOM
LONDON
NETH.
BELG.
GERMANY
POLAND
Warsaw
Prague
CZECH REP.
Vienna
SLOVAK REP.
AUSTRIA
HUNGARY
SWITZ.
FRANCE
PARIS
RUSSIA
Kiev
UKRAINE
Volgograd
KAZAKHSTAN
Aral Sea
Caspian Sea
ROMANIA
Odessa
CROATIA
BOS.-HERZ.
SERBIA & MONT.
BULGARIA
ALB.
MAC.
ITALY
Rome
Adriatic Sea
Black Sea
GEORGIA
ARM.
AZER.
Baku
TURKMEN.
PORTUGAL
SPAIN
Madrid
Lisbon
Corsica
Sardinia
Sicily
GREECE
Athens
TURKEY
Ankara
Crete
CYPRUS
MALTA
Mediterranean Sea
Algiers
Annaba
Constantine
Tunis
Sfax
TUNISIA
Chott Djerid
Rabat
Tetouan
Casablanca
Fès
MOROCCO
Marrakesh
Tripoli
Misrātah
Benghazi
Alexandria
Port Said
CAIRO
Suez
El Faiyûm
Asyût
Aswân
Nile
EGYPT
LEB.
Damascus
Tel Aviv-Jaffa
ISRAEL
Jerusalem
JORDAN
SYRIA
Aleppo
Mosul
Tigris
Euphrates
Baghdād
IRAQ
Syrian Desert
Basra
KUWAIT
TEHRĀN
Esfahān
IRAN
The Gulf
BAHRAIN
QATAR
SAUDI ARABIA
Riyadh
Medina
Jedda
Mecca
Red Sea
YEMEN
G. of Aden
Socotra (Yemen)
Ras Asir
El Aaiún
WESTERN SAHARA
Dakhla
Fdérik
Ras Nouâdhibou
ALGERIA
In Salah
LIBYA
Marzūq
Al Jawf
Tropic of Cancer
Sahara
MAURITANIA
Nouakchott
CAPE VERDE IS.
Praia
St-Louis
Senegal
C. Vert
Dakar
SENEGAL
GAMBIA
Banjul
GUINEA-BISSAU
Bissau
GUINEA
Conakry
Freetown
SIERRA LEONE
LIBERIA
Monrovia
MALI
Tombouctou
Bamako
NIGER
Agadès
Niamey
BURKINA FASO
Ouagadougou
Bobo-Dioulasso
IVORY COAST
Yamoussoukro
Bouaké
Abidjan
GHANA
Kumasi
Accra
Sekondi-Takoradi
TOGO
Lomé
BENIN
Porto Novo
NIGERIA
Kano
Maiduguri
Abuja
Ibadan
Lagos
Benue
Enugu
Port Harcourt
Bight of Benin
Gulf of Guinea
CHAD
L. Chad
Abéché
Ndjamena
Chari
Wadi Halfa
Port Sudan
Atbara
'Atbara
SUDAN
Omdurmân
Khartoum
Wad Medani
El Fâsher
El Obeid
White Nile
Blue Nile
Malakâl
Wau
Bahr el Jebel
ERITREA
Mesewa
Asmera
DJIBOUTI
Djibouti
Berbera
L. Tana
ETHIOPIA
Addis Ababa
Harer
Shabeelle
SOMALI REP.
Mogadishu
Juba
Kismayu
CENTRAL AFRICAN REP.
Bangui
CAMEROON
Douala
Yaoundé
Malabo
EQUATORIAL GUINEA
SÃO TOMÉ & PRINCIPE
Annobón
Equator
Libreville
C. Lopez
GABON
CONGO
Oubangi
Congo (Zaïre)
Mbandaka
Kisangani
CONGO (DEM. REP. OF THE)
Lualaba
Kasai
Brazzaville
Kinshasa
Pointe-Noire
CABINDA (Angola)
Matadi
Kananga
Cuango
L. Albert
UGANDA
Kampala
L. Edward
RWANDA
Kigali
L. Kivu
BURUNDI
Bujumbura
KENYA
L. Turkana
Kisumu
L. Victoria
Nairobi
Tana
Mombasa
TANZANIA
Dodoma
Zanzibar
Dar es Salaam
L. Tanganyika
INDIAN OCEAN
SEYCHELLES
Aldabra Is.
C. Delgado
COMOROS
Moroni
Mamoudzou
Mayotte (Fr.)
Antsiranana
Mozambique Channel
Mahajanga
Toamasina
Antananarivo
MADAGASCAR
Fianarantsoa
MAURITIUS
St-Denis
Port Louis
Réunion (Fr.)
Ascension I. (U.K.)
SOUTH ATLANTIC OCEAN
St. Helena (U.K.)
Luanda
ANGOLA
Lobito
Huambo
Namibe
Cunene
Cubango
C. Fria
L. Mweru
Likasi
Lubumbashi
L. Malawi
MALAWI
Lilongwe
Ndola
ZAMBIA
Lusaka
Zambezi
Blantyre
MOZAMBIQUE
Moçambique
Livingstone
Harare
ZIMBABWE
Bulawayo
Beira
NAMIBIA
Windhoek
BOTSWANA
Limpopo
Tropic of Capricorn
Gaborone
Pretoria
Johannesburg
Maputo
Mbabane
SWAZ.
Vaal
Orange
Kimberley
Maseru
LESOTHO
Durban
SOUTH AFRICA
East London
Port Elizabeth
Cape Town
C. of Good Hope
C. Agulhas
Tristan da Cunha (U.K.)

● Dakar Capital Cities

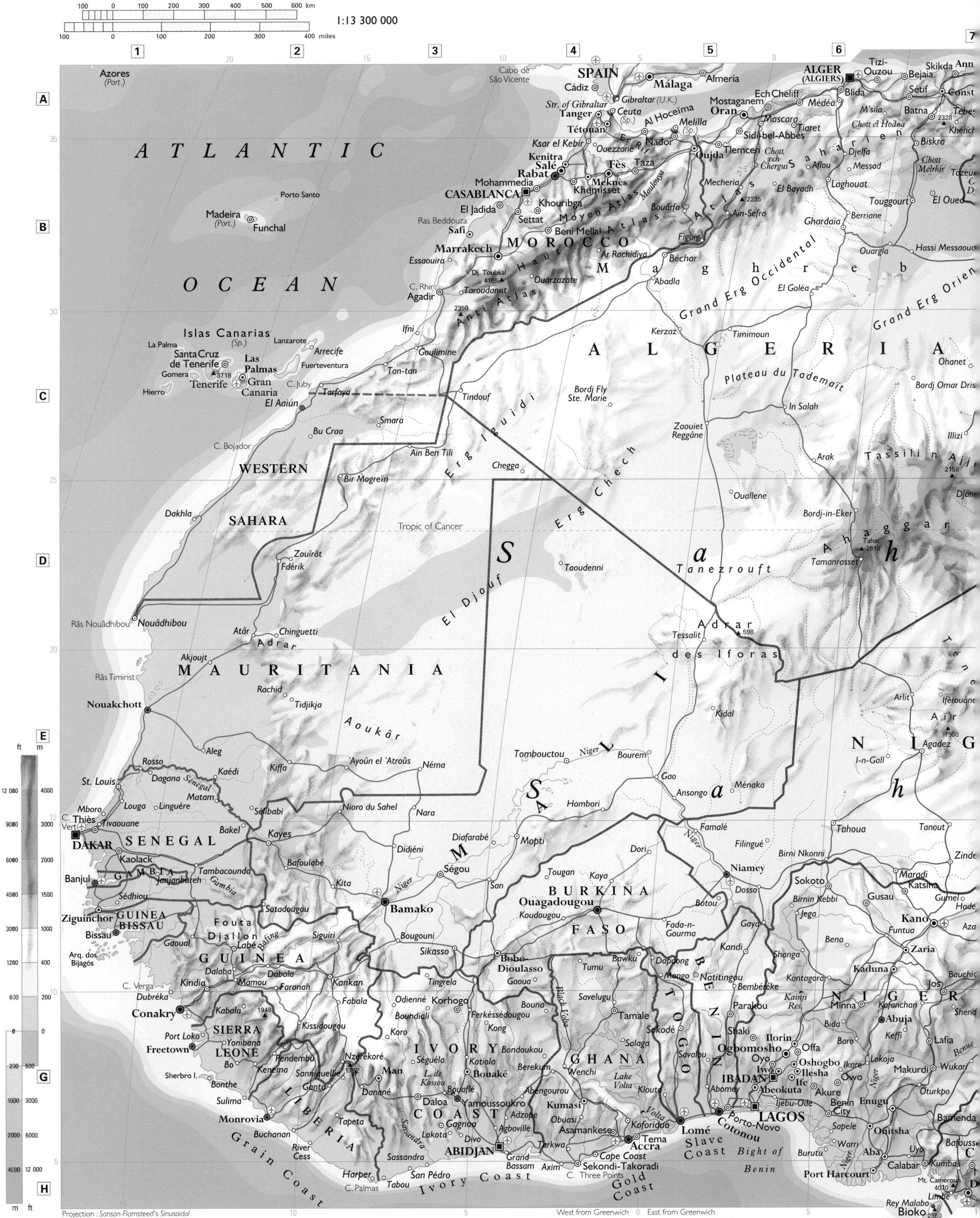
1:13 300 000
100 0 100 200 300 400 500 600 km
100 0 100 200 300 400 miles
ATLANTIC
OCEAN
Azores (Port.)
Madeira (Port.)
Funchal
Porto Santo
Islas Canarias (Sp.)
La Palma
Santa Cruz de Tenerife
Gomera
Hierro
Tenerife
Las Palmas
Gran Canaria
Lanzarote
Arrecife
Fuerteventura
C. Juby
Tarfaya
El Aaiún
SPAIN
Cádiz
Málaga
Almería
Gibraltar (U.K.)
Str. of Gibraltar
Ceuta (Sp.)
Tanger
Tétouan
Al Hoceïma
Melilla (Sp.)
Nador
Ksar el Kebir
Ouezzane
Er Rif
Kenitra
Salé
Rabat
Fès
Taza
Meknès
Khemisset
Mohammedia
CASABLANCA
El Jadida
Khouribga
Settat
Ras Beddouza
Safi
Beni Mellal
Marrakech
MOROCCO
Moyen Atlas
Haut Atlas
Anti Atlas
Essaouira
Dj. Toubkal 4165
Ouarzazate
Ar Rachidiya
C. Rhir
Agadir
Taroudannt
2359
Ifni
Goulimine
Tan-tan
Oujda
Moulouya
Bouârfa
Figuig
Béchar
Abadla
Kerzaz
Tindouf
Smara
Bu Craa
C. Bojador
WESTERN SAHARA
Aïn Ben Tili
Bir Mogreïn
Dakhla
Zouîrât
Fdérik
Râs Nouâdhibou
Nouâdhibou
Atâr
Chinguetti
Adrar
Akjoujt
Râs Timirist
MAURITANIA
Rachid
Tidjikja
Aoukâr
Nouakchott
Aleg
Rosso
Kaédi
Kiffa
'Ayoûn el 'Atroûs
Néma
St. Louis
Dagana
Sénégal
Matam
Louga
Linguère
Sélibabi
Mboro
Thiès
C. Vert
Tivaouane
DAKAR
SENEGAL
Bakel
Kayes
Kaolack
Banjul
GAMBIA
Janjanbureh
Tambacounda
Gambia
Sédhiou
Ziguinchor
GUINEA BISSAU
Bissau
Arq. dos Bijagós
Fouta Djallon
Gaoual
GUINEA
Bafing
Dalaba
Mamou
Dabola
Faranah
Kindia
C. Verga
Dubréka
Conakry
Kabala
1948
SIERRA LEONE
Port Loko
Yonibana
Freetown
Bo
Kenema
Sherbro I.
Bonthe
Sulima
Monrovia
LIBERIA
Buchanan
River Cess
Grain Coast
Harper
C. Palmas
Pendembu
Kissidougou
Nzérékoré
1752
Sanniquellie
Ganta
Tapeta
Kankan
Siguiri
Kita
Satadougou
Bafoulabé
Bamako
Niger
Bougouni
Sikasso
Fabala
Ségou
San
Nioro du Sahel
Nara
Diafarabé
Mopti
Didiéni
Tombouctou
Bourem
Gao
Ansongo
Ménaka
Hombori
MALI
Kidal
Tessalit
Adrar des Iforas
598
Taoudenni
El Djouf
Tropic of Cancer
Erg Iguidi
Erg Chech
Chegga
Tanezrouft
SAHARA
Sahel
ALGERIA
ALGER (ALGIERS)
Tizi-Ouzou
Bejaia
Skikda
Blida
Médéa
Sétif
Batna
Ech Cheliff
Mostaganem
Oran
Mascara
Tiaret
Sidi-bel-Abbès
Tlemcen
Chott ech Chergui
Chott el Hodna
M'sila
Djelfa
Aflou
Messad
Biskra
Chott Melrhir
Touggourt
El Oued
Laghouat
Mecheria
Aïn-Sefra
2235
El Bayadh
Saharien Atlas
Ghardaïa
Berriane
Ouargla
Hassi Messaoud
Maghreb
Grand Erg Occidental
Grand Erg Oriental
El Goléa
Timimoun
Plateau du Tademaït
In Salah
Zaouiet Reggâne
Bordj Fly Ste. Marie
Ouallene
Bordj-in-Eker
Arak
Tassili n Ajjer
2158
Illizi
Djanet
Ohanet
Bordj Omar Driss
Ahaggar
Tahat 2918
Tamanrasset
Ténéré
Arlit
Iférouâne
Aïr
1900
Agadez
I-n-Gall
NIGER
Tahoua
Tanout
Zinder
Birni Nkonni
Maradi
Katsina
Filingué
Niamey
Dosso
Famalé
Dori
BURKINA FASO
Ouagadougou
Koudougou
Tougan
Kaya
Fada-n-Gourma
Botou
Bobo-Dioulasso
Gaoua
Dapaong
Mango
Natitingou
Kandi
Gaya
Tingrela
Odienné
Boundiali
Korhogo
Ferkéssédougou
Kong
Bouna
IVORY COAST
Séguéla
Katiola
Bondoukou
Bouaké
L. de Kossou
Bouaflé
Yamoussoukro
Daloa
Gagnoa
Lakota
Divo
Agboville
Adzope
Abengourou
ABIDJAN
Grand Bassam
Sassandra
San Pédro
Tabou
Ivory Coast
Man
Danané
Koro
GHANA
Tumu
Bawku
Black Volta
Savelugu
Tamale
Salaga
Berekum
Wenchi
Lake Volta
Kumasi
Obuasi
Asamankese
Koforidua
Tarkwa
Axim
Cape Coast
Sekondi-Takoradi
C. Three Points
Accra
Tema
Gold Coast
Volta
Kloute
TOGO
Sokodé
Savalou
BENIN
Bembéréke
Parakou
Abomey
Lomé
Cotonou
Porto-Novo
Slave Coast
Bight of Benin
LAGOS
NIGERIA
Sokoto
Birnin Kebbi
Gusau
Jega
Kano
Funtua
Bena
Zaria
Shanga
Kontagora
Kainji Res.
Kaduna
Minna
Kafanchan
Jos
Abuja
Bida
Keffi
Lafia
Shaki
Ilorin
Ogbomosho
Offa
Oyo
Oshogbo
Iwo
Ilesha
IBADAN
Ife
Ikare
Owo
Lokoja
Abeokuta
Ijebu-Ode
Akure
Benin City
Enugu
Makurdi
Wukari
Otukpo
Onitsha
Sapele
Warri
Aba
Uyo
Calabar
Burutu
Port Harcourt
Kumba
Mt. Cameroun 4070
Limbe
Bamenda
Bafoussam
Rey Malabo
Bioko
2850
Projection : Sanson-Flamsteed's Sinusoidal
West from Greenwich
East from Greenwich
ft m
12 000 4000
9000 3000
6000 2000
4500 1500
3000 1000
1200 400
600 200
0 0
200 600
1000 3000
2000 6000
4000 12 000
m ft

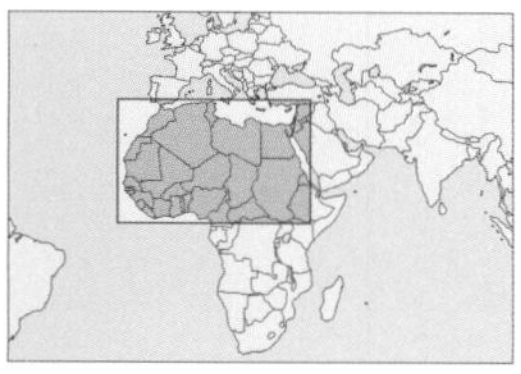

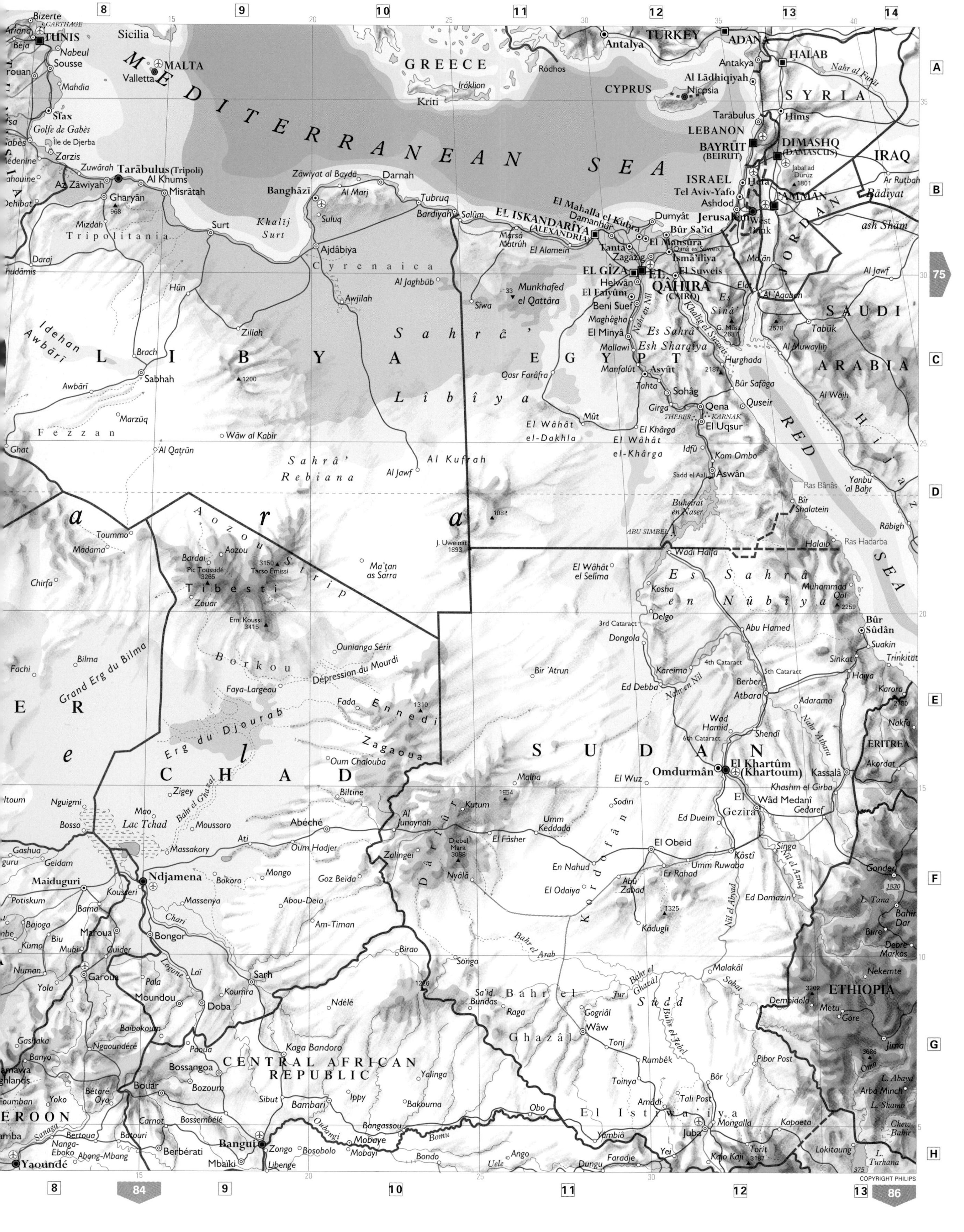

MEDITERRANEAN SEA
RED SEA
LIBYA
EGYPT
SUDAN
CHAD
CENTRAL AFRICAN REPUBLIC
ETHIOPIA
ERITREA
SAUDI ARABIA
SYRIA
LEBANON
ISRAEL
JORDAN
IRAQ
TURKEY
CYPRUS
GREECE
MALTA
Sahara
Tunis
Bizerte
Carthage
Ariana
Beja
Nabeul
Sousse
Mahdia
Sfax
Golfe de Gabès
Île de Djerba
Zarzis
Médenine
Sicilia
Valletta
Tarābulus (Tripoli)
Al Khums
Misrātah
Az Zāwiyah
Zuwārah
Gharyān
Mizdah
Tripolitania
Khalīj Surt
Surt
Banghāzī
Zāwiyat al Bayḍā
Darnah
Al Marj
Suluq
Tubruq
Bardiyah
Ajdābiya
Cyrenaica
Al Jaghbūb
Awjilah
Hūn
Zillah
Idehan Awbārī
Brach
Sabhah
Awbārī
Marzūq
Fezzan
Wāw al Kabīr
Ghat
Al Qaṭrūn
Ṣaḥrā' Rebiana
Al Jawf
Al Kufrah
Ṣaḥrā' Lībīya
Es Sahrâ Esh Sharqîya
Kríti
Iráklion
Ródhos
Antalya
Adana
Antakya
Halab
Nahr al Furāt
Al Lādhiqīyah
Nicosia
Tarābulus
Ḥimṣ
Bayrūt (Beirut)
Dimashq (Damascus)
Jabal ad Durūz
Tel Aviv-Yafo
Haifa
Ashdod
Jerusalem
West Bank
'Ammān
Ar Ruṭbah
Bādiyat ash Shām
Salûm
El Iskandarîya (Alexandria)
El Mahalla el Kubra
Damanhûr
Dumyât
Bûr Sa'îd
El Mansûra
Qanâ es Suweis
Ismâ'ilîya
Marsâ Matrûh
El Alamein
Tanta
Zagazig
El Gîza
El Qâhira (Cairo)
El Suweis
Helwân
Siwa
Munkhafed el Qattâra
El Faiyûm
Beni Suef
Maghâgha
El Minya
Mallawi
Manfalût
Asyût
Tahta
Sohâg
Girga
Qena
Thebes
Karnak
El Uqsur
Qasr Farâfra
Mût
El Wâhât el-Dakhla
El Khârga
El Wâhât el-Khârga
Idfû
Kom Ombo
Sadd el Aali
Aswân
Buheirat en Naser
Abu Simbel
Es Sînâ'
G. Mûsa
Elat
Al 'Aqabah
Ma'ân
Tabūk
Al Muwayliḥ
Al Wajh
Al Jawf
Hurghada
Bûr Safâga
Quseir
Ras Bânâs
Bîr Shalatein
Halaib
Ras Hadarba
Yanbu 'al Baḥr
Rābigh
Nahr en Nîl
J. Uweinat
Ma'tan as Sarra
Wadi Halfa
El Wâhât el Selîma
Es Sahrâ en Nûbîya
Kosha
Delgo
Muhammad Qol
Bûr Sûdân
Suakin
Sinkat
Trinkitat
3rd Cataract
Dongola
Abu Hamed
4th Cataract
5th Cataract
Kareima
Bir 'Atrun
Ed Debba
Berber
Atbara
Haiya
Karora
Adarama
Nakfa
Wad Hamid
Shendî
6th Cataract
Nahr 'Atbara
Akordat
Omdurmân
El Khartûm (Khartoum)
Kassalâ
Khashm el Girba
El Wuz
Malha
Sodiri
El Gezira
Wâd Medanî
Gedaref
Ed Dueim
El Obeid
Kôstî
Singa
Nîl el Azraq
Umm Ruwaba
Er Rahad
En Nahud
El Odaiya
Abu Zabad
Kordofân
Kâdugli
Ed Damazin
Nîl el Abyad
Gonder
L. Tana
Bahir Dar
Bure
Debre Markos
Nekemte
Dembidolo
Metu
Gore
Jima
Omo
Arba Minch
L. Abaya
L. Shamo
Chew Bahir
L. Turkana
Lokitaung
Kapoeta
Torit
Kajo Kaji
Juba
Mongalla
Tali Post
Amadi
Yambio
Yei
Faradje
Dungu
Ango
Uele
Bondo
Bôr
Pibor Post
Malakâl
Sobat
Bahr el Jebel
Bahr el Ghazâl
Jur
Sûdd
Gogriâl
Wâw
Tonj
Rumbêk
Toinya
El Istiwâ'iya
Bahr el Arab
Raga
Sa'id Bundas
Songo
Kutum
Umm Keddada
El Fâsher
Djebel Mara
Zalingei
Nyâlâ
Dârfûr
Al Junaynah
Tibesti
Aozou Strip
Aozou
Bardai
Pic Toussidé
Tarso Emissi
Zouar
Emi Koussi
Toummo
Madama
Chirfa
Grand Erg du Bilma
Bilma
Fachi
Borkou
Ounianga Sérir
Dépression du Mourdi
Faya-Largeau
Fada
Ennedi
Erg du Djourab
Zagaoua
Oum Chalouba
Biltine
Abéché
Zigey
Mao
Bahr el Ghazal
Lac Tchad
Moussoro
Nguigmi
Bosso
Ati
Oum Hadjer
Massakory
Gashua
Geidam
Maiduguri
Ndjamena
Kousseri
Bokoro
Mongo
Goz Beida
Massenya
Abou-Deïa
Am-Timan
Potiskum
Bama
Bajoga
Biu
Mubi
Maroua
Bongor
Guider
Chari
Numan
Garoua
Yola
Logone
Laï
Pala
Moundou
Sarh
Koumra
Doba
Birao
Ndélé
Baïbokoum
Ngaoundéré
Banyo
Paoua
Kaga Bandoro
Bossangoa
Bozoum
Bouar
Yalinga
Ippy
Bambari
Bakouma
Sibut
Obo
Bossembélé
Carnot
Bangassou
Mobaye
Bomu
Oubangi
Berbérati
Bangui
Zongo
Bosobolo
Mbaïki
Libenge
Bertoua
Batouri
Nanga-Eboko
Abong-Mbang
Yaoundé
Bétaré Oya
Yoko
Foumban
Sanaga
Cameroon
COPYRIGHT PHILIPS

75
84
86

1:7 100 000

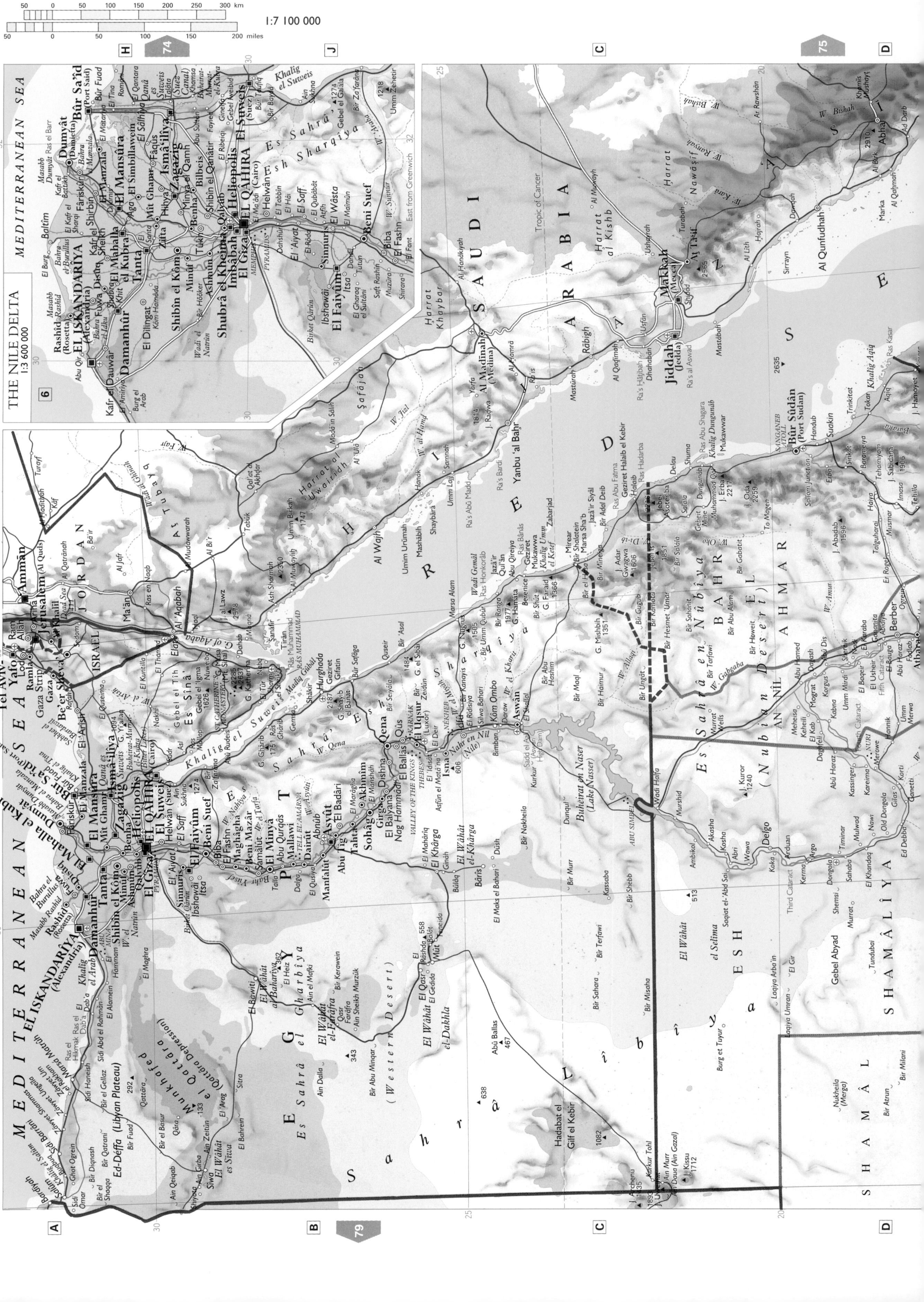
50 0 50 100 150 200 250 300 km
50 0 50 100 150 200 miles
THE NILE DELTA
1:3 600 000
MEDITERRANEAN SEA
EL ISKANDARÎYA (Alexandria)
EL QÂHIRA (Cairo)
Bûr Sa'îd (Port Said)
El Suweis
Aswân
Wadi Halfa
Jiddah (Jedda)
Makkah (Mecca)
Al Madînah (Medina)
Bûr Sûdân (Port Sudan)
Jerusalem
'Ammân
Tel Aviv-Yafo
Buheirat en Naser (Lake Nasser)
Munkhafed el Qattâra (Qattara Depression)
SAUDI ARABIA
RED SEA
JORDAN
ISRAEL
EGYPT
Sahrâ' Lîbîya
SHAMÂLIYA
Tropic of Cancer
East from Greenwich

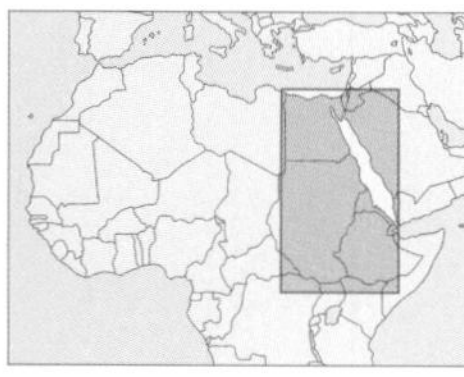

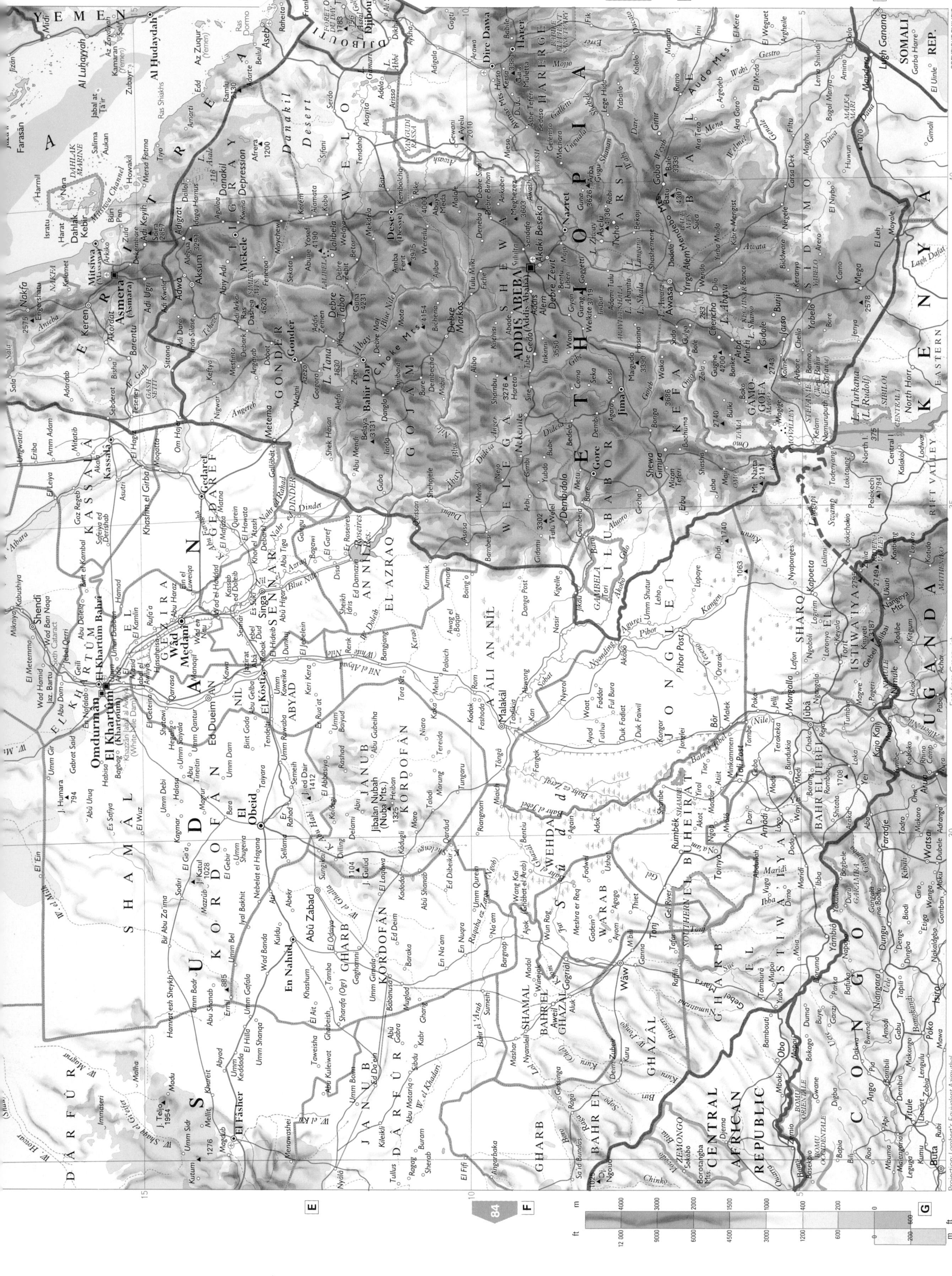
YEMEN
ERITREA
ETHIOPIA
SUDAN
KENYA
UGANDA
CONGO
CENTRAL AFRICAN REPUBLIC
SOMALI REP.
DJIBOUTI
Khartoum
Omdurman
Addis Abeba
Asmera
Djibouti
L. Tana
L. Turkana
Danakil Depression
Blue Nile
White Nile
Projection: Lambert's Equivalent Azimuthal
East from Greenwich

National Parks

Nature Reserves and Game Reserves

∴ UNESCO World Heritage Sites

1:7 100 000

78
ATLANTIC OCEAN
MAURITANIA
SENEGAL
GAMBIA
GUINEA-BISSAU
GUINEA
SIERRA LEONE
LIBERIA
IVORY COAST
MALI
BURKINA FASO
SAHARA
GULF
Grain Coast
Ivory Coast
Nouakchott
DAKAR
Banjul
Bissau
Conakry
Freetown
Monrovia
Bamako
ABIDJAN
Yamoussoukro
Bouaké
Bobo-Dioulasso
Tombouctou (Timbuktu)
Kaolack
Thiès
St. Louis
Ziguinchor
Kankan
Kindia
Labé
Kayes
Ségou
Mopti
Sikasso
Korhogo
Man
Daloa
San Pédro
Harper
Buchanan
Bo
Kenema
Nouâdhibou
Akjoujt
Tidjikja
Kiffa
Néma
Kaédi
Rosso
Tambacounda
Kédougou
Bafatá
Koutiala
Tagânt
Aoukâr
El Mreyyé
Fouta Djalon
Massif de l'Assaba
Arquipélago dos Bijagós
C. Vert
C. Verga
Cape Palmas
C. Three Points
6363

Projection : Lambert's Equivalent Azimuthal

West from Greenwich

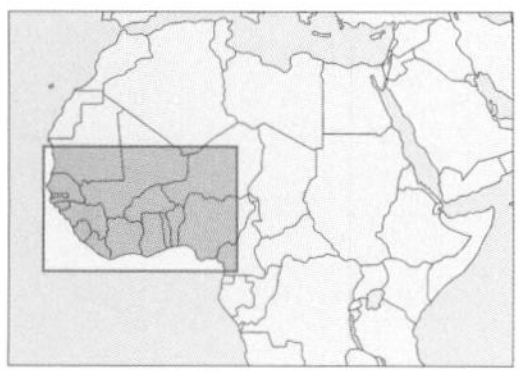

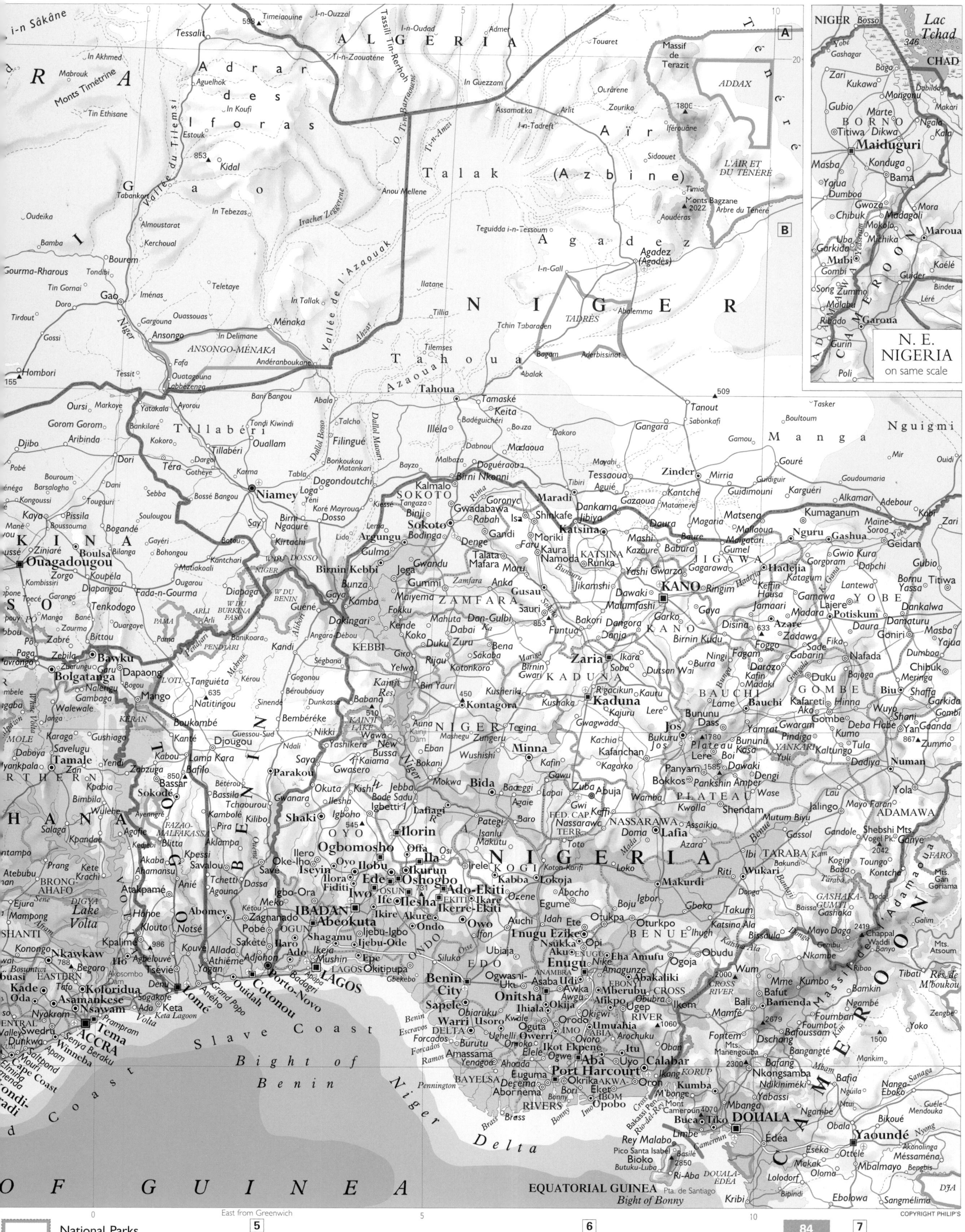
A L G E R I A
N I G E R
N I G E R I A
C A M E R O O N
G H A N A
B E N I N
T O G O
B U R K I N A F A S O
M A L I
Adrar des Iforas
Talak
Aïr
(Azbine)
Ténéré
Agadez
Tahoua
Tillabéri
Manga
Nguigmi
Niamey
Ouagadougou
Dori
Tenkodogo
Fada-n-Gourma
Zinder
Maradi
Tessaoua
Sokoto
Katsina
KANO
Zaria
Kaduna
Jos
Bauchi
Gombe
Minna
Ilorin
Ogbomosho
IBADAN
Abeokuta
LAGOS
Porto-Novo
Cotonou
Lomé
ACCRA
Tema
Kumasi
Tamale
Bolgatanga
Benin City
Onitsha
Enugu
Port Harcourt
Calabar
DOUALA
Yaoundé
Bamenda
Maiduguri
Lac Tchad
N. E. NIGERIA on same scale
Slave Coast
Bight of Benin
Niger Delta
Bight of Bonny
GULF OF GUINEA
EQUATORIAL GUINEA
Bioko
East from Greenwich
COPYRIGHT PHILIP'S

79
84

National Parks

Nature Reserves and Game Reserves

∴ UNESCO World Heritage Sites

100 0 100 200 300 400 500 600 km

1:13 300 000

100 0 100 200 300 400 miles

75

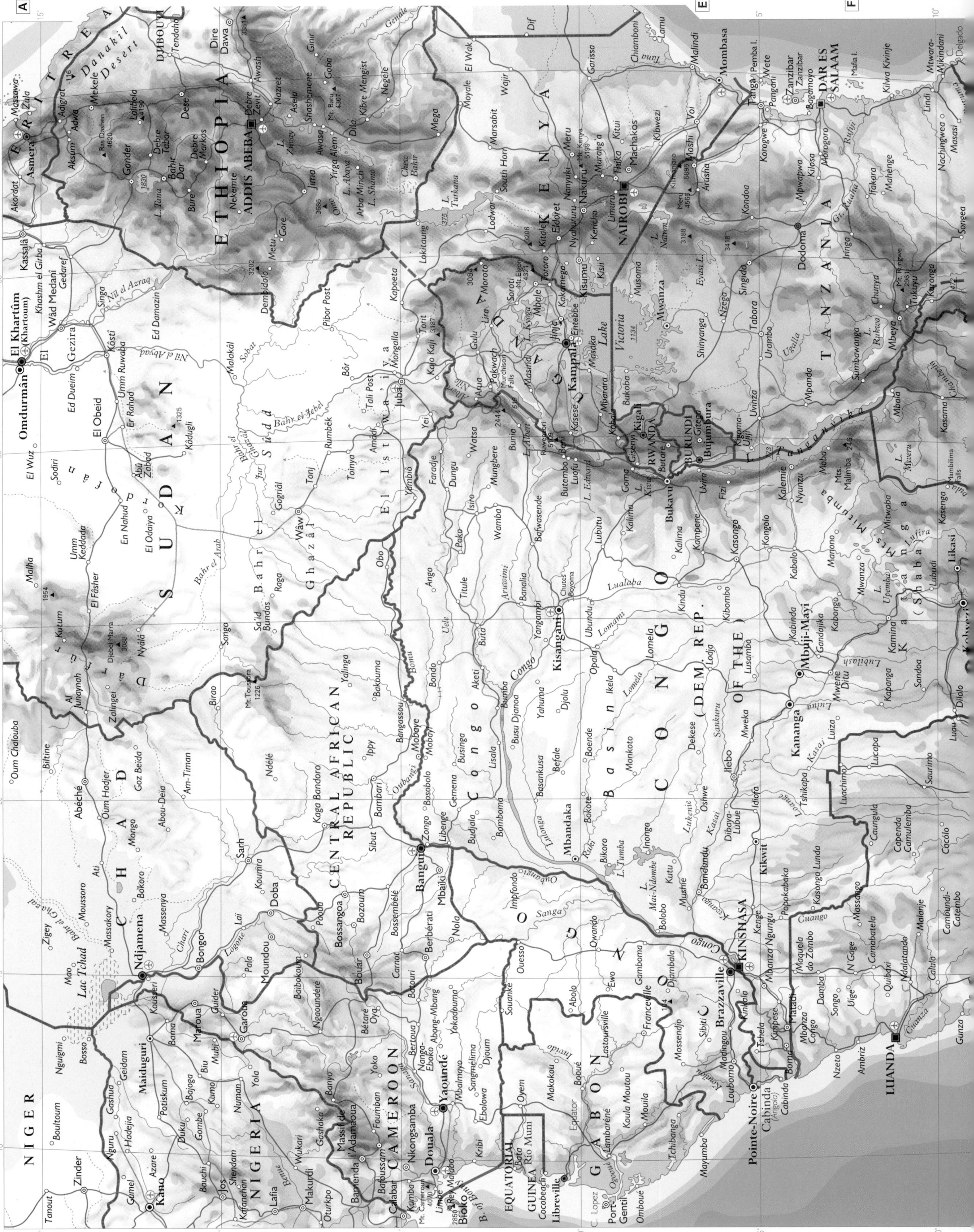
ETHIOPIA
ADDIS ABEBA
SUDAN
KENYA
NAIROBI
UGANDA
Kampala
TANZANIA
DAR ES SALAAM
Dodoma
RWANDA
Kigali
BURUNDI
Bujumbura
CONGO (DEM. REP. OF THE)
KINSHASA
CONGO
Brazzaville
CENTRAL AFRICAN REPUBLIC
Bangui
CHAD
Ndjamena
CAMEROON
Yaoundé
NIGERIA
NIGER
GABON
Libreville
EQUATORIAL GUINEA
ANGOLA
LUANDA
DJIBOUTI
ERITREA
Asmera
El Khartûm
Omdurmân
Mombasa
Lake Victoria
L. Tanganyika
Lac Tchad
Congo Basin
Lualaba
Congo
Kisangani
Lubumbashi
Pointe-Noire
Cabinda

79

78

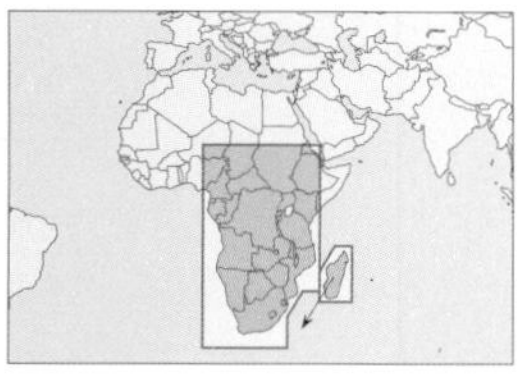

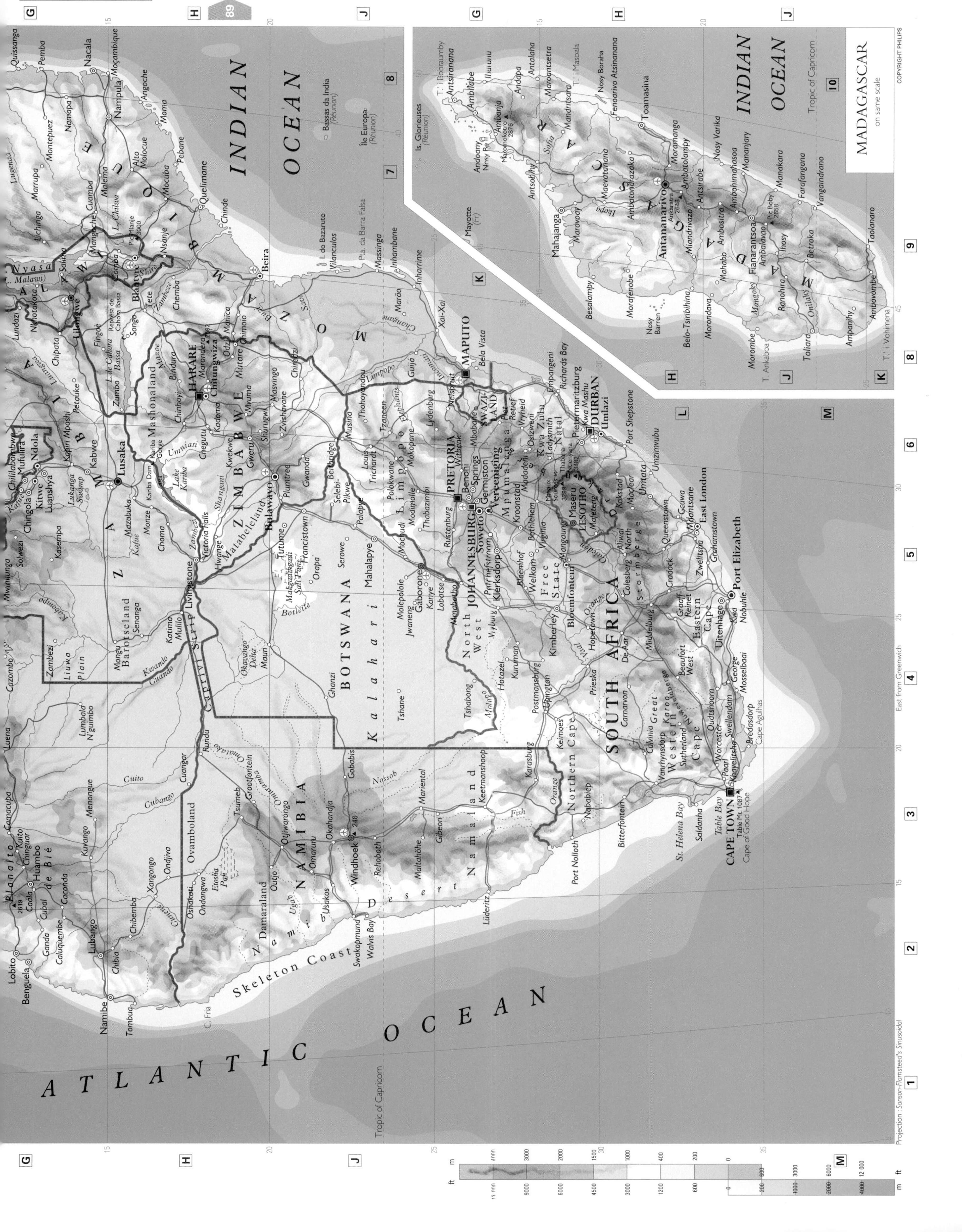
INDIAN OCEAN
ATLANTIC OCEAN
MADAGASCAR
on same scale
INDIAN OCEAN
MOZAMBIQUE
ZAMBIA
ZIMBABWE
BOTSWANA
NAMIBIA
SOUTH AFRICA
LESOTHO
SWAZILAND
Kalahari
Namib Desert
Skeleton Coast
Caprivi Strip
Mashonaland
Matabeleland
Namaland
Damaraland
Ovamboland
Barotseland
Liuwa Plain
Planalto de Bié
Okavango Delta
Makgadikgadi Salt Pans
North West
Free State
Mpumalanga
Limpopo
Kwa Zulu Natal
Northern Cape
Western Cape
Eastern Cape
Great Karoo
Lusaka
Harare
Bulawayo
Gaborone
Windhoek
Maputo
Pretoria
Johannesburg
Bloemfontein
Maseru
Mbabane
Durban
Cape Town
Port Elizabeth
East London
Beira
Antananarivo
Toamasina
Mahajanga
Toliara
Fianarantsoa
Taolanaro
Lilongwe
Blantyre
Quelimane
Nampula
Walvis Bay
Swakopmund
Lüderitz
Kimberley
Table Mt. 1087
Cape of Good Hope
Cape Agulhas
Tropic of Capricorn
East from Greenwich
Projection : Sanson-Flamsteed's Sinusoidal
COPYRIGHT PHILIPS
m
ft
12 000
9000
6000
4500
3000
1200
600
0
200
1000
2000
4000
3000
2000
1500
1000
400
200
600
3000
6000
12 000

50 0 50 100 150 200 250 300 km

50 0 50 100 150 200 miles

1:7 100 000

A B C D

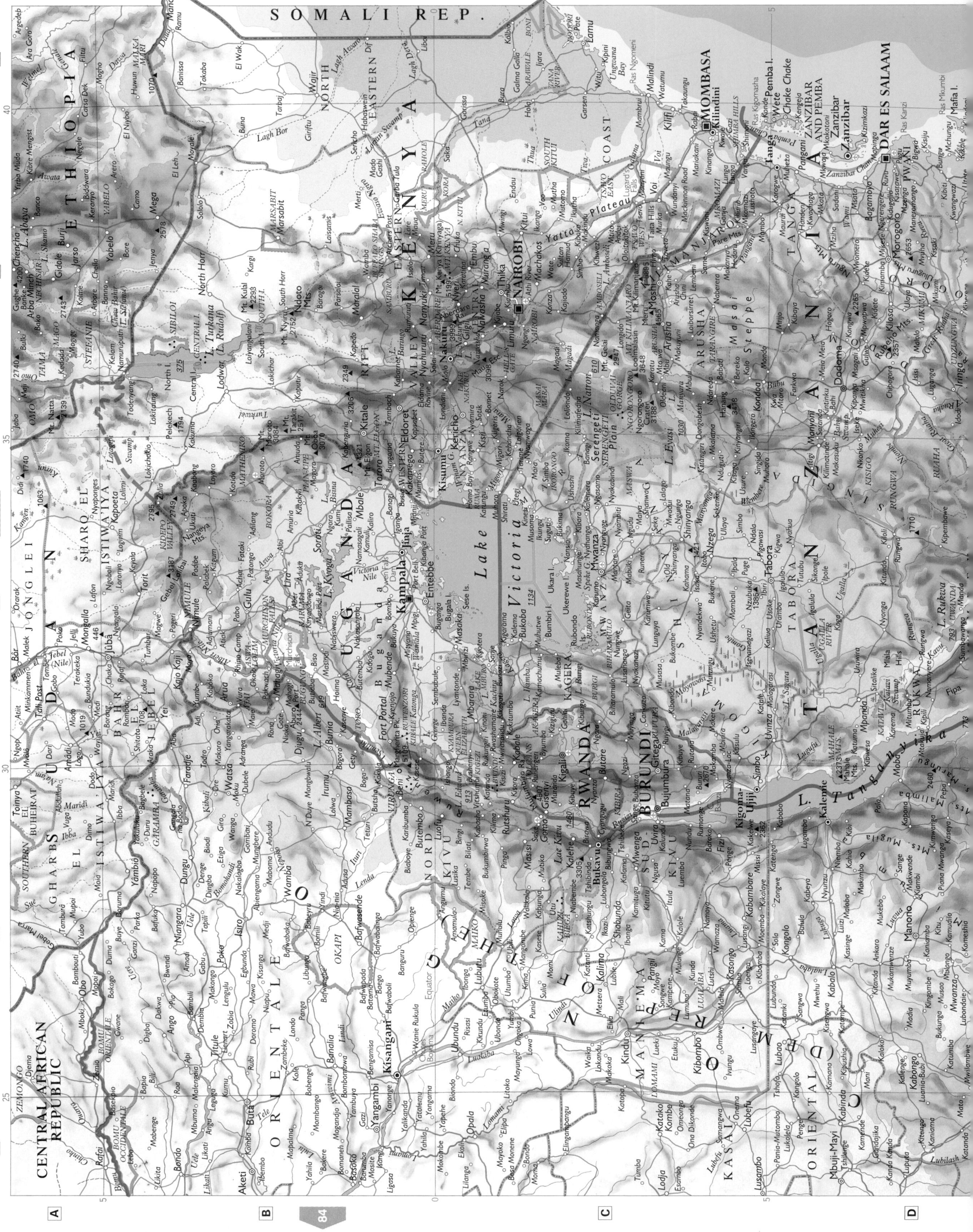
SOMALI REP.
ETHIOPIA
KENYA
UGANDA
RWANDA
BURUNDI
TANZANIA
Lake Victoria
L. Turkana (L. Rudolf)
L. Tanganyika
NAIROBI
MOMBASA
DAR ES SALAAM
Zanzibar
Kampala
Kigali
Bujumbura
Dodoma
Kisangani
CENTRAL AFRICAN REPUBLIC
ORIENTALE
NORD-KIVU
SUD-KIVU
MANIEMA
Equator

A B C D

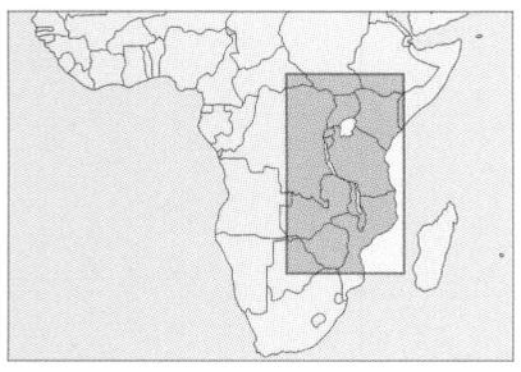

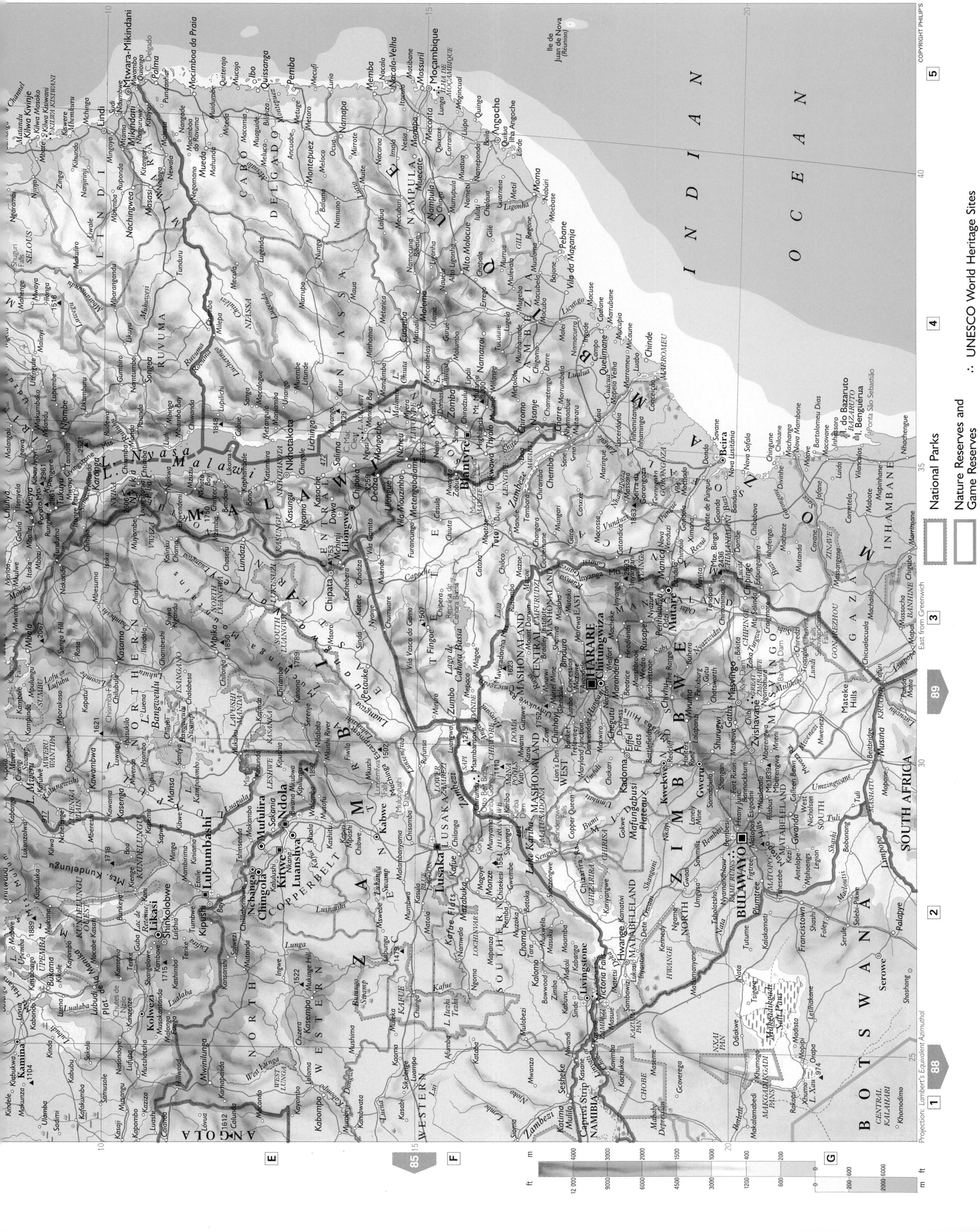
INDIAN OCEAN
MALAWI
ZAMBIA
ZIMBABWE
MOZAMBIQUE
BOTSWANA
SOUTH AFRICA
NAMIBIA
ANGOLA
L. Nyasa
L. Malawi
HARARE
Lusaka
Lilongwe
BULAWAYO
Blantyre
Beira
Lubumbashi
Chingola
Ndola
Kitwe
Mufulira
Lindi
Mocímboa da Praia
Pemba
Nampula
Moçambique
Quelimane
Chinde
Tete
Mutare
Masvingo
Livingstone
Victoria Falls
Hwange
Kabwe
Kasama
Mbeya
Songea
Lichinga
Cuamba
Angoche
Pebane
Francistown
Serowe
Palapye
Beitbridge
Musina
National Parks
Nature Reserves and Game Reserves
UNESCO World Heritage Sites
East from Greenwich
Projection: Lambert's Equivalent Azimuthal
COPYRIGHT PHILIP'S
85
88
89
E
F
G
1
2
3
4
5

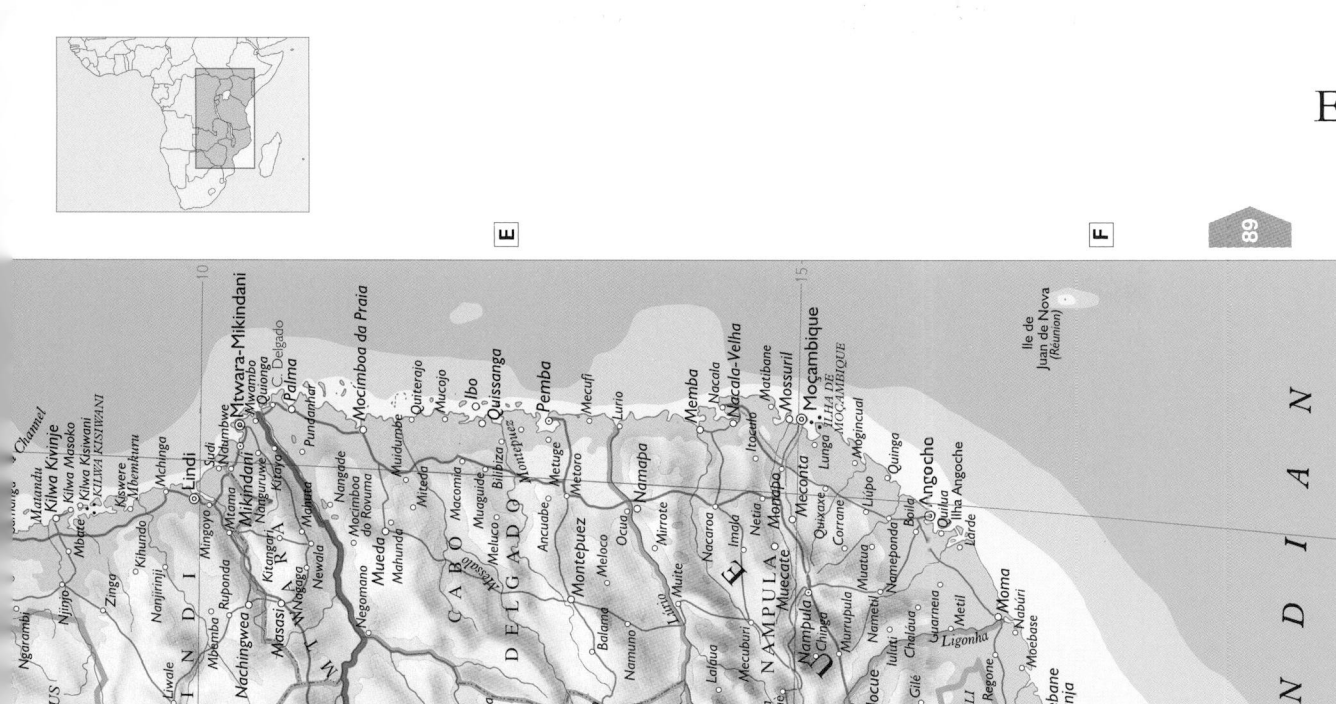

50 0 50 100 150 200 250 300 km

1:7 100 000

50 0 50 100 150 200 miles

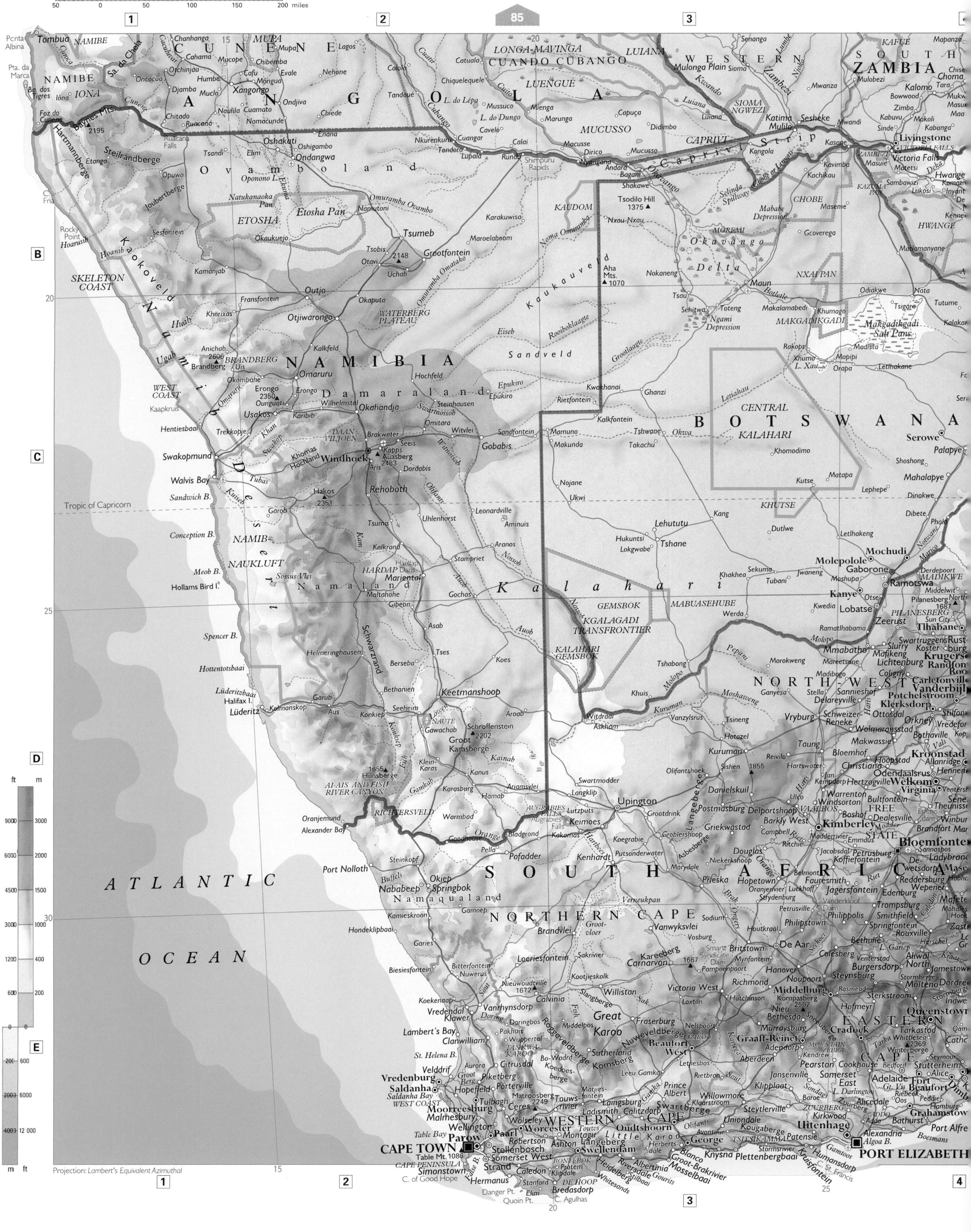

85
1
2
3
4
B
C
D
E
ANGOLA
CUNENE
NAMIBE
MUPA
IONA
Tombua
Lubango
Xangongo
Ondjiva
Ruacana Falls
Baynes Mts.
2195
CUANDO CUBANGO
LONGA-MAVINGA
LUENGUE
LUIANA
MUCUSSO
WESTERN
ZAMBIA
Livingstone
Victoria Falls
Hwange
Mulonga Plain
SIOMA NGWEZI
Katima Mulilo
Sesheke
Caprivi Strip
CAPRIVI
Kasane
Kazungula
CHOBE
HWANGE
Ovamboland
Oshakati
Ondangwa
Etosha Pan
ETOSHA
Tsumeb
Grootfontein
Otavi
2148
Kaokoveld
SKELETON COAST
Outjo
Otjiwarongo
WATERBERG PLATEAU
NAMIBIA
Brandberg
2606
Omaruru
Damaraland
Erongo
2350
Okahandja
Usakos
Swakopmund
Walvis Bay
Windhoek
2483
Rehoboth
Gobabis
Tropic of Capricorn
Sandwich B.
Conception B.
NAMIB-NAUKLUFT
Namib Desert
Hakos
2351
Hollams Bird I.
Meob B.
Spencer B.
Hottentotsbaai
Lüderitzbaai
Halifax I.
Lüderitz
Kolmanskop
Aus
Namaland
Mariental
Maltahohe
Gibeon
Keetmanshoop
Schroffenstein
2202
Grootkarasberge
Hunsberge
1655
AI-AIS AND FISH RIVER CANYON
RICHTERSVELD
Oranjemund
Alexander Bay
KAUDOM
Tsodilo Hill
1375
Aha Mts.
1070
Kaukauveld
Okavango Delta
MOREMI
NXAI PAN
Maun
Ngami Depression
MAKGADIKGADI
Makgadikgadi Salt Pans
Sandveld
Ghanzi
BOTSWANA
CENTRAL KALAHARI
KHUTSE
Kang
Lehututu
Tshane
Kalahari
GEMSBOK
KGALAGADI TRANSFRONTIER
KALAHARI GEMSBOK
MABUASEHUBE
Molepolole
Mochudi
Gaborone
Kanye
Lobatse
Ramotswa
Serowe
Palapye
Mahalapye
Zeerust
Mmabatho
Lichtenburg
NORTH-WEST
Vryburg
Kuruman
Upington
Augrabies Falls
Keimoes
Kimberley
FREE STATE
Bloemfontein
Welkom
SOUTH AFRICA
Port Nolloth
Springbok
Namaqualand
NORTHERN CAPE
De Aar
Colesberg
Middelburg
Graaff-Reinet
Beaufort West
Great Karoo
Calvinia
Vredendal
Lambert's Bay
St. Helena B.
Vredenburg
Saldanha
Saldanha Bay
Malmesbury
Paarl
Worcester
WESTERN CAPE
Table Bay
CAPE TOWN
Table Mt. 1086
Stellenbosch
Somerset West
Simonstown
Hermanus
C. of Good Hope
Danger Pt.
Quoin Pt.
C. Agulhas
Bredasdorp
Swellendam
Oudtshoorn
George
Knysna
Plettenbergbaai
Mosselbaai
Little Karoo
Uitenhage
PORT ELIZABETH
Algoa B.
EASTERN CAPE
Cradock
Queenstown
Grahamstown
ATLANTIC
OCEAN
Orange
Projection: Lambert's Equivalent Azimuthal
15
20
25
30
ft
m
9000
6000
4500
3000
1200
600
0
200
2000
4000
3000
2000
1500
1000
400
200
0
600
6000
12 000

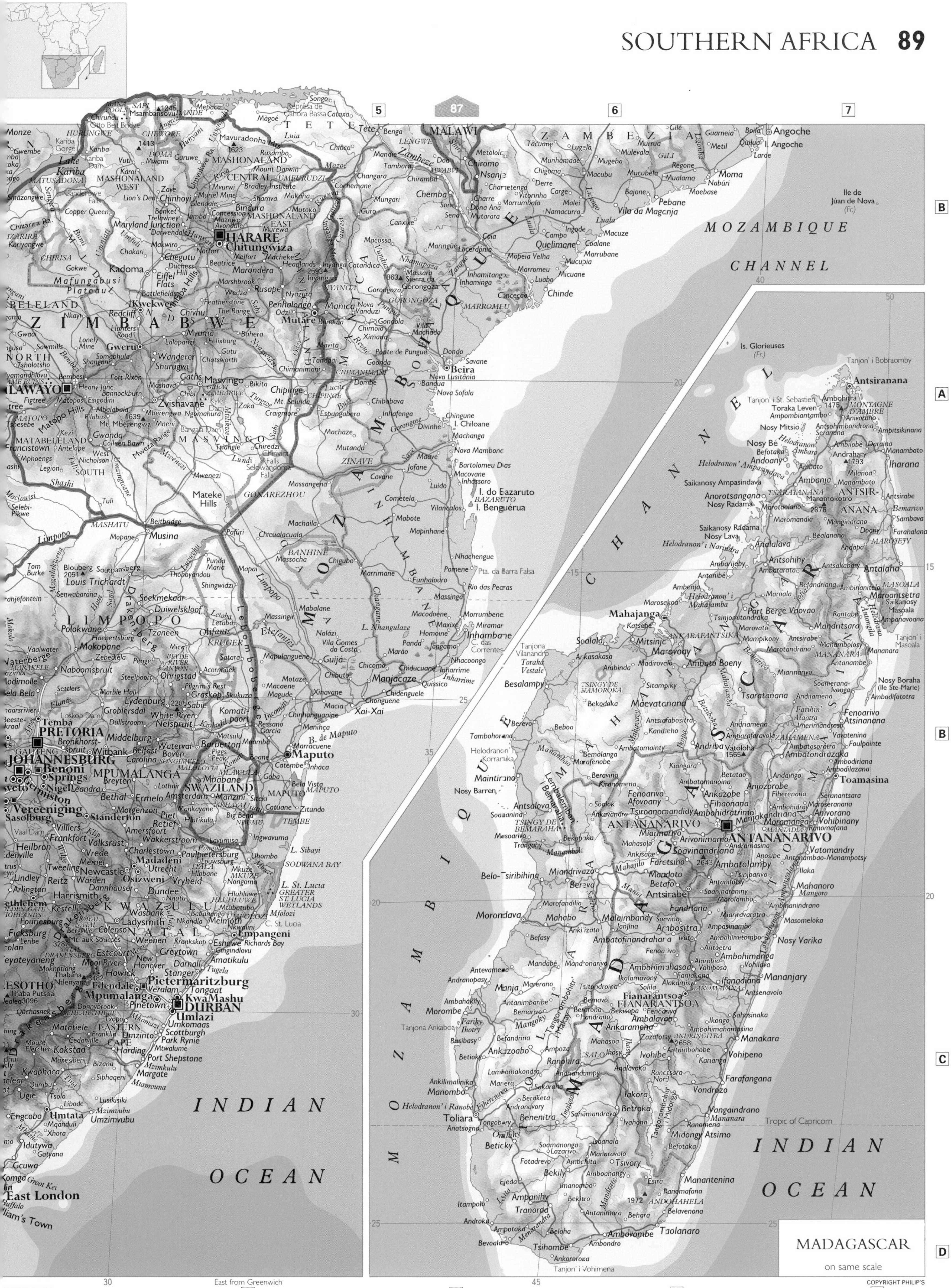
87
MALAWI
ZAMBEZIA
TETE
MOZAMBIQUE CHANNEL
MOZAMBIQUE
ZIMBABWE
HARARE
Chitungwiza
MASHONALAND CENTRAL
MASHONALAND WEST
MASHONALAND EAST
MASVINGO
Masvingo
Gweru
Kadoma
Mutare
Beira
Maputo
Xai-Xai
Inhambane
Quelimane
Chinde
Tete
Angoche
I. Angoche
Ile de Júan de Nova (Fr.)
Is. Glorieuses (Fr.)
MALAWI
LIMPOPO
MPUMALANGA
SWAZILAND
Mbabane
PRETORIA
JOHANNESBURG
Benoni
Springs
Vereeniging
Polokwane
Nelspruit
Mokopane
Louis Trichardt
Musina
Beitbridge
KWAZULU NATAL
Pietermaritzburg
DURBAN
Umlazi
Empangeni
Port Shepstone
Margate
Umtata
East London
Harrismith
Ladysmith
Newcastle
Vryheid
Dundee
LESOTHO
EASTERN CAPE
INDIAN OCEAN
MADAGASCAR
Antsiranana
Mahajanga
Toamasina
ANTANANARIVO
Antsirabe
Fianarantsoa
Toliara
Morondava
Mananjary
Manakara
Farafangana
Taolanaro
Tropic of Capricorn
MADAGASCAR on same scale
East from Greenwich
COPYRIGHT PHILIP'S

National Parks

Nature Reserves and Game Reserves

∴ UNESCO World Heritage Sites

500 0 250 500 750 1000 1250 1500 1750 km

500 0 250 500 750 1000 1250 miles

1:44 400 000

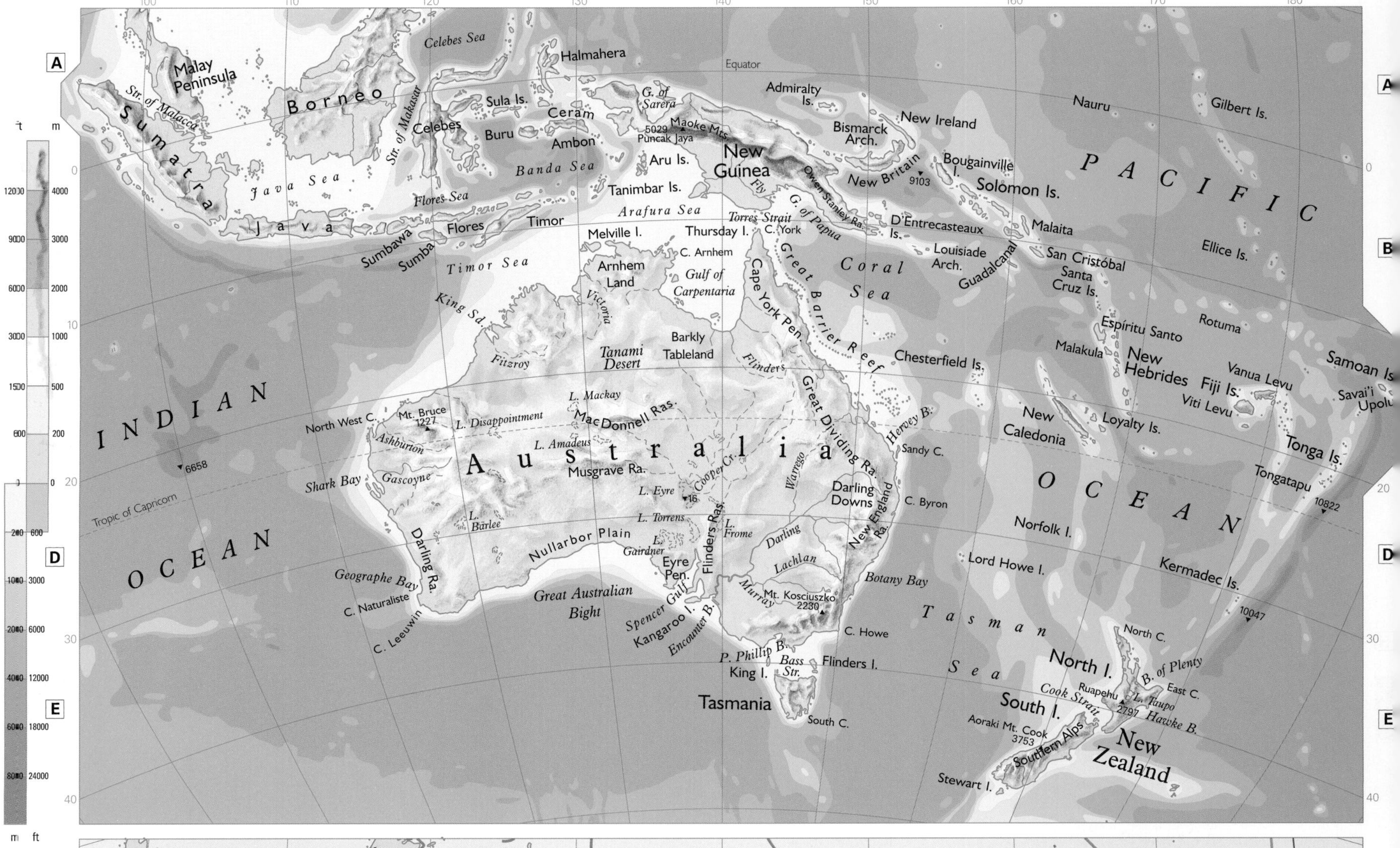

Celebes Sea
Halmahera
Malay Peninsula
Str. of Malacca
Sumatra
Borneo
Str. of Makasar
Celebes
Sula Is.
Ceram
Buru
Ambon
G. of Sarera
Maoke Mts.
5029 Puncak Jaya
New Guinea
Aru Is.
Banda Sea
Java Sea
Flores Sea
Java
Tanimbar Is.
Equator
Admiralty Is.
Bismarck Arch.
New Ireland
New Britain
9103
Bougainville I.
Solomon Is.
Nauru
Gilbert Is.
PACIFIC
Arafura Sea
Torres Strait
G. of Papua
Owen Stanley Ra.
D'Entrecasteaux Is.
Louisiade Arch.
Malaita
Guadalcanal
San Cristóbal
Santa Cruz Is.
Ellice Is.
Sumbawa
Sumba
Flores
Timor
Melville I.
Thursday I.
C. York
C. Arnhem
Arnhem Land
Gulf of Carpentaria
Timor Sea
Coral Sea
Great Barrier Reef
Cape York Pen.
Victoria
King Sd.
Fitzroy
Tanami Desert
Barkly Tableland
Flinders
Chesterfield Is.
Espíritu Santo
Rotuma
Malakula
New Hebrides
Fiji Is.
Vanua Levu
Viti Levu
Samoan Is.
Savai'i
Upolu
INDIAN
North West C.
Mt. Bruce 1227
L. Disappointment
L. Mackay
MacDonnell Ras.
Great Dividing Ra.
Hervey B.
New Caledonia
Loyalty Is.
Tonga Is.
Tongatapu
Ashburton
L. Amadeus
Australia
Sandy C.
6658
Shark Bay
Gascoyne
Musgrave Ra.
Cooper Cr.
Warrego
Darling Downs
C. Byron
OCEAN
10822
Tropic of Capricorn
L. Eyre
-16
L. Barlee
L. Torrens
L. Frome
Norfolk I.
Flinders Ras.
Nullarbor Plain
L. Gairdner
Eyre Pen.
Darling
New England Ra.
Lord Howe I.
Kermadec Is.
OCEAN
Darling Ra.
Geographe Bay
Lachlan
Murray
Botany Bay
C. Naturaliste
Great Australian Bight
Mt. Kosciuszko 2230
Spencer Gulf
Kangaroo I.
Encounter B.
Tasman
10047
C. Leeuwin
C. Howe
North C.
P. Phillip B.
Bass Str.
King I.
Flinders I.
Sea
North I.
B. of Plenty
Tasmania
Cook Strait
Ruapehu 2797
L. Taupo
East C.
South I.
Hawke B.
South C.
Aoraki Mt. Cook 3753
Southern Alps
New Zealand
Stewart I.
ft m

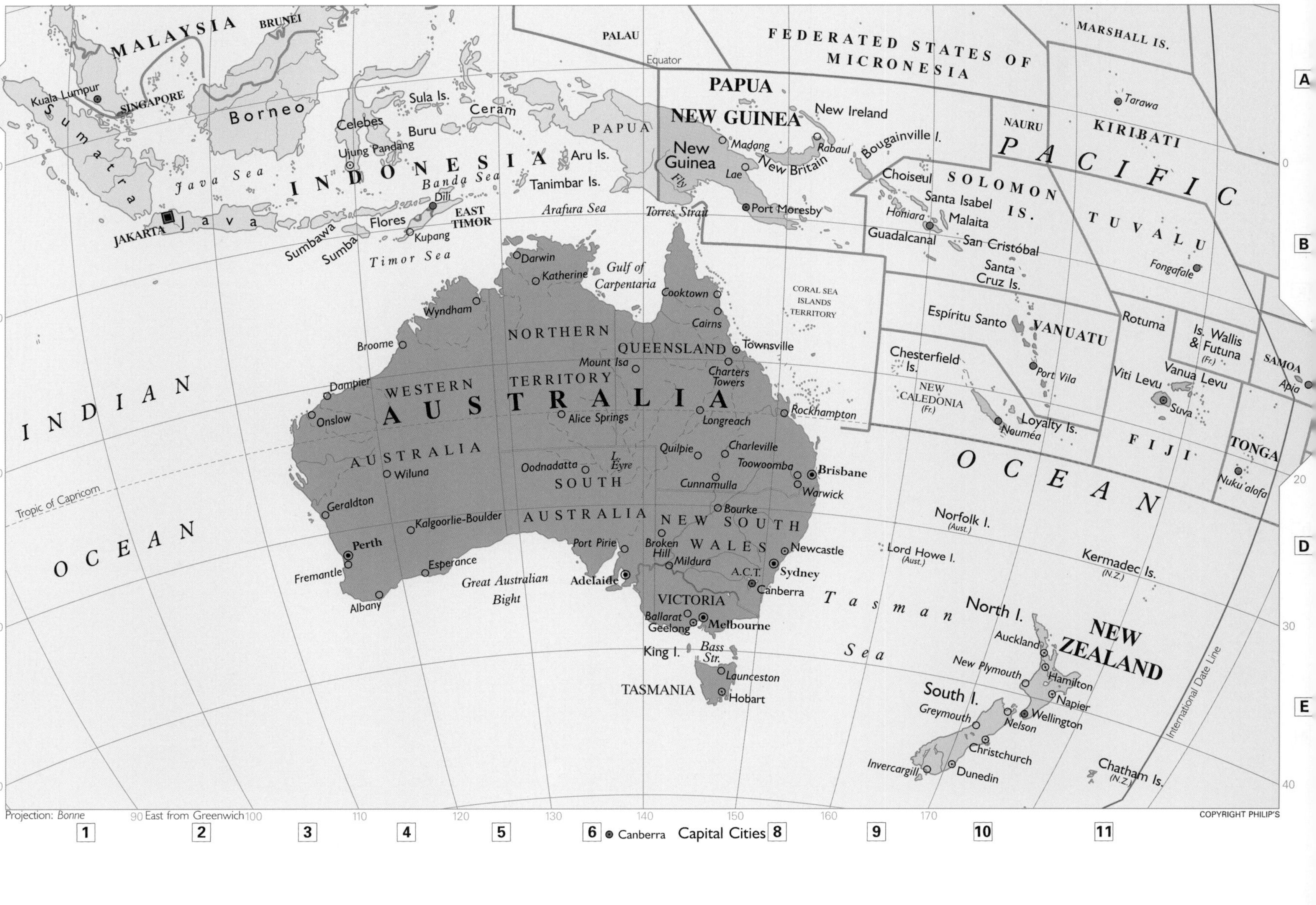

MALAYSIA
BRUNEI
PALAU
FEDERATED STATES OF MICRONESIA
MARSHALL IS.
Equator
Kuala Lumpur
SINGAPORE
Sumatra
Borneo
Sula Is.
Ceram
Celebes
Buru
PAPUA
PAPUA NEW GUINEA
New Ireland
Tarawa
NAURU
KIRIBATI
Ujung Pandang
INDONESIA
Aru Is.
New Guinea
Madang
Rabaul
Bougainville I.
PACIFIC
Java Sea
Banda Sea
Fly
Lae
New Britain
Choiseul
SOLOMON IS.
Santa Isabel
Honiara
Malaita
Tanimbar Is.
Dili
EAST TIMOR
Arafura Sea
Torres Strait
Port Moresby
TUVALU
JAKARTA
Java
Sumbawa
Flores
Kupang
Guadalcanal
San Cristóbal
Sumba
Timor Sea
Darwin
Katherine
Gulf of Carpentaria
Santa Cruz Is.
Fongafale
Cooktown
CORAL SEA ISLANDS TERRITORY
Wyndham
Cairns
Espíritu Santo
VANUATU
Rotuma
Is. Wallis & Futuna (Fr.)
NORTHERN
QUEENSLAND
Townsville
Broome
Mount Isa
Charters Towers
Chesterfield Is.
SAMOA
Apia
TERRITORY
Port Vila
Viti Levu
Vanua Levu
Dampier
WESTERN
AUSTRALIA
NEW CALEDONIA (Fr.)
Suva
Onslow
Alice Springs
Longreach
Rockhampton
Nouméa
Loyalty Is.
FIJI
TONGA
AUSTRALIA
Quilpie
Charleville
Wiluna
Oodnadatta
L. Eyre
Toowoomba
Brisbane
OCEAN
Nuku'alofa
SOUTH
Cunnamulla
Warwick
Geraldton
AUSTRALIA
Bourke
NEW SOUTH
Norfolk I. (Aust.)
Kalgoorlie-Boulder
Port Pirie
Broken Hill
WALES
Newcastle
Lord Howe I. (Aust.)
Kermadec Is. (N.Z.)
Perth
Mildura
Sydney
Esperance
A.C.T.
Fremantle
Great Australian Bight
Adelaide
Canberra
VICTORIA
Albany
Tasman
North I.
NEW ZEALAND
Ballarat
Geelong
Melbourne
Auckland
King I.
Bass Str.
Sea
New Plymouth
Hamilton
Launceston
TASMANIA
South I.
Napier
Hobart
Greymouth
Wellington
Nelson
International Date Line
Christchurch
Invercargill
Dunedin
Chatham Is. (N.Z.)
Canberra Capital Cities

Projection: Bonne

90 East from Greenwich

1:5 300 000

50 0 50 100 150 200 km

50 0 50 100 150 miles

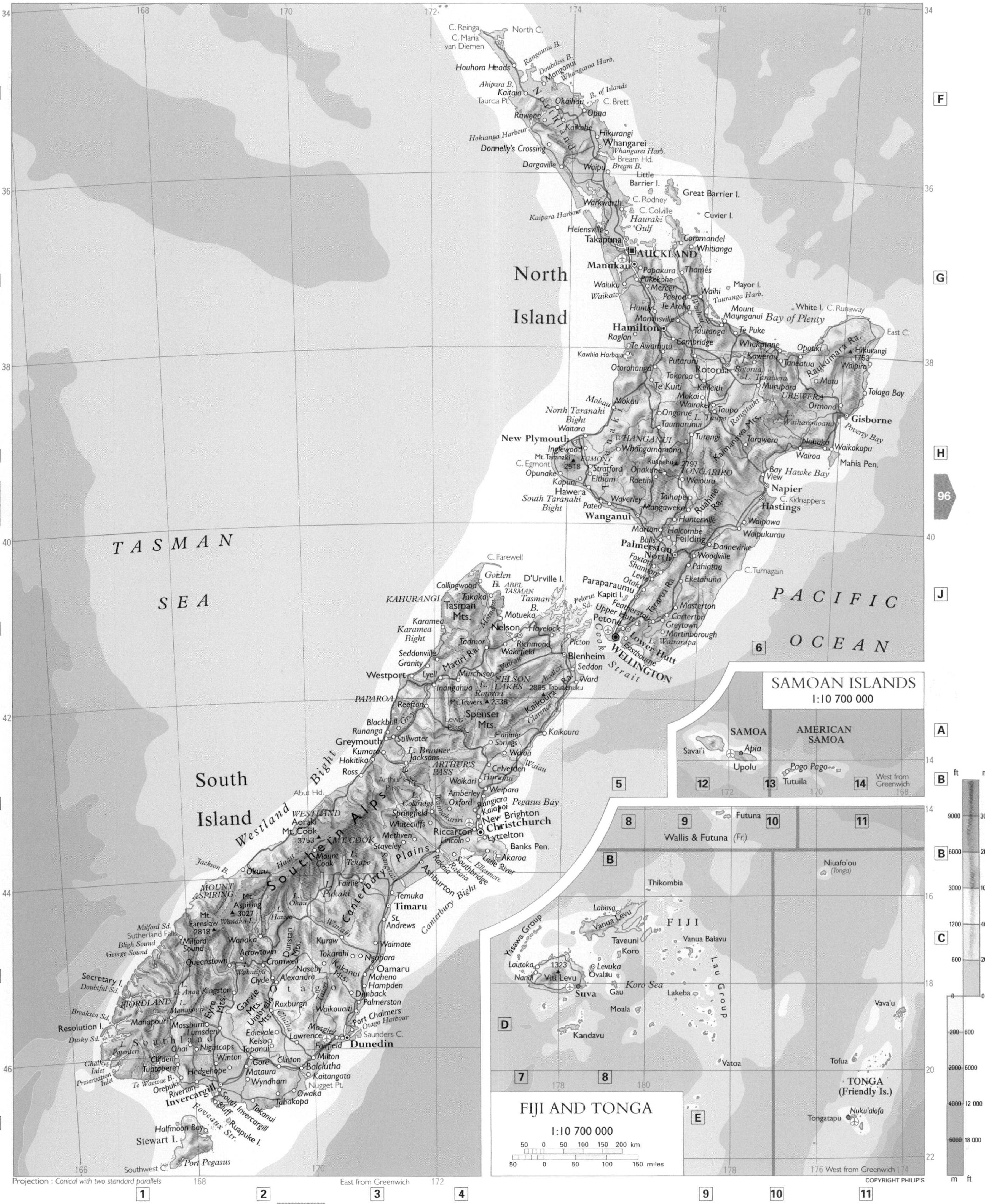

North Island
South Island
TASMAN SEA
PACIFIC OCEAN
C. Reinga
North C.
C. Maria van Diemen
Rangaunu B.
Houhora Heads
Doubtless B.
Mangonui
Whangaroa Harb.
Ahipara B.
Kaitaia
Taurca Pt.
B. of Islands
C. Brett
Okaihau
Opua
Rawene
Kaikohe
Northland
Hokianga Harbour
Hikurangi
Whangarei
Whangarei Harb.
Bream Hd.
Bream B.
Donnelly's Crossing
Dargaville
Waipu
Little Barrier I.
Great Barrier I.
Warkworth
C. Rodney
C. Colville
Kaipara Harbour
Hauraki Gulf
Cuvier I.
Helensville
Takapuna
Coromandel
Whitianga
AUCKLAND
Manukau
Papakura
Thames
Pukekohe
Mercer
Waiuku
Waikato
Mayor I.
Waihi
Tauranga Harb.
Paeroa
Huntly
Te Aroha
Morrinsville
Mount Maunganui
Bay of Plenty
White I.
C. Runaway
Hamilton
Raglan
Tauranga
Te Puke
Cambridge
East C.
Te Awamutu
Whakatane
Opotiki
Raukumara Ra.
Hikurangi
1753
Kawhia Harbour
Kawerau
Putaruru
Rotorua
Te Teko
Waipiro
Otorohanga
Tokoroa
L. Rotorua
L. Tarawera
Murupara
Ruatoria
Te Kuiti
Kinleith
Mokau
Mokai
Wairakei
UREWERA
Tolaga Bay
North Taranaki Bight
Waitara
Ongarue
Taumarunui
Taupo
L. Taupo
Rangitaiki
Ormond
Gisborne
Waikaremoana
Poverty Bay
New Plymouth
WHANGANUI
Whangamomona
Turangi
Tarawera
Nuhaka
Waikokopu
Inglewood
Mt. Taranaki
EGMONT
2518
C. Egmont
Ruapehu
2797
TONGARIRO
Kaimanawa Mts.
Wairoa
Mahia Pen.
Opunake
Stratford
Eltham
Ohakune
Raetihi
Waiouru
Bay View
Hawke Bay
Kaponga
Hawera
South Taranaki Bight
Patea
Waverley
Taihape
Mangaweka
Ruahine Ra.
Napier
C. Kidnappers
Hastings
Wanganui
Hunterville
Waipawa
Waipukurau
Marton
Halcombe
Bulls
Feilding
Palmerston North
Dannevirke
Foxton
Woodville
Pahiatua
Shannon
Levin
Otaki
Eketahuna
C. Turnagain
Paraparaumu
Kapiti I.
Featherston
Tararua Ra.
Masterton
Carterton
Greytown
Martinborough
Upper Hutt
Petone
Lower Hutt
WELLINGTON
Eastbourne
L. Wairarapa
Cook Strait
C. Farewell
Golden B.
ABEL TASMAN
D'Urville I.
Collingwood
Takaka
Tasman B.
Pelorus Sd.
KAHURANGI
Tasman Mts.
Motueka
Nelson
Havelock
Karamea
Karamea Bight
Tadmor
Richmond
Picton
Blenheim
Seddon
Seddonville
Granity
Matiri Ra.
Wakefield
Westport
Lyell
Murchison
NELSON LAKES
Awatere
Ward
Inangahua
L. Rotoroa
2885 Tapuaenuku
PAPAROA
Reefton
Mt. Travers 2338
Kaikoura Ra.
Clarence
Spenser Mts.
Kaikoura
Blackball
Runanga
Greymouth
Stillwater
Hanmer Springs
Kumara
L. Brunner
Jacksons
Hokitika
ARTHUR'S PASS
Waiau
Ross
Culverden
Waikari
Hurunui
Amberley
Weipara
Abut Hd.
Westland Bight
Oxford
Rangiora
Kaiapoi
Pegasus Bay
New Brighton
WESTLAND
Aoraki Mt. Cook
3753
Springfield
Whitecliffs
Christchurch
Riccarton
Lyttelton
Methven
Lincoln
Banks Pen.
Southern Alps
MT. COOK
Staveley
Akaroa
Canterbury Plains
Little River
Jackson B.
Okuru
Haast
L. Ellesmere
Rakaia
Southbridge
Mount Cook
L. Tekapo
Ashburton
Fairlie
MOUNT ASPIRING
L. Pukaki
Temuka
Mt. Aspiring
3027
Timaru
L. Ohau
Canterbury Bight
Milford Sd.
Sutherland Falls
L. Hawea
St. Andrews
Mt. Earnslaw
2818
Bligh Sound
George Sound
Milford Sound
Wanaka
Dunstan Mts.
Kurow
Waimate
Arrowtown
Queenstown
Cromwell
Tokarahi
Ngapara
Secretary I.
Doubtful Sd.
Naseby
Kakanui Mts.
Oamaru
Alexandra
Maheno
Hampden
Te Anau
Kingston
Clyde
Otago
Dunback
FIORDLAND
Eyre Mts.
Garvie Mts.
Umbrella Mts.
Roxburgh
Palmerston
Breaksea Sd.
Manapouri
Waikouaiti
Resolution I.
Mossburn
Port Chalmers
Dusky Sd.
Lumsden
Mosgiel
Otago Harbour
Edievale
Lawrence
Saunders C.
Southland
Ohai
Nightcaps
Kelso
Tapanui
Fairfield
Dunedin
Clifden
Winton
Milton
Chalky Inlet
Tuatapere
Gore
Clinton
Balclutha
Preservation Inlet
Hedgehope
Mataura
Kaitangata
Te Waewae B.
Orepuki
Wyndham
Nugget Pt.
Riverton
Invercargill
Owaka
Tahakopa
South Invercargill
Bluff
Tokanui
Foveaux Str.
Halfmoon Bay
Ruapuke I.
Stewart I.
Port Pegasus
Southwest C.
SAMOAN ISLANDS
1:10 700 000
SAMOA
AMERICAN SAMOA
Savai'i
Apia
Upolu
Pago Pago
Tutuila
West from Greenwich
Futuna
Wallis & Futuna (Fr.)
Niuafo'ou (Tonga)
Thikombia
Labasa
Vanua Levu
FIJI
Yasawa Group
Taveuni
Koro
Vanua Balavu
Lautoka
1323
Levuka
Ovalau
Lau Group
Nandi
Viti Levu
Koro Sea
Suva
Gau
Lakeba
Moala
Vava'u
Kandavu
Vatoa
Tofua
TONGA (Friendly Is.)
FIJI AND TONGA
1:10 700 000
50 0 50 100 150 200 km
50 0 50 100 150 miles
Nuku'alofa
Tongatapu
176 West from Greenwich 174
East from Greenwich
Projection : Conical with two standard parallels
ft m
9000 3000
6000 2000
3000 1000
1200 400
600 200
0 0
200 600
2000 6000
4000 12 000
6000 18 000
m ft

National Parks

50 0 50 100 150 200 250 300 km

1:7 100 000

50 0 50 100 150 200 miles

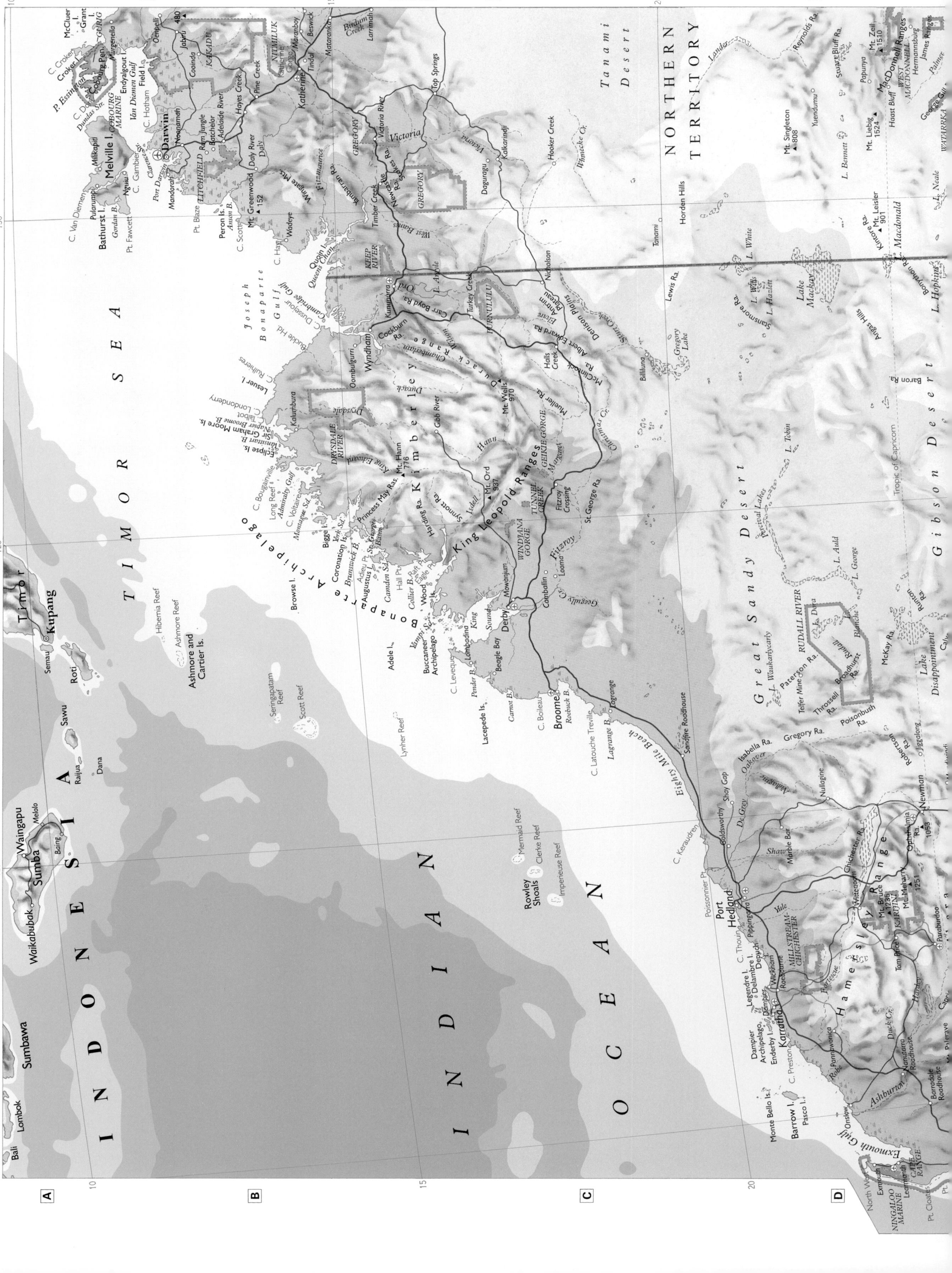
94
62
A
B
C
D
2
3
4
5
TIMOR SEA
INDIAN OCEAN
INDONESIA
NORTHERN TERRITORY
Tanami Desert
Great Sandy Desert
Gibson Desert
Kimberley
King Leopold Ranges
Bonaparte Archipelago
Joseph Bonaparte Gulf
Eighty Mile Beach
Hamersley Range
Darwin
Katherine
Wyndham
Kununurra
Halls Creek
Fitzroy Crossing
Derby
Broome
Port Hedland
Karratha
Newman
Onslow
Exmouth
Exmouth Gulf
Melville I.
Bathurst I.
Timor
Kupang
Sumba
Waingapu
Waikabubak
Sumbawa
Lombok
Bali
Roti
Sawu
Ashmore and Cartier Is.
Rowley Shoals
Lake Mackay
Lake Disappointment
Tropic of Capricorn
Barrow I.
Monte Bello Is.
Dampier Archipelago
Victoria
Ord
Fitzroy

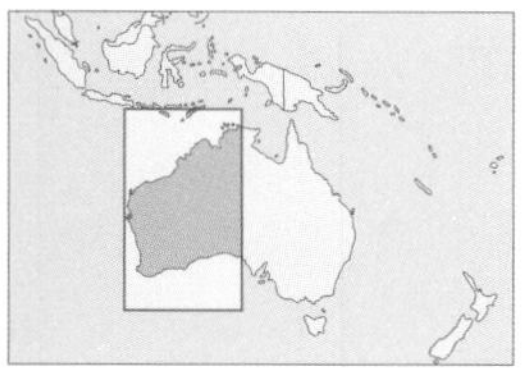

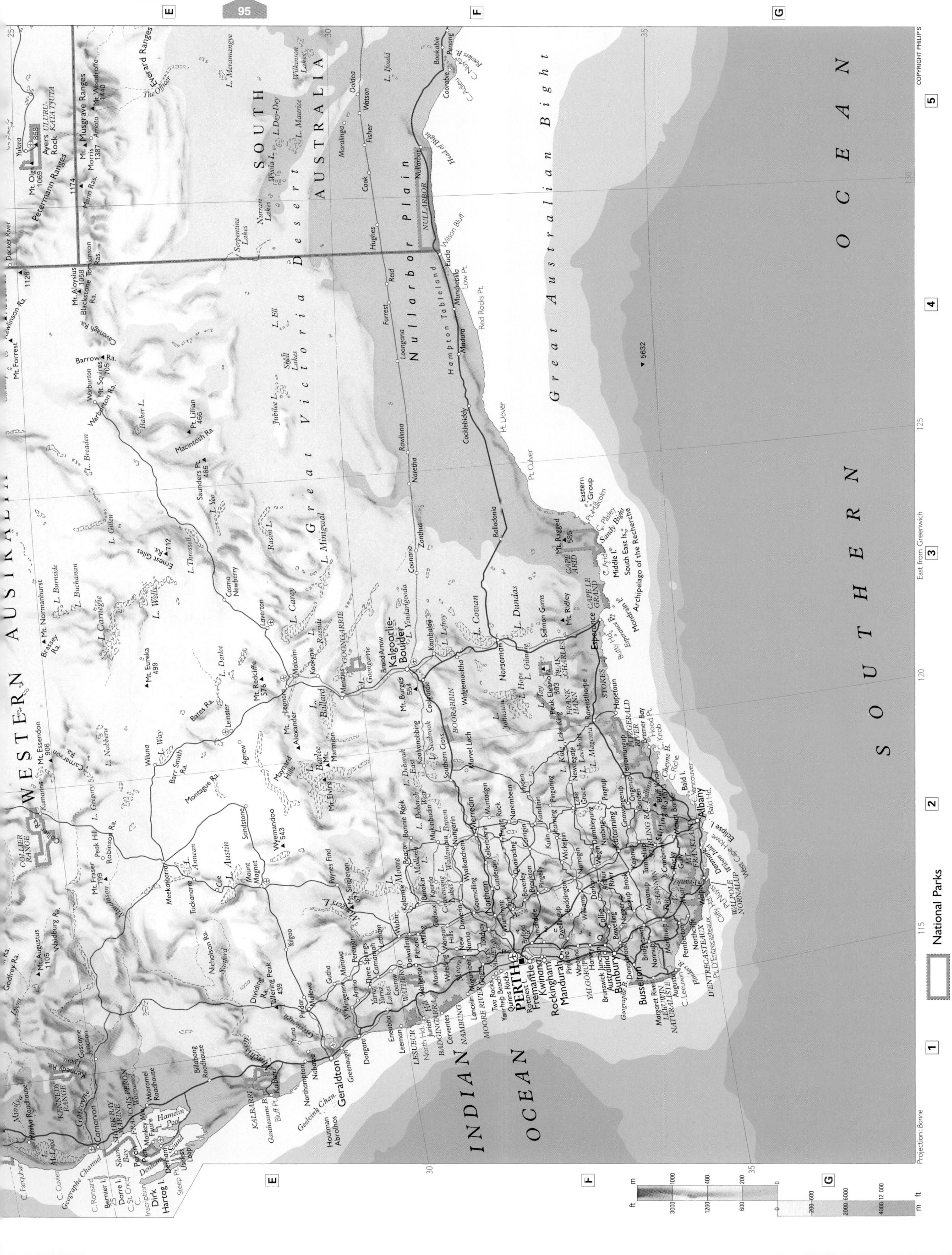

95
WESTERN AUSTRALIA
SOUTH AUSTRALIA
INDIAN OCEAN
SOUTHERN OCEAN
Great Australian Bight
Great Victoria Desert
Nullarbor Plain
Hampton Tableland
PERTH
Fremantle
Rockingham
Mandurah
Kwinana
Rottnest I.
Bunbury
Busselton
Albany
Geraldton
Carnarvon
Kalgoorlie-Boulder
Esperance
Norseman
Laverton
Leonora
Wiluna
Meekatharra
Mount Magnet
Cue
Northam
Merredin
Southern Cross
Coolgardie
Kambalda
Eucla
Madura
Cocklebiddy
Balladonia
Ravensthorpe
Hopetoun
Katanning
Narrogin
Collie
Manjimup
Pemberton
Walpole
Denmark
Augusta
Margaret River
Dongara
Kalbarri
Northampton
Shark Bay
Denham
Dirk Hartog I.
Bernier I.
Dorre I.
Houtman Abrolhos
Geelvink Chan.
C. Leeuwin
C. Naturaliste
Archipelago of the Recherche
Ayers Rock
Mt. Olga
Yulara
Petermann Ranges
Musgrave Ranges
Everard Ranges
Mt. Woodroffe 1440
Maralinga
Ooldea
Cook
Nullarbor
Head of Bight
L. Carnegie
L. Wells
L. Barlee
L. Ballard
L. Moore
L. Cowan
L. Dundas
L. Lefroy
L. Austin
L. Carey
L. Raeside
L. Throssell
L. Yeo
L. Gillen
L. Breaden
Gibson Desert
Mt. Augustus 1105
Mt. Essendon 906
Mt. Singleton 675
Mt. Ragged 585
Peak Eleanora 563
Mt. Burges 554
Wyenandoo 543
Mt. Eureka 499
Tallering Peak 439
5632
East from Greenwich
Projection: Bonne
COPYRIGHT PHILIP'S
National Parks
m
ft
1000
400
200
0
3000
1200
600
200
2000
4000
6000
12 000

50 0 50 100 150 200 250 300 km

1:7 100 000

50 0 50 100 150 200 miles

CORAL SEA
WHITSUNDAY ISLANDS
1:2 200 000
Great Barrier Reef
Gulf of Carpentaria
Cape York Peninsula
Great Dividing Range
QUEENSLAND
NORTHERN TERRITORY
Barkly Tableland
Arnhem Land
Simpson Desert
Capricorn Channel
Townsville
Cairns
Mackay
Rockhampton
Gladstone
Mount Isa
Cloncurry
Charters Towers
Longreach
Emerald
Alice Springs
Tennant Creek
Normanton
Karumba
Burketown
Weipa
Cooktown
Bowen
Proserpine
Whitsunday I.
Hinchinbrook I.
Groote Eylandt
Wellesley Is.
Mornington I.
Sir Edward Pellew Group
MacDonnell Ranges

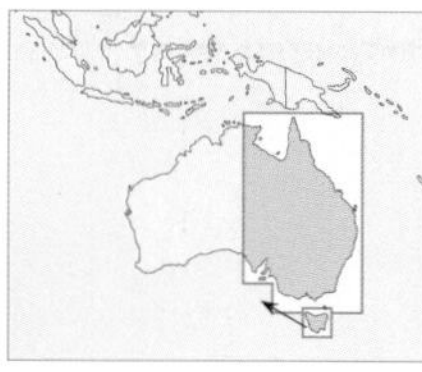

SOUTH AUSTRALIA
NEW SOUTH WALES
TASMAN SEA
TASMANIA
Bass Strait
National Parks
East from Greenwich
COPYRIGHT PHILIP'S
Projection: Bonne

Equatorial Scale 1:48 000 000

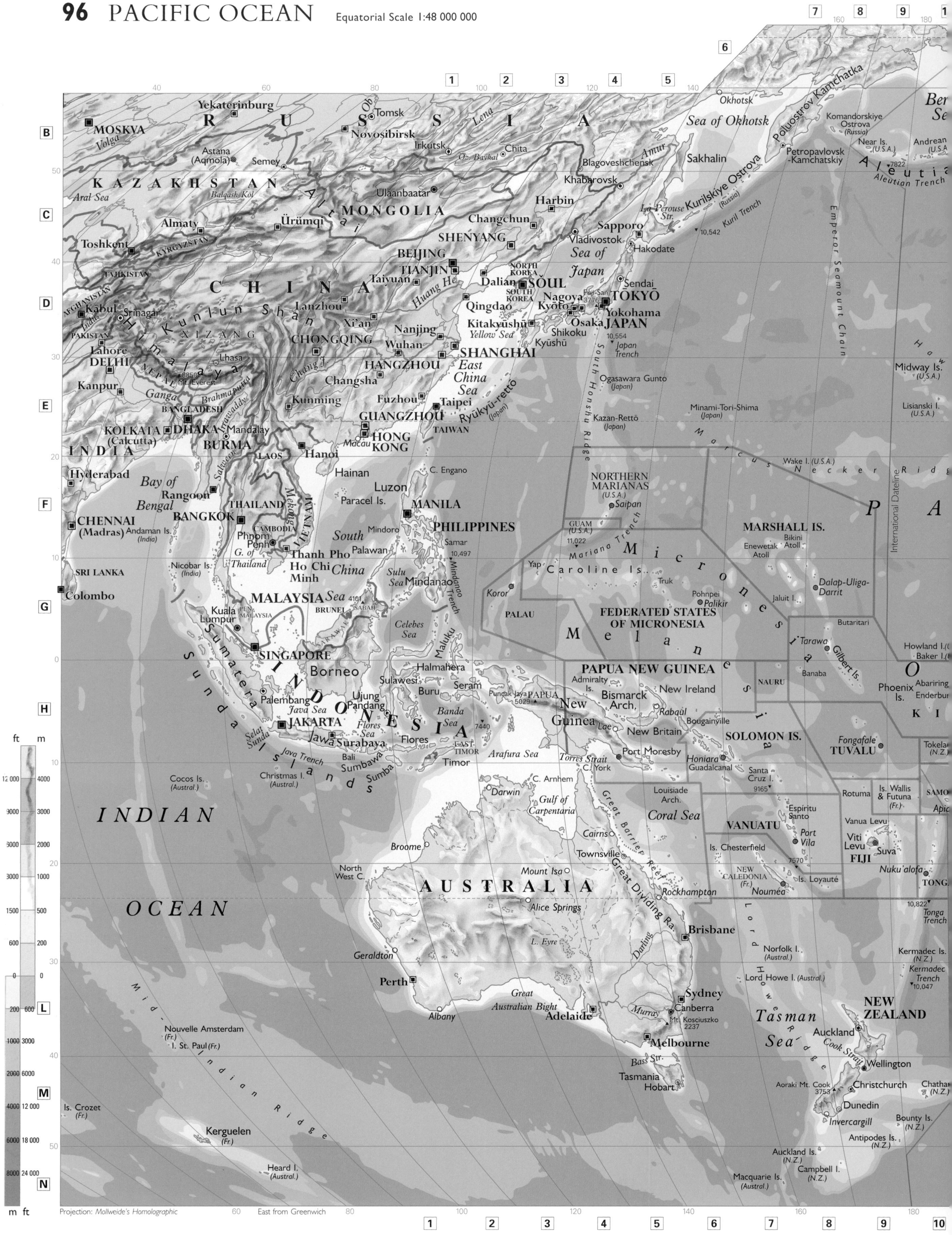
R U S S I A
MOSKVA
Volga
Yekaterinburg
Tomsk
Ob
Novosibirsk
Lena
Irkutsk
Oz. Baykal
Chita
Astana (Aqmola)
Semey
Amur
Blagoveshchensk
Khabarovsk
Sea of Okhotsk
Okhotsk
Sakhalin
Poluostrov Kamchatka
Petropavlovsk -Kamchatskiy
Komandorskiye Ostrova (Russia)
Near Is. (U.S.A.)
Andrean
Aleutian Trench
Bering Sea
K A Z A K H S T A N
Aral Sea
Balqash Köl
Altai
MONGOLIA
Ulaanbaatar
Harbin
Changchun
La Perouse Str.
Kurilskiye Ostrova (Russia)
Kuril Trench
10,542
Emperor Seamount Chain
Almaty
Ürümqi
Toshkent
KYRGYZSTAN
TAJIKISTAN
AFGHANISTAN
Kābul
Indus
Srinagar
PAKISTAN
SHENYANG
Sapporo
Vladivostok
Hakodate
Sea of Japan
BEIJING
TIANJIN
NORTH KOREA
SOUTH KOREA
Dalian
SŎUL
Sendai
Taiyuan
Huang He
Qingdao
Nagoya
Kyōto
Fuji-San 3776
TŌKYŌ
Yokohama
C H I N A
Kunlun Shan
XIZANG
Lanzhou
Xi'an
Kitakyūshū
Ōsaka
JAPAN
Yellow Sea
Shikoku
Kyūshū
10,554
Japan Trench
Nanjing
CHONGQING
Wuhan
SHANGHAI
Lahore
DELHI
Himalaya
Lhasa
NEPAL
8850 Mt. Everest
Kanpur
Ganga
Brahmaputra
BANGLADESH
Chang Jiang
HANGZHOU
Changsha
East China Sea
South Honshu Ridge
Ogasawara Gunto (Japan)
Kunming
Fuzhou
Taipei
TAIWAN
Ryūkyū-retto (Japan)
GUANGZHOU
HONG KONG
Macau
Minami-Tori-Shima (Japan)
Kazan-Rettō (Japan)
Marcus Necker Ridge
Midway Is. (U.S.A.)
Lisianski I. (U.S.A.)
Wake I. (U.S.A.)
KOLKATA (Calcutta)
DHAKA
Mandalay
Irrawaddy
INDIA
BURMA
Hanoi
LAOS
Salween
Hyderabad
Bay of Bengal
Rangoon
THAILAND
Mekong
VIETNAM
Hainan
Luzon
C. Engano
Paracel Is.
MANILA
PHILIPPINES
NORTHERN MARIANAS (U.S.A.)
Saipan
International Dateline
P A
CHENNAI (Madras)
Andaman Is. (India)
BANGKOK
CAMBODIA
Phnom Penh
South China Sea
Mindoro
Samar
10,497
GUAM (U.S.A.)
11,022
Mariana Trench
MARSHALL IS.
Bikini Atoll
Enewetak Atoll
G. of Thailand
Thanh Pho Ho Chi Minh
Palawan
Nicobar Is. (India)
Sulu Sea
Mindanao
Mindanao Trench
Yap
Caroline Is.
Micronesia
Truk
Pohnpei
Palikir
Dalap-Uliga-Darrit
Jaluit I.
SRI LANKA
Colombo
MALAYSIA
4101
SABAH
BRUNEI
Koror
PALAU
FEDERATED STATES OF MICRONESIA
Kuala Lumpur
PEN. MALAYSIA
SARAWAK
Celebes Sea
Butaritari
Tarawa
Gilbert Is.
Melanesia
Sumatera
SINGAPORE
Borneo
INDONESIA
Maluku
Halmahera
Sulawesi
Seram
Buru
Howland I. (U.S.A.)
Baker I.
PAPUA NEW GUINEA
Admiralty Is.
New Ireland
Bismarck Arch.
NAURU
Banaba
Phoenix Is.
Abariring
Enderbury
Palembang
Ujung Pandang
Puncak Jaya 5029
PAPUA
New Guinea
Banda Sea
7440
Rabaul
Lae
New Britain
Bougainville
Java Sea
JAKARTA
Jawa
Surabaya
Flores Sea
Flores
SOLOMON IS.
Sunda Islands
Selat Sunda
Java Trench
Bali
Sumbawa
Sumba
EAST TIMOR
Timor
Arafura Sea
Torres Strait
C. York
Port Moresby
Honiara
Guadalcanal
Fongafale
TUVALU
Tokelau (N.Z.)
Christmas I. (Austral.)
Cocos Is. (Austral.)
Santa Cruz I.
9165
C. Arnhem
Darwin
Gulf of Carpentaria
Great Barrier Reef
Louisiade Arch.
Coral Sea
Espiritu Santo
Rotuma
Is. Wallis & Futuna (Fr.)
SAMOA
Apia
INDIAN OCEAN
Cairns
VANUATU
Port Vila
Vanua Levu
Viti Levu
Suva
FIJI
Broome
Townsville
Is. Chesterfield
7570
Mount Isa
North West C.
NEW CALEDONIA (Fr.)
Nouméa
Is. Loyauté
Nuku'alofa
TONGA
AUSTRALIA
Alice Springs
Great Dividing Ra.
Rockhampton
10,822
Tonga Trench
Lord Howe Ridge
Brisbane
L. Eyre
Darling
Norfolk I. (Austral.)
Kermadec Is. (N.Z.)
Kermadec Trench
10,047
Geraldton
Lord Howe I. (Austral.)
Perth
Sydney
Great Australian Bight
Adelaide
Canberra
Murray
Mt. Kosciuszko 2237
Albany
Tasman Sea
NEW ZEALAND
Auckland
Mid-Indian Ridge
Nouvelle Amsterdam (Fr.)
I. St. Paul (Fr.)
Melbourne
Cook Strait
Wellington
Bass Str.
Tasmania
Hobart
Aoraki Mt. Cook 3753
Christchurch
Chatham Is. (N.Z.)
Is. Crozet (Fr.)
Dunedin
Invercargill
Bounty Is. (N.Z.)
Kerguelen (Fr.)
Antipodes Is. (N.Z.)
Auckland Is. (N.Z.)
Campbell I. (N.Z.)
Heard I. (Austral.)
Macquarie Is. (Austral.)
ft m
12 000 4000
9000 3000
6000 2000
3000 1000
1500 500
600 200
0 0
200 600
1000 3000
2000 6000
4000 12 000
6000 18 000
8000 24 000
m ft
Projection: Mollweide's Homolographic
East from Greenwich

Arctic Circle
ALASKA
(U.S.A.)
Anchorage
Bristol Bay
Gulf of Alaska
Juneau
Prince of Wales I.
(U.S.A.) Prince Rupert
Queen Charlotte Is.
(Canada)
C A N A D A
R O C K Y M t s
Edmonton
L. Winnipeg
Calgary
Regina
Winnipeg
Newfoundland
Vancouver
Vancouver I.
Victoria
Seattle
Portland
Snake
Boise
L. Superior
St. Lawrence
St. John's
N O R T H
Québec
Montréal
Ottawa
L. Huron
L. Michigan
Toronto
L. Ontario
Minneapolis
Missouri
Detroit
Buffalo
Boston
L. Erie
Salt Lake City
Colorado
Denver
CHICAGO
Pittsburgh
NEW YORK CITY
PHILADELPHIA
Baltimore
Washington D.C.
C. Mendocino
Sacramento
SAN FRANCISCO
Kansas City
St. Louis
Cincinnati
Appalachian Mts.
UNITED STATES
A T L A N T I C
Oklahoma City
Memphis
Mississippi
Atlanta
C. Hatteras
LOS ANGELES
San Diego
Phoenix
Dallas
Bermuda
(U.K.)
Ciudad Juárez
Houston
San Antonio
New Orleans
Jacksonville
Guadalupe
(Mex.)
Baja California
Golfo de California
M E X I C O
Sargasso Sea
Gulf of Mexico
Miami
Florida Str.
BAHAMAS
O C E A N
Monterrey
Tropic of Cancer
Honolulu
Oahu
HAWAIIAN IS.
(U.S.A.)
Hawaii
C. San Lucas
La Habana
C U B A
West Indies
Canal de Yucatan
Guadalajara
MEXICO
Puebla
Mérida
JAMAICA
HAITI
DOMINICAN REP.
Kingston
Leeward Is.
PUERTO RICO
(U.S.A.)
Is. Revilla Gigedo
(Mex.)
Acapulco
BELIZE
HONDURAS
Caribbean Sea
C I F I C
GUATEMALA
Guatemala
San Salvador
EL SALVADOR
NICARAGUA
Managua
BARBADOS
Windward Is.
I. Clipperton
(Fr.)
Barranquilla
Maracaibo
Caracas
San José
COSTA RICA
Colón
Panamá
PANAMA
Orinoco
VENEZUELA
Palmyra Is.
(U.S.A.)
North West Christmas I. Ridge
Teraina
Tabuaeran
Kiritimati
I. del Coco
(Costa Rica)
Medellín
Bogotá
I. de Malpelo
(Colombia)
Cali
COLOMBIA
Equator
Galápagos
(Ecuador)
Quito
ECUADOR
Jarvis I.
(U.S.A.)
O C E A N
Line Is.
Malden I.
Starbuck I.
Guayaquil
Iquitos
Amazonas
C. Paliñas
BRAZIL
Is. Marquises
Tongareva
Pukapuka
Manihiki
Vostok I.
Caroline I.
(Millennium I.)
Flint I.
East Pacific Ridge
Trujillo
PERU
LIMA
Suwarrow Is.
Is. de la Société
Tuamotu Ridge
Is. Tuamotu
Tahiti
Papeete
Cuzco
L. Titicaca
Arequipa
Nevada Ancohuma
La Paz
BOLIVIA
Cook Is.
(N.Z.)
Austral Seamount Chain
FRENCH POLYNESIA
Arica
Peru-Chile Trench
Iquique
Mururoa
Rarotonga
Is. Tubuai
Tropic of Capricorn
Antofagasta
PARAGUAY
Asunción
Ducie I.
Pitcairn I.
(U.K.)
Sala-y-Gómez
(Chile)
I. de Pascua
(Chile)
San Felix
(Chile)
San Ambrosio
(Chile)
San Miguel de Tucumán
Rapa
Porto Alegre
Córdoba
Aconcagua
Arch. de Juan Fernández
(Chile)
Valparaíso
SANTIAGO
Rosario
BUENOS AIRES
URUGUAY
Montevideo
Río de la Plata
Concepción
ARGENTINA
A N D E S
Chile Rise
SOUTH ATLANTIC OCEAN
Patagonia
Pacific-Antarctic Ridge
Falkland Is.
(U.K.)
Punta Arenas
Est. de Magallanes
Tierra del Fuego
C. de Hornos
South Georgia
(U.K.)
West from Greenwich

100 0 200 400 600 800 1000 1200 1400 km

1:31 100 000

100 0 200 400 600 800 1000 miles

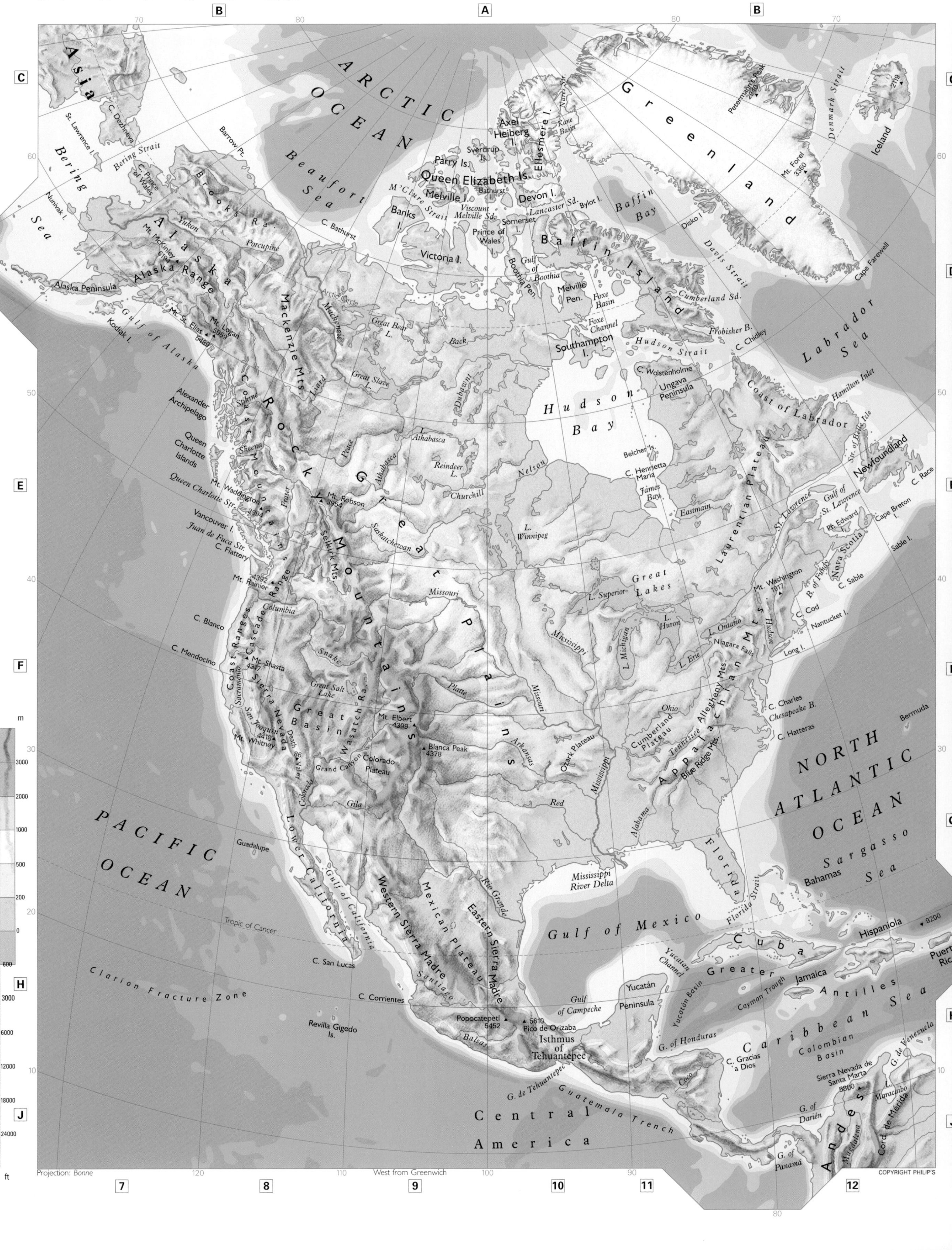
ARCTIC OCEAN
Asia
C. Dezhneva
St. Lawrence I.
Bering Strait
Bering Sea
Nunivak I.
C. Prince of Wales
Barrow Pt.
Beaufort Sea
Brooks Ra.
Yukon
Porcupine
Alaska
Mt. McKinley 6194
Alaska Range
Alaska Peninsula
Kodiak I.
Gulf of Alaska
Mt. St. Elias 5489
Mt. Logan 5959
Mackenzie Mts.
Mackenzie
Arctic Circle
Great Bear L.
Great Slave L.
Back
Liard
C. Bathurst
Banks I.
M'Clure Strait
Melville I.
Viscount Melville Sd.
Parry Is.
Queen Elizabeth Is.
Bathurst I.
Sverdrup Is.
Axel Heiberg I.
Ellesmere I.
Nares Str.
Kane Basin
Devon I.
Lancaster Sd.
Bylot I.
Somerset I.
Prince of Wales I.
Victoria I.
Gulf of Boothia
Boothia Pen.
Melville Pen.
Foxe Basin
Foxe Channel
Baffin Island
Baffin Bay
Greenland
Peterman's Peak 2940
Mt. Forel 3360
Disko I.
Davis Strait
Denmark Strait
Iceland
2119
Cape Farewell
Cumberland Sd.
Frobisher B.
C. Chidley
Hudson Strait
Southampton I.
Labrador Sea
Hamilton Inlet
Coast of Labrador
C. Wolstenholme
Ungava Peninsula
Hudson Bay
Belcher Is.
C. Henrietta Maria
James Bay
Eastmain
Laurentian Plateau
Str. of Belle Isle
Newfoundland
C. Race
Gulf of St. Lawrence
St. Lawrence
Pr. Edward I.
Cape Breton I.
Nova Scotia
Sable I.
B. of Fundy
C. Sable
Mt. Washington 1917
C. Cod
Nantucket I.
Hudson
Long I.
Niagara Falls
L. Ontario
L. Erie
L. Huron
L. Michigan
L. Superior
Great Lakes
Dubawnt
Athabasca
L. Athabasca
Peace
Reindeer L.
Churchill
Nelson
L. Winnipeg
Saskatchewan
Alexander Archipelago
Stikine
Coast Mountains
Skeena
Queen Charlotte Islands
Queen Charlotte Str.
Mt. Waddington 3994
Fraser
Rocky Mountains
Mt. Robson 3954
Great Plains
Selkirk Mts.
Vancouver I.
Juan de Fuca Str.
C. Flattery
Mt. Rainier 4392
Cascade Range
Columbia
C. Blanco
C. Mendocino
Coast Ranges
Mt. Shasta 4317
Sacramento
Sierra Nevada
San Joaquin
Mt. Whitney 4418
Death Valley -86
Snake
Great Salt Lake
Great Basin
Wasatch Ra.
Mt. Elbert 4399
Blanca Peak 4378
Platte
Missouri
Mississippi
Arkansas
Ozark Plateau
Grand Canyon
Colorado Plateau
Colorado
Gila
Red
Ohio
Cumberland Plateau
Tennessee
Allegheny Mts.
Appalachian Mts.
Blue Ridge Mts.
C. Charles
Chesapeake B.
C. Hatteras
Alabama
Florida
Bermuda
NORTH ATLANTIC OCEAN
Sargasso Sea
Bahamas
Florida Strait
Mississippi River Delta
Rio Grande
Gulf of Mexico
PACIFIC OCEAN
Guadalupe
Lower California
Gulf of California
Tropic of Cancer
Western Sierra Madre
Mexican Plateau
Eastern Sierra Madre
Santiago
C. San Lucas
C. Corrientes
Clarion Fracture Zone
Revilla Gigedo Is.
Popocatepetl 5452
5610 Pico de Orizaba
Balsas
Isthmus of Tehuantepec
Gulf of Campeche
Yucatán Peninsula
Yucatan Channel
Yucatan Basin
Cuba
Greater Antilles
Cayman Trough
Jamaica
Hispaniola
-9200
Puerto Rico
G. of Honduras
Caribbean Sea
Colombian Basin
C. Gracias a Dios
Coco
G. de Tehuantepec
Guatemala Trench
Central America
G. of Darién
G. of Panamá
Sierra Nevada de Santa Marta 5800
G. de Venezuela
Maracaibo
Magdalena
Cord. de Mérida
Andes
ft m
9000 3000
6000 2000
3000 1000
1500 500
600 200
0 0
200 600
1000 3000
2000 6000
4000 12000
6000 18000
8000 24000
m ft
Projection: Bonne
West from Greenwich
COPYRIGHT PHILIP'S

1:31 100 000

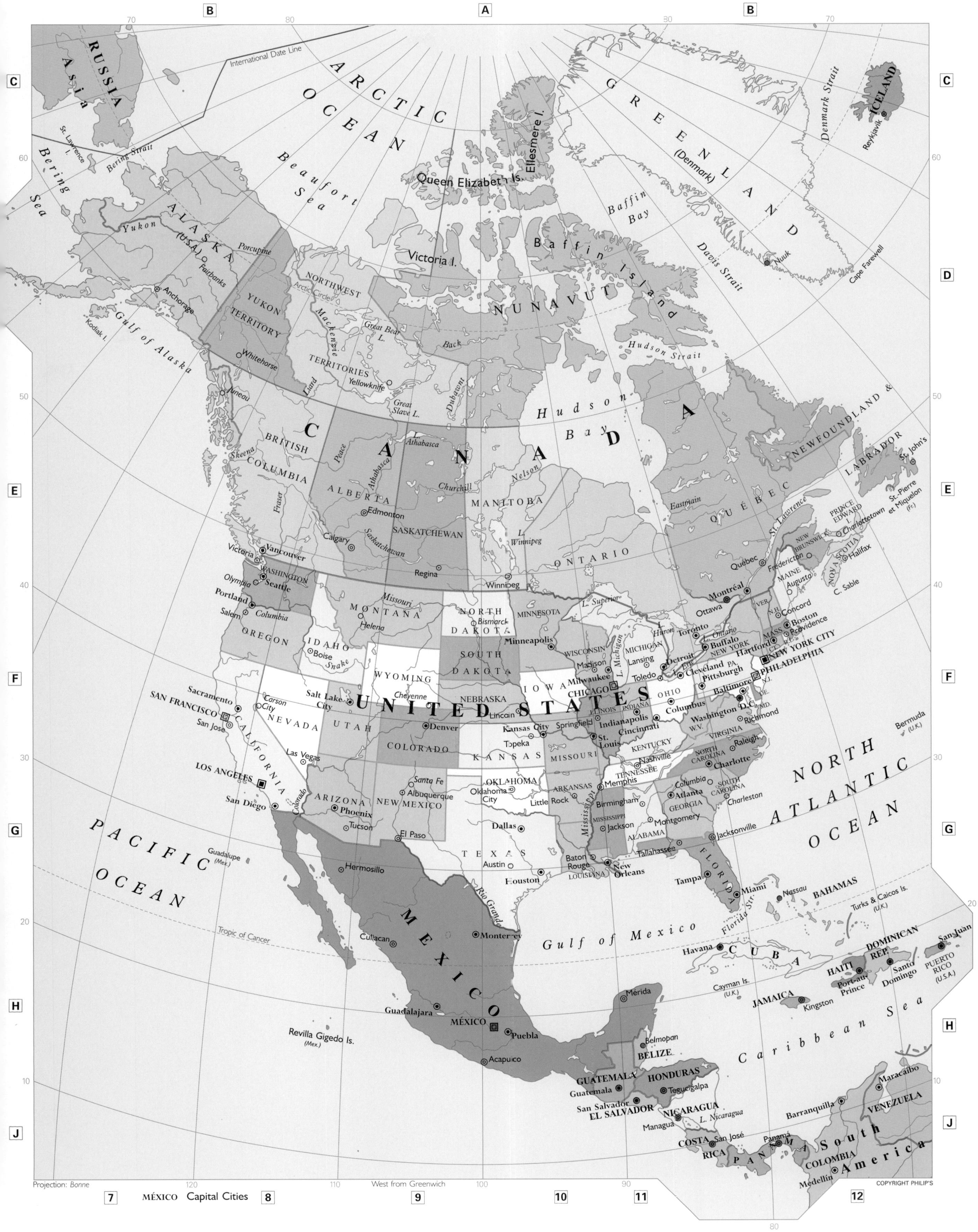
100 0 200 400 600 800 1000 1200 1400 km
100 0 200 400 600 800 1000 miles
ARCTIC OCEAN
International Date Line
RUSSIA
Asia
Bering Sea
Bering Strait
St. Lawrence I.
Beaufort Sea
Queen Elizabeth Is.
Ellesmere I.
GREENLAND
(Denmark)
Denmark Strait
ICELAND
Reykjavík
Baffin Bay
Baffin Island
Davis Strait
Nuuk
Cape Farewell
Victoria I.
NUNAVUT
Hudson Strait
Hudson Bay
ALASKA
(U.S.A.)
Yukon
Porcupine
Fairbanks
Anchorage
Kodiak I.
Gulf of Alaska
YUKON TERRITORY
Whitehorse
Juneau
NORTHWEST TERRITORIES
Arctic Circle
Mackenzie
Great Bear L.
Back
Yellowknife
Great Slave L.
Liard
Dubawnt
CANADA
BRITISH COLUMBIA
Skeena
Fraser
Peace
L. Athabasca
Athabasca
ALBERTA
Edmonton
Calgary
SASKATCHEWAN
Saskatchewan
Regina
Churchill
Nelson
MANITOBA
L. Winnipeg
Winnipeg
ONTARIO
QUÉBEC
Eastmain
NEWFOUNDLAND & LABRADOR
St John's
St.-Pierre et Miquelon (Fr.)
PRINCE EDWARD I.
Charlottetown
NEW BRUNSWICK
NOVA SCOTIA
Halifax
Fredericton
C. Sable
St. Lawrence
Québec
Montréal
Ottawa
Victoria
Vancouver
WASHINGTON
Olympia
Seattle
Portland
Columbia
Salem
OREGON
IDAHO
Boise
Snake
MONTANA
Missouri
Helena
NORTH DAKOTA
Bismarck
SOUTH DAKOTA
MINNESOTA
Minneapolis
L. Superior
WISCONSIN
Madison
Milwaukee
L. Michigan
MICHIGAN
Lansing
L. Huron
Detroit
L. Erie
L. Ontario
Toronto
Buffalo
NEW YORK
Hartford
Boston
Concord
Providence
Augusta
MAINE
VER.
N.H.
MASS.
CT.
R.I.
NEW YORK CITY
PHILADELPHIA
N.J.
PA.
Pittsburgh
Cleveland
Toledo
OHIO
Columbus
Baltimore
Washington D.C.
MD.
DEL.
Richmond
W.V.
VIRGINIA
WYOMING
Cheyenne
IOWA
CHICAGO
NEBRASKA
Lincoln
UNITED STATES
Salt Lake City
UTAH
NEVADA
Carson City
Sacramento
SAN FRANCISCO
San Jose
CALIFORNIA
Denver
COLORADO
Kansas City
Topeka
KANSAS
ILLINOIS
INDIANA
Indianapolis
Springfield
St. Louis
Cincinnati
KENTUCKY
MISSOURI
Nashville
TENNESSEE
Memphis
NORTH CAROLINA
Raleigh
Charlotte
SOUTH CAROLINA
Columbia
Charleston
Atlanta
GEORGIA
Las Vegas
LOS ANGELES
San Diego
Colorado
ARIZONA
Phoenix
Tucson
NEW MEXICO
Santa Fe
Albuquerque
El Paso
OKLAHOMA
Oklahoma City
ARKANSAS
Little Rock
Birmingham
MISSISSIPPI
Mississippi
Jackson
ALABAMA
Montgomery
Dallas
TEXAS
Austin
Houston
Baton Rouge
LOUISIANA
New Orleans
Tallahassee
Jacksonville
FLORIDA
Tampa
Miami
Bermuda (U.K.)
NORTH ATLANTIC OCEAN
PACIFIC OCEAN
Guadalupe (Mex.)
Hermosillo
Rio Grande
MEXICO
Culiacan
Monterrey
Tropic of Cancer
Gulf of Mexico
Florida Str.
Nassau
BAHAMAS
Turks & Caicos Is. (U.K.)
Havana
CUBA
DOMINICAN REP.
Santo Domingo
HAITI
Port-au-Prince
San Juan
PUERTO RICO (U.S.A.)
Cayman Is. (U.K.)
JAMAICA
Kingston
Caribbean Sea
Mérida
Guadalajara
MÉXICO
Puebla
Acapulco
Revilla Gigedo Is. (Mex.)
Belmopan
BELIZE
GUATEMALA
Guatemala
HONDURAS
Tegucigalpa
San Salvador
EL SALVADOR
NICARAGUA
Managua
L. Nicaragua
COSTA RICA
San José
PANAMA
Panamá
Maracaibo
VENEZUELA
Barranquilla
COLOMBIA
Medellín
South America
Projection: Bonne
West from Greenwich
COPYRIGHT PHILIP'S
MÉXICO Capital Cities

100 0 100 200 300 400 500 600 km

1:13 300 000

100 0 100 200 300 400 miles

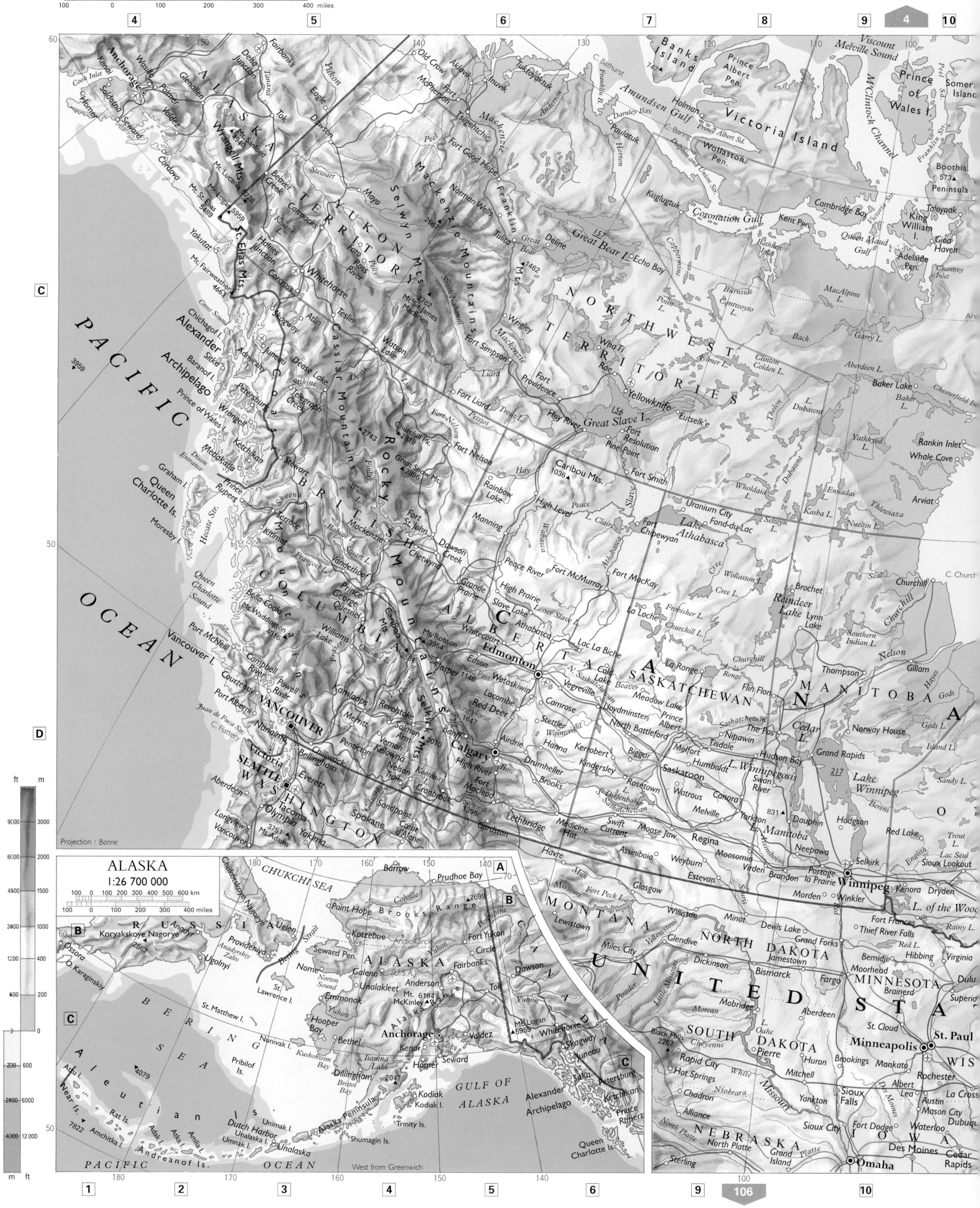
4
5
6
7
8
9
10
C
D
PACIFIC OCEAN
ALASKA
YUKON TERRITORY
NORTHWEST TERRITORIES
BRITISH COLUMBIA
ALBERTA
SASKATCHEWAN
MANITOBA
WASHINGTON
MONTANA
NORTH DAKOTA
SOUTH DAKOTA
NEBRASKA
MINNESOTA
IOWA
UNITED STATES
Victoria Island
Banks Island
Prince Albert Pen.
Prince of Wales I.
Viscount Melville Sound
M'Clintock Channel
Amundsen Gulf
Coronation Gulf
Queen Maud Gulf
Boothia Peninsula
King William I.
Great Bear L.
Great Slave L.
Lake Athabasca
L. Winnipegosis
Lake Winnipeg
L. Manitoba
L. of the Woods
Reindeer Lake
Mackenzie Mountains
Selwyn Mts.
Cassiar Mountains
Rocky Mountains
Coast Mountains
Columbia Mountains
Selkirk Mts.
Cariboo Mts.
St. Elias Mts.
Wrangell Mts.
Alexander Archipelago
Queen Charlotte Is.
Vancouver I.
Mt. Logan 5959
Mt. Robson 3954
Anchorage
Fairbanks
Juneau
Whitehorse
Dawson
Inuvik
Yellowknife
Fort Smith
Prince Rupert
Prince George
Kamloops
VANCOUVER
Victoria
SEATTLE
Edmonton
Calgary
Lethbridge
Medicine Hat
Saskatoon
Regina
Moose Jaw
Prince Albert
Winnipeg
Brandon
Churchill
The Pas
Flin Flon
Thompson
Rankin Inlet
Baker Lake
Cambridge Bay
Kugluktuk
Minneapolis
St. Paul
Omaha
Des Moines
Sioux Falls
Bismarck
Fargo
Projection : Bonne
ALASKA
1:26 700 000
100 0 100 200 300 400 500 600 km
100 0 100 200 300 400 miles
CHUKCHI SEA
BERING SEA
GULF OF ALASKA
Aleutian Is.
Brooks Range
Alaska Range
Mt. McKinley 6194
Barrow
Prudhoe Bay
Nome
Kodiak I.
Alaska Peninsula
RUSSIA
CANADA
PACIFIC OCEAN
West from Greenwich
A
B
C
1
2
3
4
5
6
9
10
106
ft
m

11
12
13
14
15
16
B
C
D
E
Devon I.
Lancaster Sound
Baffin Bay
Nunavik
Uummannaq
Ilulissat
Qasigiannguit
Ammassalik
GREENLAND
(KALAALLIT NUNAAT)
(Denmark)
Kong Frederik VI's Kyst
Brodeur Peninsula
Arctic Bay
Nanisivik
Bylot I.
Borden Pen.
Pond Inlet
C. Adair
Clyde River
Qeqertarsuaq
Kangerlussuaq
Sisimiut
Maniitsoq
Nuuk
Qeqertarsuatsiaat
Paamiut
Arsuk
Qaqortoq
Nanortalik
Narsaq
Nunap Isua
Davis Strait
Baffin Island
C. Raper
Home B.
Qikiqtarjuaq
C. Dyer
Cumberland Peninsula
Pangnirtung
Hoare B.
C. Mercy
Cumberland Sd.
Fury and Hecla Str.
Igloolik
Hall Beach
Simpson Pen.
Kugaaruk
Melville Peninsula
Committee B.
Air Force I.
Prince Charles I.
Foxe Basin
Nettilling L.
Rae Isthmus
Repulse Bay
NUNAVUT
C. Dorchester
Amadjuak L.
Foxe Pen.
Wager B.
Roes Welcome Sd.
Southampton I.
Coral Harbour
Bell Pen.
Foxe Channel
Cape Dorset
Salisbury I.
Nottingham I.
Iqaluit
Hall Peninsula
Meta Incognita Peninsula
Kimmirut
Frobisher Bay
Resolution I.
Hudson Strait
Chesterfield Inlet
Coats I.
Mansel I.
Ivujivik
Salluit
Kangiqsujuaq
Quaqtaq
C. Chidley
Akpatok I.
Labrador Sea
ATLANTIC OCEAN
Péninsule d'Ungava
Kangirsuk
Ungava Bay
Puvirnituq
Kangiqsualujjuaq
Hebron
Hudson Bay
Ottawa Is.
Kuujjuaq
Nain
Inukjuak
Hopedale
C. Harrison
Sleeper Is.
King George Is.
Baker's Dozen Is.
Sanikiluaq
Belcher Is.
C. Tatnam
Kuujjuarapik
L. Minto
Caniapiscau
Schefferville
Smallwood Res.
Labrador
North West River
Happy Valley-Goose Bay
Churchill Falls
Rigolet
Cartwright
NEWFOUNDLAND & LABRADOR
Port Hope Simpson
Belle Isle
St. Anthony
Peawanuck
Winisk
C. Henrietta Maria
Chisasibi
L. Caniapiscau
Labrador City
Fermont
Gagnon
St-Augustin
Natashquan
Havre-St-Pierre
Î. d'Anticosti
Bonavista
Gander
Lewisporte
Carbonear
St. John's
Deer Lake
Grand Falls-Windsor
Corner Brook
Newfoundland
Stephenville
Channel-Port aux Basques
Marystown
Placentia
C. Race
James Bay
Akimiski I.
Wemindji
Attawapiskat
Fort Albany
Charlton I.
Eastmain
Waskaganish
Sept-Îles
Port-Cartier
Gulf of St. Lawrence
Cabot Str.
ST-PIERRE et MIQUELON (Fr.)
Moosonee
Chibougamau
Baie-Comeau
Gaspé
Matane
Îs. de la Madeleine
C. North
Cape Breton I.
Glace Bay
Sydney
Port Hawkesbury
Nakina
Hearst
Cochrane
Matagami
Amos
Dolbeau-Mistassini
Chicoutimi
Jonquière
Roberval
Rimouski
Rivière-du-Loup
Edmundston
Campbellton
Bathurst
Chatham
P. EDWARD I.
Summerside
Charlottetown
Antigonish
New Glasgow
Nipigon
Greenstone
Kapuskasing
Timmins
Kirkland Lake
Rouyn-Noranda
Val-d'Or
La Tuque
Québec
Lévis
NEW BRUNSWICK
Moncton
Amherst
Truro
NOVA SCOTIA
Sable I. (Nova Scotia)
Thunder Bay
Marathon
Chapleau
Wawa
New Liskeard
Mont-Laurier
Shawinigan
Trois-Rivières
Joliette
St-Hyacinthe
Thetford Mines
Grand Falls
Woodstock
Fredericton
Saint John
Kentville
Dartmouth
Halifax
Digby
Bridgewater
Liverpool
Yarmouth
C. Sable
Lake Superior
Sault Ste. Marie
Elliot Lake
Sudbury
North Bay
MONTREAL
Granby
Sherbrooke
MAINE
Bangor
Augusta
Lewiston
Portland
Houghton
Marquette
Ironwood
Manitoulin I.
Parry Sound
Pembroke
Hull
Ottawa
Cornwall
Burlington
Montpelier
VERMONT
NEW HAMPSHIRE
Concord
Manchester
Rhinelander
Escanaba
Menominee
Manistique
Petoskey
Lake Huron
Georgian Bay
Huntsville
Barrie
Peterborough
Kingston
Belleville
Owen Sound
Traverse City
Wausau
Green Bay
Cadillac
Oshawa
TORONTO
L. Ontario
Syracuse
MASS.
BOSTON
C. Cod
Appleton
Sheboygan
Saginaw
Kitchener
Hamilton
Rochester
Albany
Springfield
Providence
Grand Rapids
Flint
London
Niagara Falls
Buffalo
NEW YORK
Hartford
CONN.
R.I.
Milwaukee
Lansing
Sarnia
L. Erie
Elmira
Binghamton
New Haven
Madison
Racine
Kenosha
Rockford
CHICAGO
DETROIT
Windsor
Erie
Jamestown
Scranton
Bridgeport
NEW YORK
Gary
South Bend
Toledo
CLEVELAND
PENNSYLVANIA
Newark
N.J.
Allentown
Trenton
ILLINOIS
INDIANA
OHIO
West from Greenwich

107

50 0 50 100 150 200 250 300 km

1:6 200 000

50 0 50 100 150 200 miles

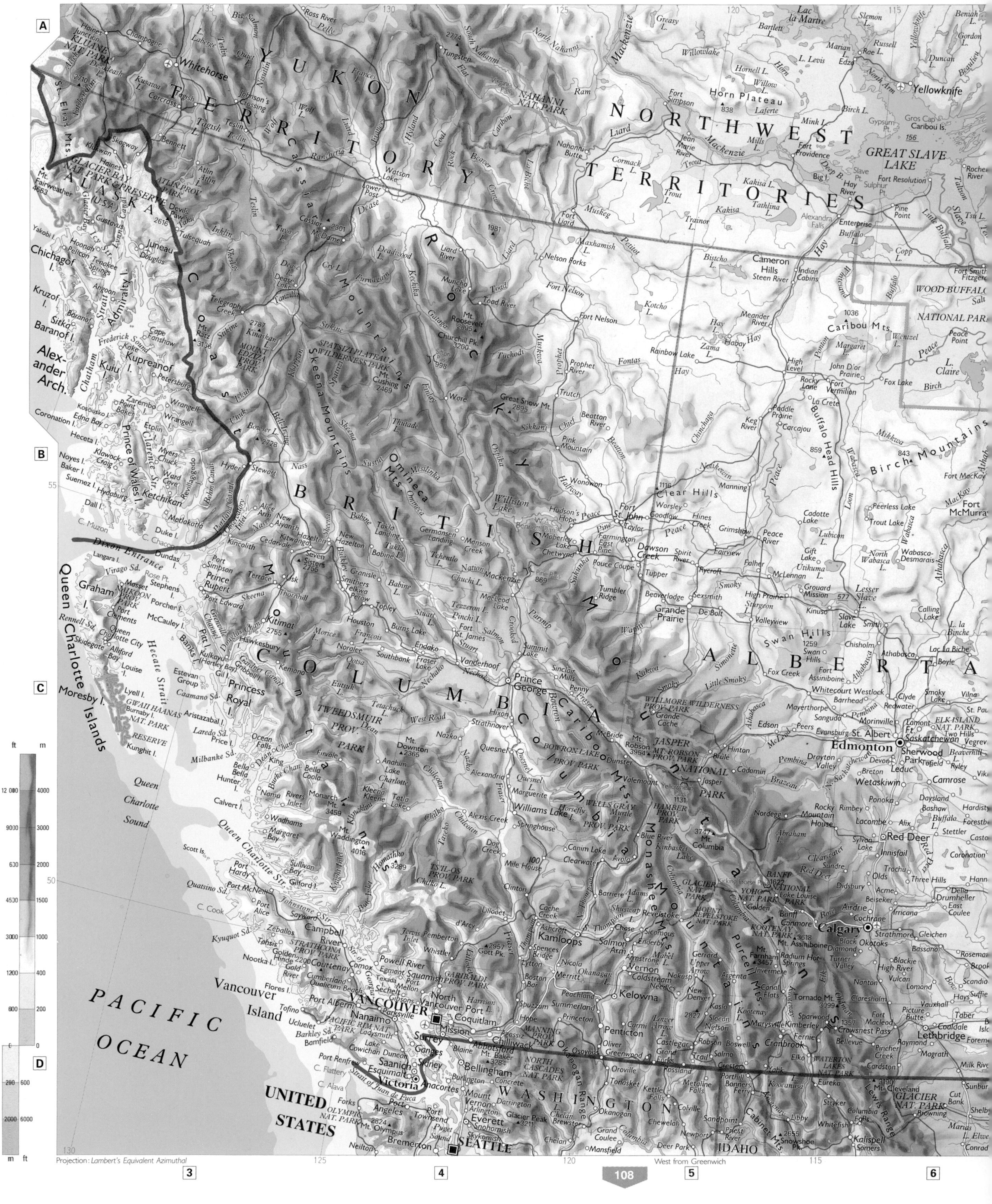
1
2
3
4
5
6
100
A
B
C
D
YUKON TERRITORY
NORTHWEST TERRITORIES
BRITISH COLUMBIA
ALBERTA
ALASKA (U.S.A.)
WASHINGTON
IDAHO
UNITED STATES
PACIFIC OCEAN
GREAT SLAVE LAKE
Whitehorse
Yellowknife
Edmonton
Calgary
Prince George
Kamloops
Kelowna
Vancouver
VANCOUVER
Victoria
SEATTLE
Bellingham
Juneau
Ketchikan
Prince Rupert
Kitimat
Fort St. John
Dawson Creek
Grande Prairie
Fort Nelson
Watson Lake
Red Deer
Lethbridge
Penticton
Nanaimo
Vancouver Island
Queen Charlotte Islands
Queen Charlotte Sound
Graham I.
Moresby I.
Dixon Entrance
Coast Mountains
Rocky Mountains
Skeena Mountains
Omineca Mts.
Cariboo Mts.
Columbia Mts.
Monashee Mts.
Purcell Mts.
Selkirk Mts.
Birch Mountains
Caribou Mts.
Swan Hills
Clear Hills
Horn Plateau
St. Elias Mts.
KLUANE NAT. PARK
GLACIER BAY NAT. PARK & PRESERVE
NAHANNI NAT. PARK
WOOD BUFFALO NATIONAL PARK
JASPER NATIONAL PARK
BANFF NATIONAL PARK
WELLS GRAY PROV. PARK
TWEEDSMUIR PROV. PARK
STRATHCONA PROV. PARK
PACIFIC RIM NAT. PARK
GWAII HAANAS NAT. PARK RESERVE
OLYMPIC NAT. PARK
NORTH CASCADES NAT. PARK
GLACIER NAT. PARK
WATERTON LAKES NAT. PARK
Mt. Robson 3954
Mt. Waddington 4016
Mt. Columbia 3747
Mt. Baker 3285
Mt. Olympus
Mt. Fairweather 4663
Strait of Juan de Fuca
Hecate Strait
Mackenzie
Liard
Peace
Fraser
Athabasca
ft
m
12 000
9000
6000
4500
3000
1200
600
4000
3000
2000
1500
1000
400
200
0
200
2000
600
6000
135
130
125
120
115
55
50

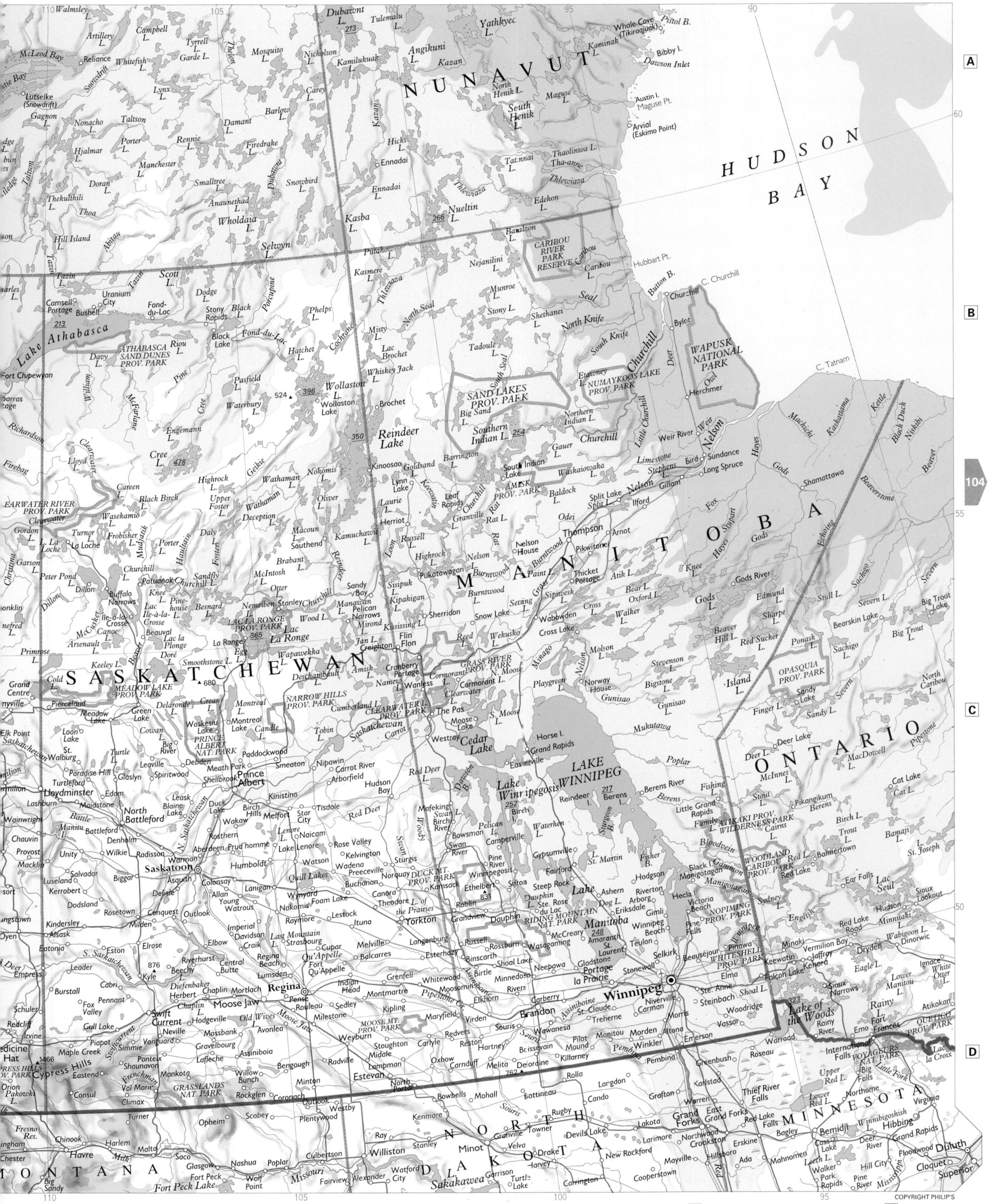
7
8
9
10
11
A
B
C
D
104
112
NUNAVUT
HUDSON BAY
MANITOBA
SASKATCHEWAN
ONTARIO
NORTH DAKOTA
MINNESOTA
MONTANA
LAKE WINNIPEG
Lake Athabasca
Reindeer Lake
Lake Winnipegosis
Lake Manitoba
Cedar Lake
Lake of the Woods
Wollaston L.
Dubawnt L.
Yathkyed L.
Nueltin L.
Kasba L.
Southern Indian L.
Churchill
Thompson
The Pas
Flin Flon
Prince Albert
Saskatoon
Regina
Moose Jaw
Swift Current
Yorkton
Brandon
Winnipeg
Dauphin
Portage la Prairie
Kenora
Dryden
Lloydminster
North Battleford
Minot
Williston
Grand Forks
Bemidji
Duluth
WAPUSK NATIONAL PARK
PRINCE ALBERT NAT. PARK
RIDING MOUNTAIN NAT. PARK
GRASSLANDS NAT. PARK
VOYAGEURS NAT. PARK
CARIBOU RIVER PARK RESERVE
ATHABASCA SAND DUNES PROV. PARK
SAND LAKES PROV. PARK
NUMAYKOOS LAKE PROV. PARK
LAC LA RONGE PROV. PARK
MEADOW LAKE PROV. PARK
NARROW HILLS PROV. PARK
CLEARWATER L. PROV. PARK
GRASS RIVER PROV. PARK
OPASQUIA PROV. PARK
ATIKAKI PROV. WILDERNESS PARK
WOODLAND CARIBOU PROV. PARK
NOPIMING PROV. PARK
WHITESHELL PROV. PARK
DUCK MT. PROV. PARK
MOOSE MT. PROV. PARK
QUETICO PROV. PARK
Cypress Hills
COPYRIGHT PHILIP'S

National Parks

50 0 50 100 150 200 250 300 km

1:6 200 000

50 0 50 100 150 200 miles

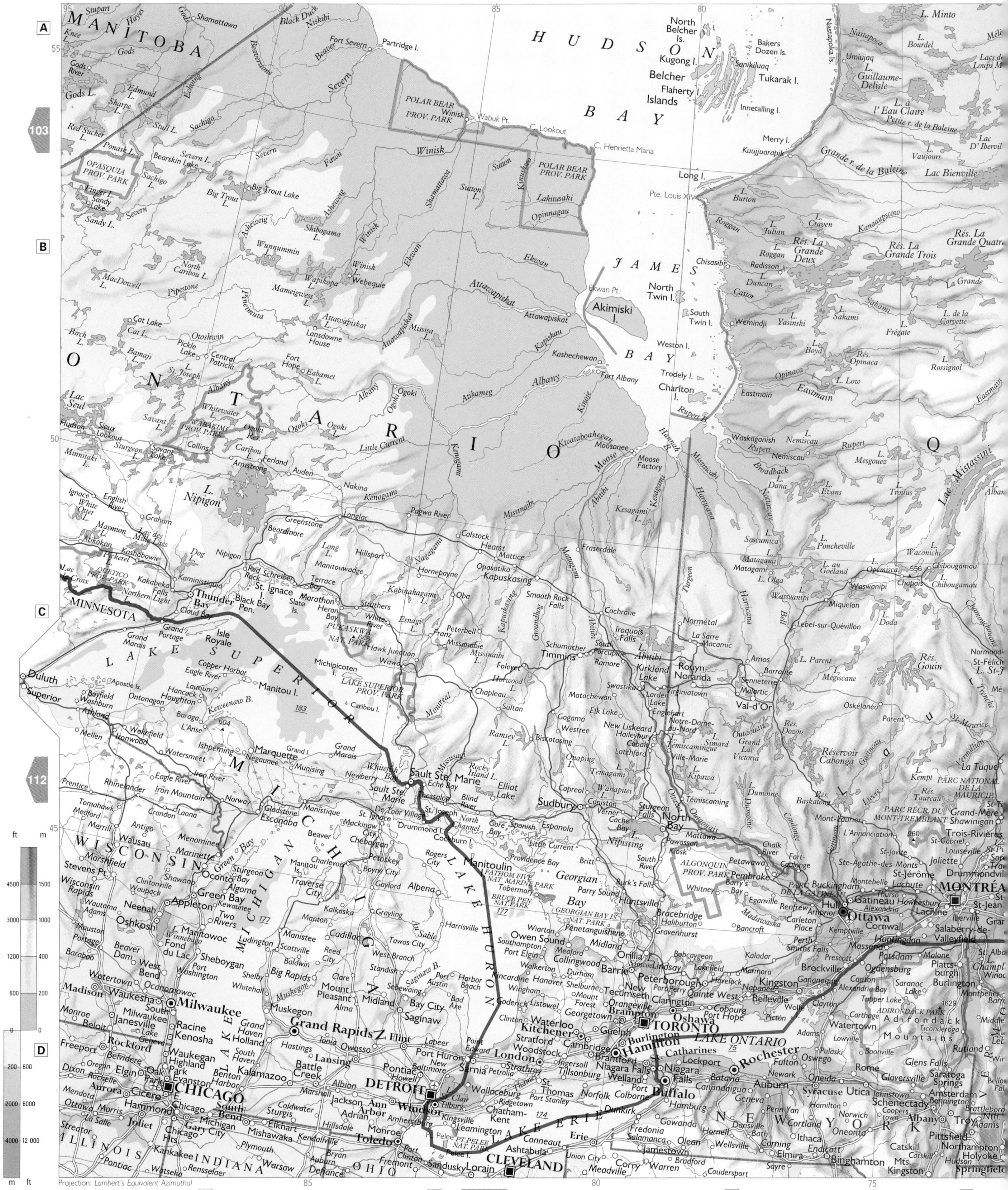
1
2
3
4
5
A
B
C
D
MANITOBA
ONTARIO
HUDSON BAY
JAMES BAY
LAKE SUPERIOR
LAKE MICHIGAN
LAKE HURON
LAKE ERIE
LAKE ONTARIO
MINNESOTA
WISCONSIN
MICHIGAN
ILLINOIS
INDIANA
OHIO
NEW YORK
POLAR BEAR PROV. PARK
OPASQUIA PROV. PARK
WABAKIMI PROV. PARK
QUETICO PROV. PARK
PUKASKWA NAT. PARK
LAKE SUPERIOR PROV. PARK
ALGONQUIN PROV. PARK
FATHOM FIVE NAT. MARINE PARK
BRUCE PEN. NAT. PARK
GEORGIAN BAY IS. NAT. PARK
PT. PELEE NAT. PARK
PARC NATIONAL DE LA MAURICIE
PARC RÉCR. DU MONT-TREMBLANT
ADIRONDACK PARK
Belcher Islands
Akimiski I.
Manitoulin
Isle Royale
L. Nipigon
Lac Seul
Lac Mistassini
Thunder Bay
Sault Ste. Marie
Sudbury
Timmins
Kapuskasing
Moosonee
Rouyn-Noranda
Val-d'Or
North Bay
OTTAWA
MONTREAL
TORONTO
Hamilton
Kingston
London
Windsor
DETROIT
CHICAGO
CLEVELAND
Buffalo
Rochester
Milwaukee
Grand Rapids
Toledo
Duluth
Green Bay
Syracuse
Albany
1500
1000
400
200
0
200
600
2000
6000
4000
12 000
ft
m
103
112
114
Projection: Lambert's Equivalent Azimuthal

National Parks

101

6
7
8
9
A
B
C
D
LABRADOR SEA
NEWFOUNDLAND & LABRADOR
Labrador
Newfoundland
QUÉBEC
Smallwood Reservoir
Churchill Falls
Happy Valley-Goose Bay
North West River
Labrador City
Wabush
Fermont
Schefferville
Nain
Hopedale
Makkovik
Postville
Cartwright
Mealy Mts.
Rés. Manicouagan
Sept-Îles
Port-Cartier
Baie-Comeau
Havre-St-Pierre
Natashquan
Kegaska
La Romaine
St-Augustin
Blanc-Sablon
L'Anse aux Meadows
St. Anthony
Str. of Belle Isle
Î. d'Anticosti
Dét. de Jacques-Cartier
Dét. d'Honguedo
GULF OF ST. LAWRENCE
St. Lawrence
Pén. de la Gaspésie
Mts. Chic-Chocs
Gaspé
Percé
Rimouski
Matane
Chicoutimi
Jonquière
La Baie
Rivière-du-Loup
Edmundston
Québec
Lévis
Sherbrooke
Thetford Mines
Îs. de la Madeleine
Cabot Strait
PRINCE EDWARD ISLAND
Charlottetown
Summerside
NEW BRUNSWICK
Moncton
Fredericton
Saint John
Bathurst
Campbellton
NOVA SCOTIA
Halifax
Dartmouth
Truro
Yarmouth
Bay of Fundy
Cape Breton Island
Sydney
Glace Bay
Corner Brook
Gros Morne Nat. Park
Long Range Mts.
Gander
Grand Falls-Windsor
St. John's
Avalon Peninsula
Bonavista
Channel-Port aux Basques
ST-PIERRE et MIQUELON (France)
Sable I. (Nova Scotia)
ATLANTIC OCEAN
MAINE
Bangor
Augusta
Portland
UNITED STATES
BOSTON
Manchester
Worcester
Lowell
West from Greenwich
55
50
45
70
65
60

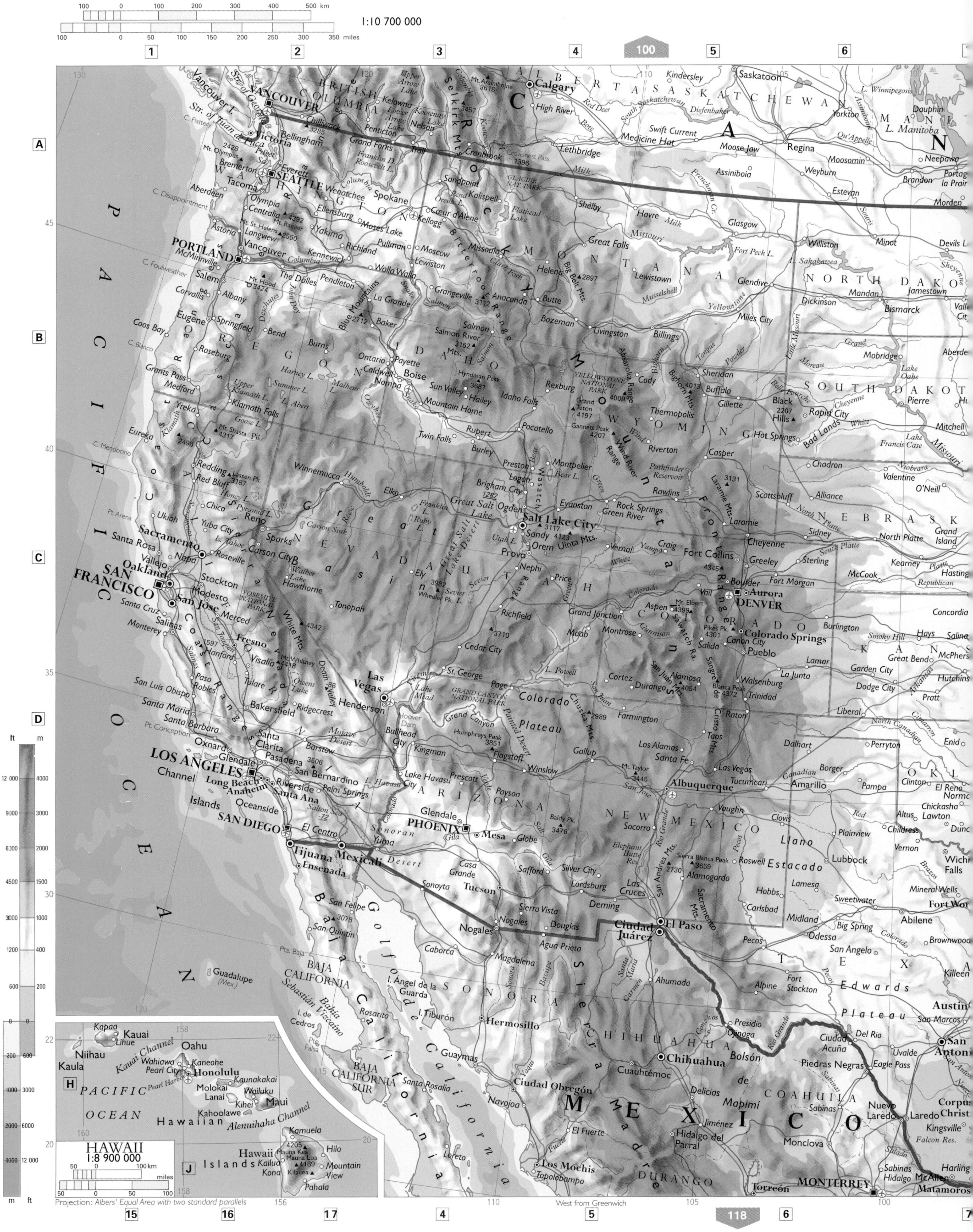
1:10 700 000
km
miles
100
118
PACIFIC OCEAN
CANADA
MEXICO
UNITED STATES
BRITISH COLUMBIA
ALBERTA
SASKATCHEWAN
MANITOBA
WASHINGTON
OREGON
IDAHO
MONTANA
WYOMING
NORTH DAKOTA
SOUTH DAKOTA
NEBRASKA
KANSAS
CALIFORNIA
NEVADA
UTAH
COLORADO
ARIZONA
NEW MEXICO
TEXAS
OKLAHOMA
BAJA CALIFORNIA
BAJA CALIFORNIA SUR
SONORA
CHIHUAHUA
COAHUILA
DURANGO
Rocky Mts.
Great Basin
Colorado Plateau
Sierra Nevada
Coast Ranges
Cascade Range
Sierra Madre
Golfo de California
Llano Estacado
Edwards Plateau
Bolsón de Mapimí
Sonoran Desert
Mojave Desert
Great Salt Lake
Vancouver
VANCOUVER
Victoria
SEATTLE
Tacoma
Olympia
Spokane
PORTLAND
Salem
Eugene
Boise
Calgary
Saskatoon
Regina
Great Falls
Helena
Billings
Bismarck
Pierre
Rapid City
Casper
Cheyenne
Salt Lake City
Reno
Sacramento
SAN FRANCISCO
Oakland
San Jose
Fresno
Bakersfield
LOS ANGELES
SAN DIEGO
Las Vegas
PHOENIX
Tucson
Albuquerque
Santa Fe
DENVER
Colorado Springs
El Paso
Ciudad Juárez
Tijuana
Mexicali
Hermosillo
Chihuahua
MONTERREY
Torreón
San Antonio
Austin
HAWAII
1:8 900 000
Kauai
Oahu
Honolulu
Molokai
Lanai
Maui
Kahoolawe
Hawaii
Hawaiian Islands
Niihau
Kaula
Kapaa
Lihue
Hilo
Kailua Kona
Mauna Kea 4205
Mauna Loa 4169
Pearl Harbor
Kauai Channel
Alenuihaha Channel
ft
m
12 000
9000
6000
4500
3000
1200
600
4000
3000
2000
1500
1000
400
200
0

Projection: *Albers' Equal Area with two standard parallels*

West from Greenwich

101
119
120
8
9
10
11
12
13
A
B
C
D
E
F
CANADA
ONTARIO
QUEBEC
ATLANTIC OCEAN
GULF OF MEXICO
BAHAMAS
Lake Winnipeg
Lake Superior
Lake Michigan
Lake Huron
Lake Erie
Lake Ontario
Lake of the Woods
Lake Nipigon
Winnipeg
Thunder Bay
Sault Ste. Marie
Sudbury
North Bay
Ottawa
MONTRÉAL
Québec
Trois-Rivières
Sherbrooke
TORONTO
Hamilton
Kitchener
London
Windsor
Chicoutimi
Jonquière
Rimouski
Edmundston
Saint John
NEW BRUNSWICK
MAINE
Bangor
Augusta
Portland
New England
BOSTON
Providence
Hartford
NEW YORK
Albany
Syracuse
Rochester
Buffalo
PHILADELPHIA
Harrisburg
PITTSBURGH
BALTIMORE
WASHINGTON D.C.
Richmond
Norfolk
Virginia Beach
Newport News
CLEVELAND
Toledo
Columbus
Cincinnati
DETROIT
Lansing
Grand Rapids
CHICAGO
Milwaukee
Madison
Minneapolis
St. Paul
Duluth
Des Moines
Iowa City
Indianapolis
Louisville
Lexington
Nashville
Knoxville
Memphis
Chattanooga
Charlotte
Raleigh
Greensboro
Columbia
Charleston
Savannah
ATLANTA
Birmingham
Montgomery
Mobile
Jackson
New Orleans
Baton Rouge
Shreveport
Little Rock
Tulsa
Kansas City
ST. LOUIS
Springfield
Topeka
DALLAS
Arlington
HOUSTON
Beaumont
Galveston
Jacksonville
Tallahassee
Orlando
TAMPA
St. Petersburg
West Palm Beach
Fort Lauderdale
MIAMI
Key West
Nassau
MINNESOTA
WISCONSIN
IOWA
ILLINOIS
INDIANA
OHIO
MICHIGAN
PENNSYLVANIA
WEST VIRGINIA
KENTUCKY
TENNESSEE
NORTH CAROLINA
SOUTH CAROLINA
GEORGIA
ALABAMA
MISSISSIPPI
LOUISIANA
ARKANSAS
MISSOURI
FLORIDA
VERMONT
NEW HAMPSHIRE
Appalachian Mts.
Ozark Plateau
Mississippi River Delta
Straits of Florida
Florida Keys
COPYRIGHT PHILIP'S

50 0 50 100 150 200 km

1:5 300 000

50 0 50 100 150 miles

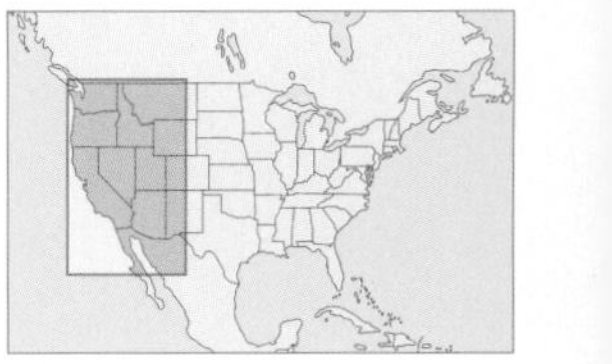

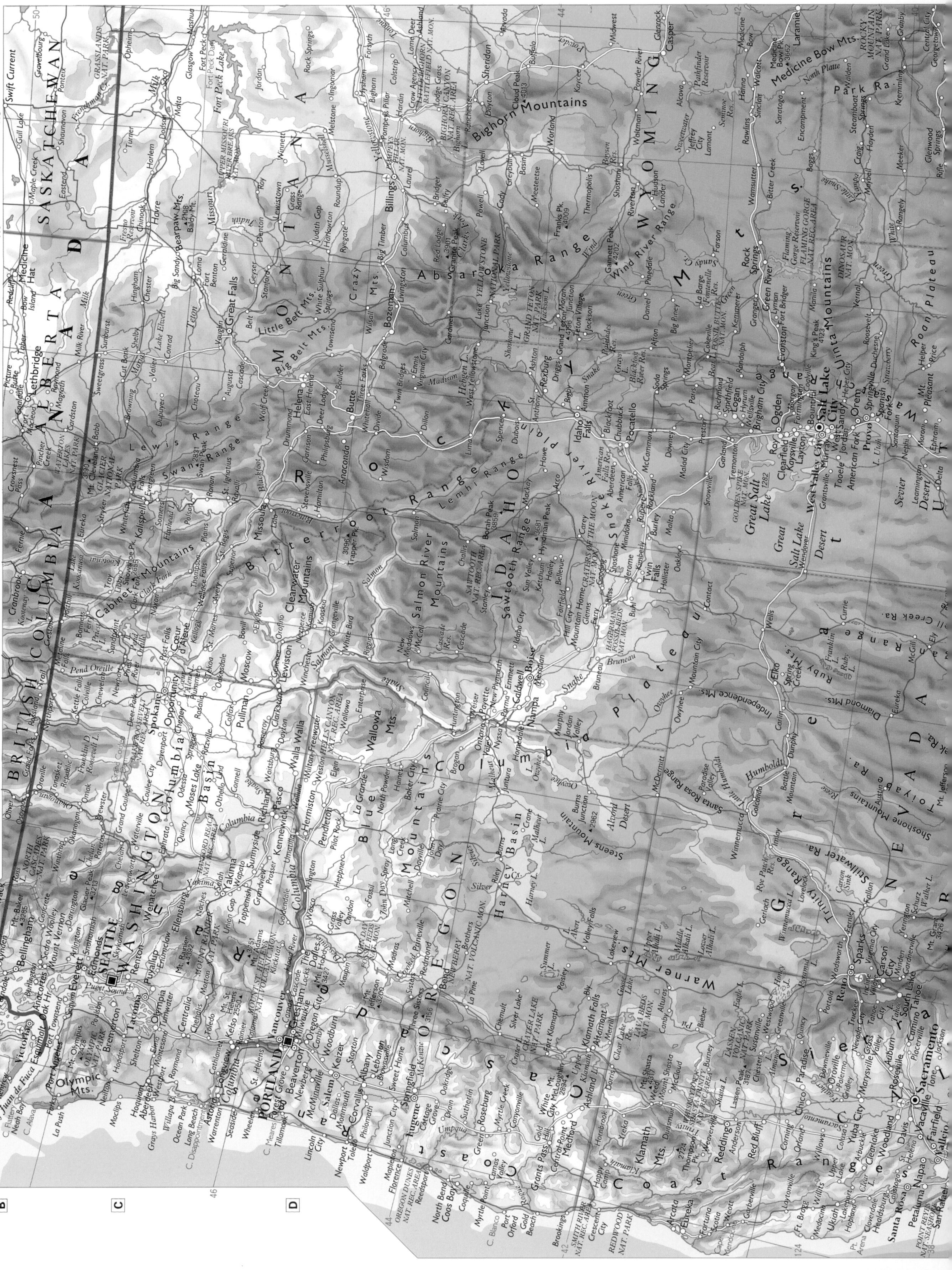
A
B
C
D
E
F
112
102
1
2
3
4
5
6
7
8
9
10
SASKATCHEWAN
ALBERTA
BRITISH COLUMBIA
MONTANA
WYOMING
IDAHO
WASHINGTON
OREGON
NEVADA
Bighorn Mountains
Absaroka Range
Wind River Range
Salmon River Mountains
Sawtooth Range
Bitterroot Range
Lemhi Range
Lewis Range
Swan Range
Cabinet Mountains
Clearwater Mountains
Blue Mountains
Wallowa Mts.
Snake River Plain
Columbia Basin
Harney Basin
Great Salt Lake
Great Salt Lake Desert
Uinta Mountains
Medicine Bow Mts.
Park Ra.
Steens Mountain
Santa Rosa Range
Independence Mts.
Ruby Mts.
Shoshone Mountains
Toiyabe Ra.
Stillwater Ra.
Warner Mts.
Cascade Range
Klamath Mts.
Olympic Mts.
VANCOUVER
SEATTLE
PORTLAND
Salem
Eugene
Spokane
Boise
Salt Lake City
Billings
Helena
Great Falls
Missoula
Butte
Bozeman
Casper
Laramie
Pocatello
Idaho Falls
Twin Falls
Ogden
Provo
Reno
Carson City
Sacramento
Redding
Medford
Bend
Yakima
Walla Walla
Lewiston
Tacoma
Olympia
Victoria
Lethbridge
Medicine Hat
Swift Current
Sheridan
Rock Springs
Elko
Winnemucca
Klamath Falls
Eureka
Pendleton
Kennewick
Pasco
Richland
Wenatchee
Bellingham
Everett

COLORADO
NEW MEXICO
ARIZONA
TEXAS
CHIHUAHUA
SONORA
MEXICO
BAJA CALIFORNIA
PACIFIC OCEAN
Golfo de California
Colorado Plateau
Painted Desert
Mojave Desert
Sonoran Desert
Grand Canyon
Death Valley
LOS ANGELES
SAN DIEGO
PHOENIX
Las Vegas
Albuquerque
Santa Fe
El Paso
Ciudad Juárez
Chihuahua
Hermosillo
Tucson
Tijuana
Mexicali
Fresno
Bakersfield
San Jose
Flagstaff
National Parks
Projection: Albers' Equal Area with two standard parallels
West from Greenwich
COPYRIGHT PHILIP'S

CENTRAL AND SOUTHERN CALIFORNIA AND WESTERN WASHINGTON

1:2 200 000

108
109
WESTERN WASHINGTON REGION
on same scale
PACIFIC OCEAN
BRITISH COLUMBIA
CANADA
Vancouver Island
Strait of Georgia
Strait of Juan de Fuca
WASHINGTON
OREGON
Olympic Mountains
OLYMPIC NATIONAL PARK
Cascade Range
VANCOUVER
Victoria
SEATTLE
Tacoma
Olympia
Mt. Rainier 4392
Mt. St. Helens 2550
Mt. Adams 3751
Vancouver
PORTLAND
Astoria
Columbia
White Mts.
Inyo Mts.
Sierra Nevada
Reno
Sparks
Carson City
Lake Tahoe
Mt. Whitney 4419
YOSEMITE NATIONAL PARK
KINGS CANYON NATIONAL PARK
SEQUOIA NATIONAL PARK
Sacramento Valley
SACRAMENTO
San Joaquin Valley
Stockton
Modesto
Merced
Fresno
Visalia
Diablo Range
Coast Ranges
Santa Lucia Range
SAN FRANCISCO
Oakland
San Jose
Santa Rosa
Monterey
Salinas
Santa Cruz
Paso Robles

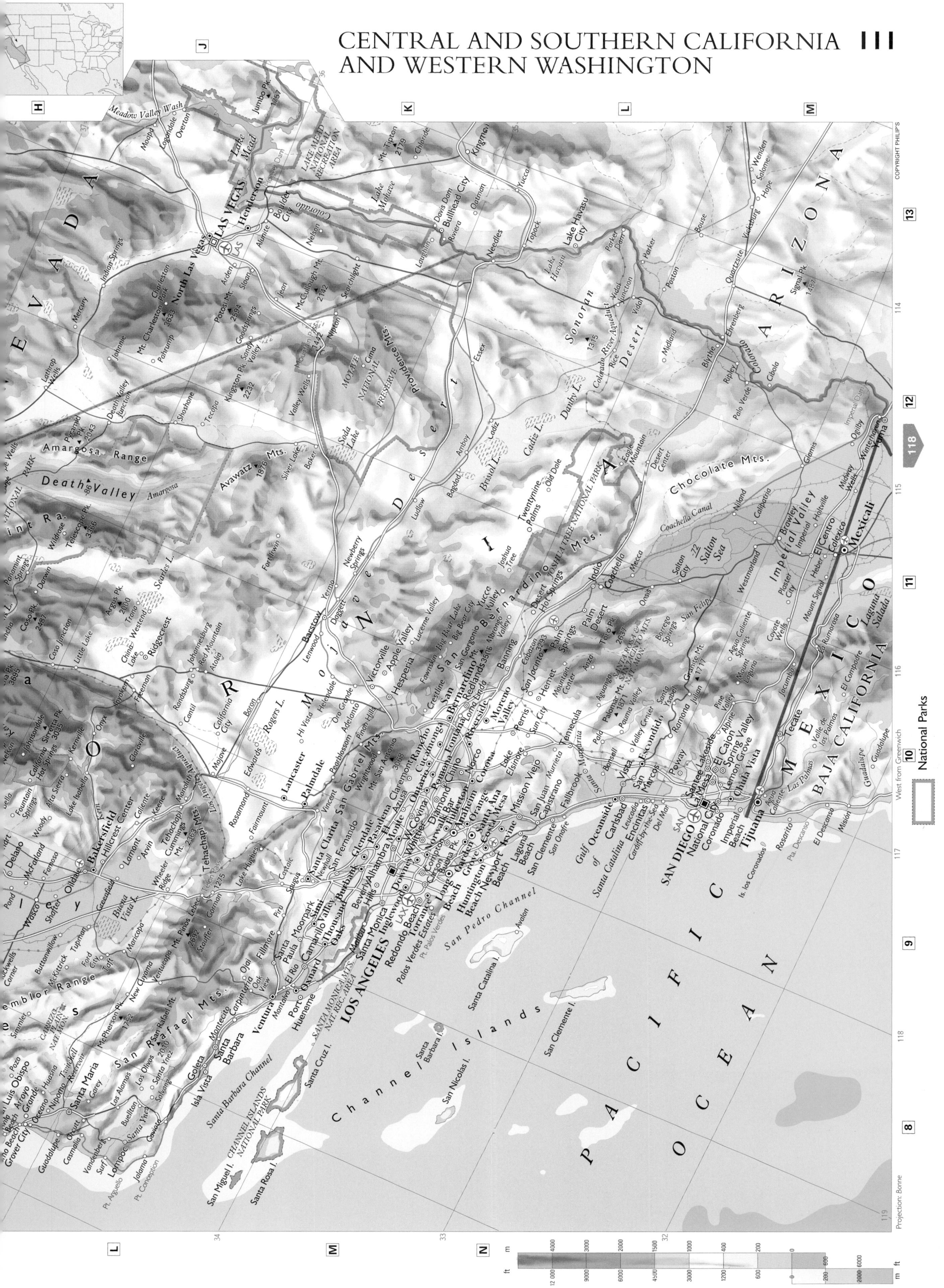
NEVADA
ARIZONA
CALIFORNIA
MEXICO
BAJA CALIFORNIA
PACIFIC OCEAN
Mojave Desert
Sonoran Desert
LAS VEGAS
LOS ANGELES
SAN DIEGO
Bakersfield
Santa Barbara
Tijuana
Mexicali
Death Valley
Amargosa Range
San Bernardino Mts.
San Gabriel Mts.
Chocolate Mts.
Salton Sea
Imperial Valley
Channel Islands
Santa Catalina I.
San Clemente I.
San Nicolas I.
Santa Cruz I.
Santa Rosa I.
San Miguel I.
CHANNEL ISLANDS NATIONAL PARK
JOSHUA TREE NATIONAL PARK
MOJAVE NATIONAL PRESERVE
LAKE MEAD NATIONAL RECREATION AREA
Lake Mead
Lake Mohave
Lake Havasu
Gulf of Santa Catalina
Santa Barbara Channel
San Pedro Channel
National Parks
West from Greenwich
Projection: Bonne
COPYRIGHT PHILIP'S
118

50 0 50 100 150 200 km

1:5 300 000

50 0 50 100 150 miles

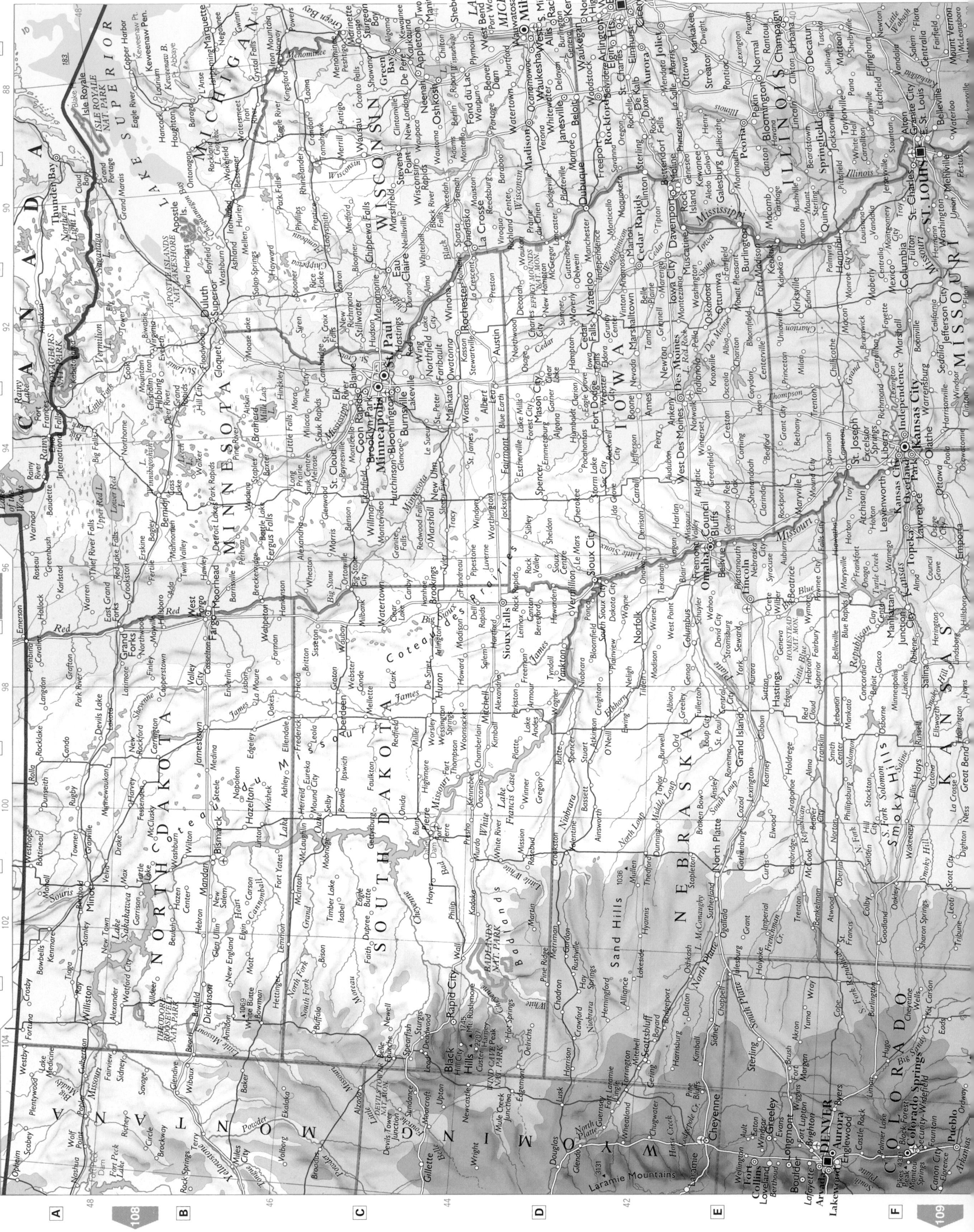
CANADA
LAKE SUPERIOR
LAKE MICHIGAN
MINNESOTA
WISCONSIN
MICHIGAN
NORTH DAKOTA
SOUTH DAKOTA
IOWA
ILLINOIS
NEBRASKA
MISSOURI
KANSAS
COLORADO
WYOMING
MONTANA
CHICAGO
Milwaukee
Minneapolis
St. Paul
Des Moines
Omaha
Kansas City
ST. LOUIS
DENVER
Sioux Falls
Fargo
Bismarck
Duluth
Madison
Lincoln
Topeka
Rapid City
Cheyenne
Sand Hills
Black Hills
Laramie Mountains
Smoky Hills
Coteau des Prairies
ISLE ROYALE NAT. PARK
BADLANDS NAT. PARK
THEODORE ROOSEVELT NAT. PARK
WIND CAVE NAT. PARK
Lake of the Woods
Thunder Bay
Mississippi
Missouri
Red
Platte

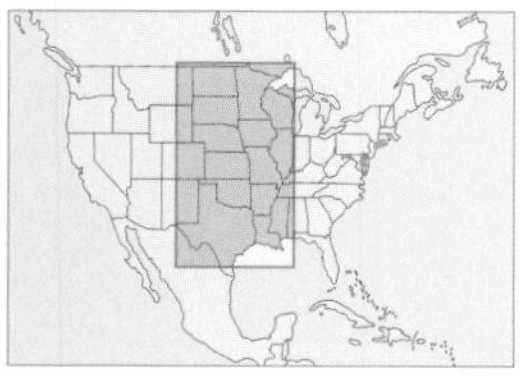

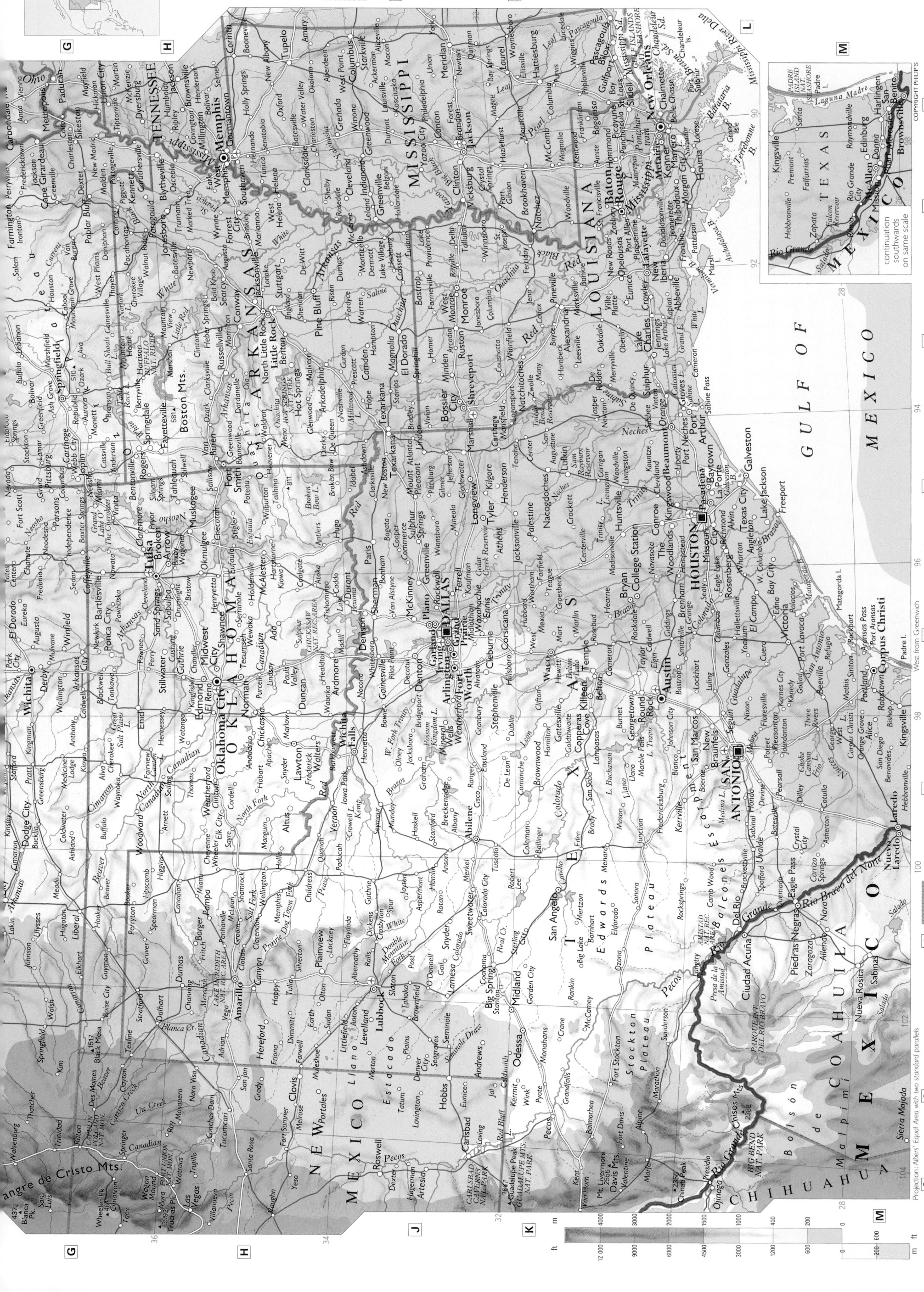
GULF OF MEXICO
MISSISSIPPI
LOUISIANA
ARKANSAS
OKLAHOMA
TEXAS
NEW MEXICO
TENNESSEE
MEXICO
COAHUILA
CHIHUAHUA
Dallas
Houston
San Antonio
Austin
Oklahoma City
Tulsa
Little Rock
Memphis
New Orleans
Baton Rouge
Jackson
Shreveport
Fort Worth
Corpus Christi
Lubbock
Amarillo
El Paso
Wichita
Springfield
National Parks
Projection: Albers' Equal Area with two standard parallels
continuation southwards on same scale
COPYRIGHT PHILIP'S
West from Greenwich
115
118

1:5 300 000

50 0 50 100 150 200 km

50 0 50 100 150 miles

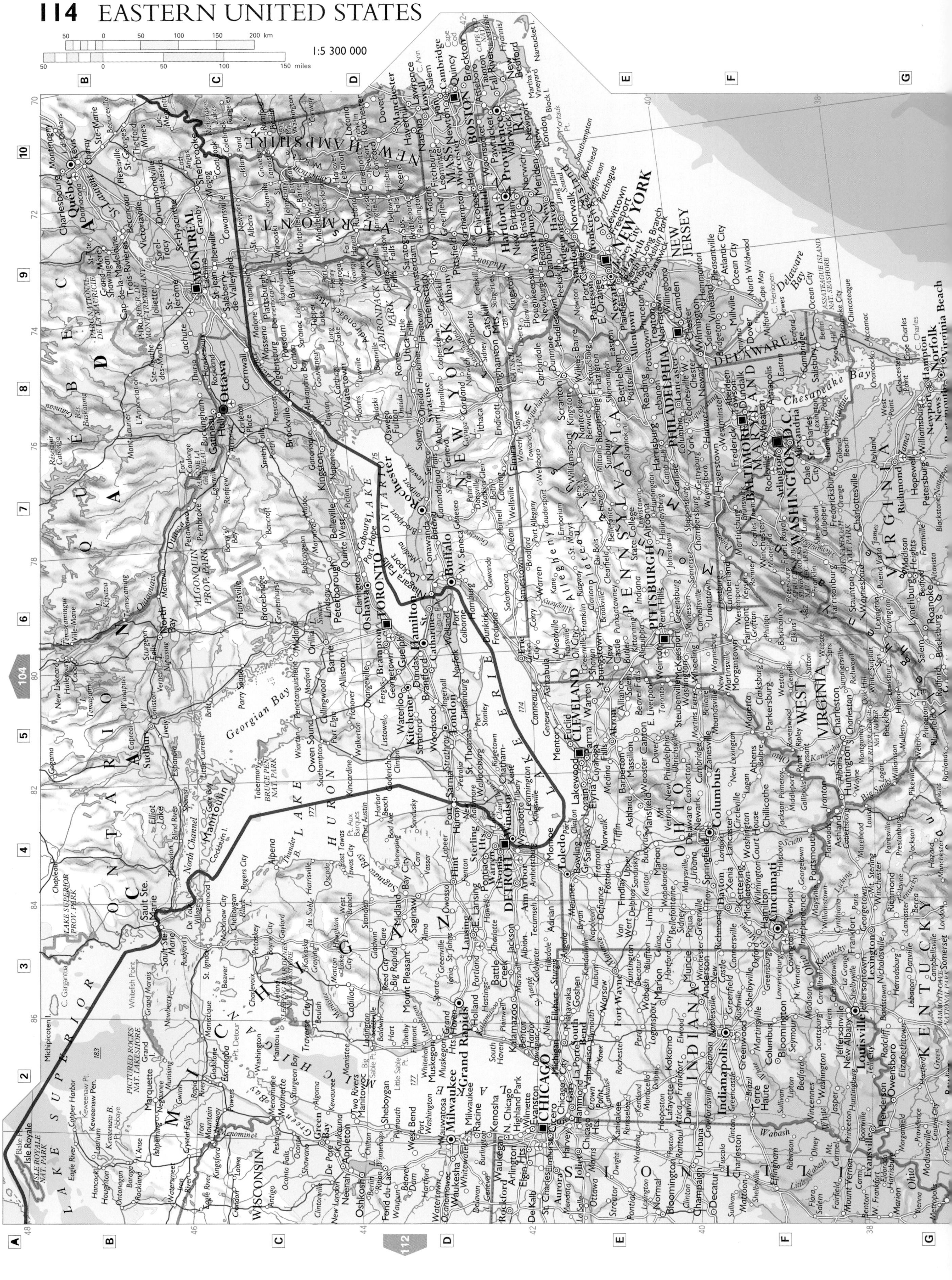
ONTARIO
QUEBEC
MICHIGAN
WISCONSIN
ILLINOIS
INDIANA
OHIO
KENTUCKY
WEST VIRGINIA
VIRGINIA
PENNSYLVANIA
NEW YORK
NEW JERSEY
DELAWARE
MARYLAND
VERMONT
NEW HAMPSHIRE
MASS.
R.I.
CONN.
LAKE SUPERIOR
LAKE MICHIGAN
LAKE HURON
LAKE ERIE
LAKE ONTARIO
Georgian Bay
Chesapeake Bay
Delaware Bay
WASHINGTON D.C.
NEW YORK
PHILADELPHIA
BALTIMORE
PITTSBURGH
CLEVELAND
DETROIT
CHICAGO
TORONTO
MONTRÉAL
Ottawa
Québec
BOSTON
Buffalo
Milwaukee
Columbus
Indianapolis
Cincinnati
Louisville
Grand Rapids

104
112

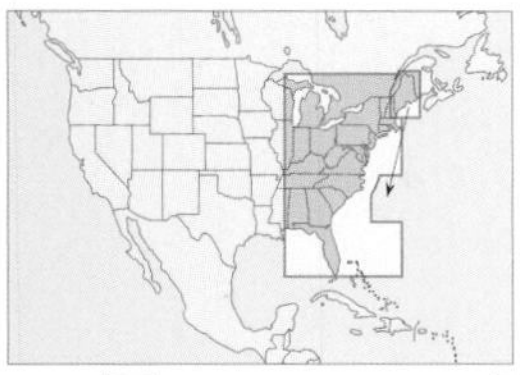

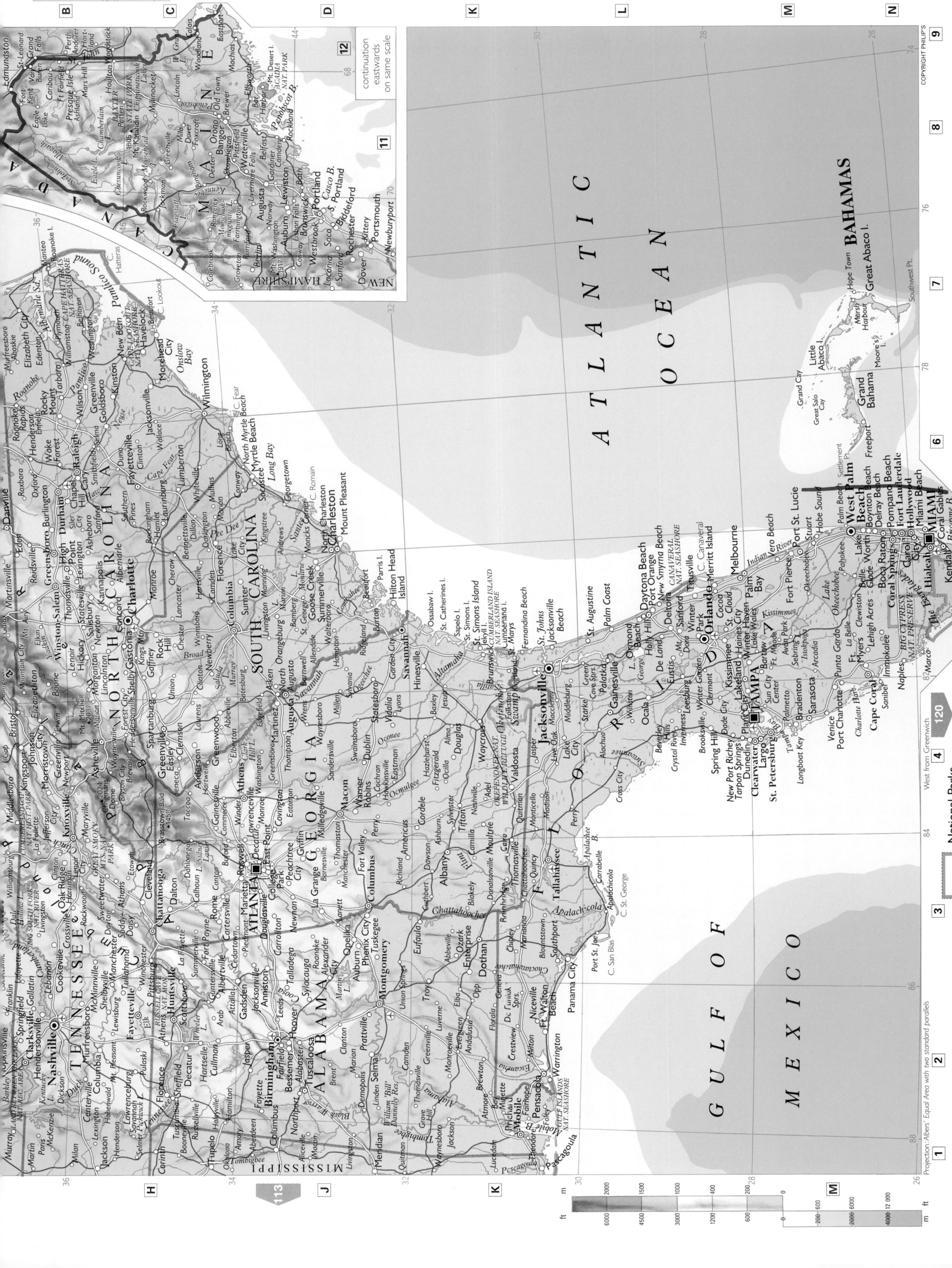
ATLANTIC OCEAN
GULF OF MEXICO
BAHAMAS
TENNESSEE
NORTH CAROLINA
SOUTH CAROLINA
GEORGIA
ALABAMA
FLORIDA
MISSISSIPPI
MAINE
NEW HAMPSHIRE
ATLANTA
MIAMI
Jacksonville
TAMPA
Orlando
Charlotte
Savannah
Nashville
Birmingham
Montgomery
Tallahassee
Charleston
Raleigh
Portland
Great Abaco I.
Grand Bahama
continuation eastwards on same scale
National Parks
West from Greenwich
Projection: Albers' Equal Area with two standard parallels
COPYRIGHT PHILIP'S

1:2 200 000

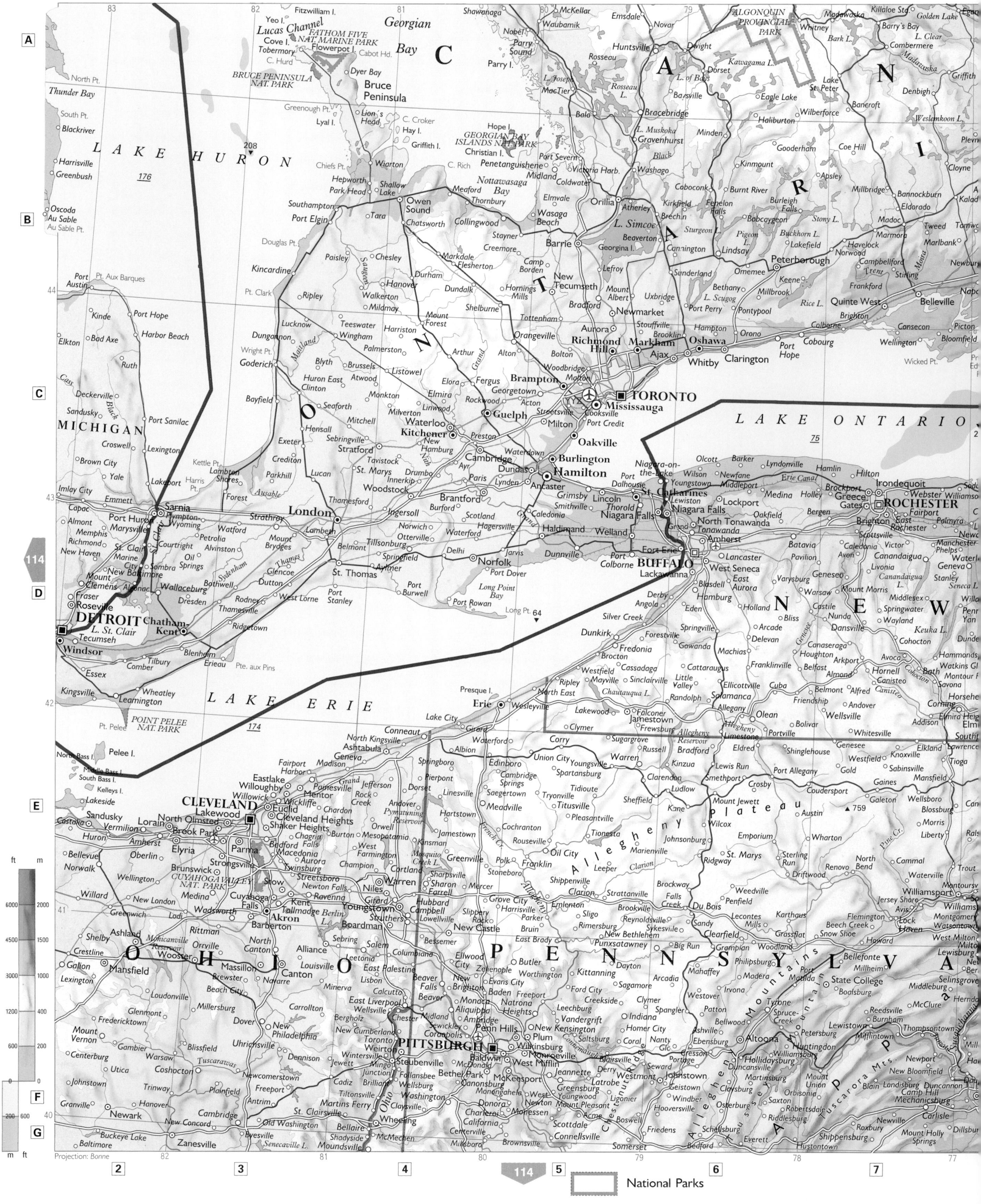
LAKE HURON
Georgian Bay
Bruce Peninsula
BRUCE PENINSULA NAT. PARK
FATHOM FIVE NAT. MARINE PARK
GEORGIAN BAY ISLANDS NAT. PARK
ALGONQUIN PROVINCIAL PARK
ONTARIO
LAKE ONTARIO
LAKE ERIE
MICHIGAN
OHIO
PENNSYLVANIA
NEW YORK
Allegheny Plateau
Allegheny Mountains
TORONTO
Mississauga
Hamilton
Burlington
Oakville
Brampton
Kitchener
Waterloo
Guelph
Cambridge
London
Brantford
St. Catharines
Niagara Falls
BUFFALO
ROCHESTER
DETROIT
Windsor
Sarnia
Port Huron
CLEVELAND
Akron
Canton
Youngstown
Erie
PITTSBURGH
Oshawa
Peterborough
Barrie
Orillia
Owen Sound
Chatham-Kent
POINT PELEE NAT. PARK
CUYAHOGA VALLEY NAT. PARK
Projection: Bonne

National Parks

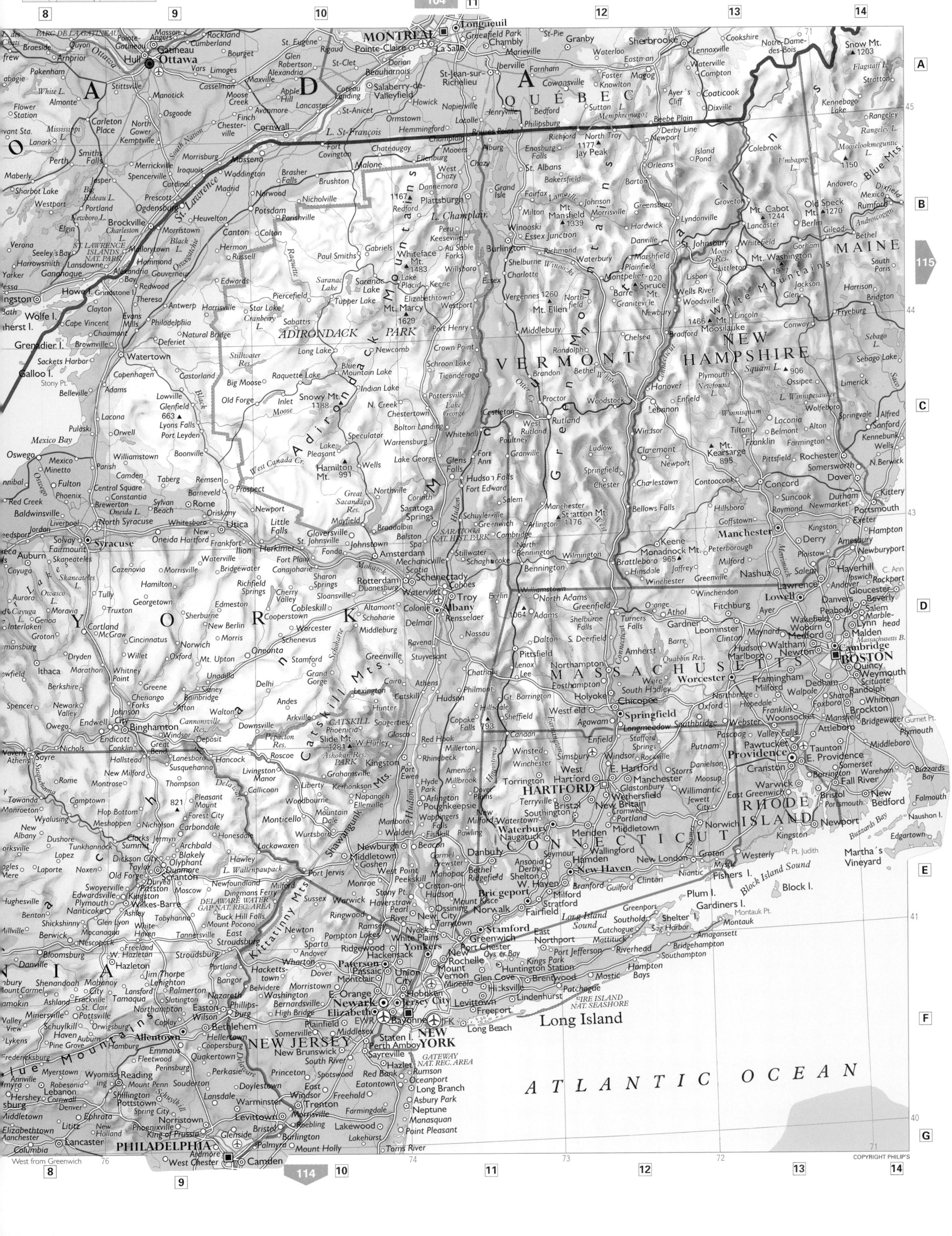
104
114
115
8
9
10
11
12
13
14
A
B
C
D
E
F
G
MONTREAL
Ottawa
Gatineau
Hull
Longueuil
Sherbrooke
Granby
QUÉBEC
CANADA
MAINE
NEW HAMPSHIRE
VERMONT
MASSACHUSETTS
CONNECTICUT
RHODE ISLAND
NEW JERSEY
NEW YORK
ADIRONDACK PARK
Adirondack Mountains
Green Mountains
White Mountains
Catskill Mts.
Blue Mountains
Kittatinny Mts.
Shawangunk Mts.
L. Champlain
Lake George
Mt. Marcy 1629
Mt. Washington 1917
Mt. Mansfield 1339
Syracuse
Utica
Watertown
Binghamton
Albany
Schenectady
Troy
Burlington
Montpelier
Rutland
Concord
Manchester
Portsmouth
Boston
Cambridge
Worcester
Springfield
Lowell
Providence
Hartford
New Haven
Bridgeport
Stamford
Yonkers
Paterson
Newark
Jersey City
New York
Elizabeth
Trenton
Allentown
Bethlehem
Scranton
Wilkes-Barre
Reading
Philadelphia
Camden
Lancaster
Long Island
Block Island Sound
Martha's Vineyard
Nantucket
ATLANTIC OCEAN
FIRE ISLAND NAT. SEASHORE
GATEWAY NAT. REC. AREA
DELAWARE WATER GAP NAT. REC. AREA
West from Greenwich
COPYRIGHT PHILIP'S

50 0 50 100 150 200 250 300 km

50 0 50 100 150 200 miles

1:7 100 000

109

1
2
3
4
A
B
C
D
A R I Z O N A
N E W M E X I C O
U N I T E
T E
TUCSON
Yuma
Gila
Gila Bend
Miami
Globe
Christmas
Elephant Butte Reservoir
Roswell
Lubbock
Hobbs
Carlsbad
Big Spring
Midland
Sweetwater
Odessa
Lordsburg
Deming
Las Cruces
WHITE SANDS NAT. MON.
CARLSBAD CAVERNS NAT. PARK
GUADALUPE MTS. NAT. PARK
ORGAN PIPE CACTUS NAT. MON.
SAGUARO NAT. PARK
CIUDAD JUÁREZ
EL PASO
TIJUANA
MEXICALI
Tecate
San Luis Río Colorado
Ensenada
La Misión
Sierra de Juárez
Santo Tomás
San Telmo
Santo Domingo
San Quintín
El Rosario
Sierra San Pedro Mártir
BAJA CALIFORNIA
DESIERTO CENTRAL DE BAJA CALIFORNIA
Desierto de Altar
GRAN DESIERTO DEL PINACATE
Sonoyta
Puerto Peñasco
El Golfo de Santa Clara
San Felipe
B. de San Jorge
El Desemboque
Concepción
Caborca
Altar
Nogales
Bisbee
Naco
Douglas
Agua Prieta
Cananea
Imuris
Magdalena
Santa Ana
Arizpe
Cucurpe
Fronteras
Nacozari
Ascensión
Janos
L. de Guzmán
Sabinal
Guadalupe Bravos
Van Horn
El Porvenir
Lucero
Villa Ahumada
Nuevo Casas Grandes
Galeana
Moctezuma
Buenaventura
El Sueco
Alpine
Sanderson
Pecos
Río Grande
Río Bravo del Norte
Golfo de California
S O N O R A
El Dátil
Benjamin Hill
La Libertad
Carbó
Moctezuma
Rayón
Ures
Hermosillo
Mazatán
Tiburón
Kino
I. San Esteban
I. San Lorenzo
Tepoca
Punta Prieta
Rosarito
Bahía de Los Angeles
I. Ángel de la Guarda
Canal de Ballenas
San Fernando
I. San Luis
I. de Cedros
Bahía Sebastián Vizcaíno
I. Natividad
Pta. Falsa
Guerrero Negro
El Arco
OJO DE LIEBRE
Desierto de Vizcaíno
Sierra Vizcaíno
San Ignacio
Santa Rosalía
Laguna San Ignacio
SAN IGNACIO
Pta. Abreojos
Mulegé
I. San Marcos
Punta Concepción
Guaymas
Empalme
Torres
Tecoripa
Pocito Casas
Sahuaripa
Suaqui
Onavas
Yécora
Movas
Nuri
Ciudad Obregón
Tóri
Esperanza
I. Lobos
Navojoa
Álamos
Huatabampo
Yávaros
Chínipas
Ojinaga
Presidio
BIG BEND NAT. PARK
El Pueblito
C H I H U A H U A
CHIHUAHUA
Aquiles Serdán
Ciudad Guerrero
Cuauhtémoc
General Trías
Julimes
Meoqui
Delicias
Saucillo
Naica
Ciudad Camargo
Bolsón de Mapimí
Madera
Temosachic
CUMBRES DE MAJALCA
CASCADA DE BASSASEACHIC
Bocoyna
Creel
Carichic
Nonoava
BARRANCA DEL COBRE
Urique
Batopilas
Jiménez
Sierra Mojada
Hidalgo del Parral
Santa Bárbara
San Francisco del Oro
Carillo
Escalón
Valle de Zaragoza
COAHUILA
Ciudad Acuña
Del Rio
Piedras Negras
Eagle Pass
Zaragoza
Nava
Allende
Nueva Rosita
Sabinas
Melchor Múzquiz
Progreso
Cuatrociénegas
Frontera
Monclova
Lampazos
Sabinas Hidalgo
Reata
Serranías del Burro
Boquillas del Carmen
RÍO BRAVO
San Carlos
Presa de la Amistad
MONTERREY
Saltillo
Ramos Arizpe
CUMBRES DE MONTERREY
Conejos
Francisco I. Madero
Tlahualilo
Mapimí
San Pedro de las Colonias
Gómez Palacio
TORREÓN
Lerdo
Matamoros
Parras
Nazas
Sierra Madre Occidental
La Purísima
Loreto
I. Carmen
I. Santa Catalina
BAJA CALIFORNIA SUR
Santo Domingo
Llano de la Magdalena
Sierra de la Giganta
Ciudad Constitución
San Carlos
C. San Lázaro
I. Santa Magdalena
B. Magdalena
I. Santa Margarita
I. San José
I. Espíritu Santo
B. de la Paz
La Paz
San Juan de la Costa
I. Cerralvo
San Pedro
Ensenada de los Muertos
Todos Santos
Sa. San Lázaro
C. Pulmo
Cabo San Lucas
San José del Cabo
C. San Lucas
Tropic of Cancer
Ahome
Topolobampo
Los Mochis
Guasave
Guamúchil
B. de Santa María
Fuerte
El Fuerte
San Blas
Choix
Sinaloa de Leyva
Mocorito
Navolato
Altata
Culiacán
Eldorado
Quila
Cosalá
S I N A L O A
D U R A N G O
Durango
Canatlán
Tepehuanes
Santiago Papasquiaro
Tamazula
El Salto
Mezquital
Guanaceví
El Palmito
Villa Ocampo
La Cruz
Dimas
Mazatlán
Concordia
Villa Unión
Rosario
Escuinapa
PUERTO DE LOS ANGELES
Z A C A T E C A S
Zacatecas
Fresnillo
Sombrerete
Chalchihuites
Río Grande
Jerez de García Salinas
Valparaíso
Juan Aldama
Francisco I. Madero
Camacho
Concepción del Oro
Mazapil
Melchor Ocampo
Galeana
San Tiburcio
Matehuala
Charcas
El Venado
Salinas
Cerritos
San Luis Potosí
Pinos
S A N L U I S P O T O S Í
N A Y A R I T
Acaponeta
Tecuala
Santiago Ixcuintla
Tepic
Compostela
I. Isabela
Islas Tres Marías
B. de Banderas
Puerto Vallarta
C. Corrientes
Aguascalientes
Calvillo
Encarnación de Díaz
Lagos de Moreno
LEÓN
Guanajuato
Irapuato
Celaya
Salamanca
GUADALAJARA
Tlaquepaque
Ocotlán
La Barca
La Piedad
Zamora
Sahuayo
Jiquilpan
Zacapu
Morelia
Pátzcuaro
Uruapan
Zitácuaro
Tacámbaro
Apatzingán
Ario de Rosales
Huetamo
Ciudad Altamirano
J A L I S C O
Ameca
Mascota
Talpa de Allende
Tomatlán
Autlán
Ciudad Guzmán
Sayula
L. de Chapala
Chamela
Barra de Navidad
Manzanillo
COLIMA
Colima
Tecomán
M I C H O A C Á N
Coalcomán
Lázaro Cárdenas
Zihuatanejo
Petatlán
G U E R R E R O
P A C I F I C O C E A N
Is. de Revillagigedo (Mexico)
I. San Benedicto
I. Roca Partida
I. Socorro
110
105
30
25
20
West from Greenwich
Projection: Bi-polar oblique Conical Orthomorphic

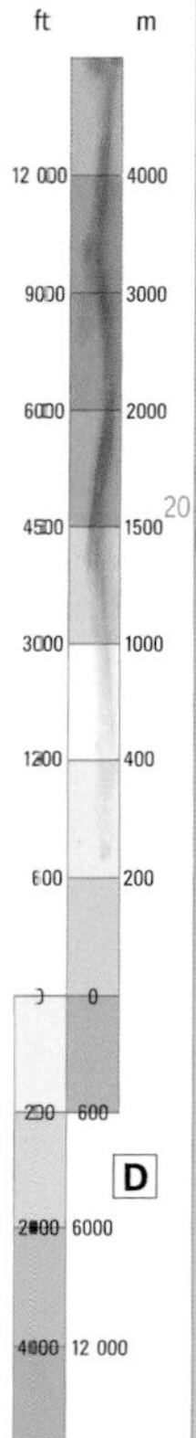
ft
m
12 000
4000
9000
3000
6000
2000
4500
1500
3000
1000
1200
400
600
200
0
200
600
2000
6000
4000
12 000
m
ft

National Parks

State names in Central Mexico

1 DISTRITO FEDERAL
2 AGUASCALIENTES
3 GUANAJUATO
4 HIDALGO
5 MÉXICO
6 MORELOS
7 QUERÉTARO
8 TLAXCALA

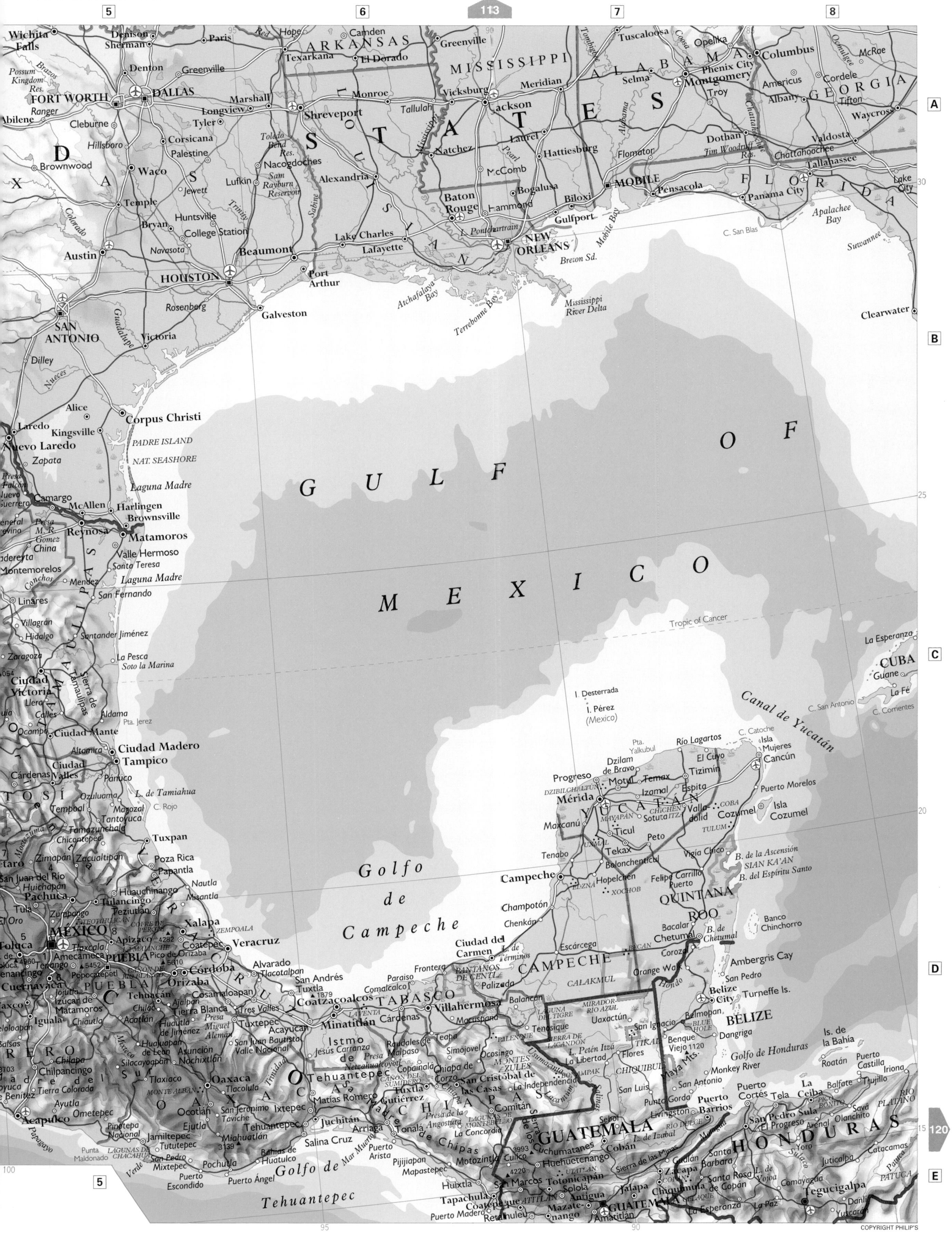
113
120
5
6
7
8
A
B
C
D
E
ARKANSAS
MISSISSIPPI
ALABAMA
GEORGIA
LOUISIANA
FLORIDA
TEXAS
UNITED STATES
Wichita Falls
Denison
Sherman
Paris
Hope
Camden
Texarkana
El Dorado
Greenville
Tuscaloosa
Opelika
Columbus
McRae
Denton
Greenville
FORT WORTH
DALLAS
Marshall
Monroe
Vicksburg
Meridian
Selma
Montgomery
Phenix City
Americus
Cordele
Abilene
Ranger
Longview
Shreveport
Tallulah
Jackson
Troy
Albany
Tifton
Cleburne
Tyler
Waycross
Hillsboro
Corsicana
Toledo Bend Res.
Natchez
Laurel
Hattiesburg
Dothan
Valdosta
Palestine
Nacogdoches
Jim Woodruff Res.
Chattahoochee
Tallahassee
Brownwood
Waco
Lufkin
Sam Rayburn Reservoir
Alexandria
McComb
Flomaton
Jewett
Bogalusa
MOBILE
Pensacola
Panama City
Lake City
Temple
Baton Rouge
Hammond
Biloxi
Gulfport
Apalachee Bay
Bryan
Huntsville
College Station
Lake Charles
Lafayette
L. Pontchartrain
NEW ORLEANS
Austin
Navasota
Beaumont
Breton Sd.
C. San Blas
Suwannee
HOUSTON
Port Arthur
Atchafalaya Bay
Terrebonne Bay
Mississippi River Delta
SAN ANTONIO
Rosenberg
Galveston
Victoria
Clearwater
Dilley
Nueces
Alice
Corpus Christi
Laredo
Nuevo Laredo
Kingsville
PADRE ISLAND NAT. SEASHORE
Zapata
Laguna Madre
Camargo
McAllen
Harlingen
Brownsville
Reynosa
Matamoros
Valle Hermoso
Santo Teresa
Laguna Madre
Montemorelos
Mendez
San Fernando
Linares
Villagrán
Hidalgo
Santander Jiménez
Zaragoza
La Pesca
Soto la Marina
Ciudad Victoria
Sierra de Tamaulipas
Aldama
Pta. Jerez
Ciudad Mante
Altamira
Ciudad Madero
Tampico
Ciudad Valles
Pánuco
L. de Tamiahua
C. Rojo
Tempoal
Tantoyuca
Tuxpan
Poza Rica
Papantla
Nautla
Misantla
Pachuca
Tulancingo
MÉXICO
Xalapa
Veracruz
Coatepec
Córdoba
Orizaba
Pico de Orizaba
PUEBLA
Toluca
Cuernavaca
Alvarado
Tlacotalpan
San Andrés Tuxtla
Coatzacoalcos
Minatitlán
Tehuacán
Tierra Blanca
Tuxtepec
Acayucan
Iguala
Chilpancingo
Oaxaca
Istmo de Tehuantepec
Tehuantepec
Matías Romero
Juchitán
Salina Cruz
Acapulco
Ometepec
Pinotepa Nacional
Puerto Escondido
Pochutla
Puerto Ángel
Golfo de Tehuantepec
GULF OF MEXICO
Golfo de Campeche
Tropic of Cancer
I. Desterrada
I. Pérez (Mexico)
Canal de Yucatán
CUBA
La Esperanza
Guane
La Fé
C. San Antonio
C. Corrientes
C. Catoche
Isla Mujeres
Cancún
Río Lagartos
El Cuyo
Tizimín
Dzilam de Bravo
Progreso
Motul
Temax
Izamal
Espita
Mérida
YUCATÁN
Valladolid
Puerto Morelos
Isla Cozumel
Cozumel
Maxcanú
Ticul
Sotuta
Tekax
Peto
Tenabo
Campeche
Hopelchén
Felipe Carrillo Puerto
QUINTANA ROO
Champotón
Chenkán
Bacalar
Chetumal
B. de Chetumal
Banco Chinchorro
Ciudad del Carmen
L. de Términos
Escárcega
CAMPECHE
Corozal
Orange Walk
Ambergris Cay
San Pedro
Frontera
Palizada
TABASCO
Villahermosa
Cárdenas
Comalcalco
Paraíso
Balancán
Tenosique
Uaxactún
Flores
La Libertad
L. Petén Itzá
Belize City
Belmopan
BELIZE
Turneffe Is.
Dangriga
Benque Viejo
Maya Mts.
Golfo de Honduras
Is. de la Bahía
Roatán
Puerto Castilla
Trujillo
La Ceiba
Tela
Puerto Cortés
San Pedro Sula
El Progreso
Puerto Barrios
Livingston
L. de Izabal
Punta Gorda
Monkey River
San Antonio
CHIAPAS
Tuxtla Gutiérrez
San Cristóbal de las Casas
Comitán
Ocosingo
Palenque
Tonalá
Arriaga
Tapachula
Huixtla
Motozintla
GUATEMALA
Cobán
Huehuetenango
Quetzaltenango
Sololá
Antigua
Mazatenango
Retalhuleu
Escuintla
Jalapa
Chiquimula
Zacapa
Santa Bárbara
Santa Rosa de Copán
HONDURAS
Yoro
Olanchito
Juticalpa
Catacamas
Comayagua
Tegucigalpa
Danlí
Puerto Madero
Puerto Arista
95
90
100
25
20
15
30

1:7 100 000

JAMAICA
1:2 700 000
a
CARIBBEAN SEA
Montego Bay
Lucea
Falmouth
Runaway Bay
St. Ann's Bay
Wakefield
Galina Point
Port Maria
South Negril Pt.
Negril
Cambridge
The Cockpit Country
Mount Denham 985
Ocho Rios
Dry Harbour Mountains
Moneague
Annotto Bay
Port Antonio
Savanna-la-Mar
Maggotty
Don Figuero Mts.
Linstead
The Blue Mountains
John Crow Mts.
Black River
Mandeville
Santa Cruz Mts.
Spanish Town
Portmore
2256 Blue Mountain Peak
KINGSTON
Morant Point
May Pen
Great Pedro Bluff
Alligator Pond
Portland Bight
Morant Bay
Port Morant
Portland Point
GULF OF MEXICO
Canal de Yucatán
I. Desterrada
I. Pérez (Mexico)
U. S. A.
L. Okeechobee
West Palm Beach
Fort Myers
Boca Raton
Fort Lauderdale
Naples
C. Romano
Everglades
Hialeah
EVERGLADES NAT. PARK
MIAMI
C. Sable
Florida Bay
Dry Tortugas (U.S.A.)
Key West
Florida Keys
Straits of Florida
West End
Freeport
Grand Bahama
Little Abaco I.
Hope Town
Great Abaco I.
Northwest Providence Channel
Northeast Providence Channel
Bimini Is.
Berry Is.
Eleuthera
Nassau
New Providence
Nicolls Town
Adelaide
Andros Town
Andros Island
Great Bahama Bank
Santaren Channel
Cay Sal Bank
Great Guana Cay
Great Exuma I.
Jumento Cays
Duncan Town
Canal Viejo de Bahama
LA HABANA (Havana)
Mariano
Guanabacoa
Santa Cruz del Norte
Canal Nicholas
Matanzas
Cárdenas
Jovellanos
Colón
Sagua la Grande
Guanajay
Bahía Honda
La Esperanza
Los Palacios
San Antonio de los Baños
Batabanó
Güines
Jagüey Grande
Pinar del Río
Guane
San Luis
C. San Antonio
La Fé
C. Corrientes
Nueva Gerona
I. de la Juventud
CUBA
Caibarién
Placetas
Santa Clara
Cienfuegos
Trinidad
Sancti Spíritus
Morón
Cayo Romano
Ciego de Avila
Júcaro
Tunas de Zaza
Florida
Camagüey
Nuevitas
Puerto Manatí
Arch. de los Canarreos
Arch. de Jardines de la Reina
Santa Cruz del Sur
Victoria de las Tunas
Gibara
HOLGUÍN
Golfo de Guacanayabo
Bayamo
Manzanillo
Sierra Maestra
1994
SANTIAGO DE CUBA
C. Cruz
Greater
Cayman Islands (U.K.)
Cayman Brac
Little Cayman
George Town
Grand Cayman
7680
Is. Santanilla (Swan Islands) (Honduras)
Pedro Cays (Jamaica)
Bajo Nuevo (Colombia)
CARIBBEAN
Progreso
Dzilam de Bravo
Punta Yalkubul
Río Lagartos
C. Catoche
Cancún
DZIBILCHALTÚN
Mérida
Motul
Temax
Tizimín
El Cuyo
Izamal
Espita
El Díaz
YUCATÁN
Maxcanú
Sotuta
MAYAPÁN
CHICHÉN ITZÁ
Valladolid
Puerto Morelos
Calkini
Ticul
Isla Cozumel
Cozumel
Tenabo
UXMAL
Tekax
Peto
Campeche
Bolonchenticul
Hopelchén
Vigía Chico
Champotón
San José Carpizo
Felipe Carrillo Puerto
B. de la Ascensión
SIAN KA'AN
B. del Espíritu Santo
Chenkán
QUINTANA ROO
Ciudad del Carmen
L. de Términos
MEXICO
Pedro Antonio Santos
PANTANOS DE CENTLA
Palizada
CAMPECHE
Bacalar
Chetumal
B. de Chetumal
Banco Chinchorro
Corozal
Balancán
CALAKMUL
Orange Walk
Ambergris Cay
MIRADOR-RÍO AZUL
Hondo
San Pedro
Tenosique
LAGUNA DEL TIGRE
PALENQUE
Uaxactún
Belmopan
Belize City
Turneffe Is.
Ocosingo
SIERRA DE LACANDÓN
L. Petén Itzá
San Ignacio
TIKAL
BELIZE
Flores
BLUE HOLE
Benque Viejo
Middlesex
La Independencia
MONTES AZULES
La Libertad
1120
Dangriga
CHIQUIBUL
Maya Mts.
Comitán
Golfo de Honduras
San Luis
San Antonio
Monkey River
Is. de la Bahía
Punta Gorda
Sebol
Sierra de los Cuchumatanes
3993
GUATEMALA
Livingston
Puerto Barrios
Puerto Cortés
Roatán
Puerto Castilla
C. Camarón
Cobán
L. de Izabal
RÍO DULCE
Tela
La Ceiba
PICO BONITO
Balfate
Trujillo
Iriona
Punta Patuca
Brus Laguna
Laguna Caratasca
Huehuetenango
San Marcos
Totonicapán
UTATLÁN
Sierra de las Minas
Motagua
San Pedro Sula
El Progreso
Savá
Olanchito
Arenal
RÍO PLÁTANO
Mosquitia
C. Falso
C. Gracias a Dios
Puerto Cabo Gracias á Dios
Kisalaya
Coco (Segovia)
HONDURAS
Quetzaltenango
Sololá
Antigua
Jalapa
Zacapa
Gualán
Santa Bárbara
Yoro
Juticalpa
Catacamas
Patuca
PATUCA
Chiquimula
Santa Rosa de Copán
El Jaral
L. de Yojoa
Comayagua
Mazatenango
Retalhuleu
Coatepeque
Ayutla
Amatitlán
GUATEMALA
Escuintla
San José
Santa Ana
La Esperanza
La Paz
Tegucigalpa
Ahuachapán
Sonsonate
Suchitoto
Cojutepeque
Yuscarán
Danlí
Bonanza
Cayos Miskitos (Nicaragua)
Pta. Gorda
Puerto Cabezas
Acajutla
Nueva San Salvador
SAN SALVADOR
Zacatecoluca
Nacaome
Choluteca
Ocotal
Coco
Somoto
Siuna
SASLAYA
Usulután
San Miguel
La Unión
EL SALVADOR
Cord. Isabelia
Tuma
Tungla
I. de Providencia (Colombia)
Cayos Roncador (Colombia)
G. de Fonseca
Puerto Morazán
El Sauce
Estelí
Jinotega
Matagalpa
San Pedro del Norte
Prinzapolca
Río Grande
Chinandega
Muy Muy
NICARAGUA
Corinto
León
Boaco
Siquia
I. de San Andrés (Colombia)
La Paz Centro
L. de Managua
Santo Domingo
Punta de Perlas
MANAGUA
Masaya
Juigalpa
Rama
Is. del Maíz (Nicaragua)
Cayos de Albuquerque (Colombia)
Diriamba
Granada
Bluefields
Jinotepe
Lago de Nicaragua
I. de Ometepe
Cord. de Yolaina
El Bluff
Pta. Mico
Rivas
San Juan del Sur
B. de Salinas
GUANACASTE
C. Santa Elena
SANTA ROSA
G. de Papagayo
La Cruz
San Carlos
Los Chiles
San Juan
B. de San Juan del Norte
San Juan del Norte
Liberia
PALO VERDE
Cord. del Guanacaste
COSTA RICA
TORTUGUERO
C. Velas
Santa Cruz
Nicoya
Carmona
Puntarenas
Pen. de Nicoya
C. Blanco
G. de Nicoya
Cord. Central
Alajuela
Guápiles
Siquirres
Esparza
San José
Cartago
Limón
Pta. Mona
Bribri
Bocas del Toro
L. de Chiriquí
Pandora
Cord. de Talamanca
AMISTAD
3837
3374
Almirante
Puerto Quepos
Chirripó Grande
Buenos Aires
Volcán Barú
Chiriquí Grande
G. de los Mosquitos
B. de Coronado
Puerto Cortés
San Vito
Boquete
CORCOVADO
Pen. de Osa
Golfito
La Concepción
David
Serranía de Tabasará
G. Dulce
Puerto Armuelles
Remedios
Santiago
Pta. Burica
G. de Chiriquí
COIBA
I. de Coiba
I. Jicarón
Soná
I. de Cebaco
Punta Mariato
Chitré
Pen. de Azuero
Tonosí
CERRO HOYA
Las Tablas
Pocri
Pta. Mala
Panama Canal
Pta. Manzanillo
Nombre de Dios
Portobelo
CHAGRES
L. Gatún
Colón
Balboa
PANAMÁ
Archipiélago de San Blas
Serranía del Darién
Golfo del Darién
La Chorrera
Chepo
Chimán
Penonomé
Río Hato
Arch. de las Perlas
San Miguel
I. del Rey
Aguadulce
Golfo de Panamá
La Palma
Yaviza
G. de Urabá
Garachiné
El Real
DARIÉN
Jaqué
I. de San Bernardo
G. de Morrosquillo
CARTAGENA
Montería
PACIFIC OCEAN
GUADELOUPE AND MARTINIQUE
1:1 800 000
b
Pte. de la Grande Vigie
Port-Louis
Grande-Terre
Pointe Allègre
Petit-Canal
La Désirade
Moule
Ste-Rose
Pointe-à-Pitre
Pointe-Noire
Pointe des Châteaux
Gosier
Ste-Anne
Basse-Terre
Bouillante
Îles de la Petite Terre
GUADELOUPE (Fr.)
GUADELOUPE
Soufrière 1467
Capesterre-Belle-Eau
Marie-Galante
Basse-Terre
Trois-Rivières
St-Louis
204
Capesterre
Grand-Bourg
Pte. des Basses
Îles des Saintes
c
Cap St-Martin
Basse-Pointe
1463
Le Prêcheur
Montagne Pelée
Ste-Marie
Presqu'île de la Caravelle
St-Pierre
La Trinité
St-Joseph
Le Robert
Schœlcher
Le François
Fort-de-France
Le Lamentin
Rivière-Salée
Le St-Esprit
MARTINIQUE (Fr.)
Rivière-Pilote
Le Marin
Pte. d'Enfer

Projection: Conical with two standard parallels

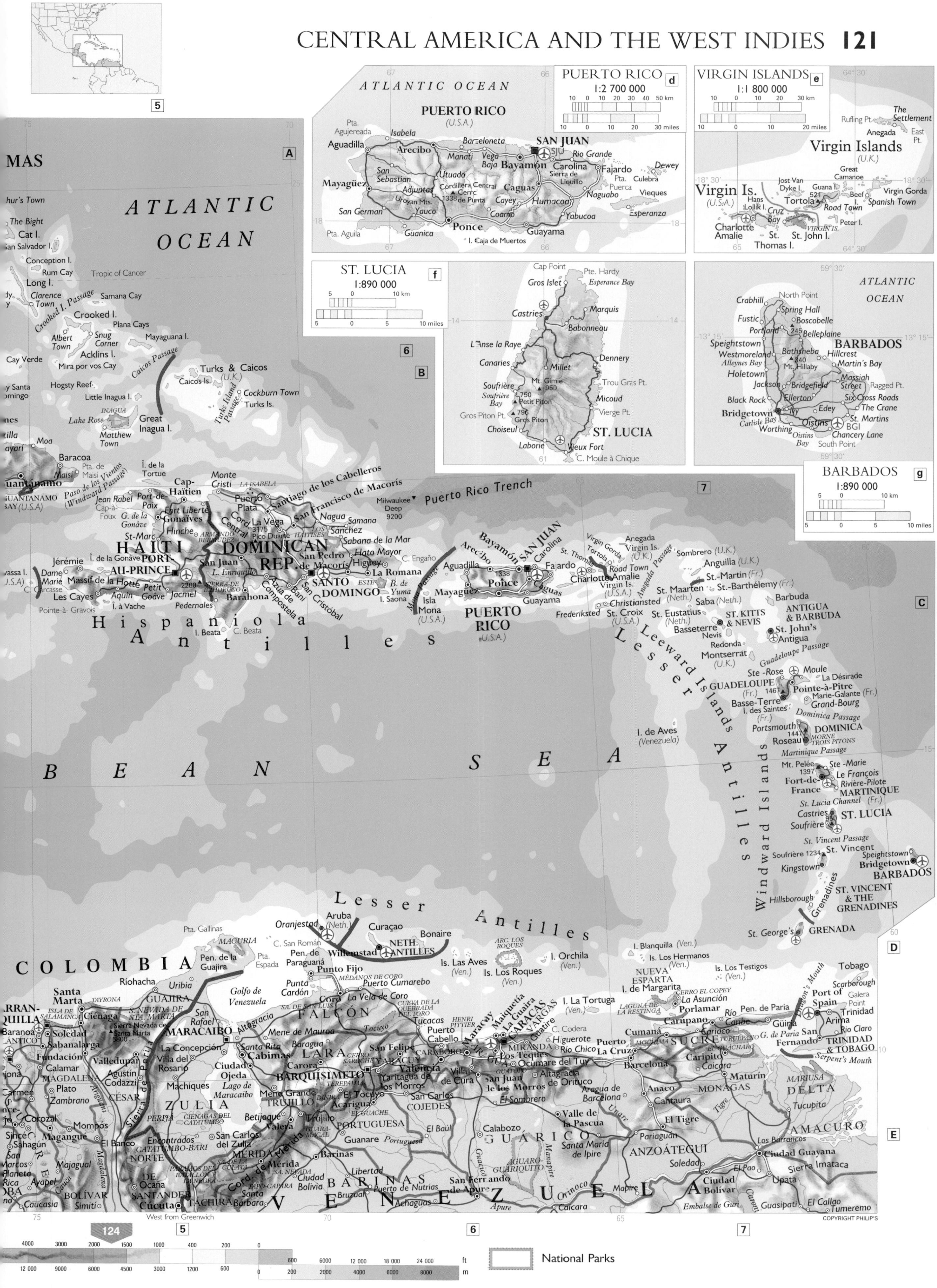
PUERTO RICO d
1:2 700 000
ATLANTIC OCEAN
PUERTO RICO
(U.S.A.)
Aguadilla
Isabela
Arecibo
Barceloneta
SAN JUAN
Bayamón
Carolina
Rio Grande
Fajardo
Mayagüez
San Sebastian
Utuado
Cordillera Central
Caguas
Humacao
Naguabo
Culebra
Vieques
San German
Yauco
Ponce
Guayama
Guanica
Coamo
Yabucoa
Esperanza
I. Caja de Muertos
VIRGIN ISLANDS e
1:1 800 000
Virgin Islands
(U.K.)
Virgin Is.
(U.S.A.)
Anegada
The Settlement
Tortola
Road Town
Virgin Gorda
Spanish Town
Charlotte Amalie
St. Thomas I.
St. John I.
Cruz Bay
Peter I.
ST. LUCIA f
1:890 000
Cap Point
Gros Islet
Castries
Marquis
Babonneau
L'Anse la Raye
Canaries
Dennery
Millet
Soufrière
Mt. Gimie
950
Petit Piton
Gros Piton
Micoud
Choiseul
Laborie
Vieux Fort
ST. LUCIA
C. Moule à Chique
ATLANTIC OCEAN
BARBADOS
North Point
Crabhill
Speightstown
Holetown
Bathsheba
Mt. Hillaby
Bridgetown
Oistins
South Point
BARBADOS g
1:890 000
MAS
ATLANTIC OCEAN
Tropic of Cancer
Turks & Caicos
(U.K.)
Cockburn Town
Great Inagua I.
Matthew Town
Baracoa
Guantánamo
Puerto Rico Trench
Milwaukee Deep 9200
HAITI
DOMINICAN REP.
PORT-AU-PRINCE
SANTO DOMINGO
Santiago de los Caballeros
San Francisco de Macorís
Cap-Haïtien
Pico Duarte 3175
La Romana
Hispaniola
Antilles
PUERTO RICO
(U.S.A.)
Mona Passage
Virgin Is.
(U.S.A.)
Anguilla (U.K.)
St.-Martin (Fr.)
St.-Barthélemy (Fr.)
Saba (Neth.)
St. Eustatius (Neth.)
ST. KITTS & NEVIS
Basseterre
ANTIGUA & BARBUDA
St. John's
Montserrat (U.K.)
GUADELOUPE (Fr.)
Pointe-à-Pitre
Basse-Terre
DOMINICA
Roseau
MARTINIQUE (Fr.)
Fort-de-France
ST. LUCIA
Castries
St. Vincent
Kingstown
BARBADOS
Bridgetown
ST. VINCENT & THE GRENADINES
GRENADA
St. George's
Leeward Islands
Windward Islands
Lesser Antilles
I. de Aves (Venezuela)
BEAN SEA
Aruba (Neth.)
Oranjestad
Curaçao
Bonaire
Willemstad
NETH. ANTILLES
COLOMBIA
Santa Marta
Riohacha
MARACAIBO
Golfo de Venezuela
Lago de Maracaibo
CARACAS
Valencia
BARQUISIMETO
Maracay
Cumaná
Barcelona
Maturín
Port of Spain
TRINIDAD & TOBAGO
Tobago
Trinidad
Isla de Margarita
Ciudad Guayana
Ciudad Bolívar
Orinoco
VENEZUELA
Mérida
Barinas
Cúcuta
West from Greenwich
National Parks
COPYRIGHT PHILIP'S

1:31 100 000

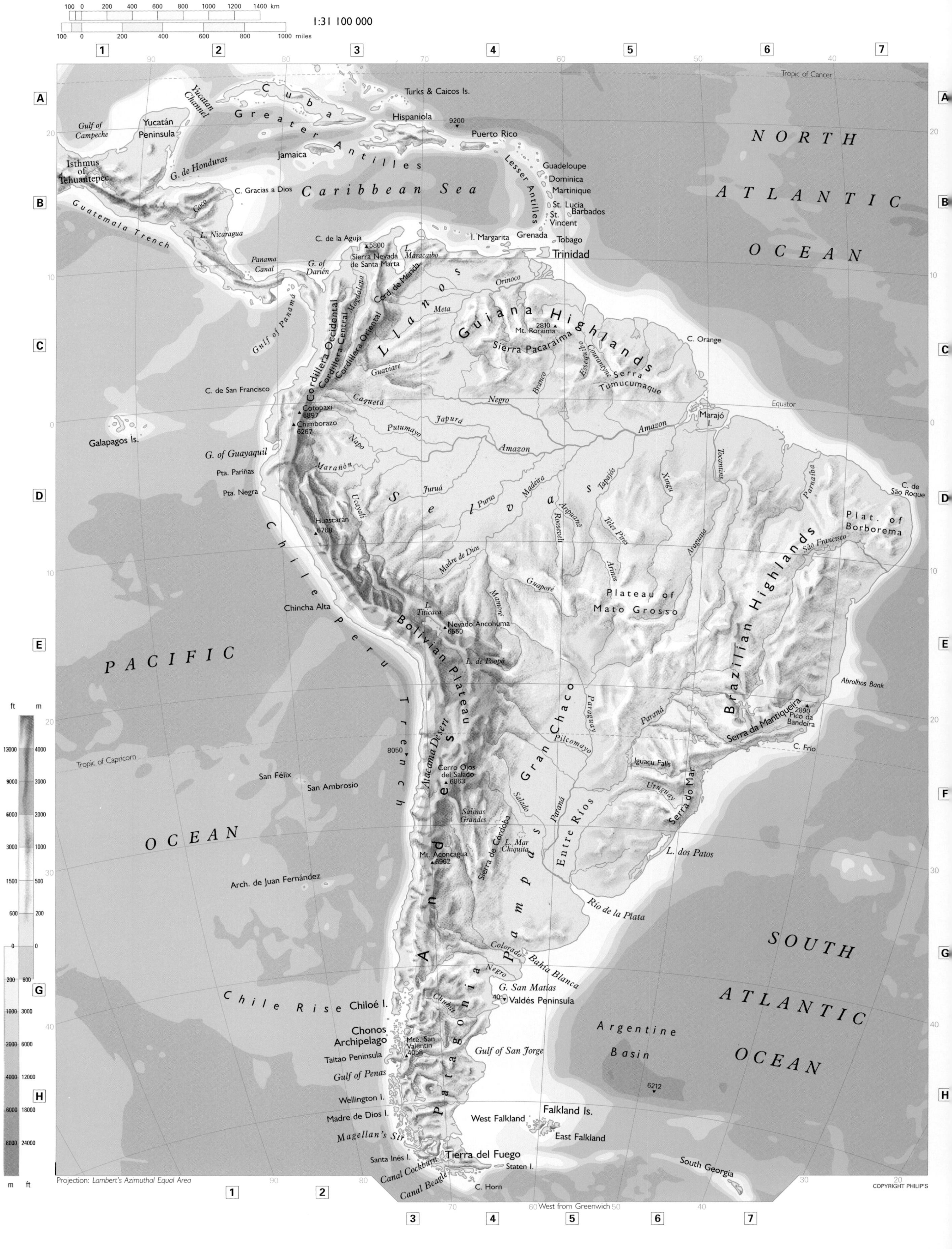
Tropic of Cancer
Turks & Caicos Is.
Yucatan Channel
Cuba
Greater Antilles
Hispaniola
9200
Puerto Rico
Gulf of Campeche
Yucatán Peninsula
Isthmus of Tehuantepec
G. de Honduras
Jamaica
Lesser Antilles
Guadeloupe
Dominica
Martinique
St. Lucia
St. Vincent
Barbados
Grenada
Tobago
Trinidad
NORTH ATLANTIC OCEAN
C. Gracias a Dios
Caribbean Sea
Coco
Guatemala Trench
L. Nicaragua
C. de la Aguja
5800
Sierra Nevada de Santa Marta
L. Maracaibo
I. Margarita
Panama Canal
G. of Darién
Cord. de Mérida
Orinoco
Magdalena
Llanos
Meta
Guiana Highlands
2810
Mt. Roraima
Sierra Pacaraima
Essequibo
Courantyne
Serra Tumucumaque
C. Orange
Gulf of Panamá
Cordillera Occidental
Cordillera Central
Cordillera Oriental
Guaviare
Branco
C. de San Francisco
Caquetá
Negro
Equator
Marajó I.
Cotopaxi 5897
Chimborazo 6267
Japurá
Putumayo
Amazon
Galapagos Is.
Napo
G. of Guayaquil
Marañón
Tocantins
Pta. Pariñas
Pta. Negra
Juruá
Purus
Madeira
Tapajós
Xingu
Parnaíba
C. de São Roque
Selvas
Ucayali
Aripuanã
Roosevelt
Teles Pires
Huascarán 6768
Plat. of Borborema
Chile Peru Trench
Madre de Dios
Arinos
Araguaia
São Francisco
Brazilian Highlands
Guaporé
Plateau of Mato Grosso
Mamoré
Chincha Alta
L. Titicaca
Nevado Ancohuma 6550
Bolivian Plateau
L. de Poopó
PACIFIC OCEAN
Gran Chaco
Paraguay
Paraná
Abrolhos Bank
2890
Pico da Bandeira
Serra da Mantiqueira
Pilcomayo
C. Frio
8050
Atacama Desert
Tropic of Capricorn
Iguaçu Falls
San Félix
San Ambrosio
Cerro Ojos del Salado 6863
Uruguay
Serra do Mar
Salado
Entre Ríos
Salinas Grandes
Sierra de Córdoba
L. Mar Chiquita
L. dos Patos
Mt. Aconcagua 6962
Andes
Pampas
Arch. de Juan Fernández
Río de la Plata
Colorado
Bahía Blanca
SOUTH ATLANTIC OCEAN
Negro
G. San Matías
Valdés Peninsula
40
Chile Rise
Chiloé I.
Chubut
Patagonia
Argentine Basin
Chonos Archipelago
Mte. San Valentín 4058
Gulf of San Jorge
Taitao Peninsula
Gulf of Penas
6212
Wellington I.
Madre de Dios I.
West Falkland
Falkland Is.
East Falkland
Magellan's Str.
Santa Inés I.
Tierra del Fuego
Staten I.
Canal Cockburn
Canal Beagle
C. Horn
South Georgia
West from Greenwich
ft
m
0
200
600
1000
1500
2000
3000
4000
6000
8000
9000
12000
18000
24000

Projection: *Lambert's Azimuthal Equal Area*

1:31 100 000

NORTH ATLANTIC OCEAN
SOUTH ATLANTIC OCEAN
PACIFIC OCEAN
Caribbean Sea
Tropic of Cancer
Tropic of Capricorn
Equator
Havana
CUBA
BAHAMAS
Turks & Caicos Is. (U.K.)
HAITI
DOMINICAN REP.
Port-au-Prince
JAMAICA
Kingston
San Juan
PUERTO RICO (U.S.A.)
Virgin Is. (U.K.)
ST. KITTS & NEVIS
ANTIGUA & BARBUDA
Basse-Terre
GUADELOUPE (Fr.)
DOMINICA
Fort-de-France
MARTINIQUE (Fr.)
Castries
ST. LUCIA
ST. VINCENT
Kingstown
BARBADOS
Bridgetown
GRENADA
St. George's
Port of Spain
TRINIDAD & TOBAGO
Aruba
Curaçao
MEXICO
BELIZE
GUATEMALA
Guatemala
HONDURAS
Tegucigalpa
San Salvador
EL SALVADOR
NICARAGUA
Managua
COSTA RICA
San José
Panamá
PANAMA
Gulf of Panamá
G. of Darién
C. de la Aguja
Barranquilla
Cartagena
Maracaibo
Barquisimeto
Caracas
Valencia
Cúcuta
San Cristóbal
Medellín
Bucaramanga
VENEZUELA
Orinoco
Ciudad Guayana
Georgetown
GUYANA
Paramaribo
SURINAME
Cayenne
C. Orange
FRENCH GUIANA
Essequibo
Bogotá
Cali
Magdalena
COLOMBIA
RORAIMA
Branco
AMAPÁ
Galapagos Is. (Ecuador)
Quito
ECUADOR
Guayaquil
G. of Guayaquil
Putumayo
Napo
Japurá
Iquitos
Marañón
Amazon
Manaus
Santarém
Marajó I.
Belém
São Luís
Fortaleza
C. de São Roque
Natal
AMAZONAS
PARÁ
Tapajós
Xingu
Tocantins
MARANHÃO
Teresina
CEARÁ
RIO G. DO NORTE
PARAÍBA
Parnaíba
PIAUÍ
Campina Grande
PERNAMBUCO
Recife
ALAGOAS
Maceió
SERGIPE
Aracaju
Juruá
Purus
Madeira
ACRE
Pôrto Velho
Chiclayo
Trujillo
Chimbote
Ucayali
PERU
Callao
LIMA
Cuzco
Madre de Dios
RONDONIA
BRAZIL
Araguaia
TOCANTINS
BAHÍA
São Francisco
Salvador
MATO GROSSO
Mamoré
L. Titicaca
Arequipa
La Paz
BOLIVIA
Cochabamba
Santa Cruz
Sucre
Cuiabá
GOIÁS
DIS. FED.
Brasília
Goiânia
MINAS GERAIS
Belo Horizonte
ESPIRITO SANTO
Vitória
Iquique
Paraguay
MATO GROSSO DO SUL
Ribeirão Prêto
Juiz de Fora
Campos
Paraná
SÃO PAULO
Campinas
R. DE J.
Niterói
SÃO PAULO
RIO DE JANEIRO
Antofagasta
PARAGUAY
Pilcomayo
Asunción
PARANÁ
Curitiba
Salta
San Miguel de Tucumán
Resistencia
Corrientes
SANTA CATARINA
Uruguay
RIO GRANDE DO SUL
Pôrto Alegre
Salado
San Félix (Chile)
San Ambrosio (Chile)
Córdoba
Santa Fe
Paraná
San Juan
Pelotas
Viña del Mar
Valparaíso
SANTIAGO
Mendoza
Rosario
URUGUAY
Arch. de Juan Fernández (Chile)
BUENOS AIRES
Montevideo
La Plata
Río de la Plata
Talca
Concepción
Bahía Blanca
Mar del Plata
Colorado
CHILE
ARGENTINA
Valdivia
Negro
Viedma
Puerto Montt
Chubut
Comodoro Rivadavia
Gulf of San Jorge
Gulf of Penas
West Falkland
FALKLAND IS. (U.K.)
Stanley
East Falkland
Magellan's Str.
Punta Arenas
Tierra del Fuego
C. Horn
South Georgia (U.K.)
West from Greenwich
Projection: Lambert's Azimuthal Equal Area
LIMA Capital Cities

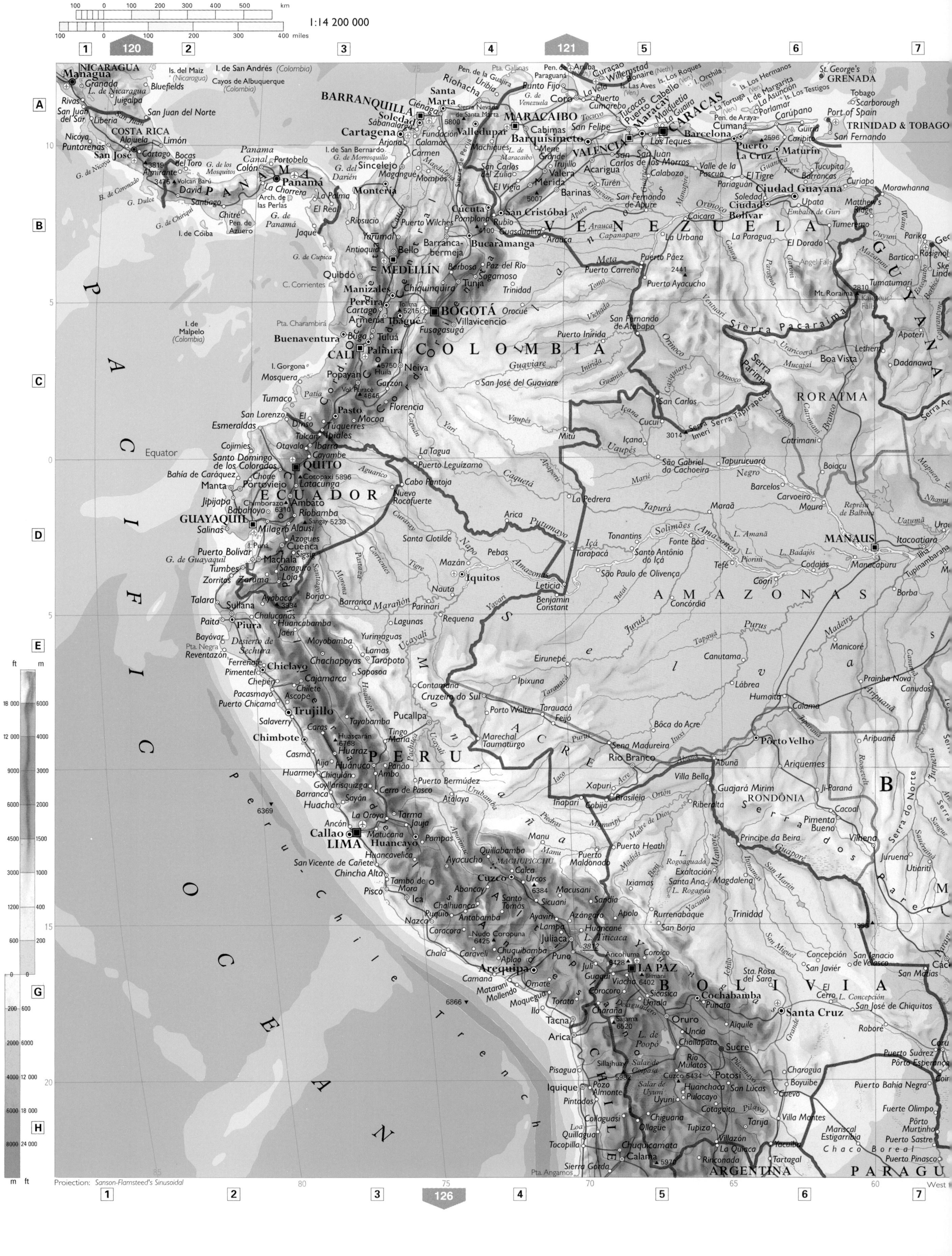
1:14 200 000
km
miles
Projection: Sanson-Flamsteed's Sinusoidal
ft
m
PACIFIC OCEAN
Peru-Chile Trench
Equator
NICARAGUA
COSTA RICA
PANAMA
COLOMBIA
VENEZUELA
GUYANA
ECUADOR
PERU
BOLIVIA
CHILE
ARGENTINA
PARAGU
AMAZONAS
RORAIMA
ACRE
RONDÔNIA
TRINIDAD & TOBAGO
GRENADA
Managua
San José
Panamá
BARRANQUILLA
Cartagena
MARACAIBO
Barquisimeto
VALENCIA
CARACAS
Ciudad Guayana
MEDELLÍN
BOGOTÁ
CALI
QUITO
GUAYAQUIL
Trujillo
Callao
LIMA
Arequipa
LA PAZ
Cochabamba
Santa Cruz
Sucre
Potosí
MANAUS
Iquitos
Porto Velho
Rio Branco
Boa Vista
Sierra Pacaraima
Serra Parima
Amazonas
Orinoco
Lago Titicaca
Chaco Boreal

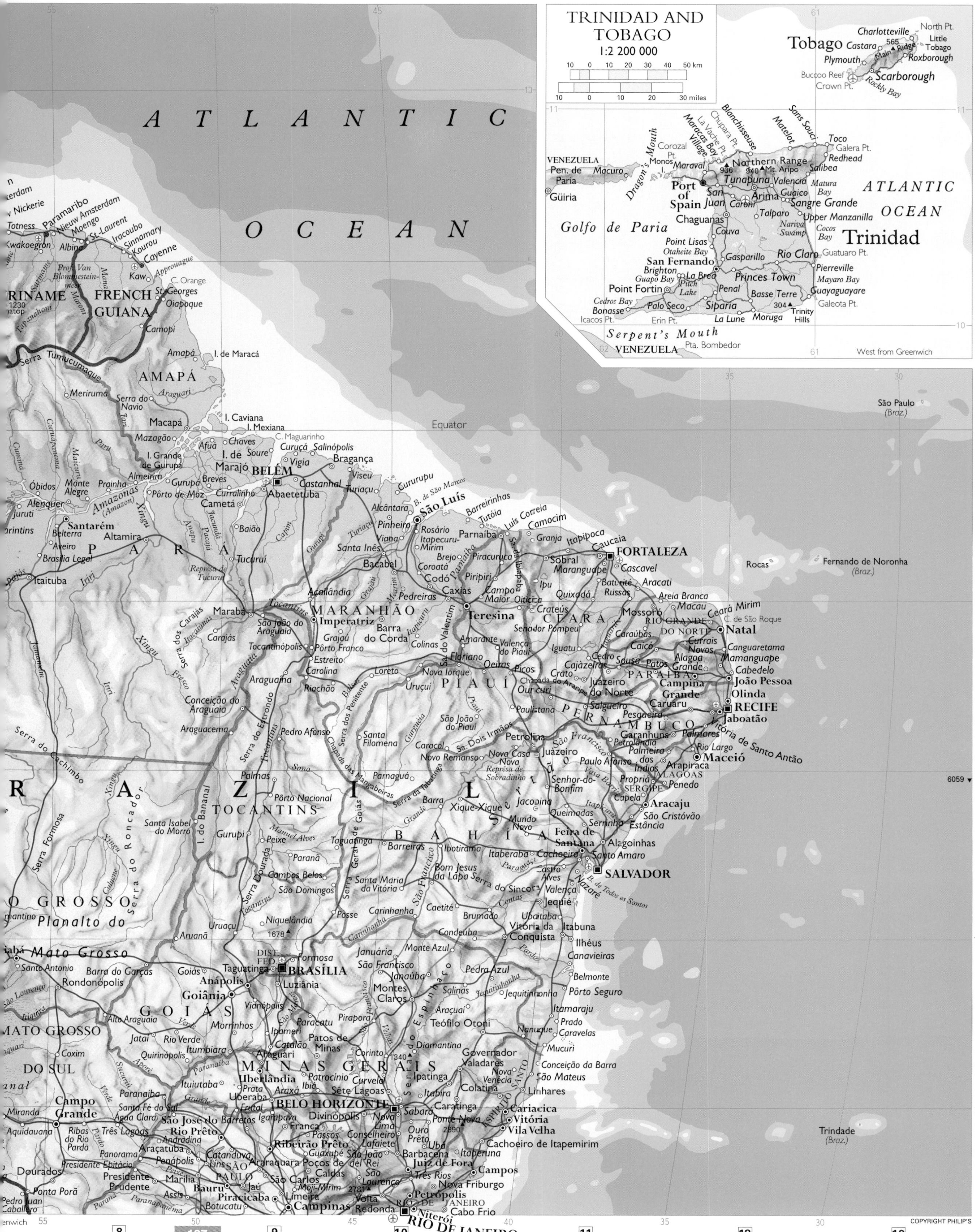
TRINIDAD AND TOBAGO
1:2 200 000
km
miles
West from Greenwich
Tobago
Charlotteville
North Pt.
Little Tobago
Castara
Main Ridge
Roxborough
Plymouth
Scarborough
Buccoo Reef
Crown Pt.
Rockly Bay
Blanchisseuse
Sans Souci
Matelot
Toco
Galera Pt.
Redhead
Northern Range
Mt. Aripo
Salibea
Maracas Bay Village
La Vache Pt.
Chupara Pt.
Corozal Pt.
Monos I.
Dragon's Mouth
VENEZUELA
Pen. de Paria
Macuro
Güiria
Maraval
Port of Spain
Tunapuna
Valencia
Matura Bay
San Juan
Caroni
Arima
Guaico
Sangre Grande
Talparo
Upper Manzanilla
Chaguanas
Nariva Swamp
Cocos Bay
Couva
ATLANTIC OCEAN
Golfo de Paria
Point Lisas
Otaheite Bay
San Fernando
Gasparillo
Rio Claro
Trinidad
Guatuaro Pt.
Pierreville
Brighton
Guapo Bay
La Brea
Pitch Lake
Princes Town
Mayaro Bay
Point Fortin
Penal
Basse Terre
Guayaguayare
Cedros Bay
Bonasse
Palo Seco
Siparia
Trinity Hills
Galeota Pt.
Icacos Pt.
Erin Pt.
La Lune
Moruga
Serpent's Mouth
Pta. Bombedor
ATLANTIC
OCEAN
Equator
Paramaribo
Nieuw Amsterdam
Nieuw Nickerie
Totness
Moengo
St.-Laurent
Albina
Iracoubo
Sinnamary
Kourou
Cayenne
Kaw
C. Orange
St.-Georges
Oiapoque
SURINAME
FRENCH GUIANA
Camopi
Amapá
I. de Maracá
AMAPÁ
Serra Tumucumaque
Merirumã
Serra do Navio
Macapá
I. Caviana
I. Mexiana
Mazagão
Chaves
C. Maguarinho
Curuçá
Salinópolis
I. Grande de Gurupá
Afuá
I. de Marajó
Soure
Vigia
Bragança
Almeirim
Gurupá
Breves
BELÉM
Castanhal
Viseu
Óbidos
Monte Alegre
Prainha
Pôrto de Moz
Curralinho
Abaetetuba
Turiaçu
Cururupu
Alenquer
Amazonas (Amazon)
Cametá
B. de São Marcos
Alcântara
São Luís
Barreirinhas
Tutóia
Luís Correia
Camocim
Santarém
Belterra
Altamira
Baião
Pinheiro
Rosário
Itapecuru-Mirim
Parnaíba
Granja
Itapipoca
Caucaia
FORTALEZA
Viana
Santa Inês
Brejo
Piracuruca
Sobral
Maranguape
Cascavel
P A R Á
Aveiro
Brasília Legal
Tucuruí
Represa de Tucuruí
Bacabal
Coroatá
Codó
Piripiri
Itaituba
Açailândia
Pedreiras
Caxias
Campo Maior
Ipu
Quixadá
Baturité
Russas
Aracati
Areia Branca
Macau
Ceará Mirim
C. de São Roque
Natal
Marabá
São João do Araguaia
Carajás
MARANHÃO
Imperatriz
Barra do Corda
Grajaú
Teresina
CEARÁ
Crateús
Senador Pompeu
Mossoró
RIO GRANDE DO NORTE
Caraúbas
Currais Novos
Canguaretama
Mamanguape
Tocantinópolis
Pôrto Franco
Estreito
Carolina
Colinas
Amarante
Valença do Piauí
Floriano
Oeiras
Picos
Iguatu
Caicó
Cedro
Sousa
Cajàzeiras
Patos
Alagoa Grande
Campina Grande
Cabedelo
João Pessoa
Olinda
RECIFE
Jaboatão
Caruaru
Serra dos Carajás
Araguaína
Loreto
Nova Iorque
Uruçuí
PIAUÍ
Crato
Juàzeiro do Norte
PARAÍBA
Chapada do Araripe
Ouricuri
Salgueiro
Pesqueira
Riachão
Conceição do Araguaia
Paulistana
PERNAMBUCO
Palmares
Vitória de Santo Antão
Garanhuns
Araguacema
Pedro Afonso
São João do Piauí
Santa Filomena
Petrolina
Juàzeiro
Petrolândia
Palmeira dos Índios
Rio Largo
Maceió
Caracol
Sa. Dois Irmãos
Nova Casa Nova
Represa de Sobradinho
Novo Remanso
Paulo Afonso
Arapiraca
ALAGOAS
Penedo
Serra do Cachimbo
Palmas
Parnaguá
Senhor-do-Bonfim
Propriá
SERGIPE
Capela
Aracaju
São Cristóvão
Estância
BRAZIL
Pôrto Nacional
TOCANTINS
Barra
Xique-Xique
Jacobina
Queimadas
Serrinha
Mundo Novo
Santa Isabel do Morro
Serra do Roncador
Gurupi
Peixe
Taguatinga
Barreiras
Ibotirama
BAHIA
Feira de Santana
Alagoinhas
Santo Amaro
Itaberaba
Cachoeira
SALVADOR
B. de Todos os Santos
Nazaré
Paraná
Campos Belos
São Domingos
Santa Maria da Vitória
Bom Jesus da Lapa
Castro Alves
Valença
Jequié
Sincorá
Serra Formosa
Niquelândia
Pôsse
Carinhanha
Caetité
Brumado
Ubaitaba
Itabuna
Vitória da Conquista
Ilhéus
MATO GROSSO
Planalto do Mato Grosso
Uruaçu
Aruanã
Condeúba
Januária
Monte Azul
Canavieiras
Formosa
DIST. FED.
BRASÍLIA
Taguatinga
Luziânia
São Francisco
Janaúba
Pedra Azul
Belmonte
Santo Antônio
Barra do Garças
Rondonópolis
Goiás
Anápolis
Goiânia
Montes Claros
Salinas
Jequitinhonha
Pôrto Seguro
GOIÁS
Vianópolis
Pirapora
Araçuaí
Itamaraju
Prado
Caravelas
Alto Araguaia
Morrinhos
Paracatu
Teófilo Otôni
Nanuque
Mucuri
Jataí
Rio Verde
Ipameri
Patos de Minas
Corinto
Diamantina
Governador Valadares
Conceição da Barra
São Mateus
Coxim
Quirinópolis
Itumbiara
Catalão
Araguari
MINAS GERAIS
Nova Venécia
Linhares
DO SUL
Uberlândia
Patrocínio
Curvelo
Ipatinga
Colatina
Ituiutaba
Prata
Araxá
Ibiá
Sete Lagoas
Itabira
ESPÍRITO SANTO
Campo Grande
Paranaíba
Uberaba
Frutal
BELO HORIZONTE
Sabará
Caratinga
Cariacica
Vitória
Vila Velha
Miranda
Santa Fé do Sul
Água Clara
São José do Barretos
Igarapava
Divinópolis
Nova Lima
Ponte Nova
Aquidauana
Ribas do Rio Pardo
Três Lagoas
Rio Prêto
Andradina
Franca
Passos
Conselheiro Lafaiete
Ouro Prêto
Ubá
Itaperuna
Cachoeiro de Itapemirim
Araçatuba
Ribeirão Prêto
Barbacena
Juiz de Fora
Campos
Dourados
Presidente Epitácio
Penápolis
Catanduva
Lins
Araraquara
Poços de Caldas
São João del Rei
Três Rios
Nova Friburgo
Ponta Porã
Presidente Prudente
Marília
SÃO PAULO
Jaú
São Carlos
São Lourenço
Petrópolis
Bauru
Assis
Piracicaba
Limeira
Moji-Mirim
Volta Redonda
Campinas
RIO DE JANEIRO
Niterói
Cabo Frio
Pedro Juan Caballero
Botucatu
Rocas
Fernando de Noronha (Braz.)
São Paulo (Braz.)
Trindade (Braz.)
6059
2787
2890
1678
1340
COPYRIGHT PHILIP'S

1:7 100 000

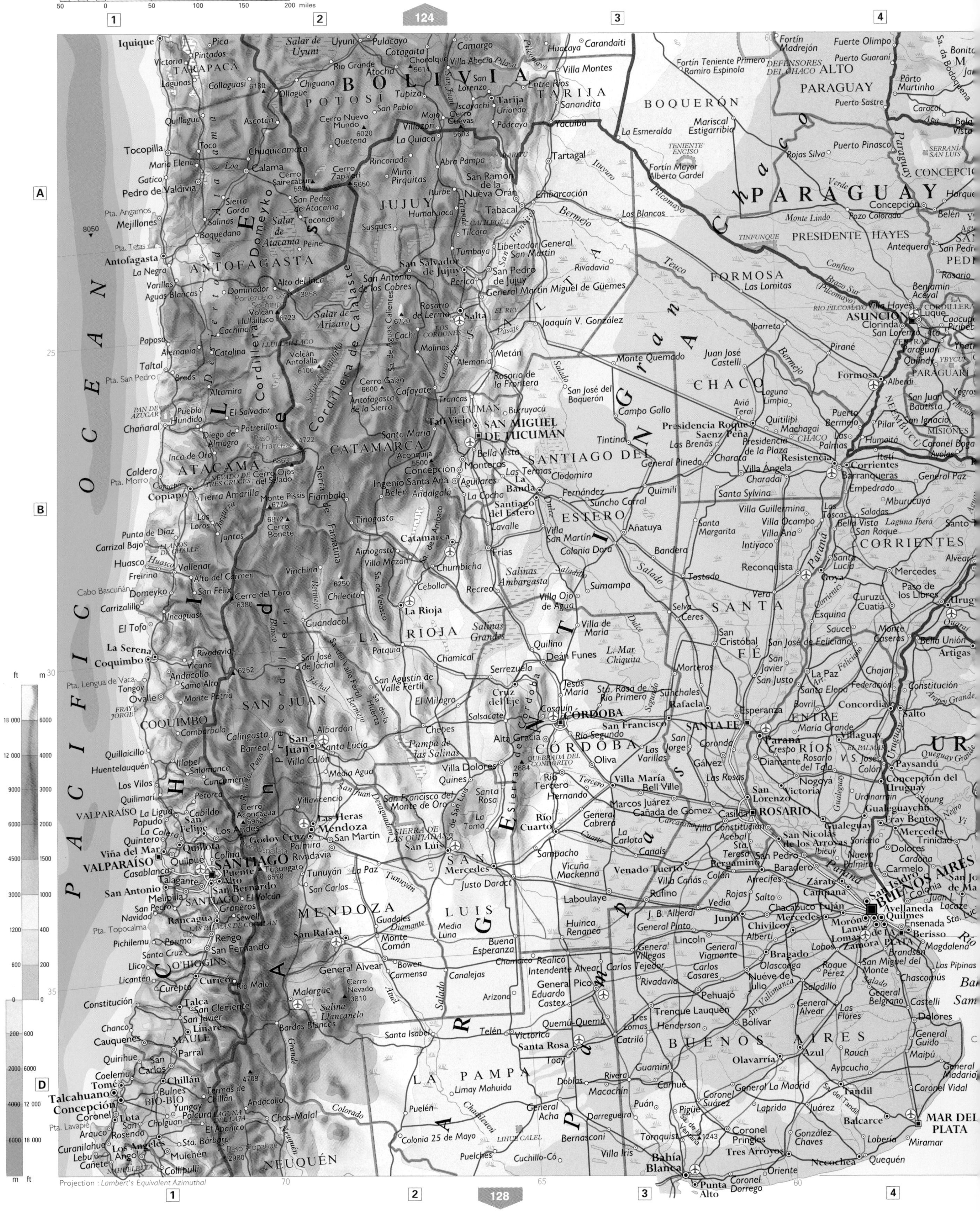
124
PACIFIC OCEAN
BOLIVIA
PARAGUAY
CHILE
ARGENTINA
Gran Chaco
Pampa
Andes
Cordillera Domeyko
Desierto de Atacama
TARAPACÁ
ANTOFAGASTA
ATACAMA
COQUIMBO
VALPARAÍSO
SANTIAGO
O'HIGGINS
MAULE
BIO-BIO
POTOSÍ
TARIJA
BOQUERÓN
ALTO PARAGUAY
PRESIDENTE HAYES
FORMOSA
CHACO
JUJUY
SALTA
TUCUMÁN
CATAMARCA
SANTIAGO DEL ESTERO
LA RIOJA
SAN JUAN
CÓRDOBA
SANTA FÉ
CORRIENTES
ENTRE RÍOS
MENDOZA
SAN LUIS
LA PAMPA
BUENOS AIRES
NEUQUÉN
Iquique
Antofagasta
Copiapó
La Serena
Coquimbo
Valparaíso
SANTIAGO
Talca
Concepción
Talcahuano
Chillán
Los Angeles
ASUNCIÓN
SAN MIGUEL DE TUCUMÁN
Salta
San Salvador de Jujuy
Córdoba
Rosario
Santa Fe
Paraná
Mendoza
San Juan
San Luis
BUENOS AIRES
La Plata
Mar del Plata
Bahía Blanca
Corrientes
Resistencia
Formosa
Santa Rosa
Río Cuarto
San Rafael
Tupungato 6570
Cerro Aconcagua 6962
Salar de Uyuni
Salar de Atacama
Salinas Grandes
Pampa de las Salinas
Paraná
Paraguay
Pilcomayo
Bermejo
Salado
Uruguay
Colorado
Projection : Lambert's Equivalent Azimuthal
128

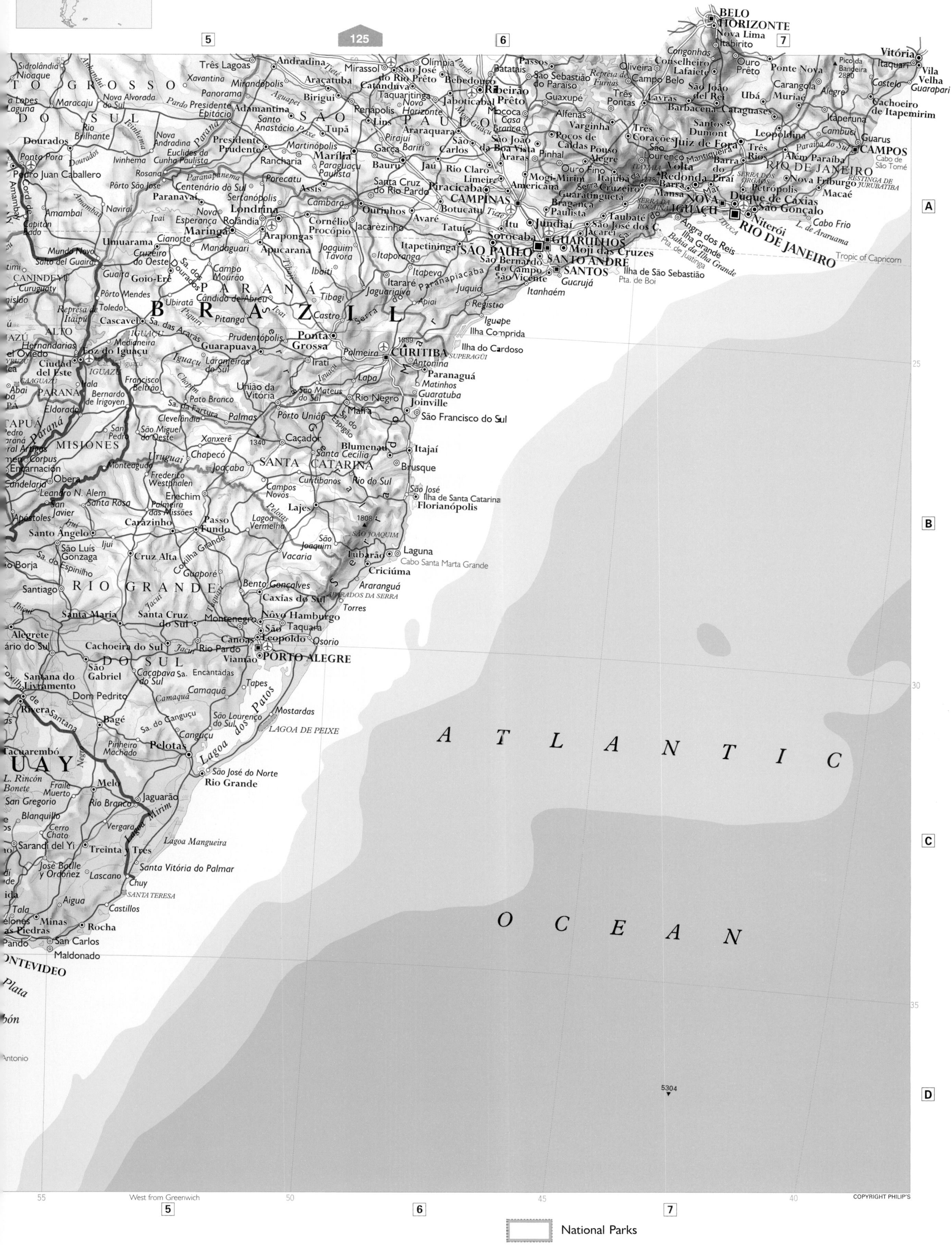

125
5
6
7
A
B
C
D
BELO HORIZONTE
Nova Lima
Itabirito
Vitória
Vila Velha
Guarapari
Cachoeiro de Itapemirim
Itaperuna
Campos
Cabo de São Tomé
Macaé
Cabo Frio
Nova Friburgo
Petrópolis
Niterói
São Gonçalo
Duque de Caxias
Nova Iguaçu
RIO DE JANEIRO
Volta Redonda
Barra Mansa
Juiz de Fora
Barbacena
Conselheiro Lafaiete
Congonhas
São João del Rei
Lavras
Três Pontas
Varginha
Poços de Caldas
Pouso Alegre
Itajubá
Guaratinguetá
Taubaté
São José dos Campos
Jacareí
Moji das Cruzes
Guarulhos
SÃO PAULO
São Bernardo do Campo
Santo André
Santos
São Vicente
Guarujá
Ilha de São Sebastião
Angra dos Reis
Ilha Grande
Tropic of Capricorn
Sorocaba
Jundiaí
Campinas
Piracicaba
Limeira
Americana
Mogi-Mirim
Rio Claro
São Carlos
Araraquara
Ribeirão Prêto
Franca
Passos
Bauru
Jaú
Marília
Lins
Birigui
Araçatuba
Andradina
Três Lagoas
Presidente Prudente
Presidente Epitácio
Assis
Ourinhos
Avaré
Itapetininga
Tatuí
Botucatu
Londrina
Maringá
Arapongas
Apucarana
Cornélio Procópio
Umuarama
Cianorte
Campo Mourão
Paranavaí
Dourados
Ponta Porã
Pedro Juan Caballero
Guaíra
Toledo
Cascavel
Foz do Iguaçu
Ciudad del Este
Guarapuava
Ponta Grossa
CURITIBA
Paranaguá
Joinville
São Francisco do Sul
Blumenau
Itajaí
Brusque
Florianópolis
Ilha de Santa Catarina
Lajes
Tubarão
Criciúma
Laguna
Cabo Santa Marta Grande
Araranguá
Torres
Caxias do Sul
Bento Gonçalves
Passo Fundo
Erechim
Chapecó
Joaçaba
Caçador
Santo Ângelo
Cruz Alta
Santa Maria
Santa Cruz do Sul
Novo Hamburgo
São Leopoldo
Canoas
PORTO ALEGRE
Viamão
Lagoa dos Patos
Pelotas
Rio Grande
Bagé
Santana do Livramento
Rivera
Alegrete
Uruguaiana
Melo
Jaguarão
Lagoa Mirim
Chuy
Treinta y Tres
Rocha
Maldonado
San Carlos
Castillos
MONTEVIDEO
B R A Z I L
P A R A N Á
SANTA CATARINA
R I O G R A N D E D O S U L
S Ã O P A U L O
RIO DE JANEIRO
URUGUAY
MISIONES
A T L A N T I C
O C E A N
5304
1808
1340
West from Greenwich
55
50
45
40
25
30
35
COPYRIGHT PHILIP'S

National Parks

1:14 200 000

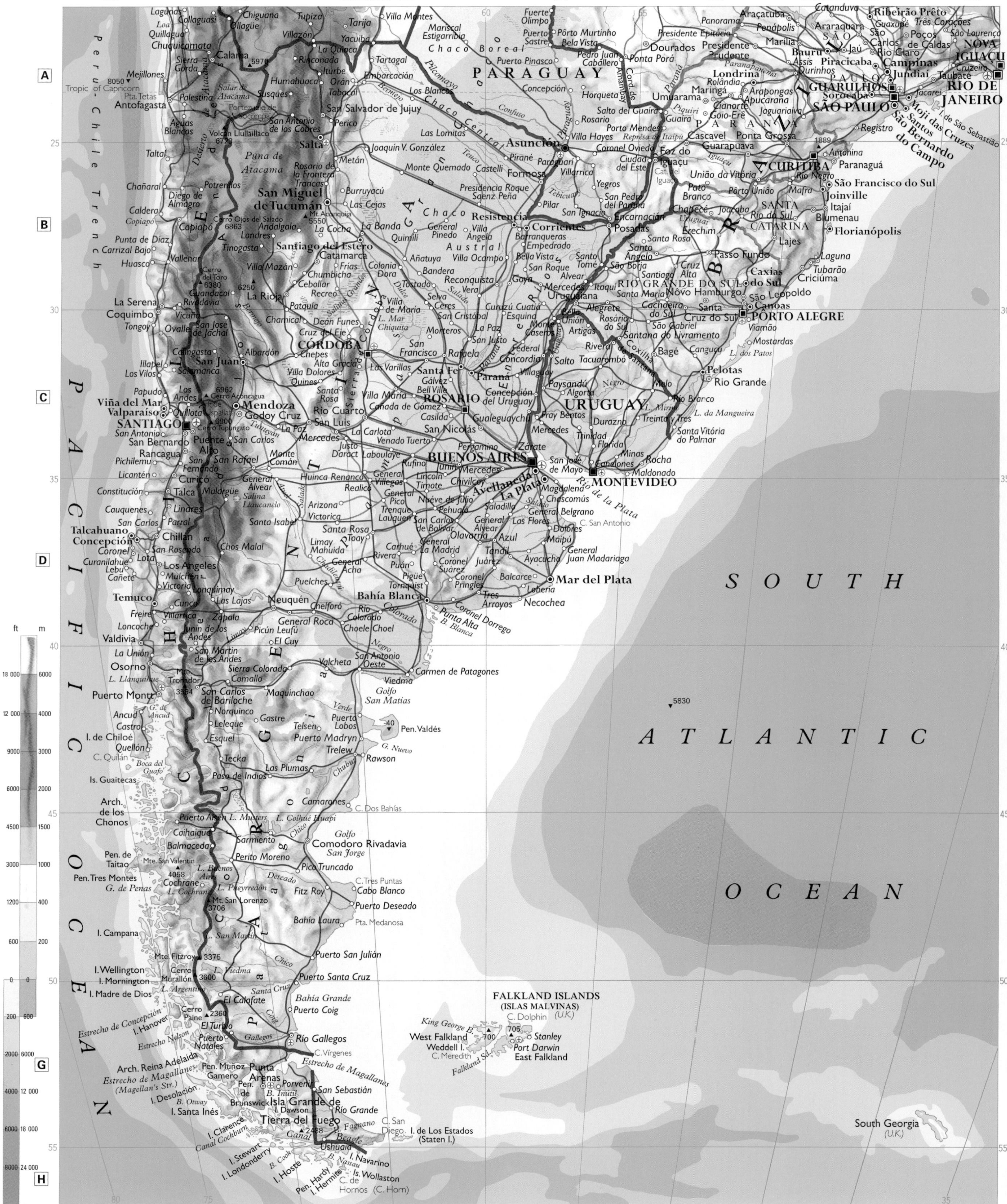
126
127
PARAGUAY
URUGUAY
BRAZIL
ARGENTINA
CHILE
SOUTH ATLANTIC OCEAN
PACIFIC OCEAN
Peru-Chile Trench
Tropic of Capricorn
FALKLAND ISLANDS
(ISLAS MALVINAS)
(U.K.)
South Georgia
(U.K.)
BUENOS AIRES
MONTEVIDEO
SANTIAGO
Asunción
SÃO PAULO
RIO DE JANEIRO
PÔRTO ALEGRE
CURITIBA
CÓRDOBA
ROSARIO
Mendoza
San Miguel de Tucumán
Mar del Plata
Bahía Blanca
Comodoro Rivadavia
Río Gallegos
Punta Arenas
Ushuaia
Stanley
Antofagasta
Valparaíso
Concepción
Puerto Montt
Isla Grande de Tierra del Fuego
Estrecho de Magallanes
Golfo San Matías
Golfo San Jorge
Pen. Valdés
Río de la Plata
Chaco Boreal
Chaco Central
Chaco Austral
Puna de Atacama
Desierto de Atacama
Cerro Aconcagua 6962
5830
RIO GRANDE DO SUL
SANTA CATARINA
PARANÁ
SÃO PAULO
Projection: Sanson-Flamsteed's Sinusoidal
West from Greenwich
COPYRIGHT PHILIP'S

INDEX TO WORLD MAPS

How to use the index

The index contains the names of all the principal places and features shown on the World Maps. Each name is followed by an additional entry in italics giving the country or region within which it is located. The alphabetical order of names composed of two or more words is governed primarily by the first word and then by the second. This is an example of the rule:

Mīr Kūh, *Iran* **71 E8**
Mīr Shahdād, *Iran* **71 E8**
Mira, *Italy* **41 C9**
Mira por vos Cay, *Bahamas* . . **121 B5**
Miraj, *India* **66 F2**

Physical features composed of a proper name (Erie) and a description (Lake) are positioned alphabetically by the proper name. The description is positioned after the proper name and is usually abbreviated:

Erie, L., *N. Amer.* **116 D4**

Where a description forms part of a settlement or administrative name however, it is always written in full and put in its true alphabetic position:

Mount Morris, *U.S.A.* **116 D7**

Names beginning with M' and Mc are indexed as if they were spelled Mac. Names beginning St. are alphabetised under Saint, but Sankt, Sint, Sant', Santa and San are all spelt in full and are alphabetised accordingly. If the same place name occurs two or more times in the index and all are in the same country, each is followed by the name of the administrative subdivision in which it is located. For example:

Jackson, Ky., *U.S.A.* **114 G4**
Jackson, Mich., *U.S.A.* **114 D3**
Jackson, Minn., *U.S.A.* **112 D7**

The number in bold type which follows each name in the index refers to the number of the map page where that feature or place will be found. This is usually the largest scale at which the place or feature appears.

The letter and figure which are in bold type immediately after the page number give the grid square on the map page, within which the feature is situated. The letter represents the latitude and the figure the longitude. A lower case letter immediately after the page number refers to an inset map on that page.

In some cases the feature itself may fall within the specified square, while the name is outside. This is usually the case only with features which are larger than a grid square.

Rivers are indexed to their mouths or confluences, and carry the symbol → after their names. The following symbols are also used in the index: ■ country, ⊠ overseas territory or dependency, □ first order administrative area, △ national park, ⌓ other park (provincial park, nature reserve or game reserve), ✈ (LHR) principal airport (and location identifier).

How to pronounce place names

English-speaking people usually have no difficulty in reading and pronouncing correctly English place names. However, foreign place name pronunciations may present many problems. Such problems can be minimised by following some simple rules. However, these rules cannot be applied to all situations, and there will be many exceptions.

1. In general, stress each syllable equally, unless your experience suggests otherwise.
2. Pronounce the letter 'a' as a broad 'a' as in 'arm'.
3. Pronounce the letter 'e' as a short 'e' as in 'elm'.
4. Pronounce the letter 'i' as a cross between a short 'i' and long 'e', as the two 'i's in 'California'.
5. Pronounce the letter 'o' as an intermediate 'o' as in 'soft'.
6. Pronounce the letter 'u' as an intermediate 'u' as in 'sure'.
7. Pronounce consonants hard, except in the Romance-language areas where 'g's are likely to be pronounced softly like 'j' in 'jam'; 'j' itself may be pronounced as 'y'; and 'x's may be pronounced as 'h'.
8. For names in mainland China, pronounce 'q' like the 'ch' in 'chin', 'x' like the 'sh' in 'she', 'zh' like the 'j' in 'jam', and 'z' as if it were spelled 'dz'. In general pronounce 'a' as in 'father', 'e' as in 'but', 'i' as in 'keep', 'o' as in 'or', and 'u' as in 'rule'.

Moreover, English has no diacritical marks (accent and pronunciation signs), although some languages do. The following is a brief and general guide to the pronunciation of those most frequently used in the principal Western European languages.

		Pronunciation as in
French	é	day and shows that the e is to be pronounced; e.g. Orléans.
	è	mare
	î	used over any vowel and does not affect pronunciation; shows contraction of the name, usually omission of 's' following a vowel.
	ç	's' before 'a', 'o' and 'u'.
	ë, ï, ü	over 'e', 'i' and 'u' when they are used with another vowel and shows that each is to be pronounced.
German	ä	fate
	ö	fur
	ü	no English equivalent; like French 'tu'
Italian	à, é	over vowels and indicates stress.
Portuguese	ã, õ	vowels pronounced nasally.
	ç	boss
	á	shows stress
	ô	shows that a vowel has an 'i' or 'u' sound combined with it.
Spanish	ñ	canyon
	ü	pronounced as w and separately from adjoining vowels.
	á	usually indicates that this is a stressed vowel.

Abbreviations

A.C.T. – Australian Capital Territory
A.R. – Autonomous Region
Afghan. – Afghanistan
Afr. – Africa
Ala. – Alabama
Alta. – Alberta
Amer. – America(n)
Arch. – Archipelago
Ariz. – Arizona
Ark. – Arkansas
Atl. Oc. – Atlantic Ocean
B. – Baie, Bahía, Bay, Bucht, Bugt
B.C. – British Columbia
Bangla. – Bangladesh
Barr. – Barrage
Bos.-H. – Bosnia-Herzegovina
C. – Cabo, Cap, Cape, Coast
C.A.R. – Central African Republic
C. Prov. – Cape Province
Calif. – California
Cat. – Catarata
Cent. – Central
Chan. – Channel
Colo. – Colorado
Conn. – Connecticut
Cord. – Cordillera
Cr. – Creek
Czech. – Czech Republic
D.C. – District of Columbia
Del. – Delaware
Dem. – Democratic
Dep. – Dependency
Des. – Desert
Dét. – Détroit
Dist. – District
Dj. – Djebel
Domin. – Dominica
Dom. Rep. – Dominican Republic
E. – East
E. Salv. – El Salvador
Eq. Guin. – Equatorial Guinea
Est. – Estrecho
Falk. Is. – Falkland Is.
Fd. – Fjord
Fla. – Florida
Fr. – French
G. – Golfe, Golfo, Gulf, Guba, Gebel
Ga. – Georgia
Gt. – Great, Greater
Guinea-Biss. – Guinea-Bissau
H.K. – Hong Kong
H.P. – Himachal Pradesh
Hants. – Hampshire
Harb. – Harbor, Harbour
Hd. – Head
Hts. – Heights
I.(s). – Île, Ilha, Insel, Isla, Island, Isle
Ill. – Illinois
Ind. – Indiana
Ind. Oc. – Indian Ocean
Ivory C. – Ivory Coast
J. – Jabal, Jebel
Jaz. – Jazīrah
Junc. – Junction
K. – Kap, Kapp
Kans. – Kansas
Kep. – Kepulauan
Ky. – Kentucky
L. – Lac, Lacul, Lago, Lagoa, Lake, Limni, Loch, Lough
La. – Louisiana
Ld. – Land
Liech. – Liechtenstein
Lux. – Luxembourg
Mad. P. – Madhya Pradesh
Madag. – Madagascar
Man. – Manitoba
Mass. – Massachusetts
Md. – Maryland
Me. – Maine
Medit. S. – Mediterranean Sea
Mich. – Michigan
Minn. – Minnesota
Miss. – Mississippi
Mo. – Missouri
Mont. – Montana
Mozam. – Mozambique
Mt.(s) – Mont, Montaña, Mountain
Mte. – Monte
Mti. – Monti
N. – Nord, Norte, North, Northern, Nouveau
N.B. – New Brunswick
N.C. – North Carolina
N. Cal. – New Caledonia
N. Dak. – North Dakota
N.H. – New Hampshire
N.I. – North Island
N.J. – New Jersey
N. Mex. – New Mexico
N.S. – Nova Scotia
N.S.W. – New South Wales
N.W.T. – North West Territory
N.Y. – New York
N.Z. – New Zealand
Nac. – Nacional
Nat. – National
Nebr. – Nebraska
Neths. – Netherlands
Nev. – Nevada
Nfld. – Newfoundland
Nic. – Nicaragua
O. – Oued, Ouadi
Occ. – Occidentale
Okla. – Oklahoma
Ont. – Ontario
Or. – Orientale
Oreg. – Oregon
Os. – Ostrov
Oz. – Ozero
P. – Pass, Passo, Pasul, Pulau
P.E.I. – Prince Edward Island
Pa. – Pennsylvania
Pac. Oc. – Pacific Ocean
Papua N.G. – Papua New Guinea
Pass. – Passage
Peg. – Pegunungan
Pen. – Peninsula, Péninsule
Phil. – Philippines
Pk. – Peak
Plat. – Plateau
Prov. – Province, Provincial
Pt. – Point
Pta. – Ponta, Punta
Pte. – Pointe
Qué. – Québec
Queens. – Queensland
R. – Rio, River
R.I. – Rhode Island
Ra. – Range
Raj. – Rajasthan
Recr. – Recreational, Récréatif
Reg. – Region
Rep. – Republic
Res. – Reserve, Reservoir
Rhld-Pfz. – Rheinland-Pfalz
S. – South, Southern, Sur
Si. Arabia – Saudi Arabia
S.C. – South Carolina
S. Dak. – South Dakota
S.I. – South Island
S. Leone – Sierra Leone
Sa. – Serra, Sierra
Sask. – Saskatchewan
Scot. – Scotland
Sd. – Sound
Serbia & M.. – Serbia & Montenegro
Sev. – Severnaya
Sib. – Siberia
Sprs. – Springs
St. – Saint
Sta. – Santa
Ste. – Sainte
Sto. – Santo
Str. – Strait, Stretto
Switz. – Switzerland
Tas. – Tasmania
Tenn. – Tennessee
Terr. – Territory, Territoire
Tex. – Texas
Tg. – Tanjung
Trin. & Tob. – Trinidad & Tobago
U.A.E. – United Arab Emirates
U.K. – United Kingdom
U.S.A. – United States of America
Ut. P. – Uttar Pradesh
Va. – Virginia
Vdkhr. – Vodokhranilishche
Vdskh. – Vodoskhovyshche
Vf. – Vírful
Vic. – Victoria
Vol. – Volcano
Vt. – Vermont
W. – Wadi, West
W. Va. – West Virginia
Wall. & F. Is. – Wallis and Futuna Is.
Wash. – Washington
Wis. – Wisconsin
Wlkp. – Wielkopolski
Wyo. – Wyoming
Yorks. – Yorkshire

A

B

C

D

E

F

G

H

I

J

K

L

M

O

P

Q

R

S

T

U

V

W

X

Y

Z

KEY TO EUROPEAN MAP PAGES

Large scale maps (>1:2 500 000)

Medium scale maps (1:2 800 000 – 1:9 900 000)

Small scale maps (<1:10 000 000)

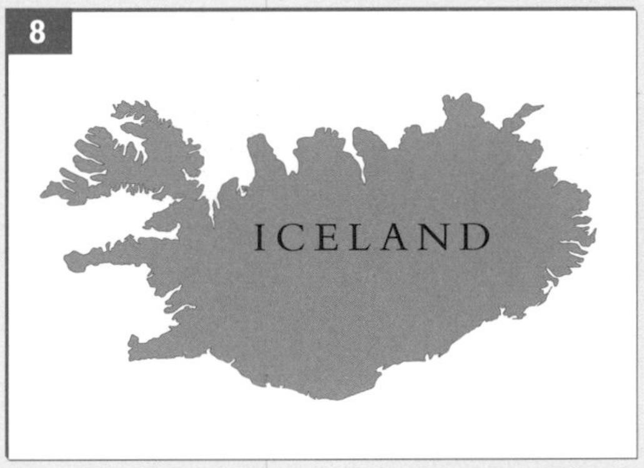

8
ICELAND

Arctic Circle

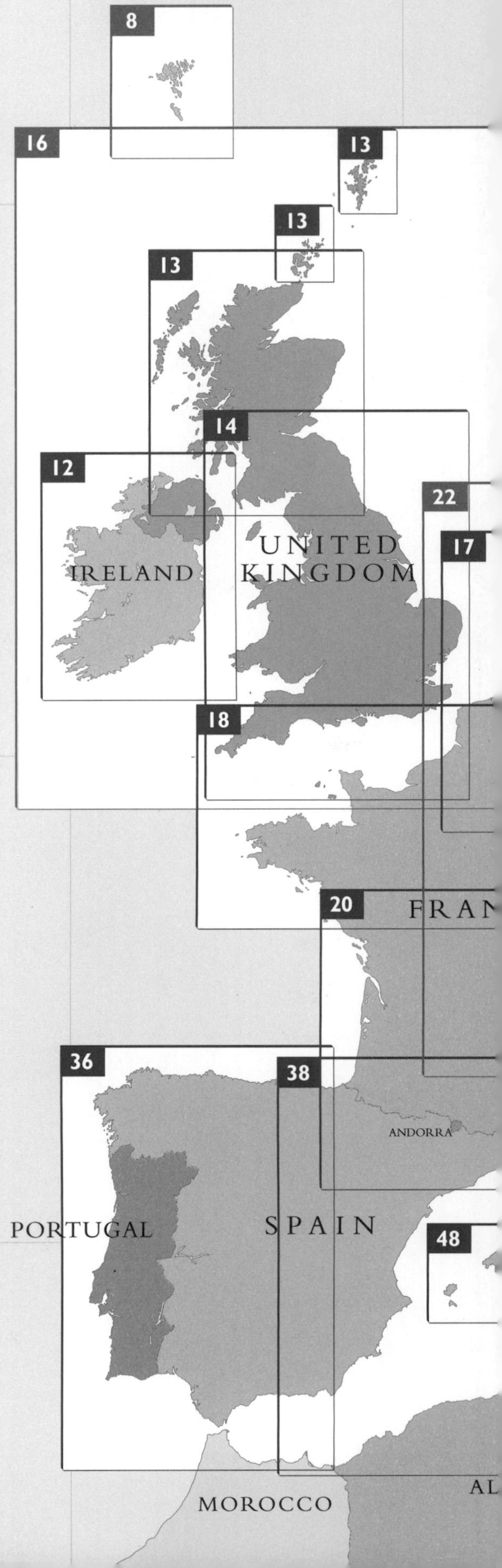

8
16
13
13
13
14
12
22
17
IRELAND
UNITED KINGDOM
18
20
FRAN
36
38
ANDORRA
PORTUGAL
SPAIN
48
MOROCCO
AL

World Country Index